*The Woman Who Turned Into a Jaguar,
and Other Narratives of Native Women
in Archives of Colonial Mexico*

The Woman Who Turned Into a Jaguar, and Other Narratives of Native Women in Archives of Colonial Mexico

Lisa Sousa

STANFORD UNIVERSITY PRESS
STANFORD, CALIFORNIA

Stanford University Press
Stanford, California

© 2017 by the Board of Trustees of the Leland Stanford Junior University.
All rights reserved.

No part of this book may be reproduced or transmitted in any form or by any means, electronic or mechanical, including photocopying and recording, or in any information storage or retrieval system without the prior written permission of Stanford University Press.

Printed in the United States of America on acid-free, archival-quality paper

Library of Congress Cataloging-in-Publication Data
Names: Sousa, Lisa, author.
Title: The woman who turned into a jaguar, and other narratives of native women in archives of colonial Mexico / Lisa Sousa.
Description: Stanford, California : Stanford University Press, 2017. | Includes bibliographical references and index. | Description based on print version record and CIP data provided by publisher; resource not viewed.
Identifiers: LCCN 2016021290 (print) | LCCN 2016020106 (ebook) | ISBN 9781503601116 (e-book) | ISBN 9780804756402 (cloth) | ISBN 9781503613621 (paper)
Subjects: LCSH: Indian women—Mexico—Social conditions. | Mexico—Social conditions—To 1810. | Mexico—History—Spanish colony, 1540–1810.
Classification: LCC F1219.3.W6 (print) | LCC F1219.3.W6 S68 2017 (ebook) | DDC 305.48/897072—dc23
LC record available at https://lccn.loc.gov/2016021290

Typeset by Newgen in 10/12 Sabon

To Kevin, Isabella, and Vincenzo, with love

Contents

List of Figures, Tables, and Maps   ix
Acknowledgments   xiii

1. Introduction   1
2. Gender and the Body   19
3. Marriage Encounters   50
4. Marital Relations   84
5. Sexual Attitudes and Concepts   110
6. Sexual Crimes   148
7. Duties and Responsibilities   177
8. Household and Community   225
9. Rebellious Women   262
10. Conclusion   296

Glossary   309
Notes   313
References   373
Index   393

Figures, Tables, and Maps

FIGURES

1.1. Offerings to the goddess Chicome Coatl at Cinteopan revealing the gendered division of labor in Nahua society 2

2.1. Drunkard who transformed into a rabbit 23

2.2. Nahualli forms of a commoner 25

2.3. Calendar reader naming a newborn and explaining his fate 27

2.4. Midwife ritually bathing a baby boy with the symbols of masculinity lying beside the basin 34

2.5. Symbols of femininity introducing text that describes the bathing ritual for a baby girl performed by a midwife 35

2.6. Midwife performing the bathing ceremony 36

2.7. Ñudzahui noblemen and noblewomen making offerings at a temple 44

2.8. Xochihuaque, or cross-dressed man and woman 47

3.1. Image submitted to the Holy Office of the Inquisition showing Martín Xochimitl being tried for polygyny with the four sisters who were his "wives" 60

3.2. Marriage prognostication warning of violence 66

3.3. Marriage prognostication warning of violence 67

3.4. Marriage prognostication warning of violence 68

3.5. Cihuatlanque discussing marriage negotiations with a young man 69

3.6. Nahua marriage ceremony   72

3.7. Beginning of indigenous-Christian marriage in 1532   78

3.8. Nahua-Christian marriage ceremony   82

4.1. Ñudzahui yuhuitayu showing the joint rule of the male yya toniñe (*left*) and the female yya dzehe toniñe (*right*)   96

4.2. Lienzo of Tabaá (*detail*)   97

4.3. Land titles showing San Francisco Caxhuacan's leading couples and its patron saint   98

5.1. Ixnextli-Xochiquetzal as the embodiment of sexual transgression and discord   115

5.2. Vagabond shown coming and going   116

5.3. Xochiquetzal with symbols of illicit sex   121

5.4. Sixteenth-century prostitute, revealing the indigenous association between drinking and sex   124

5.5. Sixteenth-century depiction of an evil youth who is prone to the vices of drunkenness and lust   125

5.6. Prostitute holding flowers, symbolizing sexual excess and seduction   127

5.7. Prostitute holding flowers and wearing a floral garment   128

5.8. "Wicked old man" depicted wearing a flowered cape (*left*) and procurer with flowery speech (*right*)   128

5.9. Ñudzahui primordial couple   129

5.10. Feathered serpent in birth scene from a Ñudzahui pictorial manuscript   130

5.11. Tlazolteotl with feathered serpent   131

5.12. Tetlanochili, or procuress   143

6.1. Prognostication warning that adultery would ruin the marriage   151

6.2. Death by stoning as punishment for adultery   160

6.3. Punishment for adultery   161

6.4. Punishment for adultery   163

Figures, Tables, and Maps

6.5. Pictorial submitted in a land dispute showing a man executed for adultery (*bottom left*) 164

6.6. Yope custom of biting off the noses of adulterers as punishment for their transgressions 165

7.1. Middle-aged Nahua woman 179

7.2. Merchants, identified by cloth and other precious trade goods 183

7.3. Spinner 184

7.4. Tailor 185

7.5. Man using metate 189

7.6. Man heating a substance over a fire 189

7.7. Nahua ticitl advising a pregnant woman, before an assembly of household members and kin, on how to take care of herself during pregnancy 195

7.8. Nahua ticitl massaging a pregnant woman's abdomen to position the baby and prepare the mother for birth 196

7.9. Nahua ticitl enclosing a woman, whose baby cannot be delivered, in the temascalli to await death 197

7.10. Female ticitl in front of Quetzalcoatl 200

7.11. Ticitl attending to victims of a smallpox epidemic 201

7.12. Nahuatl-language document with pictorial image presented in a dispute over tribute labor 220

7.13. Tribute list depicting cloth paid in tribute to Aztec rulers in preconquest times 222

8.1. Mid-sixteenth-century Nahua household showing a married couple and their children 234

8.2. Nahua household and its land 235

8.3. Aztecs' ancient origins, showing a couple in a cave 236

8.4. Woman making dye in the household patio 238

8.5. Mothers and fathers training and disciplining their daughters and sons 240

8.6. Male and female plaintiffs presenting their case to judges 252

8.7. Women and men appealing to judges in front of Moteucçoma's palace   253

9.1. Six Monkey engaged in warfare   264

9.2. Page from the pictorial manuscript presented in litigation by Tepetlaoztoc over excessive labor demands on the community   269

9.3. Page from the pictorial manuscript presented in litigation by Tepetlaoztoc over excessive labor demands, showing cloth as payment in kind   269

TABLES

2.1. Fates and personality traits associated with the calendar   28

4.1. Sampling of couples tried for amancebamiento in the archbishopric of Mexico City, 1582–1584   101

6.1. Punishments for adultery in preconquest times   159

7.1. Nahuatl-language terminology based on *toltecatl* (artisan) from the Florentine Codex   187

7.2. Nahuatl-language terminology based on *imati* (be skilled, expert) from descriptions of artisans in the Florentine Codex   187

7.3. Nahuatl-language Terminology based on *tlananamactia* (make things meet or match) from descriptions of artisans in the Florentine Codex   188

7.4. Nahuatl-language terminology based on *tlapalhuia* (paint or dye something) from descriptions of artisans in the Florentine Codex   188

7.5. Nahuatl-language terminology based on *tliloa* (outline in black) and *icuiloa* (write, paint) from descriptions of artisans in the Florentine Codex   188

7.6. Some Nahuatl terms for midwife   194

7.7. Ticitl identified in Ruiz de Alarcón's 1629 treatise on heathen superstitions   203

MAPS

1.1. Central Mexico   5

1.2. Mixteca Alta and Sierra Zapoteca regions of Oaxaca   6

Acknowledgments

I am eternally grateful to the many individuals and institutions that have supported this project. I am thankful that I had the opportunity to study with my mentor, the late Jim Lockhart, as an undergraduate and a graduate student at UCLA. Jim inspired me to pursue the study of indigenous cultures and languages of Mexico as a graduate student. His passion for learning from native- and Spanish-language sources that were produced at the local level, and often by ordinary people, his incredible work ethic and integrity, and his vast knowledge of early Latin America and early modern Spain continue to inspire me. At UCLA, I had the privilege to study with other gifted teachers and scholars, including E. Bradford Burns, José Moya, H. B. Nicholson, and Ruth Bloch, all of whom influenced my intellectual formation in profound ways. In addition, I studied Mesoamerican pictorial writing systems and colonial art in graduate seminars with Jeanette Favrot Peterson and John Pohl. Jeanette's careful analysis of continuity and change in sixteenth-century murals, paintings, and pictorial writings and her polished presentation style set a high standard. John Pohl's seminar on the Codex Borgia group introduced me to fundamental aspects of the pictorial writing system and inspired me to think creatively about the ways in which marital relations were depicted in divinatory manuscripts.

I also owe special thanks to many friends and colleagues who shared their research and offered suggestions that have enriched this study. Michel Oudijk and Bas Van Doesburg have been kind hosts, both in Holland and Mexico, and have generously shared resources and their knowledge of indigenous communities of pre-Hispanic, colonial, and contemporary Oaxaca. Michel also generously shared a photograph that he took of the Lienzo of Tabaá and gave permission to reproduce it here. In Oaxaca and Mexico City, María de los Ángeles Romero Frizzi, María Castañeda de la Paz, Bill Autry, and John Monaghan made my research visits informative and enjoyable. Ronald Spores offered his encouragement and expertise in the nascent stages of this project. I have fond memories of many wonderful conversations with Ron about Mixtec history and archaeology in the archive and on trips to the Mixteca Alta where he shared his passion for the contemporary communities and cultures of the region. Eulogio Guzmán warmly opened his home in Mexico City to Kevin and me for a summer and was an enthusiastic guide to archaeological sites, museums, and the best food in the Valley of Mexico. He also shared his facsimiles of codices, and offered insights on representations of women based on his vast knowledge of pre-Columbian Mesoamerica. I owe very special thanks to my wonderful friends in Oaxaca, Andrés and Marcelena, and their sons Victor and Luis and their families, who shared their experiences and their knowledge of Triqui language and culture over many years. I thank them for their warmth and hospitality. I also offer special thanks to my dear friend Stafford Poole, whose enthusiasm for the history of early Mexico is infectious and whose vast knowledge, especially of the history of the church and the Guadalupe devotion, is inspiring. I thank the Zapotexts group at UCLA, and especially Pam Munro, Kevin Terraciano, Michael Galant, Aaron Sonnenschein, Brooke Lillehaugen, and Xochitl Flores, for collaborating with me on the study of colonial Zapotec (Tíchazàa).

I also thank Elizabeth Boone, Louise Burkhart, León García Garagarza, Kymm Gauderman, Bob Haskett, Robinson Herrera, Rebecca Horn, Maarten Jansen, Susan Kellogg, Cecelia Klein, Aurora Pérez Jiménez, Matthew Restall, Susan Schroeder, Barry Sell, Pete Sigal, David Tavárez, and Stephanie Wood. I have learned a great deal from all of them, and I have enjoyed presenting my work on panels with them at national and international conferences. Several of my colleagues at Occidental College have read and commented on sections of this manuscript, including Maryanne Horowitz, David Kasunic, Adelaida López, Amy Lyford, Alexandra Puerto, Dolores Trevizo, and Kristi Upson-Saia. I appreciate their thoughtful feedback and comparative perspectives on the work.

I sincerely thank Sonya Lipsett-Rivera and an anonymous reader, who reviewed the manuscript for Stanford University Press. I appreciate their willingness to share their time and expertise. The book is much stronger because of their critiques and recommendations. In addition, I thank the editors at Stanford University Press for their work on this project, especially Norris Pope for his strong support of the book in its early stages, and Nora Spiegel and Margo Irvin for their guidance through the publication process. I also thank Jay Harward and his colleagues at Newgen.

Completion of this project would not have been possible without the support of various institutions and their knowledgeable staff members.

Acknowledgments

A National Endowment for the Humanities fellowship allowed me to research and write several chapters of the manuscript. Sabbatical leaves, conference funding, and research grants from Occidental College enabled me to conduct research in Mexico and to expand the scope of the book. In addition, I appreciate the assistance I received from the directors and staff members at the Archivo Judicial de Oaxaca, especially Gonzalo Rojo and the current director Israel Garrido, and the Archivo General del Estado de Oaxaca in Oaxaca City, the Archivo General de la Nación in Mexico City, and the Archivo General de Indias in Seville. I thank the many institutions that granted permission to reproduce images of Mesoamerican pictorial writings from their collections and publications: the Akademische Druckund Verlagsanstalt in Vienna; the Archivo General de la Nación in Mexico City; Biblioteca Medicea Laurenziana, Florence; the Bibliothèque nationale de France, Paris; the Bodleian Library at Oxford University; the British Museum in London; The John Carter Brown Library in Providence; the Museo de Américas in Madrid; and the University of California Press in Berkeley.

Finally, I thank my family for their love and encouragement. My grandmother Epifania and my mother Sandi inspired my deep interest in Mexican history with their stories about our family's past. My mother taught me to embrace life and to accept any invitation to travel. I thank my mom and stepfather Louie for their support and encouragement. My father Mack and my sister Marnie taught me the meaning of inner strength, courage, humility, and love, and they are both deeply missed. I am forever indebted to my husband and best friend, Kevin Terraciano, who has been by my side from the beginning of this project. Kevin read multiple drafts of the manuscript, checked translations, made suggestions concerning sources, and encouraged me to pursue this work through times of loss and sadness as well as happier times filled with parenting distractions. We have had the good fortune to travel and research together throughout Spain and Mexico. His passion for history and his great sense of humor have made this journey exciting and fun. Our children Isabella and Vincenzo have shown endless patience, goodwill, and curiosity while Kevin and I have worked at the archive in Oaxaca, traveled through the Mixteca Alta, visited museums, given lectures, and discussed research at the dinner table. This book is dedicated to Kevin, Isabella, and Vincenzo, who know best that this work has been a labor of love.

The Woman Who Turned Into a Jaguar,
and Other Narratives of Native Women
in Archives of Colonial Mexico

CHAPTER ONE

Introduction

When illustrating the offerings that Nahuas made to the goddess Chicome Coatl at her temple at Cinteopan, the indigenous artist beautifully rendered the complementary and interdependent relations of men and women (see Figure 1.1). His drawing shows young men presenting corn stalks, representing their agricultural labor, and young women carrying *atole* (a corn beverage), symbolizing their responsibility for preparing food and drink. The gifts highlight men's and women's gender duties and mutual obligations to their households, communities, and deities. The distinctive clothing and hairstyles mark their gender, age, and status. The location of the women in the lower register of the image, seated, and of men in the upper register, standing, corresponds to native cosmologies in which the earth (lower) is conceived of as female and the sky (upper) as male. The balanced composition of the image and the symmetry in the presence and number of men and women reveal the parallel and complementary organizing principles of indigenous social and gender relations.

Archival narratives from colonial Mexico both confirm and contradict the idealized view of gender relations in the ritual depicted in the temple of Cinteopan. The rich historical record in Mexico reveals a broad range of Mesoamerican women's daily activities, which were vital to the social, economic, and spiritual life of the community. As tribute-paying commoners, they can be seen spinning yarn, weaving cloth, grinding corn, making tortillas, and providing service in the homes and on the lands of native elites and Spaniards. They emerge as market vendors, some with significant investments in native and Spanish goods. Many women appear as property owners, who inherited and bequeathed lands and belongings. They stand out as wives who, if necessary, tried to force their husbands to fulfill marital obligations. Some even appear as legitimate native rulers, or *cacicas*, of their local states. Other indigenous women confronted and fought with outsiders to protect the people and resources of their communities throughout central and southern Mexico. And yet so many of their stories are unknown to us and remain to be told.

This book offers a social and cultural history of indigenous gender relations in colonial Mexico from these many different perspectives, beginning with the Spanish conquest in the 1520s and ending in the first half of the eighteenth century. I examine cross-cultural patterns in women's roles and status, focusing primarily on four native groups in highland Mexico: the Nahua people of central Mexico, who spoke Nahuatl; the Ñudzahui (Mixtec) people of the Mixteca Alta in northwestern Oaxaca; and the Bènizàa (Zapotec) and Ayuuk (Mixe) peoples of the Sierra Zapoteca in

Figure 1.1. Offerings to the goddess Chicome Coatl at Cinteopan revealing the gendered division of labor in Nahua society

SOURCE: Florentine Codex, bk. 2, fol. 28. Florence: Biblioteca Medicea Laurenziana, Med. Palat. 218, c. 82. By concession of the Ministry for Heritage and Cultural Activities; further reproduction by any means is forbidden.

eastern Oaxaca. I do not claim to address the histories of all indigenous groups in highland Mexico. I do not include the Maya of Yucatan, Chiapas, and Guatemala, or the many other culture and language groups of Mesoamerica, such as the Otomi. Nonetheless, at the time of the conquest, the groups that are the focus of the study—the Nahua, Ñudzahui, Bènizàa, and Ayuuk—were among the most populous, sedentary civilizations in Mesoamerica, and they shared countless defining social, cultural, and political traits, despite differences in language and sociopolitical organization. The peoples of highland Mexico also shared a common history under colonial rule. In the first two or three generations after the conquest, the Spaniards introduced far-reaching changes in native communities by establishing town councils, parishes, and a new tribute system, and by bringing a new material culture, domesticated animals, and diseases. Much of this history of native women and men under colonial rule considers, on the one hand, pragmatic acceptance, adoption, and adaptation of Spanish institutions, concepts, and practices and, on the other hand, rejection and resistance that has often been overlooked.

The broad geographical and temporal scope of this study enables me to trace similarities and differences in women's roles and status among some of the major culture groups of central Mexico and Oaxaca.[1] The long period from 1520 to 1750 corresponds to the periodization of several important works on native society and culture at the corporate level. Furthermore, with some notable exceptions, much of the recent scholarship on Mexican women has focused on either the postclassic period (pre-1519) or the late colonial (post-1750) and Independence (1810–1820s) periods, leaving the first two centuries of colonial rule to a handful of scholars.[2] This work seeks to help fill in this gap.

In writing this book, I have five principal objectives. First, I seek to contribute to Mesoamerican women's history by considering indigenous women from across the social spectrum, both commoners and elites, especially in rural communities where most indigenous people lived in this period. The existing scholarship on gender in the colonial period focuses overwhelmingly on Spanish and *casta* (racially mixed-heritage) women's status in the family and marriage, and especially on elite urban women.[3] Despite their very significant contributions to the study of women, these works examine women's status within a framework of Spanish custom and morality and do not specifically address indigenous gender relations. For some groups, including the Bènizàa and the Ayuuk, little or nothing has been written on indigenous women's lives under colonial rule. This book breaks new ground by integrating their experiences into a broader discussion of gender relations in central Mexico and Oaxaca. My focus on women does not overlook the fact that women's status must be considered in relation to men's. In fact, the historical record confirms that the household was the basic social unit in which men and women lived their lives as partners much more so than as individuals.

Second, I examine the formation and expression of gender identity in highland Mexico. I show how a binary gender system was imposed through roles, rituals, and behavior as a way to order and streamline the more complex realities of gender ambiguity, instability of the body, and variation in personal traits. I consider how concepts of femininity and masculinity influenced the idealized roles of women and men, and how gender ideology was tied to social, political, and economic power. I consider how gender dynamics shaped interactions in the household and community and among indigenous peoples and other ethnic groups.

Third, I place social relations in the household at the center of analysis. In doing so, I seek to shift the focus away from colonial institutions, such as the *cabildo* (municipal council), and predominately male actors, both Spanish and indigenous, in order to better understand the contributions that women made to their societies and cultures and to provide a more intimate, internal view of communities.

Fourth, I consider the impact of Spanish institutions, social customs, and cultural attitudes on indigenous gender relations and women's status. I am especially interested in how Christianity, monogamous marriage, patriarchal gender attitudes, the colonial tribute system, and legal culture, for example, altered social relations in communities. Spaniards, mestizos, and Africans are not as prominent in this study, reflecting the milieus that I encountered in the sources, which originated mainly in native communities. Nonetheless, this investigation considers the presence and influence of nonindigenous people in *cabeceras* (head towns) and nearby cities, and thus sheds light on interethnic relations and interactions in New Spain.

Fifth, I show how understanding indigenous women's history is vital to our understanding of the early modern Atlantic World. Aside from Malinche and Pocahontas, native women are rarely mentioned in narratives on the colonial encounter and the development of new societies in the Americas. Many scholars have not fully appreciated the fact that indigenous women and men produced the wealth in Mexico (and many other places) that stimulated further European expansion, settlement, and immigration; financed the early African slave trade; and established the patterns of economic production based on the exploitation of cheap labor and the extraction of natural resources that were key components of the emerging Atlantic World.

This study draws on a rich collection of archival, textual, and pictorial sources to identify and trace changes in women's economic, political, and social status in colonial native societies and to consider the extent to which Spanish gender and sexual ideologies influenced native attitudes and practices in the first several generations after contact. These sources represent more than a hundred communities in central and southern Mexico (see Maps 1.1 and 1.2). The records were written in native languages (mainly Nahuatl and, to a lesser extent, Tíchazàa and Ñudzahui) and in Spanish. Native-language sources reveal categories and concepts that are often obscured by Spanish or English translations and therefore

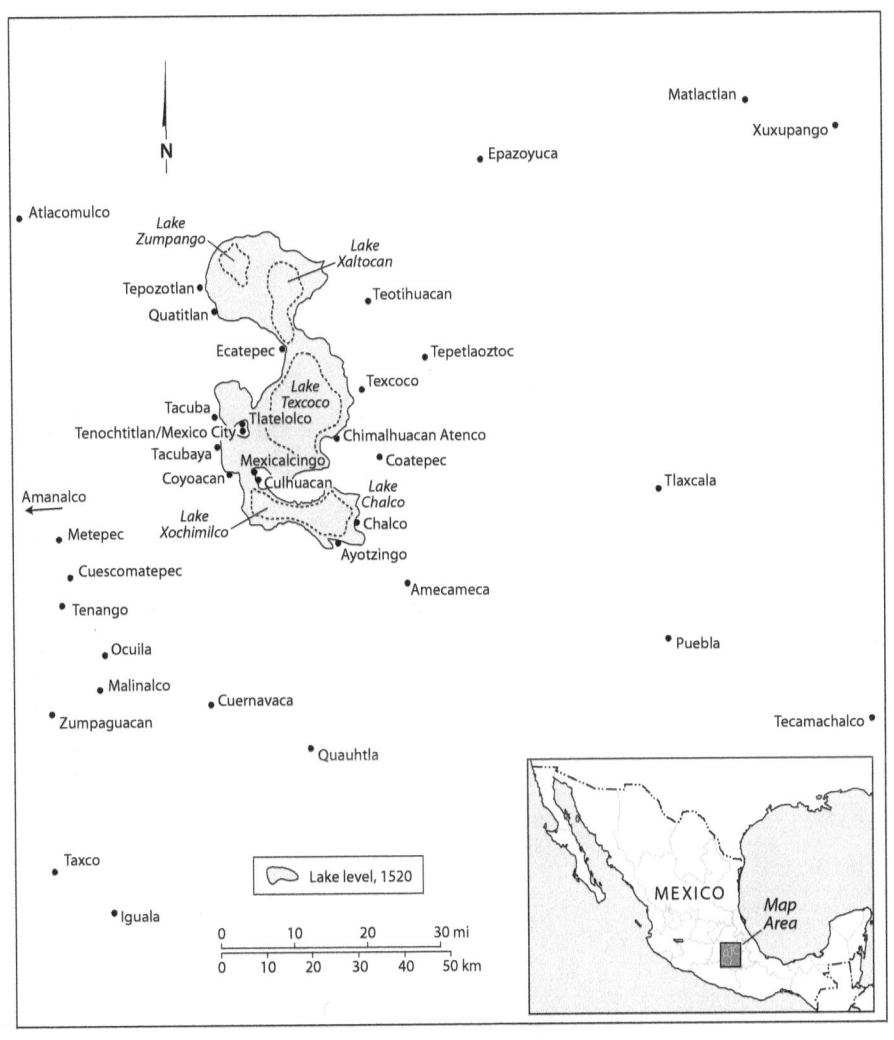

Map 1.1. Central Mexico

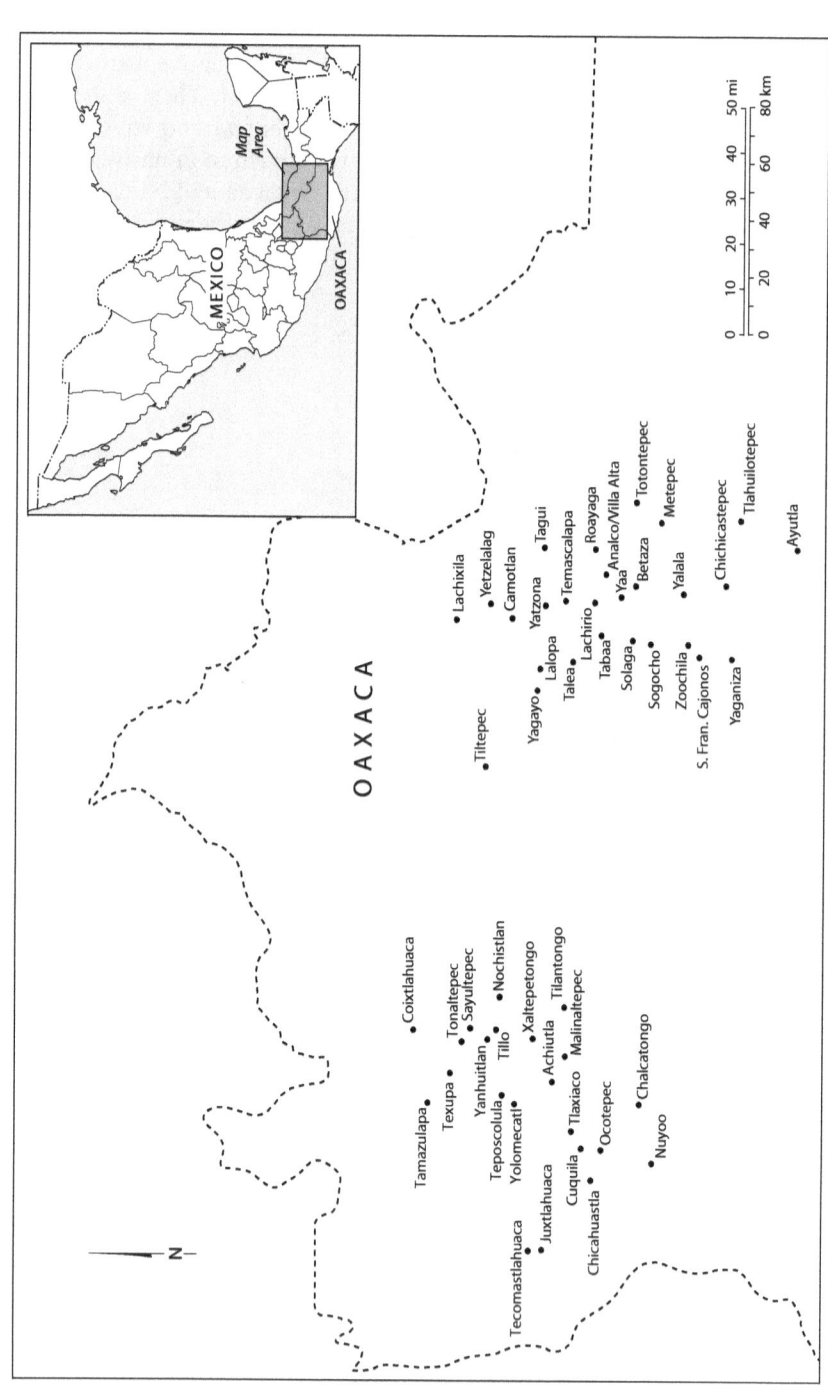

Map 1.2. Mixteca Alta and Sierra Zapoteca regions of Oaxaca

are critical to this study. Whenever possible, I have tried to use documents generated by indigenous peoples themselves rather than rely on the commentaries of Spanish observers. My sources include indigenous- and Spanish-language formal texts and speeches, confessional manuals, *doctrinas*, grammars, criminal records, last wills and testaments, land documents, inquisitorial proceedings, late sixteenth-century questionnaires (*Relaciones geográficas*), and pictorial writings. Many of the texts, although written after the conquest, refer to ancient traditions, society, and history, contributing a wealth of information on the postclassic and early colonial periods.

Most of the sources used in this study, however, were written at least two generations after the conquest and so reflect some degree of Spanish influence. After the initial decades of contact, most indigenous people of highland Mexico operated in a native-Christian context, often making it difficult to distinguish between Spanish-Christian and native ideals. Still, in most cases the community remained the locale of indigenous cultural practices and Mesoamericans vastly outnumbered Spaniards outside of cities, especially in southern Mexico. Therefore we can reasonably observe many indigenous patterns in the record that reflect native concepts and practices, particularly in regions where few Spaniards settled. Changes in ideology and social relations are less pronounced than changes in native governing institutions. I argue that it is possible to identify and trace patterns in indigenous gender relations and ideologies across the colonial period, aware that native cultures and value systems responded to dynamic, complex processes of change. Indeed, the same ideals and morals that were affirmed in formal speeches and life-cycle rituals were contested in household conflicts and disputes mediated by native and/or Spanish officials.

Since all the sources from this period were written by men, male perspectives color commentaries on society and gender in New Spain. Nevertheless, by reading these accounts critically, we can use them to reconstruct in part the roles and status of women. Even when shaped by colonial legal formulas, careful reading of the documents sheds light on gender relations and women's legal and economic status. Women's voices can be recovered in testaments, petitions, and testimonies from a variety of archival collections.[4] Although we might expect that women in this period appealed to the patriarchal ideology of Spanish magistrates and priests, we see many examples of their assertion of gender rights and articulation of marital expectations that did not conform to the attitudes of colonial elites. I use thousands of observations drawn from incidental information, especially from criminal records, to discern patterns of labor, social networks, and gender dynamics. I have tried as much as possible to integrate these voices and insights into the text by using abundant examples and quotes.

The book's title, *The Woman Who Turned Into a Jaguar*, is derived from a Zapotec man's 1684 court testimony in which he tried to justify his assault on his wife that led to her death. His captivating tale of the *nahualli* (a person who has the ability to transform into an animal) transformation of his wife, discussed in Chapter 2, exemplifies the many types of surprises that historians find in the colonial record. It also reveals the persistence of indigenous concepts and practices one hundred and fifty years after the Spanish invasion and how documents generated in colonial courts can diverge significantly from legal formulas and the calculated strategies of Spanish lawyers. In this case, the Zapotec man's testimony elicited scorn and skepticism from the Spanish judge, revealing a clash of worldviews between indigenous community members and colonial authorities that appears time and time again in the colonial record. Finally, the story offers a reminder that the perspectives of witnesses and authors shape testimonies, statements, and texts in the colonial archive.

Competing narratives in the historical record articulate different perspectives that confirm and contradict, complement and complicate, formal texts and prescriptions of gender roles and behavior. Many previous studies of native women in preconquest and colonial Mexico have turned first and foremost to prescriptive texts, such as speeches in the Florentine Codex; some do not venture far beyond these sources in their analysis. Such texts represent conservative, idealized roles that fail to provide a comprehensive view of women's activities, and yet they still reveal values essential to reconstructing aspects of native ideology. Preconquest and colonial pictorial manuscripts provide another dimension to topics represented in the many genres of alphabetic writings.[5] By reading a wide variety of sources, I have exposed certain biases and filled in gaps left by other records. Thus, archival documents, formal texts, and images, when read against each other, shed light on a range of views and conflicting perspectives of gender rights and obligations. The use of many different source types allows me to consider multiple criteria in the analysis of gender relations. I liken my methodology of integrating fragments of information from different perspectives to a woman's work of spinning thread and weaving cloth. The sources are the raw materials, which I sort and spin into threads of evidence, and then weave into patterns that tell a coherent, complex story of indigenous women's lives.[6]

This project has been informed by historiographical developments in two veins of colonial Mexican scholarship: women's history and ethnohistory. Ethnohistorical, and especially indigenous-language based, studies have emphasized the complexity and diversity of Mesoamerican culture before and after the conquest and have revealed the many forms of adaptation that indigenous social and political structures underwent at the corporate community level under colonial rule, in the face of massive depopulation and Spanish demands for wealth and labor. I have been particularly influenced by the work of my mentor, James Lockhart, and his many collaborators and students who have used indigenous-language notarial records, including last wills and testaments, land titles, and election records, to reveal social categories, political structures, and modes of organization, and to show how Spaniards built upon preexisting indigenous institutions to establish colonial rule.[7] I have also benefited from the studies of the evolution of Nahua cultural expression and language change through philological analyses of native-language annals, theater, speeches, and the like.[8]

In addition, this book has been shaped by the growing literature on women's history and gender studies in pre-Hispanic and colonial Latin America. There is an impressive corpus on women, gender, and sexuality in Spanish America that, although mainly focused on Spanish and casta women, sheds light on gender ideology, marital relations, honor systems, and women's economic activities and legal status.[9] Studies using native-language archival records to examine the family and land tenure in sixteenth-century Mexico, sociopolitical organization, and other topics, broke new ground by documenting women's agency.[10] The work of scholars in art history, archaeology, and anthropology on women in pre-Hispanic Mesoamerica, and that of historians of sexuality in colonial Mexico have also helped me think through some of the complexities and ambiguities of gender ideology.[11] The chapters of this book offer contributions to this rich scholarship in ethnohistory, women's history, and gender and sexuality studies.

THE PEOPLE AND THE SETTING

In an early seventeenth-century Nahuatl-language model dialogue intended for the instruction of friars in the art of Nahuatl rhetoric, the author includes the speech of an elder noblewoman (*cihuapilli*) who laments the collapse of the nobility, massive depopulation, and disruption to the social order brought about by Spanish colonial rule. She reminisces:

Back when I was growing up there was an infinite number of them [rulers and nobles]. And how many noble houses there were, the palaces of the former nobles and rulers! It was like one big palace. There were countless (minor) nobles and lesser relatives, and one could not count the commoners who were dependents, or the slaves; they were like ants. But now everywhere our Lord is destroying and reducing the land; we are coming to an end and disappearing.

In iquac nihualnozcali huel . . . centzontli; yhuan quezqui catca in tecpilcalli in intetecpan pipiltin tlatoque catca in iuh ce in tecpancalli, amo çan tlapohualtin tepilhuan in teixhuihuan catca: auh amo onmopohuaya in tetlan nenque macehualtin, noce in tlatlacotin; yuhquin tzicatl onoc. Auh in axcan ye nohuian motlalpolhuia motlalcanahuilia in totecuiyo ye tontlami ye tipolihui.[12]

Although the speech is rhetorical, it is not difficult to imagine Nahua elites, who saw their power, prestige, and wealth diminish under colonial rule, making such a profound statement. The cihuapilli goes on to recall the hierarchy of nobles who were clearly distinguished from commoners and slaves, and the many distinct peoples who lived in various city-states throughout the Valley of Mexico. She describes the gender-specific socialization and training of elite girls and boys educated by elder women and elder men, respectively, in temple schools. The ruling class, in her memory, maintained order by meting out harsh punishments for moral transgressions. The society that she remembers had clearly defined roles and places for nobles and commoners, men and women, and elders and youth.

The cihuapilli's speech reveals the organizing principles of Mesoamerican societies and reflects some of the dramatic changes that marked the first century of colonial rule. Sedentary groups lived in densely populated states, called *altepetl* by the Nahua, *ñuu* by the Ñudzahui, and *yetze* by the Bènizàa, that were scattered across the hills and valleys of highland Mexico.[13] The Ayuuk term is not yet known because these people used Nahuatl as a lingua franca during the colonial period and therefore adopted the term *altepetl* in their documents.[14] The population of these states ranged from several hundred to tens of thousands. Mexico Tenochtitlan, the largest Nahua altepetl at the time of contact, had as many as 200,000 inhabitants. These Mesoamerican states shared a number of characteristics, including clearly defined borders; a ruling dynasty, defined elite, and social hierarchy; a tribute system; a sacred temple or natural feature that was home to the principal local deity (or deities); and a shared ethnic identity and belief in a common origin and history within each state.[15] The peoples of highland Mexico practiced similar forms of pictorial writing and shared agricultural and ritual calendars.

There were other significant differences among the Mesoamerican peoples of highland Mexico. For example, although the Ñudzahui ñuu were structurally similar to the Nahua altepetl, the two developed unique governing institutions that are especially relevant to this study. Ñudzahui elites and commoners recognized both male and female rulers (masc. *yya toniñe*; fem. *yya dzehe toniñe*), whereas the Nahuas showed an overwhelming preference for male rulers (sing. *tlatoani*).[16] The right to rule in the Mixteca was based on the principle of direct descent from a ruling male and female, with noble status outweighing considerations of gender. The term *cihuatlatoani* (female ruler) did exist in Nahuatl in the sixteenth century, but the rulership was held by a man at the time of conquest and, in any case, female rule was an exception and may have occurred only as a result of disruption in dynastic descent.[17] The Bènizàa peoples also favored male rule, although the Zapotec language (Tíchazàa) also apparently included terms to designate female rulers, *coquitao xonaxi*, and noblewomen, *coqui xonaxi* or *xonaxi xini joana*.[18]

As suggested in the cihuapilli's speech quoted previously, in addition to status differences, gender and age were fundamental social categories that shaped an individual's roles and responsibilities. For example, participation in life-cycle and sacred rituals, tribute duties, and the division of labor were all determined by considerations of gender and age. In turn, gender and status were constructed through labor regimes, dress and adornment, and speech and gestures.

Spaniards gravitated toward the socially stratified and politically complex indigenous groups of highland Mexico who offered natural resources, material wealth, and labor. The Spanish-led conquest of Mexico Tenochtitlan in 1521 gave way to a protracted war in "New Spain" that lasted for decades. The conquest of the Mixteca Alta region of Oaxaca was complete by the 1530s; the Bènizàa, Ayuuk, and other groups in the Sierra Alta were not "pacified" until the 1550s.[19]

The political, religious, and economic institutions vital to sustaining Spanish rule were built on indigenous communities.[20] In the immediate postconquest period, the tribute system of the altepetl, ñuu, or yetze formed the basis of the *encomienda*, a grant of tribute and labor given to a Spaniard (called an *encomendero*) as a reward for his participation in the conquest or his service to the crown. The encomienda became the principal tie between the native and European populations in the early colonial period. During the mid-sixteenth century, the *cabildo*, or Spanish-style town council, which was staffed by native noblemen, was established in the most prominent states of the region, which were designated *cabeceras* or "head towns" in the new administrative order. The cabildo provided some continuity in terms of the political authority of nobles, and it established a system of indirect rule. Each state was also designated a parish, and by the 1620s the largest and/or wealthiest states had monastery complexes, often built on the ruins of the preconquest ceremonial center.

As the cihuapilli's speech suggests, contact with Europeans and Africans brought on waves of epidemics that decimated the indigenous populations of Mesoamerica. Labor abuses, the brutality of warfare, and disease reduced them by approximately 90 percent in the first century of colonial rule. It is important to note, however, that, despite this massive depopulation, the indigenous peoples constituted the majority of the population in New Spain throughout the colonial period.[21] This incredible fact had implications for the possibility of indigenous cultural vitality across time.

More than any other native group in New Spain, the Nahuas of central Mexico came into immediate and sustained contact with Spaniards, most of whom settled among Nahuas in the Valley of Mexico and surrounding areas, where the prospects of profit were greatest, near trade routes that linked the mining regions of the north with the Atlantic port. In contrast, relatively few Spaniards went to more remote regions, such as Oaxaca. In the Mixteca Alta, for example, in the colonial jurisdiction of Teposcolula less than 5 percent of the total population was non-native by the end of the eighteenth century.[22] In Villa Alta, the center of Spanish settlement in the Sierra Alta, there were only around a hundred and fifty Spaniards by the mid-eighteenth century.[23] Many types of change resulted from the extent and nature of contact with the European population. Indigenous groups in regions where the Spanish presence was minimal were less affected over time than groups in central Mexico, especially the Basin of Mexico. Still, no group was immune from Spanish competition or influence.

Studies of indigenous societies under colonial rule have shown that managed change initiated by the Spaniards occurred mainly at the corporate level.[24] Aside from dogged efforts to eliminate polygyny, Spaniards did not attempt to reorganize the native societies of central Mexico and Oaxaca at the household level—in reality, they could not have done so. People continued to live in nuclear or multifamily residences throughout the colonial period. Nor did Spaniards attempt to redefine social relations in the household. Women continued to own land, pay tribute, participate in the local economy, and possess legal status, although women's status was certainly affected over time. Furthermore, Spaniards did not need to reorient the division of labor practiced by sedentary peoples of Mesoamerica as Europeans did among semisedentary and nonsedentary groups of northern Mexico and much of North America.[25] The Mesoamerican division of labor in which men farmed and women wove cloth and carried out other activities, corresponded to European notions of appropriate gender roles. In fact, Spaniards profited by leaving the division of labor intact and by exploiting preexisting tribute mechanisms to extract wealth. The survival of fundamental aspects of social organization contributed to forms of indigenous cultural maintenance and recreation, even under the strains of colonial rule. I argue that Mesoamerican concepts of family, marital obligation, and sexuality exhibited remarkable continuity throughout the colonial period, even in areas of extensive contact with Spaniards. Over the course of several generations, Spanish gender systems, marital roles and expectations, and attitudes toward sex exerted a notable impact on native attitudes and practices, but the changes did not simply replace indigenous lifeways. Only after centuries of sustained interaction did changes in native values and gender relations become apparent, but they were often uneven and seldom comprehensive.

SOCIAL AND GENDER RELATIONS

Many Mesoamerican groups possessed distinct responsibilities and privileges, yet not one was entirely independent or self-sufficient. Despite social differentiation and hierarchy, each group was recognized as an integral part of the whole. Power struggles and fissures erupted between and within groups, but social relations were articulated in idealized terms of reciprocity and complementarity. In other words, the distinct contributions of each group or individual were considered necessary for the survival of the community. Reciprocal exchange through feasting and tribute created balance and maintained cooperation across social boundaries. Although nobles enjoyed a privileged status, they were obligated to provide for commoners. Elders and youth were other interdependent, paired groups that performed distinct yet complementary roles in the ritual life of the community. The fundamental principles of reciprocity and complementarity, as well as hierarchy, also shaped gender relations in highland Mexico.

Scholars have used *complementary* to describe several cultural characteristics of Mesoamerica.[26] In some contexts, the term refers to the combination of male and female traits in a single god or the pairing of male and female deities in Mesoamerican religion. This combination is sometimes discussed in terms of *duality*. *Complementary* also describes the way that men and women "completed" each other to achieve a certain status, such as adulthood, and it refers to the gendered tasks that men and women jointly performed to produce goods and services for the community. In this study, I use *complementary* (or *complementarity*) to describe a system in which men and women possessed distinct roles and responsibilities considered necessary for the well-being of their households and communities. Complementary social relations were naturalized and projected back into time immemorial through gendered mythologies of the deities. Susan Kellogg defines the concept concisely: "Complementary gender relations were frequently expressed through parallel structures of thought, language, and action in which males and females were conceived of and played different yet parallel and equally necessary roles."[27] These parallel structures are evident in Mesoamerican kinship systems, certain institutions, the division of labor, the socialization of children, cosmology, and the organization of ritual. Images drawn by native artists frequently depict men and women assembled in separate groups, like the image discussed in this chapter's opening, graphically revealing how space and labor were conceived as parallel, gendered spheres.

In many cases, however, concepts of complementarity, duality, and parallelism failed to promote full equality between men and women and, in fact masked gender hierarchy, inequality, and difference. For example, males almost exclusively occupied the most visible positions of local authority in all regions considered here except the Mixteca. Family structure and the organization of labor also reflect a degree of male dominance. Throughout central Mexico and Oaxaca, most heads of household were male. Although their authority over the legal and economic matters of the adult members of the household was circumscribed, men appear to have organized the labor of other household members. The colonial record reveals numerous cases of violence against women in indigenous highland Mexican communities, in which hierarchies of status differentiated the experiences of the elite and commoners. Despite these findings, however, based on my analysis of a wide variety of sources from more than a hundred Mesoamerican communities, I do not accept the characterization of gender relations in Mesoamerica as patriarchal.[28]

Patriarchy is a system that clearly elevates men above women and invests political, social, and economic power in the hands of the eldest males of households. Although it has assumed many different forms in response to specific cultural and historical contexts, some of its general features include the following tendencies: deriving a woman's social identity from her affiliation with the family patriarch, either her father or her husband; in the European context, investing authority in the eldest male; denying women independent legal status so that they cannot produce or witness legal documents or legally represent themselves in court; and denying women economic equality so that they cannot own property or carry out economic transactions without permission from a legal guardian (usually a husband or father). Evidence of these fundamental characteristics of patriarchy does not appear in the sources that I use to analyze Mesoamerican gender systems.

Finally, in some contexts gender had no bearing on one's rights and responsibilities, especially in terms of legal status and economic activities. Community membership, either through birth or marriage, and adulthood—not gender—determined who had economic and civic rights and responsibilities. Thus, women, like their male counterparts, could hold land, order their own testaments, witness legal documents, initiate criminal and civil suits, and participate in local rituals. They also shared the obligations of paying tribute as required of all community members. In a more abstract sense, Mesoamericans did not make essentializing distinctions between male and female personality traits. Both men and women could be considered, for example, hard-working, capable, providers or dishonest, adulterous drunks. Mesoamericans believed that a person's characteristics and fate were determined primarily by his or her date of birth, not biology.

Evidence of native women's status and activities in central Mexico and Oaxaca that emerges in the data collected for this study suggests the existence of overlapping gender systems of complementarity (along with the related concepts of duality, parallelism, and segregation) and hierarchy. In certain legal and economic contexts, gender was not a determining factor in gaining access to resources or institutions. The competing dimensions and discrepancies in these ideologies defy simplification and point to openings for conflict over gender rights, obligations, and status.

CHAPTER OVERVIEW

The chapters of this book examine multiple themes that, when considered together, provide a balanced and complex view of gender relations in highland Mexico in colonial times. Chapter 2 draws on theories of the body, gender performativity, and dress to show how gender was inscribed on the body to create the appearance of difference, which in turn shaped all social relations. The chapter considers, on the one hand, the fluidity of the body and gender identity and, on the other hand, the rituals and daily practices that imposed a binary system of gender. I am especially interested in the cultural construction of gender and the ways in which complementarity and parallelism shaped daily interaction.

Chapters 3 and 4 explore interrelated themes concerning marriage, a nearly universal institution in native communities practiced by nobles and commoners alike. Chapter 3 analyzes betrothal and nuptial ceremonies and practices. It also considers how Spanish attempts to eradicate native practices of serial monogamy and polygyny, and to enforce Christian monogamous marriage, altered indigenous concepts and customs. Chapter 4 first analyzes the social, political, and economic significance of native marriage to shed light on marital expectations and obligations. It then examines marital conflicts and domestic violence that developed in failed relationships. Formal and informal attempts to resolve disputes illustrate cultural expectations and attitudes about one's rights within a relationship. My analysis reveals a complex process of negotiation among husbands and wives, their households and social networks, and local native officials, in which women sometimes aired their grievances before the community. Spanish legal and ecclesiastic magistrates became involved in conflicts that turned extreme or violent, usually when a woman was beaten or killed.

Chapters 5 and 6 address sexuality. Chapter 5 examines indigenous sexual ideology and attitudes based on my analysis of Mesoamerican metaphors and symbols used to discuss and represent sexual matters. It also considers how Spanish friars adopted some of these indigenous concepts in their efforts to promote Christian morality and, in turn, how Spanish mores, Christian teaching, and colonial law affected native sexuality. Chapter 6 studies sexual crimes, including adultery and rape, and their prosecution in preconquest and colonial times. Adultery and rape were considered serious transgressions, and illicit sexuality was a central concern of indigenous moral teachings. My findings suggest that Spanish attitudes regarding virginity had very limited influence on indigenous values and customs in highland Mexico in the colonial period.

Chapters 7 and 8 reconstruct the organization of labor and the way that shared labor arrangements and other acts of sociability among households shaped community relations. Chapter 7 addresses the gendered division of labor in the household and in the community. I compare women's daily activities as described in archival records with idealized descriptions of their lives in prescriptive texts from the period, revealing significant discrepancies between observed and prescribed behavior. Whereas idealized sources locate women's work exclusively in the home, I show that women's duties, including laundering, selling in markets, working in fields, and healing the sick, took them out of the household on a daily basis. I also demonstrate that men, especially artisans, frequently worked within the home. My discussion of work thus challenges the gendering of "public" and "private" space that is implied in prescriptive texts. In addition, I use descriptions of artisans and symbolic analysis of the goods that women produced to understand the value placed on women's work. I also consider how increasing Spanish demands for labor and tribute and the development of a money economy shaped women's roles and status.

Chapter 8 investigates household relations, focusing on family organization, ritual kinship, and residence patterns. My analysis of economic, ritual, and political activities carried out in the household advances arguments in Chapter 7 refuting assumptions of a strong division between public and private space. I argue that household and community were in fact two interrelated spheres. Because women's work and activities were often conducted in the home, assessing the nature of household and family structure is essential for understanding the relative position of women in Mesoamerican societies. The chapter also examines how ritual kinship created multidimensional webs of relations among households and provided important social networks for women.

Chapter 9 studies women's participation in public protests and acts of civil disobedience, including riots. I show how threats to the integrity of the household and community, including increased demands for tribute and labor, led men and women to seek legal redress, to protest, and at times to rebel against colonial authorities. Women often organized acts of resistance, such as refusing to pay tribute, and assumed leading roles in local riots. This chapter argues that women engaged in local political and economic struggles and that their defense of homes, communities, and allies reveals a broader consciousness among women that has not been explored in previous studies.

Chapter 10 reiterates the book's major arguments and places the study's contributions in the context of existing scholarship on Mesoamerican ethnohistory and women's history. The chapter considers the evidence for both major changes and continuities in indigenous social and gender relations in rural communities of central Mexico and Oaxaca between 1500 and 1750, brought about by increasing contact with other cultures and institutions. Finally, I include a glossary of native- and Spanish-language terms used in the book.

Throughout, I use terms that the subjects of this study would use to describe themselves and their languages, as well as the names more commonly used in the literature: *Nahua* for the peoples of central Mexico who spoke Nahuatl; *Ñudzahui* for the peoples and language of the Mixteca Alta, also known as Mixtec; *Bènizàa* for the peoples of the Sierra Alta, commonly referred to as Zapotec, who spoke Tíchazàa; and *Ayuuk* for the people of the Sierra Alta, also called Mixe, who used Nahuatl as a lingua franca to write colonial documents. Men and women of highland Mexico most often would have referred to themselves as members of a particular community. For the sake of simplicity, I use placenames that are used today, aware that indigenous groups used (and in some cases continue to use) their own names in their own languages. At times I use *native* or *indigenous* to distinguish between the original individuals and groups of highland Mexico and the Spanish, African, and mixed-race populations. These distinctions were central to colonial legal, political, and economic institutions in Spanish America, as *yndios* and *yndias* were burdened with certain obligations, judged in special courts, restricted from various privileges, or designated to fill local offices, among other things.

I have reproduced many indigenous-language terms and passages in this work. All passages follow the original orthography, with spacing adjusted to grammatical norms established in the sixteenth century. Overbars and abbreviations are resolved, but no punctuation has been added to the original passages. I use italics for the first use of foreign-language terms in each chapter. When I use native-language transcriptions and translations that have been published by other scholars, I indicate this reproduction in the footnotes.

CHAPTER TWO

Gender and the Body

In 1686, Marcial de la Cruz, a Bènizàa man from San Francisco Cajonos, appeared before local native officials and confessed to the murder of his wife, Catalina María.[1] He explained that he had fled the community and drifted for two years after killing Catalina in 1684, but that he had summoned the courage to face the authorities because he was worried about the house and land that he had left behind. Marcial recalled that on the day of her murder Catalina traveled to the neighboring community of San Mateo to request his release from prison, where he had been detained because of a dispute over a mule. After she won his freedom, the couple began their journey back to San Francisco. Along the way, Marcial decided to stop to bathe in the river, but Catalina continued on her way. Later, Marcial hurried to catch up, but he could not find her anywhere. Suddenly a jaguar jumped out from behind a large maguey plant poised to attack. Fearing for his life, Marcial commended himself to God and held out the rosary he wore around his neck to fend off the ferocious animal. He picked up a club and struck the jaguar three times. At the very moment that the jaguar collapsed and died, Marcial heard a voice say to him in Tíchazàa, "Cuckold, don't kill that woman," and before his very eyes the jaguar transformed into his wife.

Marcial's fantastic account provides an example of the Mesoamerican belief in nahualism, or the ability of a person to transform into an animal, fire, or meteor.[2] Nahualism is just one aspect of a broader complex of ideas about the instability of the human body and its connections to the natural world and the sacred calendar. Tonalism and gender mutability share central aspects of this ideological complex. Previous investigations based on colonial sources and modern ethnography examined the origins and evolution of nahualism and tonalism in Mesoamerican thought; however, none considered the implications of these beliefs about the instability of the body for understandings of native constructions of gender. Discussions of gender mutability have not linked the concept to broader understandings of the body's dynamic nature.

Recent gender studies have shown that the body is a symbolic construct that has different historical and cultural significations, and that discourse on the body shapes conceptions of appropriate male and female roles and behavior. In some Western cultures, for example, changing beliefs about women's bodies have influenced perceptions of women's "nature," resulting in radically differing interpretations over time. In turn, essentialist assumptions have been used to justify women's exclusion from certain arenas of activity and expression. But how is difference constructed in cultures that believe the body to be capable of transfiguration and gender to be sometimes ambiguous? How are gender roles determined when the body is not a stable entity that can be easily categorized or definitively assigned a set of male or female characteristics? If not based on essentialist understandings of male and female bodies, what were native peoples' explanations of men's and women's personalities, inclinations, and potential based on? How was gender marked and performed?

This chapter analyzes aspects of indigenous gender ideology and concepts of the body as expressed in life-cycle rituals, native-language metaphors and terminology, and beliefs pertaining to the calendar, tonalism, and nahualism. These traditions are articulated in Nahuatl-language formal texts that describe preconquest beliefs and mythology and in archival narratives from the Bènizàa-Ayuuk (Zapotec-Mixe) area of Villa Alta and the Ñudzahui (Mixtec) region of the Mixteca Alta. The first part of the chapter discusses the instability of the body, drawing on indigenous beliefs about body transformation and gender flexibility. It also addresses native beliefs that locate the origin of personality in the calendar. The second part examines the construction of gender through labor, drawing on Nahua and Bènizàa rituals as two central case studies. It considers clothing and adornment and speech and behavior, all of which served as mechanisms to stabilize the body and impose identity.

I argue that the peoples of highland Mesoamerica developed a binary gender system to establish order in a world in which body instability and uncertain gender difference could threaten civilized existence. Individuals were placed in complementary pairs, including couplings of male/female, elder/youth, and noble/commoner, that were fundamental to sociopolitical organization. Thus, rituals that reinforced gendered responsibilities, labor regimes, and modes of behavior maintained the social order.

THE BODY AND TRANSFORMATION

In ancient and colonial times, Mesoamericans believed that certain phenomena could cause a radical and complete physical transformation of the body from one form to another. The body was dynamic and vulnerable to the complex interaction of celestial forces and human action. The passage of time, natural phenomena, ritual acts, and the use of intoxicating substances all might stimulate metamorphosis. Furthermore, the body was not a discrete entity, but rather was linked to the bodies of one's parents and to a companion animal.

Popular beliefs recorded in the sixteenth century reveal particular concern with pregnant women and children, perhaps because the instability of the body made them especially susceptible to astronomical irregularities. Precautions that a pregnant woman or a new mother should take reflect a general understanding that the body was influenced by natural forces. A Nahua adage stated that if a woman went out of the house during an eclipse of the moon, her unborn child might be turned into a mouse.[3] Linking a mother's visual experience with the physical state of the baby in her womb, another adage cautioned a pregnant woman to avoid looking at a hanged person so that her baby would not be born with the umbilical cord wrapped around its neck.[4] Among the Bènizàa people, a pregnant woman was admonished to avoid looking at a dying person.[5]

A mother's strong influence over the physical well-being of her child continued after she gave birth. A Nahua woman with a newborn, for example, was warned that her child's face would be pockmarked if she burned corncobs.[6] While we might anticipate an association between the physical experience of a mother and that of her child, the Zapotecs also believed that an unborn child endured what his or her father endured. If a father carried a load or was beaten, the fetus would suffer the same physical trials.[7] According to popular lore, a baby's body was inextricably linked to his or her parents' bodies, before and after birth. Nahuatl terms, including *teizti* (nails), *teixquamul* (eyebrows), *tetenzon* (beard), and *teuitzio* (spine), that describe the child as a fragment of the mother and father reinforce a physical connection between parent and child.[8]

Like natural phenomena, a failed ritual could stimulate a physical transformation in women and children. Concerns expressed about the New Fire festivities, which commemorated the end of a fifty-two-year calendar cycle, reveal the dire consequences of ritual transgressions and unsuccessful ceremonies. According to colonial descriptions of the preconquest New Fire tradition, people in all the altepetl of central Mexico extinguished their hearth fires and a high priest drilled a fire on the breast of a sacrificed man which runners then carried on torches to each community. Thus, local authorities created and distributed fire, investing the ritual with political and social implications. Symbolically, the ceremony fostered solidarity through the distribution and sharing of vital resources among commoners and nobles of each altepetl. According to Nahuatl accounts, children who fell asleep during the New Fire ceremony would transform into mice and pregnant women might turn into vicious beasts if the fire were not drawn.[9] Pregnant women and children risked becoming inhuman, their altered states representing the destruction of civilization. Such beliefs about the potential dangers of failed rituals link the destabilization of the human body with social disorder.

In her study of gender ambiguity, Cecelia Klein shows that rituals marking certain transitional times of the year included cross-dressing and dances that featured backward movements and leaping, symbolically upending the rigid division between male and female. She argues that "as a symbol of inversion, of reversal, and of the in-between, gender ambiguity was enormously important in Nahua ideology because it could reinstate social and cosmic order, thereby guaranteeing renewal, maturity, prosperity, and good health."[10] In liminal times, then, Nahuas used gender ambiguity to choreograph cosmic chaos that could be overcome only through the reestablishment of proper social and sacred relations.

Throughout Mesoamerica, indigenous peoples used hallucinogens and alcohol to induce revelations and physical transformations. Men and women consumed a variety of substances, including mushrooms, peyote, tobacco, *ololiuhqui* (*Turbina corymbosa*, a psychoactive plant,), and alcohol for ritual and divinatory purposes. Drinking was widespread at rituals and feasts in part because it was believed to put people in the proper state to commune with deities. However, because alcohol and hallucinogens were so powerful their use was highly regulated through restrictions and moral codes. Figure 2.1 and its corresponding text represent a belief in the power of pulque to transform a person. Drawn by a Nahua *tlacuilo* (painter, scribe), it shows a man scolding a person who turned himself into a rabbit by drinking too much. Rabbits were associated with bestial, dissolute behavior, including drunkenness.[11] If read literally, the image suggests radical physical metamorphosis from human to animal through the use of alcohol and hallucinogens. Concepts of nahualism and tonalism exemplify Mesoamerican beliefs in the complete transformation of the body.

Gender and the Body 23

Figure 2.1. Drunkard who transformed into a rabbit
SOURCE: Florentine Codex, bk. 6, fol. 209v. Florence: Biblioteca Medicea Laurenziana, Med. Palat. 219, c. 213v. By concession of the Ministry for Heritage and Cultural Activities; further reproduction by any means is forbidden.

Nahualism

Nahualism was a central aspect of transformation ideology in Mesoamerican thought. In its broadest sense, it was the belief that some men and women, or *nahuallis*, had the ability to shape-shift into animals or natural phenomena and transform other people and things as well. A nahualli was both the person who possessed supernatural abilities and his or her assumed form.

The etymology of the Nahuatl term sheds little light on this complex concept. Karttunen explains that *nahualli* is derived from *nahua*: "The basic sense appears to be 'audible, intelligible, clear,' from which different derivations extend to 'within earshot, near,' 'incantation' (hence many things to do with spells and sorcery), and 'language.'"[12] Andrews offers a somewhat different interpretation, tracing the origin of the term to *tlanahua*, which he translates as "to interpose something (between self and public, skin and outer clothing, man and gods, the natural and the supernatural, and so forth)."[13] According to Andrews and Hassig, *nahualli* has a broad range of meanings that go beyond the English sorcerer and magician.[14] Compounds based on the root *nahual-* appear in various forms in Molina's sixteenth-century Nahuatl-Spanish dictionary associated with hiding, disguising, and deceiving.[15] It is this sense that possesses the closest affinity to the concept of the nahualli.[16]

Sacred myths tell of indigenous deities, including the Nahua *teteoh* (pl., god or goddess) Quetzalcoatl, Huitzilopochtli, Tetzcatlipoca, and

Titlacahuan, that had the ability to transform themselves into human form so they could cause scandals and commit treachery.[17] According to one story, Titlacahuan changed himself into a Huaxtec man to seduce the daughter of the ruler of Tula.[18] He also took the form of a warrior, an old woman, or an old man.[19] Many of the deities combined male and female attributes, demonstrating their gender ambiguity.[20] They also tampered with the natural world. Quetzalcoatl, for example, turned cacao trees into mesquite trees, and Titlacahuan once made good food bitter.[21]

Who were nahuallis, and how did they acquire their supernatural powers? Men and women, nobles and commoners, could be nahuallis. Several colonial accounts attribute the nahualli's ability to assume an alternate form to his or her birth date. The Florentine Codex states that those born on the day One Rain would be nahuallis:

And also it was said that a noble who was born on this day became a nahualli, an astrologer. That is to say, she/he was not human. She/he hid her/himself in something, she/he turned her/himself into something. Perhaps she/he possessed a wild beast nahualli, and so forth. And if she/he were a commoner, likewise it was her/his lot to appear in the form of a turkey, or a weasel, or a dog, whatever was her/his alternate form; she/he became her/his nahualli.

No yoan mitoaia: in aquin ipan tlacatia pilli, naoalli mochioaia tlâciuhqui, quitoznequi: amo tlacatl, itla quimonaoaltiaia, itla ic mocuepaia, aço tequannaoale. Etc. auh intla maceoalli, no iuhqui itequiuh catca, aço totoli, aço coçamatl, anoço chichi, ipan moquixtiaia, in çaço tlein inecuepaliz, ynaoal mochioaia.[22]

Those born on the day of One Wind would also be nahuallis.[23] Clearly, a person born under the day signs of rain and wind, elements that transform the landscape, would be endowed with the power to metamorphose themselves and others.

Other central Mexican calendrical manuscripts attest to the nahualli's power being derived from his or her birth date. The Codex Telleriano-Remensis, a mid-sixteenth-century pictorial manuscript with Spanish glosses, states that those born on the day of One Death would be nahuallis who could transform themselves into various animals or cause it to appear that a person's body was breaking into pieces, "as if each arm and leg were detached."[24]

Death, like the elements that brought about changing weather patterns, effected a radical transformation of the body. The Florentine Codex identifies the ability to disassemble the body as a special trait of female nahuallis, suggesting that women could not only reproduce bodies but also take them apart.[25] Those born on One Wind worshipped Quetzalcoatl, and those born on One Death worshipped Tetzcatlipoca, both legendary nahuallis. Thus, both the deity and the day name influenced the behavior of those born under that sign. A hierarchy of animals corresponded to noble/commoner distinctions: nobles had powerful animals as their nahuallis, whereas commoners had dogs, turkeys, or weasels (see Figure 2.2).[26] Significantly, no difference was reported between the animal forms that women and men assumed.

In his treatise on native religion, Hernando Ruiz de Alarcón provided several accounts of nahuallis, although much of his information on the subject was in the form of hearsay from Spaniards, including priests, who apparently lent credence to this indigenous belief. Ruiz de Alarcón recounted how on one night two priests were in their cell when a bat entered through the window. The priests threw things at it to drive it away. The next day, an "old Indian woman" came to the convent and asked one of them why they had tried to kill her, explaining that she was the bat. The priest ordered her to wait while he went for his companion, but when he returned she had vanished without a trace.[27] In this account, Ruiz de Alarcón attested to the understanding that women, like men, could transform and to the continuing belief in colonial times that the body was an unstable entity.

Tonalism

Like nahualism, tonalism linked the human body with supernatural and earthly forces. The term *tonalli*, derived from *tona* (for the sun to shine, to be warm), is associated with the sun and day. It can also denote a day sign, a person's destiny associated with his or her birth date, or one of three animistic entities that a person possessed.[28] Tonalism, the belief in

Figure 2.2. Nahualli forms of a commoner
SOURCE: Florentine Codex, bk. 10, fol. 21v. Florence: Biblioteca Medicea Laurenziana, Med. Palat. 220, c. 23v. By concession of the Ministry for Heritage and Cultural Activities; further reproduction by any means is forbidden.

a "companion animal" with which a person shared the same fate and earthly sensations, was widespread throughout Mesoamerica. In this aspect, it was closely related to nahualism.[29]

Ruiz de Alarcón also used the term *nahualli* to describe a companion animal that lived a parallel and interrelated existence with a person. He wrote of one native woman who, while she was in the home of a Spaniard weaving with other women, suddenly fell over and cried out, "Simón Gómez has killed me!" When Simón Gómez was detained and questioned, he admitted that he had killed a cayman, which happened to be the woman's companion animal, near the river. The woman's family informed local officials that they wanted to press charges against him for her murder.[30] Whether or not the events they describe actually occurred, Ruiz de Alarcón's stories represent a narrative genre reflecting the belief that each person's physical well-being was linked to that of a specific animal so that if that animal were harmed or killed the person would suffer the same wounds or death. Mesoamerican beliefs attributed simultaneous existences to people that transcended a single, fixed physical state. Indigenous understandings of gender ambiguity and formation were based to some extent on this same idea of mutability.

The absence of a concept in Mesoamerican thought of an independent, stable body suggests that essential personalities and inherent qualities could not be attributed to the individual based on biological difference. How then, given the lack of essential identities, were personality traits determined?

SACRED CALENDARS, PERSONALITY, AND FATE

Mesoamericans attached great significance to their ancient calendars, which linked time to space, the natural world, and the sacred realm. Calendar readers specialized in assessing various symbols to determine whether a day would bring good fortune or bad, when a person should travel, when a couple should marry, when fields should be harvested, and so forth. The symbolic associations of each day sign, not essentializing identities based on attributes assigned to sexed bodies, shaped the fates and personalities of those who were born on a given day.

The parents of a newborn consulted a calendar reader, who named the infant and foretold his or her future. Because each day of the calendar represented the unique convergence of earthly and celestial forces, the birth date situated the newborn within a broad web of influences that determined his or her fate and characteristics. Consequently, Nahua parents sometimes postponed naming and bathing rituals until a lucky day in the cycle arrived so that the child would be assigned a favorable tonalli (day sign, fate).³¹ The Nahuas believed that those born on the days of Five House and Six Lizard would not prosper, so they waited to perform the bathing ritual on the favorable day of Seven Serpent.³² Fate, like the body or gender identity, was not fixed, but could be manipulated by cautious parents. Even those born on propitious days had to adhere to ritual prescriptions to maintain their good fortune. Calendar rituals thus not only predicted the fate of the child; they reinforced morality and emphasized ritual and social obligations.

A Nahua artist's depiction of the naming ritual in the sixth book of the Florentine Codex shows a calendar reader consulting a book of days and informing a woman of her infant's fate (Figure 2.3). A large sun looms between the reader and the woman, serving as a homonym for *tonalli* meaning sun, day, warmth, and fate. The image suggests that the mother played a leading role in the rituals involving her child at this early stage of life. The reader promised male and female infants who shared a birth date a similar destiny and personal traits; however, commentary on the fate associated with specific days frequently referred to the gendered duties that each child would perform. Examples of destinies associated with the calendar are presented in Table 2.1, which shows that those born on the day of One Rabbit were promised great success—men would become accomplished warriors, and women would prosper

Figure 2.3. Calendar reader naming a newborn and explaining his fate
SOURCE: Florentine Codex, bk. 6, fol. 168v. Florence: Biblioteca Medicea Laurenziana, Med. Palat. 219, c. 172v. By concession of the Ministry for Heritage and Cultural Activities; further reproduction by any means is forbidden.

TABLE 2.1. *Fates and personality traits associated with the calendar*

Day	Destiny	Remarks on class and gender
One Wind	Nahualli	Commoners born on this day also will perform rituals
One Rabbit	Rich, good workers	Men will be great warriors; women will prosper in the market; also men and women will be prone to drunkenness
One Serpent	Rich	Men will be wealthy and honored warriors or respected rulers; women will be "great providers, rich"
One Monkey	Rich, skilled artisans	
One Flint Knife	[Successful]	Men will be successful warriors; women will be "forceful, they will be capable in all things and will make their goods well"
One House	Unfortunate, lazy, prone to adultery	
One Eagle	Brave, shameless	
One Vulture	Elderly or die at young age	
One Deer	Fortunate	
One Ocelot	Unfortunate, prone to adultery	
One Reed	Unfortunate	
One Flower	[Skilled]	Men will be entertainers; women will be skilled embroiderers
Four Dog	Lucky at raising dogs	
Six Dog	Evil, gossiping, will dishonor elders, sickly	
Eight Death	Prone to adultery, thievery, gossiping	
Eight Rain	Prone to adultery	
Nine Flower	Prone to adultery	

SOURCE: Sahagún 1996, bk. 4.

in the market; those born on the day of One Serpent would likewise be favored and honored—men would be fortunate, wealthy, renowned warriors, or respected rulers, and women would be wealthy, able providers and skillful administrators who would "properly gather, hide away, save, and distribute to their children" (*vel quintlaçalhuiz, quintlapachilhuiz, quintetzontiz, quintlatlamachiz in ipilhoan*).[33] Similar futures were predicted for men and women born on the days of Ten Rabbit, Eleven Water, Twelve Dog, and Thirteen Monkey.[34] Because males and females who shared a birthday also exhibited similar character defects, those born on the days One House, One Ocelot, Eight Death, Eight Rain, and Nine Flower tended to be adulterers and those born on the day of One Rabbit were prone to drunkenness.

People were also associated with the animals of their day signs. According to the Florentine Codex, a person born on the day of Four Dog would have good luck raising dogs because "the dogs share his or her day sign with him or her" (*itonalecapooa in itzcuinti*).[35] In more general terms, the physical appearance and traits of the day sign animal extended to the people born on that day. The belief that those with the birthday of One Vulture would soon grow old was surely based on an association between the hunched bird and the slouched posture of the elderly.

The late sixteenth-century *Relaciones geográficas* contain many references to the importance of the sacred calendar in forecasting a person's destiny, corroborating evidence in the Florentine Codex. According to the *Relación* of Epazoyuca, *tonalpouhque* (calendar readers) used their "paintings" to determine the type of work a baby would perform, whether he or she would be rich or poor, and whether he or she would die unhappy.[36] The communities of Cuezala, Ichcateupan, Utatlan, and Tetela reported the tradition of a native priest bathing and naming the child.[37]

Córdova discussed the many uses of the Bènizàa calendar in his late sixteenth-century grammar. One use was the assignment of calendrical names to children. Córdova explained that the tonalpouhque used the numerical portion of the name when making predictions based on the calendar and when casting lots. For example, the calendar reader would add the numbers of the names of a potential bride and groom and then cast lots, using the sum to determine whether or not the couple would be compatible.[38]

The ritual uses of the calendar described by Córdova continued in Bènizàa and Ayuuk communities of the Villa Alta jurisdiction into the eighteenth century. In 1704, the *cacique* (male indigenous ruler) and *cabildo* (municipal council) officials of Lachirio confessed that the people of the community consulted their calendar readers when they wanted to name a baby and determine if he or she would be lucky or unfortunate, live in the community after marriage, and have children.[39] In the same year, Bènizàa men and women of Yatoni, Yatzona, and Taguí were among the people of the many yetze of the region who admitted to taking their babies to a native priest, who consulted a book of days to determine the child's name and predict his or her luck.[40] In the Ayuuk community of Yacochi, in 1704, a man named Jacinto Martín with the calendrical name of Macpao reported that his sons Luis Martín, Pedro Martín, and Jacinto Martín went by the names of Moxm, Meqca, and Tlaodhocpi, respectively, revealing the continued use of the ancient calendar in Ayuuk towns of the Sierra Alta.[41]

Less information on the calendar and its uses has come to light for the Mixteca Alta region, although, archival records reveal the continued use of calendrical names into the middle of the eighteenth century, even in the prominent towns of Teposcolula and Yanhuitlan, which had been the most influenced by contact with Spaniards. Among the many Mixtec individuals who appeared in colonial records were Pedro Coñoo (Three/One Monkey), Juan Nahoaco (Eight Flower), María Cunquaa (Two Deer), Melchor Xaquehuy (Seven Alligator), Pedro Naxa (Eight Eagle), and Diego Hernández Nachi (Eight Wind).[42] These names attest to the enduring significance of the Ñudzahui calendar and birth rituals.

Mesoamericans clearly recognized biological differences between males and females. However, the inherent instability of the body and gender ambiguity undermined the development of an essentialist gender system, and calendrical forces played a powerful role in determining characteristics and behavior. To create social order, a binary system was imposed in which gender was inscribed on the body through labor and ritual roles, dress and adornment, and coded behavior and speech.

GENDER MARKERS AND IDENTITY

Formal speeches, rituals, and native-language metaphors shed light on the cultural construction of gender in preconquest and colonial Mexico. The sources that most consciously present idealized male and female roles are the many sixteenth- and seventeenth-century Nahuatl-language speeches made at birth, coming-of-age, and marriage rituals that were compiled by Spanish friars to further their evangelization efforts. Equivalent speeches from Mixtec, Zapotec, and Mixe communities were apparently not collected or are no longer extant, but archival sources from central Mexico and Oaxaca frequently contain information about men and women's daily activities, labor, ritual roles, and behavior, as well as the expectations placed on them, that illuminate gender ideology throughout highland Mexico.

In Mesoamerica, gender was acquired during childhood through socialization, ritual, and the adoption of certain mannerisms and dress. Nahuatl terms for preadolescent children were gender neutral (most commonly *pilli*), and sex was first assigned in terms for young men (*telpochtli*) and for young women (*ichpochtli*). Similarly, in the Tíchazàa language children of both sexes were *pini*[43] and adolescents were *peniguijo* (masc.)[44] and *penicoconi* (fem.).[45] These designations reveal that indigenous peoples of highland Mexico understood gender as a process of formation throughout childhood and that it became fixed by mastery of

Gender and Labor

A gendered division of labor shaped the roles of men and women in central Mexico and Oaxaca in which different responsibilities constituted an essential component in gender identity. In the most basic and idealized arrangement, men practiced warfare and agriculture and women wove textiles and prepared food and beverages. (In reality, men and women shared many tasks and the division of labor was not entirely rigid, as discussed in Chapter 7). Men's and women's duties were conceived of as distinct yet complementary. Scholars have drawn on the Florentine Codex, especially the midwife's speeches in the sixth book, to explain the socialization of children into the gendered division of labor. Here I elaborate on these traditions by introducing additional information drawn from other sections of the Florentine Codex and from a broader range of sources.

Historical and mythical interpretations of the past justified and reaffirmed the division of labor among the Nahuas and made gender distinctions appear timeless and natural. In the third quarter of the sixteenth-century, Nahua writers traced the origins of the division of labor to their Chichimec ancestors:

If there is something to eat, they bake it, roast it, or perhaps stew it in a pot. The men do not do the work; only the women, because they take great care of their eyes, [they do not expose them to the smoke]. They say that it damages their eyes, for these Chichimeca see very far and very accurately, for when they shoot an arrow at something, not two or three times do they shoot it, only once. Even if it is very small, they do not miss it; even if it is very far away, they are able to pierce it with an arrow. They do not miss it, nor do they shoot at it many times.

auh in aço itla tlaqualli quixca, quitleoatza, anoço quipaoaci: amo iehoan quitequipanoa in oquichtin, can iehoan in cioa: ipampa cenca quimalhuia in imixtelolo, amo quititlani in poctli, quil quimixtlacoa, ca cenca veca tlachia inique, y, chichimeca: ioan cenca tlatlamelauhcaittani, ca in tlein quimina, amo oppa, expa, quitlaxilia çan cen: in manel cenca tepiton, amo quineoa, in manel noço veca ca, vel quimina, amo quineoa, amo no quezquipa in quintlaxilia.[46]

While it is unlikely that nomadic groups had such clearly defined gender roles, the Nahuas projected a complementary organization of tasks onto their ancestors in which women were responsible for cooking and men were responsible for hunting (and by extension warfare).

In preconquest and colonial times, midwives performed birth rituals that initiated an infant into a gendered role shaped by the cultural expectations and needs of the ethnic state. A female *ticitl* (healer, midwife) conducted the ceremony in the presence of community members who stood to benefit from the future protection and production of the next generation. The ethnic state had a vested interest in promoting a binary gender system since tribute production and organization depended on the joint contributions of married couples and tribute obligations corresponded to gendered labor.

According to Nahua writers who described the bathing ritual in the sixteenth century, the midwife informed the baby boy that his duty was to provide military support to the altepetl; she presented him with a bow, arrows, and a shield to signify his obligation to become a warrior.[47] This emphasis on warfare reflects the importance of military service for men, especially in preconquest central Mexico.[48] When the ticitl initiated the baby girl, she counseled her that her duties would be carried out in the household and that she would be responsible for preparing food and producing textiles:

Only inside the house was she to dwell, only inside the house was her home; it would not be necessary for her to go anywhere else. And that is to say that her duty was [preparing] drink and food. She was to prepare beverages, to make food, to grind maize, to spin, and to weave.

çan vel calitic, inemia, çan vel calitic ichan, amo monequi in campa iaz: ioan quitoznequi, vel itequiuh, in atl, in tlaqualli: achioaz, tlaqualchioaz, teciz, tzaoaz, hiquitiz.[49]

Significantly, the midwife used the noun *tequitl* (*motequiuh*, your duty; *itequiuh*, his or her duty) to highlight the duties that the newborn would assume in his or her adult life. Her speech indicates that indigenous peoples placed more emphasis on responsibilities than on rights. Thus, the baby girl's family prepared symbols of the socially determined labor of women for the ticitl to give to the child. As the Florentine Codex explains, "if a little girl were to be bathed, they prepared for her all of her women's gear: the spindle whorl; the weaving batten; the palm basket; the spinning bowl; the skeins; and the comb" (*auh intla cihoatzintli maltiz: quicencavilia in ixquich icioatlatqui, in malacatl, in tzotzopaztli, in tanatl, in tzaoalcaxitl, in quatzontli, ixiiotl*).[50] The midwife's words and the family's gifts emphasized specific labor assignments as the basis of masculine and feminine identities.

Descriptions of similar customs in the *Relaciones geográficas* corroborate evidence from the Florentine Codex and affirm that specific types of labor underlay the construction of gender throughout central Mexico. According to the *Relación* from Tetzcoco, at birth a shield, a *macana* (a club with obsidian blades), and a bow and arrows were presented to baby boys; a spindle and distaff and other tools for spinning and weaving were given to baby girls.[51] In Meztitlan, the Nahua ticitl led a procession of children when she took the infant to bathe it. If the child were male, six boys carried an axe or tumpline and a bow and arrow symbolizing the baby's future duties of farming, transporting goods, and providing military service. If the child were female, six girls carried weaving and spinning implements representing her future tasks of producing thread and cloth for the household and community.[52]

Images painted by native artists in the sixteenth century depict the assignment of gender-specific duties as a central aspect of the birth ritual. An illustration in the Florentine Codex shows a ticitl seated in the household patio with a child and his mother.[53] The foreground prominently displays symbols of masculinity—a shield, a bow and arrow, and a loincloth and cape—to indicate that the child is male (Figure 2.4). A less elaborate drawing of weaving and spinning implements and a *huipilli* (woman's shift) accompanying the text identifies appropriate ritual items to celebrate the birth of a female.[54] This simpler illustration serves as shorthand, pointing to where the section on women begins; at the same time, it underscores the symbolic potency of clothing and equipment to convey gender in pictorial writing (Figure 2.5).

Nahua painters of the Codex Mendoza also portrayed the ticitl instructing the newborn child in his or her gender role in their depiction of a birth ceremony. Figure 2.6 shows a midwife carrying a four-day-old baby (indicated by the four rosettes above the cradle) toward a basin of water that sits on a bed of reeds. Symbols of the trades and duties of men represent the potential future of the child. A shield and four arrows indicate the obligation to provide military service, and various symbols signify the work of a carpenter (an axe head and a piece of wood), a feather worker (a feather), a scribe (a writing instrument and the symbol of a painter), and a silversmith (a tube for blowing fire and silversmith insignia).[55] The accompanying text explains that the ticitl presents the symbol and tool of his father's trade to the baby boy. On the other side of the mat lie the symbols of women's labor: a broom, a basket, and a spinning whorl.[56]

At the time of the bathing ritual, the ticitl created a bond between the child and his or her respective place of work. Both the Florentine Codex and the Codex Mendoza describe the midwife burying the umbilical cord of a girl near the hearth or the grinding stone to signify that her duties were to be in the household. The umbilical cord of a male child was entrusted to a warrior, who buried it on the battlefield to bind the infant to his socially defined destiny. The *Relaciones geográficas* also provide

Figure 2.4. Midwife ritually bathing a baby boy with the symbols of masculinity lying beside the basin

SOURCE: Florentine Codex, bk. 6, fol. 170. Florence: Biblioteca Medicea Laurenziana, Med. Palat. 219, c. 174. By concession of the Ministry for Heritage and Cultural Activities; further reproduction by any means is forbidden.

accounts confirming the widespread Nahua practice of burying umbilical cords in places associated with the gendered division of labor. In their *Relación*, Tetzcocan informants report burying a boy's umbilical cord in the land of their enemies so that he would be dedicated to warfare, and burying a girl's cord near the hearth so that she would be dedicated to her household, "as they thought [women] were obligated."[57] The informants note that Nahua mothers train their daughters to weave cloth, produce thread, and prepare food near the hearth; however, they concede that some girls are more "inclined to play instruments, sing, and dance"—that is, to perform roles associated with temple life.[58] This suggests that the true purpose of the umbilical cord ritual was to reinforce socially

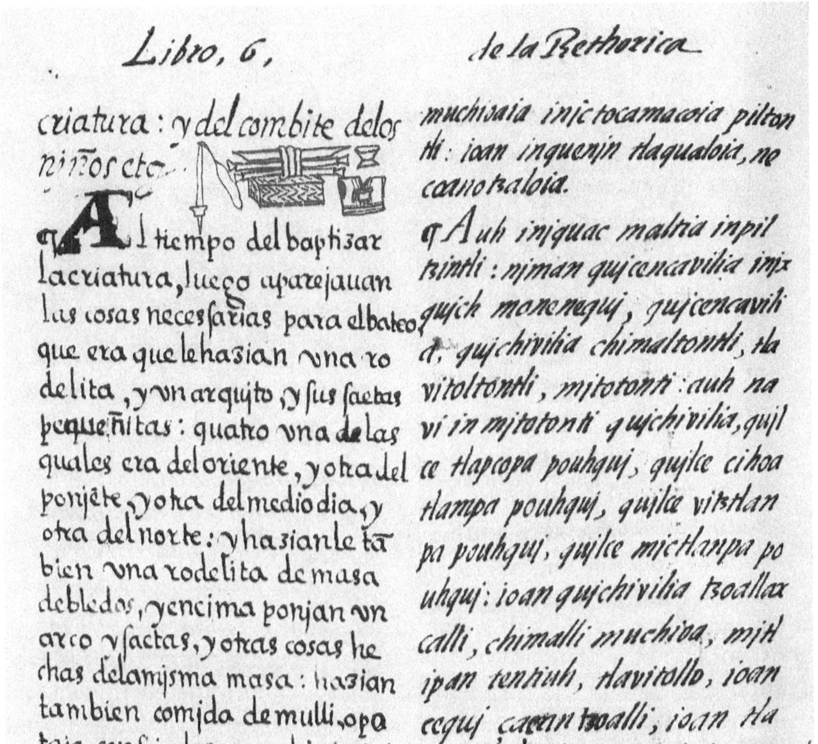

Libro, 6, de la Rethorica

criatura: y del combite delos niños etc.

Al tiempo del baptizar la criatura, luego aparejauan las cosas necessarias para el bateo que era que le hazian una rodelita, y un arquito, y sus saetas pequeñitas: quatro una de las quales era del oriente, y otra del poniente, y otra del mediodia, y otra del norte: y hazianle tã bien una rodelita de masa de bledos, y encima ponjan un arco y saetas, y otras cosas hechas de la mjsma masa: hazian tambien comjda de mulli, o potaje con frisoles, y mahis tostado y su masteleio y su mantica: y a los pobres no les hazian, mas del arco y las saetas, y su rodelilla algunos tamales, y mahis tostado. Y si era hembra la que se baptizaua aparejauanla todas las alhajas mugeriles, que eran aderezos para texer y para hilar como era uso, y rueca, y lançadera y su petaquilla, y vaso pa hilar etc. y tambien ju vipilejo y sus naoas, pequeñjtas. Y despues

¶ Auh iniquac maltia inpiltzintli: niman qujcencavilia injxqujch monenequj, qujcencavilia, qujchivilia chimaltontli, tlavitoltontli, mjtotontli: auh navi in mjtotontli qujchivilia, qujlce tlapcopa pouhquj, qujlce cihoatlampa pouhquj, qujlce vitztlampa pouhquj, qujlce mictlampa pouhquj: ioan qujchivilia tzoallaxcalli, chimalli muchioa, mjtl ipan tentiuh, tlavitollo, ioan eequj çacen tzoalli, ioan tlaqualli, molli, ioan eheio izqujtl, ioan iecavi imaxtlaton, itilmatoli: auh injcnotlaca, çan ixqujch intlavitolli, mjtotontli, ioan chimaltontli inqujchivilia, aço ioan tamalli, ioan izqujtzintli. Auh intlacihoatzintlimaltis: quj cenavilia injxqujch icacahat quj, in malacatl, in tzotzopaztli, in tanatli, in tzoaleaxitl, inquatzontli, ixijotl, ycuetonj, tivipil

muchioaia injc tocamacoia piltontli: ioan inquenin tlaqualoia, no caano tzaloia.

Figure 2.5. Symbols of femininity introducing text that describes the bathing ritual for a baby girl performed by a midwife

SOURCE: Florentine Codex, bk. 6, fol. 170v. Florence: Biblioteca Medicea Laurenziana, Med. Palat. 219, c. 174v. By concession of the Ministry for Heritage and Cultural Activities; further reproduction by any means is forbidden.

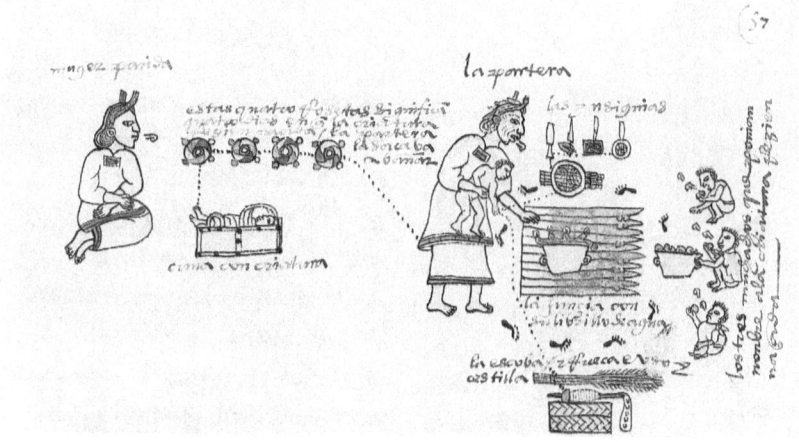

Figure 2.6. Midwife performing the bathing ceremony
SOURCE: Codex Mendoza, fol. 121. Bodleian Libraries, University of Oxford, Ms. Arch. Selden A1. Berdan and Anawalt 1992, 121. Reproduced with permission from University of California Press Books.

constructed gender roles in which tasks essential to the survival of the household and the community—military service, agriculture, textile production, and food preparation—were allocated appropriately to men and women. Nahuas recognized that it was necessary to symbolically bind individuals to their respective places of service because nothing inherently inclined them to those places.

Thus, the bathing ritual was a rite of initiation that called on both male and female children to carry out their gender-specific tasks for the good of their households and communities. However, its impact on adult observers should not be overlooked, for they were the comprehending audience. The ceremony served to remind them of their place in society, and it obligated Nahua parents to socialize their children to fulfill their prescribed gender roles.

Indigenous birth rituals persisted into the colonial period and captured the attention of Spanish chroniclers. In his *History of the Indians of New Spain,* fray Toribio de Motolinía described the bathing ceremony but interpreted its significance in a Christian light when recounting that the newborn boy received a shield and an arrow and the baby girl received a broom: "This ceremony seemed to be a sort of symbol of baptism and meant that the baptized were to fight against the enemies of the soul and to sweep and clean their souls and consciences so that, by baptism, Christ might enter."[59] It would seem that sympathetic Spaniards were forced to find Christian meaning in rituals dating to the preconquest era, just as

Mesoamericans sought to understand European beliefs and customs in a framework of indigenous concepts.

Material objects that marked gender and status distinctions retained their relevance in the afterlife. According to Nahua lore, those who died passed through the place of obsidian-bladed winds on their journey to the ninth underworld, known as Mictlan (Place of the Dead). Since they would need their earthly possessions and food for the journey, men were cremated with their shields, obsidian-bladed clubs, war trophies, and capes; women, with their baskets and weaving implements.[60] According to the *Relación geográfica* of the Chontal community of Coatepec, because the deceased would need their belongings in death, nobles' jewels and clothing were buried with them and slaves were sacrificed to serve their masters in the afterlife.[61] Equivalent practices were reported among the Cuitlatecas of Tetela and among the Ixcucas, Chontals, and Nahuas of Teloloapan, who buried their rulers with food, clothing, and slaves.[62]

Nahua legends of supernatural occurrences warned that deceased women who needed their *cihuatlatquitl* (women's gear) might return to earth to retrieve it. The Florentine Codex records the Nahua belief that women who died in childbirth went to live in the sky and each day carried the sun from the center of the sky to the west. When the sun set, the women returned to earth to demand their women's gear, which included "the spindle whorl, the weaving batten, and the palm basket" (*in malacatl, in tzotzopaztli, in tanatli*).[63] They sought out their husbands and demanded their "skirts, shifts, and all the women's gear" (*in cueitl in vipilli in ixquich cioatlatquitl*).[64]

Sixteenth-century Nahuatl terminology sheds light on the association of gender and labor. *Cihuatlatquitl* (women's gear) was a general term for weaving and cooking implements, and *oquichtlatquitl* (men's gear) was a term for agricultural tools.[65] In native ritual, cihuatlatquitl and oquichtlatquitl respectively represented women and men. During preconquest times, female and male slaves to be sacrificed for the celebrations of Izcalli were customarily paraded through the temple plaza carrying gender-specific equipment to represent their masculinity and femininity.[66] Furthermore, the terms *cihuatl* (woman) and *oquichtli* (man), used in compounds with other nouns, reinforced gender-specific duties in Nahuatl texts. In a speech in the Florentine Codex, noble parents inform their daughter that it will be her womanly duty (*mocioatequiuh*) to prepare food and beverages[67] They describe spinning and weaving as womanly duties (*cioatequitl*) as well.[68] In contrast, other parts of the Nahuatl text of the Florentine Codex equate warfare with masculinity. In one example, a warrior hangs the hair of a captured enemy in his house, and "with it he [calls] himself a man" (*ic moquichitoa*).[69]

The association between gender and labor was so strong that weaving and spinning implements, such as the spindle whorl, were synonymous with women and the female body. A Nahua riddle in the Florentine Codex asks, "What is that which becomes pregnant in just one day? The spindle whorl."[70] Another puzzles: "What are those things that at their dancing places they give stomachs, they make pregnant? They are spindle whorls."[71] Thus, the tools of women's labor represented womanhood and [re]production and weaving gear symbolized "woman" as a social category.

Because gender was mutable and not necessarily linked to a sexed body, certain types of labor served to reassign it. In an account of a Nahua mother and father apprenticing their son to a merchant, one parent worries: "What will I make of him? Is he a woman? Perhaps I should place the spindle whorl and the weaving batten in his hands" (*tle nicchioaz cuis cihoatl aço malacatl tzotzopaztli imac nictequiliz*).[72] This hypothetical question offers an example of Nahuatl rhetorical inversion in which the parents mean to emphasize that the boy is in fact masculine enough to become a long-distance merchant. Nevertheless, it underscores the dynamic nature of gender formation in young children and adolescents, and poses the possibility that gender could be manipulated to the extent that a son would become a woman by using spinning and weaving tools.[73]

Because warfare was a symbol of masculinity, women provided a metaphor for defeated warriors and enemies. Nahuas emasculated their enemies by labeling them women and likened the weapons of their enemies to tools used in women's work. Nahuatl-language incantations recorded by Ruiz de Alarcón during the early seventeenth century, which are undoubtedly of ancient origin, contain gender-based insults. In several examples, the speaker calls his enemies his "sisters" and disregards their weapons as those of women. An incantation to bolster courage and strength against bandits during travel exemplifies the Nahuatl rhetorical convention, with the speaker envisioning his potential attackers as his sisters who come bearing fluffed cotton and thread (*ini ichca tlahuitec ini icpateuh*).[74]

However, variations in gender symbols undermined rigid and absolute categories. For example, women's labor, and weaving in particular, could serve as a metaphor for hunting. In one incantation recited by a deer hunter as he sets the snare, the net is metaphorically referred to as the weavings of Cihuacoatl, a legendary female warrior.[75] In a related incantation collected by Ruiz de Alarcón, a deer hunter likens the net to a woman's huipilli and ribbons.[76] Similarly, the ticitl employed warfare imagery in her speech, likening the mother to a brave jaguar warrior carrying a captive in her womb. As she delivered the baby, the midwife was said to let out great war cries, symbolizing that the mother had performed valiantly in battle.[77]

Mesoamerican coming-of-age ceremonies reaffirmed gender roles first articulated by midwives in the birth ritual and reinforced the sacred nature of the division of labor. When Nahua mothers and fathers of the highest nobility counseled their adolescent children on proper behavior and responsibilities, they described the ideal traits of both young men and women, including modesty, moderation, and self-discipline. However, they emphasized a strict division of labor that was at the core of their gender identity. Noble parents admonished their daughters to learn the arts of cooking, preparing beverages, weaving, and spinning, and they advised their sons to dedicate themselves to political service, warfare, craft production, and agriculture.[78]

Like Nahua rituals of central Mexico, Bènizàa ceremonies in the Sierra Alta region of Oaxaca reveal complementary principles and a gendered division of labor. During idolatry investigations conducted between 1704 and 1705 in the Villa Alta jurisdiction, native officials provided extensive information on the survival of indigenous beliefs and rituals and the uneven incorporation of Christian concepts and practices.[79] Their statements reveal a cosmography shaped by gender duality and reciprocity, with a gendered division of labor ritually reinforced and sanctified.

Gender Roles in Bènizàa Rituals

Villa Alta idolatry investigations provide accounts of ceremonies that were usually held twice a year to ensure good health, abundant crops, sufficient rain, and protection from ferocious animals. Additional offerings would be made during times of epidemics or drought or when land disputes arose with neighboring communities. Witnesses distinguished between rituals organized by the community for the benefit of all and those sponsored by individuals to address their own concerns. This analysis focuses mainly on community ceremonies in order to shed light on the gendered organization of Bènizàa ritual and to show how gender complementarity influenced Christian practice in some communities.[80] A ceremony in Betaza illustrates a highly symbolic ritual life among Bènizàa people.[81]

To prepare themselves for participation in community ceremonies, the men and women of Betaza fasted, abstained from sex, and bathed for thirteen days. During this time, they also confessed to native priests or *maestros* (teachers), as religious specialists are called in the Spanish-language documents. Cabildo officials collected money from the people to purchase turkeys, feathers, incense, and other items needed for the ritual. Men and women gathered at a sacred site to watch male priests and their young assistants sacrifice turkeys or dogs; occasionally, the priests performed heart sacrifice on a deer. The blood from the beheaded animals was splattered on native bark paper, feathers, and small tortillas made by the priests' wives. Participants also sprinkled tobacco on bark paper from the small gourds they carried. The ritual leaders incensed the offerings with copal as they dedicated the sacrifice. Then they gave each person a tortilla, first tearing off a piece for the deity. Following the ritual, the men and women feasted on the sacrificial animals and tortillas and drank pulque. Later they adorned their hair with brightly colored feathers and sang and danced to the *teponaztli* (log drum). Interestingly, the teponaztli player wore a feather in his hat that was normally placed on the image of Our Lady of the Rosary in the church.

The ritual described by the Zapotec *principales* (prominent people) of Betaza reinforced fundamental social divisions based on age, status, and gender. Organized by local officials for good health and a successful harvest, it established the cabildo members and other nobles as intermediaries between the sacred and earthly realms. The continued well-being of the community depended on the leadership capabilities of these officials and nobles and on the cooperation of commoners who participated in and contributed to the rituals. Men and women performed ritual roles that corresponded to and reinforced the Mesoamerican gendered division of labor; their cooperative effort allowed the community to feed its deities and its people during the ritual act and subsequent feast. The fact that the spouses who led the ceremonies worked as teams underscores the importance of the married couple as the basic social unit in Mesoamerican society.

Age distinctions influenced ritual roles and served to promote intergenerational cooperation and solidarity—for example, the native priests' assistants were young boys who had learned the traditions of their ancestors as apprentices. Such distinctions stand out in records from other Bènizàa rituals, which specify that the elders would be the first to eat, drink, or take tobacco. In some communities, elders were also assigned to carry the sacrificial blood to other sacred sites in the area. In these ways, the ritual symbolized and reenacted complementary relations between nobles and commoners, men and women, and young and old that were vital for the community's health and prosperity.

Elsewhere in the Villa Alta jurisdiction, a somewhat different pattern of gender complementarity emerges in the organization of rituals. As in

Betaza, cabildo officials in Roayaga organized community sacrifices at least twice a year, collecting money from community members to purchase newborn dogs, turkeys, incense, wax, feathers from Chiapas, and stones called *guiag cachi* (precious stones).[82] The men gathered at a sacred site to watch the maestro and his assistants behead the animals. They offered blood, feathers, and incense to a stone image and prayed for good health, abundant crops, and rain. In the meantime, the women and children gathered in the church to burn candles. Afterwards, everyone reconvened to feast, drink, and dance.

The organization of ritual in Roayaga, in which women performed Christian acts of worship while men sacrificed animals at a sacred site, reveals the pairing of complementary principles—male/female, center/periphery, Bènizàa/Christian—so common in Mesoamerica. The fact that men performed the more traditional ceremonies and women conducted the Christian rites provides an interesting counterpoint to the conventional view of native women as more culturally conservative than men. In this example, women appear to be cultural negotiators between the Bènizàa and Christian worlds. The Roayaga case also suggests that the church became gendered as female space, which contradicts the prevailing view of the church as a male enclave. Perhaps the gendering of space corresponded to a distinction between sacred space within and outside the community center. Whereas men frequently ventured out to work in the fields, women's daily activities primarily placed them in and around the community center, where their households, the market, and the church were located. These daily activities may have influenced perceptions of gendered sacred space.

Idolatry records from the Sierra Alta document women's participation in Zapotec ceremonial life, but their roles as ritual specialists are more difficult to reconstruct because all defendants and witnesses were male and investigations focused on male ritual practitioners. Even when women were named as ritual specialists or as those who ingested *cuana betao* (sacred herb, *Turbina corymbosa*) or other hallucinogens in order to prognosticate, they were not usually arrested or questioned. For example, a Spanish priest reported having heard that in Latani a woman named Catarina de Aquino was being trained as a *maestra*. However, when ecclesiastical officials went to Latani to investigate, they did not question Aquino or even ask about her. Moreover, because all of the defendants were male, the records provide little specific information about women's equivalent practices or about life-cycle rituals and healing ceremonies that we associate with female spiritual leadership. References to women's activities in the church at Roayaga are terse compared with the detailed descriptions of men's ceremonies at the community's sacred sites.

Despite these limitations, the idolatry records of the Sierra Alta reveal glimpses of a worldview in which women and men fulfilled complementary roles in the performance of rituals that linked them to their ancestors and their deities and that ensured the future of their communities.

Dress and Gender Identity

The performance of gender was enhanced by specific clothing and adornment. In the bathing ceremony, when the Nahua ticitl presented tools symbolizing the gendered tasks of newborn children, she also gave a baby boy a loincloth and a cloak and gave a baby girl a skirt and a huipilli (see Figures 2.4, 2.5, and 2.6).[83] As a potent symbol of gender identity, clothing represented men and women in ritual contexts. In preconquest times, several days before the ritual in which Nahuas honored the god Yacatecutli, merchants placed offerings before the god's image: capes and loincloths were hung on staffs representing the number of male slaves to be sacrificed; huipiles and skirts were hung to represent the number of female slaves.[84] Thus, the garments stood in for the body.

Sixteenth-century texts continued to employ gender-specific clothing as a metaphor for male and female bodies. Nahuatl-language sources refer to women by the doublet *in cueitl, in huipilli* (the skirt, the shift). A sixteenth-century description of native marriage customs explains that a boy's mother and father would arrange his marriage when he reached sexual maturity so that he would not become involved in a scandal. The parents feared that unless their son had a wife, "he may have sex with a woman [skirt, shift]; he may commit adultery" (*ma cana cueitl, vipilli tepan ca, ma cana tepan ia*).[85] In his Nahuatl-language translation of a European witchcraft treatise, *Tratado de hechicerías y sortilegios*, published in 1553, fray Andrés de Olmos adopts this convention. Admonishing his flock to avoid committing sins of the flesh, he urges: "Do not thoughtlessly pursue, do not thoughtlessly desire a woman [the skirt, the shift], do not with this enter the servitude of the Devil" (*ma ylihuiz tictoca, ma ylihuiz tiquelehui yn cueytl, uipilli ma yc ytlan ticalac yn Diablo*).[86] In one passage, Olmos pairs metaphors based on women's clothing (*in cueitl, in huipilli*) and weaving equipment (*in malacatl, in tzotzopaztli*) to represent the female body, warning the Nahua neophytes: "And also he [the Devil] greatly deceives those who covet and greatly desire a woman [the skirt, the shift], who pursue a woman [the spindle whorl, the weaving batten] in sin" (*No yoan cenca quimiztlacauia yn teyxeleuiya ye cenca queleuia yn cueytl uipilli yn cenca quitoca yn malacatl yn tçotçopaztli tlatlacoltica*).[87] Similar conventions were used to describe the male body. When a father advised his son to avoid excessive sex, he drew an analogy between sexual vitality and a cloak customarily worn by indigenous men:

"The cloak wetted, washed, and tightly wrung, dries out quickly; you will be just the same after you have given yourself repeatedly to earthly pleasures" (*in tilmatli paltic, in tlapactli, in cenca motequipatzca, in motetepatzca: ca hiciuhca oaqui: no tiuhqui, in otoconmotetequimacac tlalticpacaiotl*).[88] In formal speeches, at least, Nahuas seem to have avoided making explicit references to the body and instead used metaphors of clothing and gear in referring to sexual intercourse.[89]

Evidence from the Villa Alta jurisdiction attests to the persistence of clothing as a signifier of gender identity in the eighteenth-century. Tensions escalated between the Bènizàa communities of Betaza and Yalálag when Spanish ecclesiastics entered the region in 1704 to extirpate idolatries. After Yalálag relinquished its deities and provided information on continuing indigenous sacred practices elsewhere, resentment ran high. On one occasion, don Pedro de Paz, a noble of Betaza, fought with a *regidor* (councilman, a member of a municipal council) of Yalálag, casting aspersions on the masculinity of Yalálag's nobles for having surrendered their deities to the Spaniards when they should have "fought for them to their last drop of blood." Don Pedro quipped that the men of Yalálag did not deserve to wear pants and sarcastically suggested that it would be more appropriate for them to put on their wives' skirts. His insult made a direct association between dress, masculinity, and local leadership, which was the purview of males in the region at this time.[90]

In addition to clothing, hairstyles and other bodily adornment distinguished women from men and indicated status. Throughout highland Mexico, unmarried young girls wore their hair long and loose while married women wore theirs braided and often wrapped with yarn on the head in a variety of styles. Nahua women also dyed their hair with a special black mud or indigo. Indigenous women wore body paint in preconquest and early colonial times, making designs on their hands, neck, and torso that, depending on the ritual occasion, might associate them with specific goddesses. Noblewomen used yellow ochre or bitumen to paint their faces, cochineal to color their teeth, and a mixture of burnt copal incense and dye to stain their feet.[91] The extent to which commoner women colored their hair, painted their faces, or stained their teeth remains unclear. Elite women, like their male counterparts, sometimes wore elaborate headdresses, particularly when they performed ritual roles.

Unlike clothing, which clearly signified rank as well as gender, jewelry was often gender neutral and conveyed elite status. Both men and women wore earrings, bracelets, nose ornaments, labrets, and necklaces made of gold, silver, shell, bone, turquoise, crystal, amber, and other stones. Such adornments represented nobility in Nahuatl-language texts. The sons of noblemen were thus "the greenstones, the bracelets, the precious items" (*in chalchiuhtin, in maquiztin, in tlaçoti*).⁹²

Like the Nahuas, Ñudzahui elites developed elaborate dress traditions to convey social rank. The highest rulers, both male and female, had their septums pierced so that they could wear nose ornaments of silver, gold, or stone. They possessed a vast array of elite costumes that signified their power and prestige. Preconquest-style codices show noblemen and noblewomen wearing feathered headdresses, pectorals, ear spools, and arm and leg bands, and carrying ritual regalia.⁹³ For example, a scene in the Codex Nuttall shows named nobles approaching temples to make offerings (Figure 2.7). The women wear the traditional wraparound skirt and rounded *quechquemitl* (woman's garment similar to a poncho) as well as costume elements that display their royal status such as nose ornaments, animal or feathered headdresses, headbands, ear spools, wrist cuffs, and pectorals. They carry incense burners, sit on jaguar thrones, and gesture toward others as if speaking, further revealing their elite status and ritual roles. The men are also dressed in fine garments. Like the women, they

Figure 2.7. Ñudzahui noblemen and noblewomen making offerings at a temple
SOURCE: Codex Nuttall, fol. 42, facsimile edition. Vienna: Akademische Druckund Verlagsanstalt; Madrid: Sociedad Estatal Quinto Centenario; Mexico City: Fondo de Cultura Económico, 1992.

sport feathered headdresses, ear spools, and pectorals. They also wear gender-specific clothing, including loincloths, sandals, and calf bands, and carry shields, arrows, and staffs.

The great attention to detail in descriptions and depictions of nobles' garments reveals the importance of clothing as a symbol of social status. But dress conveyed a message that was far more complex than simple conspicuous consumption. Quetzal feathers, shells, precious stones, and so forth, were acquired through vast long-distance trade, tribute, or gift-exchange networks with nobles in distant places. Thus, many of the luxury materials used in elite clothing attested to a noble's wealth (to purchase prestige goods), power (to demand tribute), and status (to acquire goods through political and social alliances). The materials were precious and rare, like the nobles themselves.

Gendered Speech and Behavior

Unlike European romance languages, indigenous languages were not gendered. Nahuatl, Ñudzahui, and Tíchazàa did not assign gender to nouns, distinguish between male and female pronouns, or require gender agreement.[94] However, speech conventions that signified and emphasized gender identity did develop in many Mesoamerican languages. Kinship terminology in Nahuatl, Ñudzahui, and Tíchazàa reflected the age and gender of the point of reference (ego) in relation to the person being referred to or addressed. For example, parallel terminology existed that distinguished male from female ego. Nahua women used specific terms, such as *conetl* (child) and *pihtli* (older sister), which identified the point of reference as female. Fray Antonio de los Reyes listed separate Ñudzahui terms for the brothers and sisters of men and women in his *Vocabulario*.[95] Similarly, in his Tíchazàa dictionary, fray Juan de Córdova provided distinct words for relatives used by men and women.[96]

Morphology also marked men and women's speech. For example, Nahuas inflected the vocative differently. In his seventeenth-century grammar of the Nahuatl language, Horacio Carochi explained that the masculine vocative was formed by reducing the absolutive ending of a noun and adding *-e*. Women used the standard possessed or unpossessed noun form minus the normal subject prefix.[97] Carochi also noted the female custom of inserting *-tica* between the noun stem and the reverential ending of certain kin terms to emphasize affection when addressing both males and females. For example, women would say *nopiticatzin* (my older sister) instead of the standard *nopitzin*, and *nahuiticatzin* (my aunt) rather than *nahuitzin*.[98] Moreover, men and women used different forms in speaking of gender groups. According to Carochi, when a man spoke about another man he would say *ce toquichtin* (one of us men), using the plural subject prefix and the noun. Women, however, would say *ce cihuatl* (a woman) rather than *ce ticihua* (one of us women) when speaking among themselves.[99]

Reyes, in his grammar of the Ñudzahui language published in 1593, discussed the numerous ways that men and women's speech differed. Like the Nahuas, Ñudzahui men and women employed different forms of the vocative: the vocative suffix used by women was *-ya*; that used by men was *-y*.[100] Reyes also described certain female forms of address to children; women employed these same forms to express disdain and anger when speaking to their husbands or other adults.[101] Furthermore, men and women used different particles when referring to a third person of the opposite sex.[102] In this way, Ñudzahui speech conventions, like those of Nahuatl and Tíchazàa, reinforced and rearticulated gender identity.

Gendered mannerisms and behaviors are more difficult to uncover in the historical record. However, pictorials catalogue men and women throughout Mesoamerica sitting differently according to local custom. Among the Nahuas, an adult woman sat with her legs together and tucked to the side with her hands folded in her lap; men sat on little seats, stools, or reed mat thrones with their knees folded up under their capes. In the Mixteca Alta, women customarily sat on their haunches or on stools; men sat on stools only. Women from the coastal region are depicted in codices sitting cross-legged. These coded ways of carrying the body further signified conformity to a particular gender identity.

Belief in the instability of the body and the mutability of gender shaped the understanding that cross-gendering was possible in Mesoamerica. Through the performance of labor, dress and adornment, and specific styles of speech, individuals could alter their gender identities.

Cross-Gendering

The relationship between gender and biological sex was not always obvious in the cultures of highland Mexico. The sexed body itself was a social construction. Presumably, the midwife assigned socially constructed gender roles to babies at birth based on genital difference, but Mesoamerican understandings of physiological distinctions may have been very different from those of Europeans. In his survey of the biological basis of gender difference, Monaghan finds that many contemporary Mesoamerican groups made little distinction between male and female genitalia.[103] He argues that the principal biological difference that Mixtec women and men observed was a woman's ability to become pregnant. Furthermore, the ticitl's criteria for assessing children who were sexually ambiguous are not known. The tradition of cross-gendering of both ambiguously and unambiguously sexed individuals found among indigenous groups throughout the Americas suggests flexibility between the sexed body and gender identity. As Klein concludes: "Pre-Hispanic Nahuas viewed gender as both complex and mutable and did not expect it to necessarily conform to a person's physiology and sex."[104] Through particular performances, in either ritual or everyday settings, gender could be redefined.

Although there is limited evidence on cross-gendering among the sedentary groups of highland Mexico in the colonial period, terminology and descriptions of social types in the Florentine Codex shed some light on the subject. In the discussion of a person categorized as a *xochihua* (literally, possessor of flowers) Nahua authors seem to identify a cross-gendered person. Both the brief description and the single depiction of xochihua in the Florentine Codex suggest that men or women could change their gender by adopting the opposite gender's clothing, hairstyle, speech patterns, and behavior. Highlighting the importance of speech as a gender marker, the text begins: "The xochihua has feminine speech, has a feminine way of talking, [and if a woman] has masculine speech, has a masculine way of talking" (*in suchioa cioatlatole, cioanotzale, oquichtlatole oquichnotzale*).[105] The accompanying illustration uses dress, hairstyles, and pose to signify gender, showing two seated individuals, one dressed as a man and

Figure 2.8. Xochihuaque, or cross-dressed man and woman
SOURCE: Florentine Codex, bk. 10, fol. 25v. Florence: Biblioteca Medicea Laurenziana, Med. Palat. 220, c. 27v. By concession of the Ministry for Heritage and Cultural Activities; further reproduction by any means is forbidden.

the other dressed as a woman, with speech scrolls emerging from their mouths (see Figure 2.8). The "woman" wears a traditional hairstyle, and the "man's" hair is cropped with bangs in the European fashion of the time. The "woman" is seated with her legs folded back behind her in the custom befitting a proper Nahua matron. The flower (*xochitl*) between the two is a phonetic indicator that the man and woman are *xochihuaque* (possessors of flowers).[106] The image and the text suggest that gender has trumped biology, that the person dressed and speaking as a man is a biologically sexed female and the person dressed and speaking as a woman is a biologically sexed male.

The Codex Tudela provides additional evidence that clothing and labor were central to cross-gendering. The anonymous author of the text accompanying the images in this early colonial manuscript remarks in Spanish: "In Mexico there were men dressed in the clothing of women; they were sodomites and did the tasks of women, which is weaving and spinning."[107] Although the relationship between cross-gendering and homosexuality may not have been as clear as the author assumes, the passage highlights the role of clothing and labor in the construction of gender identity.

One of the limitations of colonial sources is that they do not illuminate how cross-dressers were perceived, particularly outside of ritual contexts, so our understanding of alternative gender remains limited. Part of the problem begins with the term *xochihua*, which is used only in the Florentine Codex where it refers to a person who seduces people, including a procurer (see Chapters 5 and 6). This raises the question of whether xochihua was a type of "third sex" or had a more general meaning, such as a seducer of people. It seems to me that Nahua men who dressed, spoke, and worked as women were considered women and that women who dressed, spoke, and worked as men were considered men.

Not unlike nahuallis, cross-gendered individuals escaped the confines of the body to present themselves as what contemporary Westerners would consider "the opposite sex." Significantly, Nahuatl-language descriptions of the nahualli and the xochihua use similar terminology, linking the two concepts. According to the Florentine Codex, the nahualli was a xochihua, conveying the idea that both types confused people and made them lose their bearings with the use of the verbs *teyolmalacachoa* (spin around people's hearts) to describe the nahualli and *teixmalacachoa* (spin around people's eyes, faces) to characterize the xochihua.[108] Similarly, the Florentine Codex explains that the cross-dresser and the nahualli deceive people and cause them to change their minds, using the related terms *teyolcuepa* (turn people's hearts) and *teixcuepa* (turn people's faces, eyes).[109]

CONCLUDING REMARKS

Mesoamericans possessed an understanding of the body and its relationship to the natural world very different from modern, Western understandings. Concepts of nahualism, tonalism, and gender mutability shared a common assumption that the body was unstable and capable of transformation through ritual, celestial phenomena, consumption of hallucinogens and alcohol, and performance of particular roles. Mesoamericans did not assign essential attributes to males and females, but rather believed that personality traits and fate were tied to the sacred calendar and the birth date. Masculinity and femininity were not inherently connected to a sexed body, but were acquired during childhood through the development of labor skills, the adoption of dress and adornment, and the mastery of speech and gestures.

Cross-gendering highlights the way that clothing, labor, and speech conventions—rather than the body—provided the basis of gender identity. Duality and the pairing of opposites were organizing principles in Mesoamerican cultures. The binary gender system attempted to impose order on a world in which the body was vulnerable to natural and supernatural phenomena and in which sexual ambiguity might complicate gender identity. On the one hand, this system seems rather rigid; on the other hand, cross-gendering provided a degree of flexibility that allowed some individuals to negotiate their gender identities. The performance of gender, rather than the body alone, determined a person's sex. For all intents and purposes, a man who performed the tasks and behaviors of women became a woman and vice versa.

CHAPTER THREE

Marriage Encounters

In the autumn of 1538, fray Juan de Zumárraga, the Bishop of Mexico City and an apostolic inquisitor, summoned Francisco, a Nahua noble of Coyoacan, to appear before him after learning that Francisco had committed bigamy by marrying twice in the church.[1] In their testimonies, Francisco and his two wives told the same story. Francisco had married his first wife, Ana, around 1531. After the death of their only child in about 1534, he informed Ana that he had married another woman, named María, and told Ana that she was free to look for a new husband. When he appeared before the Bishop, Francisco admitted that although he had heard the friars preach many times it was a grave sin to remarry while one's first spouse was still living, he did so anyway.

Determined to make an example of the wayward noble, the apostolic inquisitor demanded that half of Francisco's belongings be confiscated and that he pay for the cost of the proceedings. Zumárraga also ordered that Francisco be led through the city on a mule by a town crier, who would announce his crime as they made their way to the marketplace. There Francisco was to suffer the penalty of one hundred lashes on his bare back. The Bishop demanded that Francisco return to his first wife Ana, despite the fact that he and María had a daughter together and another child on the way. Although Francisco had married in the church, he rejected the Christian premise that marriage created a lifelong union. Francisco's trial and humiliating punishment highlight conflicts between Mesoamericans and Spaniards over marriage concepts, the indigenous population's reinterpretation of Christian ritual, and the power of the church to impose its will, however sporadic and limited it was in the early colonial period.

This chapter considers the encounter between traditional indigenous practices and Christian marriage in colonial highland Mexico. The first section examines differing nuptial concepts and ceremonies of indigenous groups and Spaniards, and considers ecclesiastics' attempts to promote indissoluble, monogamous Christian marriage as a cornerstone of their broader evangelization project. The second section reconstructs indigenous weddings and traces the development of local indigenous-Christian ceremonies. The study of marriage reveals how colonial discourse and policy altered the intimate relations of native men and women.

MARRIAGE PRACTICES

Mesoamericans developed a variety of institutions to formalize marriage and sexual relationships. The friars expressed grave concerns over practices that violated Christian morality and the sacrament of holy matrimony. From the first decades of the colonial period onward, they debated the status of indigenous relationships and methods for imposing marriage in the church.

Serial Monogamy

Mesoamerican men and women practiced serial monogamy, a system in which divorce and remarriage were permitted when a husband and wife faced irreconcilable differences. In his grammar of 1578, fray Juan de Córdova lists several grounds for divorce among the Bènizàa people (Zapotecs), which might apply to other Mesoamerican groups as well, including the inability to have children; laziness and failure to perform duties, especially on the part of the wife; adultery, especially by the wife; unequal status; incompatibility of calendrical names; belligerence leading to constant arguing; and sexual abuse of a wife.[2]

Evidence in mundane records from highland Mexico corroborates Córdova's observation that Nahuas, Ñudzahuis (Mixtecs), and Ayuuks (Mixes) shared similar attitudes. Although the Catholic Church permitted divorce on rare occasions, it was nothing more than a separation, granted on either a temporary or a permanent basis.[3] Once separated a husband or wife were not allowed to remarry until the death of the first spouse. Some friars used this fundamental difference toward lifelong union to argue that native societies had not had true marriage before the arrival of Christianity.[4]

Polygyny

In addition to serial monogamy, a small number of indigenous nobles and commoners practiced polygyny in preconquest and early colonial Mexico.[5] As an institution that formalized political and economic arrangements, polygyny consolidated a complex network of relations and resources, with multiple wives ensuring that a man's goods, houses, and lands would be protected and maintained in his absence.[6] According to Motolinía, it had financial benefits for the husband, who profited from the labor of his wives.[7] Moreover, historians of sexuality have suggested that polygyny allowed "warrior societies" to reconstitute their populations despite elevated male mortality rates.[8] Although Mesoamerican ethnic groups were not warrior societies, they were frequently at war on the eve of the Spanish conquest and nobles played a prominent role in this highly ritualized warfare. More important, numerous wives produced multiple heirs, thereby increasing the likelihood of the survival and prosperity of the lineage.

Respondents to the *Relaciones geográficas* expressed their concern with reproduction, attributing dramatic population decline to the abandonment of polygyny. "The reason that there were more people in other times is because each Indian had the women that he wanted and they gave birth to many [children]," explained the people of Xuxupango. "Now that they have no more than one, and they live with reason, justice, and matrimony, they don't give birth to many [children]."[9] Informants from nearby Chila and Matlactlan drew a similar conclusion: "Because each Indian had the women that they wanted without anyone impeding them, they had many children and multiplied."[10] While the image of unregulated sexual relationships is certainly an exaggeration, it sheds light on how indigenous men, at least, may have viewed Christian marriage as an unwanted, destructive introduction.

The religious argued that monogamous Christian marriage was essential for regulating sexual relations. In his Nahuatl-language sermons, fray Juan de la Anunciación preached that marriage allowed individuals to live in a "sacred way," and fray Bernardino de Sahagún asserted that marriage was necessary to avoid "liv[ing] wickedly."[11] Fray Alonso de Molina advised the Nahua couple who came to church seeking the sacrament that those who married for the love of God would be redeemed.[12] In New Spain as in Europe, the church promoted the marriage of Saint Joseph and the Virgin Mary as the model of an ideal union.[13]

Canon law dictated a series of impediments that established the terms of acceptable unions and sexual relations.[14] The most serious of these, *dirimente* impediments, provided grounds for denying marriage or for invalidating an existing union, regardless of whether the marriage had been consummated or the couple had produced children. Prior marriage (when the spouse was still living); previous public engagement; being underaged (younger than fourteen for boys and twelve for girls); being a pagan or having joined the clergy (which was not an option for indigenous men);

and consanguineal, affinal, or ritual kinship were among the *impedimentos dirimentes*.

The friars envisioned a system in which native church officials would assist in the enforcement of canon law. This was a practical solution to the shortage of ecclesiastics, especially those trained in indigenous languages, which was a problem that persisted throughout the colonial period. Fray Toribio Motolinía described the role of local aides as early as the 1530s, reporting that in every community friars trained native assistants, called *licenciados* (licentiates) because of their expertise in impediments and canon law regarding marriage. The licenciados investigated kinship and other matters that might provide grounds for denying a couple the sacrament.[15] In addition, they sorted out the relationships between a man and his multiple wives in difficult cases of polygyny and made recommendations to the friars on how best to resolve the matter.[16] Although Motolinía's claim that licenciados were functioning throughout the region by this early date was overly optimistic, his commentary reflects the Franciscans' ambitious plans to work through local nobles and officials to promote Christianity and the celebration of the sacraments.

Molina's *Confesionario mayor en la lengua mexicana y castellana*, a Nahuatl-Spanish confessional manual published in 1569, illustrates the church's attempts to impose Christian marriage, as stipulated by canon law, on the Nahuas of central Mexico.[17] It contains instructions on preparing a Nahua couple for Christian marriage and a brief description and illustration of the wedding ceremony. Molina directed the text to both the Spanish priest and native church officials, like those described by Motolinía, who would interview the betrothed and their witnesses. If the bride and/or groom were not from the altepetl, the notary was to notify the priest in the candidate's home community so that he could investigate whether impediments existed and announce the banns, making the couple's intention to marry public. Thus, the *Confesionario* includes instructions and model dialogues between the priest, local officials, the couple, and their witnesses. An early seventeenth-century indigenous-language document concerning a marriage dispensation that was issued to two Ñudzahui nobles confirms the prominent role played by the native *fiscal* (church steward) as Motolinía and Molina envisioned. The fiscal interviewed the witnesses to the marriage, announced the banns on three consecutive Sundays, and mediated between the nobles and the Spanish priest.

Molina opened the section on marriage in his *Confesionario mayor* with a warning that an impediment would invalidate a union. Seeking to discover impedimentos dirimentes, the fiscal and notary asked the bride and groom their ages, status, whether they had been baptized, and whether they had exchanged the marriage promise with anyone else.[18] Investigation of status prevented the possibility that a person might marry based on false information about his or her spouse; such a discovery would invalidate the required consent and annul the marriage.[19] The couple was also asked if their union was consensual, since, as a sacrament, marriage could only be entered into freely and voluntarily.

The new requirements of the church that dictated acceptable marriage partners and patterns led to tensions between ecclesiastics and their indigenous parishioners, especially in the first few generations after the conquest, when native responses to Christianity were characterized by an uneasy mixture of acceptance, ambivalence, misunderstanding, and hostility.

Conflicts over Marriage Practices

The ability to divorce and remarry, according to Mesoamerican custom, was a central point of contention between indigenous peoples and Spaniards. In the eyes of the church, such behavior constituted polygyny or bigamy, and many indigenous couples found themselves facing these charges in the first few decades after the conquest. This was the dilemma of Francisco, the Nahua noble who was punished for marrying twice in the church.[20] Francisco openly acknowledged the church's prohibition against divorce and remarriage, yet ultimately acted according to indigenous custom.

A trial over the brutal murder of Juana Xochitl in 1558 reveals the clash between Christian definitions of marriage and indigenous practices.[21] Martín Tilantzin, a Nahua of Acatepec, responded to the fundamental difference between local traditions and Christian doctrine when he appealed to indigenous cabildo and church officials to dissolve his marriage, arguing that he had never wanted to marry his wife, Juana Xochitl, in the church because he wanted the freedom to leave her if their relationship soured, as permitted by native custom. The altepetl authorities were not persuaded by his reasoning and upheld the marriage. Denying him permission to leave his wife, a fiscal told him: "Look, Martín Tilantzin . . . she is your woman and it has been a long time since you took her and in our law you married until one of you dies. It is not possible for you to separate from each other." Significantly, the indigenous official referred to canon law as "our law," reflecting differing levels of understanding and acceptance of Christian doctrine regarding marriage in native communities. Tragically, Martín Tilantzin resorted to killing his wife to end their lifelong union so that he could marry his lover.[22]

In areas of extensive evangelization, divorce and remarriage were denied, but this did not preclude simple abandonment, which continued to provide escape from an undesired marriage. It is difficult to assess precisely how common or permanent abandonment was in highland Mexico, since such cases were only occasionally documented in archival records.[23] When abandonment did occur, an unhappy spouse would return to his or her parents' household or move to another community. However, those who left home without the spouse's consent risked harsh punishment at the hands of native and Spanish magistrates.

For example, when a Ñudzahui man complained in 1615 that his wife had abandoned him, the Spanish *alcalde mayor* ordered her to return to her husband and suffer the penalty of twenty lashes.[24] Indigenous witnesses often cited marital problems, abuse of authority, and excessive demands for tribute and labor as reasons for desertion of home and family.[25] Economic problems may have been the last straw in difficult marriages. Members of opposing political factions in communities also frequently complained that people fled their towns because their rivals were incompetent and unjust administrators. Although such charges may exaggerate the problem, it is clear that colonial pressures, including the increasing demands of local Spaniards, the crown, and the church for labor and tribute, posed significant challenges to many households.

Sometimes, those who separated formed new partnerships, living together outside of wedlock and often having children together. Martín Tilantzin and Juana Xochitl did just that. According to Nahua witnesses, they had not lived as husband and wife for at least three years, during which he resided in another pueblo where he had relationships with two other women. Apparently, Juana had moved on, too, since she was in the later stages of pregnancy at the time of her murder.[26]

Spanish and indigenous sources on marriage practices in preconquest times often highlighted the different conceptions of Christian and native marriage by underscoring the indigenous option of terminating a commitment. The *Relación geográfica* of the Nahua altepetl of Meztitlan reported that "either side undid these marriages at will, when they wanted, or when they became angry or exasperated with each other."[27] In emphasizing the ability to divorce, however, respondents of Meztitlan's questionnaire seem to overstate the ease with which unhappy couples parted. To contest a marriage was to challenge the authority and wisdom of one's parents, community elders, local diviners, and native authorities who had arranged and sanctioned it.[28] The Spanish jurist Alonso de Zorita commented on the gravity of the situation based on his observations of the indigenous judicial system in the sixteenth century:

When a divorce case was heard—which was rare—the [native] judges attempted to reconcile the parties. They harshly scolded the guilty party, and they asked the pair to recall the good will with which they had entered into marriage; they urged them not to bring shame on their parents and relatives who promoted the marriage; the judges also reminded them that people would point the finger of blame at them, for it would be known that they had been married. Many other things the judges said in order to reconcile them.[29]

Zorita may have misrepresented the extent to which pre-Hispanic marriage traditions resembled Spanish practices. However, criminal records corroborate his observation. When couples complained to indigenous officials, they were often counseled to forgive each other and to learn to live in peace.[30] The permanence of Christian marriage undoubtedly contributed to the magistrates' tendency in colonial times to attempt to resolve marital conflicts and to encourage feuding couples to stay together.

Because of their understanding that indigenous unions could be terminated, ecclesiastics emphasized the permanence of marriage in their sermons and speeches. In his Tíchazàa doctrina of 1567, fray Pedro de Feria stated that God had ordered that "marriage is to be entirely solid, as stone is solid, as wood is solid, and never, ever is it to be undone" (*caca nalibitete quelahuechagañaa, cica tilibi quie cica tilibi yaga, chela yaca zochij, yaca zabiquela quibilla*).[31] In a speech to a wedding party in his early seventeenth-century Nahuatl-language religious manual, fray Bartolomé de Alva began with this very point: "Here is what you are to understand. You are taking each other for always and cannot abandon one another tomorrow or the next day even if you have a change of heart" (*auh ca nican ca in anquicaqui, ca ye içenimayan, in ammana, ca ámo moztla, huiptla anmocahuazque, in manel anmoyolcuepazque*).[32] His emphatic statement no doubt reflected the friars' continuing frustrations over their inability to convince indigenous people to accept this fundamental aspect of Christian marriage, even a century after the introduction of Christianity.

Polygyny violated the church's doctrine on marriage. Ecclesiastics viewed it as a moral weakness, a grave insult to God, and a rejection of Christianity. They complained that polygyny was a significant impediment to the conversion of the nobility, neglecting to mention the practice among commoners.[33] For example, fray Diego Durán described polygyny as a noble's privilege, along with wearing cotton clothing and sandals, using tobacco, eating special foods, drinking pulque, and participating in rituals and dances.[34] In their writings, friars berated intransigent caciques who would not abandon their multiple wives. In 1537, Motolinía went so far as to frame the problem as a status-based sexual struggle, suggesting that humble men could not find eligible women to marry because native rulers "stole" women, some living with as many as two hundred wives.[35] The term *stole* in this exaggerated assessment characterized polygyny as not only immoral but criminal. Charges of polygyny condemned the authority of indigenous leaders and, when cast in terms of social rank, allied the friars with the commoner majority. This position served to justify their intrusion in local politics and custom.

The violation of the prohibition of marriage between people related by consanguinity, affinity, or spiritual kinship is another major theme in church texts and marital investigations. Molina's confessional manual placed more emphasis on this concern than on any other. According to his model, the native fiscal and the Spanish priest were to ask the betrothed and their witnesses five separate times whether the bride and groom were related. The priest would warn them that lying warranted strong punishment, including excommunication. The banns were read on three consecutive Sundays and holy days of obligation. The attention devoted to kinship as an impediment may have resulted from the ability of closely related kin to marry in indigenous society, which the friars observed in the first decades after the conquest, especially among the nobility. The importance placed on this theme in the confessional manuals explains the friars' frustration with those who married while knowingly violating impediments; these cases revealed deception by the couple and collusion between family and community members who did not make the impediment known. As with many other aspects of Christianity, native neophytes selectively accepted marriage doctrine.

In the early seventeenth century, Alva revealed the friars' persistent preoccupation with the marriage of blood and ritual kin in his speech to a couple seeking the sacrament. He asked, "Are you relations, [either] through the church [or] through blood? Because," he warned, "[in such a case] the marriage will count for nothing" (*aço quen anmonotza, in aço Teoyotica, tlapalotica, yeyca ca acan ompohuiz, in nenamictiliztli anquichihuazque*).[36] Like Molina, Alva chastised the witnesses, threatening them with severe consequences, including eternal damnation, if they failed to reveal an impediment.

Do you know of something, which is in detriment of, and an impediment to, the marriage? Then speak up, because if you do not you will incur God's disdain. What do you come to say here: are you just drunk? It is not true? Or do you just lie? For it is your nature that you always are accustomed to doing so. Do not let the devil confuse you with something, for you will go to hell if the marriage is thus impeded, and all that which will afflict those who are getting married will become your burden of responsibility. Open well your eyes!

aço itla anquimmachillia inic ytlacahui, inic tzotzoni in nenamictiliztli niman xiqualyto çan, yeyca intlacamo ca ipan anhuetzizque in itlatelchihualtzin Dios aço çan oamechtlahuantique inic nican tlen anquitotihuitze? Acaço nelli? Aço çan amiztlacati, ca ye amoyeliz inic mochipa yuhqui anquichihuani, ma ytla ic amechtlapololti, in tlacatecolotl, ca mictlan anyazque intla ytla ic tlatlacahuiz in nenamictiliztli amomamal mochihua in ixquich motolinizque in monamictia huel xitlapocan in amixtelolo.[37]

Alva's patronizing tone reveals a tension between Nahuas and Spaniards over fundamental marriage concepts and illustrates the friars' willingness to use sarcasm, insults, threats, and coercion to force indigenous parishioners to adhere to canon law. A Ñudzahui fiscal issued a similar warning to witnesses to the marriage of two nobles: "If you lie, the owl-person, the devil, will take your souls to hell, and in hell your souls will burn, suffer, and be tormented."[38] While not quite as condescending as Alva's, this admonishment shows how the hypothetical dialogues of the doctrinas shaped local discourse on marriage.[39]

A case involving María and Tomás, a member of the ruling family of Tecoaloya, illustrates the church's intrusion into the married lives of indigenous couples when friars identified an impediment. In 1548, fray Juan de Estella denounced Tomás for polygyny. When called to testify, the couple explained that María had been married to Tomás's first cousin before the Spanish conquest. When the cousin died, she and Tomás celebrated indigenous nuptials. After the conquest, the friars of Toluca ordered them to separate, refusing to recognize their ten-year marriage because according to canon law their affinity automatically annulled it. The friars first baptized them and then married Tomás to a woman named Magdalena. When Magdalena fell victim to one of the epidemics that ravaged the native population, Tomás reunited with María and insisted that she was his only wife.[40] This case reveals the hypocrisy of the imposition of Christian marriage. Tomás and María's renewed relationship clearly indicated that he had not entered freely into the sacrament of marriage with Magdalena, as required by canon law. Thus, to avoid violating the impediment against marriage among affines, the friars instead dismissed the principle of free will when they forced Tomás to marry Magdalena. The reunion of Tomás and María shows that they continued to regard one another as husband and wife and that they maintained the validity of their indigenous marriage despite the friars' orders.[41]

The friars' willingness to make exceptions for some nobles but not for others contributed to the persistence of marriage among blood and spiritual kin.[42] When in 1622 the church issued a marriage dispensation that allowed two Ñudzahui second cousins to wed, other nobles must have assumed that in certain circumstances such marriage was acceptable. Indeed, disruptions to noble lines due to epidemics, warfare, and other colonial hardships created a crisis in succession and might explain why two closely related nobles, or *toho*, were allowed to marry.

In the first few decades after the conquest, friars used carefully choreographed public punishments to demonstrate the church's power to enforce Christian marriage. Through the mid-sixteenth century, ecclesiastical judges issued harsh penalties, including public shaming, whippings, and fines for the crime of polygyny. As he became increasingly frustrated with the friars' inability to end polygynous marriage, Bishop Zumárraga proposed an audacious plan to the Council of the Indies in 1536 "to build houses ... where young girls are cared for who escape the wicked clutches of the caciques and it is necessary that Your Majesty give authority to take daughters five years and older from their homes." He feared that "the only other remedy is to hang most of the indigenous leaders."[43] The reader will recall that in 1538 Francisco, the noble of Coyoacan, was publicly humiliated, given a hundred lashes, fined, and ordered to return to his first wife when he was found guilty of polygyny.[44] A year later, Martín Xochimitl, led through the market by a town crier who announced his crime, was lashed for having sexual relations with four sisters (see Figure 3.1).[45] Apostolic inquisitors intimidated men by threatening to burn them at the stake if they continued to live with their "concubines," and in some cases they followed through with their threats.[46]

The Franciscans' use of exemplary punishments and their willingness to break up indigenous families must be understood within the larger context of campaigns to extirpate idolatry and break the will of incorrigible nobles who threatened to undermine the Christian mission.[47] The struggle over marriage and sexuality was part of a "spiritual conquest," in which friars used violence, threats, and coercion to bring an end to traditional beliefs and practices that challenged Christianity. In 1539, in one of the most notorious inquisitorial investigations in New Spain, don Carlos, a high lord in Tetzcoco, was tried for crimes against the faith.[48] Francisco, a young noble who had been working with the friars in Chicanautla to evangelize the local population, appeared before Zumárraga, bishop and apostolic inquisitor; speaking through interpreters fray Antonio de Ciudad Rodrigo, fray Alonso de Molina, and fray Bernardino de Sahagún, he reported that don Carlos had challenged the teachings of the friars and had advocated a return to the ways of his ancestors. A full investigation ensued. Two of the main allegations were that don Carlos had continued to engage in idolatry after a number of images were discovered

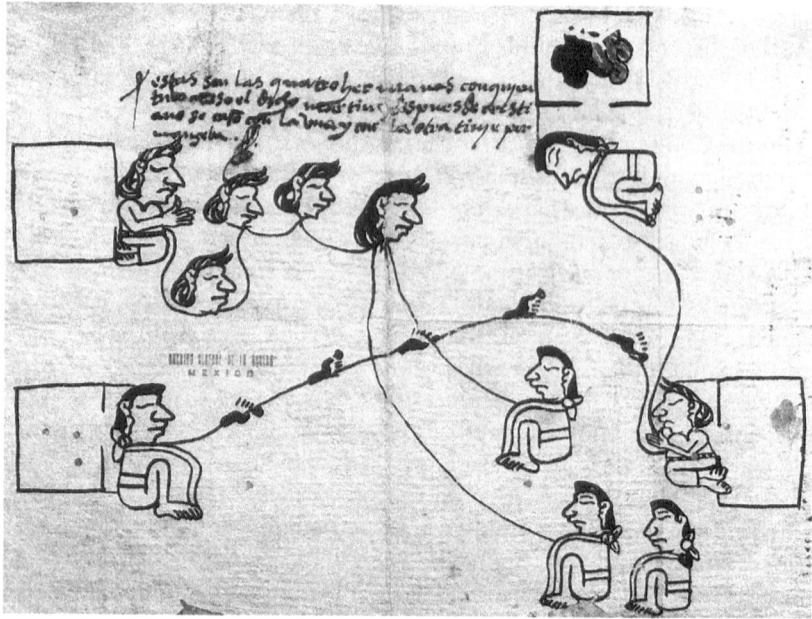

Figure 3.1. Image submitted to the Holy Office of the Inquisition showing Martín Xochimitl being tried for polygyny with the four sisters who were his "wives"
SOURCE: Archivo General de la Nación, Mexico, Inquisición, vol. 36, fol. 314.

in his home, and that he had committed concubinage and incest after being married in the church.

The investigation turned up little concrete evidence of don Carlos's idolatries. However, multiple witnesses recalled that he had denounced the church's teachings on morality and monogamy. Doña María, don Carlos' sister, testified that he had told her that if her husband wanted other women as his concubines, she should tolerate them and not question her husband because that was how their grandfathers and grandmothers had lived. Another witness corroborated doña María's testimony, adding that don Carlos pointed to the Spaniards' double standards of morality: "Let's see, brother. What does a woman do to a man, or what sin is it to have her, what sin is it to drink? Is it that the Christians don't have a lot of women, and they don't get drunk? And it is only us whom they try to stop so that we don't have women and we don't get drunk, but not the Christians."[49]

Perhaps worst of all in the eyes of his judges, don Carlos practiced what he preached. He defied the church's definition of appropriate sexual relations by continuing to keep his niece, doña Inés, as his concubine even after he had married another woman in the church, and he repeatedly tried to have sex with his deceased brother's widow. Because don Carlos had alienated the local nobility, including his own family members, his lawyers were not able to muster an adequate defense and he was found guilty and burned at the stake. This inhumane punishment is striking considering the lack of evidence of idolatry brought against him. In the end, don Carlos was executed because he refused to accept Christian monogamy and because he challenged the authority of the friars.

Despite intimidation and harsh punishment, many polygynists openly defied priests' warnings and threats even after don Carlos' execution. A 1540 case concerning don Juan, the cacique of Iguala, reveals that accusations of polygyny were often intertwined with charges of other crimes against the faith.[50] Don Juan allegedly offered food and copal to deities in his home and practiced ancestor worship by offering food, cacao, pulque, and flowers to a statue of his deceased sister. He practiced other ancient rituals, arranging, for example, ceremonies that included *voladores* (pole flyers). He even required the boys who flew on the pole to draw blood from their ears and tongues. He disregarded the Christian faith by refusing to have his son baptized, ordering the nobles to eat meat on Ash Wednesday, and by blessing the commoners himself. Although he had been married in the church, he was charged with making a mockery of Holy Matrimony and Christian teachings on sexuality by forcing sex on several women, including two of his wife's sisters and a young girl. According to his accusers, he went so far as to rape two of the women in the church and continued to live openly with his many women.

In a similar case in the same year, an exasperated fray Andrés de Olmos complained that for six years he had tried in vain to convince don Juan, the cacique of Matlactlan, to abandon idolatry and polygyny.[51] Despite the numerous warnings and persistent prodding from local friars, don Juan continued to live with his multiple wives. The fact that fray Andrés himself had married don Juan in the church spurred his anger over the cacique's disrespect. Like don Juan of Iguala, the ruler of Matlactlan challenged the friars' authority over matters of the spirit and the flesh even as the friars threatened harsh punishment and burning at the stake.

Others simply concealed the truth from the friars who married them in the church. Martín Xochimitl confessed that he had failed to inform the friar about his affiliation with his bride's three sisters because he knew these relationships were sinful in the eyes of the church.[52] Doña Inés, the concubine of don Carlos of Tetzcoco, admitted that she had heard the friars say many times that it was forbidden to have sex with a relative but had done so anyway and "offended God."[53] These statements reveal a strategy of participating selectively in rituals of the new faith while interpreting sexual morality within a traditional indigenous framework.

The ecclesiastics' attack on polygyny not only caused conflicts between Spaniards and indigenous peoples but also created tensions between men and women. Little direct evidence of women's opinions on the subject survives; however, the aforementioned trials of don Juan of Iguala and of don Carlos of Tetzcoco provide glimpses of noblewomen's reactions to polygynous relationships. Doña Ana, don Juan's wife and a noblewoman in her own right, denounced her husband before the apostolic inquisitor in 1540.[54] She accused him of committing idolatry and of forcing sexual relations with his sister, her sister, her aunt, and other women in the community. Whether or not doña Ana's accusations were true, it is clear that she used Christian doctrine, even specifically citing the church's prohibition against sex between siblings, to escape her marriage to the cacique. In a key part of her statement, she complained that her husband treated her like a "dog," ignoring her and cloistering himself with his concubines. The term *dog* carried sexual and social connotations and is synonymous with the pejorative sense of *commoner* in this context. Thus doña Ana stressed that her husband failed to recognize her elevated status.

It would seem, at least from this one case, that a legitimate wife might tolerate her husband's concubines as long as he treated her with respect and dignity. His failure to do so, however, could lead to serious resentment and hostility, which in this case culminated with doña Ana's accusations. Similarly, when doña María, the sister of don Carlos, a lord of Tetzcoco, testified before the Inquisition, she criticized don Carlos for treating his wife as a "slave" because he was dedicated to his concubine, doña Inés. She recalled that she and don Carlos once had a heated exchange because he had chastised her for rejecting polygyny and thereby abandoning the ways of their ancestors. She objected to polygyny as she denounced her brother to the ecclesiastical officials, as did several other women who also testified in the case.[55] These trials illustrate the way that women sometimes found a powerful ally in the church.[56] After indigenous people were exempted from the Inquisition's jurisdiction in 1571, native officials, Spanish royal magistrates, or specially commissioned ecclesiastical judges pursued the investigation of sexual matters in the community.

The question of how to advocate Christian marriage among polygynists generated considerable debate. Whereas the Franciscans and Dominicans tried to force nobles to accept monogamy, the Augustinians simply refused to baptize men and women in polygynous marriages, baptism being a requirement for participating in the other sacraments.[57] Ultimately, the friars were forced to compromise. Polygynists would be baptized only if they agreed to live with one wife in a monogamous relationship.[58] In fact, early colonial censuses and archival records show that rulers, nobles, and commoners who had been baptized and married in the church continued to live with their multiple wives, indicating that the friars were not entirely successful in convincing their parishioners to adopt monogamy.[59] Most nobles eventually abandoned polygynous marriage, but it was a gradual process fraught with conflict. One way that the friars spread Christian marriage was by promoting participation in church ceremonies as a privilege.

MARRIAGE CEREMONIES

Writing in the mid-sixteenth century, fray Diego Durán revealed conflicts with his indigenous parishioners over marriage concepts and practices when he complained: "After I married some young men and young women, with all the solemnity and ceremonies that the sacrament demands, after leaving the church, they went to a house of some elder men and elder women and they married them again, with the ancient ceremonies and rites."[60] Differing nuptial rituals reflected the values of New Spain's multiethnic society. The language, gestures, and behavior of participants and the use of multivalent symbols articulate social and sacred ideologies. The ritual process reflects and reinforces a society's conceptualization of ideal social and sacred relations and marks life-cycle events for all. In New Spain, where language barriers often hindered communication between friars and the indigenous population, ritual acts took on added significance. All of the Nahua nuptials that Durán witnessed in the mid-sixteenth century began with the arrangement of the marriage.

Arranging a Marriage

In preconquest and colonial times, as in many native communities today, marriage was arranged by the parents of the bride and groom or another household member.[61] Both men and women participated in marriage negotiations and, according to some colonial accounts, elders played a role as well. For example, according to the *Relación* of Ichcateopan, a Chontal and Nahua community, those who wished to marry "went to the elders who were in charge of this and they told them that they were looking for a woman, that they wanted to marry."[62] Similarly, a man hoping to marry in the Tlapanec community of Ayutla consulted with two elders in order to find a woman of his status.[63] Marriage negotiations considered various issues, such as when the marriage would take place, the type and quantity of gifts to be exchanged between the bride and groom's households, and where the newlyweds would live.[64] The inability to resolve the location of the newlyweds' residence could be devastating for a young couple; cases in which the bride repeatedly returned to her parents' home were not unusual.[65]

Most men and women married young, probably between the ages of ten and fifteen and, on average, around twelve.[66] According to Nahua accounts, the groom's parents arranged his marriage when he became sexually active.[67] Archival documents suggest that there was usually little age difference between the bride and groom. In contrast, Spanish men, especially nobles, tended to marry much later than women, often marrying women who were significantly younger.[68]

Most people in highland Mesoamerica practiced class endogamy.[69] Córdova underscored the importance of status in the choice of marriage partners when he reported that Bènizàa couples sometimes divorced when it was learned that either the husband or the wife had misrepresented his or her status to achieve social mobility. Pretension to noble descent presented more of a problem for elites, who tended to marry exogamously, because a pretender from a distant community could manipulate his or her status.[70] While nobles sought to marry within their class in order to strengthen their lineages and to build alliances through marriage, polygyny and concubinage provided opportunities for unions across status divisions.[71]

In preconquest and colonial times, before proposing marriage, a young man and his family consulted a ritual specialist who determined through various means whether or not the couple should marry and when the marriage should take place. For example, Nahua calendar readers advised parents to perform the nuptials on a day deemed favorable for marriage: *acatl* (reed), *oçomatli* (monkey), *cipactli* (alligator/crocodile), *quauhtli* (eagle), and *calli* (house).[72]

Preconquest and colonial pictorial manuscripts, such as the Codex Borgia, the Codex Laud, and the Codex Vaticanus B (writings considered the product of altepetl in the eastern Nahua area), contain sections used for marriage prognostication that present a variety of scenarios and potential outcomes.[73] Each illustration is numbered from two to twenty-six by a series of dots. The prognosticator added the numbers of the bride and groom's calendrical names (the addition of two names with numbers between one and thirteen totaled a number between two and twenty-six) to determine the scene that applied to them.[74] Common features in the marriage prognostication scenes include male and female couples (their positions and gestures are highly significant); sky symbols representing the sun, the moon, or an eclipse[75]; children and other representations of fertility and lineage (trees, birds); numbers from two to twenty-six;

animals or parts of animals; clothing, hairstyle, headdresses, jewelry, and body paint; accoutrements of the gods; and objects, mainly vessels and bloodletting instruments. These constituted a rich visual vocabulary of morality that served as mnemonic devices for the prognosticator, who interpreted this iconography in terms of the mythical structures and metaphors that shaped formal, moral discourse.

While a complete analysis of each scene in the three manuscripts is outside of the scope of the present study, it is worth noting that several scenes address issues that frequently arose in wedding speeches and discourses on marriage in colonial texts and archival records. Scenes portraying violence, gossip, and bickering illustrate some of the destructive aspects of marriage, while others symbolizing harmony, prosperity, and fertility signify a successful marriage. In interpreting the scenes, the marriage prognosticator expounded on a variety of challenges that a young couple might face. Thus the scenes represent moral narratives.

As an example of marriage prognostication conveying moral lessons, let us briefly consider scenes from the three manuscripts that show couples whose marriages would be plagued by violence. Figures 3.2, 3.3, and 3.4, from the Borgia, Laud, and Vaticanus B codices, respectively, portray a husband (fatally) wounding his wife. Figure 3.2, from the Codex Borgia, corresponds to the fate of the couple whose names totaled six, depicting the man attacking his wife with an axe. The man's appearance associates him with the god of dance, Huehuecoyotl, suggesting that moralizing tales about the deities were invoked in the marriage prognosticator's didactic speeches.[76] Huehuecoyotl was associated with, among other things, the destructive aspects of excessive sex.[77] The wife's appearance and posture symbolize discord; her hair is disheveled (a Nahua pictorial convention for representing disorder and uncivilized behavior), and she has turned her back to her husband, signifying conflict. The deer head (a metaphor for dissolute behavior) on her skull reveals her disloyalty and sexual excess. The symbol of the moon, which occupies the center of the illustration, indicates a bad omen. Figure 3.3, from the Codex Laud, shows a man spearing his wife in an illustration that corresponds to the couple whose names add up to twenty-three. Other symbols in the illustration reinforce the notion of separation and conflict: the footprints, a Mesoamerican glyph representing travel, suggest that they will part, while the crossbones above them foreshadow death. Similarly, the Codex Vaticanus B (Figure 3.4) predicts a dreadful future for couples whose names total twenty-three. The man attacks his wife with an obsidian-bladed club; as in the equivalent scene from the Codex Laud, death is foretold by the skull and bone. Furthermore, the woman wears spools of cotton thread in her hair, evoking the costume of the goddess of sexuality,

Figure 3.2. Marriage prognostication warning of violence
SOURCE: Codex Borgia, fol. 59. Facsimile edition. Vienna: Akademische Druckund Verlagsanstalt; Madrid: Sociedad Estatal Quinto Centenario; Mexico City: Fondo de Cultura Económico, 1993.

Tlazolteotl, who like Huehuecoyotl was associated with excessive sexuality. The multivalent symbols in these scenes suggest that the diviner's narrative addressed the relationship between illicit sexual relations and violence in marriage.

Evidence from Oaxaca shows that Mixtec, Zapotec, and Mixe people also consulted a prognosticator, who determined whether or not a marriage would be successful and when the ceremony should take place. According to the *Relaciones geográficas* of Justlahuaca, Mixtepec, Ayusuchiquilazala, Xalapa, and Zacatepec, the parents of a betrothed noble Ñudzahui couple presented cloth, jewels, and feathers to native priests, who communicated with their deities to determine whether the couple

Figure 3.3. Marriage prognostication warning of violence
SOURCE: Codex Laud, fol. 37, facsimile edition. Vienna: Akademische Druckund Verlagsanstalt; Madrid: Sociedad Estatal Quinto Centenario; Mexico City: Fondo de Cultura Económico, 1994.

should marry and whether they would have children to succeed them in the rulership.[78] Bènizàa priests cast lots and may have used calendars or paintings of marriage scenes similar to those in the Codex Borgia, Codex Laud, and Codex Vaticanus B.[79] Córdova's *Arte del idioma zapoteco* explains how the prognosticator added up the numbers of the couple's calendrical names to predict whether they would have children and the sex of the offspring.[80] The *Relación* of the Bènizàa yetze of Tecuicuilco confirms Córdova's account.[81] Records from an investigation of idolatries in the Zapotec Sierra in 1704 attest to the persistence of such traditional practices. The people of Teotlasco, Latani, Xuquila, Yatoni, Yalálag, Betaza, and Yacochi, among others, confessed that they performed sacrifices and consulted a calendar reader for the best time to celebrate a marriage and bring the bride to the groom's home.[82] Traditional forms of sacred knowledge continued to influence the daily lives of Bènizàa and Ayuuk

Figure 3.4. Marriage prognostication warning of violence
SOURCE: Codex Vaticanus B, fol. 34, facsimile edition. Vienna: Akademische Druckund Verlagsanstalt; Madrid: Sociedad Estatal Quinto Centenario; Mexico City: Fondo de Cultura Económico, 1993.

men and women of the region after nearly two centuries of contact with Christianity.

Once the young man and his family had received a favorable prediction, they initiated negotiations with the bride's family. High-ranking Nahua nobles employed marriage negotiators, or *cihuatlanque* (sing. *cihuatlanqui*; literally "one who asks for a woman") to make arrangements with a potential bride's family.[83] A Spanish section of the Florentine Codex clearly identifies these "honored old women" who spoke with the young woman's parents.[84] Furthermore, in a different description of the marriage arrangements in the Florentine Codex, the Nahuatl couplet *in ilamatque, in cihuatlanque* pairs "the old women, the bride negotiators," and the accompanying illustration depicts the negotiators as women (see Figure 3.5).[85] They are larger in size than the young man, indicating their high status and older age, and the speech scrolls and hand gestures reveal their authority in the negotiations.

Molina's Nahuatl dictionary includes the term *huehueyo* for a marriage negotiator (*casamentero*), a construction apparently based on the noun *huehueh* (old man, elder) with a possessive prefix and abstract derivational suffix (*-yotl*), which suggests that men might also specialize in arranging marriages.[86] Ñudzahui and Tíchazàa terms for marriage negotiators in sixteenth-century dictionaries attest to this office in Oaxaca as well, but they do not indicate whether it was held by men or women.[87] A

Figure 3.5. Cihuatlanque discussing marriage negotiations with a young man
SOURCE: Florentine Codex, bk. 6, fol. 106. Florence: Biblioteca Medicea Laurenziana, Med. Palat. 219, c.110. By concession of the Ministry for Heritage and Cultural Activities; further reproduction by any means is forbidden.

model of a Nahuatl speech (ca. 1570–1580) that the cihuatlanque would make when representing a ruler contains many elements of high Nahuatl rhetoric and conveys the formality of marriage negotiation. The metaphorical language suggests that the role of the cihuatlanque was reserved for those who were truly gifted in the art of Nahuatl speech, and it sheds light on just how prestigious this position was for the women and men who held it.

Perhaps more commonly, a boy's mother and father visited the prospective bride's house to present gifts of food and clothing, which were symbols of life and wealth in Mesoamerican cultures. If the girl's mother and father accepted the marriage proposal, they made their own offering of food and clothing within a few days.[88] Thus a cycle of gift exchange formalized the marriage proposal and initiated reciprocal relations among households.[89] For example, among the Mazatec of Tzicaputzalco, a young man's parents slaughtered turkeys and sent them to the parents of the prospective bride. Receipt of the turkeys signified acceptance of the proposal. The groom's family provided a banquet for the bride's relatives, and her family reciprocated by sponsoring a feast for them.[90] Similarly, among the Chontal of Coatepec, when a man's family desired marriage, they held a great feast for the family of the prospective bride. When the meal was finished, they asked for the girl. Her parents returned the favor by hosting a feast.[91] Accounts from the Juxtlahuaca jurisdiction of the Mixteca discuss gifts of cloth and banquet foods, including turkeys, deer, and rabbit supplied by the groom's family during the marriage negotiations.[92]

Several accounts of marriage in the *Relaciones* suggest that the offering of food and other items to the bride's parents compensated them for the loss of her labor. In some respects, the bride literally was exchanged for these goods because she was brought to the groom's house after her parents received food, textiles, and other luxury goods, depending on the couple's status. An account from Xalapa, for example, states: "When the cacique was to marry a cacica of another town, they took many gifts of cloth, skirts, huipiles, and gold jewelry, and of turkeys, deer, and rabbit: they gave all of the gifts to the girl's parents, and the father and mother gave them their daughter, and they brought her to where her future husband was [residing]."[93] Similarly, the response of the people of Ichcateopan to the royal questionnaire specified that the bride and groom fasted for five days before they were allowed to have sex. On the sixth day, she was given to the groom so he could sleep with her and at that time her relatives received food.[94] However, the goods exchanged did not simply amount to a bride price or some equivalent of a European dowry. Viewing the offering of goods as payment diminishes the multidimensional nature of gifting in native society. The presentation of a gift did not represent a final payment, but rather involved the expectation of an equivalent gesture in the future. Many of the symbolic acts associated with marriage negotiation were to be found in the wedding ceremony.

Marriage Celebrations

In preconquest times, indigenous peoples celebrated weddings with great formality and, depending on wealth and status, elaborate festivities. Rituals from highland Mexico shared many central elements and symbols despite regional variations. Among Nahuas, Mixtecs, Zapotecs, and other indigenous groups of the region, formal speeches, gift exchange, and feasting and drinking were central to the legitimation of marriage.

The nuptials began when the bride traveled ceremoniously to the groom's home, where the wedding took place. An image from the Codex Mendoza, a pictorial manuscript drawn by Nahua artists around 1540 with Spanish-language glosses, depicts the procession and ceremony (Figure 3.6). Various aspects of the Nahua ritual highlight the transition from childhood to adulthood that the bride and groom achieve in marriage. The procession represents the transition of the bride, who leaves her household as a child and by the end of the ceremony in the groom's household becomes a woman.[95] The continued celebration of the marriage through the night confirms the transitional state of the young couple.[96] The culmination of festivities in the early morning harmonizes with the Nahua belief that the sun provided moral order to the world.[97] In the same way, the institution of marriage regulated sexual, social, and economic relations in the community. The *Relación geográfica* from the Chontal and Nahua community of Ichcateopan corroborates the Codex Mendoza account in reporting similar processions in which elders carried the bride on their shoulders to her groom's house.[98]

In the Codex Mendoza illustration, during the procession to the groom's house a woman carries the bride on her back, as if she were a child, accompanied by women bearing pine torches. The woman is identified as an *amanteca*, a term used for a midwife and healer as well as skilled laborer, and her enhanced size suggests that she is older and/or of higher status. The bride arrives at the groom's house bathed in the light of the pine torches, symbolizing the regeneration and *tonalli* (heat, light, life force) that the marriage will bring to the couple and their households.

The Nahua bride wears a sign of liminality with her face paint, which associates her with the Nahua goddess of sexuality, Tlazolteotl, literally "trash goddess" (from *tlaçolli*, trash, and *teotl*, deity). Tlazolteotl was said to have ruled over dust and trash (*in teuhtli, in tlaçulli*) and by extension disease.[99] She was associated with fertility, sexuality, and sexual

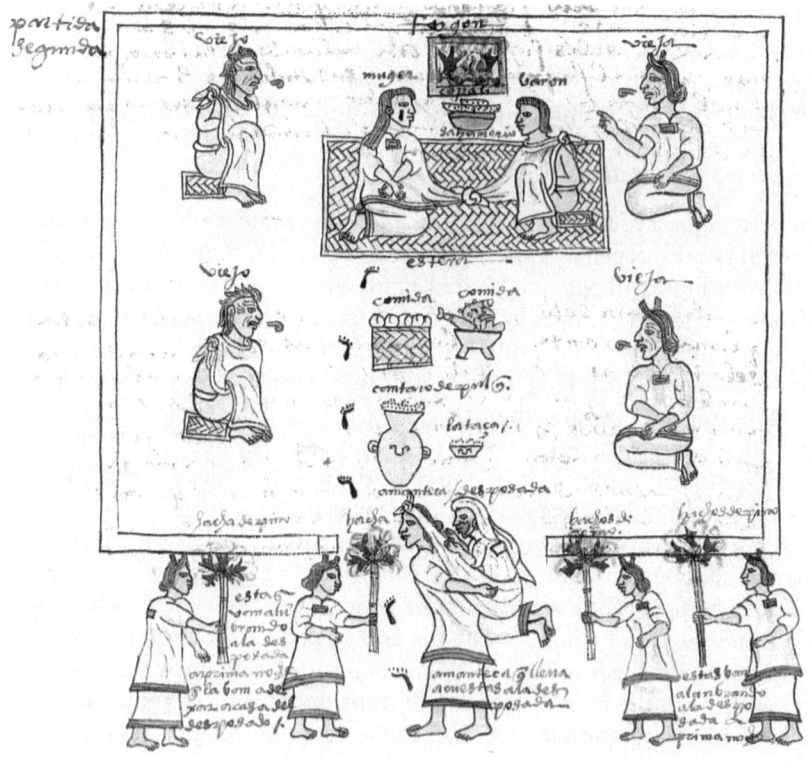

Figure 3.6. Nahua marriage ceremony
SOURCE: Codex Mendoza, fol. 61. Oxford: Bodleian Libraries, University of Oxford, Ms. Arch. Selden A1; Berdan and Anawalt 1992, fol. 61. Reproduced with permission from University of California Press Books.

excess, including adultery. The woman carrying the bride/Tlazolteotl on her back performs the role of a god(dess) bearer. Her face paint functions as a multivalent symbol that expresses Nahua concerns for reproduction in marriage and associates the bride with the realm of deities and with pollution.

When the bride arrived at the groom's house, the couple was seated together on a reed mat, which was both a bed and, for the nobility, a symbol of authority in Mesoamerica. Elders, respected guests, and the bride and groom's parents wished them well and counseled them on their duties in marriage. The Codex Mendoza shows two older men and two older women flanking the couple, capturing this moment in the ceremony; the artist depicts their advanced age by their wrinkled faces and indicates their roles as orators by placing speech scrolls in front of their mouths. The late sixteenth-century *Relación* of the Nahua altepetl of Tetzcoco describes a scene such as the one illustrated in the Codex Mendoza, reporting that representatives of rulers from distant altepetl would attend weddings of nobles in order to congratulate the married couple.[100] Accounts of Ñudzahui marriage ceremonies also mention the custom of making speeches to the newlyweds.[101] The *Relación* of Xalapa, for example, states that when the cacica arrived at the cacique's house, "many nobles and elders and the most ancient of the *ñuu* gathered and made their speeches."[102]

Family members and honored guests expressed their hope that the couple would bear children.[103] In one example from an early seventeenth-century Nahuatl-language speech made during a wedding ceremony, an honored guest congratulates the bride and considers the fact that she may produce an heir to the throne. Speaking to her in metaphorical terms, he comments: "I wonder if we will also be so fortunate that a jewel and plume of ours will split and break off from you, will bloom and blossom out from your womb and throat, the sprout and blossom of the lord ruler, the Tlacateuctli" (*aço ça nen no tocnopiltiz inic motechtzinco tzicuehuaz tlapaniz in tocozqui in toquetzal, aço xotlaz aço cueponiz in moxillantzinco in motozcatlantzinco in itzmolinca in icelica in ixotlaca in tlacatl in tlatoani in tlacateuctli*).[104]

Rituals involving clothing stand out in descriptions of marriage in highland Mexico. Records from the Nahua, Mixtec, and Zapotec regions report that the groom's cape and the bride's huipilli were tied together while they were seated on the mat.[105] This act is also depicted in the Codex Mendoza image (Figure 3.6). In some accounts of Nahua marriage ceremonies, an elder female healer performs this highly symbolic act, and the gloss "amanteca" in the illustration of the procession in the Codex Mendoza attests to the participation of a midwife as the bride bearer.[106] As discussed in Chapters 2 and 5, gender-specific clothing stood in for the male and female bodies in Nahuatl-language metaphors, and the Nahuatl term *nemecatiliztli* (tying oneself [to someone]) meant to "have sexual relations with someone."[107] Thus the couple's seat on the mat/bed, the tying of their garments, and the participation of midwives represents their sexual union.

Gifts of clothing continued the reciprocal relations of the bride and groom's households first established during the marriage negotiations, symbolizing their lives as adults and as husband and wife.[108] According to Nahua tradition, the groom's mother put a new huipilli on the bride and placed a new skirt before her; then the bride's mother adorned the groom with a new cape and laid a new breechcloth before him. Clothing exchanges are also reported in accounts of Ñudzahui wedding ceremonies.[109]

Just as clothing was used in a variety of ways throughout the wedding ceremony, offerings of food and drink were central to Mesoamerican ritual expression. The Codex Mendoza highlights their significance by showing food and drink at the center of the composition. According to the *Relación* of the Ñudzahui ñuu of Juxtlahuaca, the bride and groom fed each other a piece of tortilla and some meat after their garments were tied together.[110] Zapotec couples reportedly drank two vessels of pulque while they sat together on the mat.[111] Eating and drinking together symbolized the couple's intimacy and obligation to provide for one another (see Chapter 5 for a discussion of the sexual symbolism of food). During the Nahua ceremony, the groom's mother fed her daughter-in-law and her son tamales from the same bowl to demonstrate that the groom's family's accepted the responsibility of nurturing the young woman who was joining their home.[112] This act underscored the mother-in-law's duty to protect her daughter-in-law and to care for her as if she were her own child.

Following the ceremony, the bride and groom retired to their quarters and their guests ate, drank, and danced for as many as four days.[113] According to the Florentine Codex, older women sat outside the newlyweds' room drinking. When the couple emerged four days later, the festivities concluded with one last round of speeches, feasting, and drinking in what was called the *huexiuhtlahuana* (parents-in-law get drunk) ceremony, which provided the newlyweds' mothers with a final opportunity to counsel them on their duties and obligations.[114] The speaking roles of the women represented a symbolic exchange of children; the groom's mother (and other female relatives) addressed the bride, and the bride's mother spoke to the groom.[115] By reminding the bride and groom of life's difficulties and their responsibilities to each other, the mothers asserted their authority over their son-in-law or daughter-in-law, who until that time had answered primarily to his or her own parents.

Fundamental ideals of gender parallelism and complementarity shape the Codex Mendoza illustration and sixteenth-century accounts of the marriage ritual. The spatial relationship between the couple in the Mendoza image suggests equality in age and status, and the alignment of male and female elders and their equivalent speeches reveal their equal roles in the ritual. The elder women sit facing the bride, and the elder men sit facing the groom, suggesting parallel lines of gender authority as the elders prepare the young couple for their new roles. The speeches and ceremonial acts reinforced a gendered division of labor and formalized cooperative work and resource arrangements between households. These accounts of the marriage ceremony portray idealized social relations between husband and wife, elders and youth, and the families of the bride and groom.

Despite broad similarities in the marriage rituals of indigenous groups in central Mexico and Oaxaca, distinct regional and cultural variations existed. For example, only Nahua sources mention that the marriage ceremony was celebrated in front of the hearth.[116] The Nahuas also adorned the newlyweds with colored plumes.[117] On the other hand, only one account, of a marriage celebration in the Ñudzahui town of Mixtepec, recalls priests performing autosacrifice by drawing blood from their tongues and ears to offer to their deities.[118] Likewise, a single report on practices in Juxtlahuaca describes the Ñudzahui bride and groom giving each other gifts of flowers.[119] It is unclear whether inconsistencies in the sources reflect true variations or whether they represent details of the full ceremony omitted from other descriptions. In any case, these variations evoke symbolic references to fertility, life, wealth, and mutual obligation typical of marriage ceremonies throughout highland Mexico.

The local rulers, nobles, and commoners who witnessed the marriage ritual legitimated the union and signified that the newlyweds would be recognized as husband and wife.[120] Nuptials initiated the couple into the community as a tribute-paying unit, thereby formalizing relations between household and community. When a cacique and cacica married in the Ñudzahui ñuu of Ayusuchiquilazala, "many Indian men and Indian women gathered, noblemen and noblewomen and commoners," showing that commoners, who were to serve and obey the ruling couple, were not excluded from the ceremony.[121] Rather, communal feasting reinforced cooperative relations and mutual obligations across class lines. And because the ruling elite often married exogamously, feasting at the marriage ceremony allowed people of the bride and groom's places of origin and allied communities to establish positive relations.

When pieced together, the evidence drawn from many different sources portrays the richness of indigenous marriage customs. Every gesture, every gift, every speech, and even every silence, conveyed symbolic meaning. The friars who sought to change nuptial practices among peoples who held time-honored traditions faced a daunting task.

Indigenous-Christian Marriage Practices

Throughout the colonial period, indigenous people increasingly celebrated marriage in the church; however, early accounts of requests for the marriage sacrament, like enthusiastic reports of mass baptisms, are surely exaggerated. According to Motolinía, the Franciscans were besieged by parishioners seeking to marry in the church. In 1537, he boasted:

> There are days when they [Franciscans] marry a hundred couples, and other days, two, three, or even five hundred, and as the priests are so few it gives them a great deal of work, for it happens that one priest may have many to confess, baptize, betroth and marry, and besides he has to preach and say mass and do other things that cannot be neglected.[122]

Motolinía reiterated the high demand for the sacrament among native neophytes when he stated that the friars betrothed and married from two hundred to a thousand couples a day in the various altepetl of central Mexico. However, the scarcity of priests trained in indigenous languages in this early period makes this claim highly unlikely. Baptism, instruction in the fundamental tenets of the faith, and extirpation of idolatries were the friars' immediate priorities. Some ecclesiastics were reluctant to administer the sacrament of marriage to neophytes whose understanding of Christianity was limited. Sarah Cline's study of a circa-1540 census from the Morelos region shows that, at least in some areas of central Mexico, Christian marriage remained limited even a generation after the conquest. In a data set of information on more than three hundred joint family and nuclear households, Cline found evidence of only one couple having married in the church.[123] Although the number of indigenous people who married in this way appears to have been limited in the first few decades after the conquest, it is clear that the friars promoted Christian marriage in their sermons and ceremonies.

The friars recognized and used the power of ritual in the colonizing process.[124] They believed that if they could attract nobles to Christianity by offering participation in church sacraments and festivities as a privilege, then the commoners would follow. Motolinía acknowledged the friars' strategy:

> In order to uproot the old feasts, they [the friars] celebrate the Christian festivals with great pomp, not only in the services and administration of the sacrament, but also with dances and entertainment; all of this is necessary to wean them away from the evil customs into which they were born.[125]

This account of what Motolinía purports to be the first Nahua-Christian wedding, held in Tetzcoco in 1526, shows that friars carefully choreographed the ceremony as a display of power and prestige in the new colonial order to encourage holy matrimony among native neophytes.[126] He recalls that don Hernando, brother of the cacique of Tetzcoco, and seven other nobles "who had been brought up in the house of God" and their brides were the first indigenous couples to marry in the church. The elaborate festivities included a mass followed by feasting and dancing in the cacique's home. Both Spaniards and indigenous nobles attended the ceremony and brought gifts for the couples.[127] Motolinía admitted that the friars staged impressive services in order to promote Christian marriage, writing: "Because this wedding was to be an example for the whole of New Spain, the full and solemn nuptial mass was used, with benedictions and pledges and a ring, as the Holy Mother Church commands."[128]

Initially, the sacrament was administered selectively to young indigenous men and women who had been educated by the friars to accept monogamy as the norm.[129] Indigenous participants were not naïve about the very real political struggles of the period. As Patricia Don points out in her study of Franciscan evangelization efforts in New Spain in the first generation after the conquest, the Tetzcocan cacique Ixtlilxochitl agreed to his brother's marriage in a calculated attempt to appease Franciscan desires that indigenous nobles express devotion to the new faith.[130]

Indigenous sources recall the introduction of holy matrimony at a later date. According to the Nahua writer don Domingo Chimalpáhin, Christian marriage began in 1529 when twelve Franciscans, and especially fray Martín de Valencia and fray Toribio de Motolinía, forced the tlatoani of Itztlacozauhcan Amaquemecan Chalco, don Tomás de San Martín Quetzalmazatzin Chichimecateuctli, to abandon his multiple wives. Don Tomás chose to marry doña Catalina Chimalmantzin, the Lady of Tlalmanalco Chalco, who was his sister-in-law and the widow of his older brother. Most likely, this was the first marriage in Chalco, not in New Spain, for Motolinía would not have reported that the first marriage had taken place in Tetzcoco if that had not been the case.[131] The Codex Mexicanus dates the beginning of Christian marriage in the church to 1532. The fact that this institution is depicted alongside the invasion of the Spaniards, the conquest of Mexico Tenochtitlan, epidemics, the arrival of Franciscans, and the coming of the first viceroy testifies to the importance of the new wedding ritual in Nahua social memory of the early contact period (see Figure 3.7).

Several aspects of Christian marriage would have resonated with native audiences, providing a common ground for its acceptance by the indigenous people of highland Mexico. As in preconquest times, spiritual authorities prepared couples for marriage. The colonial native fiscal, whose job was to initially interview couples to determine who could and could not marry, filled a role that had been performed in preconquest times by the calendar readers and prognosticators who counseled the prospective

Figure 3.7. Beginning of indigenous-Christian marriage in 1532
SOURCE: Codex Mexicanus, fol. 78. Bibliothèque nationale de France.

bride and groom and determined their compatibility. The couple's family and friends continued to participate as witnesses to the Christian ceremony, although the broader roles that they performed in indigenous weddings would have been circumscribed.

The priest's repeated use of terms such as *nopilhuane* (my children) and *notlaçopilhuane* (my beloved children) to address the couple and their witnesses, invoked kinship terms to legitimize the friar's role in the creation of alliances between families.[132] Molina instructed the bride and groom to come to the church on the day of their marriage with their hands and faces washed and their clothing clean and neatly arranged. These directions clearly expressed the church's prohibition against the use of body paint and adornment in the ceremony, but they coincided with the Mesoamerican custom of bathing before any ritual and of donning new garments as part of an indigenous wedding. Gift exchange, feasting, and dancing, as described in Motolinía's account of the wedding in Tetzcoco, resonated with native spiritual practices and forms of legitimating agreements and transactions.

In addition to ceremonial similarities, friars emphasized similarities in the purpose of Christian and native nuptials, especially the importance of producing offspring within a family. Molina reminded his parishioners: "And another thing, one is to be married for having children, not for earthly pleasure, which would just be in vain" (*Oc cenca ye yeuatl ypampa yn nepilhuatiliztli nenamictilo: amo yehuatl ypampa yn çan nenquizqui tlayelpaquiliztli*).[133] This admonition aligned with Nahua expectations that a couple would have children who would bring new life to a household and, among the nobility, would serve as heirs to the rulership.[134] Similarly, in his 1634 Nahuatl-language confessional manual, Alva advised the couple:

You shall serve God, the devil not setting down between and among you the dust and refuse of sin, [for] you will be like dogs nipping at one another as you always are accustomed to doing. Just go along in life peacefully and calmly in service to God, and if He gives you children love them, then raise them in His service.

anquimotlayecoltlizque in Dios amo tle teuhtli tlaçolli amotzalan amonepantla quitlalitiez in tlacatecolotl, in iuhqui anchichime anyezque anmoquaquatiezque, in yuhqui mochipa anquichihuani, çan paca yocoxca amotlatocazque in ipan ytlayecoltilocatzin in Dios, auh intla oamechmomaquilia amapilhuan, anquintlaço-tlazque, niman ipan anquinhuapahuazque in itlayecoltilocatzin.[135]

By juxtaposing the negative social consequences of intercourse as sin with the loving creation of a family in the service of God, Alva asserted that sex should be only for procreation and not to fulfill desire. He conjured the image of the snapping dog to warn of conflict associated with unregulated sex. Marriage for lust, he warned, was sure to bring social discord and bickering.

The emphasis on procreation as one of the fundamental purposes of marriage appears in Tíchazàa-language Christian marriage texts as well. In his 1567 doctrina, Feria begins his discussion of the seventh sacrament with an explanation:

When our Lord God created our very first father and mother, Adam and Eve, truly he ordered marriage, which is called matrimony. He issued the commandment among people so that people will multiply along with the generations here in the world.

Chi pezaa Bejoannana Dios bixoce xiña nîtolij tono Adan la, Eva la, chicalijni coleepeani quela huechagaña (nila matrimonio), colaquini ticha pea lahui loo beniati quela matrimonio, niani quita le loo beniati, laa tia beniati tuatij q[ue] chelayoo.[136]

Alva and Feria's admonishments reinforced indigenous beliefs in the importance of marriage as an institution that regulated sexual relations.

Native-language ecclesiastical texts reveal that the friars and their indigenous aides incorporated some local traditions into the Christian ceremony. In Molina's *Confesionario*, the priest usurps the role of Nahua elders, reminding the bride and groom of their duties in marriage: "Through reciprocity you are to help one another with [things] on earth, you are not to be idle" (*ynic nepanotl ammopalehuizque yn itechpa tlalticpac, amo nenca*),¹³⁷ and counseling the groom: "It is a man's duty to work very hard to acquire what is needed to eat and drink for himself, his wife and his children" (*ca ytequiuh yn oquichtli ynic cenca tlatequipanoz, ynic quimixnextiliz yn itech monequiz yn quiquaz yn quiz yn yeuatl yuan yn iciuauh no yeuantin yn ipilhuan*).¹³⁸ He also articulates the wife's duties: "And likewise the woman is to greatly help her husband: it is her obligation to guard the belongings, to be in the house, to live in the house, to sweep, to wash, to spin, to weave, to grind [corn], to make food, [and] to raise children" (*Auh çano yuhqui yn cihuatl, ynic cenca quipaleuiz yn inamic: ca ynauatil ynic uelquipiez yn tlatquitl: cali yez cali nemiz, tlachpanaz, tlapacaz, tzauaz, hiquitiz, teçiz, tlaqualchiuaz, tlacauapauaz*).¹³⁹

Feria's Tíchazàa-language doctrina similarly articulates a gendered division of labor that made sense to indigenous parishioners. He admonishes the couple to cooperate, to complete "the work that is necessary to the life of this world" (*quela chiña ni naquiña quela nabanni tuatij quechelayoo*), reflecting their idealized complementary roles¹⁴⁰: "If it is just a man alone, he truly cannot do all things that are necessary to living in the world because he truly cannot spin cotton or weave cloth or make tortillas or do other types of work similar to this work" (*Tebela tobi quiquieci beni niguio, yagacalij cònini quitao loo ni naquiña quela nabanni quechelayoo quelani yagaca chahui cochijni xylla la cabani quela la cotoni guera xoba la la cónini cechacuee loo chiña leçaa chiña nitij*).¹⁴¹ In turn, the woman must have the help of a man for, according to Feria, "in the same way, a woman truly cannot carry burdens far on the road, she cannot plow the land, she cannot build her house, she cannot go far to the market, because this is man's work" (*Laani cica benigonà yagaca chàhui còani yohua neza cito, yaca cànani yo, yaca cozaani lichini, yaca çani queya cito: quelani xichiña beniniguio naca nitij*).¹⁴²

Although it is possible that Molina and Feria's indigenous assistants influenced the ideology and terminology of the dialogues on marriage, it is most probable that the inclusion of Mesoamerican customs in the ceremony followed a Christian tradition of using local practices to assert church authority. In fact, the Christian ceremony had evolved over the course of centuries and had incorporated many local customs, including the presentation of a ring to the bride, which derived from Roman practices of alliance building, and the joining of hands, which was a feature of the ancient Jewish ceremony.¹⁴³

While ecclesiastics incorporated concepts of complementarity into native-Christian marriage ceremonies, they also promoted a more hierarchical relationship between the couple by insisting on a wife's submission to her husband. In his discussion of marriage, Feria told the women who were gathered in the church: "If at any time they [your husbands] become angry with you and slap you or they pull your hair or they strike your body, you are not to leave your spouses at that time, but you spouses are to reconcile with them ... you are to speak well to them, let there be no more words because, thus, Our Lord God orders it" (*Tebela zochij quitòxoni lato la càpani lato la caxeni quichaquiquieto la quiñeni latito yagaca quitona lechelato chicani cani q[ue]olayaga leçaato colohuichachahuito leçaato quinnitiloogaticha q[ue]lani cica tij tenapea bejoãnana Dios*).[144] Similar sentiments were incorporated into a model speech that a Nahua mother was to make to her daughter, in which she would explain that Christian unions were different from traditional marriages: "But today when you marry in a sacred way, if indeed you should become jealous, if indeed your husband beats you, if indeed he afflicts you, in no way will you be able to leave him," insisting that "he is your lord, he is your spouse in a sacred way. It is ordained by our mother the Holy Church. It is also ordained by God. It is a sacrament. No one at all will be able to break it."[145]

Feria and Molina's statements place equal emphasis on the indissoluble bond of marriage and female submission in the relationship. A major difference between indigenous and Spanish practices of marriage, then, was that Christian doctrine denied women the option of leaving an abusive relationship.[146]

Despite many similarities in the ceremonies, an analysis of the iconography of the Codex Mendoza image and of a 1569 woodcut illustrating the Christian marriage of a native couple in Molina's *Confesionario* reveals the differences between Christian and Mesoamerican concepts of marriage and gender relations (see Figure 3.8).[147] The woodcut represents the church's view of the proper social order in the mid-sixteenth century. In it, the Spanish friar, positioned in the center of the composition and larger than the indigenous parishioners, is the most prominent figure. All native participants are subordinated to the friar, who represents authority in the colonial ethnic and cultural hierarchy. In contrast, the elders, the keepers of wisdom and knowledge in indigenous tradition, who are prominent in the Codex Mendoza depiction of the marriage ceremony, are absent in the woodcut and therefore silenced. Colonial authority was to be vested in Spanish Christian males rather than in community male and female elders and parents who guarded the ancient rites. Symbols of reciprocity in the Mendoza illustration, including the food and drink that signified the binding of social and economic relations between husband and wife and their respective households, are also missing from the image

Figure 3.8. Nahua-Christian marriage ceremony
SOURCE: Molina's *Confesionario mayor,* 1565, fol. 57. Courtesy of John Carter Brown Library, Brown University, Providence, Rhode Island.

in Molina's book, as are the bride's face paint, the procession at dawn, and the participation of elders and the midwife.

The 1569 woodcut reveals the church's insistence on the transformation of indigenous ritual and the restructuring of social relations, but it represents an ideal more than reality. The friars' frustration over their inability to eradicate ancient practices stemmed in part from their lack of understanding of the broader social, economic, and political significance of marriage.

CONCLUDING REMARKS

In the first generations after the Spanish conquest, priests sought to replace indigenous polygyny and serial monogamy with indissoluble, monogamous Christian marriage based on canon law. The imposition of Christian marriage was inextricably linked to larger campaigns to eradicate idolatry. The use or threat of violent punishments, including flogging, burning, and hanging, in the first decades of colonial rule represented a spiritual war over marriage and sexuality waged on the bodies of those who resisted the new morality. As Don notes in her study of the Franciscans' early evangelization efforts, "in some ways, the struggle between the friars and the native leaders on the question of sexual and marital conduct presented a more highly charged power struggle than idolatry."[148] Coercion, intimidation, and persecution slowly eroded traditional practices of polygyny and divorce in indigenous communities.

To promote Christian marriage, ecclesiastics (with the help of their indigenous aides) incorporated some aspects of native nuptials into the Catholic ritual and significantly altered others. Yet, even such adapted ceremonies could not replace the symbolic acts performed during indigenous weddings that served to reinforce fundamental social relations based on age, gender, and status. The friars did not comprehend the social, economic, and political significance of the marriage union in Mesoamerican cultures. Reluctant to give up their marriage customs, Nahua, Ñudzahui, Bènizàa, and Ayuuk couples often practiced parallel rituals. As with other European introductions, indigenous peoples adapted Christian nuptials to their own local traditions and beliefs. Furthermore, the Christian ritual represented a realignment of social relations under colonial rule that promoted the subordination of indigenous peoples and their leaders to the authority of the friars, the subordination of a wife to her husband, and more generally the subordination of local custom to Christian European culture. The rigid teachings of the church on marriage and sexuality imposed a model of heterosexual monogamous marriage as the only acceptable union and procreative intercourse as the only sanctioned expression of sexuality. As a result, the marriage encounter in colonial Mexico engendered conflict, compromise, and new practices.

By the late colonial period, *criollo* painters were incorporating images of indigenous weddings and rites into their picturesque depictions of Mexican village life. In her study of eighteenth-century paintings of popular festivals, Ilona Katzew concludes that "the incorporation of indigenous traditions as part of a wedding scene held a powerful meaning: it demonstrated that the native population of New Spain fully partook of an important Christian sacrament, thereby conveying the notion of a 'civilized' land."[149] Indeed, efforts to impose Christian marriage were part of a long, protracted struggle that the friars deemed a "spiritual conquest." Although painters were able to convince their patrons in Mexico City and Spain that this conquest was complete, the friars and their indigenous parishioners often continued to understand matters of marriage and sexuality in very different terms.

CHAPTER FOUR

Marital Relations

On November 20, 1651, Cecilia Chávez filed criminal charges against Miguel Morales, don Nicolás de Velasco, and Juan de la Cruz.¹ She claimed that Morales, her son-in-law, had severely beaten her daughter, María Chávez, as they returned in the evening to Temascalapa from the home of their compadre, Juan Martín, and comadre, María de Acevedo. María had fled to her compadres' house in Yalahui earlier that morning, with her one-year-old son tied in a rebozo on her back, after Miguel had beaten her and threatened to kill her when he returned from his cornfield. Miguel found María there that evening, and after his compadres scolded him for mistreating her, he insisted that she return home with him. Her comadre convinced her to come out of the room where she was hiding by promising her that "Our Lord God and the Holy Virgin, his mother, would save her from the harm that her husband would like to do to her" and assuring her that Miguel was a Christian.²

Once beyond sight of Yalahui, Miguel unleashed his fury on his wife, beating her so badly that she was covered with bruises and barely breathing. By the time he carried her back to Temascalapa, she was dead. Miguel denied his crime, insisting that María had had a history of heart problems and that she had slipped and fallen into a ravine, causing her death. The officials of Temascalapa summoned don Nicolás Velasco, *alcalde* (judge, serves on municipal council), and Juan de la Cruz, regidor, of Yalahui to help them sort out the matter. They had accepted Miguel's story and did not intend to investigate further. For that reason, Cecilia Chávez asserted that they were complicit in the crime and guilty of a cover-up. When interrogated, Miguel maintained his innocence and only begrudgingly admitted to a history of domestic violence. Juan de la Cruz seemed to have a change of heart, testifying several days later that he was "certain" that Miguel had killed María, for he had heard Miguel complain many times in Yalahui that María "was lazy, and didn't know how to serve or weave."³

This record of a grieving mother's pursuit of justice for her daughter exposes a contested discourse on marital expectations and gender violence. It also highlights women's networks and their use of the court system to prosecute men for crimes of assault and battery and wife murder. This chapter analyzes dozens of similar cases in the archival record in relation to other types of evidence on marital behavior in central Mexico and Oaxaca. The first section of the chapter analyzes rituals, metaphors for marriage, and marital expectations to shed light on the social, economic, and political significance of marriage in native societies. The second section focuses on those who lived in informal unions but shared many of the experiences and expectations of married couples. The third section examines multiple cases of wife beating and uxoricide in indigenous communities in order to understand some of the tensions that led to domestic violence and to examine community responses to crimes against women.

THE SIGNIFICANCE OF MARRIAGE

Marriage was a fundamental institution in Mesoamerica. Many of its different dimensions shaped the expectations that a husband and wife had of one another and that formed the basis of a couple's relationship with their families, their communities, and colonial institutions.

Social Dimensions of Marriage

Marriage in Mesoamerica signified social maturity. It was a rite of initiation that marked one's passage from childhood to adulthood, and one's full membership in the community with all of the responsibilities that this privilege entailed. Mesoamerican languages included terminology for the marital status of young adults but none for the concept of virginity. An unmarried young man was a *telpochtli* in Nahuatl, a *dzuchi* in Ñudzahui (Mixtec), and a *penixitobi* in Tíchazàa (Zapotec), while an unmarried young woman was an *ichpochtli* in Nahuatl, a *dzuchi* in Ñudzahui, and a *pinichápa* in Tíchazàa.[4]

Marriage speeches articulated the change in status associated with marriage. The groom's Nahua kinsmen began their speeches by explaining to the noble bride that with marriage she would assume the full responsibilities of an adult woman: "Now with this you have settled in among the old women; already you begin the life of an old woman. Now leave childishness entirely behind; you are no longer to be like a little child" (*in axcan, ca ic intech tompachivi in ilamatque: ie toconpeoaltia in ilamanemiliztli: axcan xiccencaoa in pipillotl, in coconeiutl: aiocmo tiuhquin tipiltontli tiez, aiocmo iuhquin ticonetontli tiez*).[5] Expressing seemingly universal sentiments, the groom's mother-in-law informed him that his careless days of childhood were behind him:

Do not take [marriage] lightly, because it is now your world and your special realm; your life is now different. Your attitude is no longer to be frivolous, because you have already left behind the misbehavior of youth—drunkenness, laughter, and joking. Now you are a married man.

macaçamo xommauilmati, ca ie motlalticpac, ca ie mixcotian, ca ie centetl in monemiliz, ca aiocmo aviliez in moiollo, ca ie oticcauh in telpuchtlavelilocaiutl in neivintiliztli, in vetzquiztli, in camanalli, ca ie titlapaltzintli.[6]

Native-language terms for widows and widowers underscore marriage as the ideal state. In Nahuatl, these terms were *icnociuatl* and *icnooquichtli*, the standard terms for female and male, respectively, but modified by *icnotl*, meaning humble, poor, orphaned, a concept expressed in the Tíchazàa *huizabi*.[7] Such terminology suggests abandonment, poverty, and diminished social status for surviving spouses.

Marriage also united a man and a woman who ideally would have children, enabling the social reproduction of the household. This was such an important aspect of the union that the depiction of children often immediately follows marriage presentation scenes in Ñudzahui and Aztec pictorial histories.[8] As we have seen, ritual acts, such as the tying of the bride and groom's garments and speeches made during the marriage negotiation and ceremony, emphasized the couple's responsibility to have children.[9] Family members honored a woman with feasting, drinking, and formal speeches when she became pregnant. According to the Florentine Codex, elder noblemen praised the couple's good fortune when a woman's pregnancy was announced and the husband's parents advised their daughter-in-law to take care of herself and cautioned her against harming her unborn child.[10] All gathered again when the expectant mother was in her seventh or eighth month to choose a midwife and arrange for the delivery, formalizing arrangements with another round of speeches, feasting, and drinking.[11]

Because married couples were expected to have children, those who did not stood out in colonial censuses. Scribes who compiled Nahuatl-language censuses from Cuernavaca in the Morelos jurisdiction around 1540 noted a couple's failure to conceive. In some cases they remarked that a couple had only recently married; in others they provided more explicit information, stating that a couple did not have children because the man was "impotent" (*tetzicatl*).[12] The census takers felt compelled to explain childlessness because for married couples it was considered an aberration.

The Cuernavaca census suggests that childless couples remained together, but other sixteenth-century sources indicate that childlessness caused considerable tension.[13] According to Córdova, this was the principal reason for divorce among the Bènizàa people (Zapotec).[14] Indeed, concern over reproduction was expressed from the very beginning, when the parents of the bride and groom consulted a prognosticator to learn whether the betrothed couple would be compatible. Furthermore, documentary evidence provides examples of men who ended relationships when a child died at birth. The reader will recall that Francisco, a Nahua noble who was tried for polygyny in 1538, ended his marriage to his first wife at the very time when their baby was stillborn.[15] Similarly, in 1558 a Nahua woman of Igualapa named Catalina Cozcaquaxochitl confessed that she had been having an affair with Martín for over a year and that he had promised to marry her. She became pregnant by him, but their baby was born dead. After the stillbirth, Martín ended the relationship and refused to see her.[16] It seems that, at least in some cases, indigenous men considered a failed pregnancy grounds for terminating a relationship. The difference was that unlike the examples in the Morelos census, the men were not impotent.

Marriage shaped the social identity of husbands and wives, who were associated with and defined by each other. Men and women often identified themselves and were identified by others in relation to their spouses in colonial courts and documents. This was especially the case for women, who were almost always labeled as "the wife of" someone according to the typical wording of testimony and legal documentary formulas.[17] On the other hand, archival records sometimes identify a man in terms of his wife. For example, male petitioners or witnesses often stated their community affiliation and identified their marriage partner when they presented themselves in court. Perhaps because the indigenous people of central Mexico and Oaxaca did not use surnames that would have clarified familial and marital relationships, qualifying terms such as "husband of" and "wife of" were necessary.

Although witnesses also often stated their marital status, occupation, and age in court, these identifiers were far less frequently mentioned than community affiliation. For example, in a typical case from the Mixteca Alta, Cecilia López was named with no mention of her marital status; however, in documents from related proceedings, she was identified as Pedro López's wife. In both cases, her community membership was recorded, suggesting that her pueblo affiliation was more central to her identity and status than was her association with her husband.[18]

Evidence from civil proceedings suggests, however, that by the end of the sixteenth century men increasingly represented their wives in court. For example, based on her study of legal disputes over land and inheritance in Tenochtitlan, Susan Kellogg concludes that "by the seventeenth century, the legal identity of women had become increasingly intertwined with that of their husbands."[19] This in part contributed to women's declining legal and economic status at the heart of the viceroyalty. Kevin Terraciano comes to a similar conclusion in his discussion of the decline in political power of Ñudzahui (Mixtec) *cacicas* (female indigenous rulers) in Oaxaca. He says, "The Spanish principle of *conjunta persona* [joint person], when applied to members of the *yuhuitayu* [Ñudzahui complex state formed by the marriage of a male ruler and a female ruler], acknowledged the rights of women as more than mere consorts of the cacique. However, the category entitled men to represent the yuhuitayu in legal action, even when their separate patrimonies were not at issue."[20] Furthermore, women's participation in other legal processes also declined over the course of the colonial period. The rich collection of Nahuatl-language testaments from sixteenth-century Culhuacan, published by Cline and León-Portilla, reveals that women frequently served as witnesses, always listed after the men and often identified in relation to their husbands. In his work on Ñudzahui-language testaments from Oaxaca, Terraciano found many examples of women witnessing wills, but in both regions this had declined by the first quarter of the seventeenth century as cabildo members increasingly verified legal documents.[21]

Daily attitudes preserved in the testimony of mid-eighteenth-century colonial criminal records show that marriage was considered an honorable state, perhaps because of the added responsibilities that married couples held or because of the importance placed on the institution by the church. When one woman shouted that Ana María was "a daughter of a great whore," Ana María responded: "I will not accept such defiance, I am a married woman."[22] For her, it was her marital status that elevated her above such foul insults and degrading remarks. Juana de la Cruz expressed similar sentiments in 1742 when she accused Magdalena Pascuala of "beating the other Indian women of the community *although they were married*" and of insulting them in their husbands' presence.[23] Married women expected that other members of their communities would treat them with respect.[24]

An important aspect of marriage was the social life that a couple shared. Husbands and wives frequently traveled together to attend celebrations in their communities and neighboring pueblos and to participate in church functions. Religious holidays in honor of local patron saints featured masses, dramas, feasts, dances (*mitotes*), and markets. Couples from the community and surrounding towns welcomed these opportunities to see old friends and family members, as did Juan López and María Qunuu, who met many other men and women in the plaza of Coixtlahuaca when they attended Easter vigil festivities in 1578.[25] Mitotes, or native dances, often performed with costumes, rattles, and teponaztlis (log drums), celebrated Christian events while retaining a rich underlay of indigenous sacred symbolism. Couples attended local fiestas to participate in and observe these local spectacles.[26] In addition, husbands and wives visited relatives, compadres, and friends.[27] They often assisted sick friends and relatives by going to their houses to comfort them and bring them food.[28] Drinking and eating together exemplified the ways that indigenous couples socialized and expressed intimacy.[29]

The sentiments of a Ñudzahui couple, don Géronimo García y Guzmán and doña Lázara de Guzmán, expressed in their last wills and testaments, reveal their tender concern for each other. When don Géronimo made his testament in 1672, he was sure to ask the assembled nobles to "keep my wife company," communicating his wish that she not be alone after his death.[30] Doña Lázara survived her husband by nearly twenty years, yet the passing of time did not fade the memory of their bond. She described sharing "the gift of life" with don Géronimo for sixty years; together they had twelve children, only three of whom were living as she lay on her deathbed in 1691.[31] Statements such as these provide a rare glimpse into the intimate family life of a Ñudzahui ruling couple.

Just as important as the social dimensions of the joint life of a husband and wife was the economic significance of marriage. Marriage was built on the premise of reciprocity, mutual obligation, and cooperative labor.

Economic Dimensions of Marriage

In Mesoamerican cultures, marriage was conceptualized as the union of male and female laborers who would perform gender-specific work and duties for the benefit of their household, their parents' households, and their community. At its core, marriage was based on the mutual obligations of husband and wife to sustain each other. The *Relación* of the Tlapanec community of Ayutla describes a wedding ceremony at which two elders instructed the groom to "take care in working and providing food for your wife" and admonished the bride to "take care in serving and making food for your husband."[32] A Nahua orator advised the groom to provide for his family and the bride to dedicate herself to cleaning, cooking, weaving, and managing the household.[33] In closing speeches at the *huexiuhtlauana* (parents-in-law get drunk) feast on the fourth day of the wedding festivities, Nahua mothers of the bride and groom discussed marriage as a partnership in which husband and wife performed corresponding and complementary gender-specific duties. A wife, they said, was to trade locally while a husband was to travel to distant markets to sell his goods.[34] The link between marriage and work was perhaps most forcefully made when the women of the groom's family empathized with the bride: "Poor you, you have taken on that which is like a great burden, a large packframe, which is truly heavy, which cannot be lifted" (*timotolinia ca itlan otonmaquilti, in iuhqui in vei tlamamalli, in vei cacaxtli, in vel etic, in aeoaliztli*).³⁵ From the time of the nuptials, marriage was all about work.

Discussions of prehispanic divorce customs highlight the value placed on cooperative labor arrangements in marriage. According to the *Relación* of the Nahua altepetl of San Juan Teotihuacan:

Having married some Indian man and Indian woman with the ceremonies to which they were accustomed, if perchance they did not treat each other well and they quarreled often, the principal Indian who was the overseer of the barrio where they lived called them and asked them why they were quarreling. And, being a native woman, if she complained that her husband did not provide her with that which is necessary, nor worked in his/her/their fields and farms in order to sustain himself, but went around loafing, it was grounds for their separation, and the same if the woman were an idler, and did not tend to serving her husband.³⁶

Grounds for terminating a marriage in other parts of central Mexico especially placed the burden of efficiently performing their duties on women. The *Relación* of the Mazatec community of Tzicaputzalco stated: "If she were a good woman, doing her duty, and she did not betray her husband, she lived with her husband until old age; and if she were lazy, they cast her out, and then they married another."³⁷ Similarly, Córdova reported in 1578 that the Bènizàa people cited laziness, especially the woman's, as grounds for divorce.³⁸ These comments reveal a double standard that undercut the marital concept of complementarity.

Idealized views of marital obligations and gender responsibilities shaped the words and deeds of indigenous people in their daily lives.³⁹ When Lucas Juan, a Nahua, testified in 1696 that he had proposed marriage to Sebastiana Ana because "as a widower he did not have anyone to make tortillas" for him, he expressed in no uncertain terms his understanding of a woman's role in marriage.⁴⁰ Even in the afterlife, seen throughout Mesoamerica as a journey down a road, a woman was required to provide her husband with food and drink. In 1667 a native of Teotlasingo placed a bundle of tortillas, beans, and piñol wrapped in banana leaves in his mother's grave so that "if she should meet her husband on the road, she could give them to him and alleviate [his hunger]."⁴¹ Her responsibility to feed her husband followed her into the afterlife.

The prescribed roles of husband and wife informed the narratives that people told regarding their own marriages and the relationships of others. Thus when Ana Juana, a Nahua woman of Culhuacan, ordered her testament in 1580, she voiced bitter disappointment at the lack of collaboration in her marriage:

And here is what I say concerning my husband named Gabriel Itzmalli, who is a great scoundrel. Let him never bother my son, nor let him accuse (my son) of anything. I don't know how many debts he has. He never gave me anything whatsoever, not money nor telling me "poor you," as did the three who died, two of whom were my husbands, because together we carried out the duties of life on earth. But look, this one, if he went to fetch fruit or if he went to fetch maize, he would sell it himself without showing me how much he had bought. But as to the maize he gave to me, he just measured it out.

*Auh yz catqui yhuan niquitohuan yn itechpan yn nonamic yn itoca gabriel ytzmalli ca cenca tlahueliloc ma quemaniya quitollini y notelpoch ma ytla ytech quitlami ca hamo nicmatin yn quexquich yn inetlacuil auh ca hamo ma yca [sic] onechmacac yn ma tomines y ma quitohuan timotollinaya yn iuhqu(e/i) yn momiquillique yeyntzintzin catca y nomenti y nonamictzitzinhuan catca ca nepanotl oticotlatoctiaya yn tlalticpac tonetlayecotilliz auh ynin yehuatl yntla xochiqualli oquicuito yntla noço tlaolli oquicuito ca yyoma yn quinamaca camo nechiyntitiya yn quexquich quicohua auh yn tlaolli ca ça nechtamachihuilia y nechmaca.*⁴²

This statement reveals that the values of cooperation and compassion articulated in formal speeches and rituals underlay popular marital expectations. Ana Juana fondly recalled that the three previous men in her life had comforted her and that she and they had worked together to carry out "the duties of life on earth." While we can never know whether Gabriel Itzmalli was the miserly husband that Ana Juana described, it is clear that she framed her case against him in terms of the marriage ideal in order to protect her son from him.

Native men also invoked the model marriage when they spoke in court. In 1596, a Mixtec man considered the fulfillment of labor duties when he positively assessed one woman's character, citing as evidence of her good qualities that he had seen her "serving her husband, grinding maize to make him tortillas, and weaving cloth for him."⁴³ In the case from 1651 that opened this chapter, a Zapotec regidor recalled the angry accusations that a man had made when authorities arrested him for killing his wife. Expressing classic expectations, the man confessed that he and his wife had fought because he thought she was lazy and incapable of performing the most basic tasks of weaving and serving him.⁴⁴ Men also drew on culturally sanctioned roles in discussing their own success in meeting their marriage obligations. When Juan Tomás appeared before officials in 1723 to complain that his wife repeatedly abandoned him and returned to her parents' home, he insisted that her actions were unwarranted because he had fulfilled his duty to provide food for her.[45]

Conflicts resulting from a woman's refusal to cook for her husband shed light on the way in which women sometimes challenged gender obligations and marital expectations in unhappy relationships. For example, a Nahua woman informed indigenous officials in 1619 that her husband, an escaped convict, had threatened to kill her when she refused to give him anything to eat.[46] In another case, from the Ñudzahui town of Tlaxiaco in 1636, Melchor Hernández returned home drunk from the festivities of the Magi and began beating his wife because she had hesitated to serve him the tortillas that he had asked for.[47] Similarly, Juan Gutiérrez, a Bènizàa man of Camotlan, threatened violence to enforce his concept of marital obligation in 1685. When he did not find his wife at home, he stormed over to his mother-in-law's house and quarreled with her over his wife's behavior. "It is your fault," he said. "You can order your daughter to be at home so that when I return from the countryside she can give me a tortilla."[48] His mother-in-law told him that he was crazy. By casting blame on her, Juan acknowledged her authority and continued influence over her daughter.

The identification of marriage with cooperative male and female labor was so strong that it often served as evidence of illicit relations between an unmarried couple. Thus witnesses testified in 1642 that they were certain that Francisco Jiménez was committing adultery with Juana de la Cruz, a married woman, because he had taken her to Mexico City and arranged for her to sell fruit for him in public "as if she were his legitimate wife."[49] Likewise, when Lucas Antonio was interrogated in 1752 about the accusation that Josef Antonio and Petra María were lovers, he testified that he had seen her help him in his wheat field and that they worked together all day, "just the two of them, like husband and wife."[50] Another witness swore under oath that he knew that the accused were having an affair because he had heard that Petra María wove cloth for Josef Antonio and his mother. From the indigenous perspective, then, collaboration between a man and a woman proved their sexual intimacy and commitment to one another.

The Spanish reorganization of the tribute system during the sixteenth century reinforced the interpretation of marriage as the union of male and female labor. By the late sixteenth century, each married couple constituted one tributary.[51] Moreover, widows and widowers and single men and women paid half of the tribute assessed each married couple.[52] When they identified themselves in court, people sometimes explained that they had "married in" the pueblo of their spouses, signifying that they resided and paid tribute there, not in their natal community.[53] In this way, marriage and tribute obligations shaped community membership as well as gender relations.

Political Dimensions of Marriage

In preconquest and colonial times, Mesoamerican nobles, like their European counterparts, forged alliances with other distinguished families through marriage, thereby giving their unions a political dimension. In his study of marriage patterns among some of the prominent Nahua dynasties in ancient Mexico, Pedro Carrasco identifies several types of marriage, including those between and within lineages, those among subordinates and superiors, and those among relative equals. He concludes that a variety of marriage types allowed ruling dynasties to create and strengthen alliances among altepetl, some of higher rank, others of lower rank. The influential roles of women in the marriage alliances studied by Carrasco are clear. They often brought lands and dependents to royal marriages, while sons of high-ranking men from the outside frequently succeeded to the rulership of their mothers' communities.[54] Based on her analysis of Chimalpahin's writings on prehispanic and colonial Amaquemecan Chalco, Susan Schroeder shows that the Nahua noblewomen of Chalco also formed strategic marriage alliances to enhance the political status of elite families, and that women were sometimes recognized as the founders of lineages.[55] Some Nahuas even attempted to forge alliances with the Spanish during the conquest period by marrying off native noblewomen to Spaniards.[56] Many of these Nahua strategies and patterns continued well into the colonial period.

Marriage alliances also were at the heart of Mixtec sociopolitical organization in preconquest and colonial times. As Terraciano has shown in his study of colonial Ñudzahui communities, either men or women who were direct descendants of hereditary rulers could rule over a ñuu. Two ñuu were united through the marriage of their male and female hereditary rulers, thereby creating a complex sociopolitical entity called a yuhuitayu, which lasted for the duration of the rulers' lives. At the death of the rulers, the individual patrimonies (used in the gender-neutral sense of the term) were divided and bequeathed to different heirs, who constituted new yuhuitayu through marriages to rulers of other ñuu.[57]

The sixteenth-century Spanish reorganization of the indigenous countryside into *cabeceras* (head towns) and *sujetos* (subject settlements) in many cases conflicted with indigenous concepts of political rule and autonomy. Spanish administrators subordinated some native communities to others that had been their equals. Ñudzahui nobles who contested their communities' subordinate status based their claims to autonomy on the fact that they had a ruling couple. Thus, when the *estancia* (outlying settlement) of Santiago attempted to break from Teposcolula to win recognition as a cabecera in 1583, the litigants argued that they had a cacique and a cacica, don Pedro and doña Juana. From the perspective of the Santiago nobles, this royal marriage made them a yuhuitayu and therefore far too important to be relegated to the status of Teposcolula's sujeto.[58]

An advantageous marriage and matrilocal residence continued to provide a nobleman access to office in his wife's community in central Mexico and Oaxaca in colonial times. Although a cacica was excluded from holding office on the local cabildo, she could exercise considerable influence through her husband, especially when he held office by virtue of his marriage to her.[59] Men sometimes claimed the right to the governorship or other cabildo offices based on their wives' connections. The well-known Nahua intellectual and writer don Antonio Valeriano was born in Azcapotzalco, yet he was able to rise to political prominence and become governor of Mexico Tenochtitlan from 1573 to 1599 by virtue of his marriage to doña Isabel de Alvarado, a Mexican noblewoman.[60] Following a similar pattern, don Francisco de Aranda, a Nahua noble, insisted in 1685 that although he was from Istlahuaca he was entitled to the governorship in his wife's altepetl of Atlacomulco because her father had held the office and because both he and his wife had descended from caciques.[61] Through strategic marriages, noble families could not only dominate the governorship but control officeholding in their jurisdictions. Thus in 1635 don Nicolás de San Miguel, the governor of Malinalco, was accused of fixing elections in order to place his sons-in-law and brothers-in-law in office.[62]

As in central Mexico, indigenous men in Oaxaca sometimes held office outside their natal communities because of their associations with high-ranking women and their families. In one case, Don Pablo de la Cruz, a Ñudzahui noble of Ixtepec, married doña Juana de Castañeda, the cacica of Cuquila, and resided in her ñuu. As the husband of the legitimate hereditary ruler of Cuquila, don Pablo dominated the governorship, the highest elected office on the all-male cabildo, in the early seventeenth century.[63] In another case, witnesses testified in 1633 that Juan de Mendoza's father-in-law appointed him regidor when he married into the important Mixtec ñuu of Teposcolula.[64] Similarly, Miguel de Illescas, a Bènizàa man of Santiago Lalopa, moved to San Pedro Nesiche when his sister married don Esteban Maldonado, a noble of that yetze.[65] In Lalopa, Illescas had served as regidor for three years and as alcalde for two years. Recognized as a noble in Nesiche, he was first elected regidor, then alcalde (twice), and eventually governor, thus holding the highest position on the cabildo through his association with his sister and her husband.[66] In his study of marriage alliances among Ñudzahui elites in late colonial Mexico, John Chance cautions against assuming that strategic marriages always promoted the couple's interests.[67] Nevertheless, contrary to conventional wisdom, matrilocality among the ruling elite could bring new opportunities rather than a loss of status to men who held office through their wives or other female relatives.[68]

Claims to office through marital ties illuminate indigenous conceptions of officeholding and political legitimacy. To some extent, a married couple represented the ethnic state and held office jointly.[69] This is most clearly the case in a depiction of the Ñudzahui yuhuitayu, which shows male and female rulers seated together on a reed mat (see Figure 4.1). The yya toniñe and yya dzehe toniñe are equal in size, and both occupy seats of authority. Both gesture, symbolizing their ability to issue commands, and wear the accouterments of rulers, including turquoise ear spools and golden collars. Both are identified by their calendrical and personal names.

Compared with Ñudzahui pictorial manuscripts, Bènizàa and Nahua illustrations of ruling authorities do not include women as often, but there are some important exceptions. The Lienzo of Tabaá, for example, illustrates local Bènizàa history, genealogy, and boundaries with a series of *coqui* (cacique) and *xonaxi* (cacica) couples and Tíchazàa-language glosses (Figure 4.2).[70] Most of the men and women are identified by their calendrical or personal names, and the lower row of figures shows parental (sometimes only the father's) information about the xonaxi who came from outside the community.

The convention of depicting married couples in Nahua documents representing the ethnic state continued into the later colonial period. A mid-eighteenth-century illustration accompanying land titles for the Nahua altepetl of San Francisco Caxhuacan suggests that couples held political and religious offices. It shows San Francisco, the community's patron saint, sporting wings, standing on an orb, and gazing at a crucifix that he holds in his hand. Three men and three women flank him, all of them named. In addition, one man is identified as an alcalde and the other two as regidores, indicating that the men are officials of the cabildo and the women are their wives.[71] The native artist and the nobles he depicted asserted their claims by virtue of an association with the leading couples of the community, not simply prominent men, and through their relationship to the local patron saint (see Figure 4.3). The understanding of the married couple as joint officeholders also seems to have informed the decision of the cabildo of Yanhuitlan to send gifts of silk huipiles and

Figure 4.1. Ñudzahui yuhuitayu showing the joint rule of the male yya toniñe (left) and the female yya dzehe toniñe (right)
SOURCE: Codex Becker 2, fol. 3. Facsimile edition. Vienna: Akademische Druckund Verlagsanstalt; Madrid: Sociedad Estatal Quinto Centenario; Mexico City: Fondo de Cultura Económico, 1994.

mantas to the male judges of the *Real Audiencia* ("royal court," high court that adjudicated civil and criminal matters) in Mexico City in 1677, "as if the items were intended for yuhuitayu couples."[72]

In his study of local religion in late colonial Mexico, Edward Osowski detects an underlying gender parallelism in Nahua concepts of authority.

Figure 4.2. Lienzo of Tabaá (detail)
SOURCE: Photograph courtesy of Michel Oudijk.

He shows that men and women worked together to guard and maintain community icons, even as Spanish ecclesiastics attempted to limit women's role: "From the perspective of late colonial Nahuas, women's participation in alms collection was not a sign of the breakdown of community, but the opposite." He explains that working as male and female pairs, alms collectors embodied spiritual authority and so could more successfully solicit donations. Therefore, "Women's participation was helpful to the cohesion of the community because their affiliation with male alms collectors increased donations in a time of general financial crisis in the late eighteenth century."[73] The indigenous peoples of highland Mexico continued to see some aspects of authority in terms of gender complementarity despite the fact that women's activities were not sanctioned by Spanish colonial institutions and officials.

Figure 4.3. Land titles showing San Francisco Caxhuacan's leading couples and its patron saint
SOURCE: Archivo General de la Nación, Mexico, Tierras, vol. 2912, fol. 210.

Married men held a particular political status in native communities.[74] Although only nobles held office before conquest and during the early colonial period, the larger group of married non-noble men constituted a political force by at least the mid-seventeenth century. For example, when a hundred and thirty men of Yatzona sued to have their governor and alcaldes removed from office in 1695, they identified themselves in the Tíchazàa-language petition as the "married men" and listed their names.[75] By so designating themselves, they indicated that they were married and therefore adult, tribute-paying members of the yetze. Their challenge, framed in terms of the rights and responsibilities that they assumed when they wed, underscores the sociopolitical dimensions of marriage in colonial native communities.

Relations between indigenous elites and commoners became strained in the later colonial period because of the caciques' loss of political authority, the establishment of the cabildo system, population loss, disruptions in noble lineages, and the increasing influence of Spanish culture and language on the nobility. These changes seem to have altered strategic marriage alliances, at least in some regions. Elites sought marriage partners who could enhance their wealth and status rather than help them achieve political ambitions.[76]

INFORMAL UNIONS

In 1671, the altepetl of Cuescomatepec sent a scathing letter, written in the Nahuatl language, to local Spanish magistrates informing them that Josef Rodríguez, a Spanish trader and pig farmer, was living outside of wedlock (*amancebado*) with an unnamed married indigenous woman of the community. According to Rodríguez's accusers, he had lived with this woman for twelve years and had fathered two of her children. It is likely that her husband had abandoned her, although his whereabouts were not clearly stated. They also complained that Rodríguez's pigs had killed many of their chickens and that the stench from the *pitzocalli* (literally pig house) was making the people of the town ill. Rodríguez, they asserted, overcharged the townspeople for goods and defrauded the crown by not paying the royal tax. In their effort to have him banished from the altepetl, the officials strategically invoked ordinances that prohibited non-natives living in their community, and they shaped their accusations to appeal to the Crown's interests and the Christian sensibilities of Spanish magistrates. The objections to Rodríguez, raised so long after he had come to Cuescomatepec, were most certainly motivated by economic concerns.[77] The altepetl officials' letter reveals an arrangement—that of couples living together in informal unions—that had become quite common in New Spain by this period.

Amancebamiento (living together outside of wedlock) was often the only option for couples facing an impediment to marriage such as kinship through blood or marriage. For example, María Ycuma had lived with Antón Sajo, her husband's brother, for two years after her husband's death. After she and Sajo were punished with whippings by local authorities for amancebamiento, she agreed to marry another man.[78] Prior marriage also prevented couples from celebrating the sacrament. María Jiménez, a Ñudzahui woman who had been abandoned when her husband left for Mexico City, carried on a long-term affair with Pedro López Hordóñez, a mestizo bell and trumpet maker.[79]

Many of the couples who lived together out of wedlock were interracial, which meant that inequality of ethnic and/or class status, aside from impediments, determined the likelihood that a couple would not marry.[80] Often an elite Spanish man postponed marriage while he advanced his career and socioeconomic position. During this delay, he might live with or have a long-term relationship with an indigenous, African, or casta (mixed-race) woman whom he had no intention of marrying. When this man married a Spanish woman, he often arranged his mistress's marriage to someone else. This pattern, based on Iberian custom and established in Mexico at the time of conquest, persisted throughout the colonial period.

So then, what did women have to gain from settling with a man who they knew would probably never marry them? Only rarely did women comment specifically on the intimate details of their relationships. In one such case from Teposcolula in 1597, Lucía López, a thirty-year-old Mixtec widow, very clearly spelled out the agreement she had with Juan Bautista Grimaldos, a mestizo interpreter. She confessed to Spanish authorities that for four years she had eaten and resided in Juan Bautista's house and that every night they had slept together in the same bed, where he had "carnal access" to her whenever he wanted it. She cooked, cleaned, laundered clothes, and wove cloth for him; in exchange, he paid the tribute for her and her mother. With considerable reluctance, Juan Bautista eventually promised to marry Lucía.[81]

A partial list of couples denounced by the fiscal of the archbishopric of Mexico City between 1582 and 1584 illustrates the range of social and ethnic types who lived in informal unions (see Table 4.1).[82] It provides a glimpse into the multiethnic urban society of late sixteenth-century Mexico City and shows the high degree of intermixing between indigenous women and working-class Spanish, mestizo, and native men at the heart of the viceroyalty. At the same time, the list reveals the extent to which social mobility was limited in this urban setting. Spanish, mestizo,

TABLE 4.1. *Sampling of couples tried for amancebamiento in the archbishopric of Mexico City, 1582–1584*

Male and occupation/ethnicity	Female and ethnicity
Pedro González, Spanish fruit vendor	María, mestiza
Miguel Rodríguez, mestizo	Justina, single india ladina
Nicolás Rodríguez, Spanish muleteer	Cristina, india
Juan Vásquez, mestizo tailor	María Vásquez, india
Miguel Rodríguez, mestizo	Juana, india
Cristóbal Nuñez, Spaniard	Francisca and Paula, indias
Diego Francisco, mestizo	Juana, india
Sebastián, native blacksmith	María Bautista, mestiza
Bartolomé de Morales, married mestizo tailor	Francisca de Alvarado, india ladina
Juan González, mestizo weaver	Margarita, india
Martín León, meztizo "who sells merchandise on a little table in the plaza"	María, india
Agustín, mestizo blacksmith	Agustina, india
Juan de Cháves	Felipa, negra

SOURCE: AGN, Criminal, 641, 28, Ciudad de México, 1584.
NOTE: I have retained the ethnic designations used in the document.

and indigenous men typically formed informal unions with lower-ranking women. Degrees of assimilation also determined the category of partners. Because they were "acculturated" indigenous women, the two *indias ladinas* on the list managed to form unions with mestizos, who were somewhat higher in the social hierarchy. By learning a trade, an indigenous blacksmith also elevated his status and therefore could carry on a relationship with a mestiza.

The differential treatment of Spanish, indigenous, and casta women by ecclesiastical courts reflects the official and religious view in colonial society that natives of mixed race did not possess "honor" and therefore had nothing to lose by having their names recorded in amancebamiento documents.[83] On the other hand, records of cases involving Spanish women often omitted their names or identified them by the polite term *honest woman (mujer honesta)*.[84] Names of single Spanish women inadvertently listed in the records were later redacted.

Punishments for amancebamiento varied depending on the situation and on the authority investigating the case. Indigenous officials tended to punish amancebamiento with lashes, whereas Spanish secular and ecclesiastical authorities often ordered the couple to purchase candles or oil for the church.[85] The man and woman typically were ordered not to see each other again and, in cases in which previous warnings had failed, one of the couple might be temporarily banished from the community.[86] Special circumstances might warrant harsher punishments. For example, when Lucas Juan confessed that he was having sexual relations with Sebastiana Ana, even though he had been involved with her adult daughter a few years earlier, his labor was sold for one year to an *obraje* (workshop) and hers was sold for six months.[87] The inconsistent prosecution of amancebamiento suggests that political and economic motivations, rather than moral outrage, were at the root of many denunciations.

VIOLENCE IN MARRIAGE

Despite the ideals that shaped relations between couples, native women sometimes suffered at their husbands' or lovers' hands, complaining to relatives, friends, and local and Spanish officials that their husbands had pushed, beaten, or whipped them and, in more extreme cases, attacked them with weapons or rocks. Some complaints led to formal investigation and prosecution. When a woman did not survive her husband's violence or was gravely wounded, her parents urged indigenous and Spanish authorities to punish their son-in-law. Both the plaintiff and the defendant in such a case presented three witnesses who testified to what they had seen or what they knew about the couple's relationship (hearsay was admissible in Spanish courts). Native officials judged minor cases and reported serious or especially violent crimes to a Spanish magistrate. In towns where a Spanish authority resided, or when the plaintiff feared bias from the indigenous cabildo, the Spanish alcalde mayor or a local priest might hear the case directly, with a notary taking statements from all parties through an interpreter. (In the many multiethnic communities of highland Mexico in which two indigenous languages were used, two interpreters were often employed.[88]) Criminal records generated in assault and battery and uxoricide trials disclose fascinating, disturbing, and revealing perspectives on marriage, family, and community in central Mexico and Oaxaca.

Patterns of Violence

Women of all social and economic groups were at risk of domestic violence. In their studies of crime in colonial Mexico, both William Taylor and Steve Stern find that most female victims were assaulted by husbands, lovers, or other male relatives.[89] Although Taylor's and Stern's investigations encompass a broader cross-section of society than the present work, this pattern holds true in the native communities of highland Mexico that I researched. In a sample of forty-eight cases involving wife beating from central Mexico, the Mixteca Alta, and the Sierra Zapoteca, twenty-one provide the ages of the men, of whom seventeen were less than thirty years old.[90] Age was also an important factor in the twenty-five uxoricide cases from this period. In the thirteen cases in which the husband's age was given, eleven husbands were thirty or younger.[91] This trend may be interpreted in several ways. First, it appears that the initial ten or so years of marriage, during which the couple were adjusting to new responsibilities and living arrangements, could be difficult; many couples resided with parents or other relatives, which may have escalated tensions. Second, many incompatible couples either separated by the time they reached thirty or managed to resolve their issues. Third, the dynamics within marriage were shifting: whereas young men might have been more prone to rash, violent behavior, they may have matured and become more secure with their roles as husbands as time passed. Fourth, perhaps those who had been punished for wife beating by local officials grew weary of floggings and practiced more restraint. Women also may have developed strategies for diffusing potential conflicts.

Wife beatings were handled like other battery cases. No distinction was made between violence against wives and violence against any other persons in the community, and there was no term "wife beating" per se. Instead, husbands were charged with battery, suggesting that women were considered worthy of protection not as "wives" and "mothers" but strictly as community members.[92] The Spanish term *mala vida* (bad life) was sometimes used to describe domestic violence, but it carried broader connotations of mistreatment that destroyed relationships, including verbal abuse, failure to provide, and infidelity. Although less frequently reported, women could also give their husbands mala vida, which should therefore not be conflated with wife beating.[93]

Men and women fought over a variety of issues related to marital expectations and gendered divisions of labor, but two prominent issues emerge in the narratives on violence in the criminal records. First, men justified their violence by accusing their wives of adultery. In preconquest and colonial times, adultery was considered an egregious violation of the marriage vows; jealousy was a powerful emotion offered as an excuse for an inexcusable crime. (The relationship between adultery and violence is discussed in more detail in Chapter 6). Second, men and women fought over their domestic duties, most often a husband's expectation that his wife would cook for him. As a way to pressure their men, women sometimes refused to cook when they were angry; however, men considered this a serious affront and could become violent if they believed that their wives were acting defiantly. Also, as guardians of the home, women were expected to keep track of household property and tools, and men sometimes became enraged when they felt that their wives had misplaced their belongings.[94] Conflicts over domestic responsibilities also arose when a woman questioned her husband about his whereabouts or how he had spent money.

In cases of uxoricide, men often testified that a petty dispute had escalated into a violent attack. Andrés Naqui, a twenty-two-year-old Ñudzahui man, described how he and his wife had argued and how she had thrown a cloak, an axe, and a net on the ground at his feet; this infuriated him, and he became even angrier when she refused to pick them up. He pushed her, and after they struggled for a few moments, she ran out of the house and threatened him with a rock. He found a club and hit her twice in the head. She died a few days later.[95]

What recourse did women have when their husbands assaulted them? They often turned to family and friends to help them escape violent spouses, and some attempted to use native and Spanish authorities to prosecute abusive husbands.

Responses to Violence

Male and female relatives and neighbors opened their homes to battered wives and confronted the men who beat them. In a 1558 case, a Nahua woman of Acatepec named Catalina testified that she had challenged her brother for mistreating his wife.[96] Similarly, in 1688 an Ayuuk (Mixe) woman scolded her cousin for whipping his wife's feet purportedly because she had lost two of his turkeys and a machete. She then reported the abuse to his wife's brother.[97] Sometimes a wife's male relatives used or threatened violence to curb a husband's behavior. Fearing reprisal, a man who had fought with his wife often hesitated to go to her parents' home to ask her to return to him. When questioned by authorities about mistreating his wife, a twenty-three-year-old Zapotec man named Pedro Méndez admitted that his father-in-law and brother-in-law had beaten him on several occasions for abusing his wife.[98] Similarly, Tomás Juan, a twenty-two-year-old Nahua imprisoned for assaulting his wife, alleged in 1723 that his wife's father and uncle had beaten him several times after she had complained to them about the way that he treated her.[99]

Although tensions sometimes existed between mothers-in-law and daughters-in-law, evidence from colonial criminal records often reveal a different dynamic. A mother-in-law was expected to look after her daughter-in-law's well-being and care for her as her own child. In a case from the Mixteca Alta in 1634, María López defended her daughter-in-law when her son began to fight with his wife over some tortillas that she had made for him. When her son became violent, María López scolded him, asking, "Son, why do you become angry with your wife when she has not given you occasion?" He then threw the plate of tortillas at his mother, and she criticized his ingratitude: "Well! This is how you treat your mother who gave birth to you!"[100] The frustrated man stormed out of the house. In cases of patrilocal residence, a bride's family expected the groom's household, especially the women, to protect her. When María Alávez was murdered in the Bènizàa yetze of Camotlan in 1706, her father, Pedro Alávez, blamed her death on her mother-in-law, María Viloria, and her two sisters-in-law. He chastised the three women and threatened that they would pay for her death because they had not watched out for her safety although they had all lived together.[101] Even so, Alávez admitted that he knew that María Viloria had loved his daughter because she was her daughter-in-law.

Even after remarriage, a woman often maintained close ties with the mother of her first husband. For example, in 1605 Ana de Rojas notified Ñudzahui authorities of Teposcolula that Juana López, who had once been married to her son, was missing. She told a *topile* (lesser native official) and a church singer that she suspected that Andrés López, Juana's second husband, had killed her and that they could find him at a nearby house. When officials arrived at the house, they found Ana de Rojas interrogating the man: "Where is my daughter? You have killed her. Tell the truth."[102] Significantly, Rojas continued to consider Juana López her daughter, attesting to the permanence of their bond even after her remarriage. Not only did Rojas notify the authorities and tell them where to find the murderer, she directly confronted him and demanded that he confess to the crime. Relationships between mothers-in-law and their daughters-in-law surely could be complex and difficult, but these cases demonstrate that women at times found their mothers-in-law to be important allies and intermediaries.

Defying stereotypes of the resigned Indian woman, indigenous female family members and friends intervened in marital conflicts and, at the risk of serious injury, challenged men who had attacked their wives in a violent rage. But to suggest that these confrontations played out strictly along gender lines would be a great oversimplification. Indeed, grandparents, parents, aunts, uncles, siblings, compadres, and mothers-in-law all became involved in monitoring a man's treatment of his wife, and they frequently defended a woman who was being abused by her husband. As Stern concludes, based on his analysis of violence in Morelos, "women crossing over to denunciations of female immorality, men crossing over to denunciations of male excess, relatives crossing over to stances of enmity that inverted the usual kinship alignments—these crossovers required skill in the art of gender and family politics."[103] Clearly, the objections raised by relatives of the bride and groom, neighbors, and officials demonstrate that marital violence was not condoned even if it was widespread. But cases of repeated abuse also show that breaking patterns of violence was not an easily achieved objective.

Indigenous women and their families often used the legal system to prosecute violent husbands. Because native men and women of central

Mexico and Oaxaca maintained separate accounts and possessed their own properties, goods, and monies, a woman could risk her husband's imprisonment or temporary exile from a community. Although ideally a husband and wife contributed jointly to both the household and their tribute obligations, a woman was not entirely financially dependent on her husband. Moreover, in cases where relations had become strained, financial cooperation may have already declined. Thus women's semi-autonomous financial status allowed them to pursue legal action against their husbands without completely jeopardizing their own economic well-being.[104]

When cabildo officials investigated a husband's treatment of his wife, witnesses often made a point of reporting whether in the past or not the woman had ever complained to authorities about her husband's behavior, which suggests that it was routine, rather than exceptional, for a woman to bring charges against a violent spouse.[105] When Juan López was tried for assaulting his wife, Catalina, witnesses testified that not only had she complained before but Juan's first wife had sought the intervention of local officials on many occasions. No doubt Juan's previous record of abuse and his local reputation as a violent man contributed to his harsh sentence of a hundred lashes and two months labor in the orchard of the local monastery. Women's frequent appearance in the courts, where all officials were men and the proceedings were lengthy and complex, belies their passive and naïve role as wives. Furthermore, the lack of distinction between the public and private spheres contributed to the number of cases brought to trial. Because the household was often the site of social interaction and economic exchange, relatives and passersby observed a couple's relationship and did not hesitate to report mistreatment to the authorities. The fact that many households contained multiple families also suggests that other adults would be on hand to observe the daily interactions and conflicts of a married couple. Complex webs of social and political surveillance thus limited male power.

In addition to punishing abusive husbands, local officials often granted women permission to return to their parents temporarily. In 1692, in the Bènizàa yetze of Taguí, Juan de Cháves and María de Alvaro appeared before members of the cabildo to accuse their son-in-law, Pedro Méndez, of beating their daughter, Petrona. They testified that their daughter had come to their house and told them that her husband had beaten her and threatened her life when he began to suspect that she was having an affair. Several days passed, but Pedro did not go to Petrona's house to ask her to return, fearful that her father and brothers would beat him as they had done when he had previously mistreated her. Before complaining to officials, Petrona's parents had attempted to make peace with Pedro, asking his brother, who lived in the same household, to look after their daughter.

Pedro still suspected Petrona of adultery although she denied the accusation. Unable to resolve the conflict, the disputing sides approached the Bènizàa authorities, who, after a hearing, sent Petrona home to her parents.[106] Official intervention was often only a temporary solution to buy time and make peace between a feuding husband and wife. The evidence suggests that this strategy had limited success. In some cases, including the tragic marriage of Pedro and Petrona, the abuse continued once the woman returned to her husband and sometimes became deadly.[107]

As with assault and battery, parents or other relatives of victims often pursued uxoricide cases, demanding that justice be served. For example, in 1596 Joaquin Gaitán and Francisca Hernández, parents of Magdalena Gaitán, urged Ñudzahui officials of Tilantongo to punish their son-in-law, Sebastián Gómez, for the attempted murder of their daughter. She was eight months pregnant when he poisoned her after an argument; she suffered a violent miscarriage, was stricken blind, and was on the point of death when her parents appeared before local authorities. Throughout the proceedings, both parents were named as plaintiffs in the case.[108] Similarly, in Yanhuitlan in 1577 a victim's father, two uncles, and brother brought suit against her husband.[109]

In his study of violence in colonial Mexico and Oaxaca, Taylor finds the numerous complaints of physical abuse by women "particularly remarkable because husband-wife assaults are routinely underrepresented in the criminal records of societies in which wife-beating is socially acceptable."[110] I would argue that the many cases indicate that wife beating was not socially acceptable in these societies. By filing suits against their husbands for mistreatment, women contested their subordinate status and sought to restore balance in marital relations. A woman's ability to make a claim against her husband undermined his attempt to control her absolutely. Moreover, local officials who pursued the case, and community and family members who were often the first to intervene and who served as witnesses, reaffirmed a woman's status as a valued member of society and condemned her husband's abusive behavior.

An analysis of sentences for wife beating from indigenous communities in central Mexico and Oaxaca indicates that women often succeeded in having their husbands punished; men who attacked their wives with weapons, such as knives or machetes, were sentenced to lashes, fined the costs of the proceedings, and ordered to pay the healer who treated the victim.[111] Authorities also sometimes ordered the sale of a husband's labor. For example, in 1577 a Ñudzahui man who had beaten his wife was sentenced to flogging and sent to work in the monastery for two months.[112]

Although uxoricide trial records are often incomplete and relatively few include sentences, those extant that do include judgments show that wife murder was harshly punished.[113] Of the twenty-five cases of spousal homicide that I examined, eight had sentences (in addition, two men maintained their innocence while deposing under torture and were officially cleared of the charges). Two of the guilty were condemned to death; three were sentenced to two hundred lashes and labor for periods of two to eight years[114]; one was banished from the community for a year; one was fined twenty pesos[115]; and one was sold into servitude for five years after he attempted to poison his wife.[116] As discussed in greater detail in Chapter 6, Spanish authorities excused murder only when a man could prove that he had caught his wife committing adultery.

CONCLUDING REMARKS

Even with the introduction of Christianity, indigenous people continued to interpret the social, economic, and political significance of marriage in traditional terms. Marriage represented the transition from childhood to adulthood, and marital status and affiliation largely shaped one's social identity. Marriage enabled the establishment of new households, promoted joy in the growth of families, and provided companionship and love for husband and wife. It also formalized cooperative and reciprocal labor arrangements between a man and woman and their respective households.

To understand marital relationships in strictly economic terms is to overlook a fundamental form of expressing affection, however. Providing food or clothing for a mate strengthened emotional bonds and demonstrated concern for another's well-being. When members of households worked together or pooled their resources, they expressed social solidarity in the collective effort to survive. Finally, nobles used marriage to build alliances and enhance the political power of their lineages in colonial times.

Many couples lived in informal unions outside of wedlock and shared the expectations of married couples. The inconsistent prosecution of these couples makes it difficult to estimate how frequent such arrangements were in rural native communities, but they seem to have been common. In the cases that I located in the historical record, many couples were interracial and there may have been differences in race and status that undermined their ability or desire to marry. An existing marriage also prevented a couple from formalizing their union.

When a husband and wife (or an unmarried couple) failed to live up to their partner's ideals, their relationship could deteriorate and, in some cases, become violent. Criminal cases of assault and battery and homicide reveal native attitudes toward appropriate gender roles, marital relations, and the use of violence. Although in their exhortations on the permanence of marriage the friars admonished women to remain submissive to their husbands, even in cases of violence and abuse, the criminal prosecution of wife beating suggests that domestic violence, especially if deemed excessive, was not condoned or accepted (even if common) in indigenous communities.

Women's use of the criminal justice system indicates that they expected to be taken seriously and treated fairly by native and Spanish officials. By initiating a case before the community, a woman used social pressure and legal institutions to curb her husband's cruel behavior. In his comparative analysis of attitudes surrounding gendered violence in Morelos and Oaxaca, Stern detects "hints of a wider cultural affirmation of contingent right in male-female relations" in Oaxaca, a region that remained predominantly indigenous in the late colonial period.[117] My research on the earlier period reveals similar patterns, even in central Mexico. In conjunction with other sources, criminal cases provide alternative perspectives to idealized gender roles described in formal texts and enable a more comprehensive view of indigenous women's status in early Mexico.

CHAPTER FIVE

Sexual Attitudes and Concepts

On December 19, 1593, Andrea Hernández complained to Ñudzahui (Mixtec) officials and the Spanish alcalde mayor in Teposcolula that her husband, Pedro, had been having an affair with a married neighbor named Cecilia López for over a year. Other women corroborated her accusations, testifying that they had seen Pedro and Cecilia enter each other's house on many occasions and seen them sit and eat together on a *petate* (reed mat used for sleeping and sitting). Andrea also alleged that her husband and Cecilia often mistreated her because of their infidelity. The alcalde mayor warned the promiscuous pair that they would be given a hundred lashes if they were caught meeting publicly or privately ever again, but just two days later Andrea saw her husband enter Cecilia's house. Rather than bother with officials, Andrea and five other women, including her mother, went to Cecilia's house and beat her.[1]

The accusations of adultery and assault in this case from late sixteenth-century Teposcolula illustrate how sexual attitudes and mores shaped the dynamics of marriage, household, and community relations in this part of New Spain. Indigenous peoples of highland Mexico held similar beliefs about sexuality, and they shared common concerns over the perceived dangers of excess and deviation from prescribed behavior. Formal texts and speeches are especially valuable for reconstructing indigenous sexual ideology and behavior. The vast majority, written by Christianized native noblemen under the supervision of Spanish friars, are in Nahuatl and show varying degrees of Christian influence.[2] Texts written by friars and their indigenous aides reflect the Christian sexual concepts that ecclesiastics sought to impart to native peoples as part of the larger evangelization project, yet their reliance on native terminology reveals the persistence of local concepts. Colonial criminal records are more representative than these sources in terms of region, class, and gender in that they come from areas outside of central Mexico and include women and men of all social types. They complement the formal sources and reveal popular attitudes concerning intimacy and desire.

This chapter examines indigenous sexual concepts, symbols, and metaphors, and their evolution in contact with native Christian sexual morality. Multiple perspectives in the sources show that attitudes toward sex were especially important in shaping interactions among adult men and women and in regulating behavior within and among groups in ancient and colonial times.

SEXUAL ATTITUDES

Nahuas rarely spoke directly of sex or the body in formal speeches, preferring symbolism and nuance instead. Speeches from Nahua rituals that marked the passage from childhood to adolescence suggest that sex was seen as one of the principal pleasures on earth, but it could also bring disease and social discord and therefore had to be carefully regulated.

Sexual Desires

Early colonial Nahuatl-language texts use the term *tlalticpacaiotl* (earthly pleasure) as a metaphor for sexual intercourse.[3] A sixteenth-century model speech for a ruler addressing his daughter conveys the sentiment that tlalticpacaiotl, like food, rest, and friendship, enriched life and perpetuated society:

So that we will not forever go about weeping, so that we humans will not die of sorrow, our lord gave us laughter, sleep, and crops, the source of our health and sustenance, and finally earthly pleasure so that procreation would occur.

inic amo cemicac tichocatinemizque, inic amo titlaoculmiquizque in timaceoalti: ieoatl techmomaquili in totecuio, in vetzquiztli, in cochiztli: auh ie in tonacaiutl in tochicaoaca, in tooapaoaca: auh iequene ie iehoatl in tlalticpacaiotl, inic nepixolo.[4]

Such texts recognize the desires of both men and women. It is significant that in the speech just translated the father permits his daughter to consider sexual relations a pleasure. In fact, among the terms for female genitalia is *ipaquia* (her place of joy),[5] and one name for a courtesan is *ahuiani* (one who indulges in pleasure). Perhaps influenced by Spaniards who spoke of the *debito matrimonial* (marriage debt), Nahuas considered sexual satisfaction a marital obligation.[6] In a speech to his adolescent son, a father refers to the "earthly pleasures that you owe to your spouse" (*tlalticpacaiotl, inic timaceoalti in monamic*).[7] He warns that, because of his inability to satisfy her needs, a wife might come to "abhor" and "detest" her husband (*ie cuel mitzihiia, ie cuel mitztlaelitta*) and even seek a lover: "Perhaps, even if it is not her intention, she will go to another; she will betray you because you have quickly ruined yourself, you have exhausted yourself" (*acaço y iatlamatia mopan iaz, mitzontlaximaz: ca nel noço otonmiciuhcapolo, ca otonmotlami*).[8]

In the Nahua father's speech are two legends that acknowledge the sexual appetites of both men and women. In one, a preconquest tale about the sustained sexual longing of women throughout their lives, two old women accused of adultery with younger men were brought before the ruler Neçahualcoyotzin, who asked how it was that they still "want earthly pleasure" (*anquinequi in tlalticpacaiotl*).[9] The women explained that, while men may become impotent, women have inside of them "a cave, an abyss, whose only function is to await that which is given, whose only function is to receive" (*ca oztotl, ca tepexitl in totech ca; ca çan tequitl imacoca quichia, ca çan tequitl tlacelia*).[10] As receptors, women were passive but not passionless. The second legend is that of an old man accused of adultery who explained that he still "required earthly pleasure" because he had been prudent in sexual relations and had not wasted his semen when he was young.[11] While the father's speech and other Nahua moralistic narratives concede the intimate desires of both men and women, they emphasize the importance of moderation.

Following Nahuatl conventions of polite discourse, the body, like the sexual act, was discussed in metaphorical terms. In the legend of the old women who committed adultery, the vagina is a cave, playing on the Mesoamerican conception of the earth as female and illuminating one dimension of "earthly pleasure." In another part of the Nahua father's speech, he says to his adolescent son, "It is as though you are a maguey, you will sprout a stalk, you will ripen" (*in ma iuhqui timetl, tiquiiotiz, titeteçaviz*).[12] Although Nahuas considered sex a tlalticpacaiotl, they also believed that it could destroy life and social relations.

Sex and Contamination

The Nahuas thought that a man had a fixed amount of semen, which he would have to expend sparingly over the course of his lifetime. Nahuatl-language speeches and texts often warn of the dangers of excessive sexual activity that would exhaust a man's supply too quickly and lead to impotence. Terms such as *mocauani* (one who is depleted) and *tlatzivi* (idle) are used to describe impotent men. Thus, a father would warn his son that he would shrivel and die if he became sexually active prematurely, just like a maguey that had been tapped too early.[13]

You are like a bored maguey, you are like a maguey: soon you will cease to flow. Perhaps while you are still in your full manhood, you already will have exhausted yourself, you can no longer say anything, no longer do anything to your spouse.

Auh in mahan titlachictli, in mahan timetl: çan cuel in timocaoaz timeia, aço quin vel ica toquichtli, in o cuel tonmotlami, in aoc cuelle tiquilvia, in aoc cuelle ticaitia monamic.[14]

In some ways, a man's marriage and his very life depended on his ability to perform sexually. It also was thought that the immoderate use of aphrodisiacs would quickly exhaust a man's semen and therefore lead to an early death.[15] Interestingly, the Nahuas recognized semen as a life-giving fluid, yet they understood it as necessary not just for creating new life but for sustaining the life of the male and his female partners.

Although moderation in sex and monogamy were the prescribed norms, polygyny and concubinage contradicted Nahua rhetoric. Despite warnings, it is clear that many did not heed recommendations of moderate sex. For example, in 1540 the Nahua cacique of Matlactlan admitted that he had five concubines living in his home and several others in different houses; native witnesses estimated that he had as many as twenty.[16] Privileged status and/or wealth may have allowed some noble and commoner men to exceed prescribed sexual norms.[17] In fact, demonstrations of virility may have symbolically enhanced political and social power.

Nevertheless, stories of the sexual excesses of rulers sometimes served as cautionary tales. In his chronicle of the Mexica, Chimalpahin writes that the great altepetl of Tlatelolco came to an end in the year 1473 "because of concubines." Its ruler, Moquihuixtli, was married to Chalchiuhnenetzin, the sister of the ruler of Mexico Tenochtitlan, Axayacatzin, but he surrounded himself with his concubines and entirely rejected her. He took her gifts from her brother and gave them to his women, he stopped sleeping with her, and he beat her. The disgraced and downtrodden Chalchiuhnenetzin informed her brother of Moquihuixtli's abuse and of his plans to make war on the Mexica. This news angered Axayacatzin and he declared war on Tlatelolco.[18] Chimalpahin's account is a parable warning that inappropriate sexual relations, including concubinage among the nobility, could unleash social and political chaos.

As Alfredo López Austin observes, Nahuas believed that excessive sex was dangerous because during the sexual act the *tonalli* (life force) and the *ihiyotl* (breath) were liberated from the body, which left it vulnerable to illness.[19] They also prescribed moderation because they considered sex to be a source of contamination. Male and female bodies were not pollutants per se, but they carried polluting residues and odors after sex.[20]

A sixteenth-century Nahua nobleman's speech to his adolescent daughter expounds on the corrupting aspect of sexual activity: "Do not desire earthly pleasures. Do not wish to know of that which is called the place of excrement, the place of trash" (*ma çan cuel tontlaelevi in tlalticpac, ma çan cuel tontlamatiznec, in mitoa, in cuitlatitlan, in tlaçultitlan*).[21] Popular belief reflected this preoccupation. It was said that those who lived together outside of wedlock, along with adulterers, thieves, and gamblers, would contaminate ritual offerings (*quitlaçollotiz*),[22] and that pulque makers who did not abstain from sex during production would make the beverage "sour" (*xocoiaz*).[23]

The Nahua goddess of sexuality, Tlazolteotl (*tlaçolli*, trash; *teotl*, here goddess), illustrates the association between sex and contamination.[24] Tlazolteotl was also called Tlaelquani, or one who eats filth.[25] In preconquest times, adulterers confessed their transgressions to her and did penance in her honor to avoid punishment.[26] The goddess Xochiquetzal was also associated with sexual excess.[27] A depiction of Xochiquetzal-Ixnextli in the Codex Telleriano-Remensis symbolizes sexual transgression and discord (see Figure 5.1). She is seated backward on a throne with her head turned around and her hair disheveled; she is weeping. Unlike most images of central Mexican women, this one shows Xochiquetzal's breast exposed. She holds a container full of what an anonymous scribe in a Spanish gloss describes as *mierda* (excrement), representing all bodily excretions. According to native pictorial traditions, Xochiquetzal's posture and appearance represent discord.

Native artists depicted a restless, irresponsible person with his or her hands, head, and/or feet directed backward. For example, an illustration of a vagabond in the early colonial manuscript known as the Codex Mendoza shows a man with his hands and feet facing backward as if to signify that he is constantly coming and going (see Figure 5.2).[28] In her study of gender ambiguity, Cecelia Klein has shown that preconquest, colonial, and modern ethnographic sources use twisted bodies, backward-facing feet, and backward dancing and walking to represent moral disorder, evil, and a variety of illicit sexual behaviors, including adultery, homosexuality, and bisexuality.[29] This concept may also be related to the concept of double-crossing in the Nahuatl verb *maxaloa* (commit adultery) and to the reflexive form of the verb *cuepa* (turn oneself around or turn into something). *Mocuepa* is used in Nahuatl moralizing speeches such as when a Nahua father rhetorically warns his daughter "And if truly you turn yourself around, will you become a goddess?" (*Auh tla nel timocuepaz: cuix titeutiz*).[30] The term as used in the text clearly carries a sexual connotation and may suggest something similar to the English "to be twisted."[31] Unkempt hair further signifies transgression and uncivilized

Figure 5.1. Ixnextli-Xochiquetzal as the embodiment of sexual transgression and discord
SOURCE: Codex Telleriano-Remensis, fol. 11r. Bibliothèque nationale de France.

Figure 5.2. Vagabond shown coming and going
SOURCE: Codex Mendoza, fol. 70r. Bodleian Libraries, University of Oxford, Ms. Arch. Selden A1. Berdan and Anawalt 1992, fol. 70r. Reproduced with permission from University of California Press Books.

behavior. The Codex Telleriano-Remensis image of Xochiquetzal can be read as the embodiment of conflict, disharmony, and sexual excess.

In a Nahuatl-language model speech, a noble warns his adolescent son about having sex with women too early:

You will interrupt your development, you will stunt your growth, your tongue will be white, your mouth will become swollen, puffed; you will go about tasting your snot; you will be pale, you will go about on earth pale; your snot will be dripping; you will go about coughing; you will be weak, weakened, emaciated; you will become a tuft of hair. You will possibly linger on earth a short time, very soon you will be old, old and wrinkled.

timozcallopuztequiz, ticacamacpil, tinenepiliztacapil tiez, ticamaçapil, ticanponaton timuchioaz moiacacuitlapil ticpalotinemiz, tipinectontli tiez, tipineoatinemiz in tlalticpac, moiacacuitl chipintinemiz, titôtôlcatinemiz, tiiâiacatontli, tivivitoctontli tiez, tiquequetotzpil, timamalichtontli timuchioaz: hacaço ie tiquezquilvitia in tlalticpac, çan cuel iça tivevepil, tivevexolochton.[32]

In his treatise on native spirituality and healing, written in 1629, Ruiz de Alarcón claimed that pollution-induced diseases affected male and female adults and children; even an unborn child could be harmed in the womb.[33] These diseases fell into two main categories: *tlaçolmiquiztli* (filth-death) and *netepalhuiliztli* (the state of being dependent on someone).[34] A sexual transgressor, especially an adulterer or a man with many concubines, transmitted tlaçolmiquiztli diseases when he or she came into contact with others. The Florentine Codex records that adulterers, who were particularly dangerous because of their sexual transgressions, would kill turkey chicks with their "filth" (*quintlaçolmictia*) if they came near them.[35] Netepalhuiliztli diseases were spread by those who had become sad and melancholy from coveting another's spouse or possessions. The healing rituals for these diseases emphasized the native belief in the polluting effects of sex. The victim was purified with incense and cleansed through bathing or *tetlaçolaltiloni* (the means of washing someone with regard to filth).[36] Significantly, the curing incantations recorded by Ruiz de Alarcón were addressed to Tlazolteotl and other goddesses. Thus immoral thoughts and acts brought disease to oneself as well as to others in the household and community.[37]

Nahuatl descriptions of prostitutes and adulteresses exemplify native beliefs in the destructive effects of excessive and illicit sexuality.[38] Many of the noun constructions used metaphorically to describe prostitutes contain *micqui*, (a dead person). Nahuatl-language texts describe the prostitute as *tlacamicqui* (a dead person), *xochimicqui* (a sacrificed captive), *teomicqui* (a sacrificed captive), and *miccatzintli* (a poor dead person).[39] An adulteress also is deemed *omic, omomiquilli* (dead, a dead person).[40] These references suggest associations between a richly attired captive who impersonated a deity before his or her sacrifice and the prostitute adorned with face paint, an elegant coiffure, and perfume. According to the Florentine Codex, prostitutes, like god impersonators, were frequently intoxicated. Furthermore, both slaves and prostitutes were bought and sold in the market.

Because intercourse was considered a contaminating act, ritual preparation and penance required sexual abstinence. For some ceremonies, only priests and priestesses practiced chastity; for others all ritual participants, sometimes the entire community avoided sex. Responses to questions in the *Relaciones geográficas* regarding ancient religious customs frequently mention that men and women of the noble and commoner classes abstained from sex to prepare themselves for spiritual exercises.[41] Reports of severe punishments for those who broke vows of chastity underscore a belief in the polluting effects of sex and the subsequent damage that prohibited intercourse might cause. Native nobles recalled that, in preconquest times, priests who failed to keep their vows were burned, strangled, or shot with arrows.[42] The *Relación* of the Bènizàa (Zapotec) community of Tecuicuilco corroborates the Nahua data, citing the case of a priest who had failed to abstain from sex and pulque and was executed.[43] While such accounts may be exaggerated in order to fashion an image of a more austere and well-ordered past, they nevertheless locate pollution in the sexual act. An investigation of religious practices in the Sierra Alta reveals the continued importance of sexual abstinence as part of ritual preparation in the Bènizàa, Ayuuk (Mixe), and Chinantec communites in the early eighteenth century.[44]

Indigenous-language sources and colonial criminal records discuss sexuality overwhelmingly in heterosexual terms and only rarely comment on homosexuality. The silence suggests a number of possibilities. We might conclude that homosexuality was not a serious moral concern or a threat to socioeconomic relations in the way that adultery was and so did not attract the attention of local officials. A second possibility is that if homosexuality was a concern, it was policed at the household, not the community, level. A third possibility is that cross-gendering and transvestism regulated homosexual relations by recasting a same-sex couple as heterosexual, although here we must be cautious not to conflate gender identity and sexual orientation. In any case, I agree with Sigal that it seems unlikely that a sexual identity equivalent to "homosexual" existed in the indigenous communities of preconquest and early colonial highland Mexico.[45]

Discussions of sex in formal texts and speeches are often couched in metaphorical terms, and sexual symbols were used in images of intimate relations to encode daily interaction between native men and women with meaning; such sexual signifiers entered into popular discussions and expressions of intimacy.

SEXUAL SYMBOLS AND METAPHORS

In indigenous metaphorical speech and iconographic systems, food and drink, flowers, feathers, and reed mats have sexual connotations. Moreover, since native peoples also sexualized communication and interaction between men and women, sight and speech were symbolically invested with sexual potency. Preconquest and colonial visual and verbal expression reveals the richness and persistence of this symbolism.

Food and Drink

Throughout Mesoamerica, native peoples associated food and drink with fertility, (re)production, and sex. The sharing of food and drink, like sex, was the foundation of intimacy between a man and a woman and a central aspect of marriage ceremonies in the communities of highland Mexico. Sahagún's Nahua informants likened sexual intercourse to eating in recalling instructional speeches, ritual preparation, and calendrical prognostications. Speaking metaphorically, Nahuas said that the masters of the youth "ate in secret" (*ichtacaquaia*) when they arranged a rendezvous with a woman.[46] Parallel phrases in speeches and texts that juxtapose eating and intercourse also conflate the two. For example, the Florentine Codex prognostication of the fate of a man born on the day of One House warns: "Perhaps he will commit adultery; perhaps he will sleep with, he will have sex with, another's woman (*cueitl, vipilli*); perhaps he will eat another's food, he will eat upon departing from another's place" (*aço tetlanximaz, aço tetlan aquiz, aço cueitl, vipilli tepan canaz, aço tetlaqualiz, tetlan quateuiz*).[47] Eating conveyed the man's inclination to commit adultery. Linguistic evidence illuminates the conceptual relationship between eating and sexual intercourse. The Nahuatl verb *yecoa* means "to taste, sample food or drink" or "to copulate with someone."[48]

Sixteenth-century models of speeches that Nahua parents delivered to their adolescent children also employed metaphors of eating for sexual relations. In one a father instructs his son to avoid excess, likening oversexed behavior to that of a dog, a symbol of lasciviousness gulping its food: "[But] you are not to waste yourself quickly; you are not to devour, to gobble earthly pleasures as though you were a dog" (*iece amo timiciuhcapoloz, amo iuhqui tichichi, ticquativetziz, ticquetzontivetziz in tlalticpacaiotl*).[49,50] In advising his son to practice moderation, even with his wife, the father says: "Although she is your spouse, your flesh, with whom you will live, with whom you will go about, it is as with food—you are not to eat it quickly; that is to say, you are not to live in filth; you are not to give yourself to it excessively"(*ma nel monamic, monacaio, in itlan tinemiz, in itlan tiaz: in mahan tlaqualli, amo tiquiciuhcaquaz, quitoznequi, amo titlahelnemiz, amo ticmotequimacaz*).[51] Finally he speaks of sex as food when he warns his son that if he becomes incapable of satisfying his wife, he will "starve her to death" (*ticapizmictia*).[52] Food, like sex, was one of life's necessities to be shared with one's spouse. Sexual desire was like hunger—if not fulfilled, it could lead to premature death.

References to fasting and sexual abstinence in the same passages in the Florentine Codex, the *Relaciones geográficas*, and colonial criminal and Inquisition records also associate food, drink, and sex. The Florentine Codex states that before a ritual rulers, officials, and warriors fasted for five nights, during which they abstained from their wives and slept in the *calpulli* temple (a calpulli is a subunit of an altepetl).[53] Similarly, in an account of the ceremonies for Panquetzaliztli, Sahagún's informants told him that in preparation, "they greatly honored fasting. All of the people abstained, especially those who were the bathers. No one slept with a woman, and none of the women slept with a man" (*cenca quimaviztiliaia in neçaoaliztli: vel ixquich tlacatl, motzitzquiaia: oc cenca iehoantin, in tealtique: aiac cioacochia, auh in cioa, ano ac oquichcochia*).[54] Narratives of the preparations for the feast of Quecholli also combine abstinence from sex, food, and pulque. To avoid contaminating offerings and ritual items, people fasted and abstained while they made the spears that would be used in a festival: "And when spears were being made, no one slept with a woman. And the old men did not drink pulque; they did not get drunk. They abstained; they abstained from pulque" (*Auh in iquac tlacatia mitl, aiac cioacochia; auh in vevetque, amo quia in vctli, amo tlaoanaia, motlacaoaltiaia, quimocaoaltiaia in vctli*).[55] Finally, from the Florentine Codex on the feasts of Macuilxochitl and Xochipilli: "When they were fasting, if one of us men slept with a woman, or a woman slept with a man, it was said 'they destroyed their fasting with filth'" (*yn iquac neçauililoia, intla aca toquichti ipan cioacochiz, anoço cioatl, ipan oquichcochiz: mitoaia, quintlaçulmictia, yn neçaoaliz*).[56] Sex was a food that spoiled the fast.

In addition to contaminating ritual offerings, breaking a fast or a vow of abstinence carried long-term personal consequences. Because their inability to keep ritual commitments was linked with their control of sex, women born on the day Seven Flower were warned that they would become great whores if they broke their fast.

Indicating that it was not a good [day sign], it was said, when if some embroiderer broke her fasting, it was said, then she deserved infamy and a bad name, that she would just live in vice and become a prostitute. For it was said the embroiderers lived in great vice and became prostitutes.

auh inic amo qualli, mitoaia, iquac intla aca tlâmachchiuhqui, yneçaoaliz quitlacoaia, mitoa: vncan quimomacevia aviliquizcaiotl, aviltocaitl: inic çan âavilnemiz, âavienitiz, ca mitoa, tlaquauh avilnemia, mâaviltiaia in tlamachchiuhque.[57]

This warning is ambiguous since "fasting" could very well mean sexual abstinence. In any case, the inability of women born on Seven Flower to fulfill their sacred obligations undermined their success as embroiderers. Images of the goddess Xochiquetzal that show her with symbols of sexual excess and of women's work embody the fate predicted for them (see Figure 5.3).

Like Sahagún's Nahua aides, native respondents to the *Relaciones geográficas* and witnesses in idolatry trials consistently equated sexual abstinence and fasting. Residents of Ucila, for example, abstained from sex and did not eat chile, salt, or any other prized foods before rituals.[58] Similarly, those of Chinantla abstained and ate only once daily for one hundred days before their principal feast.[59] In Camotlan, Chinantla, and Lalana in the Zapotec Sierra in the early eighteenth century, inhabitants also observed food restrictions and sexual prohibitions for ceremonial

Figure 5.3. *Xochiquetzal with symbols of illicit sex*
SOURCE: Codex Telleriano-Remensis, fol. 22v. Bibliothèque nationale de France.

purposes and the local calendar reader instructed them when to start and how long to maintain their penances.[60]

In colonial adultery investigations, Nahua, Ñudzahui, Bènizàa, and Ayuuk witnesses accused men and women who ate together of sexual intimacy. Drawing from the case that opened this chapter, two Ñudzahui women of Teposcolula testified in 1593 that Pedro Hernández and Cecilia López were certainly lovers because the women had seen them eating together.[61] Similarly, when don Agustín Maldonado and Inés Pérez were tried for adultery in the Mixtec community of Tamazulapa in 1626, one witness was convinced of their affair because he had seen them sleeping and eating together; a second said that he had seen the couple drinking together.[62] In 1657, Bènizàa residents of Lalopa, in a homicide investigation involving a local man accused of murdering his wife, testified that the man had been sexually involved with another woman because they had seen the two eating together.[63] Trying to prove his innocence, the man's mother and stepfather employed the same strategy, insisting that their son and his wife had been on good terms because they had seen the couple eat dinner together and then lie down on their mats. As for the other woman, the parents explained that she had given them food because she was their comadre and that her gesture did not reflect any intimacy with their son.

The act of eating together could intimate sexual relations even among household members. In 1667, a jealous, young Zapotec wife accused her husband of committing incest with his stepmother, offering as evidence the fact that the two routinely ate together. The man explained that he had given his stepmother tortillas and *atole* (a corn beverage) only because she was his father's wife. Local native officials took the charges seriously and investigated.[64] The symbolic significance of a shared meal shaped the daily interactions of native men and women, who had to be careful about the messages they might send if they offered food to or shared it with a member of the opposite sex other than a relative or spouse.

The linking of sex and food in native society derived in part from the duties that a husband and wife shared and the obligations that they owed each other. Food was a prized, sacred commodity.[65] Thus sharing food was an act of love and respect. Cooking meals was laborious and time-consuming for women, making food even more valuable because of the effort invested in its preparation. In 1692, a Bènizàa woman of Taguí associated labor obligations with sexual pleasure when she assaulted a woman whom she suspected of sleeping with her husband. She dragged the woman by her hair to a *metate* (grinding stone) and demanded that if she was going to have sex with her husband, she should grind maize for his tortillas, too.[66] The duties and rewards of marriage converged when it came to food and sex.

Drinking, like eating, symbolically established and extended all social relations, but among adult men and women it took on a deeper significance. Couples often drank pulque together in their own homes or in the homes of other couples, friends, or relatives.[67] Consequently, social drinking was seen as a part of courtship.[68]

While couples ideally ate and drank in moderation, excessive drinking, like gluttony, was associated with a voracious sexual appetite and illicit sex. This is illustrated in pictorials and Nahuatl-language text descriptions of prostitutes. For example, according to the Florentine Codex, a Nahua mother reminded her adolescent daughter that only *ahuianime* (women of pleasure) indulged in pulque and jimson weed.[69] To the Nahuas, the prostitute evoked terms such as *tlahuana* (she/he gets drunk), *xocomicqui* (she/he is a drunkard), and their derivations, including *tequixocomicqui* (one who has the occupation of habitually drinking), *tlatlahuana* (she/he continually gets drunk), and *tlahuanqui* (one who gets drunk).[70]

Figure 5.4, an illustration from the Florentine Codex, shows a prostitute offering a drink to a man in exchange for money. It is a hybrid of native and Spanish sexual symbolism. As Jeanette Peterson points out, the prostitute wears red shoes, a European convention for a harlot.[71] Also, her posture mimics European poses of the time and she is facing front rather than in profile, representing the influence of three-dimensional European art style on Nahua artists. She sells her body for money, a Spanish introduction. At the same time, this image reveals underlying indigenous symbols. The couple is shown at the crossroads, a place of danger and transgression.[72] Clearly drink, sex, and the prostitute's sale of her body are all connected here, as they are in Figure 5.5, which shows an "evil youth" (*telpochtlahueliloc*) holding a jug and offering a cup to a woman. The accompanying Nahuatl text makes clear that the young scoundrel indulges in alcohol and women.[73]

Colonial criminal records from Oaxaca and central Mexico reflect many of the attitudes toward sex and seduction expressed by the Nahua writers and artists who contributed to the Florentine Codex. A 1588 case of assault against Ana Hernández Tajasos, a fifty-year-old Ñudzahui woman, took an unexpected turn when don Gabriel de Guzmán, the cacique and governor of Yanhuitlan, accused her of prostituting her own daughter.[74] A thirty-five-year-old Ñudzahui woman testified that she had seen people bringing large jugs of pulque to Ana's house and many women of loose morals drinking there. Other native witnesses also alleged that there was frequent drinking at Ana's house, proving that she was a procuress. Generally, natives who testified in adultery cases equated excessive drinking with licentiousness. In 1643, don Miguel Caros, a

124 Sexual Attitudes and Concepts

Figure 5.4. Sixteenth-century prostitute, revealing the indigenous association between drinking and sex

SOURCE: Florentine Codex, bk. 10, fol. 70. Florence: Biblioteca Medicea Laurenziana, Med. Palat. 220, c. 72. By concession of the Ministry for Heritage and Cultural Activities; further reproduction by any means is forbidden.

Nahua noble of Coyoacan, presented several witnesses who attested to his wife's infidelity, alleging that she had gotten drunk on pulque with don Miguel's rival.[75] Regardless of the truth of such accusations, the link between drinking and sexual impropriety in formal speeches, popular imagination, cultural practice, and legal testimony echoes Florentine Codex descriptions of prostitutes and lewd young men.

Flowers, Feathers, and Reed Mats

In metaphorical speech and iconography, flowers, feathers, and reed mats appear as symbols of potency, fertility, and (re)production.[76] As with food and drink, the enjoyment of flowers was subject to restrictions. According to the Florentine Codex, people did not deserve to smell the centers of flowers; that honor belonged to the god Titlacahuan alone.[77] Those

Figure 5.5. Sixteenth-century depiction of an evil youth who is prone to the vices of drunkenness and lust
SOURCE: Florentine Codex, bk. 10, fol. 24v. Florence: Biblioteca Medicea Laurenziana, Med. Palat. 220, c. 26v. By concession of the Ministry for Heritage and Cultural Activities; further reproduction by any means is forbidden.

who violated such restrictions challenged the social and moral order. As symbols of fertility and productive sexuality, flower imagery was evoked in speeches at native life-cycle rituals. Nahua elders and honored guests spoke of children as flowers when they addressed a bride and groom at the marriage ceremony, telling the bride that if she were fortunate, she would have children who would "bloom and flower" from her "womb and throat" (*aço xotlaz aço cueponiz in moxillantzinco in motozcatlantzinco*).[78] In some communities, the bride and groom exchanged flowers during the wedding ceremony, as did Mixtec couples of Xalapa, for example.[79] Late colonial paintings depict native couples wearing flower garlands as they leave the church or grooms carrying flower staffs.[80]

Flowers, like food and drink, had both positive and negative connotations. While they might represent reproduction in certain contexts, they symbolized the destructive aspects of sexual excess and illicit relations in others. Nahuatl-language expressions in the Florentine Codex suggest the negative connotations in, for example, the Nahuatl phrase "I caress one with flowers (*nictexochitzotzona*)," meaning "I seduce him/her."[81] Similarly, the expression "I destroy one with flowers (*nitexochipoloa*)" means "to entice one with drink, with food, with flowers, with tobacco, with capes, with gold."[82] In both cases, flowers signify temptation, decadence, and forbidden pleasures.

The giving of flowers as an act of intimacy appears in the historical record. When doña María, the widow of the cacique of Tetzcoco, testified against don Carlos Ometochtzin Chichimecatecuhtli in 1539, she recalled that on two or three occasions he had sent her flowers to seduce her, but claimed that she had rejected them.[83] Molina's Nahuatl dictionary includes the term *xochihuia* (from *xochitl*, flower), which means "to enchant, to seduce the woman with pleasing words in order to take her to another place, or to bewitch her."[84] A cross-dresser was also called a "possessor of flowers," or *xochihua*, and the illustration accompanying this description in the Florentine Codex shows a flower between a seated couple (see Chapter 2 for further discussion and Figure 2.8 of the cross-dresser). The Nahua association of sexual diseases with certain flowers, including the white amaryllis and the poinsettia, confirms the potentially destructive nature of flowers.[85]

Several illustrations in the Florentine Codex show prostitutes holding flowers to represent promiscuity (Figures 5.6 and 5.7).[86] Flowered clothing, although sometimes worn by indigenous men and women without inherently negative connotations, conveys overt sensuality and seduction when worn by prostitutes and the "wicked old man" (*ueue tlahueliloc*) (see Figure 5.7 and the left panel of Figure 5.8). Significantly, an illustration of the procurer depicts his enticing speech (*xochihuiliztli*) as a small flower (see the right panel of Figure 5.8 and refer to Figure 3.2). In the Nahuatl-language description of the prostitute, "she appears like a flower" (*mosuchiquetza*).[87]

Feathers, another symbol of fertility and reproduction, were used frequently in ceremonies and worn by nobles and ritual participants. Alessandra Russo has shown that feathers represented *tonalli* or a person's essence or "shadow" in preconquest and colonial featherworks and costumes.[88] Understanding feathers as a symbol of a person's essence or life force explains why in some Nahua myths they symbolize impregnation, sexual vitality, and reproduction. According to one myth, Coatlicue, a goddess and the mother of Mexica's principal god, Huitzilopochtli, became pregnant when she placed a ball of downy feathers at her waist and they slipped into her dress.[89] Nahuatl speeches, written down during the sixteenth century, were filled with feather imagery. For example, Nahua nobles customarily made speeches to young women when they became pregnant for the first time. The pregnant woman's

Figure 5.6. Prostitute holding flowers, symbolizing sexual excess and seduction
SOURCE: Florentine Codex, bk. 10, fol. 39v. Florence: Biblioteca Medicea Laurenziana, Med. Palat. 220, c. 41v. By concession of the Ministry for Heritage and Cultural Activities; further reproduction by any means is forbidden.

parents congratulated her on the impending birth, telling her that the "All-Pervasive" (a term used for a deity in preconquest times and the Christian god in the colonial period) "wants to place a life inside of you, to provide you with a necklace, to provide you with a fine feather" (*a mitic quimaquiliznequi in ioliliztli; mitzmocozcaiotiliznequi, mitzmoquetzallotiliznequi*).[90] Significantly, in a late sixteenth-century description of a marriage ceremony in the Nahua community of Epazoyuca, the bride and groom were bedecked in feathers, symbolizing their association with reproduction.[91]

The Ñudzahui creation myth depicted in the preconquest Codex Vindobonensis shows a primordial couple establishing the first yuhuitayu on earth. Both the male and the female share the name One-Deer, and both wear ear spools, necklaces, and garments that convey their nobility and equal status. Also, their large feather headdresses represent their roles as the progenitors of the Ñudzahui deities and people (see Figure 5.9).

Figure 5.7. Prostitute holding flowers and wearing a floral garment
SOURCE: Florentine Codex, bk. 10, fol. 39v. Florence: Biblioteca Medicea Laurenziana, Med. Palat. 220, c. 41v. By concession of the Ministry for Heritage and Cultural Activities; further reproduction by any means is forbidden.

Figure 5.8. "Wicked old man" depicted wearing a flowered cape (left) *and procurer with flowery speech* (right)
SOURCE: Florentine Codex, bk. 10, fol. 24v. Florence: Biblioteca Medicea Laurenziana, Med. Palat. 220, c. 26v. By concession of the Ministry for Heritage and Cultural Activities; further reproduction by any means is forbidden.

Figure 5.9. Ñudzahui primordial couple
SOURCE: Codex Vindobonensis Mexicanus I, obverse 51. Vienna: Osterr Nationalbibliothek. Facsimile edition. Vienna: Akademische Druckund Verlagsanstalt; Madrid: Sociedad Estatal Quinto Centenario; Mexico City: Fondo de Cultura Económica, 1992.

Among the most prominent fertility images in Mesoamerica is the feathered serpent, or Quetzalcoatl (Nahuatl, *quetzalli*, quetzal feather; *coatl*, snake). The extensive iconography and mythology surrounding Quetzalcoatl has numerous meanings, and in certain contexts the feathered serpent served as a sexual symbol. Scholars frequently associate Quetzalcoatl with the phallus; however, in his study of a modern Mixtec community, Monaghan finds that the people of Nuyoo associate it with female genitalia.[92] Representing the union of earth (snakes/female) and sky (birds/male), the image embodies duality and bisexuality. Significantly, in preconquest and early colonial codices it is frequently undulating through the legs of a woman, clearly connoting fertility and reproduction. Figure 5.10, from a preconquest Ñudzahui manuscript known as the Codex Nuttall, shows a woman named Three Flint who has just given birth. The newborn is still attached to her by the umbilical

Figure 5.10. Feathered serpent in birth scene from a Ñudzahui pictorial manuscript
SOURCE: Codex Nuttall, fol. 16. Facsimile edition. Vienna: Akademische Druckund Verlagsanstalt; Madrid: Sociedad Estatal Quinto Centenario; Mexico City: Fondo de Cultura Económico, 1992.

cord and blood pools beneath her. A feathered serpent winds around behind her and through her legs, and the position of its head mimics hers. The snake follows her as she enters the earth through a cave. In the Codex Laud, the feathered serpent appears in a scene with the goddess Tlazolteotl-Ixcuina, identified by the weaving implements in her headdress and in her hands and by the crescent moon on her skirt and her nose ornament (see Figure 5.11). The serpent passes through her legs, and the head of Ehecatl, the god of wind and a manifestation of Quetzalcoatl, peers from its mouth.[93] Ehecatl is shown adjacent to Tlazolteotl as a body of water in which the latter is submerged in a birthing position.[94]

Like flowers, feathers, food, and drink, the reed mat had a variety of meanings in native verbal and visual expression. Throughout

Figure 5.11. Tlazolteotl with feathered serpent
SOURCE: Codex Laud, fol. 32. Facsimile edition. Vienna: Akademische Druckund Verlagsanstalt; Madrid: Sociedad Estatal Quinto Centenario; Mexico City: Fondo de Cultura Económico, 1994.

Mesoamerica, it was a symbol of authority. In native pictorial manuscripts, murals, painted ceramics, and sculptures, rulers are shown seated on reed mats or high-backed mat "thrones." Nobles and commoners alike used mats to sit and sleep on. As discussed in Chapter 3, for example, in the marriage ceremony the mat, symbolized the couple's union and sexual intimacy. In Ñudzahui codices, ruling couples were often depicted sitting together on a reed mat and gesturing to one another. As Terraciano argues, in this context the mat was more than simply the seat of authority; it represented the "conjugal bed" of the ruling couple and their legacy of producing heirs to the rulership. Thus in Ñudzahui manuscripts the mat was both a political and a social symbol that represented the intimate relationship between the royal pair.[95]

Native-language terminology makes a metaphorical association between sex and the mat. Verb constructions meaning "have sex" are based on indigenous words for mat. Among Tíchazàa terms meaning "have sex," Córdova's dictionary lists *taañee penigonná* (*taha*, mat; *ñee*, with; and *penigonná*, woman).[96] Alvarado's dictionary provides a similar construction, using *yuhui* (mat): *yoyuhuindiña* (mat someone).[97] Nahuatl constructions for sexual relations do not mention the mat explicitly, although it is implied in references to the place of sleep. For example, Molina lists *niteteca* (I lay someone down) and *ytlan nicochi* (I sleep next to him/her) among terms for intercourse, and native pictorials express sexual intimacy by showing a man and woman lying together, suggesting these terms.[98] In an illustration from the Codex Mendoza, an adulterous couple lies together under a blanket facing each other, a pose that, according to native pictorial conventions, symbolizes consent (see Figure 6.2).

According to testimony in archival records, when a man and a woman sat or lay down together on a mat, they were expressing their sexual intimacy. Thus the statements of common people provide insight into the popular understanding of these multivalent symbols. When called to testify about accusations of adultery, native witnesses sometimes evoked the image of the reed mat to suggest indiscretion. In the example from Teposcolula that opened this chapter, a witness incriminated a couple in an affair by testifying that she had seen them sitting together on a reed mat.[99] Similarly, in 1626 two witnesses in an adultery trial in Tamazulapa testified that they had seen the alleged lovers sleeping together on a petate.[100] Like couples sitting together on a mat, men and women who spoke to or looked directly at one another raised suspicions.

Speech, Sight, and Seduction

The cultures of Mesoamerica possessed rich oral traditions. Speaking was invested with considerable power, and nobles distinguished themselves from commoners by the use of reverential, metaphorical language. Colonial records attest to a highly developed genre of speech for intimacy and courtship. In some contexts, speaking represented intercourse. In a moralizing speech, a Nahua father advises his son that if he foolishly wastes his semen by indulging in sex at an early age, his later sexual performance will suffer; the time will come "when you are no longer able to say anything, no longer able to do anything to your spouse" (*in aoc cuelle tiquilvia, in aoc cuelle ticaitia monamic*), making the association between sex and speech explicit.[101] Discourses on acceptable sexual behavior and descriptions of transgressors in the Florentine Codex articulate the relationship between speech and seduction. An evil youth is characterized as a womanizer and a smooth talker. He is deemed "a keeper of mistresses, a talker; he lives in concubinage" (*mecaoa, notzale momecatia*).[102] The illustration of the prostitute in the Florentine Codex (Figure 5.4) reinforces the sexual power of speech by showing a client kneeling before and offering money to a prostitute; a speech scroll emerges from his mouth indicating that he propositions her with pleasing words. Nahuatl-language descriptions of the procurer and the procuress also emphasize their abilities to deliver arousing discourses (see Figure 5.8). In fact, it is through speech alone that the procurer is said to have led clients astray:

The procurer is a mouse, a charmer, a windbag, an enticer, a possessor of flowers, one who seduces people with flowery words, one who flatters people with pleasing words, one who poisons people. He entices, he poisons people; he stretches out long-winded speeches; he summons people with spells, he lays ambushes for people.

in tetlanochili quimichi tensuchitl, hecatlatole, tecoconauiani, suchioa, tetensuchiuiani, tetensuchitzotzonanii, tepauiani: tecoconauia, tepauia, hecamecatl quiteca, tenaoalnotza tetlachichiuilia.[103]

The procuress, too, uses speeches, incantations, and spells to lure clients:

She is a charmer, a sweet-talker, a smooth-talker; she is of pleasing, agreeable speech, soft-spoken. Her words are flowers, sweet, pleasing. She is an artful, skilled speaker, a master of discourse. She is one who flatters, tricks, and induces people with pleasing words; she is one who entices, entrances, and lulls people with incantations. She is a cajoler, one who summons people with spells, one who destroys people with sorcery, one who places obstacles so that others will stumble. She stretches out long-winded speeches, converses deceitfully, tricks people with pleasing words; she lulls one with words. She perverts, provokes, confuses, corrupts people; she fools people; she induces people, she induces people with spells; she lulls people with incantations; she entrances people.

tensuchitl, camasuchitl, camasuchiecacal, tenuelic, tlatoluelic, tlatoliamanqui, suchitl uelic auiiac itlatol, camatoltecatl, tentoltecatl, tentlamatini, tetencoxouiani tetensuchitzotzonani, tecoconauia, tecochtecani, tecochtlacani, tetamooalchalpoloani, tenaoalnotzani, tenaoalpoloani, tetlanaoaltequiliani, hecamecatl quiteca: tenaoaltza, tetensuchitzotzona, tetencoxouia, teiolmalacachoa, teiollochololtia, teiolcuepa, tetlacuepilia, teca mocacaiaoa, tecoconauia, tenaoalcoconauia, tecochtlaça, tecochteca.[104]

Such long and eloquent speeches emphasize the seductive nature of speech and the power that procurers and procuresses wielded because of their command of language.

Criminal testimony from highland Mexico affirms the perceived sexual power of speech. In 1594, in the Mixtec town of Tlaxiaco, for example, an outraged husband attacked a man after his wife told him that the man "had spoken to her about love."[105] In 1650, a Nahua mother of Amanalco complained to local officials that a young married man frequently spoke to her daughter, attempting to persuade her to commit adultery with him.[106] In some criminal cases, indigenous witnesses testified about their own seduction. Couching her confession in Christian terms, a Ñudzahui widow admitted in 1630 that when she met a married man in the market "he wooed her, telling her to offend God with him ... and as a miserable sinner she conceded to his pleasure."[107] Her testimony reflects both the influence of Christianity on popular conceptions of sex and sin and the persistence of indigenous beliefs about the power of speech in seduction.

Speaking and sexual intimacy were so strongly associated that a husband might accuse his wife of indiscretions based solely on the fact that he had found her talking to another man. In the Nahua community of Ayapango in 1765, a noble accused his wife of committing adultery when he found her "speaking to a man in a very suspicious place," and he asked local officials to punish her.[108] In extreme cases, a jealous husband became violent, attacking his wife and her suspected lover with a club, a knife, a machete, or stones. In 1590, for example, a thirty-year-old Ñudzahui man repeatedly stabbed his wife and her sister when he found them conversing with another man.[109] The two terrified women survived the attack, but other women were not as lucky. In 1623, a Nahua cobbler killed his wife in Teposcolula because he found her "speaking" with his master.[110] The extreme violence in these cases was rare, but envy provoked by a wife's conversation with other men was not. The intense jealousy of husbands who found their wives speaking to other men underscores the intimacy of speech.

Conversely, in order to prove their innocence, those who insisted that they had been wrongly accused of adultery testified that they had never spoken to their alleged lovers. For example, in 1578, when one Ñudzahui man complained that his wife had cheated on him with a local noble, both of the accused declared that they had never had relations, nor had they ever spoken to each other.[111] Similarly, in 1612, don Agustín Maldonado and Angelina de Peralta claimed that they had remained faithful to their spouses, specifically stating that they had never "communicated" with each other.[112] The denials of native defendants do not merely assert a lack of familiarity but specifically refute charges of sexual intimacy.

Like speech, sight was invested with social and sexual power. Mesoamerican prescriptions for proper conduct regulated the act of looking between men and women, nobles and commoners. These concepts overlapped with European ideals and were especially promoted by elites. Commoners and nobles were not to look directly at the ruler, and men and women were not to make eye contact with members of the opposite sex other than their spouses. Thus a noble Nahua father warned his son that to look into the eyes of a married woman was to commit adultery:

You are not to look at people, you are not to gaze into the eyes of people, you are not to stare, you are not to look into the face of or stare at one who is honored, especially at a woman, and finally especially at someone's wife, for it is said that he who stares at, gazes into the eyes of another's wife commits adultery.

Auh amo titehittaz, amo teixco titlachiaz, amo titececemittaz: amo iixco, icpac titlachiaz, amo ticcecemittaz in mavizti: oc cenca ie in cioatl, oc cenca iequene iehoatl in tecioauh: ca mitoa, teixtlaxima in aquin quicecemitta, ixco tlatlachia in tecioauh.[113]

The perception that direct eye contact conveyed sexual intimacy meant that unmarried men and women had to be reserved in their interactions. Linguistic evidence from Oaxaca suggests a similar understanding of the sexual power of sight. Alvarado provides several terms in his Ñudzahui *Vocabulario* under the Spanish entry *echar los ojos en mugeres con mala intencion* (to cast one's eyes upon women with bad intentions).[114] Córdova's Tíchazàa dictionary also has an entry, *ojos desonestos luxuriosos derramados* (dishonest, lustful, darting eyes), suggesting a connection between sight and seduction.[115] An inappropriate gaze penetrated social boundaries between men and women, nobles and commoners.

Sixteenth-century Nahua legends treat sight as a sexual experience. One, from the Florentine Codex, tells of the daughter of the ruler, Huemac, who became sexually aroused when she saw a Huaxtec chile vendor walking naked in the market. Her desire became so all-consuming that Huemac had little choice but to arrange a marriage between the two, despite the fact that the Huaxtec was a social inferior.[116] Another myth tells of two messengers who were sent by the ruler Quetzalcoatl to find out who was bathing in the place where he normally bathed.[117] When the messengers reached the spot, they saw two women bathing, became distracted, and never returned. Quetzalcoatl sent another messenger who, on seeing the women, also failed to return. Such myths warn that arousal brought about through looking could prevent one from completing his or her duties.

The Florentine Codex description of the harlot also links sight and sexual desire. According to Nahua writers: "She makes herself beautiful; she arrays herself well; she is very attentive [to her appearance]. She appears like a flower, looks stylish, dresses herself stylishly; she looks at herself in a mirror, she carries a mirror in her hand" (*moieiecquetza, moiecchichioa, mocecenmati, mosuchiquetza, motopalquetza, motopalchichioa, motezcauia, matezcauia*).[118] Furthermore, she gestures with her hands, head, and eyes. Significantly, according to Sahagún's Nahua aides, "she beckons people with her eyes, she makes eyes at people, she closes one eye at one, she winks" (*teixnotza, teicopiluia, teixcapitzuia, teixcapitzaluia, teixtlaxilia*).[119] The prostitute adorns herself and uses her eyes to attract attention. The adulteress, however "blinds people" (*teixpepechoa*).[120]

Metaphors for sex and desire suggest that Mesoamericans understood sexual relations as completely sensual. All five senses—taste, smell, sight, hearing, and touch—are evoked in discussions of intimacy. Metaphors and verbs linking intercourse with eating and drinking refer to the sense of taste. The sense of smell is evoked in descriptions of the prostitute who wears perfume and the loose woman who freshens her breath by chewing chicle. Flowers in descriptions of sexual desire, and references to them incorporated in verbs related to seduction, also provide a pleasing scent, and admonitions about excessive and illicit sexual activity warn of the damaging effects of bad odors and pollution. The sense of sight emerges in descriptions of the prostitute who makes people look at her by using face paint, coloring her teeth, fixing her hair, and gesturing with her hands and eyes in the marketplace. Flowers and feathers are also worn to enhance one's appearance. Descriptions of the procuress, procurer, prostitute, and lascivious youth, who all seduce people with their speeches, refer to the sense of hearing as an arousing experience. Interestingly, touch is the most opaque sense in Nahua formal speeches and metaphors. The myth of the impregnation of Coatlicue, which describes a soft ball of feathers falling inside her dress and down along her body, is the most direct reference to tactile seduction in the texts considered so far. Nahua writings depict sexual pleasure, in moderation and with the right partner, as a fully sensual experience.

The imposition of Christianity introduced new sexual attitudes, beliefs, and practices and generated debate among those who sought to establish a native-Christian moral dialogue in New Spain.

INDIGENOUS-CHRISTIAN SEXUALITY

By the mid-sixteenth century, friars began to publish religious texts in Spanish and native languages to promote conversion. We have seen that Christian marriage was a major preoccupation of ecclesiastics engaged in the evangelizing mission. The friars appealed to native sensibilities and morality by incorporating fundamental indigenous concepts into the Christian-native marriage ceremony as long as they did not violate Christian teachings. Similarly, church texts show that friars used some indigenous sexual concepts, especially those related to pollution, in their sermons and catechisms, but refused to compromise in defining the parameters of appropriate sexual relations.

From colonial times to the present, Mesoamerican narratives on deviance and morality have been shaped by indigenous and Christian concepts. In her study of Nahuatl-language church-sponsored texts, Louise

Burkhart describes a complex dialogue between indigenous nobles and Spanish friars that informed sixteenth-century moral discourse. In the Nahua worldview, "moral excesses [were] associated with liminal times and places."[121] Crossroads, the periphery, and things affiliated with the periphery, such as animals and insects, all signified moral danger, and night was a time of deviance and immorality.[122] Burkhart concludes that the Christian association of the Devil with the periphery and night reinforced Nahua concepts of the moral dimensions of time and space.[123]

James Taggart, in identifying many of these same concepts in his study of contemporary Nahua narrative, outlines a symbolic system of oppositional pairs that represent ethical and unethical behavior.[124] Time and space are invested with moral significance in a cosmology that combines Christian and indigenous ideology. According to Nahua belief, the sun, which in the colonial period became associated with Jesus Christ, creates moral order.[125] Because of their relationship to the sun, light, heat, and daytime have positive connotations; the center is also believed to be a place of organized, moral life. Conversely, Nahua storytellers identify deviance with the Devil, the periphery, and night (and by extension cold and darkness). Thus, as Taggart observes, "the widely held belief was that the Devil causes internal conflict in Nahuat society and is responsible for human mortality."[126] Contemporary Nahuas, like their colonial ancestors, emphasize moderation and therefore consider excessive drinking, extreme emotions, and uncontrolled sexual passions as threats to the moral order.[127]

Modern ethnography from Oaxaca reveals a comparable evolution of indigenous Christian moral ideology. According to John Monaghan, Mixtecs of Santiago Nuyoo consider Jesus and Tachi (wind, a supernatural that incorporates some aspects of the Devil) "complementary opposites" or "halves." Since the time of creation, Tachi has been the antithesis of Jesus. "Where Jesus—the Sun—grew hot (*itni*), the Tachi grew cold (*viji*). Where Jesus was truthful (*nijia*), the Tachi became deceitful (*shinaʻvi*). Where Jesus acted virtuously (*vaʻa*), the Tachi acted badly (*nduvaʻa*). Where the work of Jesus was good, that of the Tachi was sinful (*kuachi*) or envious (*yatuni* or *uʻvini*)."[128] Jesus is associated with day; Tachi, with night.[129] Monaghan also observes a belief in the "amoral and asocial world" of the tinumi, a people who lived on the periphery in caves when there was no sun or agriculture and before people settled into households and practiced marriage. The belief that the era of the tinumi ended and Christian life began when the sun appeared confirms an association between the sun, Jesus, and moral order.[130]

In her study of ecclesiastical texts, Burkhart discusses the friars' adoption and adaptation of several Nahuatl terms to convey Christian concepts. *Tlatlacolli* (derived from *tlatlacoa*, make a mistake) meant sin and was used in a broad sense without any clear moral connotation; it did not have *sin*'s specific meaning of having knowingly and willingly engaging in an act that violated Christian principles. The friars similarly extended Ñudzahui terms to describe Christianity in their efforts in the Mixteca Alta. Terraciano shows that the term *quachi* was used in doctrinal texts and sermons to mean sin. Like tlatlacolli, quachi had a wide array of uses but lacked a strong moral sense.

One of the earliest church texts printed in Mexico was fray Pedro de Córdova's *Christian Doctrine for the Instruction and Information of the Indians in the Manner of History*, published in Spanish in 1544. Córdova's language was direct, suggesting that the major concern at this time was conveying the basic tenets of the faith. The text itself is gendered, with all questions and warnings addressed to the male neophyte. In his discussion of the sixth commandment, that you shall not fornicate, Córdova explained that a man who even "desires" to be with another woman or who "frolics" with a woman other than his wife breaks this commandment.[131] He reiterated prohibitions against sexual desire in his brief consideration of the ninth commandment, that you shall not covet the wife of your neighbor. While it would be worse to actually lie with a married woman, simply to desire to do so would also violate the commandment.[132]

Córdova devoted a major part of his discussion of the sixth commandment to the "even greater sin" of two men lying together: "These sinners not only will go to Hell but also Justice will burn them there in a very great fire . . . Justice will destroy you and burn you and kill you if you commit this sin."[133] To emphasize the dire consequences of homosexual acts, he threatened that the punishment would continue in the afterlife: "Each one of you who commits this sin will be carried away to Hell by the devil, and because of it you will be given great torture."[134] In fact, some men had been burned at the stake in early modern Spain for being homosexuals, a sentence that was also carried out on occasion in New Spain.[135]

Molina's *Confesionario mayor* of 1569, which was to achieve major significance, was relatively early, very detailed, and written in Nahuatl, a lingua franca of highland Mexico. The text included questions for both male and female parishioners and was clearly intended as a model to be used by friars in the confessional. Molina devoted a great deal of attention to the relationship between sexual partners. As discussed in Chapter 3, in preconquest times natives married close relatives. Molina's concern with carefully enumerating forbidden relationships reflected his awareness of this practice. He warned that it was a mortal sin (*yn temictiani tlatlacolli*) for a man to have sex with a woman who was a relative through marriage or ritual kinship and that it was a violation of the sixth commandment to engage in sex with a woman who was married or single or had taken a vow of chastity, such as a widow, a nun, or a *beata* (a laywoman who had taken religious vows). Betraying a particularly Spanish perspective, Molina interrogated parishioners: "Did you have sex with some woman who was not baptized or with some Jew or Chichimec?" (*Cuix ica ytech otacic, yna y amo moquatequia ciuatl, yn judia, yn chichimecatl?*)[136] The question seems especially ridiculous considering that the former act was very common given the large percentage of the native population who remained unbaptized at this time and that the latter act was very unlikely since Jews and infidels (here Chichimecs) were prohibited from entering New Spain. Molina warned that a person who broke the commandment by having sex outside of marriage could not resume sexual relations with a spouse until absolution had been granted by a priest. Molina also asked if the sex had been consensual, expressing concern that a male parishioner had forced a woman to have sex even when she told him to stop.[137]

The *Confesionario* raises two interrelated issues that reflect Spanish preoccupations that would come to influence indigenous sexual ideology over the next two centuries. First, the doctrina emphasized the importance of a woman's virginity in several questions directed to a man concerning the status of his partner. Whereas Spaniards esteemed the ideal of female virginity before marriage, Mesoamericans did not, at least before the sixteenth century. In fact, Mesoamerican languages lack an equivalent term for *virgin*. Second, Molina asked the man whether he had seduced the woman with a pledge to marry her but then had failed to keep his promise.[138] This question reflects the importance that Spaniards placed on the marriage promise (*palabra de casamiento*). Once the couple had exchanged such a promise, they customarily began to have intercourse even though the wedding had not yet taken place. If either party reneged on the agreement, by backing out or by announcing marriage to another person, the aggrieved lover could force the other to marry. A betrayed woman could also sue a man for having taken her virginity.[139]

Like Córdova, Molina was concerned that Nahuas understand that both deeds and thoughts were to be regulated to ensure the proper expression of sexuality. In his discussion of the sixth commandment, he asked, "How many times did you think dirty thoughts of lust?" (*In iquac aço quezquipa tiquilnamique tlahelpaquiliztlalnamiquiliztli*).[140] He focused on sexual dreams, asking whether the man spilled his seed during sleep and whether he enjoyed thinking about it on waking.[141] Whether or not a person took pleasure from sensual thoughts and dreams determined whether the act constituted a sin. Even when men had sex with their wives, they had to monitor their thoughts. Molina warned that a man who fantasized about another woman while having sex with his wife committed a mortal sin.[142]

At the heart of these concerns was the church's contention that the fundamental purpose of sexual relations should be procreation. Sex between unmarried men and women was condemned because it would not lead to reproduction in a proper, stable family unit. Even worse, from the church's perspective, was a relationship between members of the same sex that would not lead to reproduction at all. These concerns led to a number of questions aimed at both men and women about masturbation in Molina's confessional. Intimate married relations raised additional concerns. Molina explained that a husband and wife who committed sodomy or impeded conception violated the church's teachings on procreation. Sex between a married couple was frowned on during the later stages of pregnancy for fear that the fetus would be harmed. Molina explained that it was "a very grave sin" (*vey tlatlacolli temamauhti*) if a man caused birth complications because he had insisted on having sex with his wife.[143]

Despite the aggressive conversion and evangelization tactics the friars used in the first century after contact, indigenous peoples of highland Mexico continued to struggle with fundamental aspects of confession. In part this was due to the fact that they were only required to confess once a year. In addition, many parishes were underserved, and even when a friar was present, he may have lacked adequate skills in the local native language(s) to communicate effectively. In his confessional manual, written in the early seventeenth-century, Alva revealed the frustration that friars had experienced in teaching Nahuas to confess properly. He advised that natives first reflect on their sins:

Then begin talking to your confessor revealing your sins to him, beginning with the great and mortal sins, afterwards mentioning the small ones (perhaps you spoke ill of another or laughed at him or made jokes about him, etc.). Do not speak nonsense, do not hide and wrap up your sins with a [multitude of obscure?] words, for thus you will put your confessor in danger and the confessor will not rightly understand you, he will become impatient with it since your language is another thing altogether. Has everyone been reared and raised in it? For it is very difficult.

auh niman tipehuaz in ticpolihuiliz ticpantlaxiliz in moteyolcuiticauh yca tipehuaz in huehuei in temictiani tlatlacoli, zatepan tictenehuaz tepitoton, in azo teca otimononotz otihuetzcac oticamanalo &c. Auh ámo titlatolzaçacaz ámo tlatoltica tictlatiz ticquimiloz in motlatlacol, ca ic ticohuetiliz in moneyolcuitiliz, auh ca ámo melahuac mitzcaquiz in moteyolcuiticauh ca zan ic ticxiuhtlatiz, canel oc zentlamantli in amotlatol; cuix mochi tlacatl ipan omohuapauh omozcalti? Ca cenca ohue.[144]

Alva's admission that the Nahuatl language was "very difficult" suggests that many confessors could not understand Nahuas in the confessional. It also reflects some concern that Nahuas did not state their sins clearly, nor did they organize them according to Christian definitions of mortal and venal. Alva expressed his concerns that the confessional was ineffective in changing sexual attitudes and practices:

You natives, even though you are cohabiting for two [or] three years already with a woman and sinning with her every day and every night, when the priest and confessor questions you about how many times you have sinned with her, you just reply: "Two times, three times." And you all make the same [sort of] confession, and with this you really damage your confession.

In amehuantin anmaçehualtin, in manel ye oxhuitl, ye xihuitl, anquimomecatititicate çe çihuatl, in çeçeyohual ytech antlatlacoticate, in iquac amechtlatlania, in teopixqui teyolcuitiani in quezquipa inahua[c] oantlatlacoque; zan anquinaquilia, ca opa, yexpa, auh huel amoçentlatol in anmochtin, auh ca yehuatl in huel ic anquitlacoa in ámoneyolcuitiliz.[145]

We might interpret this passage as evidence of subterfuge that the Nahuas used to comply with the demands of confessing by downplaying their sins, and indeed this scenario is plausible. However, as we have seen, the rules of polite Nahuatl discourse required that Nahuas speak of sexual relations and the body in metaphorical terms. And to show respect for friars, many would have used symbolic and complex linguistic forms. There was clearly a cultural clash between the formal, coded language for sexual matters and the direct, if not crude (from the Nahua perspective), language of the friars in the confessional and the pulpit. On the most basic level as well, it suggests lingering confusion over the concept and categories of sin.

Alva warned parishioners that they should not blame others for their deeds or omit any sin that they had committed, assuring them that confession would be absolutely confidential.[146] Here he revealed a fundamental problem: if a parishioner confessed a sin and the friar assigned some forms of penance, others would discover that that person had erred. As we will see, those who acted immorally brought shame on themselves, their spouses, and members of their households. The broader social consequences of immorality and deviance in Nahua culture undermined the church's attempts to promote "individualization" in the confessional.[147]

Like Molina, Alva incorporated Nahuatl concepts of sexuality to express the seriousness of sin. He referred to the sinful dirtiness and blackness (*in icatzahuaca, in tliliuhca*) that sullied the soul and associated transgression with mud and dust: "It is also possible for me to slip and slide in the mud [of sin] and get myself more mixed up in the muck [of sin] than you" (*ca no huelitiz in nalahuaz ninoçoquipetzcoz yhuan oc qualca ninoçoquineloz in ámo tehuatl . . .*).[148] Also, he relied on the Nahua association of transgressions with stench when he spoke of sin: "Do not be afraid [or] ashamed for God has placed me here to wash away your sinful stink and rottenness" (*ámo ximomauhti ámo xipinahua, ca ic nican nechmotlalillia, in Dios in nicpapacaz in miyaca in mopalanca*).[149] The priest's absolution was a cleansing act, similar to ritual bathing in preparation for Mesoamerican ceremonies. Furthermore, in his discussion of the sixth commandment, Alva invoked Nahua concepts of sexual pleasure using the terms *aahuilnen, tlaticpac tlatlacolli*, and *tlailpaquiliztli*: "Have you licentiously enjoyed yourself? Have you given yourself over to earthly sin and lust?" (*Cuix otaahuilnen? Cuix otimomecati in tlalticpac tlatlacolli tlailpaquiliztli?*).[150] Significantly, he reformulated earthly pleasure (*tlalticpacayotl*) as earthly sin (*tlalticpac tlatlacolli*).

In addition, Alva employed concepts of moral time, referring to "the dark and obscure night in which you still live" (*in za ie noma tlai[o] huayan mextecomac, annemi*).[151] Christianity, he promised, would enlighten the native neophyte whom he invited into the fold: "Come, my wretched child, who the devil still today maintains in the darkness of sin and the gloom [of ignorance]" (*Tla xihualauh nopiltze, timotolinia, in oc noma ça ye axcan tlayohuayan mextecomac mitznemitia in tlacatecolotl*).[152] Drawing on the Mesoamerican worldview associating the sun with order and morality, he likened the sun to the true faith: "Ah, O foolish ones, the sun [of the true faith] has come upon you, [the true faith] has dawned on you, and you still want to live in the darkness of sin and the gloom of ignorance" (*Iho, xolopitine in axcan ye o ámopan tonac ye o [a]mopan tlathuic auh oc noma anquinequi in tlayohuayan mixticomac a[n]nemizque amicampa amotepotzco*).[153]

Like Alva's linking of the Devil with the "darkness of sin" and the "gloom of ignorance," the Florentine Codex attributed sexual misconduct to the Devil in a description and illustration of the *tetlanochili* (procuress), described with a parallel phrase as "a diablo, a tzitzimitl" (*in diablo, in tzitzimitl*); like sorcerers, supernaturals, and the Devil, she was said to "deceive," "derange," "provoke," and "destroy."[154] Figure 5.12 shows the procuress enticing a woman to commit prostitution. The Devil instructs her, even pointing to the woman who is to be deceived. By depicting the Devil as standing close behind the woman, the artist conveys the description in the text: "She is truly the eyes, the ears, the messenger of the Devil, of the tzitzimitl" (*uel iix, uel inacaz, uel ititlan in diablo, in tzitzimitl*).[155] The Devil is a European caricature, complete with horns, cloven hooves, a tail, and long hair, but the setting and characters are indigenous. The scene is set in the countryside, reflecting an indigenous belief in the periphery as a place of danger and transgressions. Like Christians, Mesoamericans from preconquest times to the present have associated evil with the left.[156] In Figure 5.12, the procuress approaches her victim from the left (from the viewer's perspective) and the Devil stands to the far left as the procuress points the gullible woman in that direction. This hybrid image suggests the adoption and adaptation of the Christian Devil into indigenous concepts of deviance by the last quarter of the sixteenth century, at least by the artists of the Florentine Codex.

Elsewhere, to show that people associated the Devil with jealousy, sexual tension, drinking, and violence, I use criminal cases from indigenous

Figure 5.12. Tetlanochili, or procuress

SOURCE: Florentine Codex, bk. 10, fol. 41, Florence: Biblioteca Medicea Laurenziana, Med. Palat. 220, c. 43. By concession of the Ministry for Heritage and Cultural Activities; further reproduction by any means is forbidden.

communities of central Mexico and Oaxaca in which native defendants attributed their devious acts to the Devil's deception.[157] The statements of indigenous defendants and witnesses in colonial records preserve the spontaneous words of common people rather than the speech of educated nobles who contributed to the production of formal texts under the supervision of friars. There is the possibility that Spanish lawyers prompted their clients to invoke God and the Devil in their confessions to win sympathy from Spanish judges; however, this excuse did not provide extenuating circumstances. By comparing references to the Devil in archival documents with descriptions of antisocial and immoral behavior in formal native-language sources, I show how ordinary indigenous men and women imagined the Devil as a continuation of their belief in supernaturals, including the *tlacatecolotl* (Nahuatl for a type of sorcerer; literally owl person) and *tzitzimitl* (Nahuatl for a lesser deity associated with the western sky that visited earth to torment people).[158] A few detailed examples demonstrate how indigenous people sometimes blamed the Devil for distorting reality and for inspiring suspicions, anger, and hate when conflicts did occur.

Two uxoricide trials illustrate popular conceptions of the Devil's dementing influences. The first is a case introduced in Chapter 3 involving Martín Tilantzin, a Nahua from Acatepec, who in 1558 confessed that he had murdered his wife of approximately fifteen years and the mother of his two children.[159] Martín admitted that he followed his wife to her cacao orchard and confronted her with his suspicion that she had become pregnant "by three men who had had dealings with her."[160] In the heat of argument, he took off his belt and used it to hang his wife, leaving her body in the countryside, where it was later discovered by a man hunting rabbits. One of the arresting officials attempted to account for this brutal crime by blaming the murderer's malicious thoughts and acts on the Devil, who must have tricked Martín into hating his wife. By this account, only a generation after the introduction of Christianity, the Devil had been invested with the power to deceive, to inspire destructive emotions, and to provoke violence, at least in the center of New Spain where Spanish influence was most profound in this early period.

Although separated by considerable time and distance, a similar case occurred in Lalopa in 1657, when a woman appeared before Bènizàa officials and accused her son-in-law, Jacinto Manzano, of killing her daughter, María de Vargas.[161] Apparently, the couple had not lived together for some time. Her mother became alarmed when Jacinto sent someone to her house one morning to ask if María, who was nine months pregnant, had given birth, because she knew that her daughter had agreed to meet Jacinto the night before. Local authorities arrested Jacinto, but he refused to cooperate. After holding him in jail for a few days, they whipped him as they questioned him. Jacinto eventually confessed to the crime and led authorities to María's body. He admitted that he had lured his wife to the countryside on the night of the murder by suggesting that they go to the remote shrine (*ermita*) of Our Lady to light candles so that the Virgin would protect her during childbirth. On the way, the Devil "persuaded" him that he had not fathered the child that she was carrying, and with that thought he strangled her and threw her body into a ravine.

Both cases demonstrate that native witnesses and defendants blamed the Devil for inspiring jealousy and convincing men to commit murder. They also link the Devil to the murderers' own adulterous relations and desires to escape their marriages. Betraying their sexual double standards, Martín Tilantzin and Jacinto Manzano, men who suspected the worst of their wives, admitted to having had intimate relationships with other women. Several witnesses in the case against Martín recalled that he had repeatedly approached native officials, asking them to terminate his marriage so that he could marry a woman in a neighboring community. His inability to persuade them and his desire for his mistress, it was said, caused him to detest his wife. Similar statements were made in the case against Jacinto. Don Juan de la Cruz, the governor and cacique of Lalopa, testified that when asked why he had killed María, Jacinto replied "that he had no other cause or basis than the temptation of the demon, who had tempted him for four years."[162] Don Juan explained that Jacinto had mistreated his wife and carried on an affair with María Sánchez, for which he had been punished repeatedly. Sexual temptation and jealousy, both inspired by the Devil, had led to discord and violence.

The testimony of indigenous men and women in criminal records reveals the extent to which illicit sexual relations came to be understood within a Christian-native moral ideology. Even though many friars were skeptical about the impact that Christian morality was having on the native population, criminal testimony suggests that many men and women classified certain behaviors as violations of the church's teachings. When Spanish officials investigated an assault in Yanhuitlan in 1588, several witnesses denounced one of the defendants, Ana Tajasos, as a procuress who prostituted women from her home. Inés Hernández described Ana as a "bad Christian of bad living and ill-repute" who was the reason that "many people had committed sins in offense of God, Our lord."[163]

Occasionally, indigenous defendants framed their confessions of deviant or immoral behavior in Christian terms. Andrea Hernández, a thirty-year-old widow, admitted that she sold pulque from her home in Teposcolula; she insisted, however, that she did so to earn money to raise her many children, not "to offend God," as the friars would have asserted in their sermons.[164] When witnesses spoke of "offending God," they often referred to adultery.

Christian concepts such as sin, temptation, and weakness of the flesh also enter the archival discourse on crime and morality. When Pedro López Hordónez confessed his infidelity, he drew on a Christian moral framework, describing himself as "a weak man, tempted by the flesh," and he swore that he would never reunite with his lover and "offend God" with her again.[165] Juana de Trujillo, a twenty-six year-old widow, used similar language when she admitted to her affair with the married Andrés de Sosa in 1630. She explained that he had courted her, asking to "offend God with her" and that "as a miserable sinner" she conceded to his wishes. She described her relationship with him as an offense against God, internalizing church doctrine when she called herself a miserable sinner. When Andrés killed the official who had caught the lovers together in a cave, Juana looked on in horror. She criticized Andrés, telling him that he had committed "a great sin" by taking the official's life and vowing to tell the truth about him.[166]

When María García testified about a murder that was committed in Tamazulapa, she said she had walked in on the defendant and found him holding an axe and standing over the bodies of his wife and another man lying on the floor covered in blood. He told her that he had found the man on top of his wife "committing a sin."[167] In the Chinantec community of Teotalsingo, indigenous witnesses testifying that a local man was having an affair with his mother-in-law adopted a Christian framework by stating that he had "offended God" with her in the cactus field behind the house.[168] In Xinastla, in 1695, Pedro Martín attacked his lover, María López, a twenty-four year-old widow, when she told him that she wanted to end their adulterous relationship because she planned to marry another man. María admitted that as a "weak" person, she had become involved with Pedro, but she insisted that she wanted to serve God by marrying. Pedro stated that he flew into a jealous rage when María rejected him and insisted that she "no longer wanted to offend God" with him. She even "swore to God and the cross" that she wanted to marry another man and end her relationship with Pedro. Her testimony suggests that indigenous women and men had absorbed the Christian message that marriage regulated sexual relations and served God.[169]

CONCLUDING REMARKS

As in preconquest times, indigenous parents in colonial Mexico delivered moralistic speeches about sexuality to their adolescent children. These speeches and the language used to describe sexual relations in archival records reveal an entire cultural complex of intimate behavior. The principal concern in the texts was the necessity for moderation in sexual relations. Excessive intercourse, adulterous relations, and the use of aphrodisiacs could all lead to impotence, illness, and violence. Flowers, food, feathers, speech, and sight were invoked in metaphors and as symbols to represent sexuality in alphabetic and pictorial texts, and they continued to resonate in the narratives and actions of indigenous people in colonial times.

Clearly, Christian concepts of sin, temptation, and the Devil seeped into the narratives of indigenous people who described illicit sexual relations and crime. However, this was a slow and limited process, and we would be remiss to assume that Christian ideology entirely eclipsed indigenous concepts of morality and sexuality. As Sigal points out in his study of sexuality in Nahua ritual and cosmology, modern scholars have placed too much emphasis on the ability of friars to change ideas and practices through the confessional. By the friars' own admission, the sacrament of confession had limited effect on indigenous concepts of appropriate behavior in large part because of differences in cultural attitudes, reliance on native ideas in the Nahua-Christian moral dialogue, sporadic contact between priests and parishioners, and the inability of many confessors to master native languages. Spanish Christian moral and sexual values influenced, but did not completely change, indigenous attitudes and practices.

CHAPTER SIX

Sexual Crimes

In 1596, officials from Coixtlahuaca informed the alcalde mayor that sixteen-year-old Diego López Cachi had been imprisoned for murdering Luis Coquixi after he had caught Luis sleeping with his wife, Isabel Xaco.[1] Enraged by the sight of Isabel and Luis together, Diego struck the sleeping man with a digging stick and then bludgeoned him to death with a rock. He grabbed his wife and tried to strangle her, but she managed to get away and call for help. When Isabel's mother heard her daughter screaming, she grabbed her son-in-law by the sleeve and told him that he was not going anywhere until the officials arrived. He brusquely replied, "I will not flee. I have killed Luis Coquixi because I found him here inside [the house] with my wife and I am also going to kill her." His defiant attitude and threats suggest that he assumed a right to seek vengeance according to native custom and Spanish law. Ultimately, Diego López Cachi was absolved of the death of Luis Coquixi.[2]

This dramatic case of betrayal and vengeance highlights indigenous attitudes toward illicit sexuality and the understanding of a husband's rights over his wife in colonial Mexico. Here I examine the criminalized sexual relations of adultery, rape, and taking a woman's virginity by considering the definitions of various acts, the circumstances surrounding the crimes, and native reactions to transgressions. As with the murder of Luis Coquixi, household members, community officials, and Spanish magistrates and friars all played a significant role in the condemnation and punishment of sexual crimes. Over time, Spanish cultural norms and law influenced the ways that indigenous men and women made gendered claims in cases concerning illicit sexuality, even when demands for justice were framed in explicitly native terms.

SEX IN MARRIAGE

Colonial indigenous moral texts prescribed that sexual union take place within marriage and warned against prostitution and adultery. Once a marriage had been arranged, the couple might begin to live together (usually with the bride's family) and to initiate sexual relations.³ Occasionally, the sources suggest that these codes of conduct were not enforced rigidly in preconquest times. A passage in the Florentine Codex hints that premarital sex was not uncommon among Nahua youth, and a description of life in the temple schools indicates that a young man might have sex with several young women but then choose only one of them when it was time for him to marry.⁴ In fact, native languages lacked a precise term for virgin in this period; those that most closely approximate this concept are *ichpoctli* in Nahuatl, *penicoconi* in Tíchazàa (Zapotec), and *ñaha quachi* in Ñudzahui (Mixtec), all of which translate to unmarried young woman.⁵ Premarital sex may have been tolerated and even condoned, but once married, men and women were expected to be faithful. Catholic indoctrination undoubtedly strengthened the emphasis on monogamous marriage and sex for procreation in colonial formal discourse.

ADULTERY

Infidelity constituted a major violation of marriage vows and threatened to disrupt the ideal of reciprocal economic and sexual relations between husband and wife. It also created conflict among members of the community. Throughout the colonial period, Meosamerican men and women sought punishment of disloyal spouses through violence or legal action. Their frequent complaints to authorities and family members reveal the importance that indigenous peoples placed on fidelity in marriage. Evidence from ethnohistorical sources on reactions to adultery and the punishment of adulterers in preconquest and colonial times speak to the gravity of this crime.

According to native definitions, adultery was committed when a married man or woman had sexual intercourse with a person other than his or her spouse and was not contingent on the woman's marital status alone, as in many other societies.⁶ Sexual relations between married men and unattached (unmarried or widowed) women were considered to be adulterous.⁷ For example, in 1612 in Tamazulapa a married man was prosecuted for committing adultery with a widow.⁸ Furthermore, because the marital status of either the man or the woman could influence whether or not sexual activity was prohibited, native officials frequently specified the status of both parties in adultery cases. For example, Juan de Zarate, a Ñudzahui man, was imprisoned for being with a "married Indian woman."⁹ Juan Bautista, a Bènizàa (Zapotec) alcalde, was accused of trying to rape a "married woman" in 1695.¹⁰ In 1650, a Nahua woman complained to local authorities that a neighbor had pursued her single daughter and that "he summoned her and requested [sexual relations] of her, persuading her to have an illicit relationship with him, being that he is married."[11] In this regard, native custom resembled Christian doctrine, which also defined adultery as an illicit sexual union between two adults, at least one whom was married.[12]

Native-language terminology somewhat illuminates concepts of adultery, but more systematic linguistic investigation is required. Many of the terms in Nahuatl are quite opaque, consisting of a verb plus the relational word *-tlan*, meaning, among other things, next to, under, or among in idiomatic phrases. Prefixed to *-tlan* is the indefinite personal possessor *te-*, and a basic unresolved question is whether *tetlan* means on the offended party or with the adulterous party. Apparently the latter is the original meaning because it definitely applies in one expression, *tetlan aqui* (literally enter among people) which means both "to have sex with someone who is sleeping" and "to commit adultery."[13] A seemingly cognate expression meaning to commit adultery is *tetlan yauh* (literally "go among people").[14]

The most common word for adultery in Nahuatl-language dictionaries and texts is puzzling. Although usually written as *tetlaxima*, it appears in one source as *tetlaxxima*,[15] in which the first *x* must be an assimilated *n*, so that an earlier form would have been *tetlanxima*, with the same *tetlan* as in other expressions.[16] Less ambiguous is the verb *maxaloa*. Here the object of the verb is the spouse against whom adultery is committed, and the meaning in Molina's *Vocabulario* is to betray a spouse of either gender by having sex with someone else.[17] The root of the word has to do with forking, crossing, doubling; thus *maxaloa* is akin to the English *double-cross*. *Mocuepa*, the reflexive form of the verb *cuepa*, which means "turn oneself around" or "turn into something" is used in Nahuatl moralizing speeches, for example, when a father rhetorically asks his daughter, "And if truly you turn yourself around, will you become a goddess?" (*Auh tla nel timocuepaz: cuix titeutiz*).[18] As used in the text, the term clearly carries a sexual connotation and, like maxaloa, suggests twisting, crossing, or turning.

Young men and women were warned of the evils of adultery when they were betrothed. For example, the marriage prognostication pages of the Codex Borgia contain scenes warning of the dangers of infidelity. Figure 6.1 shows a man committing adultery; he turns away from his wife and grabs the other woman's breast, evoking the Nahuatl verb *chichihualtzitzitzquia*.[19] His twisted posture reveals his dishonesty and depravity, and may convey a verb such as maxaloa or mocuepa. The man's mistress also has her head turned back. Their positions are similar to depictions of punishments for adultery, foreshadowing their fate

Sexual Crimes 151

Figure 6.1. Prognostication warning that adultery would ruin the marriage
SOURCE: Codex Borgia, fol. 59. Facsimile edition. Vienna: Akademische Druckund Verlagsanstalt; Madrid: Sociedad Estatal Quinto Centenario; Mexico City: Fondo de Cultura Económico, 1993.

(refer to Figure 6.3). The man's extra-long snake loincloth signals his masculinity, while his mistress's nudity conveys overt sexuality. Both women wear flowers in their hair, symbolizing fertility and seduction. The man's wife grabs him by the hair, mimicking the pose of Mexica warriors shown in pictorial manuscripts and sculptures taking captives. This image suggests terms for a sacrificed captive (*xochimicqui, teomicqui*) that describe the prostitute, although in this case the captive is the husband. The reference to warfare highlights the violence and social disruption that betrayal often caused. The eclipse in the center of the frame indicates moral danger.

Indigenous people considered adultery a serious violation and a great offense to the adulterer's spouse. According to native belief, a couple remained together after death and their obligations to each other continued in the next world. Consequently, those whose spouses had abandoned them for another suffered in this life and beyond. While concerns about the afterlife might linger, they were secondary to the real, immediate threat that infidelity posed to the household and the community. A wife's extramarital relations could produce children who would not have legitimate claims to the household's property or resources. An unfaithful husband could dissipate a family's resources on his lover and illegitimate children, and commit violence against his wife. Adultery was a special concern among nobles, whose children stood to inherit lands and privileges, including the right to exact tribute and labor from the community's commoners.

Perhaps influenced in part by Christian attitudes, the Nahua authors of the Florentine Codex condemned the separation of sex for pleasure and sex for reproduction. A passage in the Codex reflects disapproval of women who became pregnant through adulterous relations and warns of the turmoil and controversy that illicit relations might bring about.

The scandalous woman is an adulteress, one who commits adultery, a toy, a joke, a laugh, a mockery. She has no name, no reputation; she is dead, deceased. She is a bearer of bastards; she aborts. She causes people to have differences among themselves. She commits adultery; she is adulterous. She cheats, deceives, blinds people.

in tetzauhcioatl, ca tetlaxinqui tepaniani, auilli camanalli, uetzquiztli, netopeoalli, aoc tle itoca, aoc tle itenio, omic, omomiquili, ichtacapiloa, motlatlaxiliani, açaze quimixnamictia, tetlaxima, tepan iauh, teixtzcautlaxilia, teixtzacupepechoa, teixpepechoa.[20]

Like the prostitute, the adulteress "is dead, deceased," she is deceptive; she causes conflict.

Criminal records from the later colonial period also condemn pregnancy outside of marriage (from either previous or adulterous relationships) because they were a source of conflict between a husband and wife. For example, in 1665 a Bènizàa woman of Lachirio named María Magdalena informed municipal officials that her husband had killed her baby and attacked her. She explained that before she married her husband, she had told him that she was pregnant with another man's child. He assured her that he understood and that he still wanted to marry her. After the child's birth, however, the couple fought frequently. When the baby died one night in its sleep, she accused her husband of murder; a few days later he retaliated, going after her with a machete.[21]

The social stigma against illegitimate birth is highlighted in a 1699 case from the Bènizàa town of Yalahuí against Juana Hernández for infanticide. Juana, a thirty-five year-old widow, denied the charge and explained that she miscarried after she fell while collecting firewood. She insisted that the child had been stillborn, but admitted that she had buried it without telling anyone what had happened because she did not want to bring shame to her father, who was a noble in the community. Juana's father responded to the illegitimate pregnancy in grave terms. Casting her pregnancy out of wedlock in a Christian moral framework, he admitted that, when he learned what had happened, he beat Juana "for the sin that she committed which left her pregnant." The defendant and witnesses in this case made it explicit that an illegitimate child brought shame to the woman and to the other members of her household.[22]

Perhaps because of the economic dimensions of marriage, people conflated the crimes of adultery and theft. This may suggest that adultery and stealing were equivalent offenses; however, the frequency with which the two were mentioned in the same breath indicates that adultery was seen as theft of a particular type.[23] The Codex Telleriano-Remensis relates that adulterers and thieves received their final punishment on the same day.[24] The Florentine Codex explains that those born on the day of Eight Death were prone to the crimes of adultery and stealing.[25] Recollections of preconquest crime and punishment in the late sixteenth-century *Relaciones geográficas* and discussions of infidelity in colonial criminal records frequently associate the two offenses. According to the *Relación* of Atlatlauca and Malinaltepec, "they punished with great rigor adultery and theft" and "nobody could pardon the [sentence of] death of anyone who committed these two crimes."[26] A similar pairing of these transgressions occurs in the *Relación* of Juxtlahuaca: "They punished adultery with great rigor, so that they did not remain with their lives, and the same with those who stole, and their goods went to the cacicazgo."[27] Betrayed spouses, too, considered adultery a theft. In a rare Ñudzahui-language murder note, Pedro de Caravantes confessed to killing his wife because he caught her fornicating with the sacristan. He insisted on his innocence and exculpated himself by blaming his wife's lover, calling the man a "great thief" who had stolen his wife and brought shame on him, leaving him no choice but to kill her.[28]

As victims of "theft," betrayed spouses sometimes expected material compensation. In preconquest times, the Bènizàa community of Iztepec required adulterers to reimburse their spouses, specifying that a wife pay her husband in cloth.[29] The belief that a wronged spouse deserved payment might explain the rationale behind certain acts of revenge described in the criminal records. For example, in 1610 a Ñudzahui woman from Teposcolula, María Méndez, and her sister beat a woman whom they suspected was having an affair with María's husband. They stole two balls of wool yarn before they fled the scene, thereby avenging María's offense and symbolically recovering what had been taken from her.[30]

In addition to its economic costs, adultery carried considerable social consequences. In court testimony, witnesses often distinguished between public and illicit extramarital relationships; flaunted affairs brought the most contempt. Betrayal cast shame on adulterers, their spouses, and even other household members, and gossip spread scandals that sullied the reputations of adulterers and their families. As a result, real and suspected adultery in central Mexico and Oaxaca frequently provoked violence. A betrayed husband or wife, often with the help of family members, might assault the unfaithful spouse and his or her lover to punish them for past indiscretions and to deter them from committing the offense again. For example, in 1613 one Ñudzahui man who did not find his wife at home became suspicious that she was meeting secretly with a local mulatto resident; although he was mistaken, he beat her in a jealous rage when she returned home.[31] Suspicious men also used violence to intimidate their wives into confessing an adulterous affair. In 1723, twenty-two-year-old Juan Tomás beat his wife, Angelina María Vicenta, so that she would admit her betrayal. Ironically, he had become suspicious when his wife did not visit him while he was in jail in Atengo for wife beating. Apparently, he did not learn much from his incarceration.[32]

Natives frequently interpreted wife beating as evidence that a man had taken a lover and had grown to despise his wife. For example, a Ñudzahui official of Yanhuitlan notified the Spanish alcalde mayor in 1609 that Tomás Hernández mistreated his wife because he was sleeping with Inés López.[33] Often witnesses speculated that the man's lover had ordered him to beat his wife. Some men reacted violently when their wives questioned them about their activities. In the Mixtec town of Teposcolula in 1631, a woman filed criminal charges of adultery and wife beating against her husband after they fought when she asked him where he had slept the previous three nights.[34]

Although many suspicions of betrayal were unfounded, the number of adultery accusations in judicial archives suggests that infidelity was not uncommon.[35] Extant judicial records surely represent only a portion of the actual number of marital transgressions, since many betrayed spouses, who had either resolved their issues through informal negotiation or resigned themselves to the situation, never brought official charges. Or perhaps some illicit relations escaped the vigilant eyes of the community and the reprimands of local and Spanish authorities. The social consequences of infidelity explain the need to condemn it in moralizing speeches and myths and the use of harsh punishment as a deterrent. Local officials' involvement in the resolution of conflicts over adultery underscores the integration of the household and community in native society.

Circumstances Surrounding Adulterous Relations

For a variety of reasons, married men and women often were forced to live without their spouses, either temporarily or permanently, and this pattern may have contributed to the incidence of adultery. Over the course of the colonial period, many people abandoned their communities and spouses to escape tribute obligations, to avoid excessive labor demands, to find work in Spanish enterprises, or to flee from local conflicts or oppressive authorities. Even men who did not forsake their homes often worked on projects that required them to leave the community for weeks or months at a time. Furthermore, in patrilocal arrangements some women in unhappy marriages returned to their natal communities, essentially deserting their spouses. Men also left failed relationships, and abandonment constituted a type of de facto divorce.

Successive epidemics created more widows and widowers than had existed in preconquest times, perhaps contributing to those who remained becoming sexually involved with married partners. Illicit relationships frequently crossed class boundaries, but this fact does not suggest that sex was a social equalizer. On the contrary, as in many other times and places in history, men used their greater status and wealth to persuade women to engage in sexual relations with them but higher-status native women apparently did not openly form sexual unions with significantly lower-status men.

The sources reveal that many adulterous relationships were long-term.[36] Even after being punished by native officials, Spanish authorities, and ecclesiastics, many couples remained intimate. A man who regularly had business in a neighboring community might develop an association with a woman there. Likewise, the temporary or permanent absence of a husband gave a woman the opportunity to engage in extramarital affairs; however, the presence of household members may have restricted the freedom of women, especially in the case of postmarital patrilocal joint residences.

Adulterers typically met in the home of one of the partners or in the home of a friend or relative. Sometimes they arranged a rendezvous outside of the community, where they would not arouse suspicion or be caught. Lovers met in caves, maize plots, maguey fields, and anywhere else away from the watchful eyes of the community. A few representative cases from central Mexico and Oaxaca reveal the social dynamics of adultery in native communities. In 1612, don Agustín Maldonado, a married Ñudzahui noble, confessed that he had committed adultery with Catalina Xañuu, a young Ñudzahui widow who made her living weaving huipillis and *naguas* (skirts).[37] As a literate noble of the estancia of San Pedro, the twenty-eight-year-old don Agustín held office on the municipal council in the head town of Tamazulapa, to which he made frequent trips. He also owned property and kept livestock there. On the night that he was arrested, he had bought some pulque to drink with Catalina. According to his confession, he had been involved with the twenty-seven-year-old widow for two weeks. Don Agustín and Catalina's affair is representative in several regards. First, it involved a relationship between a widowed woman and a man who regularly operated outside of his own community and beyond the immediate view of his wife and family but not his social peers. Second, it shows how men and women established unions that crossed class boundaries but were formed through secondary relationships such as adultery or polygynous marriage. Third, don Agustín and Catalina were only one year apart in age, reflecting the tendency to form unions with a similar-age partner. In general, age differences between husband and wife and between sexual partners varied little. Fourth, the case reveals native social customs in that don Agustín brought pulque to share with Catalina as an act of intimacy.

Two additional seventeenth-century cases from the Villa Alta jurisdiction represent typical patterns of adultery in native communities of colonial highland Mexico. In 1659, a Bènizàa man of San Francisco Cajonos named Josef Luis returned home from mass to find his wife, María Magdalena, with her lover, Jacinto Gabriel. Nineteen-year-old Jacinto confessed that he and María Magdalena had been having an affair for three years, but he insisted that they had kept their relationship a secret. On the day of his arrest, Jacinto had entered María's house, believing that her husband was gone.[38] Similarly, in the Ayuuk (Mixe) community of Amatepec in 1699, Catalina Teresa and Josef Mateo were caught committing adultery by a community official. Catalina confessed that her husband had left town to attend a distant market and so her lover of three years had come to spend the night with her.[39] Both cases illustrate the opportunity for a native woman to carry on a long-term relationship in her own home because of her husband's frequent travels. The Ayuuk and the Bènizàa couples admitted that they had been involved for three years, suggesting that these were not casual relationships.

The native disdain for adultery raises many questions about responses to it. What recourse did a betrayed man or woman have against an unfaithful spouse? How did household members and community officials participate in the condemnation of adulterers? How did Spanish law influence native custom in the punishment of adultery? Under what circumstances did adultery lead to violence, and did men and women both resort to it? Finally, what roles did jealousy and violence play in the control of sexuality? The following section considers these questions.

Responses to Adultery

Native officials frequently heard charges of adultery from both local men and women. Occasionally local authorities caught people committing adultery, but they mainly acted on tips or the complaint of a betrayed spouse. Sometimes officials were attacked during the performance of their duty, and such violence contributed to the odious nature of the crime.[40] Shortly after an arrest, all concerned parties, including spouses, parents, household members, and other witnesses who could testify to the charges were summoned. Officials who mediated household disputes and punished adulterers had reason to condemn an act that caused such upheaval and ill will in the community. In addition, married couples were the foundation of the colonial tribute system, and cabildo officers had a vested interest in maintaining the total number of community tributaries and the smooth delivery of payment at the household level.

Household members or relatives of the offended spouse participated in punishment of a convicted adulterer, revealing the broader social implications of one's actions within the family and community.[41] For example, the *Relación* of Teotihuacan states that in preconquest times relatives of an offended spouse would club the adulterer to death.[42] In a case from the Ñudzahui community of Yanhuitlan in 1603, the parents of twenty-year-old María Pérez complained to community officials that their son-in-law, Domingo Hernández, and his father had beaten María because of a rumor that she had committed adultery.[43] A traumatized María testified that her husband and father-in-law had not only beaten her with a stick but had attacked her with scissors and had held her head over the fire (perhaps chile smoke) as they threatened to kill her.[44] The frequency with which family members became involved in physical confrontations over adultery reveals that the crime brought shame to the entire household.

Parents of adulterers also appeared before officials to testify and beg forgiveness on behalf of their children. A sixteenth-century pictorial from the Codex Tudela drawn by a native artist (refer to Figure 6.6) depicts parents as intermediaries between disputing couples and local officials. The mothers of Yope adulterers are shown pleading with officials, their tears representing a native gesture of humility. Colonial court records corroborate such images. Parents routinely appeared with their children to bear witness to adultery and other marital disputes. For example, in 1657 María and Miguel de Santiago testified on behalf of their son, who stood accused of adultery and uxoricide, denying that their son had murdered his wife so that he could be with another woman. Ultimately, native and Spanish officials were not persuaded, and the murderer's parents were sentenced to the public shaming of wearing *corozas* (conical hats) for their alleged consent to their son's extramarital relationship.[45]

Typically, the betrayed husband or wife told officials that the couple no longer maintained a *vida maridable* (married life), which meant that they no longer had sex or worked, ate, or lived together. Witnesses often verified the charges, pointing out that they no longer saw the couple sharing their meals. Conversely, friends and neighbors might testify that they had seen the accused adulterers eating, drinking, sleeping, and working together, or entering each other's house.

Native officials weighed the evidence and considered the penalty, often with the advice of the betrayed spouse, who could request a specific punishment. This practice reflects aspects of traditional conflict resolution, in which each party represented his or her case and the plaintiff bargained for fair compensation. Spanish magistrates and priests sometimes prosecuted cases of adultery, especially when an extramarital affair led to violence, although their presence in most native communities outside of the Valley of Mexico was limited and irregular.

Punishments for Adultery

Because adultery frequently led to conflict and violence in the household and the community, and because it violated Christian and native moral codes, officials harshly punished those convicted of the crime. Table 6.1 lists various punishments for adultery in the postclassic period according to pictorial documents and sixteenth-century texts and questionnaires, including Spanish chronicles, the Florentine Codex, and the *Relaciones geográficas*. The severity of the reported punishments reveals the perceived gravity of the crime. The *Relación* of Guaxilotitlan in particular seems exaggerated with its report of adulterers being executed and their bodies cannibalized.[46] More typically, in *Relaciones* from central and southern Mexico, including those of Ayutla, Atlatlauca and Malinaltepec, Coatepec, Tlacotepec, Cuezala, Teloloapan, Guaxilotitlan, Cempoala, and Epazoyuca infidelity is said to have merited a death sentence.[47] One mid-sixteenth-century Nahuatl text warned that if a man took someone else's wife, "the woman would be his companion in death" (*auh in cioatl imiquiztevical iez*).[48] In many places, adulterers commonly had their heads crushed with stones, which is why they were often called *quatepitzic* (pulverized heads) and *quatexamac* (smashed heads) in Nahuatl.[49,50] In preconquest times, adulterers purportedly could confess to a local priest or priestess, who acted as an intermediary with Tlazolteotl, the Nahua goddess associated with lust and sexuality; offenders could do penance rather than face death.[51]

Several sixteenth-century codices from central Mexico confirm penalties of death by stoning as reported in the *Relaciones geográficas*. As seen previously, the Codex Mendoza shows a man and a woman executed for the crime of adultery with their eyes closed, conveying that they are dead; rocks next to their heads and the Spanish gloss indicate that they had been stoned.[52] The punishments for theft and drunkenness are depicted

Sexual Crimes

TABLE 6.1. *Punishments for adultery in preconquest times*

Place	Ethnicity	Punishment
Ayutla	Tlapaneca	Death
Atlatlauca, Malinaltepec	Mixtec	Death
Guaxolotitlan	Zapotec	Death and cannibalizing
Itztepexic	Zapotec	Marriage ended; adulterer sent back to his or her parents
Iztepec	Zapotec	Nose and ears cut off; adulterer made to pay offended spouse nine mantas
Juxtlahuaca	Mixtec	Death
Mixtepec	Mixtec	Death
Ayusuchiquilazala	Mixtec	Death
Xalapa	Mixtec	Hanged and beaten; put in chile smoke; sold into slavery
Zacatepec	Mixtec	Made slave of cacique
Teotihuacan	Nahua	Clubbed to death by offended spouse's family
Cempoala	Nahua	Head smashed with rocks until death
Epazoyuca	Nahua, Otomi, Chichimec	Head smashed with rocks until death
Huexutla	Nahua, Tepehua	Death if adulterer is noble; payment if adulterer is commoner
Coatepec	Chontal	Death
Tlacotepec	Tepuzteca	Head smashed with rocks until death
Utatlan	Tepuzteca	Death by stoning if adulterer is noble; death by shooting with arrows if adulterer is commoner
Tetela	Cuitlateca	Nose cut off; adulterer made to pay offended spouse nine mantas; all of wife's goods given to her husband
Teloloapan	Ixcuca, Chontal, Nahua,	Death
	Yope	First offense, nose cut off; second offense, death by stoning[a]
	Nahua	Death by stoning[b]
	Nahua	Death by strangulation and stoning[c]

SOURCE: Punishments for adultery come from the *Relaciones geográficas* except where indicated.
[a]Punishment information from the Codex Tudela.
[b]Punishment information from the Codex Mendoza.
[c]Punishment information from the Codex Telleriano-Remensis.

adjacent to the execution image, revealing that all three crimes constituted a complex of interrelated, immoral behaviors and confirming associations between these crimes in other sources, as described earlier (see Figure 6.2).

The Codex Telleriano-Remensis and the Codex Borbonicus, which both contain divinatory and calendrical information, also depict punishments for adultery. Figure 6.3, from the Telleriano-Remensis, shows a woman executed by strangulation and a man by stoning. The couple's heads face backward, a pose that in other illustrations indicates

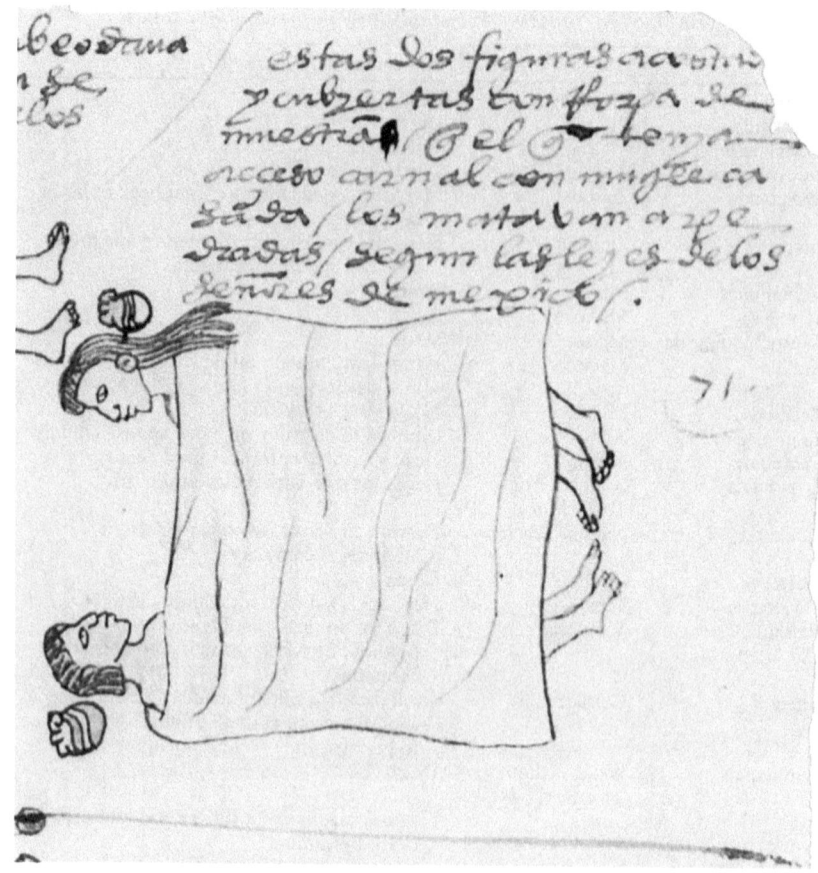

Figure 6.2. Death by stoning as punishment for adultery
SOURCE: Codex Mendoza, fol. 71. Bodleian Libraries, University of Oxford, Ms. Arch. Selden A1. Berdan and Anawalt 1992, fol. 71. Reproduced with permission from University of California Press Books.

deviousness and depravity (see also the Xochiquetzal image representing discord in Figure 5.1, the vagabond in Figure 5.2, and the Borgia illustration of the unfaithful husband in Figure 6.1). The woman's messy hair symbolizes the disarray associated with excessive sex and drunkenness (see also Xochiquetzal as a symbol of discord in Figure 5.1). The Codex Telleriano-Remensis image may refer to a case involving both adultery and incest. According to the *Historia Mexicana por sus pinturas*, a collection of myths and information about preconquest central Mexico attributed to fray Andrés de Olmos, incest was punished by strangulation with a rope.[53] Significantly, the Nahuatl term *mecatl* means both rope

Figure 6.3. Punishment for adultery
SOURCE: Codex Telleriano-Remensis, fol. 17. Bibliothèque nationale de France.

and lineage; thus the rope used to strangle an offender may symbolize the crime of incest as well. Interestingly, the Spanish text at the bottom of the page mentions only that women were executed for adultery, although the figures are clearly glossed as a man and a woman. Like the Mendoza and Telleriano-Remensis codices, the Codex Borbonicus shows a man and woman who have been stoned to death. The Spanish gloss vaguely states that those born during this time would die for being *mentirosos* (liars). The image conveys far more than the text, with nude bodies and twisted positions symbolizing adultery as the crime and stoning as the mode of execution (see Figure 6.4).

Preconquest codices that functioned as moralizing texts and colonial accounts that sought to promote the image of a well-regulated prehispanic society may have exaggerated the severity of punishments for adulterers. However, a rare colonial document confirms such reports, indicating that reported punishments were not simply fabricated in nostalgic remembrance of a moralistic past. A Nahua noble submitted an early sixteenth-century pictorial document as evidence in a suit over land and privilege, tracing his connection to several other nobles and summarizing the history of the land in dispute. One portion of the illustration shows that the noble's father had been stoned to death for adultery (see Figure 6.5); a Spanish gloss was added, probably when the document was submitted as evidence.[54]

In some native communities, adultery was punished by bodily mutilation. In the Zapotec town of Iztepec, an offended spouse could request that the adulterer's nose and ears be cut off and that the adulteress pay her husband nine lengths of cloth (*mantas*).[55] Likewise, in the Cuicatec town of Tetela an adulterer's nose was sliced off and all his goods were given to his co-defendant's husband.[56] The Codex Tudela shows the same practice among Yopes for the first offense, explaining that the betrayed man customarily bit off the nose of his wife and her lover; this act of revenge is graphically illustrated in a corresponding image (see Figure 6.6).[57] Disfigurement painfully revealed both adulterers' transgressions for the remainder of their lives and marginalized them from the rest of society.

Adulterers suffered public shaming in myriad ways. The Bènizàa community of Itztepexic reportedly sent an adulteress home to her parents, rejecting her and demonstrating to others that she was a "bad woman."[58] In the Nahua community of San Juan Teotihuacan, a man could pardon his wife's offense and spare her life, but they would separate; if they reunited, he was considered an accomplice in her vile behavior and therefore subject to death.[59] Some accused adulterers were sold into perpetual slavery. Those who betrayed their spouses in the community of Xalapa

Sexual Crimes 163

Figure 6.4. Punishment for adultery
SOURCE: Codex Borbonicus, fol. 12. Facsimile edition. Vienna: Akademische Druckund Verlagsanstalt; Madrid: Sociedad Estatal Quinto Centenario; Mexico City: Fondo de Cultura Económico, 1991.

were whipped, exposed to chile smoke, or sold as slaves.[60] In Zacatepec, another Mixtec town in the Juxtlahuaca jurisdiction, the ruler enslaved unfaithful spouses and confiscated all their belongings.[61]

Various communities reported punishments based on class distinctions. In Huexutla, a noble who slept with one of the ruler's concubines was sentenced to death; a commoner who committed the same crime

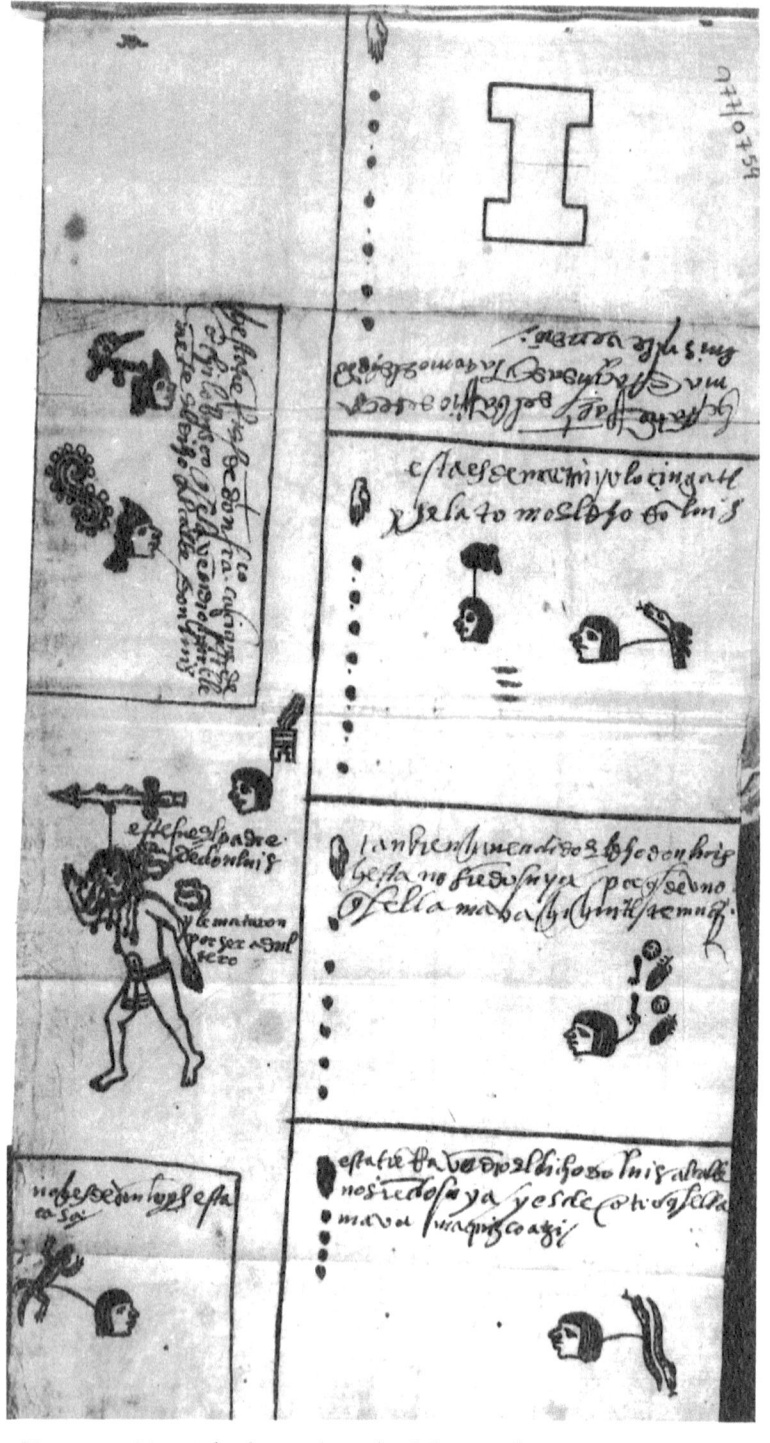

Figure 6.5. Pictorial submitted in a land dispute showing a man executed for adultery (bottom left)
SOURCE: Archivo General de la Nación, Mexico, Tierras, 19, pt. 2, fol. 79.

Figure 6.6. Yope custom of biting off the noses of adulterers as punishment for their transgressions
SOURCE: Codice Tudela, fol. 75. Madrid: Museo de Américas.

was spared but his family had to give "many gifts to placate the ruler's anger."[62] This discrepancy in punishments reflects the indigenous expectation that nobles who were to act as examples to commoners be held to a higher standard of morality in the preconquest era. Sometimes the punishment varied but the ultimate outcome was the same. Thus Utatlan, a Tepuztec community, mandated that a nobleman who committed adultery with another noble's wife be stoned to death while a commoner offender was killed with arrows.[63]

Undoubtedly, many adulterers escaped punishment because of negotiations with their spouses and families. Several descriptions of punishment for adultery in the *Relaciones geográficas* state that compensation in material goods could be used to reestablish harmony between a couple. However, these examples only mention a payment of cloth to the woman's husband or to local rulers; they do not state whether a woman could demand compensation from her husband. A woman clearly had the right to request her husband's punishment, and the archival record shows that many women did so over the course of the colonial period.

Although many criminal records do not include final judgments and sentences, an analysis of patterns found in complete cases shows that punishments for adultery were not as harsh in colonial times as those recalled by native informants or depicted in preconquest and early colonial pictorial sources. Usually couples were released after a warning and a penalty.[64] In 1612, a noble of Tamazulapa and his lover were sentenced to a fine of four pesos each.[65] Native officials ordinarily also gave prisoners several lashes at the time of their arrest just for being involved in a scandal. Thus an element of physical punishment remained, but it did not exact the ultimate price. Regardless of the final judgment, the importance of bringing charges before the community cannot be overstated. Men and women who accused their spouses of infidelity rallied public opinion in their favor and brought shame to transgressors. Furthermore, witnesses frequently recalled prior offenses and previous marital conflicts. Complaints made before the community brought obvious immediate benefits in the short term, but the threat of multiple accusations enabled betrayed husbands and wives to call on established social networks to curb the behavior of their spouses.

In adultery cases resulting in a violent crime, offenders received much harsher sentences. For example, when a man murdered his unfaithful wife in the Zapotec community of San Francisco Cajonos in 1659, her lover was convicted of adultery. He received two hundred lashes and his goods were confiscated to pay for the legal proceedings, but the murdered woman's husband went unpunished.[66] Similarly, in the Ayuuk community of Amatepec, an official was killed when he discovered a couple rendezvousing in the countryside in 1699. The man fled, but his lover remained in the community and later confessed to committing adultery; she was sentenced to fifty lashes.

Status and wealth shaped the boundaries of acceptable interaction in the community and the likelihood of prosecution. When Luis de Peralta suspected his wife and don Agustín, a nobleman and a local official, of committing adultery, he complained to native authorities. He told them that when he caught don Agustín at his house, he let him go because he respected him as an alcalde of the community, but he confiscated his cloak and hat for evidence.[67] People sometimes asserted that nobles and wealthy people received preferential treatment from local officials. A native of Tamazulapa complained that his wife had been living with a noble of the community but he could not force her to desist nor was she ever punished "because she had the favor of the justices of the community, the governor, and the alcaldes for being a rich Indian woman."[68] Similarly, a Nahua noble complained that his wife's lover, a fiscal of the church, had not been punished for committing adultery because of his prominent position.[69] Occasionally, the highest nobility were emboldened by their status, believing that they were beyond the reach of colonial law. When don Miguel de los Angeles, the heir to the hereditary rulership of Yaguivee, killed his lover's husband, he reassured the woman that the authorities would never hang a woman and boasted that his father would provide the money to hire a good lawyer to win his acquittal.[70]

Although punishments for adultery were apparently less harsh in the colonial period, the Spanish legal system condoned the murder of an adulterous couple caught in the act. A man who murdered his wife and her lover was exonerated, allowing an aspect of preconquest justice to continue in colonial times.

Adultery and Homicide

According to Spanish law, the outrage provoked in a man who caught his wife committing adultery provided extenuating circumstances for the crime of homicide.[71] Reflecting Spanish influence, one source states that in preconquest times only those caught in *flagrante delicta* were stoned to death.[72] As the sixteenth-century questionnaire for Ayutla bluntly stated: "If they found some Indians with their women [in preconquest times], they killed them both."[73] In the colonial period, native men who caught their wives in the act often attacked the lovers with machetes or clubs. In one case from a Ñudzahui community in 1624, Dionisio Pérez Xiqua caught his wife, Lucía Xiqua, and Mateo de Velasco committing adultery in a maguey field. Although Dionisio had warned Mateo to keep away from his wife, the lovers continued to arrange trysts. When Dionisio found them together this time, he stabbed both with a knife, but his wife managed to escape. The fact that Dionisio Pérez Xiqua caught the couple in the act provided extenuating circumstances for the murder, and he was released from prison and absolved of the crime.[74]

Spanish legal discourse influenced the interpretation of marital rights and morality in native communities. Spanish lawyers filed legal petitions asserting that a man had the right to kill his wife and her lover if he caught them fornicating. This legal position shaped the confessions of indigenous men when they were brought to trial. Thus when Diego Xiquio caught his wife and her lover having sex and attacked them with a machete, his Spanish lawyer argued that he had exercised "the right by which he is permitted to kill both of them with an ax."[75] When questioned about the attack, Diego readily admitted that his intention had been "to avenge his offense and to kill them both."[76] In another case, a Bènizàa man named Josef Luis fled from his home in San Francisco Cajonos in 1659 after he killed his wife and seriously wounded her lover. The lawyer who represented him submitted a request that his client be absolved of the murder because he had acted within his right: he was innocent "since he caught her in adultery, [and] the law permits that the adulterers be condemned to the penalty of death." Ultimately, Josef Luis, too, was absolved of his crime.[77]

Only rarely did criminal records document cases in which women and their lovers conspired to kill a husband so that the woman would be freed from her marriage.[78] One example concerned Josefa de Rosa, her husband, Juan de Santiago, and her uncle, Baltasar Melchor, all of whom had left Coixtlahuaca in 1701 because of a devastating drought to seek work in the Mixteca Alta. Josefa and her uncle were lovers, but they presented themselves as husband and wife to the Spanish couple who eventually hired them in Tlaxiaco. A relative became suspicious when he attended the market in Tlaxiaco and learned that no one had seen Juan for some time. Eventually, the uncle and niece confessed that they had killed Juan and buried him in the house, claiming that the murder was self-defense and denying that they had committed incest. However, because they had presented themselves as husband and wife from the beginning, several witnesses testified that the two were indeed lovers.[79]

The study of native marriage and sexuality reveals a double standard in which a wife's indiscretions were deemed more serious than a husband's. This attitude provides an example of the failure of concepts of gender complementarity to produce full equality between men and women.

Sexual Double Standards

Fray Juan de Córdova noted a sexual double standard when he commented that adultery was the reason for divorce among natives "when she was an adulteress, and *sometimes* also when he was [an adulterer]" (emphasis added).[80] Testimony in adultery cases confirms this observation, that men believed that their extramarital affairs were acceptable but their wives' were not. When Martín Tilantzin was tried for his wife's murder in the Nahua community of Acatepec in 1558, he openly admitted that he had been involved with other women; native officials even summoned two of his lovers to testify.[81] One of them provided further evidence of Martín's philandering when she recalled that he had told her, "I have had relations with many women, but none has pleased me like you."[82] Martín, who had boasted about his affairs with other women, confessed that he had murdered his wife because he suspected that she had become pregnant by another man. He may have tried to appeal to the court's sensibilities by insinuating that his wife had committed adultery and that her actions provided extenuating circumstances. Regardless, he had been frank about his relations with another woman and his admission that he had become angry over his wife's alleged affairs reveals his assumptions about male sexual privilege. Similar circumstances surrounded a case from the Villa Alta. In 1657, the Spanish alcalde mayor was notified that Jacinto Manzaro had killed his wife when she was in an advanced stage of pregnancy. Although Jacinto was involved with another woman, he confessed to murder because he believed that his wife was carrying another man's child.[83]

Colonial criminal records indicate that men who carried out extramarital affairs expected their lovers to be monogamous. In one case from the Mixtec community of Tlaxiaco in 1635, a married man named Jacinto de la Cueva fatally stabbed his lover with a pair of scissors while in a jealous rage because he suspected that she had slept with and promised to marry another man.[84] Jacinto confessed that he was furious because he had seen Inés, his lover of two years, enter the other man's house and speak with him. Challenging a man's philandering by carrying on her own affairs could carry deadly consequences for his wife or his lover.

The distinction between adultery and other sexual indiscretions was not always clear in indigenous communities. From the native perspective, an adulterous act was not necessarily voluntary; therefore, the line between adultery and rape was sometimes blurred in criminal cases.

RAPE

Records of rape cases from central Mexico and Oaxaca document violence, shame, honor, and propriety in relation to women's sexuality. The fact that charges of rape were sometimes leveled against political enemies in colonial times demonstrates the association between the act and immoral, violent behavior.[85] Rape cases are somewhat rare in secular criminal records from central Mexico and Oaxaca. However, an examination of nineteen Spanish-language rape cases, dating from 1601 to 1763, suggests patterns of sexual criminal behavior and illuminates native women's status in the family and in the community.

Four Spanish terms for rape appear in documents from central Mexico and Oaxaca: *forzar, estuprar, corromper*, and *violar*.[86] *Forzar* (to force) was most frequently used to describe the rape of an adult woman who was no longer a virgin. *Estuprar* (to rape) and/or *corromper* (to corrupt or seduce) referred to the rape of a girl or young woman who was still a virgin.[87] *Violar* (to violate) was used in combination with *estuprar* and *corromper* apparently to add emphasis.[88] The phrase *contra su voluntad* (against her will) distinguishes fornication and rape.[89] All of these terms convey the woman's lack of consent.

Formal native-language texts, such as the Florentine Codex, do not discuss rape, but indigenous terms can be found in colonial dictionaries. Like the Spanish terms, their native-language counterparts convey the involuntary nature of the sexual act for the woman. In his Nahuatl dictionary Molina lists *cuitlauiltia* (to oblige to do something) and *cuitiuetzi* (to take quickly, snatch).[90]

Actions leading to rape charges help to reconstruct local concepts of sexual assault. In some cases, a woman complained of attempted rape when a man grabbed her clothing. Clothing, which stood in for the body in metaphors, also stood in for the body in rape accusations. In the Ñudzahui community of Teposcolula in 1594, a Nahua muleteer was tried for attempted rape because he grabbed a woman's huipilli.[91] Similarly, in 1697 Juliana Martín, a Bènizàa woman, accused her brother-in-law of attempted rape when he grabbed her dress.[92] Cases like this one underscore the importance of proper decorum and reserved behavior between men and women in indigenous communities.

In all of the nineteen cases examined for the present study, the victim knew her attacker, who typically lived in the same community; in two cases both defendant and victim lived in the same household. In Ayozingo in 1736, María del Carmen, a single Nahua woman, accused a married man of raping her and, following Spanish custom, sued for compensation for the loss of her virginity; she and the accused lived and worked on the estate of a prominent Spaniard.[93] In Ecatepec in 1748, thirty-year-old Manuel Antonio was accused of raping his godfather's twelve-year-old daughter; Manuel had been orphaned as a child, and his victim's father had taken him in and raised him.[94] If incestuous rape occurred within a household, it apparently was not reported to native or Spanish officials.

Victims of rape ranged in age from adolescent girls to young single women and adult married women. Although the ages of victims and defendants are not always given in the record, a pattern emerges suggesting that defendants were usually older. In the trials for which ages were recorded, the youngest victim was eight and the oldest was twenty-six. Defendants ranged from twenty to thirty-seven.

Sexual assault cases tried in indigenous communities reflected racial differences between victims and their perpetrators in only three of the nineteen investigations studied. In one trial, a thirty-six-year-old married Spaniard was prosecuted for raping a ten-year-old Nahua girl; however, the case was dropped after three midwives testified that the girl had not lost her virginity and she retracted her story.[95] In a second investigation, a Nahua man was accused of raping an unmarried Spanish woman; he was sentenced to a fine and his labor was sold for four years to raise the money for it.[96] In a third case, a mestizo raped a young Nahua woman.[97] Certainly rape occurred across racial boundaries, and further examination of criminal records from multiethnic centers, such as Mexico City, will undoubtedly bring more cases to light. Spaniards, mestizos, and mulattos may have entered native communities and raped women, but records of their crimes have not come to light; either the cases went unreported or they were resolved through informal negotiation. In 1666, for example, Bènizàa officials in Lachirio admitted that they had given the African slave of a local Spaniard fifty lashes because some of the women complained that he had raped them; there is no record of a trial, and the case entered the written record only after the slave accused officials of committing idolatry.[98]

An important exception are cases involving the sexual harassment, assault, and rape of indigenous women and men by Spanish priests. This disturbing reality is well documented in ecclesiastical records and native-language petitions.[99] Often sexual solicitation and assault were part of a larger pattern of abuse that included corporal punishment, usurpation of land, exploitation of labor, and demands for excessive fees. While the charges against priests may have been exaggerated as a strategy to push for a priest's removal from a community, they nevertheless reveal clerical abuse of authority and the unequal power relations between indigenous community members and local ecclesiastics (and Spaniards in general).

Rape and Adultery

One significant finding based on the analysis of criminal records from central Mexico and Oaxaca is that indigenous peoples did not always make a clear distinction between adultery and rape. In some cases, terms for adultery and rape were used interchangeably in the documents. For example, in 1721 a Nahua woman named Francisca María filed a petition for her husband's release from jail in Chiconauhtla. She stated that he had been imprisoned because another local woman had complained to local officials that he had "committed adultery" with her twice two years prior. Another document, however, stated that the man had been charged with rape (*haverla forzado*).[100] Francisca María may have attempted to recast his crime as a less serious offense to increase the likelihood that her petition would be granted. Nevertheless, the variation in terminology shows that the boundaries between rape and adultery were not always clear.

The response of some husbands to their wives' rape further suggests that the violation of a wife was conflated with adultery. A woman's marital status sometimes took precedence over her lack of consent in the definition of the crime. In these cases husbands considered themselves to be victims of adultery and did not acknowledge that their wives had suffered sexual assault. When Gregorio López raped Isabel Conquihui in 1601, her husband, Domingo García, filed criminal charges with the Ñudzahui officials in Yanhuitlan. Isabel testified that Gregorio had dragged her to a cornfield, where he had sex with her against her will (*contra su voluntad*). Since she was a little drunk on the night of the assault, she had not been able to defend herself. When she returned home and told her husband what had happened, he beat her with a club.[101] Similarly, a Ñudzahui man named Pedro de Ontiveros attacked his wife with a knife after an attempted rape in 1634. When Pedro de Ontiveros found the cacique of Cuquila attempting to wrestle his wife to the ground, he stabbed him and slashed his wife, even though she shouted that the cacique had not succeeded in committing any "misfortune" (*desgracia*).[102]

Testimony taken in criminal cases and the actions of native officials suggest that rape, as an act of adultery, brought shame to the victim's husband. In 1694, Nicolás Pacheco explained to Bènizàa officials in Yaa that he had twice struck Gaspar Martín with a machete because he had caught Gaspar raping his wife. Thus he justified his act by providing evidence accepted as proof of extenuating circumstances in adultery cases. The officials took Nicolás's wife to the alcalde's house so that her husband "would not kill her." They later whipped her and her attacker, although both insisted that they had never had relations and that he had not raped her. Although Nicolás clearly stated that his wife had been raped, his anticipated actions and her punishment by local authorities reflect the equation of rape and adultery.[103] In the Bènizàa community of La Oya in 1697, Juliana Martín complained to community officials that her brother-in-law had attempted to rape her. Only later did she admit that he had succeeded in penetrating her, explaining that she had lied at first because she did not want to bring shame upon her husband, who was a regidor. After the accused man admitted that he had raped Juliana, her husband returned home and beat her.[104] The stunning lack of compassion for the woman who had endured a painful and humiliating violation demonstrates that she was blamed for her rape. Because rape was perceived as adultery, married women risked punishment when they reported the crime, which in part explains the underreporting of this violent act against women.

Resolution and Punishment for Rape

Like other criminal matters, rape cases were resolved through the formal channels of the Spanish legal system or through negotiation mediated by community officials. In most trials involving unmarried women and girls, the victim's father filed the original complaint. However, in one case from Amanalco in 1650, a young woman's mother pursued justice, although her father was still living and resided with the family.[105] As guardians, Spaniards also brought suits concerning the rape of girls who lived and worked in their households.[106] Adult women, single or married, sometimes appeared on their own to initiate rape charges; at other times a husband complained and prosecution was carried out on his behalf.[107] Following notification of a sexual assault, native and Spanish officials ordered a midwife to examine the victim to verify that the woman had been penetrated and to determine whether she required treatment. The midwife's testimony was central to the case.

Incomplete colonial criminal records prevent quantitative analysis of punishments for rape. Furthermore, punishments were not standardized, but rather depended on the circumstances of the crime. In some cases, native officials publicly whipped accused men and their alleged victims simply because there was suspicion of sexual misconduct. In the most extreme judgment, a Ñudzahui man named Domingo de Silva was sentenced to death for the "violent and forceful" rape of an eight-year-old girl in 1684.[108] More often a convicted rapist was ordered to pay a fine, reimburse medical expenses, and compensate his victim. If he could not raise the money, his labor was sold to an obraje. In Amanalco in 1650, for example, a Nahua man's labor was sold to a bakery, with the proceeds of the sale going to his victim.[109]

Some rape charges were attempts to obtain compensation for the loss of virginity. For example, in the Nahua community of Malinalco in 1696 Catalina María charged Juan Tello, a twenty-year-old man, of raping her.[110] Several witnesses questioned her virginity, and one called her a "public woman and a common prostitute." In fact, it seemed that Catalina had sent Juan Tello "love notes," and when he did not respond she sent him one last letter alleging that "he was not a man nor did he know how to do anything since he did not answer her call."[111] Throughout the case Catarina María insisted that she did not want to marry Juan but simply wanted him to pay for the loss of her virginity. Perhaps reacting to the testimony about Catarina's loose reputation, her brothers submitted a petition stating that Juan had promised to marry her.[112] Juan was absolved of the charges, but he was still required to pay twelve pesos to cover the costs of the proceedings.

In Ayozingo in 1736, María del Carmen accused Juan Josef, a married mestizo, of rape.[113] Juan admitted that he had deflowered María, but he insisted that she had submitted voluntarily and that he had already given her two reales. María eventually retracted her accusation and dropped the case, although it is possible that she convinced Juan to pay her something more. In a case from Mexico City, a rapist was ordered to pay his victim twenty-four pesos, considerably more than the one peso he had promised her as consolation after his attack.[114]

In her study of rape in central Mexico, Sonya Lipsett-Rivera notes that some rape cases resulted in the marriage of the victim and her attacker.[115] This pattern emerges in the sources examined for the present study as well but only in central Mexico. For example, don Juan Diego, a noble of Chiconautla, accused Matías Nicolás of raping his daughter, Margarita, and named Bartolomé Andrés and Josefa María as accomplices in the crime. According to several witnesses, Josefa María lured the girl to her house and placed her in the oratory with Matías Nicolás. Whether or not Matías had raped Margarita is unclear, but he swore that he had not because she said she did not want to have sex, and neither Josefa María nor a midwife testified in the case. Don Juan Diego beat Matías Nicolás and scolded him: "Since you took Margarita Magdalena, you will marry her."[116] By taking the girl from her parents' home, he had raised suspicion of improper conduct, which could only be remedied by legitimating the union. Matías Nicolás won his release from prison only when he promised to marry Margarita.[117]

Pregnancy resulting from rape may have contributed to the pressure on a victim to marry her attacker. Thus when don Juan Francisco learned in 1748 that his twelve year-old daughter, Petra Antonia, was pregnant, he forced her to marry her rapist, Manuel Antonio. After the rape, he consoled her by promising to marry her. Terrified, she did not tell her parents what had happened, and they learned of the crime only when they realized that she was pregnant. Petra testified that Manuel raped her the first time they had sex, but she admitted to having relations with him a few times after that initial incident. Thus rape initiated the sexual relationship between Petra and Manuel, who had grown up together in the same household. Although Manuel swore to his innocence on "a thousand crosses," he agreed to marry Petra and petitioned for his release from prison. The victim's father, don Juan, was a high-ranking man in Jalastoc who had served as alcalde and fiscal; his daughter's pregnancy out of wedlock brought shame to her family, and only by her marriage could their honor be restored.[118]

Native men sometimes justified sexual misconduct using the popular Spanish practice of exchanging a marriage promise (*palabra de casamiento*). For example, in 1763 Catarina María and Juan Cristóbal, native commoners of Tizapan, complained to the Spanish alcalde mayor that their son had exchanged the palabra de casamiento with the daughter of a local Spaniard but the Spaniard had had him tried and convicted of rape.[119] By referring to Spanish practices, they hoped to overturn their son's conviction.[120]

A 1743 case resulting from an attempted rape reflects the way that sexuality shaped community dynamics. Simona Teresa, a Nahua woman of Ecatepec, accused Hilario Juan of attempting to rape her because he knew that her husband was out of town, but she beat him with a stick and called out to the fiscal to arrest him. Hilario mustered the lame excuse that he had intended to have sex with Simona's unmarried sister, perhaps thinking that fornication would be the lesser crime. Two prominent native nobles of the community later requested that the alcalde mayor order Simona to drop the case, arguing that because she was married the scandal had caused strife in the community. The officials may have acted as mediators in trying to reestablish peace outside of the Spanish system, although they did so at the expense of justice for Simona, who had risked her own safety and reputation by bringing the crime to light.[121]

CONCLUDING REMARKS

Indigenous peoples themselves, not just friars, enforced a moral code of sexual behavior by gossiping about local scandals, reporting crimes to indigenous and Spanish magistrates, testifying in criminal trials, and in more extreme cases resorting to violence to punish misconduct, often with the help of relatives and friends. Beliefs about sexuality were constantly contested and reinforced by popular opinion, official action, legal culture, and church doctrine.

In reality, indigenous and Spanish attitudes toward sexuality converged in many respects. Both encompassed a sexual double standard that held women to a stricter code of behavior. Both placed a great deal of importance on marriage as an institution that regulated sexuality and strongly condemned adultery and rape. Among its many dangers, adultery threatened cooperative labor arrangements, which were the foundation of indigenous social and political relations. There was a preconquest precedent for the harsh punishment of adultery, including death, and Spanish legal protection for men who murdered their wives and their lovers who were caught in adultery continued the tradition.

Cases involving compensation for the loss of virginity and the question of whether the couple had exchanged a marriage promise reveal considerable Spanish influence on indigenous sexual relations. In Spanish society, men and women frequently engaged in sex once a promise of marriage had been exchanged. In cases in which an impediment to marriage existed, the man customarily paid the woman for her virginity and the money served as a dowry for her marriage to another man.[122] Significantly, the majority of cases that discuss compensation and the exchange of a marriage promise come from central Mexico, which suggests that the degree to which Spanish custom influenced native sexual attitudes in Oaxaca was limited in some respects, even by the mid-eighteenth century.[123]

CHAPTER SEVEN

Duties and Responsibilities

In 1742 in the Nahua altepetl of Ecatepec, a group of local men and women urged the native authorities to expel Magdalena Pascuala from the town. Apparently, Magdalena had developed the annoying habit of arguing with other women in the community and calling them names. To bolster their case against Magdalena, her enemies charged that neither she nor her parents paid tribute.[1] Although we might surmise that on some level this accusation was simply a strategy to arouse the concerns of local officials, a deeper analysis of this case and many others suggests that these types of complaints reflect indigenous attitudes toward work, sociality, and community membership.

Ethnographic sources from the early colonial period reveal the value that Mesoamericans placed on diligence and responsibility to community. Descriptions of different social types in the Florentine Codex frequently refer to industriousness, productivity, and prosperity as admirable traits in both men and women.[2] Ordinary Nahuas, Ñudzahuis (Mixtecs), Bènizàas (Zapotecs), and Ayuuks (Mixes) expressed similar attitudes when testifying in court during the colonial period by framing their moral assessments in terms of the individual's work ethic and community service. When questioned about a person's character, witnesses often commented that he or she was hard working, quiet, and peaceful.[3] They described how the person earned his living sowing maize or fulfilled her labor obligations by cooking for her family.[4] Conversely, community members sometimes publicly disgraced a rival by accusing him or her of being lazy or of failing to contribute to tribute obligations.[5] Because it was such a great insult to suggest that a man did not fulfill his labor duty, violence sometimes erupted when a man refused to participate or was accused of slacking off.[6]

Frequent references to work in the mundane and ethnographic record shed light on the nature and organization of labor in highland Mexico.

Studies have focused on native and Spanish labor institutions, especially the *encomienda* and *repartimiento* systems, but daily duties and responsibilities have received less attention.[7] Moreover, while scholars have recognized women's work of weaving and preparing food, the broader cultural and symbolic meanings of this type of labor have not been considered. Although the present study is not exhaustive, it examines some of the types of labor that appear most prominently in hundreds of archival documents from central Mexico, the Mixteca Alta, and the Sierra Zapoteca; sixteenth-century Nahuatl texts; and preconquest and colonial pictorial manuscripts. It also considers the impact of European introductions and colonial changes on the organization and nature of work in highland Mexico.

THE ORGANIZATION OF LABOR IN NATIVE COMMUNITIES

At the heart of indigenous attitudes toward work were concepts of obligation. Terms for work in Nahuatl, Ñudzahui, and Zapotec, *tequitl*, *tniño*, and *china*, respectively, carried broader connotations, including labor, duty, occupation, tribute, and term of office.[8] Within these societies, each person had specific roles and responsibilities according to age, gender, and status. While tequitl for a nobleman might be serving the community through officeholding, for a commoner woman it might be grinding corn. Despite the difference in these tasks, the underlying concept of obligatory service to the local state remained the same. In a Mesoamerican community, the rights and privileges of belonging were contingent on fulfilling certain duties and responsibilities.

Except for the most urbanized centers of New Spain, real specialization was limited after the sixteenth century. In the rural native communities that are the focus of this study, even most artisans also practiced some form of agriculture and daily routines entailed working at many different things. On a typical day, a woman would juggle numerous demanding tasks, such as grinding corn, preparing food, weaving cloth, carrying food to household members in the fields, weeding crops, tending chickens and turkeys, and trading in the market, all while caring for her children. In fact, the idealized image from the Florentine Codex of the "middle-aged woman" shows her balancing these multiple demands (see Figure 7.1). She sits with her backstrap loom while an infant crawls beside her as her husband looks on. The accompanying Nahuatl text states that she has a husband and children and is skilled at weaving, cooking food and preparing beverages.[9] Together the image and the text convey the multiple

Figure 7.1. Middle-aged Nahua woman
SOURCE: Florentine Codex, bk. 10, fol. 7v. Florence: Biblioteca Medicea Laurenziana, Med. Palat. 220, c. 9v. By concession of the Ministry for Heritage and Cultural Activities; further reproduction by any means is forbidden.

duties that women carried out in the course of their daily lives in highland Mexico.

Weaving and Craft Production

Scholars have long recognized weaving and cooking as the principal responsibilities of Mesoamerican women and as symbols of their femininity; however, the metaphorical, social, and economic significance of these activities has not been examined in great depth.[10] Appreciating the significance of women's work enables a better understanding of their high status as laborers.

Weaving and cloth were central to Nahua concepts of the universe and the life force. Klein shows how some Mesoamericans conceived of the cosmos as made up of cords and thread stretched to create the universe, woven into fabric, and then folded into multiple layers.[11] In Nahua metaphors, clothes and food represented vitality, and thus women, as producers of these goods provided life's basic necessities. As items of gift exchange, cloth and food reaffirmed social relations and represented care and affection for another. Nahua writers equated cloth with health and vigor when they explained the meaning of the Nahuatl expression "He departs from the earth" (*vmpa onquiçan tlalticpac*):

It is said that when we are very poor, when with difficulty we can get what we require—a poor cape, a little food. So may it be understood of one who is poor, who undergoes great trials, whose rags are much worn, much tattered. When he puts them on, they are almost used up; they are about to fall apart; his body is about to show through there. So began there the saying: "Now he is departing from the earth," or "He goes about departing from the earth."

Iquac mitoa: in cence ie titotolinia, in aiaxcan neci totech monequi, in tilmatzintli, in tlaqualtzintli: inic vel caquizti in motolinia, in cenca tlaihiiouia, in itzotzomatzin cenca oiçoliuh, cenca ie tzatzaiani, in quimoquentia ça achi inic tlatlantica ie oalcocotoniz, ie vmpa onquiçaznequi in inacaio: inic vncan peuh in mitoa. Ie vmpa onquiça in tlalticpac, anoço onquiztinemi in tlalticpac.[12]

Frayed garments stand in for the worn-out body of a person who has endured great hardship and whose life is about to end. An account of the surrender of the rulers of the Triple Alliance of Tenochtitlan, Tetzcoco, and Tlacopan to the Spanish, in which the narrators carefully describe the rulers' cloaks, also associates cloth with well-being and vigor:

Thereupon the Marqués [Cortés] sat down there. Next to him sat Malinche. And Quauhtemoc was next to the Captain [Cortés]. He had on a shining maguey fiber cape, each half of different color, with hummingbird feathers in the style of the people of Ocuillan. It was extremely dirty; that was all he wore. Coanacochtzin, the tlatoani of Tetzcoco, followed him; he wore only an ordinary maguey fiber cape, with a flowered border, with a design of radiating flowers. It too was extremely dirty. Tetlepanquetzaltzin, tlatoani of Tlacopan, came next. He likewise wore a maguey fiber cape. It also was very dirty, filthy.

niman ic oncan ommotlali in Marques, itlan ommotlali in Malintzin: auh in Quauhtemoctzin itlan ca in Capitan: in quimolpilia quetzalichpetztli, tlatlacuhuitectli, vitzitzilin hivio inic ocuiltecaio, omach catzaoac, çan quixcavitica: niman contoquilitica in Coanacutzin, tetzcucu tlatoani: in quimolpilitica, çan vel ichtilmatli, xoxochiteio, xochimoiaoac, omach no catzaoac: niman contoquilitica. Tetlepanquetzatzi, tlacuban tlatoani, çan no iuhqui in quimolpilitica in ichtilmatli, ono vel catzactix, ouel catzaoac.[13]

This passage is striking because commoners, not nobles, wore maguey cloaks and the tattered and soiled condition of the garments described certainly was not befitting the illustrious *tlatoque*, who reigned over some of the most wealthy and powerful ethnic states in the Americas. When the authors remark, "That was all he wore" in reference to Quauhtemoc and that the ruler of Tetzcoco "only" wore a common cape, they reveal that the rulers appeared without the regalia associated with their official status, such as their royal diadems, nose ornaments, ear spools, and pectorals. Thus, in the context of indigenous symbolism, the rulers' humble dress signified the poverty, disarray, and chaos brought on by the war and the demotion in rank.[14] Their disheveled appearance and miserable garments foretold the imminent demise of the native nobility of Mexico Tenochtitlan and Tlatelolco.

Because of its symbolic significance, as well as its practical value, clothing was an important item exchanged at rituals, including birth and marriage ceremonies. As discussed in Chapter 2, the midwife welcomed an infant into the world by giving a baby boy his breechcloth and cape and giving a baby girl her huipilli and skirt.[15] At the feast held in honor of a newborn noble child, the parents offered their guests tobacco, flowers, food, drink, and "gifts, cloaks, clothing, garments, capes, and loincloths" (*motlauhtizque, motilmatizque, moquentizque, motlaquentizque, motlalpilizque, momaxtlatizque*).[16] Cloth represented (re)birth in other sacred rituals, including the New Fire ceremony that commemorated the beginning of a new fifty-two-year cycle. According to the Florentine Codex, as part of the festivities men and women donned new clothing and replaced all household goods, including the hearthstones that would contain the fire when it arrived.[17] Then they offered incense and sacrificed quail to the hearth and the four directions. The ceremony represented regeneration and renewal, symbolized by new clothing, household items, and hearth fires.

As a precious item, indigenous people offered cloth to their deities and, in colonial times, to saints. The Florentine Codex describes the *huey tecuilhuitl* feast (Great Feast of the Lords), celebrated after the Spaniards withdrew from Mexico Tenochtitlan during the military phase of the conquest, and relates how the Mexica adorned all of the gods in feathers and turquoise mosaic masks and dressed them "in sacred garments, the quetzal feather garment, the yellow parrot feather garment, the eagle feather garment" (*in teuquemitl, in quetzalquemitl, in tozquemitl, quauhquemitl*).[18] Following the festivities the clothing and regalia that adorned the deities were distributed to the principal nobles in attendance. Such attention to the detail of different colors and types of garments placed on the gods highlights the sacred significance of textiles and reveals the semi-sacred status of nobles who were arrayed in the clothing of the deities.

As an army of Christian saints eclipsed the pantheon of preconquest gods in colonial times, many ancient indigenous ritual practices survived under a new guise. Fray Toribio de Motolinía described in the sixteenth century how on holy days women continued to offer cloth of different sizes and patterns that was made of cotton or rabbit fur. He noted that the women meticulously incorporated Christian iconography into their weavings, including crosses, a shield with the five wounds, the names of Jesus and Mary, and roses, and that they walked up to the steps of the church, raised their textiles, and then placed them on the ground while bowing.[19] He ecstatically concluded: "To see the recollection and devotion with which they do this is enough to bring the dead to life."[20] What

Motolinía did not acknowledge as he wrote his glowing account of the neophytes' devotion was that many indigenous people continued to offer cloth to Mesoamerican deities as well as to Christian saints during this period.

Because Spaniards persecuted worshippers of ancient deities, some rituals were driven underground. Caves, which Mesoamericans considered sacred as entrances to the underworld, temporarily provided protection from the inquisitorial gaze of Spanish friars. Some ecclesiastics and secular Spaniards and mestizos became aware of this and began to search caves for evidence of "idolatry." They often discovered cloth among the caches of religious materials and offerings.[21]

Cloth was given in political as well as sacred contexts, especially to consolidate alliances. In preconquest times, rulers and high lords exchanged textiles with merchants, who often acted as ambassadors on travels to distant regions and sometimes bought and sold goods on the nobility's behalf. According to the story of the conquest of Anahuac (the coastal region), when merchants returned victoriously to Tenochtitlan, the tlatoani, Ahuitzotzin, sent priests to welcome them and offer them many types of cloaks with elaborate designs, along with bundles of rabbit fur capes, maize, beans, and chia.[22] The merchants reciprocated when they hosted the feast during the month of Panquetzaliztli, honoring their distinguished guests by presenting the men with cloaks and loincloths and the women with huipillis and skirts.[23] Similarly, during the conquest period, before the Spaniards marched into Tenochtitlan, the Mexica tlatoani Moteucçoma offered them eight different types of *tlaçotilmatli* (precious cloaks) in an attempt to appease them and create an alliance.[24]

In addition to their symbolic and social significance, textiles had great economic value.[25] In preconquest times, cloth and cacao beans were used as units of exchange. In an illustration in the Florentine Codex, Nahua merchants are identified as traders by the cloth and other luxury goods at their sides (see Figure 7.2).[26] Indeed, cloth was synonymous with wealth. When Nahuas described the Spanish looting of Mexico Tenochtitlan, they listed woven capes first among the valuables that were plundered, lamenting: "And our enemies snatched and took whatever they came upon. Whatever they encountered they took and carried away, whether it be cloaks, large cotton capes, war devices, log drums, or upright drums." (*Auh in toiaovan tlanamoxtivi, quicuitivi in tlein ipan oquiçato, in tlein oquipantito quicui, quimotquilia in aço tilmatli, in aço quachtli, in anoço tlaviztli, in anoço teponaztli in anoço vevetl*).[27]

Woven goods retained their value during the colonial period and were traded in regional markets throughout highland Mexico to pay tribute, sponsor local festivals, and raise money for the community. Spanish

Figure 7.2. Merchants, identified by cloth and other precious trade goods
SOURCE: Florentine Codex, bk. 9, fol. 8. Florence: Biblioteca Medicea Laurenziana, Med. Palat. 219, c. 316. By concession of the Ministry for Heritage and Cultural Activities; further reproduction by any means is forbidden.

merchants also profited from the production and sale of cloth. Significantly, when people complained to colonial officials that they had been robbed, the stolen goods overwhelmingly consisted of clothing and textiles, suggesting that in a cash-starved colonial economy many people possessed more wealth in cloth than in money.[28]

Weaving remained one of the most significant and lucrative forms of craft production in New Spain. Throughout the colonial period, women continued to produce massive amounts of cloth on backstrap looms; however, the Spanish introduction of spinning wheels and foot looms modified the division of labor in certain respects. Although the extent to which men spun thread and wove in preconquest times is believed to have been limited, it is clear that they learned to spin on wheels and to weave new types of cloth on European looms, such as *sayal* (a loosely woven, low-quality cloth) and taffeta.[29] In some places, men may have been compelled to learn these trades as part of their tribute duty.[30] It is likely that male professional spinners, such as Domingo García, a Mixtec man of Santiago Iztepec, used European-style spinning wheels like the one depicted in the Florentine Codex (see Figure 7.3).[31] As with other European introductions, change proceeded from the presence of Spanish weavers and traders and therefore was restricted to certain regions. Even in those regions, women continued to weave on backstrap looms to produce cloth for household use, sale in the market, and tribute.

A growing market for European-style clothing promoted new trades and changes in clothing production. Whereas women had been primarily (perhaps solely) responsible for weaving in preconquest times, in the colonial period native men and women worked as tailors and seamstresses to fashion fitted garments complete with sleeves, collars, and buttons.[32] Illustrations of tailors and spinners in the Florentine Codex suggest a fascination with these Spanish introductions[33] (see Figures 7.3 and 7.4).

Indigenous artisans and vendors catered to the growing demand for European-style shoes. On the list of vendors in the tenth book of the Florentine Codex are the *çapatosnamacac* (Spanish-style shoe vendors), a term that uses the Spanish loan noun *zapatos* (shoes) to qualify the Nahuatl word for trader *namacac*.[34] In the Mixteca Alta, cobblers were concentrated in Teposcolula, the cabecera and seat of the *alcaldía mayor* (the town where the alcalde mayor resides), where there was notable Spanish-native cultural interaction. As in other aspects of cultural transference, Nahuas of central Mexico participated in the introduction of Spanish material culture to southern Mexico. In the early seventeenth century, for example, several Nahua shoemakers resided and worked in Teposcolula, including a craftsman employed by Rafael Hernández, an *indio ladino* (Spanish-speaking native) and resident of Teposcolula.[35]

Figure 7.3. Spinner

SOURCE: Florentine Codex, bk. 10, fol. 23v. Florence: Biblioteca Medicea Laurenziana, Med. Palat. 220, c. 25v. By concession of the Ministry for Heritage and Cultural Activities; further reproduction by any means is forbidden.

Figure 7.4. Tailor
SOURCE: Florentine Codex, bk. 10, fol. 23. Florence: Biblioteca Medicea Laurenziana, Med. Palat. 220, c. 25. By concession of the Ministry for Heritage and Cultural Activities; further reproduction by any means is forbidden.

In addition to textiles, women produced an array of goods and luxury items. In preconquest and colonial times, certain crafts were often gender-specific. Men worked as stone polishers, coppersmiths, goldsmiths, jewelers, mosaicists, codex painters, woodworkers, carpenters, stonemasons, and bricklayers. Women specialized in weaving, embroidering, and dyeing.[36] Some artisan trades were not gendered; both men and women practiced elite crafts such as featherworking, a trade synonymous with artisanship.[37]

Nahuatl-language terminology, descriptions of native craftspersons, and accounts of preconquest rituals demonstrate that some women were acknowledged as artisans of the first rank. Significantly, speeches directed to the ruler's daughter and son advised them to emulate "the artisans, the craftspersons" (*in tultecaiotl, in amantecaiotl*).[38] Featherworking was a regional specialization of Amantlan in central Mexico, where both men and women were renowned for producing exquisite plumed garments, headdresses, shields, and images. A description of the people of Amantlan pledging their children to the temple on the feast of Tlaxochimaco reveals the association between fine craftsmanship and women's work. Honoring their two principal goddesses, Xiuhtlati and Xilo, parents in Amantlan prayed that their sons and daughters might be accomplished artisans:

And if it were a woman, one asked that she would embroider well and would dye articles, rabbit fur well; she would dye the colored rabbit furs wherever they were placed; or perhaps she would dye, tint feathers in varied colors—dark green, yellow, rose red, blue, black—that she would judge the many colors, so that she would work her feathers skillfully.

auh intla cihoatl quitlaniaia inic uel tlamachioaz, ioan uellapaz tochomipaz, uel quipaz in izquican icac tlapapaltochomitl, anoço ihuitl quipaz tlatlapalpaz, tlamatlalpaz, tlacozticapaz, tlaxochipalpaz, tlatexopaz, tlaiiappalpaz, tlapaltica tlatlatlapalpoaz inic quitlatlamachiz ihuiuh.[39]

These wishes for a daughter reveal the high esteem in which female artisans were held. Interestingly, although the text refers to women as featherworkers, the accompanying illustrations show only men.[40] Nevertheless, information gleaned from both the alphabetic text and the images suggests that craft specialization often was regionally specific, but not always gender-specific.

An analysis of Nahuatl-language terminology used in descriptions of various trades illuminates the role of women as artisans. *Toltecatl* (literally, inhabitant of Tula; metaphorically, artisan) and several words derived from it connote male and female artisans. First, as a general category *toltecatl* refers to a careful, skilled worker who produces works of art.[41] It also refers to the seamstress (*tlatzonqui*; literally one who sews) and the potter, who could be male or female.[42] *Tlatoltecatlaliani* (one who arranges things as an artisan) describes the lapidary, and the scribe is said to "act as an artisan" (*toltecati*; *toltecatl* verbalized with the intransitive suffix *-ti*); men specialized in both occupations.[43] Several other terms incorporating references to the hands emphasize skill. Combining *maitl* (hand) and *toltecatl*, the spinner and the seamstress are described as *matoltecatl* (a person possessing artisan's hands) (see Table 7.1). Other derivations include *momaimati* (skilled of hand), a term applied to the goldworker (apparently always male), the seamstress, the spinner, and the potter.[44] Finally, expressing skill more generally is *ca mimati* (she/he is expert), which applies to a weaver (see Table 7.2).[45]

The Florentine Codex emphasizes the artisan's ability to arrange shapes and colors in creating designs. The verb *tlananamactia* (to make things meet or match) is the root of constructions for the work of the weaver (*tlananamictiani*, one who matches things) and the featherworker

TABLE 7.1. *Nahuatl-language terminology based on* toltecatl *(artisan) from the Florentine Codex*

Term	Meaning	Used to describe
Toltecatl	Literally inhabitant of Tula	Seamstress
	Metaphorically artisan	Potter
Tlatoltecatlaliani	One who arranges things as an artisan	Lapidary
Toltecati	To act as an artisan	Scribe
Matoltecatl	A person possessing artisan's hands	Seamstress

TABLE 7.2. *Nahuatl-language terminology based on* imati *(be skilled, expert) from descriptions of artisans in the Florentine Codex*

Term	Meaning	Used to describe
Momaimati	Skilled of hand	Goldworker
		Seamstress
		Spinner
		Potter
Ca mimati	She/he is expert	Weaver

(*tlananamactia*, he/she matches things) (see Table 7.3).[46] The same idea is expressed in the term *tlapopotiani* (one who matches or joins things; from *potia*, to pair off or join one thing to another, based on *po*, equal, mate, match) and *tlahuipana*, (he/she lines things up.)[47,48]

Other verbs conceptually link the tasks of the weaver, the featherworker, the lapidary, and the scribe. Derivations based on *tlapalhuia* (he/she paints or dyes something) a verb clearly associated with the art of painting, describe the weaver as "one who dyed with various colors" (*tlatlapaloani*) and the featherworker as "one who arranged various colors" (from *tlatlapalpohua*) (see Table 7.4).[49] Terms based on *tliloa* (he/she outlines in black) also suggest a connection between writing, painting, and other artistic forms. The coppercaster (always male) was a person who "outlines in black" (*tlatlatlilhuia, tlatliloa, tlatliloani*), and the weaver was "one who outlines designs" (*tlatlilaniani*).[50] *Icuiloa* (he/she paints or writes) describes the seamstress who "makes designs" (*tlacuicuiloa*) (see Table 7.5).[51] According to the Florentine Codex, Nahua scribes and weavers both worshipped the day of Seven Flower "so that what they undertook might be well done, that their embroidery and design would be a work of art, well made, and well painted" (*inic itla vel aizque mimatizque, toltecatizque, vellalalizque, vellacuilozque: in ipan intlamach, intlacuilol*).[52] Nahuas associated the work of scribes with that of featherworkers: scribes drew designs that provided patterns that

TABLE 7.3. *Nahuatl-language terminology based on* tlananamactia *(make things meet or match) from descriptions of artisans in the Florentine Codex*

Term	Meaning	Used to describe
Tlananamictiani	One who matches things	Weaver
Tlananamactia	He/she matches things	Featherworker

TABLE 7.4. *Nahuatl-language terminology based on* tlapalhuia *(paint or dye something) from descriptions of artisans in the Florentine Codex*

Term	Meaning	Used to describe
Tlatlapaloani	One who dyes with various colors	Weaver
Tlatlapalpohua	One who arranges various colors	Featherworker

TABLE 7.5. *Nahuatl-language terminology based on* tliloa *(outline in black) and* icuiloa *(write, paint) from descriptions of artisans in the Florentine Codex*

Term	Meaning	Used to describe
Tlatlatlilhuia, tlatliloa, tlatliloani	To outline in black	Coppercaster
Tlatlilaniani	One who outlines designs	Weaver
Tlacuicuiloa	Makes designs	Seamstress

featherworkers copied.[53] The use of similar terms demonstrates that the Nahuas understood there to be connections between writing, weaving, embroidering, featherworking, and other forms of artisanal production.

A philological analysis of the terminology used to describe craft production in the Florentine Codex suggests that little conceptual distinction was made between men and women's work. Various verb forms based on *tzotzon* (to beat or pound) refer to the activities of both men and women. For example, the gold worker was said to "pound out designs" (*tlanextzotzona*), the coppercaster "beats" (*tlatetzotzona*) copper, and the weaver "beats" (*tlatzotzona*) on her loom (to tighten the weave).[54] The weaver was also said to be "one who presses down on something" (*tlatepachoani*) and "one who beats something" (*tlahuitequini*).[55] Nahuatl terminology captures the active, physical nature of men and women's work.

Pictorial evidence reveals the many ways that producing food or textiles required the same types of labor and tools used for crafting goods. Although *metates* (grinding stones) are primarily associated with women and their task of grinding maize, men also used them to, for example, to pulverize various materials into dyes. Men are shown heating and melting raw materials over a fire in the Florentine Codex (see Figures 7.5 and 7.6) much in the same way women prepare food. The Nahua authors

Figure 7.5. Man using metate
SOURCE: Florentine Codex, bk. 11, fol. 221. Florence: Biblioteca Medicea Laurenziana, Med. Palat. 220, c. 372. By concession of the Ministry for Heritage and Cultural Activities; further reproduction by any means is forbidden.

Figure 7.6. Man heating a substance over a fire
SOURCE: Florentine Codex, bk. 11, fol. 218v. Florence: Biblioteca Medicea Laurenziana, Med. Palat. 220, c. 370v. By concession of the Ministry for Heritage and Cultural Activities; further reproduction by any means is forbidden.

associated cooking and working precious metals in describing how the artisan made a mold by combining clay and charcoal that was "kneaded and worked with the hands" (*ic quixaqualoa ic quimatzacutilia*) and that "in just the same manner as making tortillas they made it into flat cakes" (*çan oc iuhqui in quitlatlascaloa*), which were then left in the sun to harden.[56]

That the Nahuas understood and described men and women's work in similar terms challenges previous assumptions that men performed most, if not all, of the prestigious trades in Nahua society. Such generalizations are due more to assumption and a superficial reading of formal sources than to a close analysis of texts, archival documents, and philological evidence. It should be noted that the lack of a source comparable to the Florentine Codex for the Mixteca Alta and the Sierra Zapoteca makes it difficult to uncover specific usages that might equate male and female craft production in these regions. Nevertheless, notarial records from central Mexico and Oaxaca confirm a general community-level concern about women's labor and a recognition of women's contributions to the household and the community. As craftspersons, women were on par with their male peers; they could be accomplished artisans, and their expertise could bring considerable prestige.

The introduction of European goods, forms, and styles radically altered indigenous material culture in the colonial period. Over time European forms eclipsed many exquisite preconquest artistic traditions, such as featherworking, although in the early period indigenous artisans, using new materials, techniques, and iconography, produced hybrid works of art.[57] Pictorial images and archival evidence suggest that men more often than women learned to work with new European tools and media. Changes in the supply of basic materials, including cotton, feathers, rabbit fur, and precious stones, also must have altered patterns of traditional craft production.[58] I leave it to others to document the decline of pre-Columbian craft production in the colonial period. Suffice it to say that, aside from weaving, Spaniards demanded mainly unskilled labor from indigenous women, which suggests that the collapse of elite artistic traditions was one of the many factors that eliminated positions of prestige and ultimately eroded women's status in New Spain.

Cooking Food and Preparing Beverages

Normative texts describe the preparation of food and drink as one of women's principal duties. According to archival records, grinding maize, making tortillas, cooking food, and preparing chocolate, or *atole* (a corn-based beverage), were laborious and time-consuming daily tasks. In pre-Hispanic times, women played a central role in developing agriculture and methods of food preparation that enhanced nutritional value and long-term storage.[59] These responsibilities were vital to the survival of the household in colonial Mexico. Careful distribution was essential, especially when supplies were low in the months before a harvest; thus the importance of a woman's ability to regulate the supply of household resources cannot be overstated.

Tortillas were the staple of the native diet and with salt and chiles sometimes constituted the entire daily intake for humble people.[60] Women arose before dawn to begin grinding corn for the atole and tortillas that they served in the household or gave to their husbands to take to the fields.⁶¹ Using a *metlatl* (grinding stone), they ground dried corn kernels that had been soaked to make dough (*masa*). Often women carried tortillas to their husbands in the fields at midday and then worked with them during the rest of the afternoon.⁶² They also prepared *piñol*, a dried corn meal that was ideal for long trips because it was not perishable.⁶³ When a woman was sick or simply overburdened, she could count on her female relatives, comadres, or friends for help in fulfilling her indispensable cooking responsibilities.⁶⁴

The presence of a Spanish and mestizo population created new demands for European goods, including foods. Wheat mills and bakeries were among the new enterprises established to serve local Hispanic populations. In 1641 don Juan de Escobar, the governor of Malinalco, owned a mill and bakery with his wife.⁶⁵ His wife taught the men and women of the community how to bake bread, which they then sold in nearby towns. In 1665 in Lachirio, where there was a Dominican convent, Juan de Santiago and his wife, Lucía, worked as bakers.⁶⁶ Similarly, in Teposcolula and Tamazulapa, cabeceras in the Mixteca Alta where Spanish speakers resided, two Ñudzahui men, Baltasar de Contreras and Gaspar Hernández, worked as bakers.⁶⁷ Significantly, only in Spanish-style bakeries could indigenous men be seen preparing food. For the most part, men assumed roles associated with activities and technologies introduced by Spaniards.

Although according to idealized texts beverage preparation was women's work, in reality both men and women produced and sold pulque and *tepache*, native alcoholic beverages.⁶⁸ All native peoples used pulque as a sacred offering in ceremonies and drank it to achieve ritual inebriation. During times of drought, pulque provided refreshment and was a dietary supplement. Perhaps because the pulque trade was so profitable, men and women both were involved in its production and sale.⁶⁹

Sharing food was an essential part of all relationships, human and divine. In some pre-conquest cosmologies, the life of the sun depended on a reciprocal exchange of food and drink between humans and deities. As the domain of the mother and father of the sun, the battlefield was an essentially complementary place, providing an arena of human-sacred interaction. The military leaders Tlacateccatl and Tlacochcalcatl sustained the sun with food and drink.⁷⁰ In an interesting inversion of gender duties during the bathing ritual, the midwife associated the baby boy's future victories on the battlefield with sustenance: "You are to serve up drink and food to the sun, the lord of the earth" (*ticatlitiz, tictlaqualtiz, tictlamacaz in tonatiuh in tlaltecutli*).⁷¹ Sacrifice and offerings, even of human flesh and blood, were conceptualized as "drink and food."

Just as the exchange of food between humans and deities was required to maintain life, sharing food among humans was necessary to a civilized existence. The Nahuas, like other Mesoamericans, ascribed a great deal of importance to oratory and associated food and drink with eloquent speech. One sixteenth-century Nahua proverb says, "Only by drink and food did words of wisdom emerge, so that no one might live in evil. Not without purpose did they drink and eat" (*in çan atica i çan tlaqualtica, in onca quiçaia in nezcaliliztlatolli, inic aiac tlauelilocanenca, amo çan quinenquaia, amo çan quinemia, in atl in tlaqualli*).[72] Food and drink stimulated speech, enriched social interaction, and reinforced moral codes.

Ritual feasting and drinking legitimated business agreements and consummated social bonds. People frequently offered community officials some pulque and something to eat before they decided land tenure or other legal matters.[73] In preconquest times, when parents placed their children in temple schools, they showed their good faith by sponsoring a feast for the teachers: "They drank and ate; there was the mutual giving of gifts in the spirit of friendship" (*atli, tlaqua: nel motlauhtia in netlacamatcapan*).[74] It was the exchange of food and drink that was the foundation of friendship and established bonds with officials.

Food also was used to compensate services and expertise. Indigenous and Spanish officials who summoned commoners for tribute labor fed them and paid them a nominal fee. Parents generously paid the calendar reader who named their newborn child and foretold his or her fate with food and drink and turkeys.[75] The custom of giving food to a spiritual leader, healer, or midwife continued during the colonial period. For example, in 1666, in exchange for her eye treatments, Isabel López ordinarily gave a Bènizàa healer named Catalina Pérez fish, eggs, beans, or greens (*quelites*) to take home.[76] Considering the ritual context of healing in native culture, the offering of food was not simply an economic arrangement but a highly symbolic act showing respect for the healer, who served as an intermediary between earthly and sacred realms. In a similar vein, native communities were required to provide food to the Catholic priest and his retinue when in town, giving women's tribute labor for the church a holy dimension.

The sharing of food and drink continued to be a highly symbolic social and political act during the colonial period. In 1660 political opponents of the Bènizàa governor of San Pedro Nesiche accused him of protecting the interests of Spaniards to the detriment of the community. They imprisoned him, placed him in stocks, and then paraded him throughout the community on a mule. A town crier announced that he would be whipped because he had "accompanied and helped the Spaniards and he had eaten with don Joseph de Reynoso," the alcalde mayor.[77] By dining at the official's table, the governor had revealed his loyalties to the Spaniards and demonstrated his complicity in promoting their interests.

Food and drink, like cloth, symbolized material wealth. A newly elected Nahua ruler pondered the hypothetical fate of a diligent woman: "Perhaps he [our Lord] gives her valor to be rich on earth; she will have drink and food" (*in at tlalticpac, oquichiotl quimaca, mocuiltonoz in tlalticpac, oniez in iauh, itlaqual*).[78] The association of food with livelihood is perhaps best explained by the common Nahua metaphor "It is my drink, it is my food" (*ca nauh, ca notlaqual*), which meant "my property, my goods, my living" (*ca naxca, ca notlatqui, ca nonetlaiecoltiliz*).[79] This is not surprising given that the majority of native people lived at subsistence levels. The politics of class and food distribution in native communities can be glimpsed in archival records. One's access to wealth, specifically food, determined one's ability to formally express polite behavior. When a certain Martín offered to accompany a Ñudzahui noble, don Andrés de Tapia, to Diego Ramírez's house in 1578, don Andrés advised him: "Do not go. He is poor, and he does not have anything to give us for dinner."[80] This remark suggests that humble commoners had little access to the surpluses that would allow them to exchange food and other goods necessary for alliance building.

Midwives and Healers

Despite the view expressed in formal texts and reiterated by many scholars that women were to remain in the household, women's work often took them out of their homes and their labor had social and economic significance beyond the support of their families. This was especially true of the midwife and healer. The Florentine Codex preserves a set of speeches made by the midwife, a pregnant woman, and her kin that sheds light on the roles and status of the Nahua healer. The most common term for a midwife in the speeches was *ticitl*, which means a medical specialist in the general sense of healer or doctor.[81] The title is gender neutral (men were also referred to as ticitl) and does not limit the ticitl's medical knowledge to childbirth or women's health.

Certain terms reserved for elite artisans and craftspersons emphasize the ticitl's skill and expertise. Thus the expectant woman and her family addressed the ticitl as *in amantecatl* (wise one), *in toltecatzintli* (skilled one), and *amiamantecaoan totecuio* (you (pl.) artisans of our lord/lady). Some constructions refer to the ticitl's specialization in childbirth: *in tetlacachiuiliani* (one who brings about birth), *in temixiuitiani* (one who delivers), *in imac tlacatioani* (one in charge of birth), and *in ititl quiuellaliani* (one who sets the womb straight). Formal speeches contain terminology that attests to the high status accorded female healers—for example, *tlaçotitlacatzintli* (precious lady/lord), *totecuio* (our lady/lord), and *cioapilli* (noblewoman). *Teunantli* (sacred mother) and *totechiuhcauh* (our progenitress) associate the midwife with the sacred and ancestral worlds (see Table 7.6).

According to the Florentine Codex, household members and kin summoned a ticitl to advise a pregnant woman on how to care for herself during the pregnancy (see Figure 7.7). The ticitl instructed her to eat and drink well and not to fast or eat chalk or earth because the baby would absorb whatever was ingested.[82] She also warned that the woman must not become overheated in the sun or the sweatbath because excessive heat could kill the baby. Some of the healer's advice linked the mother's behavior to particular deformities in the child. Thus she admonished the expectant mother not to sleep during the day lest the child be born with unusually thick eyelids, and warned that the baby's lips would be perforated if she chewed chicle.

The ticitl also spoke of the relationship between the baby's health and the mother's emotional state, warning that a pregnant woman was to avoid feeling sad, troubled, or frightened, which might cause her to miscarry. The ticitl ordered the expectant mother not to physically exert herself by overworking, lifting heavy items, or running. She charged the elder women who organized the household's female labor with taking special care of the pregnant woman, using her authority to restructure labor obligations and ensure the mother's access to the increased nutritional resources that pregnancy required.

TABLE 7.6. *Some Nahuatl terms for midwife*

Term	Translation
Ticitl[a]; *ticitzintli*	Healer; esteemed healer
In titici, in ilamatzitzin	The healers, the old women
In tetlacachiuiliani	One who brings about birth
In temixiuitiani[a]	One who delivers
In imac tlacatioani	One in charge of birth
In amantecatl; namantecatl	Wise one; I am a wise one
In toltecatzintli; amitoletcaoan	Skilled one; [you] skilled ones (plural)
Amiamantecaoan totecuio	[You] artisans of our lord/lady (plural)
Tlaçotitlacatzintli	Precious lady/lord
Totecuio	Our lady/lord
Cioapilli	Noblewoman
In ititl quiuellaliani	One who sets the womb straight
Teunantli	Godly mother
Totechiuhcauh	Our progenitress

SOURCE: Sahagún 1996, bk. 6, fols. 127–138v.
[a]These terms are also found in Ruiz de Alarcón 1984, 159, passim.

Figure 7.7. Nahua ticitl advising a pregnant woman, before an assembly of household members and kin, on how to take care of herself during pregnancy
SOURCE: Florentine Codex, bk. 6, fol. 116. Florence: Biblioteca Medicea Laurenziana, Med. Palat. 219, c. 120. By concession of the Ministry for Heritage and Cultural Activities; further reproduction by any means is forbidden.

The ticitl also advised women to modify sexual activity during the pregnancy. She encouraged a couple to continue having sex (always in moderation) during the first trimester so that the baby would form properly, reflecting the Mesoamerican belief that the baby developed and grew through the accumulation of bodily fluids contributed by both mother and father. However, once the baby was formed, the ticitl and the couple's mothers admonished them to abstain from sex to ensure that the child was not harmed. Otherwise, the woman would have a difficult delivery and the child would be born covered "in filth," thereby revealing that its parents had continued to have sexual relations into the pregnancy's advanced stages. Male elders gave the expectant father a similar warning in a ritual when the pregnancy was first recognized.[83]

When the pregnant woman began to feel labor pains and was close to delivering, the ticitl returned to the household to assist the birth. She prepared food for the woman and quickly bathed her in the *temascalli* (sweat bath).[84] She then massaged the woman's abdomen to align the baby properly and administered herbal infusions as expellants to speed the birthing process (see Figure 7.8). Typically, an herb called *ciuapactli* (woman medicine) sufficed; however, if the labor were very difficult the midwife used an infusion of ground opossum tail that was a more intense ejectant, making sure to avoid fatal overdoses.[85] If potions failed to induce contractions, the ticitl suspended the woman and kicked her in the back to start labor. In critical cases, when after days of trying unsuccessfully to deliver the child, she even performed surgery to save the mother's life, using an obsidian blade knife to dismember the baby and remove it from the womb. In tragic cases in which all options had been exhausted and the woman's parents objected to the baby's removal, the ticitl solemnly enclosed the suffering woman in the temascalli by herself and left her to die in peace (see Figure 7.9).[86] In this sense, the temascalli became both a womb and a tomb, a symbol of both life and death.

As a spiritual leader and an intermediary between her patients and the deities, the ticitl played a sacred role in Nahua society. During the birthing process, she intervened on behalf of the pregnant woman, invoking a

Figure 7.8. Nahua ticitl massaging a pregnant woman's abdomen to position the baby and prepare the mother for birth

SOURCE: Florentine Codex, bk. 6, fol. 128v. Florence: Biblioteca Medicea Laurenziana, Med. Palat. 219, c. 132. By concession of the Ministry for Heritage and Cultural Activities; further reproduction by any means is forbidden.

Figure 7.9. Nahua ticitl enclosing a woman, whose baby cannot be delivered, in the temascalli to await death

SOURCE: Florentine Codex, bk. 6, fol. 139, Florence: Biblioteca Medicea Laurenziana, Med. Palat. 219, c. 143. By concession of the Ministry for Heritage and Cultural Activities; further reproduction by any means is forbidden.

number of female deities including Yoalticitl, Cihuacoatl, and Quilaztli. In some contexts, she personified deities through ritual speech in which the physician assumed the deity's role.[87] In incantations recorded by Ruiz de Alarcón in 1629, the ticitl took a handful of tobacco and moved it across the pregnant woman's belly, urging the deities Cuato and Caxxoch (perhaps local versions of names for Tlazolteotl) to open the birth canal and let the baby pass.[88]

The ticitl led certain rituals, such as the ceremony in which newborns were bathed and their umbilical cords were removed (see Chapter 2). Ruiz de Alarcón also described a ritual in which the ticitl circled the head of a baby four times with embers from the fire, literally giving it more heat, to honor the god of fire and strengthen the child's *tonalli* (heat, life force), which resided in the crown of the head.[89] He also described variations in the bathing ritual, which he considered to be "imitation[s] of baptism with water" performed on the fourth day after birth along with the naming ceremony.[90] An account written by don Pedro Ponce in 1892 verifies that well beyond the colonial period the ticitl continued to lead rituals involving fire, water, and gender-appropriate labor tools before the child was baptized in the Catholic church.[91]

Female ticitl participated in other life-cycle rituals, including the marriage ceremony, as discussed in Chapter 3, and the funeral procession of a woman who died in childbirth. According to Nahua tradition, women who died in childbirth became deities or *ciuateteo*, joining male warriors who had died in battle in the realm of the sky. Male warriors carried the sun from the east at dawn to the middle of the sky at the peak of the day, and the cihuateteo then carried it to the west, where it set. For a deceased woman to become a ciuateteo, her body could not be disturbed, so the ticitl protected her from young male warriors who believed that they could paralyze the feet of their enemies on the battlefield by placing a finger and/or a lock of hair of a woman who had died in childbirth in their shields. In a fascinating example of gender inversion, the relic enabled the young men to be brave and valiant in warfare. According to the Florentine Codex, the ticitl and elder women engaged in battle with the warriors over the woman's body:

And the ticitl, the old women, assembled to accompany her [the deceased woman]. They went with their shields; they went shouting, making war cries, expressing anger. It is said they went as coyotes, as enemies. It is said the young men, those whose duty was warfare, went confronting them, went skirmishing against them. They went skirmishing against them as they wanted to seize the poor woman. It was not mock battling, not plundering; when they fought they truly made war.

Auh mocentlalia in titici ilamatzitzin: inic quivica inchichimal ietiuh, tlacaoatztivi, motempapavitivi, oiouhtivi: mitoa coiouitiui, iaoui: iehoan quinnamictiui, quimicaltivi in mitoa telpupuchtin, inoc intequiuh iaoiotl inic quimicaltivi quimaniliznequi in cioatzintli: amo motlamachhuia, amo mopilhuia, in movitequi, vel nelli muiaochioa.[92]

As a spiritual leader and healer, the ticitl transcended the earthly realm, guiding the woman and her baby on a treacherous journey between life and death and mediating between the earthly and sacred realms by invoking the gods and goddesses. Leading the funeral procession, she transgressed traditional Nahua gender roles by truly engaging in battle.

In his analysis of Yucatec Maya medicinal texts and rituals, Pete Sigal has argued that male healers/spiritual leaders sometimes usurped female power through symbolic acts, such as bloodletting from the penis, which mimicked women's reproductive capacity.[93] Ramon Gutiérrez makes a similar argument in his analysis of the third-sex tradition among the Pueblo peoples of New Mexico.[94] Third-sex–gendered individuals, he concludes, emerged as powerful spiritual leaders because they embodied both the masculine and the feminine. I believe that we can extend this analysis to the female ticitl, who as a warrior woman, spiritual leader, and medical practitioner, transcended the bounds of male/female, earth/sacred realm, life/death.

The description of female healers in the tenth book of the Florentine Codex illuminates their work beyond midwifery. Paradoxically, it fails to mention midwifery at all, although, as discussed earlier, *ticitl* was widely used in the Florentine Codex as a term for midwife. Like the male physician, the female ticitl was "one who knows herbs, roots, trees, and stones" (*xiuiximatini, tlaneloaioiximatini, quauhiximatini, teiximati*).[95] As a healer, again like the male physician, she was recognized as restoring good health using a variety of cures, including massage, bloodletting, purging, herbs and medicines, rubbing with ashes, lancing, setting broken bones with splints, and prognostication. Descriptions of male and female ticitl are remarkably similar, but the Florentine Codex only mentions women curing diseases of the anus and cutting growths from the eyes. It is unclear whether these were areas of female specialization or whether the Nahua authors simply failed to discuss these practices in relation to male physicians.[96] Interestingly, Ruiz de Alarcón described two cures for eye ailments and mentioned specific women that he had encountered who used these treatments; this evidence further suggests that women specialized in curing the eyes. The Codex Magliabechiano shows a female healer seated before an image of Quetzalcoatl and casting lots with maize to determine the outcome of an illness (see Figure 7.10). According to Elizabeth Boone, the patient apparently suffers from an eye disease because of the tear on his face and, according to fray Diego Durán, Quetzalcoatl was the "advocate" for a number of maladies, including those of the eyes.[97] The broader evidence that women specialized in treating eye ailments supports Boone's reading of this image. Ruiz de Alarcón reported that female ticitl, called *tetonaltique* (women who return the fate or fortune to its place) also were experts in healing children and restoring their *tonalli* when they became gravely ill.[98]

An illustration in the tenth book of the Florentine Codex, which tells the history of the conquest from a native perspective, includes an image showing a lone female ticitl tending to men and women stricken by the first waves of smallpox epidemics to wash over central Mexico (see Figure 7.11).[99] She is surrounded by five victims whose bodies are ravaged by pustules. Most lie motionless, but the speech scroll in front of one suggests that she/he cries out in agony.[100] Also, like the depiction of the healer in the Codex Magliabechiano (Figure 7.10), the speech scroll in front of the ticitl reveals her use of incantations in healing. As one of

Figure 7.10. Female ticitl in front of Quetzalcoatl
SOURCE: Codex Magliabechiano, fol. 78r. Facsimile edition. Vienna: Akademische Druckund Verlagsanstalt; Madrid: Sociedad Estatal Quinto Centenario; Mexico City: Fondo de Cultura Económica, 1970.

only a few colonial representations of the epidemic diseases that devastated the indigenous population, the Florentine Codex image reveals the powerful and painful social memory of the consequences of contact with Europeans and the valiant efforts of female healers to comfort and care for those who suffered.

Ecclesiastics used the power of the confessional and the pulpit to intervene in traditional medical practices and discredit the knowledge of the ticitl. In his 1553 treatise on sorcery, fray Andrés de Olmos chastized natives who, "like *tlacuaches* (opposums)," sought out a *ticitl teyxcuepani* (deceitful doctor) to divine whether or not they would recover from their illnesses or to determine what they should do.[101] In his treatment of the fifth commandment in his 1569 Nahuatl-language confessional manual, fray Alonso de Molina asked a question clearly pointed at the ticitl: "Did you give to some pregnant woman beverages so that she would miscarry her child or so that [the baby] would die?" (*Aço aca ciuatl otztli oticpayti ynic quitlaçaz yn iconeuh yn iticca ynic miquiz?*) In 1634 fray Bartolomé de Alva picked up these themes in his confessional in an exchange between a friar and a tiçitl that begins with the priest asking, "Did you

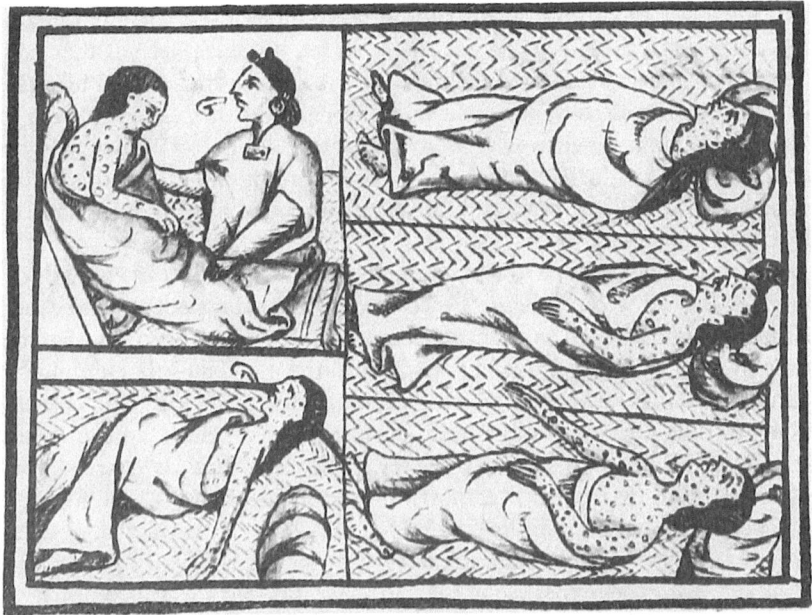

Figure 7.11. Ticitl attending to victims of a smallpox epidemic
SOURCE: Florentine Codex, bk. 12, fol. 53v. Florence: Biblioteca Medicea Laurenziana, Med. Palat. 220, c. 460v. By concession of the Ministry for Heritage and Cultural Activities; further reproduction by any means is forbidden.

give medicine [or] a potion to a young unmarried woman so that her baby would fall [stillborn] and be aborted?" (*Cuix aca ichpochtli otic, payti oticmacac patli, inic huetziz yconeuh motlatlaxiliz.*)¹⁰² He then intimidated the midwife: "Now I order you to never again do so for it is a very great sin. On account of you a creature of God, who did not enjoy salvation and holy baptism, perished in vain. You will go to hell if you again do so" (*Axcan nimitznahuatia áocmo, oc cepa yuhqui ticchiuaz, ca zenca huei tlatlacolli, ca mopampa nenpolihui in itlachihualtzin Dios, in amo quimomacehuitiuh in nemaquixtiliztli Sancto Baptizmo, ca tehuatl mictlan tiaz, intla oc çepa yuhqui ticchihuaz*).¹⁰³

Ruiz de Alarcón's 1629 account of the "idolatries" that he discovered reveals the grave concerns that Spaniards had about the persistence of indigenous spiritual beliefs and rituals even a century after the introduction of Christianity. His narrative attests to the complexity of healing concepts and practices in native communities in colonial Mexico, and his catalogue of medical practices places health in the context of social and sacred relations, with healers serving as doctors, prognosticators, and ritual leaders. Ruiz de Alarcón emphasized the use of incantations and the various methods of prognostication in healing practices, including reading patterns in fire, in maize kernels in water, in maize kernels that had been cast, and in lines on the hands. The incantations that he collected invoked ancient deities, although saints were sometimes called as well.[104] One healer mentioned was named after the goddess Xochiquetzal. The symbolic and linguistic complexity of the incantations makes this genre of speech particularly powerful, for it was intended to rally supernatural forces to intervene in wordly affairs.[105]

Of particular concern to Ruiz de Alarcón was the ticitl's use of hallucinogens, including *ololiuhqui* (*Turbina corymbosa*) and peyote and other ritual substances such as tobacco, to determine the source of illness, the type of offerings that should be made, and the medicines that should be administered. He was deeply disturbed that healers advised their sick patients to make offerings of candles, incense, flowers, cloth, cotton, food, tortillas, and beverages at sacred sites.[106] Because Ruiz de Alarcón was obsessed with extirpating "idolatries" and "superstitions," he focused on aspects of healing that he considered the work of charlatans, or even worse, the Devil. He almost completely overlooked the ticitl's pharmacological knowledge, expertise in massage therapy, and surgical skill.

Nearly as striking as Ruiz de Alarcón's dismissive tone were his frequent references to actual female healers that he observed (and apparently harassed for) performing these rituals and healing practices. Of the twenty-four individuals that he identified in connection with specific healing practices, twenty were women (see Table 7.7). The variety of cures that he attributed to them suggests the range of medical knowledge that women had. Four of the twenty-four had the honorific title "don" or "doña" or were married to someone who had it, and one woman was identified as the wife of a local alcalde, demonstrating that high-ranking individuals could be found among the ranks of the healers.

Only rarely do archival records refer to women's healing practices beyond assisting with childbirth. One example, from the Ñudzahui community of Teposcolula in 1596, concerns Isabel de Salas, who testified that she had been treating an ailing woman using medicine (*pactli*) and sweatbaths.[107] In 1666 Isabel López said that a local healer named Catalina Pérez had been coming to her house for two years to cure her eyes. Catalina testified in the case, and some of her comments reveal her high status in the community. Her first marriage, to a don Juan Pérez, produced don Diego Martín, a man identified as a "cacique" of Lachirio, and a first cousin of the "cacique and governor" of Lachirio.[108] Thus Catalina had married into and produced an heir to the community's ruling family. She also had intriguing connections with male spiritual authorities in the community. When she testified, Catalina was married to the *fiscal*, a

TABLE 7.7. *Ticitl identified in Ruiz de Alarcón's 1629 treatise on heathen superstitions*

Name	Town	Ailments treated	Prognostication/ healing methods
Female Healers			
Mariana	Iguala		Used ololiuqui to identify cause of illness
A woman	Atengo		Read hands
María Madalena	Ozomatlan		Read fire
María Madalena	Comala		Read fire
Magdalena Juana	Ohuapan		Read maize
Ana María	Xoxouhtla		Read maize in water
Francisca María	Mescaltepec		Restored tonalli to child
Catharina Juana	Tequaquilco	Headache	Applied pressure; sprinkled with water
María Salomé	Tetelpan	Eye ailment	Used cold water
Marta Monica	Teteltzinco	Eye ailment	Used mesquite sap
		Chest pain	Used herbs
A woman	Mayanala		Used cupping glasses
Catalina María	Teteltzinco	Chest pain	Used herbs
Doña Catalina Paula	Huitzuco	Chest pain in child	Applied pressure
Isabel María	Temimiltzinco		Piercing
Petronilla	Tlayacapan	Tertian fever	Used herbs
Magdalena Juana	Tepequaquilco	Urinary problem	Used herbs
Isabel Luisa	Mazatec nation	Fever	Used ololiuhqui
Magdalena Petronilla Xochiquetzal	Huitzoco	Body fatigue and pain	Massage
Justina			Used herbs; administered enema
Male Healers			
Miguel	Xicotlan		Used herbs, incantations
Domingo Hernández	Tlaltiçapan	Belly ache	Used herbs
A blind man	Tlaltiçapan	Hemorrhoids	Used herb
Martín de Luna	Temimiltzinco	Broken bone	Set in splint
		Back pain	Piercing
Don Martín Sebastían y Ceron	Chilapa	Scorpion bite	Applied tourniquet

native church official, and her brother, Gerónimo López, was allegedly a *maestro* of native religious practices.[109]

Colonial archival documents only rarely mention female healers, and they are silent on the rituals performed by midwives and spiritual leaders. Recognizing their expertise in midwifery and overlooking practices that ecclesiastics condemned, colonial authorities sometimes summoned female ticitl as expert witnesses in investigations of (attempted) homicide, rape, and assault, as illustrated in several late sixteenth- and early seventeenth-century cases from the Teposcolula jurisdiction. In the trial of Sebastián Gómez for attempted murder in the Mixtec community of Tilantongo in 1596, the Spanish alcalde mayor ordered Ana de Luna, a female healer and midwife, to testify about having discovered a poisonous substance in a beverage that Sebastián had given his wife, and about her attempts to save the dying woman.[110] Similarly, in Teposcolula in 1593 the alcalde mayor asked the midwife María García to examine a woman named Cecilia who had suffered a beating by several women who suspected her of committing adultery with Andrea Hernández's husband.[111] María testified that Cecilia was not pregnant but simply had menstrual bleeding. Her testimony provided crucial evidence, for had Cecilia miscarried, her case against Andrea Hernández would have been far more serious. In 1603 María Sisayu and María Siquahu, *yndias parteras* (midwives), examined ten-year old Mariana after her grandmother appeared before local authorities to accuse Juan de Mendoza of rape.[112] The two concurred that Mariana had not been raped or injured, nor had she lost her virginity. In Yanhuitlan in 1606, María Sahuaco, was described as a *comadre y partera y titzitl entre los yndios*, using the Nahuatl term in its original form along with two Spanish words for midwife (*comadre* and *partera*). She declared under oath before the Spanish alcalde mayor that Francisca López had been raped and required treatment.[113]

Female healers and ritual specialists enjoyed a certain amount of local authority. As the writings of Ruiz de Alarcón and other ecclesiastics demonstrate, some suffered persecution by Spanish religious and civil authorities who understood that the specialists' knowledge was shaped by a cosmology that challenged the full adoption of Christianity and a Spanish worldview. Nevertheless, many women continued to use traditional concepts of health, understanding of local plants and herbs, and sacred knowledge to heal and care for the people of their communities.[114]

Cacicas, Noblewomen, and Female Leadership Roles

Cacicas and noblewomen stood out from the majority of men and women in their communities. As privileged elites, they were attended to by personal servants who assisted them in their daily lives and accompanied them on their travels.[115] The testaments of noblewomen and civil records concerning suits over their estates reveal significant wealth, which was comparable to that of prominent men.[116] Although these records shed light on noblewomen's investments and economic status, they reveal little about their special roles and responsibilities as the leading women of the ethnic state.

Some of the richest ethnographic information on Nahua noblewomen comes from *huehuetlatolli* (speeches of the elders).[117] These sources elucidate the important roles that elite women played in the spiritual lives of their households and communities. First, noblewomen participated in ceremonies and made speeches as representatives of lineages and palaces in a variety of rituals. The highly metaphorical and reverential language that they used suggests that they studied and practiced the art of discourse. Second, noblewomen performed sacred acts in the household to maintain the cosmic order. They were instructed to pray night and day, to hold vigil at night, and to sweep the house, a symbolic act that represented spiritual cleansing. They were also to take care of the deities by washing their mouths and offering them incense.[118]

The huehuetlatolli emphasize the gendered division of labor that shaped the lives of all women. However, the labor of noblewomen was described in terms of art. The noble daughter was reminded to look after the "truly womanly task" (*in vel ic cioatequitl*) of weaving, as one speech makes clear:

Look well, really apply yourself to the truly womanly task, the spindle whorl, the weaving stick. Truly open your eyes [to see] how your sisters, your ladies, our honored ones, the noblewomen become an artisan, how they are featherworkers, how they make designs by embroidering, how they judge colors; how they apply colors. Look with diligence, really apply yourself to how heddles are provided; how leashes are provided; how the template is placed. Take care not to fail to know, not to lose [this knowledge] through neglect, not to lose [this knowledge] through carelessness.

auh ie iehoatl vel xiquitta, vel xonmopacho, in vel ic cioatequitl in malacatl, in tzotzopaztli: vel xonmixtzaiana, quenin tultecati, quenin amantecati, quenin tlatlamachicuiloa, quenin tlatlapalpoa, quenin tlatlapalaquia, in mopitzitzioan, in motecuiiotzitzioan, in totecuiiooan, in civaapipilti: quenin nexiiotilo, quenin nequatzomalo, quenin neoctacatilo, vel xonmixti, vel xonmopacho, ma timonenma, ma timonencauh; auh ma timoxiccauh.[119]

This father's speech alludes to a female culture in which elder women established an aesthetic for craft production. It also reminds his daughter that her "womanly duty" was to attend to the preparation of fine foods and drink that were made exclusively for the lords. Her knowledge of how to cook certain foods not only demonstrated her accomplishments as a woman but showed that she belonged to the elite class. Because success in this arena could enhance a young woman's reputation and status, she was to "look with diligence, really open your eyes, really apply yourself to how it is done, for thus you will live and thus you will acquire things, and thus you will be loved" (*vel xommixti, vel xonmixtzaiana, vel xommopacho, in quenin chioalo: ca ic timonemitiz, auh ca ic timotlalpializ.*

Auh ic titlaçotiz).[120] The speech emphasizes the woman's responsibility for preserving the cultural privileges and traditions of the elite.

Although noblewomen may have developed expertise in cooking specialty dishes and weaving elaborate textiles, they also supervised commoner women whom they employed as weavers and cooks in their homes and palaces. A document from 1559 reveals witnesses' elitist attitudes about the appropriate work of noblewomen. Don Domingo de Guzmán, son of the cacique and governor of Tonaltepeque and heir to the rulership, was accused of murdering his wife, doña Ana Cocuma, daughter of don Francisco de Mendoza, governor of Coixtlahuaca. As evidence that don Domingo had mistreated his wife, witnesses accused him of having forced her to grind cacao. Clearly, the onerous task of grinding was considered beneath a woman of doña Ana's status.[121]

The historical record provides many tantalizing references to Mesoamerican women's leadership roles in preconquest and early colonial times. As Kellogg has noted, Nahua women held leadership positions as market supervisors (*tianquizpan tlaiacanque*), girls' teachers (*cihuatiachcahuan*) in the temple schools (*cuicacalli*), ward leaders (*cihuatepixque*, literally women guards) and *cihuatlamacazque* (female priests). These positions had male equivalents, highlighting the parallel structure of Nahua social organization.[122]

Descriptions of the Nahua male ruler in the Florentine Codex emphasize the importance of caring for and governing commoners, supervising judges and officeholders, leading warriors, organizing and collecting tribute, overseeing the market, dancing, and presiding over rituals.[123] The equivalent categories of Nahua noblewomen suggest that women also fulfilled leadership roles. Thus, a noblewoman (*totecuiocihoatl*) was "one who deserves obedience; she is honorable, of high standing—to be heeded. A modest woman, a true woman, accomplished in the ways of women, she is also vigorous, famed, respected, fierce, stern" (*tocioatecuio tlacamachoni, tlacamachiztli, caquiztli, caconi, timalli, cioatl, nelli cioatl, acic cioatlan, niman nima pilli, tleio mauizio tequaio ihiio*).[124] Another category of noblewoman, the *cioatecutli*, was "a protector, deserving of obedience, revered, worthy of being obeyed, one who takes on responsibilities, one who bears burdens" (*macuche, teputze, mamale, tlacamachoni, imacaxtli, tlaiecultiloni, tlatquini, tlamamani*).[125]

The description of a ruler woman (*tlatocacioatl*) in the Florentine Codex is even more specific about women's leadership roles: "The tlatocacioatl is a female tlatoani, one who governors, one who leads, one who provides, one who issues orders. The good woman ruler is a provider of good conditions, a corrector, a punisher, a chastiser, a reprimander. She is heeded, obeyed; she creates order, establishes rules" (*in tlatocacioatl, ca cioatlatoani, tepachoani, teiacanani, tetlatlaluiani, tlanaoatiani. In qualli cioatlatoani: tlauelmamanitiani, atl cecec, tzitzicaztili quitecani quitlaçani, tealcececaui, tetzitzicazui, caco, nepechtequililo, tlatecpana, naoatillalia*).[126] These descriptions speak to the authority and power that some noblewomen enjoyed as rulers, leaders, and administrators. Furthermore, Nahuatl-language terminology suggests that women could assume rulership of the altepetl in the late postclassic and late colonial periods. Among most groups, however, female rulers seem to have been an exception, stepping in when a crisis of succession prevented an eligible male from ascending the throne.[127] The Ñudzahui tradition of male and female rule represents an important exception.[128]

Under Spanish colonial rule, some native noblewomen were recognized as cacicas; however, the meaning of this term varied regionally and across time. In the historical record, *cacica* might refer either to the wife of a cacique or to a woman who was recognized as a hereditary ruler in her own right. Ruling caciques and cacicas were primarily responsible for working with the cabildo to collect tribute. The Codex Sierra, a pictorial and alphabetic text from the mid-sixteenth-century Ñudzahui community of Santa Catalina Texupa, shows a cacica named doña Catalina receiving tribute in food and money.[129] A few years later, in another part of the Mixteca Alta, doña María Rojas, the cacica of Chicahuastla, negotiated the tribute that she received, the tribute paid to the governor, and the salary paid to the cabildo officials.[130] In the course of proceedings, doña María appeared with paintings, apparently now lost, that recorded the tribute arrangement she claimed to have with the community. Commoners gave her cotton mantas, turkeys, cacao, salt, firewood, and pine torches; they worked her lands, where she grew maize, cotton, and chia; and they supplied two men and two women to serve in her *aniñe* (palace) each week. Although there was a cabildo in place, between 1562 and 1573 the alcalde mayor directed all inquiries concerning tribute and cabildo salaries to doña María.

A Ñudzahui-language record from the prominent community of Teposcolula is even more explicit in its discussion of the cacica's responsibilities. When don Gerónimo García y Guzmán, the Ñudzahui cacique, made his last will and testament in 1672, he specified that his wife, doña Lázara de Guzmán "hand over the tribute to our lord king" (*saha maa ñaha dzehendi conducundaha stohondo Rey sindi*).[131] As the cacica, doña Lázara was not merely a figurehead; she had the political authority to organize tribute.

While the Spaniards recognized the rights of cacicas to collect tribute in goods, money, and labor from commoners, they excluded women from holding office on the cabildo. Based on his study of civil documents regarding *cacicazgos* (estates and privileges of caciques), Terraciano shows that Spaniards influenced native patterns of political authority. Where women were the legitimate rulers of their communities, Spaniards tended to recognize their husbands as the holders of the cacicazgos. He concludes: "Spanish legal protocol recognized women's hereditary right but gave preference to the public behavior and authority of men."[132] Nevertheless, in the Mixteca Alta region, cacicas might be paid a salary as the elected officials of the community were.[133] Although they suffered a decline in political status, Ñudzahui cacicas (*yya dzehe toniñe*) continued to control vast estates and lucrative enterprises throughout the colonial period.[134]

Several recent studies have shown that women played a prominent role in the religious life of their communities. Based on his examination of *cofradía* (confraternity) records from Mexico Tenochtitlan and Tula, Jonathan Truitt finds evidence of women's leadership roles in Catholic lay organizations.[135] According to the constitution of Tula, women were expected "to make certain that proper respect was paid to the sacraments, to approve expenditures of finances and use of goods, and to monitor behavior."[136] The organization of the confraternity of San Josef, which mandated its governance by four *cihuatepixque* (women in charge of people) and four male deputies, reveals the persistence of parallel gender structures in local institutions, although the extent of women's influence was often subject to the scrutiny of ecclesiastics.

In the late colonial period, Spanish authorities attempted to limit women's leadership in religious life, just as they had restricted women's participation in political institutions. Edward Osowski shows that in the second half of the eighteenth century Spanish ecclesiastics advocated more patriarchal arrangements in native households and barred women from serving as traveling guardians of religious icons and as alms collectors. Rather than abandon their leadership positions, women established home altars that were open to the community and worked with male *mayordomos*, who had more freedom to travel to collect alms. According to Osowski, "As guardians of the most important religious symbols of their local communities, indigenous women acted politically in public, but patriarchy literally limited the geographic range of activity."[137] Whether in terms of the cabildo or of religious institutions, Spaniards sought to limit women's sanctioned leadership roles in New Spain. Nevertheless, underlying concepts of gender parallelism predominated at the local level, and indigenous women found ways to exert their influence and authority despite formal restrictions.

Merchants and Marketing

In 1610 Inés Coco, a Mixtec woman of Santo Domingo Ticu, testified before the alcalde mayor that she had gone to the market in Teposcolula with her sister, Cecilia Sasayu, and Angelina Caquaa.[138] Upon arriving, the three women would have found a busy space bustling with people from nearby and distant communities. Among the items for sale would have been abundant local fruits and vegetables and European products, such as wheat, wine, and peaches. Perhaps the women would have stopped for a little pulque, tamales, or *mole* (sauce) sold in the market. They would have eyed the brightly woven textiles, some elaborately decorated with dyed rabbit fur and feathers, or imported fabrics, such as taffeta, velvet, and cloth from the Philippines and Brittany. Or they might have come to buy basic necessities such as maize, lime, salt, wax, baskets, or *petates* (reed or palm mats).[139]

Two major trade routes are prominent in the colonial record. The first linked the Mixteca Alta and central Mexico, bringing Nahuatl, Ñudzahui, and Spanish speakers into regular contact. The second was between the Sierra Zapoteca, Antequera and the Valley of Oaxaca, and the Isthmus of Tehuantepec, extending to Chiapas and Guatemala.[140] These routes followed the paths of preconquest merchants who had built impressive trade networks that reached from central Mexico to modern-day Costa Rica. The importance of regional market systems to both household and community economies cannot be overstated. Essential items that might not have been locally available, such as salt and cotton, were accessible through regional trading. Furthermore, as household supplies dwindled, tribute items, including maize, were redistributed through markets and made available throughout the year. As vendors, men and women controlled and distributed resources that they had produced in the household or had acquired in their communities.

In preconquest times, cloth and cacao beans were used as forms of currency, and throughout the colonial period textiles remained one of the principal items of trade. Men and women were involved in all aspects of the colonial market in cloth; however, whereas men traded cloth in both local and distant markets, women mainly traded locally or regionally. Women might travel some distance to sell their weavings, as did Ana Pérez and her sister, María Pérez, who in 1643 journeyed from their home in Achiutla to sell cotton mantas in the Teposcolula market.[141]

Thread and yarn, cloth, and woven and tailored garments were among the most important merchandise bought, sold, and exchanged in markets. Raw materials in the inventories of one merchant who sold throughout the Mixteca Alta included cotton, silk, cotton and silk thread, and rabbit fur.[142] Unfinished lengths of cloth, including *lienzo* (something like broadcloth), *jerga* (thick, coarse cloth), *paño* (wool cloth), *olandilla* (cloth from Holland), *sinabafa* (cloth similar to olandilla), *sayal* (thick, loosely woven cloth), taffeta, and damask were also sold.[143] Imported textiles and European fashions added to the rich array of goods for sale. Some merchants specialized in trading imported cloth and ornate trims, which perhaps were used to embellish traditional native garments.

In addition to indigenous goods, the inventory of one merchant who traded along the Pacific Coast at the end of the sixteenth century included silk braids, taffeta, Cordovan leather shoes, hats, and garments tailored from cloth imported from London.[144] Another trader's merchandise included such diverse goods as dyed and embroidered (*labradas*) huipillis and indigenous skirts (*naguas*) of cotton and wool; *flecos* (fringe); dyed and embroidered cloaks made of wool, cotton, and silk, some with fringe; pants made of imported cloth; collars (*cuellos*); and a pair of white shoes.[145]

Gender does not seem to have influenced specialization among market vendors.[146] Both men and women bought and sold produce, including oranges, cactus fruit, melons, and apples, as well as maize and lime—two essential ingredients for tortillas.[147] Men and women also sold meat and a variety of other agricultural goods, including cotton, cacao, hay, and *hierba buena*, an herb used to make tea.[148]

Depictions of vendors in the tenth book of the Florentine Codex show male and female vendors selling a wide array of agricultural goods, cooked food, crafts, and other products.[149] The lack of gender distinctions is in part explained by regional craft and agricultural specialization. For example, Yanhuitlan specialized in dyed rabbit fur, a trade item found in the inventories and testaments of both local men and local women in excess of what they might have owned for personal use. The people in the Zapotec region of Zumpaguacan wove petates and sold lime in regional markets.[150] Similarly, the men and women of Temascalapa customarily made pulque to sell in the markets of Papalutla and Acuescomac.[151]

The lack of specialization among male and female vendors may also be related to the fact that husbands and wives often worked together to ply their wares as merchant teams.[152] Luis de Velasco Saaqua and Juan de Chávez went to the market in the Mixtec community of Teposcolula in 1613 with their wives.[153] María Noquihui sat with her spouse, Mateo Cuixao, selling meat there.[154] Juan Guillermo and María Salomé, Nahuas from Temascalapa, traveled together to sell pulque.[155] Even fairly high-ranking merchant couples, such as Juana López and Juan de Velasco, went to local markets together.[156] The frequent references to husband and wife merchant teams in the archival record underscore the cooperative nature of labor in marriage and undermine the view that native women were relegated to the household. The organization of agricultural production provides additional evidence of cooperative labor arrangements between spouses.

Agriculture and Animal Husbandry

Mesoamerican societies developed intensive agricultural systems that used technologies such as irrigation, terracing, and *chinampas* (raised garden beds in shallow water) to produce surpluses of goods. Men were primarily responsible for preparing fields and planting crops, but women also performed all types of agricultural labor, including planting and harvesting and raising animals.[157]

Women's contributions to agricultural production have been largely overlooked, although sixteenth-century Nahuatl-language sources hint at women's farming activities. According to a Nahuatl speech, when a newly elected ruler admonished the people to work hard, he inspired them with the example of the humble woman whose fields were highly productive because of her diligence.[158] Archival records corroborate the ruler's speech with repeated references to women's participation in agriculture.

In her study of a sixteenth-century census from Morelos, Sarah Cline found occasional references to female farmers, such as "a householder named Citlal and his widowed older sister, Tecapan," who "jointly work his field and do the tribute duty."[159] Moreover, in court women described tending their lands to earn their livelihoods. When called to testify in a criminal trial in 1594, Francisca Nucu, a Ñudzahui woman of Topiltepec, stated that she supported herself by spinning thread and cultivating her fields and magueys.[160] Other women owned and worked orchards as well. One was Juana Xochitl, a Nahua of Acatepec, who tended several cacao trees on her land.[161] In 1698 many men and women of the Bènizàa pueblo of Taguí together planted corn according to local tradition.[162] Contemporary ethnographic evidence suggests that regional customs can prohibit women in certain communities from some aspects of agricultural work; however, the historical record does not reveal these restrictions, at least in places where the records refer to women working in fields or orchards.[163]

Ayuuk (Mixe) women from communities of the Sierra Zapoteca also farmed land. Ayuuk testators often specified that their sons and/or daughters were to work the lands that they were to inherit. In his Nahuatl-language testament written in 1662, for example, Gerónimo Vargas named his four daughters and two sons as heirs to lands that he had purchased, and expressed his wish that "all six of my children are to work them" (*mochi chicuace ynin nopilhuan yelemiquiz[que]*).[164] In another testament, written in 1675, Benito Jiménez bequeathed a piece of land to his seven daughters, ordering that they "provide for themselves and work this land next to the lot called Ocopaxco" (*motleyeecoltisque quiyelemiquisque yni tlali caltenco solar ytoca ocopaxco*).[165] Similarly, in 1669 the cabildo of Totontepec issued a land document that protected the rights of two women and two men. The statement declared that in accordance with the testament they possessed, "all four of them, Bárbola, María, Juan, and Simón, are to keep and work that land" (*mochi nahuintin barvula maria Juan yua simo quipiasque quiyelemiquisque yno tlali*).[166] This evidence corroborates Stephanie Wood's conclusion that rural women performed agricultural labor based on her analysis of Nahuatl-language testaments from the Toluca Valley.[167]

Once fields were planted, they had to be protected from animals and thieves. Because many landholdings were scattered and distant, some members of the household would temporarily leave the principal house to go look after their crops, sheltering in simple huts.[168] Sometimes couples went together to watch over their fields, but often women went alone or with their children. For example, in 1592 Ana Tuchuu and her children went to guard a plot so that coyotes and dogs would not eat their crops, while her husband stayed at their house in Coixtlahuaca.[169] Women were also sometimes hired to look after fields; in 1625, for example, Lucía Cunco guarded maize for Juan Jiménez, an alcalde of Izcatlan.[170]

During the harvest season, women assisted their relatives, compadres, and friends in the fields.[171] Inés Martínez, a Ñudzahui woman from Yanhuitlan, recalled that she helped Inés de la Ascención and Cecilia de Silva reap their maize crop.[172] Women frequently collected the fruits and vegetables that they needed to prepare food and drink.[173] Sometimes husbands and wives walked the countryside together to harvest herbs, plants, cotton, and flowers.[174] Men also gathered grasses and flowers for the community as part of their tribute duties.[175]

There is abundant evidence in the record that the organization of agricultural labor and trade involved close cooperation between a husband and wife. While couples worked their lands together, women often assumed primary responsibility for the sale of foodstuffs and agricultural products in the local markets. Bartolomé Manzano, a Bènizàa man of Lachirio, stated that "in his pueblo those who could sowed cane, which their wives sold in the plaza."[176] Similarly, wives and husbands worked collectively to produce cloth, first gathering wild cotton, planting and harvesting cotton crops, or purchasing cotton in the market. In some communities, such as Yatzona and Tagui, they both spun raw cotton into yarn.[177] The woman then wove the cloth and the husband traded it at a distant market or the wife sold it locally or contributed it to the household's tribute payment. Maize production followed these same principles. Men, often with assistance from their wives, planted and harvested maize; the cycle of production was completed when the women ground the maize and prepared tortillas.

Some nobles owned significant amounts of land that they used for commercial agriculture.[178] A typical example was doña Leonarda, a Nahua noblewoman of San Juan Teotihuacan, who grew maize and magueys on her ranch. She employed a married couple and their children to work the land while she maintained a separate residence in the pueblo.[179] Nobles also invested in the new European plants, trees, and animals that had dramatically changed land tenure in central and southern Mexico. When he made his will in 1622, don Juan de Guzmán, a Nahua noble, divided his orchards of European fruit trees and indigenous avocado trees between his two daughters and one son.[180] In central Mexico and the Mixteca Alta, in Spanish centers of activity where the demand for Spanish goods only increased over time, wheat became an important crop. Relatively wealthy people, such as Inés López, a Ñudzahui woman of Topiltepec who grew wheat, profited from their investments in European crops and products.[181]

Silk and cochineal were among the most lucrative agricultural products in the viceregal economy and the transatlantic trade.[182] Cochineal, a red dye used throughout Mesoamerica, was in high demand by European textile manufacturers. In the mid-sixteenth century, the meeting minutes of the cabildo of Tlaxcala record the concerns of Nahua nobles over the impact of the cochineal trade on the local economy and society. The nobles warned of impending famine because the commoners engaged only in cochineal production and no longer grew food crops. They also asserted that the new wealth generated by the dye contributed to an increase in sinful and decadent behavior and fostered abusive relationships between noblemen, commoners, and Spaniards. Especially condemned was the role that women played in the trade. The nobles suggested that women were being exploited (sexually and economically) by cactus growers and Spaniards.

Underlying such condemnation was a deep concern that the cochineal trade was inverting the social order by allowing commoners to become wealthy, which caused them to lose respect for the nobles. After much deliberation, on March 3, 1553, the Tlaxcala cabildo decreed that cochineal plantings were to be restricted to ten per person and that women were prohibited from trading cochineal in the marketplace.[183] These measures, however real or exaggerated the threat, reveal the prominent role that women played as cochineal traders and reflect the centrality of work to morality and proper social relations. Despite efforts at regulation, men and women continued to specialize in the production and trade of cochineal throughout the colonial period, as did one Bènizàa woman of Talea, who had eight pounds of cochineal among her possessions in 1674.[184]

Silk, introduced by the Spaniards in the sixteenth century, was another valuable commodity produced in native communities, especially in the Mixteca Alta. Although Spaniards, including church officials, remained its principal investors and buyers, some Ñudzahuis profited from silk as well. For example, Mateo de Higuera, a native of Achiutla, reportedly sold one hundred pesos (a great sum by the standards of the day) worth of silk to a Spaniard in 1587.[185] In some regions, small-scale producers paid their tribute in silk.[186] The silk industry created new types of employment as native women and men learned to prepare the silk for thread and cloth production.[187]

The introduction of European animals altered the native economy and provided new labor opportunities. Prior to the conquest, because of the lack of draft animals, *tlamemes* (porters) carried goods on their backs between the countryside, cities, mines, and ports. Although many continued this work during the colonial period, some became muleteers. For example, Captain don Manuel de Pedraza, a Spaniard, hired six Bènizàa men of the Cajonos jurisdiction to deliver goods to Diego Sánchez de Zamora, a merchant in Mexico City.[188] Some native men owned their own mules; others offered only their labor to those who owned the animals.

In the Mixteca Alta and the Villa Alta, women sometimes owned horses and mules that they rented to men for trade and long-distance travel. This was the case when Diego de los Reyes became ill while on an errand on behalf of a cofradía. He was forced to rent a horse from Catalina de Velasco for two tomines so he could return home.[189] In Solaga in the Villa Alta jurisdiction, María Gregoria and Catalina de Santiago earned their livelihoods by renting out mules and oxen.[190] Catalina Pérez, a Ñudzahui resident of Yanhuitlan, explained in 1614 that she owned a mule that her husband, a trader, used to travel to Guatemala.[191] The introduction of draft animals from Europe also created demands that had not existed previously. Native craftsmen were soon among those who produced horseshoes, saddles, and oxen yokes for the growing market.[192]

Before the conquest, animal husbandry had been limited to the domestication of turkeys, dogs, and bees. The introduction of sheep, goats, pigs, and chickens by the Spaniards had a dramatic impact on the ecology of the Americas and the native economy. Indigenous men found employment as shepherds in areas linked to Spanish markets and population centers. Nahuas (especially from Tepeaca) were hired by Spaniards to drive their animals from central Mexico to the Mixteca Alta.[193] Most native households engaged only in small-scale animal husbandry. However, in order to participate in the Spanish market economy, caciques and nobles invested in large-scale enterprises, and some owned several hundred sheep or goats (generically referred to as *ganado menor*). The cacique of Yanhuitlan, don Gabriel de Guzmán, for example, listed 1,340 goats and 200 kids among his possessions when he made his testament in 1591.[194]

Perhaps taking their lead from the friars who raised livestock for profit, indigenous confraternities invested in ganado menor to support their religious activities. In fact, local men and women may have learned to care for sheep, goats, and cattle while providing tribute labor to local convents. As but one example, the Cofradía de Nuestra Señora del Rosario of Sinicagua, a subject settlement of Tlaxiaco, owned livestock that both the men and women of the cofradía helped raise.[195] Typical of this shared responsibility, Mateo Juárez, his wife, and another man were sent to a neighboring community to buy saltpeter for the livestock.

Throughout central and southern Mexico, women were primarily responsible for raising turkeys and chickens to be consumed by the household, sold in the market, and used as tribute.[196] Just as men and women worked together in agricultural production and animal husbandry, they shared many responsibilities in maintaining the household.

Maintaining the Household

In her study of the symbolic relationship between women's work and ritual activities in the domestic sphere and the fate of their husbands on the battlefield, Burkhart shows that women and men played complementary, interdependent roles.[197] The sources that she examined emphasize the household as a female domain but one intimately linked to the battlefield realm. In previous chapters, we saw that Mesoamericans considered certain tasks, such as cooking and preparing beverages, as women's duties. Interestingly, however, mundane records suggest that the gendering of household labor was not entirely rigid.

Although women were primarily responsible for maintaining and guarding the household, men sometimes shared these duties. Both men and women carried water from rivers and streams to supply the household.[198] Both provided the household with fuel and fire—men cut the wood and but shared the task of gathering and carrying it with women along with obtaining coals from neighbors.[199] Both swept the household patio, but men swept the roads and the church.[200] Furthermore, both men and women laundered clothes, although this seems to have been primarily women's work.[201] One duty that appears to have been principally assigned to women was guarding and keeping track of the household's tools and goods. In fact, accusations that women had misplaced these items were often at the heart of many domestic disputes during the colonial period.[202]

Perhaps the sharing of household work was due in part to the agricultural cycle, in which farmers spent more time in their homes than in their fields during certain times of the year. Or it may reflect the reality that cooking food and preparing beverages were particularly time-consuming and therefore men and boys had to do some of the other work around the household. Also, few rural Mesoamericans distinguished between the workplace and the home. Most artisans crafted goods in the household patio or in the palaces of nobles. Although some specialized workshops began to exist in the Iberian centers of New Spain by the end of the sixteenth century, Spaniards and native nobles owned most of them.[203]

The sharing of domestic labor extended into employment as some husbands and wives worked together as servant teams in the houses of Spaniards and wealthy indigenous people. For example, Agustín and Inés de Alavéz lived and served in the house of a Mixtec merchant couple who traded indigenous and imported goods.[204] Similarly, Diego de Castro, a regidor of the Ñudzahui community of Teposcolula, and his wife employed a commoner couple to plant maize and complete household tasks.[205] Juan Cunchi and his wife, María Hernández, were in the service of Inés López, a wealthy indigenous entrepreneur who had invested in European enterprises; among their duties was transporting wheat to a mill for grinding.[206] Higher-ranking Nahua couples, such as Nicolás de Bobadilla and Teresa de la Cruz, also employed commoner husband and wife teams.[207] Of course, indigenous servant couples also found work in the houses of Spaniards as domestic and agricultural laborers. When they were driven from Coixtlahuaca by a devastating drought in 1701, Baltasar Melchor and Josefa de Rosa moved to Tlaxiaco to farm and tend sheep on the ranch of Spaniard Diego Rodríguez and his wife.[208]

Patterns of labor organization found in the household were replicated at the community level through the tribute system. In preconquest and colonial times, each household was responsible for providing labor on a rotational basis so that all commoners shared the tribute burden. Like men, women took turns providing tribute labor in a system organized by the household head.

TRIBUTE LABOR

After the conquest of New Spain, the Spaniards instituted a tribute system that was built on, but eventually transformed, preexisting local traditions. The *encomienda* was a grant from the Crown given to a Spaniard, usually as a reward for serving in the conquest, that allowed him to demand a specified amount of labor and tribute from an indigenous community, usually for life. It was based on an existing native sociopolitical unit, such as the Nahua altepetl, the Ñudzahui ñuu, or the Bènizàa yetze and was the principal tie between the Spaniards and the native population in the sixteenth century. The indigenous community kept its own authorities, lands, and ways of organizing labor, but through the cacique rotated the responsibility of providing labor and paying tribute to the *encomendero*, with the cacique keeping a portion of the tribute for himself. The functioning of the encomienda depended on the indigenous community retaining much of its original political and social structures. It would not work if those were lost, whether through depopulation or for other reasons.

The encomienda system, although built on existing native mechanisms, was fraught with tension. First, native communities were forced to pay increasing amounts of tribute and labor to the encomenderos even as their populations dwindled because of warfare, epidemics, and social dislocations. Additional requirements to pay certain taxes to the Spanish Crown and the church further increased their burden. Second, over time the Spaniards grew reluctant to accept traditional tribute items, such as warrior costumes and shields, and increasingly demanded items for consumption, such as wheat, or maize, which could be sold for a profit in indigenous markets. Tribute in kind was eventually assessed in quantities of gold, silver, or currency (although maize remained important), meaning that native men and women were forced to enter the money economy to some extent. Now they had to trade for gold, silver, or currency, which rarely circulated in their communities. Some local states rented or sold lands to non-natives to raise tribute money. Third, the Spaniards changed the way that tribute was assessed. In preconquest times, native households paid tribute as one unit based on the amount of land they held. During the second half of the sixteenth century, Spanish officials modified the system by imposing a head tax so that all men and women, including widows and widowers, had to pay the same amount regardless of their ability to do so.

The encomienda system spurred competition and sometimes created problems among Spaniards. Since it was based on a preexisting native community, the number of grants to distribute among the Spanish population was fixed. A generation after the conquest, however, newly arriving Spaniards complained that they did not have access to native labor because all native communities had already been assigned as encomiendas to other, senior Spaniards. Increased competition and the demographic collapse of the indigenous population led to the decline of the encomienda as a way to distribute labor because it gave too many privileges only to a few.

The crown stood to benefit from limiting the encomienda grant by cutting into the extensive privileges of the encomenderos. By abolishing or at least curtailing the encomienda in the name of justice (ostensibly for the natives), the crown could demand that the Indians pay more taxes. At the same time, the crown would increase its authority by limiting the powers of the local Spanish aristocracy and address the shortage of labor. The solution to the shortage of labor was the *repartimiento*, which was a system of rotational labor in which groups of native people were assigned to work for individual Spaniards for given periods of time. In this way, more Spaniards gained access to native labor. Repartimiento became the predominant labor system in central Mexico among the Nahuas during the second half of the sixteenth century and in Oaxaca among the Bènizàa, Ayuuk, and Ñudzahui populations by the last quarter. By the middle of the seventeenth century, the repartimiento gave way to individual arrangements between Spaniards and indigenous natives or mestizos based on wage labor, but this was subject to regional variation.

There can be little doubt that severe epidemics and tribute burdens led to the impoverishment of native communities over time. Although people had paid tribute in preconquest times, the rotational system of draft labor benefited their own communities—for example, building terraces on community lands. In colonial times, however, labor was often channeled toward projects outside of the community and toward enterprises from which the people did not profit. Tensions that resulted from onerous demands for tribute are explored in greater depth in Chapter 9.

Through colonial labor mechanisms, all indigenous males, except nobles and their dependents, were obligated to work for the Spaniards in building churches, planting crops, herding sheep and goats, and mining, among other tasks.[209] Maintaining churches and supporting the friars absorbed much of a community's tribute labor, especially in areas where few secular Spaniards resided. Male tributaries built and roofed churches, constructed and repaired walls, and cleaned patios.[210] Tribute labor was also employed for the many economic enterprises of the monastery, as it was in Tamazulapa, where commoners farmed wheat, herded sheep, and transported cacao from Oaxaca.[211] Indeed, the burden of tribute labor fell heavily on male commoners, especially as epidemics had reduced the indigenous population to approximately 10 percent of its preconquest total within a hundred years after the conquest.[212] Nevertheless, women's contributions to the tribute system have been overshadowed by an emphasis on the exploitation of male workers under the encomienda and repartimiento systems.[213]

Women's tribute work most often corresponded to the idealized gendered division of labor. Because tributaries traditionally were paid a small amount and fed in exchange for their labor, women were recruited to cook for men performing their service. While men roofed the church in Yate, for example, the women ground maize and made tortillas to feed them.[214] Women also prepared piñol for men who were required to travel long distances on labor projects and community business. The *tequitlatos* (tribute collectors) collected tortillas from the women of Texupa for nobles who took ashes to Teposcolula for the Easter ceremonies.[215]

Women also ground maize and cooked for the native nobility, Spaniards, and friars. In the Ñudzahui town of Cuquila, in 1633, Cecilia de Ontiveros was assigned to grind maize and make tortillas for the cacique and governor, don Pablo de la Cruz, for a week.[216] Similarly, a tequitlato distributed corn to María de Espinosa to make tortillas for the monastery of Teposcolula.[217] In 1610, Juan de Cisneros and his son, Spanish residents of Tlaxiaco, obligated the ñuu to provide a woman to grind maize and three men to serve them for eight-day periods.[218] In a case from Coixtlahuaca, the officials of San Gerónimo sent fifteen men to care for livestock and one woman to grind maize on the monastery's estancia for one-week intervals.[219] According to don Tomás de Vera, cacique of Santa María (a constituent settlement of Coixtlahuaca), the friars paid five men and one woman three reales each for their work; other workers were not paid.[220]

A Nahuatl document from 1593 dealing with tribute arrangements in Quautla and combining text and pictographs, provides tangible evidence of men's and women's contributions.[221] An image of don Francisco de la Cueva, the tlatoani, shows him sitting on a high-back reed mat throne, known as the *petlatl icpalli*, which was a Mesoamerican symbol of authority. Before him are fields of maize, beans, chile, and another plant that commoners were to cultivate on his lands. Also shown are a man and a woman who are to serve him for a week (according to the Christian calendar), indicated by the seven suns over their heads (the bird signifies that he is also to be given a turkey weekly).

In sharing tribute obligations, the men and women of a community rotated their posts on a weekly basis (see Figure 7.12). Thus males and females alike served in the homes and on the properties of indigenous nobles and Spaniards in the colonial tribute system.

Women worked alongside men on community lands and in enterprises that helped pay tribute. For example, in the second decade of the seventeenth century, the men and women of San Felipe labored in the community's salt beds, manufacturing the salt that they depended on for

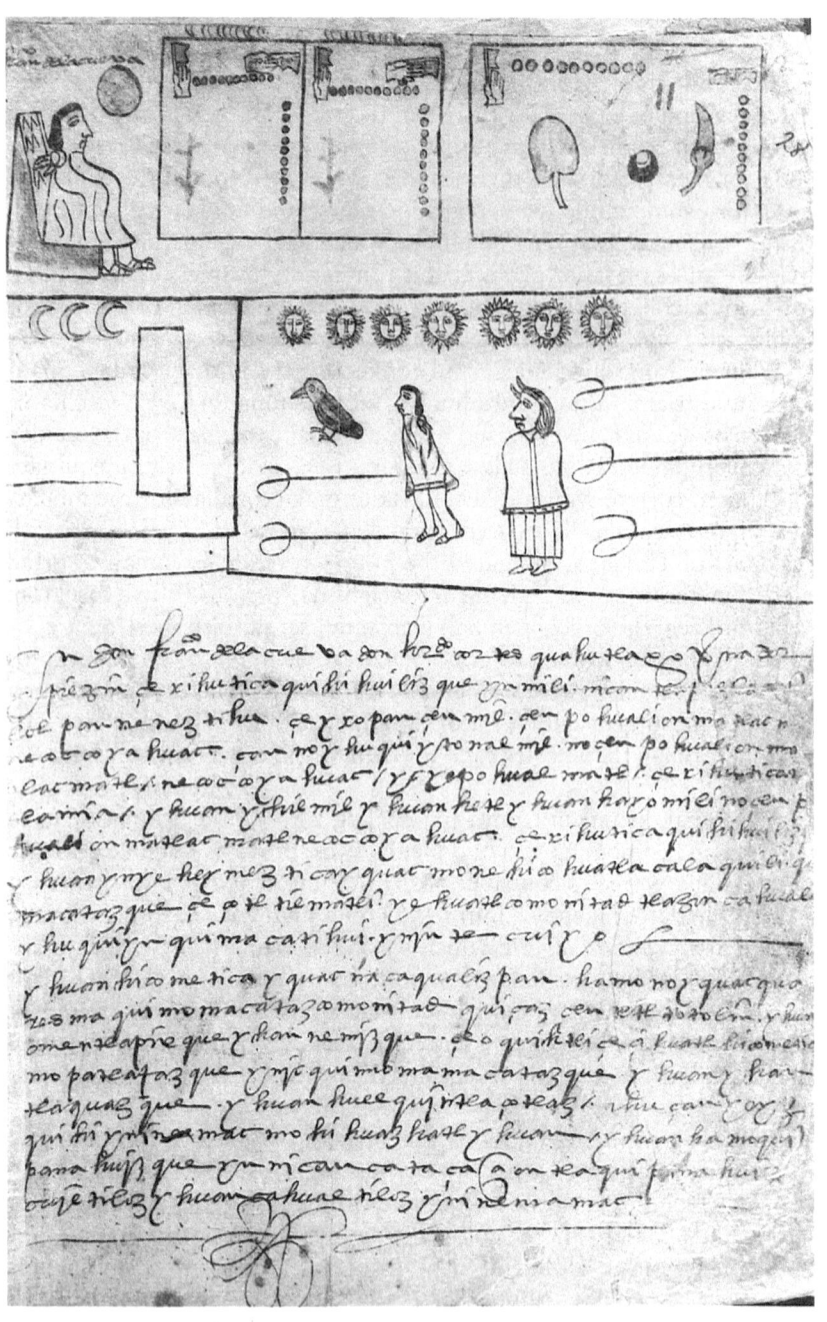

Figure 7.12. Nahuatl-language document with pictorial image presented in a dispute over tribute labor
SOURCE: Archivo General de la Nación, Mexico, Tierras, 1871, 1, Quauhtla, 1593.

subsistence and tribute payments.[222] Throughout the region, men and women planted and harvested fields of maize, beans, chile, and magueys on lands belonging both to local nobles and to the community in fulfillment of their labor obligations.

Women's most significant labor contributions were spinning and weaving. The Codex Mendoza's lists of tribute paid to the Aztec empire attest to the importance of weaving as service in preconquest times. They neatly illustrate the valuable items that were paid by subject communities from central and southern Mexico, indicated by place glyphs on the left and along the bottom of the page. Elaborately woven textiles stand out, often depicted first at the top of the page. Their colors and elaborate designs reveal the richness of native weaving traditions (see Figure 7.13). The quantities of cloth are astonishing. Feather-like symbols drawn above some types of cloth indicate that four hundred loads of these were to be paid; four flags, each with a value of twenty, above the more ornate designs indicate that eighty loads of these were to be paid.

Throughout the seventeenth century, people in many regions continued to pay tribute in yarn and cloth. Caciques and native officials distributed the cotton and thread for this purpose. For example, the governor and alcalde of Coixtlahuaca issued wool and cotton to be spun by the "community and Indian women" (*comun e yndias*) of the subject settlement of Tepeneme in 1628.[223] In the Mixteca Alta, don Pablo de la Cruz, the cacique and governor of Cuquila, distributed materials to the women of San Juan.[224] Similarly, the women of Justlahuaca spun cotton thread for tribute in 1637.[225]

Even as communities began to pay tribute in money rather than goods, funds were raised by the production and sale of cloth. Indigenous officials and nobles often worked with Spanish investors, who, in exchange for serving as intermediaries, kept a portion of the tribute supposedly for community expenses. In the Mixe town of Tonaguia, for example, Martín López, a Spanish trader, gave the residents cotton to make cloth in 1654.[226] Transactions such as these were handled by cabildo officials, who kept one of the eight reales that López paid for each length of cloth despite the fact that the weavers needed the money to live, to pay tribute, and to sponsor festivals. As late as 1696, cloth was being given as tribute in the Zapotec Sierra. When don Miguel de Santiago, the governor of Yagayo, attempted to collect tribute in money (*reales*) rather than cloth, over forty nobles and commoners opposed him.[227]

Because women were expected to contribute equally to tribute projects and assessments, local magistrates fined both men and women who failed to fulfill their labor obligations. In 1633 Teposcolula, for example, the regidor took a real from Domingo García and a skirt from his

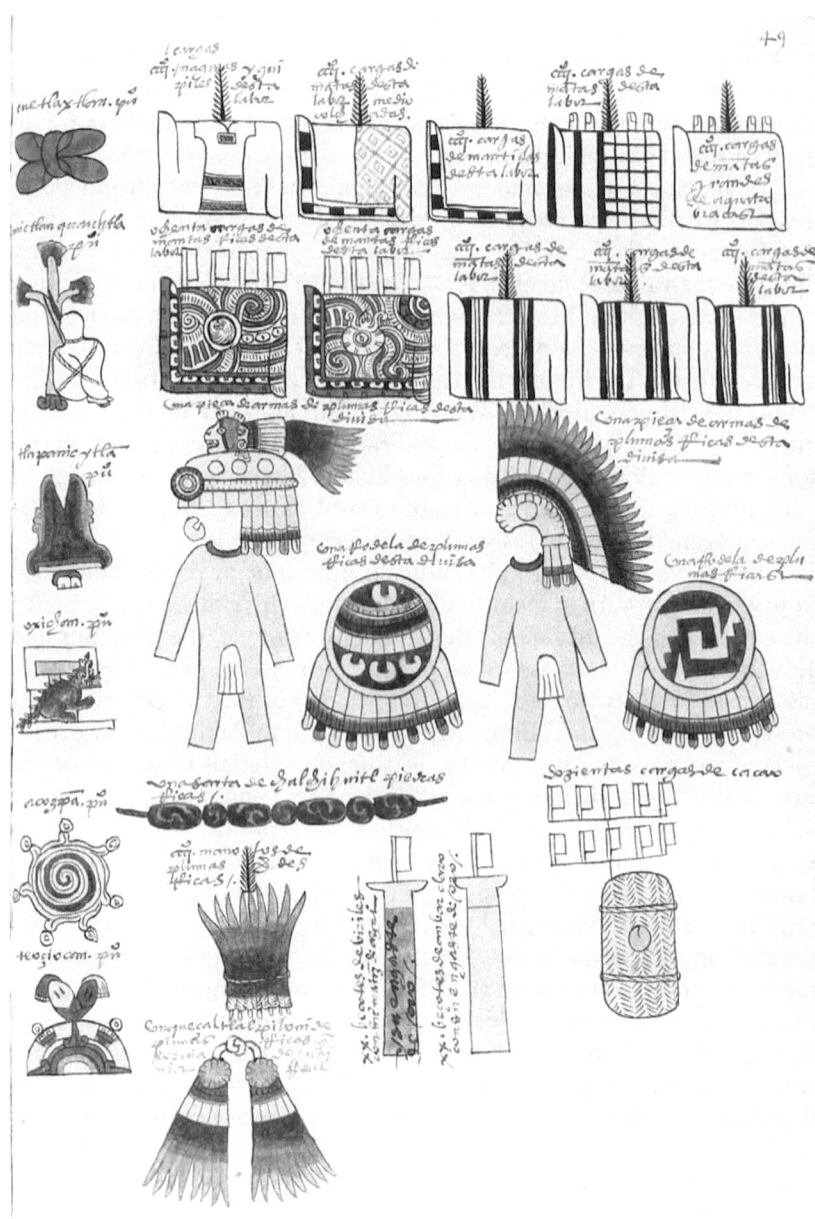

Figure 7.13. Tribute list depicting cloth paid in tribute to Aztec rulers in preconquest times
SOURCE: Codex Mendoza, fol. 52. Bodleian Libraries, University of Oxford, Ms. Arch. Selden A1. Berdan and Anawalt 1992, fol. 52. Reproduced with permission from University of California Press Books.

wife because neither had helped weed the cacique's fields.[228] Similarly, a Ñudzahui-language book of community accounts from Yolomecatl records monies paid by men and women who did not perform tribute labor in 1705.[229] The many examples in this chapter demonstrate that the organization of labor at the community level paralleled the division of labor in the household.

CONCLUDING REMARKS

Indigenous-language descriptions of preconquest society, colonial archival records, and other texts reveal that women's contributions to the community were highly valued. Because the gendered division of labor in the household was the foundation of payment of goods and organization of labor through the tribute system, women's production of food and cloth was critical to the economies of the household and the local state. Women were encouraged to take pride in their work. Skill in weaving, cooking, and healing could bring prestige and honor. The rich symbolic and social significance of food and cloth in indigenous culture both in preconquest and colonial times illuminates the great value that was placed on the fruits of women's labor.

Depending on their social status, indigenous women engaged in a variety of economic and productive activities that went far beyond the cooking and weaving described in idealized texts. Wealthy women invested in Spanish enterprises, employing humbler indigenous couples on their estates. The records show that female commoners worked in agriculture, tended animals, collected salt, gathered firewood, fetched water, laundered clothes, traded in the marketplace, and produced crafts. Some women became skilled healers respected for their knowledge of illness and remedies and for their roles as spiritual leaders. All of these activities took women out of the household on a regular basis. While some production was organized along gender lines, the archival record reveals, to a surprising degree, that many subsistence activities were carried out jointly by men and women, either as married couples or as members of a household.

Principles of mutual obligation and cooperation shaped the organization of household and community labor. Everyone contributed something for the good of the whole, and although ideally men and women had distinct roles and responsibilities, the work of both was seen as necessary to household and community well-being. Based on her study of the symbolic importance of housework among the Mexica, Burkhart insists that "the significance of women's work and the constitution of the domestic or household domain are variables that must be examined in relation to their specific cultural and historical contexts."[230] I agree, and I argue that in the context of pre-Columbian and early colonial Mesoamerica women's contributions were not secondary to men's. Couples worked together to produce agricultural goods, food, and cloth; some worked in teams as merchants and servants. These enterprises were collective and cooperative rather than individual and hierarchical.

In an examination of the many different facets of women's work, it becomes evident that the policies and practices of Spanish authorities contributed to the slow erosion in women's status over time. The decline in prestigious positions as artisans, religious leaders, and political authorities (especially among the Mixtecs) limited women's opportunities. Furthermore, the discrediting of traditional medicine by religious officials threatened healers and spiritual leaders, who were once considered wise men and women in their communities. Spanish pressures did not succeed fully, however, because underlying concepts of gender parallelism and complementarity were at the very core of social organization and household relations.

CHAPTER EIGHT

Household and Community

This sixteenth-century Nahuatl-language description of the preconquest feast of Huauhquiltamalqualiztli (Feast of Eating Amaranth Greens Tamales), celebrated by the Nahuas of central Mexico, speaks to the Mesoamerican conceptualization of "family," using *cencaltia* (to form a household) to describe the social bonds that a woman established by offering food to her kin and neighbors—an act that symbolized the mutual obligations of the household members:

She whose tamales of amaranth greens were first cooked would immediately go to give them to her housemates, her neighbors, the people next door to her house. And for her distant relatives, she first heated them. When they were ready she distributed them to people everywhere. Then they sat down to eat their tamales of amaranth greens. They went around; they rounded up, collected, assembled, and gathered their children. These formed a household.

in aquin achto oicucic ioauhquiltamal niman ic iauh quimacaz in icalpo, in icalecapo, in icalnaoac tlacatl: yoan in vecapa ivaniolqui, achto contonaltiaia. Auh in ie iuhqui, in onoviampa quitemamacac niman motlalia in quiquazque, in inoauhquiltamal, moiaoaloa, quincemololoa quinnechicoa, quincentlalia quintecpichoa in impilhoan inin cencaltia.[1]

Philological evidence drawn from colonial dictionaries and archival sources in Nahuatl, Ñudzahui (Mixtec), and Tíchazàa (Zapotec) reveals a complex of terms for the Spanish *familia* that recognizes a shared residence and communal life rather than consanguinity or common lineage. Among the terms in Nahuatl are *cenyeliztli* (being together), *cencalli* (one house), *cencaltin* (those in one house), *cemithualtin* (those in one patio), and *techan tlaca* (people who live together in a house).[2] Similarly the terms for *familia* in fray Francisco de Alvarado's 1593 Ñudzahui dictionary, *ee huahindi* (my one house), and in fray Juan de Córdova's 1578 Tíchazàa *Vocabulario*, *peni hualichia* (people of my house), refer to a common residence.³ Based on his study of Nahuatl, Lockhart concludes that the terms for family "emphasize the setting in which a joint life takes place, not the origin of the relationships between those living together."⁴ His observation captures the underlying sentiment of the terms in Ñudzahui and Tíchazàa.⁵

This chapter explores some of the many dimensions of the joint life of members of a residence and examines the ways in which alliances among households formed the basis of community. Based on his ethnographic work in the Mixteca Alta, John Monaghan sees the community as an "association of households" bound through "value laden acts."⁶ This also describes the colonial native community. As the account of the Huauhquiltamalqualiztli feast demonstrates, women were often at the center of such value-laden acts as social actors who constructed and sustained familial bonds.

Because indigenous prescriptive literature asserted that a woman's place was in the home (although this study shows that women's lives and activities were not so circumscribed), it is essential to understand the tenor of daily life in a household. I evaluate the extent to which the home was "private" and therefore gendered through an analysis of the relationship between the household and the community. It is only through the use of many different types of sources that the multifaceted nature of the household and the roles of women emerge. While censuses organized for tribute purposes highlight the productive capacity of a residential unit and the role of its (mainly) male head, they tell us little about its developmental cycle or the relationships among domestic groups. Descriptions of feasts such as the Huauhquiltamalqualiztli emphasize consumption and the social dimension of women's labor. Criminal records and didactic speeches reveal the residential compound as a moral unit, while land documents and testaments portray the household primarily as a landholding entity. This chapter employs all of these sources in order to better understand the relationships between the men and women of a household and their relationship to the broader community.

Like *community*, *household* refers to both a place and a set of social relations. Let us begin with the idea of the household as a place with an overview of the different types of compounds that were homes to families in highland Mexico.

LAYOUT OF THE HOUSEHOLD COMPLEX

The prototypical Mesoamerican domestic complex consisted of a series of one-room structures, or houses, arranged around a patio, often built against outer walls that formed an enclosure but sometimes the separate units were only clustered together. Each house had one entrance and sometimes a small storage room built on the side. More elaborate homes might have two stories; however, the second story had its own entrance and was not connected internally to the lower structure.[7] Houses for specific activities and the patio provided communal living space. Among the houses were kitchens and oratories containing ritual objects, deities, and, in colonial times, saints. The physical layout of a residential compound was fairly consistent throughout Mesoamerica and differed more in elaboration than in design.

Elite compounds followed this basic layout, but were significantly larger. Palaces contained multiple patios, each with single- or multi-room houses built around it. The impressive *aniñe* (palace) of the Ñudzahui cacique of Yanhuitlan, for example, had nine patios.[8] In preconquest and early colonial times, craftsmen were dependents of the nobility and so some space may have been used as workshops. Often at least one patio would have had enough space to hold a large assembly.[9] Other houses in noble residences were homes to local nobles, who conducted the community's business in them.[10]

Not only were elite houses larger, they also were constructed with finer building materials. The Florentine Codex describes the ruler's palace, the *tecpancalli*, as magnificently built, its walls plastered and painted, inlaid with mosaics, or decorated with carved stonework.[11] As a house that "stands constantly shining, wonderful, a marvel," (*totonaticac, maviztic tlamahuiçolli*), the architecture embodied the importance, glory, and honor of the ruling family.[12]

The needs of the family dictated the size and structure of the household complex. When a couple joined an existing household, a new structure was built to accommodate them. In the Nahua region, when a couple left a household they sometimes took down their house and moved it to a new location.[13] The flexibility of the residential unit reflects the evolving composition of the Mesoamerican household.

HOUSEHOLD COMPOSITION

In central Mexico and Oaxaca, nuclear family and joint households coexisted. Nuclear families consisted of one married couple and their unmarried children, if any, and frequently unmarried or widowed consanguineous or affinal relations and their children. Joint households were composed of at least two married couples and their children, who did not necessarily share blood ties. Each couple occupied a separate house in the compound.

Elite households had the largest and most complex residential groups, which were composed of members of all social classes—nobles and commoners, dependents and slaves—and thus were microcosms of local society. Members of extended ruling or noble families resided together in the palace. In cases of polygynous marriages, secondary wives and their children might also live in quarters there.[14] In their complexity, elite Mesoamerican households compared with contemporaneous European residential groups, which were larger than the average domestic establishment both in terms of numbers of extended biological kin and physical size.[15]

The earliest extant information on native living arrangements in colonial Mexico is preserved in several pictorial cadastral registers and a handful of Nahuatl-language censuses that date approximately from the 1540s. They provide a rare glimpse into native social organization within a generation after the Spanish conquest and reveal evidence of significant regional variation in prevalent household types. Based on his study of the Codex Vergara, a circa-1540 pictorial census illustrating several subdistricts of the Nahua community of Tepetlaoztoc, Jerome A. Offner concludes that 62 percent of households were nuclear.[16] Herbert R. Harvey arrives at the same figure working with the Codex of Santa María Asunción, a companion of the Codex Vergara.[17] In contrast, data uncovered by Pedro Carrasco from Molotla based on a circa-1540 Nahuatl-language census vary significantly from the data for Tepetlaoztoc. In Molotla, most likely a calpolli of the Nahua community of Yautepec, nearly 62 percent of residences were joint households.[18] Studying census data for Quauhchichinollan and two sections of Huitzillan, S. L. Cline finds that joint residences predominated. In Quauhchichinollan only 19 percent were single-couple households; one section of Huitzillan had 18 percent; in the other section, joint and single-couple residences were more evenly distributed, with 48 percent having just one couple.[19]

Many factors shaped the developmental cycle of the household. Natural mortality and epidemics contributed to the decreasing size of the residential group and disrupted the household in unimaginable ways. Over the course of the colonial period, men and women seeking employment or wishing to avoid tribute demands increasingly abandoned their homes and were absorbed into Spanish centers.[20] The household might contract temporarily as people left their homes for days, weeks, or months to provide tribute labor to native nobles and Spaniards. Or new opportunities might entice a couple to break away from the existing group and establish a new residence altogether. In any case, however, the flexible and tenacious nature of the household, with its inherent ability to reconstitute and fragment, helps explain the survival of indigenous social and cultural forms in the face of disaster. The conception of family as a social unit with shared obligations and privileges, more so than a lineage group, shaped the composition of the household as it fluctuated through its development cycle.

Working against the tendency to fragment were practices that allowed the household to replenish its resources, labor force, and social groupings. Marriages and the birth of children contributed new members to and extended alliances between households. Residence based on ties to female household members was neither rare nor insignificant.[21] An early sixteenth-century pictorial census (ca. 1545) known as the Codex of Santa María Asunción, provides information on each household in eleven subterritories of the Nahua community of Tepetlaoztoc. Studying its data, Harvey finds that the majority of married couples chose neolocal residences; however, among those who joined parents after marriage 77.2 percent adopted patrivirilocal residence and 19.3 percent chose patriuxorilocal residence.[22] Pedro Carrasco, in tracing ties to the household head through the wife in a number of cases in his study of joint families in Molotla, concludes that out of eighty-four cases of married dependents residing with consanguineous relatives, seventeen (20.2 percent) were close female relatives of the household head. In addition, 27 percent of married couples in joint households were affinal relatives, the majority either brothers or sisters of the household head's wife.[23]

Examining joint households in the Nahua communities of Huitzillan and Quauhchichinollan, Cline finds that daughters continued to reside with their parents more frequently than did sons after marriage; patriuxorilocal residence occurred in 27.5 percent, 27 percent, and 8 percent of the cases in Quauhchichinollan, the second section of Huitzillan, and the first section of Huitzillan, respectively. Furthermore, affinal kin resided jointly in 25 percent, 17 percent, and 20 percent of households in the two sections Huitzillan and in Quauhchichinollan, respectively.[24] The studies by Harvey, Carrasco, and Cline show that ties through female kin played an important role in establishing residence. Even when a woman lived with her husband's household, she might be joined by some of her own relatives. Therefore, patrivirilocal residence did not necessarily lead to a woman's permanent isolation or alienation from her own family.

Information on residence patterns culled from criminal records dating from the mid-sixteenth to the mid-eighteenth centuries, although not as systematic as early colonial census data, shows that residence arrangements and household types continued to vary considerably even within one ethnic region.[25] In general terms, Nahuas tended to reside patrivirilocally more often than patriuxorilocally, although the latter situation did occur regularly.[26] The records show that in Oaxaca postmarital residence among commoners was similar to that in central Mexico. The Ñudzahui people of the Mixteca Alta and the Bènizàa and Ayuuk (Mixe) people of the Sierra Alta preferred patrilocal residence, but occasionally settled matrilocally.[27]

Bènizàa and Ñudzahui nobles exhibited more marked differences in residence patterns. Whereas Bènizàa elites from the Sierra showed an overwhelming preference for patrilocality, Ñudzahui nobles seem to have had more flexible arrangements, perhaps because of the unique form of sociopolitical organization that developed in the Mixteca Alta.[28] Ñudzahui rulers and nobles established patrivirilocal, matrivirilocal, or ambilocal residences, depending on their opportunities to exploit the labor and material resources associated with the ruling privileges that the husband and wife each brought to the marriage.[29]

Like political factors, economic concerns shaped decisions regarding postmarital residence. A prospective couple's parents considered access to resources, the labor needs of their respective households, and the groom's trade when negotiating the newlyweds' living arrangements.[30] For example, sixteen-year-old Diego López Cachi married Isabel Xaco under the condition that she would make a life with him in his native community of Texupa, where his mother and father lived and where he possessed houses and lands.[31] In contrast, fifteen-year-old Domingo Hernández married María Pérez in the late sixteenth century and joined her family's household. He was a muleteer who frequently traveled, leaving his wife alone, and his occupation suggests that his natal household may not have had sufficient lands to farm.[32] These factors informed the decision that the couple would establish residence with the bride's family.[33]

Residence arrangements and household types varied considerably according to regional custom, individual circumstances, and the development cycle of the household. For many couples, postmarital residence was a temporary arrangement until they could acquire lands and establish their own households.[34] Historians, anthropologists, and sociologists have long considered residence patterns to be important determinants of women's status. In studies of colonial Mexico, it is accepted that a woman suffered a loss in status when she resided in her husband's family's household and/or community after marriage.[35] Conversely, it is argued that a woman retained her high status and her husband became subordinate in a matrilocal arrangement.[36] Given the complexity of living arrangements in central and southern Mexico however, a decline in women's status after marriage based on residence patterns cannot be assumed.

As Spores observes in his study of colonial Mixtec society, "both sets of parents usually resided in the same community, and a newly married couple could likely depend on the support of both . . . ."[37] Moreover, residence type did not clearly correspond to a woman's status. While a woman may have found stronger support within her natal household, patriuxorilocality did not necessarily ensure her higher status or improved relations with her husband. In the Mixtec community of Yanhuitlan in 1601, for example, Domingo Hernández pulled his wife to the ground by her hair and smashed her head with a rock in her parents' home as her mother and father watched in horror. This shows that wife beating might still occur in the home of the bride's parents.[38] Nor did patriuxorilocality change a woman's legal or economic status, although conversely there was no loss of status for men who joined their wives' households and communities. In fact, marriage alliances provided increased political, economic, and social power to noblemen, who benefited from their associations with elite women.[39] As discussed in Chapter 4, a noble who married into his wife's community might even hold office by virtue of this affiliation.

It has often been assumed that patrilocal residence simply isolated women; however, such a stark interpretation overlooks the ways in which marriage often served to integrate households. Regardless of postmarital residence, men and women who relocated interacted across households and communities. Women who left their birth communities after marriage often visited their "hometowns" to participate in community rituals and lifeways. To cite one of many such cases, María Coqua, a Ñudzahui woman who had taken up residence in her husband's community of San Pedro in the Mixteca Alta, traveled with her husband to her home in San Miguel to celebrate the community's feast day in 1597.[40] Also, a woman who had moved to her husband's community often returned to help her parents with labor projects. In 1625 a married Ñudzahui woman named Catalina who resided in Izcatlan returned to Yolotepec to help her father harvest his field.[41] Similarly, in 1706 María Alávez, who had married into the Zapotec community of Camotlan, returned with her husband to her natal town to help her mother and father pick maize.[42] These cases show that even in cases of patrilocal residence, a woman did not permanently sever ties to her community, even though the frequency with which she returned home might be a source of tension. In fact, in many respects her husband was drawn into her natal household and community despite the location of their residence.

The inclusive nature of the native family shaped social dynamics such that when young men and women entered their spouses' homes at marriage, they were integrated into the household and considered their in-laws' children. A sixteenth-century Nahua oratory from a marriage ceremony, in which the groom's male relatives and his mother address the bride as "my daughter," reveals the relationship between a bride and her in-laws.⁴³ Although the use of kin terms was a standard feature of Nahuatl rhetoric, in this context the terminology also served to name and acknowledge a new social relationship established as the bride joined her husband's family's home. These relations may have been tense at times, but the ideal was to bring the young woman into the household, albeit as a junior member.

A domestic group might also grow when adults, either with or without children, joined the household. Widows and widowers and their children sometimes relocated upon the death of a spouse.⁴⁴ Single or separated individuals might also move when new opportunities arose, bringing crucial resources to their new homes. For example, in her Nahuatl-language testament written in 1657, an Ayuuk woman named María Catalina left seven pieces of land and all her assets to the man who had taken her in two years earlier.⁴⁵ Those who lacked material or propertied wealth offered skills and labor. Single women sometimes resided in the homes of native employers, who provided room and board in exchange for weaving labor.⁴⁶ Destitute men and women might be forced to move to new communities, where they offered themselves as dependents of wealthy indigenous nobles and Spaniards.⁴⁷

The presence of short-term guests in a home was not uncommon as members frequently moved between households and duties. Family, friends, and even strangers added to the household, if only temporarily. Although occasional guests did not contribute to the household's functions, they developed informal ties with the "family" and contributed to the dynamic composition of the Mesoamerican household. Women sometimes slept at the houses of relatives, neighbors, and local officials, especially after arguing with their husbands.⁴⁸ People who were taking care of business or attending community celebrations lodged with extended-household and community contacts when they traveled.⁴⁹

The extension of kinship terminology in indigenous speech attests to a broad conceptualization of family that included social relations beyond the residential group. Model dialogues written down by literate Nahuas working with Spanish friars in the sixteenth and early seventeenth centuries, provide examples of the use of kin terms as a standard convention of high-Nahuatl speech.⁵⁰ Mundane criminal records corroborate the evidence in formal texts and oratory for an inclusive understanding of family. Native people called to testify in criminal cases recalled events that they had witnessed and often repeated conversations with defendants, victims, and other community members. Dialogue preserved in such records reveals the colloquial use of kin terms beyond their literal sense. For example, in 1581 a Mixtec man testified that as a gesture of peace, he had addressed the man with whom he had fought using the

Ñudzahui term for brother, *ñani*; he had tried to reason with the man, saying, "Andrés, you know, brother, we must forgive one another, we must cleanse ourselves of this" (*andres conahando ñani nanooquachiyo naquihuindoyo*).⁵¹ Significantly, the two men established peace by eating tortillas together, just as household members, ritual kin, and other social groups shared food to consolidate their bonds.

An entry in Córdova's Tíchazàa *Vocabulario* indicates broad use of kin terms among both men and women. The term *pariente* (relative) has an explanatory note: "Relative—all call each other brothers: *peeche*, the men to men, and to women, *pizanaya*, and the women to others, *pela*."⁵² The Ñudzahui grammarian fray Antonio de los Reyes also noted the use of *brother* for neighbors (*próximos*).⁵³

HOUSEHOLD RELATIONS

Each household recognized a head, usually a senior male but on some occasions a female who organized labor and delivered tribute to local magistrates.⁵⁴ The head should not be equated with a "patriarch" because he or she did not represent other household members legally; archival records never explicitly identify plaintiffs with a household head, indicating that adult members of the household engaged the legal system without the head's direct participation. Nor did the head impart his or her name and identity to other members of the group. The Nahua, Ñudzahui, Bènizàa, and Ayuuk people did not use patronymic or matronymic names (unlike the Mayas of Yucatan).⁵⁵ Evidence from native-language testaments suggests that, excluding the payment of tribute, each male and female adult had relative independence and responsibility in economic matters, so they could incur debts, extend loans, and purchase and sell goods and property without the approval of the household head.

Early colonial pictorials of the house and its occupants presented as evidence in land disputes show that the married couple—rather than a patriarchal head—was the foundation of the household. They trace the origins of the home's establishment to the time of the couple's marriage. Significantly, the couple are shown on an equal plane and facing each other, which suggests negotiation and consensus according to native pictorial conventions. Their children are drawn behind or below them.

Two pictorials of houses and lands with Nahuatl glosses provide excellent examples of this convention. Figure 8.1, a 1568 drawing from the Nahua community of Coyoacan in central Mexico, shows a nuclear family, their house lot, and outlying land.⁵⁶ The heads of the husband and wife are adjacent to the household, which the Nahuatl gloss *cali* (house)

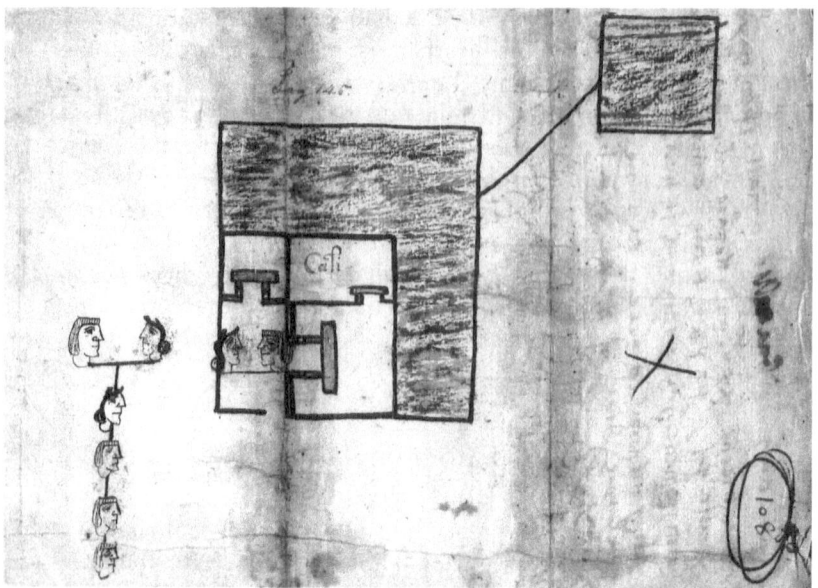

Figure 8.1. Mid-sixteenth-century Nahua household showing a married couple and their children
SOURCE: Archivo General de la Nación, Mexico, Tierras, 1735, exp. 2, 108.

identifies as a residence; it may also refer to a group that lives together.[57] Gender is distinguished by hairstyle: the woman's hair is gathered at the nape and braided into "hairhorns" on top of her head in the typical Nahua fashion; the man's hair is cropped. The heads of the mother and father are also shown outside of the structure, and their children are shown in a line below. This image and the accompanying Nahuatl-language text confirm the rights of María, a Nahua commoner, to land that she had inherited from her late husband. Figure 8.2 uses similar pictorial conventions in the plan of a household and its chinampas.[58]

Interestingly, the Nahuas projected their sixteenth-century conceptualization of the household onto their interpretation of the past. One of the native artists who illustrated fray Diego Durán's *Historia de las Indias de Nueva España y Islas de Tierra Firme* depicted an ancestral couple facing each other seated in a cave, their historic home.[59] Between the two is a bowl of food symbolizing their shared sustenance (see Figure 8.3). The anachronistic rendering underscores the understanding that a married couple constituted a household even in a structure as primordial as a cave. A closer examination of the functions of the household tells us more about native people's social interactions.

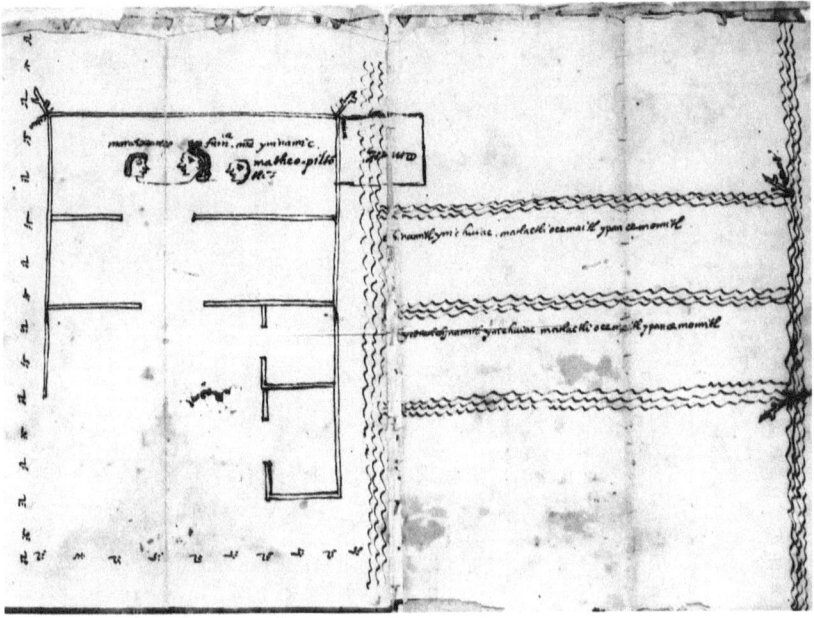

Figure 8.2. Nahua household and its land
SOURCE: Archivo General de la Nación, Mexico, Tierras, 165, exp. 4, 15.

FUNCTIONS OF THE HOUSEHOLD

The household was the site of various activities that defined the joint life of its members, whose mutual endeavors gave substance and meaning to daily life and bound them in vital ways to the broader community. Economic, social, sacred, and official activities intertwined the lives of the members of a household with its community.

Economic Dimensions of the Household

The sedentary peoples of central Mexico and Oaxaca managed labor and resources through a household-based tribute system. In exchange for payment of tribute in labor and kind, individuals received access to land and other resources. Some lands were held communally; others were privately owned. In preconquest and early colonial Mexico, tribute was based on the amount of land held privately by a household's members. Landowners and fellow household members worked their lands collectively, producing goods and providing labor to meet tribute obligations. Although some landholdings were in many ways treated as "privately" held, all land theoretically belonged to the community and was worked by individual

Figure 8.3. Aztecs' ancient origins, showing a couple in a cave
SOURCE: Biblioteca Nacional de España, vit. 24-2, following Durán 1994, plate 1.

households. Certain lands were transferred through bequest and sale and thus might be controlled indefinitely by households, with no intervention from the community as long as tribute was paid. However, the community could reclaim and redistribute fallow lands. Furthermore, the right to possess and work land was directly tied to an obligation to serve the community—individual privilege derived from public obligation—so the land held by individuals within households was in a sense both public and private.

Women and men owned land, acquiring it through inheritance, sale, and community grant. Landowners had the right to leave their property and other belongings to their preferred heirs. They could also freely alienate lands through sale. In the early colonial period, quantitative differences in landholding reflected status distinctions rather than gender preference. In the sixteenth and seventeenth centuries, men and women seem to have owned land in roughly equal amounts, although scholars have suggested that by late colonial times, women's landholding in central Mexico had declined. The extent of this decline is debated, with studies of different regions showing significant variation from the central Mexican trend.[60] For example, Terraciano found no such decline in the Mixteca Alta in the late colonial period.[61] Bènizàa and Ayuuk women in the Sierra Alta continued to hold property throughout the colonial period; however, the extent to which they possessed land in relation to men has not yet been studied.[62]

Over the course of the colonial period, the tribute system evolved to meet Spanish demands for payment in goods that could be resold in the market, including cloth and maize, and in gold or pesos.[63] Eventually, land-based assessment gave way to a general headtax on every adult man and woman, but whether in labor, kind, or money, tribute continued to be organized through the household, directly linking the household to the community. Every able-bodied man and woman in a residence contributed to the tribute payment. Important tribute activities, including spinning, weaving, grinding corn, and making tortillas, gave a "public" dimension to women's work in the home in that the product of that labor supported the colonial administration.

In addition to agricultural production, the household was the site of craft manufacturing and trade. Florentine Codex images of sixteenth-century Nahua life consistently situate craft production in a patio framed by the household walls. Figure 8.4, for example, shows a woman making dye in a native household, which is identified by its flat-roofed house and enclosed patio. Women wove cloth in the patio; both men and women spun thread and wove mats and baskets there.[64] The household was also where people bought and sold goods, including animals, cloth, and

Figure 8.4. Woman making dye in the household patio
SOURCE: Florentine Codex, bk. 11, fol. 222. Florence: Biblioteca Medicea Laurenziana, Med. Palat. 220, c. 373. By concession of the Ministry for Heritage and Cultural Activities; further reproduction by any means is forbidden.

corn.[65] In central Mexico, the Mixteca Alta, and the Sierra Alta of Oaxaca, women played a key role in the production and sale of pulque and as the proprietors of pulque taverns (*pulquerías*), where people gathered to drink and eat.[66] These daily economic activities allowed men and women to interact with others, even within the confines of the home.

Just as important as production to defining a household was the joint consumption of resources. As we saw at the beginning of the chapter, in the description of the Nahua Huauhquiltamalqualiztli feast, sharing food was synonymous with creating a household and expressing concern and affection. Archival narratives corroborate the significance of mutual feeding and clothing as the foundation of social relations. When María Tiacapan ordered her Nahuatl testament in 1581, she complained that her uncles had not looked after her when she was left orphaned. However, she fondly remembered her "dear grandmother, Juana Ana, [who] truly has acted honorably; she would come to give us little tortillas to eat that perhaps she had been given somewhere" (*yehuatl omotlamaçehui yn noçitzin juana ana tocamac quimaquillitihuitz yn cana aço onemaquilliloc tlaxcaltzintli*).[67] María clearly associated familial obligation with providing sustenance, a task ideally carried out by both men and women.

The flexible nature of the native household allowed people to bring in the destitute, widowed, and orphaned, and their generosity was recognized and respected. For example, Ñudzahui witnesses testified in 1632 that Diego Xiquio welcomed a poor local man into his house and gave him food to eat.[68] Similarly, a Ñudzahui healer of Teposcolula, Gaspar Sánchez, had a reputation as "a good person who often brought sick people to his house to cure and feed them."[69] Finally, when Andrés Jacobo testified in 1639 that he had helped his sister-in-law raise her children since his brother's death by "feeding and clothing them, teaching them to read and the Christian doctrine," he showed that familial relations were predicated on the provision of food and clothing among members.[70] His statement also sheds light on the importance of the household as a moral unit.

The Household as a Moral Unit

Among the many activities that the indigenous household jointly engaged in were the socialization of children and the moral policing of adults, although even in these matters the household was not an isolated or private entity. Often the participation and/or intervention of local authorities integrated the functions and relations of the household and the community. Of course, colonial institutions in native communities, including the church and judicial system, also contributed significantly to the discourse on morality.

The training and disciplining of children were shared by both parents. Infants remained with their mothers, but as they grew older they increasingly accompanied their same-sex parent. Images in the Codex Mendoza, a preconquest-style central Mexican pictorial manuscript, depict in idealized terms the progressive training of Nahua boys and girls from the ages of three to fourteen years. They show a mother teaching her daughter first to spin thread, then to grind maize, and eventually to weave cloth on a backstrap loom, and a father teaching his son to carry loads, to sweep, to navigate a canoe, and to fish (see Figure 8.5). It is interesting that there is no reference to caring for children as solely a woman's responsibility— not only in these images but in the idealized roles outlined in formal speeches such as those preserved in the Florentine Codex.

The socialization of children was primarily a household function; however, in preconquest central Mexico some parents, mainly of the nobility, enrolled their children in temple schools, where boys and girls were segregated and cared for respectively by elder men and women.[71] Girls were taught to weave cloth, spin cotton, dye rabbit fur and yarn, cook

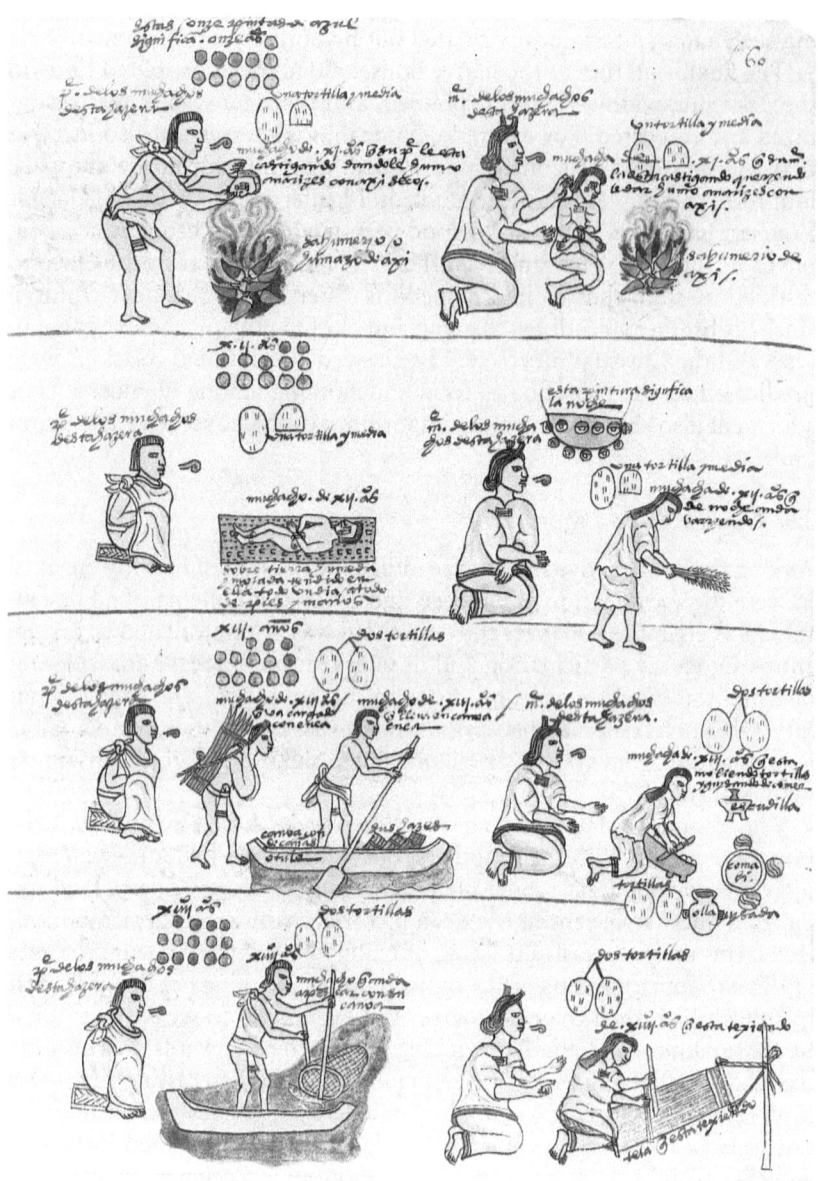

Figure 8.5. Mothers and fathers training and disciplining their daughters and sons

SOURCE: Codex Mendoza, fol. 60. Bodleian Libraries, University of Oxford, Ms. Arch. Selden A1. Berdan and Anawalt 1992, fol. 60. Reproduced with permission from University of California Press Books.

food, and prepare beverages.⁷² Boys were taught hunting techniques, received military training, or were apprenticed to painters, featherworkers, or jewelers. Some boys were apprenticed to male long-distance traders.⁷³ By entrusting their children to the temple, a noble Nahua family strengthened ties to community authorities.

In colonial times, social and professional training continued to be gender-specific, often conducted by tutors of the same sex. In a sixteenth-century model dialogue of high-Nahuatl speech, a woman speaking to an elderly woman praises her sons' tutor: "Antonio Coatecatl goes about looking after them and taking good care of them, for raising children is his special domain" (*in Antontzin Cohuatecatzintli, huel quimitztinemi huel quinmocuitlahuitinemi; ca ye ixcoca in tlacahuapahualiztli in tlacazcalitliztli*).⁷⁴ However, in most cases the education of children continued to be a function of the household. For example, don Agustín Maldonado, a Ñudzahui noble of San Pedro, a subject settlement of Tamasulapa, was actively involved in raising his children and had taught them to read.⁷⁵

The tradition of entrusting children to the temple seems to have continued in a modified form in the colonial period. The Christian church, often built on the ruins of the preconquest ceremonial center, lent prestige to the community and the nobility as the ancient temple had. Furthermore, the close association between the nobility and religious officials, Spanish and indigenous, had preconquest antecedents. Some nobles placed their children in the new temple school—the Christian church—to be educated and indoctrinated in Christianity. In central Mexico in the first decades after the conquest, some sons and (fewer) daughters of nobles were educated and converted in Franciscan schools so that they could help teach the Christian doctrine.⁷⁶ In the second half of the sixteenth century, Ñudzahui nobles, such as don Gabriel de Guzmán, cacique of the important community of Yanhuitlan, were tutored by the friars in their youth.⁷⁷ Nobles continued to build alliances with friars by entrusting their children to them in the seventeenth century. For example, in 1665 twelve-year-old Joseph de Vargas, the son of don Ciprián de Vargas, the Bènizàa cacique of Yatzona, was in the service of fray Antonio de Castro, vicar of Lachirio.⁷⁸

Model speeches for nobles to deliver to their sons and daughters in preconquest times demonstrate that parents shared the responsibility of guiding their children. They were written from a mother's and a father's perspective, with each parent taking his and her turn in admonishing the child on the importance of proper conduct and polite behavior.⁷⁹ When children were married, both mothers and fathers spoke at the wedding ceremony, mainly emphasizing the scope and importance of the newlyweds' roles as husband and wife.⁸⁰

The household also influenced the manner in which children were raised. Rather than the nuclear family, it served as the primary social unit in multifamily groups. Parents sometimes left their children in the care of household members. In 1605 Juana López and Juan de Velasco, a Ñudzahui merchant couple of Yanhuitlan, asked a tailor who worked for them and lived in their household to look after their children while they went to the market in Teposcolula to sell clothes.[81] In 1624, Lucía Xiqua, a Ñudzahui woman, asked her sister-in-law to take care of her children when she left the house.[82] When Cecilia Sasayu saw her husband drunk and fighting with another man, she went to sleep at her mother's house and left her children with other members of her household.[83]

As a moral unit, one of the most important functions of the household was the counseling and disciplining of children, which, according to normative texts, was shared by mothers and fathers. In a sixteenth-century model Nahuatl-language dialogue, an exasperated mother complains:

But especially the little first-born concerns me somewhat; he's quite mischievous and afraid of nothing at all, and when he has flown out of the house he runs howling and shouting as though he were a Chichimec. He stops nowhere, and right away goes running off. Sometimes they catch him in Tetzcohco, or even in cities farther away. Though I whip his skin with a rope and stick him in chile smoke or mistreat and afflict him even more and leave him practically dead, he will not listen at all.

çan huel yehuatl in yacapantontli achi nechtequipachoa in achi cueciuhqui in niman amo tlaimacaci in o no chipetontehuac, yuhquin ma chichimecatl motenhuitectiuh tzatzitiuh in motlaloa: auh acan ma moquetza, niman hueca altepetl ipan: immanel ye nicmecaxipehua nicchilpopochhuia, noce oc hualca ic nictolinia nictotonehua izça micqui niccahua, niman amo ic tlacaquiznequi.[84]

Although such situations are hypothetical, they shed light on the frustrations of parents and the authoritative position of mothers. The Codex Mendoza depicts a mother and father punishing a daughter and son, respectively, for misbehaving or for performing their duties poorly. The top two panels of Figure 8.5 show parents holding their childrens' faces in chile smoke, making them lie in water all day with their hands and feet tied, and forcing them to awake and sweep in the middle of the night. like the Nahua mother's dialogue, the images reveal that corporal punishment was acceptable in disciplining children and that women shared the responsibility for making their children suffer for their wrongdoings.[85] Boys and girls received similar punishments, suggesting that girls were not considered weaker than boys.

Native officials also might be involved in discipline. According to a Bènizàa cabildo record of 1689, a woman complained to local magistrates that a neighbor's adolescent daughters had wounded her eight-year-old son on the head with a rock. The officials gave the older girl twelve lashes and the younger one six.[86] In another example, from the Mixteca Alta, community officers gave fifty lashes to a boy who had stolen his grandfather's money.[87] The authority of local officials in matters concerning children undermined the concentration of authority and power in the hands of the household head. Moreover, the extension of cabildo authority into such matters blurred distinctions between households and the community.

Adult household members monitored each other's activities and punished any transgressions involving drunkenness, sex, and violence. The household was not only a site of production and communal living but also an arena of conflict in which individual and corporate interests were contested. Because an individual's actions, reputation, and fortune were tied to those of other household members, a crime or indiscretion of one brought shame to the others.[88]

A tragic homicide case from the Villa Alta region reveals the importance of family reputation. In 1676 Nicolás Gabriel, a respected man who served as lead singer in the church and who had held civil and religious offices in the community, killed his son, Pedro de los Ángeles. Witnesses testified that the two men fought frequently and that once Pedro had seriously wounded his father by hitting him on the head with the *mano* (pestle) of a *metate* (grinding stone). On the night of the murder, Nicolás found his son beating his wife in a drunken rage. Mortified by such deviant behavior, he tied Pedro to a pole and repeatedly clubbed him with an ax handle.

Despite the gruesome attack, every witness in the case, including those for the prosecution, insisted that Nicolás was highly respected in the community and explained that it was "publicly known that he killed [Pedro] for his honor because it had been proven that he had stolen two mules in the town of San Pedro, and from shame he committed the murder." Nicolás confessed that he had harshly punished his son out of shame "because the people of the community threw [Pedro's] thefts in my face."[89] To restore his own honor and that of his household, Nicolás believed that he had no choice but to punish his villainous son by taking his life. In a similar but unrelated case, Gabriel Sánchez, as he lay on his deathbed narrating his Nahuatl-language testament in 1630, spoke bitterly of the shame that his son's faults had brought to him. The Ayuuk man disowned his miscreant son, and described how he had "afflicted" him (*onechtolini*) by stealing money from the community.[90] Similarly, when Catalina López returned home from the market after being pronounced a "thief" and whipped by community officials for stealing clothes, her husband punished her to show that he did not condone her behavior.[91]

The wrongdoings and punishment of a household member could bring more harm than simply a tarnished reputation. Arrest and imprisonment disrupted labor and tribute arrangements, and the loss of a worker could be difficult, especially during planting and harvesting. To add insult to injury, family members of the incarcerated had to provide him (or her) with food. Sometimes community magistrates incarcerated or punished an alleged criminal's fellow household members or relatives. For example, in 1660 native and Spanish officials attempted to arrest the wife of a man who had escaped from prison, but community members drove the jailers away.[92] In Atengo in 1723, native officials detained the mother of a fugitive from justice in the house of a local official, where she was forced to spin thread until he appeared.[93] Wives especially suffered the consequences of their husband's criminal activities. In one example from 1632, Sebastián Xiquihui promised that he and his wife would work for a Ñudzahui noblewoman carrying water, performing household tasks, and cleaning, sowing, and harvesting her fields to repay the money that he had stolen from her.[94] In another example, the *coquitao* (hereditary ruler) of Yatzona, don Josef de Celís, and his wife served his sentence jointly when he was convicted of stealing a silver pedestal of the church monstrance in 1688. Don Josef was forced to pay for the pedestal, to labor in the mines for a year, to serve a local Spaniard for eight months and the Spaniard's son for an additional eight months, and to work in the church for three months; his wife served with him for four of those months.[95]

As a microcosm of the community, each household had its own deities and, after the conquest, Christian saints, altars, and places of worship. The perception of the house complex as sacred space extended the understanding of the household as a moral unit.

The Household as Sacred Space

Just as members of a community had openly worshipped local and pan-Mesoamerican deities in preconquest times, members of a household venerated specific gods and, in colonial times, Christ and saints. Nahua, Ñudzahui, Bènizàa, and Ayuuk men and women built houses and altars for their gods and/or saints in the household compound.[96] The sacred house was referred to as an *oratorio* (oratory or chapel) or a *casa* (house) in Spanish documents and as a *santocalli* (saint house) in Nahuatl-language records (no equivalent term has been identified in Ñudzahui or Tíchazàa). Some people even left property to their household saints, perhaps according to some ancient belief that deities were the legitimate guardians of land.[97]

Based on his extensive study of Nahuatl-language testaments, Lockhart concludes that the main purpose of the santocalli was as a residence for the household saints.[98] However, archival records show that it also provided a place to pray, drink, and perform rituals that often combined Christian and native spiritual elements. The saint's house functioned like a typical house—as a residence and as a gathering place for sacred celebrations. For example, several people in Coyoacan gathered in a household oratorio to drink pulque in honor of San Nicolás.[99] A mid-eighteenth-century document from the Nahua community of Malinalco suggests that funerary rituals were carried out in the household chapel; in this case, a family laid out a stillborn baby in the oratorio and with the help of neighbors and friends prepared the infant for burial in the church cemetery.[100] A witness in a criminal investigation from the Mixteca Alta recounted in 1681 that a sick man drank an herbal remedy and then entered the oratory, a separate structure within the compound, to pray to the saints that were kept there.[101]

Evidence from campaigns to exterminate "idolatries" in New Spain reveals the continued importance of native ceremonial practices and the integration of community and household forms of worship. In his treatise on the persistence of Nahua beliefs and practices in the early seventeenth century, Ruiz de Alarcón discussed many cases in which he found sacred objects and altars hidden in peoples' homes.[102] In the early eighteenth century, an extensive investigation of idolatries in the Sierra Alta, carried out under the direction of Oaxacan bishop fray Ángel Maldonado, uncovered local practices throughout the region.[103] The testimony of Bènizàa and Ayuuk "teachers of idolatry" (*maestros de idolatrias*), local officials, and other town members who confessed to participating in sacred ceremonies shows that some residences maintained special "houses" for the worship of the entire community and for storing non-Christian religious objects. In the Bènizàa community of Yaa, a room in Mateo Hernández' house provided a place to practice native religion and to keep the instruments used in rituals.[104] Similarly, Bernabé de Santiago of Yoeche was appointed majordomo of the community's sacred objects, which he kept in his home.[105] In Betaza, Juan Luis confessed that he had been to the houses of two local men that had special rooms for performing indigenous rites, including one that housed all the "skulls of the grandparents of the barrio."[106] Ancestor worship remained a central feature of local religion in Betaza. As Tavárez explains, records from this region discuss the ceremonial use of "effigies, ranging from carved or painted representations of individuals to 'hanks of hair' tied to pieces of cotton," referred to as *quiquiag yagtao* (heads of the Great Tree) in Tíchazàa, to signify founding lineages. These were called heads of the ancestors or grandparents in Spanish.[107]

Sacred altars and houses also contained Catholic images and objects, sometimes alongside indigenous religious articles. In his testament written in 1591, don Gabriel de Guzmán, the Ñudzahui cacique of Yanhuitlan, left a number of Christian objects to his heirs, including a silver-plated reliquary of the Agnus Dei, four icons of the Virgin Mary, three gold rosaries, and gold figures of Santiago, the Baby Jesus, cherubs, and Jesus the Savior, which he must have displayed in his household chapel.[108] Among the icons that don Felipe de Santiago, a Bènizàa noble of Yatzona, kept in 1699 were a *lienzo* (painted canvas) of Nuestra Señora de la Soledad, an image of Nuestra Señora de Guadalupe in a black frame, a framed picture of Nuestra Señora de Las Angustias, a tablet bearing the image of Santa Verónica, a lienzo of San Juan Bautista, another picture of Nuestra Señora de la Soledad, a print of Santa Catarina, and thirteen other unspecified prints. He also had a rosary, a catechism, and an image of Christ with a cross on display.[109] In his study of Nahua religious devotion in late colonial Mexico, Osowski finds that households where local saints and icons were kept and where miraculous events were reported served as community spaces. He highlights the prominent role that women played as guardians of religious images and as alms collectors, observing that in this capacity women were like "informal tlatoanis" who protected community religion even as Spanish ecclesiastics attempted to curb their participation as leaders in local devotions.[110]

In the Sierra Alta, community feasting following religious rituals provided yet another sacred dimension to the household. Typically, people gathered to eat and drink together after performing sacrifices at sites considered to be sources of power and life, such as swamps, springs, caves, or mountains. Residents of the Bènizàa town of San Miguel Talea, for example, described their traditions in 1704, including one custom in which all of the men gathered before dawn at a sacred site to watch native priests behead turkeys and scatter their blood on the ground.[111] After making offerings at all of the sacred places around the community, the men met the women at the native priest's house and together they feasted on the sacrificed turkeys. In 1704 the officials and nobles of San Bartolomé Yatoni also admitted to performing two sacrifices a year: the first when they sowed their fields; the second, on Easter.[112] They provided feathers, turkeys, and candles to their gods, all items typically used in rituals of the Zapotec region. The men assembled at the site very early in the morning to watch the maestros sacrifice turkeys as they asked their god, Betahoyona, to provide them with good health and an abundant harvest. When the sacrifice was completed, the maestros took the turkeys to their houses for the community feast. Such indigenous ceremonial practices and offerings reveal the "public" nature of households in which community feasts were held.

Commoners also sponsored meals to complete sacrifices that they made for the benefit of the household's members and for success in their daily endeavors.[113] A Bènizàa priest of Yalálag (described as a "master of idolatry" and "soothsayer") confessed that he had performed rituals for many people and recalled that he once accompanied a woman named Magdalena to her field to offer a turkey and pray to "Señor Coqui Yalálag" (Lord Ruler of Yalálag) for an abundant harvest.[114] Afterward they returned to her house and ate together. In 1665 Cristóbal Juárez and Isabel Hernández sponsored a Christmas feast in their home in Lachirio, where many people drank *pulque de plátanos* (pulque with bananas).[115]

Evidence from the Villa Alta region shows that, at least in Bènizàa and Ayuuk communities, the residential compound itself continued to be the site of offerings. Rituals similar to those performed at sacred sites were conducted in the household to ensure that the needs of the family would be met. When a native priest of Yacoche named Juan Domingo married, he sacrificed a turkey by cutting open its breast in his house.[116] Traditionally on All Saints Day, his household offered thirteen tamales and *memelas* (large, thin corn tortillas), and cut a turkey's breast and scattered its blood on the fire. Another Bènizàa priest named Josef Alonso confessed in 1704 that he frequently made offerings of dogs and turkeys for people in their homes in San Melchor Yoeche.[117] Josef Hernández, a spiritual leader in San Pablo, testified that he had learned from the cacique, don Pablo Jiménez, how to conduct a certain ritual in peoples' homes, in which he would behead turkeys and dogs and sprinkle their blood on the image (idol) and head of "our grandparent who we call Quiquiag yagtao [Head of the Great Tree]."[118] Nicolás Espino of Betaza admitted that he went to the house of Nicolás Martín Bechi to sacrifice turkeys.[119] Fabián de Vargas, another native priest from Betaza, stated that when he was sick he went to the house of his compadre, who kept the skulls of his grandparents (*quiquiag yagtao*) in his house, and sacrificed two turkeys and offered incense to the image there.[120]

Sometimes people went to other towns to bring native priests to their homes, suggesting that networks of specialists extended across community boundaries. Nicolás de Espinoza, a native of Yatee, brought Josef Bautista, a priest in San Andrés Yaa, to his house to sacrifice a turkey and dogs to Quiquiag yagtao and to skulls of his grandparents.[121] After the offering he cast lots with small sticks (*palillos*) to see whether the ritual would have a positive effect.

Although people had kept religious articles and relics in their homes in preconquest times, the persecution of idolatry and the replacement of temples with churches in the colonial period may have contributed to the tendency to safeguard ceremonial objects in residential compounds. In this way, the household became a site of resistance to efforts to extirpate local indigenous devotions. Even when Catholic icons were the focus of community spirituality, struggles ensued with Spanish priests attempting to regulate who could care for them. Tensions arose because of different ideas among Nahuas and Spaniards about the household and women's roles as leaders of sacred practices.[122] As guardians of the household, women played a significant role in these conflicts. Just as the observance of religious rituals in the home integrated the household and community, so did the practice of conducting political and legal matters there.

The Political Nature of the Household

Business pertaining to the household and community was often conducted in homes rather than in the municipal palace. Community members assembled in household compounds to witness and legitimate legal transactions, to partake in feasts marking legal and formal agreements, and to host political gatherings. Strict rules of comportment defined interactions in the local lordly palace, designated areas of restricted access, and limited contact with members of the royal household, especially the ruler's wives and children.[123] As a symbol of political rule, palaces epitomize the integration of household and community.

For the Nahuas and Mixtecs, groups whose sociopolitical organization is best understood, the ruling palace represented a political entity as well as a set of social relations. Ruling nobles of each calpolli subterritory of the Nahua altepetl traced their lineages to a *teccalli* (or *tecpan*, palace).[124] The teccalli represented the calpolli as a geographical entity and the social, economic, and political relations between the territory's commoners and nobles.[125] In fact, the word *calpolli* literally means big house, however, as with the household, it should not be imagined that close kin relations among its members amounted to a clan.[126]

Ñudzahui rulers, whether male or female, also represented distinct sociopolitical structures.[127] Each siqui, or constituent part of the ñuu (the Ñudzahui equivalent to the Nahua altepetl) had an *aniñe*, which resembled the Nahua *tecpan* and represented relations in the region as well as the ruling lineage. Other noble and commoner houses of the calpolli or siqui paid tribute to the ruling nobility of the palace, and the head of the tecpan organized tribute in the community just as the household head oversaw tribute in the household. Furthermore, rulers attended to civil and religious matters, negotiated conflicts, and organized tribute payments to the local state and then to the Spaniards after the conquest. Distinctions between the physical structure of the aniñe or tecpan and the social relations that it connoted are unclear. Noble houses literally belonged to the community and functioned as places where community members assembled to conduct business and fulfill tribute obligations. When don Francisco de Mendoza, the cacique of Tocaçahuala (a sujeto of Yanhuitlan), was elected to serve as an alcalde on the cabildo in Yanhuitlan, he maintained dual residences in the cabecera of Yanhuitlan and in his hometown. People from his community gathered and stayed at his house in Yanhuitlan when they attended the market or religious festivities in the cabecera.[128]

In early colonial times, nobles mobilized the labor and assembled resources needed to sponsor a feast. On occasion community officials collected donations to fund celebrations and organized feasts and other rituals, both native and Christian. Although ordered by Spanish authorities to eliminate community drunkenness, the magistrates could not expect to collect tribute or hope to be considered good administrators if they did not host feasts that involved drinking.[129] For example, on Easter Sunday in 1661 many men and women of the Mixe community of Tiltepec gathered at the house of Juan López, the notary, to drink pulque.[130] On the day of San Marcos in 1697, all members of the community gathered to drink at the house of the cacique, don Andrés López.[131] Sometimes officials organized feasts to show gratitude to the community when they were elected. To give thanks for their support when he was elected to the cabildo of Yatzona in 1676, a Bènizàa official invited his political allies to his house to partake of pulque and turkey.[132] Revealing the overlap of political and religious spheres, he scheduled the celebration to fall on the day after the feast day of the community's patron saint.

Native officials often conducted community business, sometimes of a spontaneous and subversive nature, in the homes of cabildo members or nobles rather than at the municipal building or church. For example, in 1703 a Bènizàa fiscal recalled that he and another church official met the alcaldes and regidores at the notary's house to decide what to do about the arrest of two local men in a neighboring community.[133] Once a crowd gathered in the compound of a local, high-ranking noble of Tabaa, don Cristóbal de Velasco, and decided to arrest the governor and three other men, whom they suspected had informed Spanish magistrates of the community's continuing non-Christian religious traditions.[134] The officials, nobles, and commoners of San Francisco Cajonos met with those of the Bènizàa communities of San Mateo, San Pablo, Santo Domingo, and San Miguel at the house of Sebastián Martín to decide the fate of two men who had been imprisoned in San Pedro after having discovered the others committing sacrifices.¹³⁵ Although the records do not specifically mention women participating in these gatherings, it is certain that they were present in the household because it was the site of much of their daily work and because their labor would have been required. Thus it is reasonable to assume that women were very much aware of the discussions taking place.

Nobles and commoners also met in individual households to conduct personal legal business, including the writing of last wills and testaments.¹³⁶ The testator would summon cabildo officials, local nobles, and as many men and women of the community as possible to serve as witnesses in keeping with a deeply rooted oral tradition.¹³⁷ The dying person would first pronounce her faith in Christianity; commend her soul to God; distribute offerings to the saints, the church singers, and the priest who would perform masses for her soul; and finally relinquish her body to the earth. The testator then bequeathed property, settled debts, and requested the repayment of loans. As with other official business, indigenous people throughout central Mexico and Oaxaca legitimated their last wills and testaments by sharing food and drink with magistrates and witnesses. Juan de la Cruz of the Ayuuk community of Totontepec, for example, served a little *tepache* (pulque mixed with other substances) to the officials who gathered at his home and, following the conventions of indigenous polite speech, apologized for not having any other gifts to offer before ordering his last will and testament.¹³⁸

The many responsibilities and activities jointly undertaken by members of a household could cause tensions when relations between household members were strained. Women and men engaged in a constant dialogue about morality, rights, and obligations through the resolution of household conflicts in a community setting.

The Community's Role in the Resolution of Household Conflicts

Local indigenous officials were responsible for investigating and negotiating civil matters in their ethnic states, such as inheritance disputes and land distribution, as well as criminal matters including robbery, fraud, homicide, assault and battery, adultery, and rape. Under colonial rule, Spanish magistrates adjudicated the more important civil and the most serious criminal cases involving native individuals, communities, and nonindigenous people; however, native officials were usually the first notified that a crime had been committed, and in subsequent investigations acted as intermediaries between Spanish administrators and community members. Because tribute and landholding were organized through the

Household and Community 251

household, the cabildo had a direct interest in resolving disputes among family members. The community could not afford to allow members to abandon their homes because of lingering conflicts and thus risk the amount of tribute they could collect. Tribute monies funded communal irrigation and construction projects, maintained the church and other municipal buildings, sponsored local celebrations, and paid officials' salaries, among other things. Moreover, local cabildo officials had a stake in the collection of tribute, since they were subject to imprisonment and the confiscation of their personal possessions if they did not submit full payment to Spanish magistrates. Communities also relied on labor provided through tribute, and even in the colonial period nobles often directly benefited from the labor of commoners who worked their lands. In all these ways, the livelihood of the community and the nobility depended on the stability of its households.

Complaints brought before officials in the colonial period ranged from very serious, such as homicide or arson, to trivial, such as an insult or the sale of adulterated cochineal. As tribute-paying citizens of the community, women theoretically had equal access to magistrates and the right to pursue civil and criminal cases. They appeared before cabildo officials to accuse their husbands of abuses, including domestic violence and adultery (see Chapter 4). They also reported cases of assault and battery, robbery, and unfair treatment by Spanish and native authorities. As mothers, they approached community leaders to file criminal charges on behalf of their children. Native men and women testified in trials and hearings about what they had seen and heard and about the character of plaintiffs and defendants. As discussed in Chapter 7, midwives and female healers often provided expert testimony, especially when a woman had been raped or when a pregnant woman had miscarried after having been assaulted.

Two illustrations of judicial administration in the Codex Mendoza link women's active use of the court in colonial times to a preconquest precedent.[139] Drawn by a Nahua artist in the early sixteenth century, Figures 8.6 and 8.7 show the two levels of justice in Mexico Tenochtitlan as instituted by Moteucçoma. Figure 8.6 depicts conflict resolution in the presence of a council of noble judges who, according to the accompanying Spanish text, were appointed by Moteucçoma to hear civil and criminal matters. The judges are shown seated on reed mat thrones, symbols of authority, and are attended by apprentices who sit behind them on humbler mats. Three men and three women, identified as plaintiffs in the Spanish gloss, present their case to the judicial council. One man and one woman represent the others, as indicated by the speech scrolls that emerge from their mouths. They are parallel to each other with no clear indication of hierarchy. Interestingly, the men and women are not clearly paired into

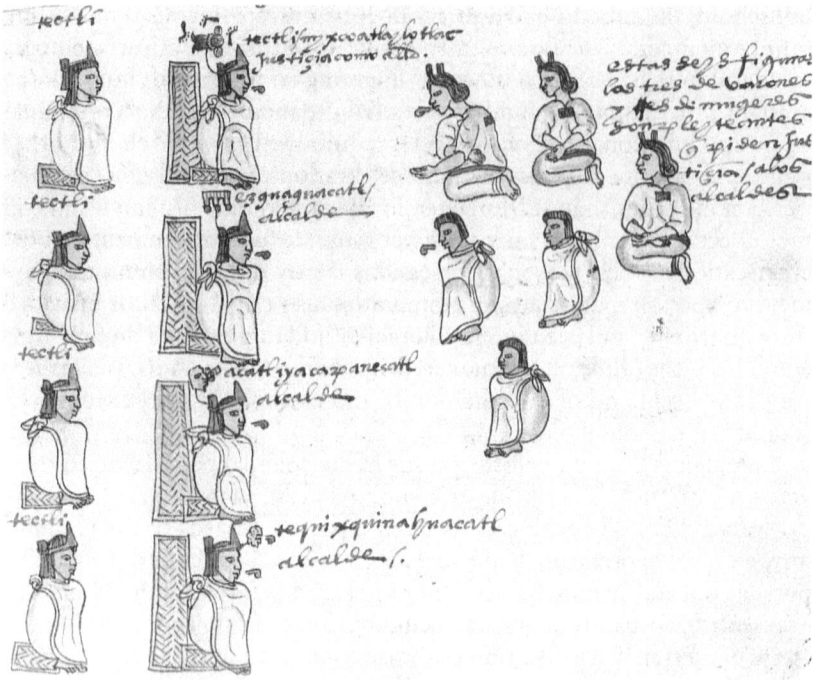

Figure 8.6. Male and female plaintiffs presenting their case to judges
SOURCE: Codex Mendoza, fol. 68. Bodleian Libraries, University of Oxford, Ms. Arch. Selden A1. Berdan and Anawalt 1992, fol. 68. Reproduced with permission from University of California Press Books.

couples; rather, the women are grouped together and the men are shown near one another, suggesting a gendered spatial organization when the parties assembled. The relationships within the group are unspecified.

Figure 8.7 shows Moteucçoma seated on the reed mat throne and wearing the diadem of Mexica rulers, presiding over the scene. At the lower right side of the illustration, four justices, identified by the Spanish gloss as *honbres sabios* (wise men), are seated on small reed mat stools. Two men and two women sit in front of the palace, appealing to the judges, and as in Figure 8.6, speech scrolls indicate that all of the men and women are actively participating in the proceedings. While the illustration suggests that in preconquest times women and men enjoyed equal access to the legal system, it is significant that all of the judges are male, indicating the institutionalization of male authority among the Nahuas in this area of government.

Colonial commentators noted the prominent role that women played as plaintiffs and representatives of the household's interests. For example,

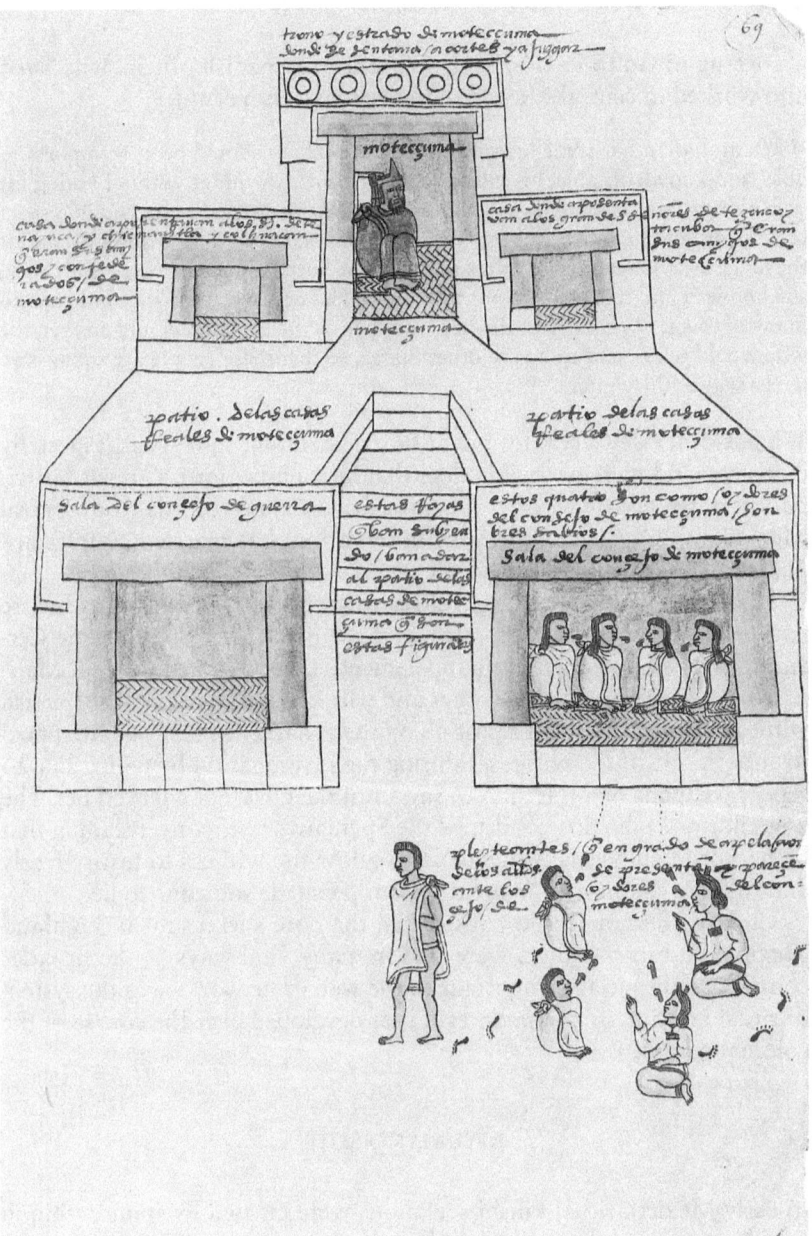

Figure 8.7. Women and men appealing to judges in front of Moteucçoma's palace
SOURCE: Codex Mendoza, fol. 69. Bodleian Libraries, University of Oxford, Ms. Arch. Selden A1. Berdan and Anawalt 1992, fol. 69. Reproduced with permission from University of California Press Books.

according to Gonzalo Gómez de Cervantes, a Spanish official who lived and worked in central Mexico in the late sixteenth century:

> When an Indian has some lawsuit, though the Indian should be very important, able, and knowledgeable, he will not appear before the judge without taking his wife along with him, and they report and say what is needed to be said in respect to the suit, and the husbands remain very silent and retired in themselves; and if the judge asks something he wants to know, the husband replies: "here is my wife, she knows"; and this to the point that I have had occasion to ask an Indian, and many of them, "What is your name?" and before the husband would answer, the wife would tell it; and so it is in other things, so that these people are submissive to the will of the woman.[140]

While Gómez de Cervantes might be exaggerating somewhat, especially in his concluding remark, it is clear that he found women's active participation in the courts worthy of comment. Criminal records from central Mexico and Oaxaca confirm his observation that married couples appeared together as plaintiffs to pursue cases.

Some criminal proceedings reflect women's active campaigns before native and Spanish officials, such as those described by Gómez de Cervantes. For example, when Juan Clemente killed Juan Agustín in Malinalco in 1626, the victim's mother and wife pressed charges.[141] A Spanish witness testified that Juan Agustín's mother, María Magdalena, attempted to suborn one of the witnesses during the investigation by telling him to repeat what she had told him to say, until the governor silenced her. The governor of Malinalco confirmed the Spaniard's testimony, recalling that he had ordered María Magdalena to allow the witness to testify freely and told her that it was "a great sin" to persuade someone to lie.

Clearly, the household constituted the core social unit in highland Mexico, and its members were tied in many vital ways to the broader community. Especially important to the web of networks was the system of ritual kinship, or *compadrazgo*, that developed over the course of the colonial period.

RITUAL KINSHIP

In early Mexico, ritual kinship relations were created by sponsorship in Christian ceremonies, including baptism and marriage. While the church considered ritual kinship primarily a spiritual bond, in reality it was much more. Such multidimensional alliances fulfilled many of the same functions as the household, extending economic, social, and moral networks beyond the immediate residential group.

The Formation of Kinship Ties

Although colonial compadrazgo relations were established by joint participation in Christian rites, some aspects of ritual kinship may have been rooted in preconquest indigenous tradition. For example, according to sixteenth-century Nahuatl-language accounts, in preconquest times, the Nahuas chose "aunts" and "uncles" for their children at the time of the Izcalli feast, which was celebrated during the eighth month of the sacred calendar. Nahua mothers, who were responsible for choosing their children's guardians, played a prominent role in creating ritual kin relations:

> The mothers would look for an experienced warrior, or a war leader, or a leader of youth; those with children wanted them to act as uncles. Also they sought a woman who would act as an aunt. They gave to the man a pard cloak or a coyote cotton cloak. Also, presents were given, gifts were bestowed upon the woman . . . And there was eating and drinking when they returned to their homes.
>
> *auh in tenanoan ce quitemooaia, iehoatl in tiacauh aço tequioa, anoço telpochiaqui iuh quintlanenequia impilhoaque inic tetlatizque: no ce quitemoa cioatl in teavitiz, quitlauhtiaia: in oquichtli in quimaca, aço quappachtilmatli, anoço coioichcatilmatli: auh no motlauhtiaia, no quitlauhtiaia in Cioatl . . . auh in oniaque inchan, niman ie ic tlatlaqualo, haatlioa.*[142]

The celebrants concluded the ceremony by singing, dancing, and drinking pulque at the temple.

Acts of sociality that extended and legitimated social relations during the Izcalli feast and other preconquest rituals of alliance, including gifting, feasting, and drinking, continued to be used to formalize compadrazgo ties during the colonial period. For example, in the Mixe community of Ocotepec in 1694, Lucía Ana and Juan de Escobar invited the entire community to eat and drink with them in celebration of their grandchild's birth and to honor their daughter's compadres.[143] They considered the pulque that they served to be a "gift to the compadres."[144] Moreover, just as song and dance punctuated the end of the Nahua Izcalli festival, the Ayuuk celebration concluded with singing and dancing to the *teponaztli* (log drum). That the maternal grandparents sponsored the feast suggests that, at least in some cases, ritual kin relations continued to be initiated by women and their natal households.

Like marriage, compadrazgo relations integrated newcomers into an existing community. The life of Diego Hernández demonstrates the ability of ethnic "outsiders" to move into a community and develop ties through ritual kinship.[145] A Nahua trader born in Cholula, Diego settled in Teposcolula in the late sixteenth century, where he and his wife became compadres with a local Ñudzahui couple, Lucas Hernández and Catalina

Hernández. Although Diego's high status as a long-distance trader with ties to prosperous Nahua and Hispanic centers may have facilitated the couple's acceptance, their experience demonstrates that ethnic difference did not necessarily marginalize a person when he or she relocated. Rather, compadrazgo networks, like other forms of social relations, were constantly created and maintained in and across native households and communities.[146] Ritual kinship relations across communities were not only formed by nobles, who had the greatest geographic mobility and the most extensive social, political, and economic ties; they were also widespread among commoners.[147]

Economic, Social, and Moral Alliances

By finding occasions to share a meal together, whether on holidays or in the course of everyday life, compadres maintained and reaffirmed their kinship ties. For example, on Easter Sunday in 1581, Catalina Hernández prepared a traditional Oaxacan feast of turkey mole, tamales, tortillas, and chocolate for her compadre and comadre.[148] Similarly, in 1652 Juan Nicolás, invited his compadres and neighbors in the Nahua community of Coyoacan to gather in the oratory of his household compound to eat and drink pulque in honor of the feast of San Nicolás.[149] Everyday business provided opportunities to strengthen bonds between ritual kin.[150] When a compadre or comadre stopped by to visit, his or her hosts would be sure to offer a meal and pulque as a formal expression of their mutual obligations and friendship.[151] Compadres also brought food to one another when they were sick.[152] Kinship relations were reinforced through terms of address. Thus the terms *compadre* and *comadre* named the relationship between two people, just as kin, gender, and age markers did among other social groups.[153]

Women and men occasionally commented on the affection that ritual kin felt for each other. In 1603, Andrés Bautista described the relationship between his wife and her godmother, recalling that they "were great friends and loved each other very much."[154] Various witnesses who testified in a trial held in the Zapotec community of San Francisco Cajonos in 1678 recalled that compadres Francisco Pérez and Juan Martín had always been good friends.[155] While few people had occasion to articulate their feelings for their compadres in the written record, their actions speak volumes. The many situations in which compadres assisted one another in the course of daily life attest to the strength of the emotional bonds that united ritual kin.

Beyond providing companionship, compadres gave one another economic and moral support. They helped each other with daily work and contributed their labor during peak times of planting and harvesting.

Thus when Juan Clemente, a native of Malinalco, wanted to sow his field in 1626, he asked his compadre and comadre for help and promised to repay them in the future.[156] Women also called upon comadres to help them weave cloth and grind corn for tortillas.[157] Ana Pérez's compadre guarded her house and fields while she attended mass in a neighboring community.[158] Some formed explicit economic ties by loaning their compadres money and by selling goods in local markets for them.[159] In their study of Nahuatl-language testaments from the Metepec jurisdiction in the early nineteenth-century, Myriam Melton-Villanueva and Caterina Pizzigoni found evidence of godparents leaving land in their wills to godchildren along gender lines.[160] Some godparents were even granted custody of their godchildren upon the death of the mother or father.[161]

Compadres often served as intermediaries in marital conflicts and other violent situations. A case from Villa Alta reveals the dynamics between compadres and shows how ritual kin represented a vital aspect of women's networks. In 1651 María Chaves, a Bènizàa woman, fled to the house of her compadres after her husband beat her and threatened her life.[162] When he showed up at the house demanding that his wife return home, both his compadre and his comadre confronted him about the abuse. His comadre, Marta de Acevedo, demanded: "Compadre, why do you mistreat and beat my comadre?"[163] Other witnesses testified to the stern reprimand that Marta gave him. In a similar case from central Mexico, a woman sent a young boy to call her compadre for help when her husband attacked her in a jealous rage in 1723.[164] Like other relatives, compadres chastized men who mistreated their wives and provided refuge to battered women. Women also relied on their compadres' intervention when they found their husbands in danger. For example, Cecilia Sasayu, a Ñudzahui resident of Yanhuitlan, ran to her compadre for help when her husband began to brawl with another man.[165]

A compadre or comadre might even perform one of the most important functions of parents or other family members—arranging a marriage. In Xinastla in 1695, Juan Francisco took responsibility for arranging the marriage of his comadre, María López, a young widow, who placed her future in her compadre's hands when she asked him to look for a man for her to marry.[166]

Many people turned to their ritual kin for support on difficult occasions, including matters of life and death. When Ñudzahui officials of Tamazulapa notified Margarita that her husband had been murdered, her comadre accompanied her to the scene of the crime and consoled her.[167] Similarly, Miguel García rushed to his comadre's side when he learned that his compadre had died. He helped the grieving widow prepare the body for burial and carried it to the church.[168] Comadres and *madrinas* (godmothers) with expertise as healers and midwives often aided their ritual kin in times of sickness. A case from the Mixteca Alta tells of one gravely ill Ñudzahui woman who entrusted herself to her madrina, who attempted to cure her with herbal remedies and a steam bath in 1603.[169] Antonia María, a midwife, attended her goddaughter, Sebastiana María, after a serious fall caused her to miscarry and threatened her life.[170]

As confidants, compadres assisted one another even in the most delicate of situations, as a detailed exchange between two nobles preserved in a 1685 criminal record from the Mixteca Alta shows. When doña Marta de Zúñiga was the recipient of an unwelcomed advance, she turned to her compadre, Luis de Betanzos, for help. Because she was the Ñudzahui *yya dzehe toniñe* (indigenous female ruler) of Yanhuitlan, one of the most important communities in the Mixteca Alta region, and the wife of the powerful don Domingo de San Pablo y Alvarado, she hoped to avoid a scandal. As Doña Marta began to tell how Pablo, a dependent of the household, got drunk on pulque the night before, stumbled into the room where she slept, and tried to rape her, she prefaced her story with an assurance: "Only to you, my compadre, do I speak of [what happened]." She recalled that she fled from the room and locked the drunken man inside, where he was still confined when her compadre arrived. Perhaps to assert her innocence or to show her contempt for the rogue, she told Luis, "If I'd had a dagger or knife I would have killed him." She then politely asked him, "Compadre, would you do me the favor of whipping this Indian [i.e., commoner], Pablo, who is locked in there because last night he tried an offensive act with me?" Her loyal friend agreed to punish the man: "Comadre, I will go to hear mass because as you see, it's Sunday, and then I will come back and do what you order." When he returned, doña Marta gave Luis de Betanzos a cup of *atole* (a beverage made of ground maize) and showed him to the kitchen, where Pablo was being held. Luis proceeded to tie up the accused man and give him a hundred lashes. Witnesses recalled that the avenging compadre even stopped whipping Pablo now and then and talked awhile so he could rest. When he finished, he left Pablo "tied up like a penitent" and bleeding. Later the cacica ordered a *regidor* (councilman on the cabildo) to take the man and leave him on the mountain of San Sebastián to die so that her husband would not find out what had happened.[171]

Throughout the entire episode, doña Marta and Luis de Betanzos addressed one another as compadre and comadre, and the cacica was careful to offer her compadre something to drink when he returned to the palace. The conventions of polite speech and behavior seem almost comical given the awkward circumstances; nevertheless, they were ingrained in the behavior of compadres, especially among the nobility. This extraordinary case illustrates the depth and intensity of ritual kinship ties, for Doña Marta entrusted her secret and the man's punishment to her compadre and he discreetly carried out her wishes.

Ritual kinship networks provided trustworthy allies who served as witnesses on each other's behalf in civil and criminal cases when necessary. Compadres shared genuine friendships, but because they also relied on ritual kin for labor and support, they had a vested interest in keeping them out of trouble with authorities who might impose jail sentences or fines. Both native men and women were called to testify in trials involving serious criminal charges ranging from theft to murder. For example, a mestizo resident of Yanhuitlan, accused of carrying a musket without a license and of having an affair with a local native woman, presented his comadre, a Mixtec woman, as his witness.[172]

Like their humble counterparts, nobles counted on the allegiance of ritual kin when they faced political and personal challenges in court. Andrés Jacobo, a Nahua *fiscal* (church official) had his compadre, governor don Joseph Buenaventura, testify when he tried to win custody of his deceased brother's children in a civil court in Tacubaya.[173] In the second half of the seventeenth century, the Bènizàa yetze of Yatzona was plagued by factional disputes among the ruling nobility, leading to numerous accusations of criminal misconduct. In 1687 don Pablo de Vargas was tried for stealing funds from the town, and in 1695 the Spanish alcalde mayor heard charges against don Francisco de Paz for a litany of offenses, including collecting special taxes, taking fish and herbs from the people to give to his Spanish lawyer, granting the position of maestro to his *tonto* (dimwitted) relative, neglecting the church, ordering that cloth be woven for Spaniards and, ironically, being too litigious.[174] Both men counted their compadres among the list of influential witnesses that they summoned in their defense. Not surprisingly, don Francisco's compadre attested to his innocence and characterized him as a cacique of good customs and a God-fearing Christian. Compadres might also serve as executors of and witnesses to last wills and testaments, expanding their participation in the legal matters of their ritual kin.[175]

Ritual kinship, as a vital part of indigenous social networks, strengthened bonds across households and in some cases across communities. These relationships were critical in enabling indigenous men and women to cope with the challenges of everyday life.

CONCLUDING REMARKS

A household was created through the union of a man and a woman, whether their home was within the residential compound of parents or at a new site. Household members, whether or not blood relatives, formed a family united by their collective experiences of working and living together. Depending on the complexity of the household unit, the presence of other adult relatives or nonkin extended the network of alliances beyond the household and sometimes across community boundaries. Marriage and ritual kinship formalized ties between households, while informal arrangements were sustained by mutual support, collaborative labor, and shared resources.

The Mesoamerican household constituted a unit of production and consumption in which members pooled resources and shared the fruits of their labor. But it was also much more. To a certain extent, the household might be considered a landholding and craft-producing entity, with its members jointly working lands and paying tribute on them, often with textiles. In addition to these economic functions, the household was a moral unit in which adults indoctrinated children in the culture's fundamental values and norms of behavior and in which members monitored one another's activities and transgressions. Of course, the household also constituted a social group whose members shared the joys and difficulties of everyday life. And it was a spiritual place where worship and ritual activities were carried out and where indigenous deities and, in colonial times, Christ, the Virgin, and the Catholic saints, were revered. Among the nobility, the palace was the seat of local rulership, invested with political meaning. Conflict resolution was a dynamic arena for the discussion of cultural values and the articulation of social expectations that integrated the household and the community.

Civil and criminal records document the daily involvement of native authorities in household and local conflicts and offer insights into the dynamics of marriage, family, and community in central Mexico and Oaxaca. Local officials heard disputes within and among households over civil matters involving lands and inheritance and dealt with routine matters such as requests for access to land. They also presided over criminal matters and in so doing decided important issues, such as whether a man or woman should be removed from a household or whether a battered wife could return home to her parents. The extent to which native officials involved themselves in domestic disputes reveals the integration of the household and community. Moreover, criminal and civil records underscore the active role of native women in legal proceedings.

Clearly, the household was the locus of daily life, and therefore women were not isolated, even when they worked in their homes. Burkhart concludes in her study of the symbolic importance of housework in postclassic Mexica society:

To judge women's status by their "public" importance is to miss an essential point: the "public" hardly existed except as a series of replications and inversions of the "private," and vice versa. Concepts of home and home life existed, but these constructs were seen as integrated with the rest of society and cosmos, subject to the same laws and the same disruptions.[176]

My analysis of the economic, social, spiritual, and political life of household builds on Burkhart's observation and shows that the multidimensional nature of the residential compound allowed it to be integrated with the community in significant ways. Thus it should not be understood as a strictly "private sphere."

Ritual kinship allowed indigenous men and women to formalize bonds of friendship and create support networks that extended beyond the confines of the household complex. Ritual kin proved to be faithful allies in good times and bad, with women especially counting on their compadres to help them with their work, to support them in times of need, and to protect them from abusive husbands.

During the colonial period, the enormous strains placed on native households by, among other hardships, devastating population loss, decreasing local autonomy, increasing tribute and labor demands sometimes resulted in collective responses. Although native families and communities exhibited a profound capacity for adapting to and accommodating Spanish demands, the long-term result of these pressures was increasing impoverishment. The economic burdens and social disruptions that native men and women experienced left them little choice at times but to resist the demands of local and Spanish officials. Women played major roles in these confrontations with colonial authorities, both as participants and leaders of local uprisings.

CHAPTER NINE

Rebellious Women

In 1612, a Spanish official ordered several Ñudzahui (Mixtec) nobles to arrest don Tomás de Rojas and four other indigenous magistrates of Santiago Nuyoo on charges that, without proper authority, they had obligated the women of the neighboring community of Justlahuaca to weave cotton cloth.[1] When the men arrived in Nuyoo and announced their business, don Tomás told them to wait. When he finally appeared, one of the men tried to seize him by his cloak. The besieged noble called for help, and all of the women who were working in his palace ran to his aid. They surrounded don Tomás so that the men could not get to him and fought off the outsiders with clubs, fists, and chile powder to blind them. They wounded one intruder so badly that blood flowed from his mouth, nose, and hand, and threw another official to the floor, repeatedly kicking and clubbing him. The outsiders fled the community without taking don Tómas into custody.

The people's devotion to don Tomás did not stop there. A few days later, the Spanish official sent a contingent of Spaniards and a Dominican friar to deliver the viceroy's order that the community recognize and obey don Pedro de Sotomayor, don Tomás' cousin, as hereditary ruler of Santiago Nuyoo.[2] Don Tomás challenged his cousin's ascension to the rulership of Nuyoo, claiming that he alone was the cacique of the ñuu (Ñudzahui ethnic state), entitled to the right to demand labor from the subject community of Justlahuaca. Many men and women gathered in the town square to hear the mandate; they attacked the outsiders with sticks and stones, shouting that they refused to obey the viceroy's decree or accept don Pedro as their ruler. When the friar attempted to calm the crowd, they showed blatant disregard for his authority and pelted him with rocks. Don Tomás and the other officials fled to the church to evade arrest. The Spaniards managed to apprehend several people, but a group from Nuyoo armed with bows and arrows stopped them from taking anyone away. At least for a time, the rebellious women and men had managed to protect the integrity of their community.

The actions of the women (and men) in Nuyoo in 1612 were not entirely unusual. In his study of violence in late colonial Mexico, William Taylor finds that women participated in virtually all *tumultos* (riots) and even led 25 percent of community uprisings.[3] Tumultos were often powerful expressions of local identity and of community solidarity. The patterns that Taylor observes in the late colonial period are evident in the sixteenth century as well. From the time of the conquest, native women struggled alongside men to protect their homes, lands, and communities from real or perceived threats.

Using pictorial manuscripts, civil suits, and criminal records from archives in Oaxaca City, Mexico City, and Seville, this chapter examines indigenous women's participation in community uprisings, lawsuits, and other acts of civil disobedience between 1540 and 1750 in highland Mexico. I do not attempt to quantify the revolts or legal suits. Rather, I use more than fifty cases from indigenous communities throughout central Mexico, the Mixteca Alta, and the Sierra Zapoteca to illustrate women's motives and roles in challenging the subordinate status of indigenous people under colonial rule.[4] I recognize that rioting was just one strategy that women and men employed to remedy their grievances and that there were many subtler, and often more effective, forms of resistance. Nevertheless, the prominent roles that women played as leaders and participants in local uprisings has received limited attention since Taylor noted their frequent involvement. This chapter examines women's active participation in tumultos in the context of their involvement in legal suits and factional politics, and in relation to their labor and livelihood.

PRECONQUEST AND EARLY COLONIAL PRECEDENTS

In postclassic Mesoamerica, warfare was considered the ultimate masculine activity. However, women's regular participation in uprisings during the colonial period suggests that it was not without some preconquest precedent. There is evidence that women played a formal role in war, especially as rulers of local states. Perhaps the best-documented case is that of 6-Monkey, whose life story is most fully recounted in the Codex Selden (Añute), a pictorial manuscript that records the history of some of the prominent ñuu in the Mixteca in the postclassic period.[5] The codex shows 6-Monkey at various points in her life consulting with priests, going into and coming out of hiding, marrying 11-Wind, and leading the conquest of other Ñudzahui ñuu. She is depicted carrying a shield and taking a captive, conveying her role as both a ruler and a warrior (see Figure 9.1). Whether she literally engaged in battle is unclear, but as the local ruler she would have played a defining role in the decision to go to war to protect and advance the interests of her community. Other Ñudzahui female rulers would have faced similar situations. Clearly, 6-Monkey exemplifies an active, powerful *yya dzehe toniñe* (Ñudzahui female ruler), but she is exceptional among women.

More commonly women responded as a group in times of conflict. Preconquest Nahua annals from central Mexico mention two instances when women fought: in 1428 two Tepanec women battled Mexica warriors alongside Tepanec men, and in 1473 Tlatelolcan women fought Mexica invaders.[6] Their ventures into the masculine realm of warfare represented an inversion of gendered spheres of power.

Chronicles of the conquest of Mexico discuss women mobilizing to confront the Spaniards and their allies during the final siege of Tenochtitlan. According to fray Diego Durán, when the Spaniards threatened to retake the island, Cuauhtemoc's military forces had already suffered significant losses due to warfare, disease, and flight from the city.

Figure 9.1. Six Monkey engaged in warfare
SOURCE: Codex Selden (Añute) 8, Bodleian Libraries, University of Oxford, MS. Arch. Selden, A.2.

Cuauhtemoc called on women to dress as warriors and take up posts on the rooftops around the city; he then rallied his remaining men and Tlatelolcan allies to resist the invading forces. The women fought valiantly alongside the men to make one last attempt at defending their home, but ultimately the Spaniards and their allies prevailed.[7] In another pivotal retelling of the final days of the conquest, Tlatelocan women continued to battle the Spaniards and their allies when the Mexica abandoned the fight and let the southern portion of the island fall into Spanish hands. The Nahuatl-language Annals of Tlatelolco record women's fierce resistance to the Spanish invasion of the altepetl. By the time the fighting reached the great marketplace, the Tlatelolcan warriors were "entirely vanquished" but the women refused to surrender: "That was when the Tlatelolca women all let loose, fighting, striking people, taking captives. They put on warriors' devices, all raising their skirts so that they could give pursuit" (*ye ycuac y mocentlazque micalque tlatilulca çiua teuiuiteque tlamamaque tlauiztli onactinenque yn i[n]cue moch cacoquistique ynic vel tetocaya*).[8] These spontaneous interventions during times of crisis, recorded in Nahuatl-language texts and Duran's ethnographic account, prefigure women's physical engagement and stubborn resistance in riots of the colonial period.

COLONIAL STRATEGIES

The documentary record reveals that women tended to rebel against local and Spanish authorities to defend their resources, lifeways, and labor. An increase in the tribute assessment, the removal of a noble from office, disruption of cultural practices and customs, or a disagreement with Spanish friars over church matters were grounds for resistance. Disputes with neighboring indigenous communities over land and resources also led to violent clashes, particularly when attempts to resolve conflicts through the legal system failed. Turmoil over hereditary rights, tribute demands, and the subordination of subject settlements to cabeceras (head towns) engendered deep divisions within colonial communities that could lead to fighting between internal factions to advance their agendas.[9] In turn local officials sometimes accused rival or recalcitrant men and women of inciting rebellion, of being *rebeltosos* or *reboltosas* (rebellious).[10]

Investigations of alleged insubordination sometimes reveal political networks that included powerful women who provided financial resources and leadership to a cause. For example, in 1641 the alcalde mayor investigated the accusation that Pedro de Zarate had organized people to oppose the Ñudzahui nobles of Yanhuitlan.[11] Several witnesses described Zarate as "a rich and powerful Indian" who welcomed "litigious Indians" into his house day and night and helped them bring suit against local officials. Among those named as his closest collaborators was Ana de Meneses, a wealthy Ñudzahui widow.[12] Together Pedro and Ana financed lawsuits and supported Diego de la Cruz, Zarate's cousin, who resided in Mexico City where he pursued their legal cases. These efforts apparently paid off; their critics claimed that they had succeeded in having two officials removed from office; a regidor named Juan de Meraz was forced to leave the cabildo in Yanhuitlan and don Fernando Santoty was relieved of his post of alcalde mayor of Oaxaca.[13] This case provides evidence of women's political influence and shows how women asserted their will by forming alliances with prominent men.

Disagreements with Spanish and native officials over tribute reveal women's gendered interests and demonstrate their attempts to unify as a group to oppose unreasonable demands that threatened them. In 1649 the Spanish *teniente* (deputy) testified that he had confronted doña María de Mendoza and all of the women of the Ñudzahui ñuu of Achiutla, "whose names were too numerous to list," who occupied the plaza in Teposcolula. The Spaniard told the women that they had two hours to return to their homes and warned that they would face serious punishment if they continued to seek justice for the abuses of the alcalde mayor, who they asserted was constantly "demanding things from [them]." Doña María, apparently a cacica or high-ranking *toho dzehe* (noblewoman), led the women in their protest and emerged as their spokeswoman. She may have been responsible for organizing the women's tribute, and in that capacity she led their struggle to seek recourse against the rapacious Spanish magistrate.

Another example of women who fought to protect their gendered labor had occurred in the same area of the Mixteca Alta in 1633. Ñudzahui officials of Teposcolula charged Juana de Mendoza and Magdalena de Alvarado with disobeying the alcaldes and regidores and inciting rebellion.[14] Defending herself, Juana explained that she had only tried to convince some of the women to refuse to provide labor and personal service in response to an increase in the cloth tribute that financed the festival for the local patron saint. She strategically downplayed her activities as an agitator and leader in the hopes of clearing herself of the charges, but continued to challenge the authority of local officials and campaign for tribute reductions. She appeared in the record in 1639, again accused of being reboltosa.[15]

Magdalena de Alvarado used similar tactics to protect herself when she was questioned about her role in the same conflict. Appealing to Spanish sensibilities and assumptions in order to diminish her responsibility, she said that "as a woman" she had been persuaded to defy cabildo authorities by Lorenzo de la Cruz, a local noble who had encouraged the women to resist the tribute increase.[16] In fact, she was not so naïve. Magdalena understood that Spanish judges could overrule the orders of the ñuu cabildo, so when local magistrates were not responsive to the women's requests to reduce the tribute, she appealed to the alcalde mayor. She testified that she "wanted to excuse herself of the duties that the alcaldes assign them, so she colluded with the other 'yndias' of her pueblo with the intention of using the alcalde mayor to try to resist what the alcaldes had mandated."[17] Her statement reveals not only an acute awareness of the multiple levels of the colonial bureaucracy but also a strategy of using the Spanish judge to undermine the authority of native officials. The very system that instituted the exploitation of women's labor, Magdalena knew, simultaneously curtailed the autonomy of indigenous officials. But she firmly denied that she had been rebellious, insisting that she had advocated before the officials "with good words." She distinguished between her actions, which she felt had been dignified, and those of rioters, who used offensive words to express their resistance. The case suggests that community factions were at times organized along gender lines and emerged over women's duties and responsibilities.

In his study of the Cuernavaca region, Robert Haskett finds ample evidence of women's leadership roles.[18] One case involved doña Josefa María Francisca, a Nahua noblewoman who led a faction that agitated for twenty years to abolish the obligation to send people to Taxco to fulfill the mining repartimiento. According to one witness, "She makes the speeches and leads in pursuing the litigation."[19] As a wealthy widow, like Ana de Meneses of Yanhuitlan, doña Josefa used her personal wealth to finance legal suits in the viceregal capital. Significantly Ana de Meneses, doña María de Mendoza, Juana Mendoza, Magdalena Alvarado, doña Josefa, and many more women like them, engaged in long-term campaigns to seek justice for themselves and their communities. Their protracted struggles reveal an understanding of the colonial bureaucracy, strategic alliance building, and an ongoing commitment to challenging onerous demands.

Use of the Legal System

Whenever possible, communities or factions within pueblos appealed to colonial authorities to address their grievances. Some natives even wrote directly to the crown, but their eloquent appeals for justice often fell on deaf ears.[20] When a burden became too much to bear, native communities initiated lawsuits over a broad variety of issues, including requests for restoration of traditional political authority, a reduction in tribute, exemption from providing labor, punishment of Spaniards who mistreated natives verbally and physically, and compensation for damages to lands and crops.

Scholars have shown that indigenous leaders and officials quickly learned to use the legal system, often to their own personal advantage or to the benefit of the ethnic states that they represented. Ethelia Ruiz Medrano's study of indigenous communities from early colonial times to the present, using both written and pictorial evidence, demonstrates that pueblos engaged in a complex process of political negotiation. She concludes: "In some cases the history of the pueblos, as appropriated by the pueblos themselves, serves as an important marker of identity as well as a political weapon by which the pueblos can improve their present condition and gain hope for the future."[21] This participation in legal proceedings throughout the colonial period, informed by community memory, gave rise to a hybrid juridical and political system that to some extent accommodated local practices within the larger framework of Spanish American law.[22] In turn this participation shaped social memories of interactions with colonial authorities that later resurfaced in local riots and disputes.

If they hoped to succeed, litigants were forced to hire Spanish lawyers to bring their cases before the *Real Audiencia* (Royal Court) or the viceroy.[23] They needed to be patient and persistent because the court was slow and certain types of evidence and testimony had to be gathered. As costs mounted and cases dragged on, some litigants inevitably lost their resolve and grew impatient. Communities did sometimes win favorable settlements, but it was often at great expense, and lasting justice ultimately depended on the opposing party's compliance with court rulings.

Legal suits filed by indigenous communities frequently registered multiple complaints, including unfair tribute practices and abusive behavior.[24] The case records document the heavy toll that male commoners especially paid; however, they also frequently denounce the exploitation of women as spinners, weavers, cooks, and domestic servants. A pictorial manuscript painted by an indigenous artist on behalf of the Nahua altepetl of Tepetlaoztoc in the mid-sixteenth century reveals early clashes between native communities and Spaniards over the payment of labor and goods in the first few decades after the conquest. For example, Figure 9.2 shows women grinding maize and the enormous number of men (twelve hundred) required to carry goods as porters.[25] Other pages in the manuscript document exorbitant amounts of cloth paid in tribute, illustrating the high demand for women's labor.[26] Figure 9.3 shows eleven mantles woven with flowers, a load of *mantas ricas*, and four loads of simpler cloth that were paid to the Spanish encomendero, who redistributed the goods in

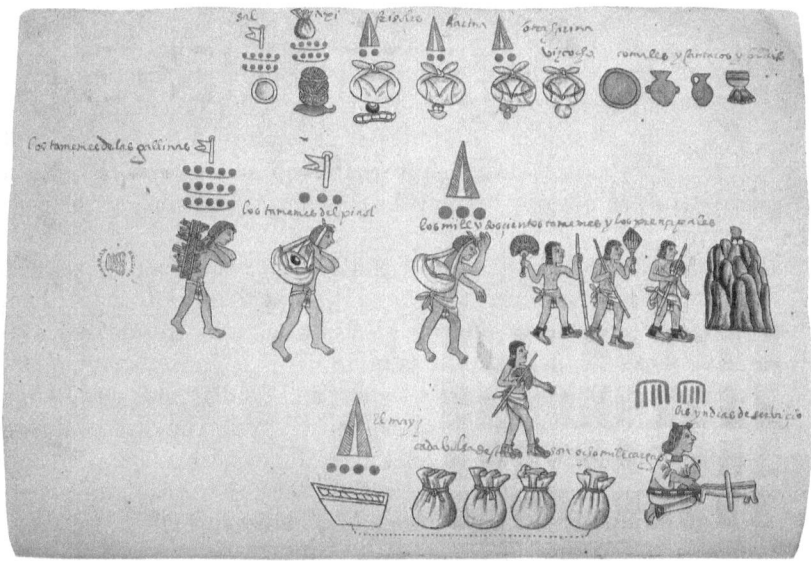

Figure 9.2. Page from the pictorial manuscript presented in litigation by Tepetlaoztoc over excessive labor demands on the community
SOURCE: Codex Tepetlaoztoc (Codex Kingsborough), fol. 12. British Museum, London.

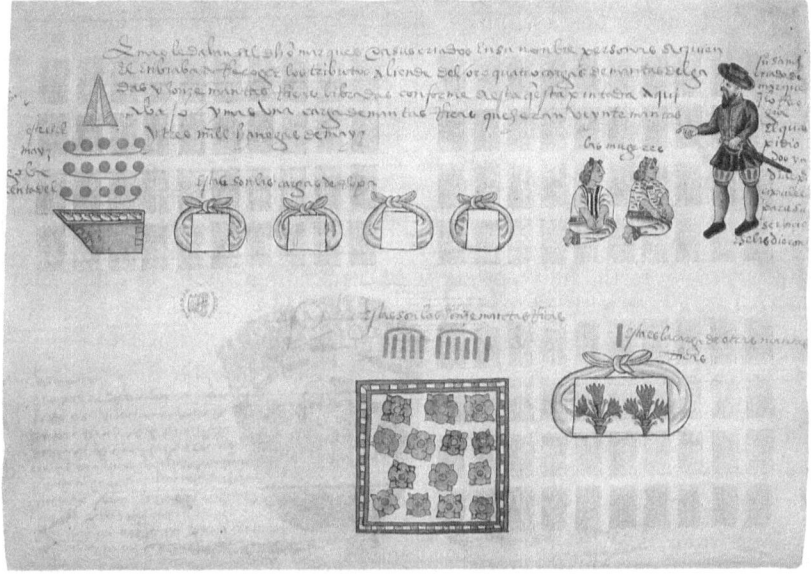

Figure 9.3. Page from the pictorial manuscript presented in litigation by Tepetlaoztoc over excessive labor demands, showing cloth as payment in kind
SOURCE: Codex Tepetlaoztoc (Codex Kingsborough), fol. 8. British Museum, London.

the market for a profit. In addition, the image shows two *indias principales* (Indian noblewomen) who were given to Juan Sánchez, a servant of Cortés, "for his service." Manuscript depictions of the beating and execution of local nobles demonstrate that indigenous people challenged the use of violence as a way to force the community to comply with Spanish demands.

Although male nobles and officials initiated civil suits, petitions sometimes named women and men as plaintiffs, recognizing both as partners in protest. For example, documents filed in a suit over tribute in Tlaxiaco in 1633 specifically mention as plaintiffs the "Indian commoners and Indian women" (*macehuales e yndias*) and "Indian men and Indian women" (*yndios e yndias*) of the community.[27] Even when women were not specifically named, frequent references in lawsuits to spinning and weaving underscore the importance of their work to the economic well-being of their households and communities and their vested interest in litigation.

Women were barred from holding seats on the local cabildo; nevertheless, they sought to influence which men would hold office. For example, several women appeared among the plaintiffs in a complaint in Teposcolula in 1641.[28] Pedro de Chávez, Reymundo Hernández, María de la Cruz, Elena Hernández, and Elena López alleged that although Reymundo de Zarate, a principal, had been elected *alguacil mayor* (head constable) by the pueblo, Pedro Hernández had the *vara* (staff) of office. They demanded that the alcalde mayor intervene and return the staff to Zarate. In this case, women took an active part in the struggle over local electoral politics.

The confrontation in Justlahuaca that opened this chapter illustrates a typical labor dispute heard in colonial courts: a Ñudzahui noble of Santiago Nuyoo used his power to force women to spin cotton for his own profit. However, the noble privilege of demanding labor was often intertwined with local politics. In this 1612 case, rivals of don Tomás de Rojas accused him of distributing cotton to the women in Justlahuaca and ordering them to spin thread.[29] Don Tomás's right to make these demands was contested as a result of an inheritance dispute over the rulership. The women had a stake in his political status, which structured the relations of Nuyoo with other indigenous communities in the Mixteca and affected its labor obligations, specifically. If don Tomás could compel the women of Justlahuaca to spin thread, the women of Nuyoo would likely be freed from the task. In this case, the colonial labor regime pitted commoner women of different communities against one another.

While many cases involved inter- or intra-community disputes, others involved lawsuits against Spanish alcaldes mayores for obligating women to spin cotton and wool and weave cloth. For example, in Achiutla in 1601, Ñudzahui men and women complained that the alcalde mayor, working through local officials, forced them to spin cotton, work silk, and weave textiles for his own gain.[30] In 1613 the town council of Teposcolula filed charges against the alcalde mayor for compelling people to spin large quantities of cotton and coercing them to sell cochineal at a low price.[31] In 1647 three major Ñudzahui communities again accused an alcalde mayor of Teposcolula of ordering women to spin cotton without compensation.[32] In the Villa Alta district in the mid-seventeenth century, as many as four thousand indigenous people denounced the abusive policies of a particularly avaricious alcalde mayor.[33] Exploitative repartimiento and tribute practices by Spanish alcaldes mayores in Tehuantepec, Nexapa, and Villa Alta led to extensive petitioning and widespread rebellions in Oaxaca in 1660.[34]

Most often women and men resorted to violence only after they had exhausted other means of redress. In a riot over tribute in Mexico City in the mid-sixteenth century, don Luis Santa María Cipac told an angry crowd that the cabildo had on numerous occasions tried to persuade the Audiencia to reduce the tribute obligation but to no avail:

And when we [the cabildo officials] heard what the commoners would have to pay in tribute, then because of this we conversed, all of us went before the Royal Audiencia and before the lord judges. And many times we appealed it; in vain we countered it, and it could not be done. And many times we assembled in the cabildo to discuss it, but it was not possible that it [our appeal] would endure, it [the new tribute assessment] was confirmed. Yesterday again it was judged, on Wednesday, 13 of July, in the year of the birth of our lord Jesus Christ, mentioned above. And another time it ended with their decision to reject [our request].

yn iquac oticacque ynic tlacalquizque in machehualtzintli niman yc otitononotzque timochintin otiaque yn ixpantzinco Audiencia Real yvan ymixpantzinco in tlatoque oydores auh miecpa in apelacion oticchiuhque yn oc nen yc titlacuepa aocmo veliti yhuan miecpa inic otitocentlalique in cabildo hitic ynic otitononotzque çan niman aoc hueliti yehica ohuelchicahuato oneltic auh yalhua ye quene ohueltzontec miercoles ypan XIII de julio auh in xihuitl çan ye no yehuatl in tlacpac omoteneuh yn itlacatilitzin yn totecuyo Ixesucristo auh yn iquac otzonquiz yn intlacuepaliztlatol.[35]

According to don Luis, the justice system had failed the Mexica and Tlatelolca time after time because Spanish judges refused to consider their appeals and so there was no remedy.

The Oaxacan uprisings in 1660, precipitated by the murder of the alcalde mayor in Tehuantepec, exemplify the despair of cabildo officials and community members caused by authorities' indifference to their suffering. Before the rebellion, officials from the region had sent numerous contingents to Mexico City seeking justice, but they had been denied entrance to the Audiencia chambers, lawyers had refused to sign their petitions, and judges had declined to hear their cases. The officials of Nexapa wrote to the archbishop of Oaxaca, their one staunch ally, to ask if they should send yet another group to Mexico City, confiding: "Once again no one will help us; only God and you, our sainted bishop."[36] Their exasperation recalls the frustrations of the cabildo of Mexico Tenochtitlan a century earlier when they, too, lost hope that their problems would be resolved through the legal system.

An incomplete record of an uprising in Tlaxiaco in 1598 reveals the many protest strategies that the community had employed prior to the disturbance.[37] In their terse confessions, several of those arrested for participating admitted to having donated money to bring a case against the Spaniards for "mistreatment." Only after their attempts to seek legal recourse had failed did they revolt and break down the doors of the jail.

Patterns of Violence

When they did resort to violence, indigenous rebels relied on whatever weapons they could find and used their sheer numbers to overwhelm Spanish or native officials from outside the community. Most often they threw rocks and brandished clubs, but many also engaged in pushing and shoving, fistfighting, and kicking.[38] In the case from Nuyoo that opened this chapter, the Ñudzahui women even used ground chile powder to blind royal officials, and in a conflict with neighboring communities, the Bènizàa (Zapotec) women of San Andrés Yaa threw dirt in their enemies' faces. Sometimes opponents were attacked with cactus branches. Many riots led to attacks on sites of royal authority, especially the local jail. Rioters often broke down the doors of the jail or set fire to the municipal palace; sometimes they vandalized the homes of Spanish crown and church officials.

Indigenous-language terminology for uprisings emphasizes the violence that was often directed against officials and sites of government. Variations of the verb *tlatetepachoa* (throw stones) appear frequently in Nahuatl-language sources concerning rebellions.[39] While throwing stones at officials and government buildings was in fact a common act of defiance, it was also highly symbolic. Stoning was the punishment administered by indigenous officials to adulterers, drunkards, and thieves in preconquest times, all crimes associated with immorality and deceit. By stoning the palace and colonial authorities, those who were discontent turned the justice system on its head and symbolically punished the officials for their excesses and deception. In his *Vocabulario*, Molina lists the words *comonia* and *tlaltecuinaltia*, both meaning start a fire, which brings to mind the depiction of a burning temple to convey the conquest of a place in pictorial writings.[40] In colonial uprisings, the municipal palace, the jail, and the homes of authorities were often set on fire, suggesting a symbolic conquest and a temporary inversion of the political order. Forms of *comonia* and *tlaltecuinaltia* also mean "agitate people" and "make people fired up." Other verbs reveal the rioters' anger and frustration. In colonial annals, *ixnamicoa* (confront someone) and *huel tlatohua* (protest strongly) convey the acts of challenging magistrates and social superiors and of shouting defiantly at them.[41]

The sources often describe the people becoming angry using the verb *qualania* and threatening violence by striking their mouths with their hands while shouting, or making battle calls (*netenhuiteco*).[42] Whereas Spanish sources tend to describe protesters as unruly mobs harassing royal officials because they have lost respect for the King's justice, indigenous-language sources more clearly show men and women taking action because of their pent-up frustrations, deep resentments, and justified anger.

The prominent role that women played in physical and verbal confrontations is striking. Women fought and often occupied the front lines, goading the enemy with taunts. In a dispute over land in the Villa Alta region, one man recalled that a woman had approached him and pulled his moustache before a more serious assault began.[43] During riots women hurled insults, and witnesses frequently commented on their use of fighting words.[44] In one clash, women called the people clearing a contested meadow "dogs."[45] When a conflict erupted in Atepec in 1659, the Spanish official reminded a crowd of enraged Bènizàa women that he was the *corregidor* (chief Spanish judicial and administrative officer of a district) and that he held the royal staff of office. Ana la Caxona, who led (*capitaneava*) the protestors, defiantly responded that he was not a corregidor "but rather a piece of trash" and threatened: "Give us our alcalde, or we will kill you!" When the governor attempted to intervene and calm the crowd, she jeered: "Go on, dog! Since you eat and drink with the corregidor, you defend him."[46] Similarly, Ñudzahui women in San Miguel in 1719 unleashed a torrent of insults at Spanish officials and threatened to refuse to pay tribute if the officials did not release their cacique.[47] The uproar was so intimidating that the teniente summoned all Spanish residents with their weapons and placed in *deposito* (the practice of detaining women in the household of a local Spaniard) "the women who shouted the most and lost respect for the royal justice." In 1722 the women and men of Santiago Tiyyu besieged Spanish officials who had entered the town looking for the governor, stoning them and shouting: "We want nothing more than that all of you die."[48] The fact that women became more infuriated when Spanish officials reminded them that they represented royal justice reveals their sense that the system did not serve them. Rioters' words, intended both to offend officials and to spur on fellow protestors, reflect intense dissatisfaction with the colonial system, especially with local Spanish officials.

Indignant crowds also taunted royal authorities in the famous 1692 Mexico City uprising. According to don Carlos de Sigüenza y Góngora, a prominent *criollo* (American-born Spaniard), who witnessed the unrest, the trouble began when native women became outraged over the viceroy's mismanagement of the maize supply at the granary, uttering "insolent, impudent, vulgar words." As pushing and shoving began, the women's shouts became raucous. After one woman was seriously injured, more than two hundred others rushed to protest in front of the viceroy's palace. A rowdy crowd assembled, and according to Sigüenza y Góngora, the women "instigated [the riot]," suggesting their leading role in mobilizing resistance with persuasive speeches. Soon a full-scale uprising was under way and the multiracial throng threw stones at the Spaniards, set several government buildings on fire, and looted merchants' shops, all the while shouting: "Death to the virrey! Death to the virreina! Death to the corregidor! Death to the Spaniards! Death to bad government!"[49] Their provocative cries for the execution of the viceroy and his wife suggest that they saw them as a ruling couple. Thus the indigenous demonstrators, if we are to believe Sigüenza y Góngora, expressed a racialized understanding of colonial inequities, when calling for "death to the Spaniards and *gachupines* (those who have come from Spain), who are eating our maize!" Sigüenza y Góngora also attributed a clear political consciousness to the women, who he claims shouted in Nahuatl: "At them, ladies! Let us go joyfully to this war, and if God wishes that the Spaniards be destroyed in it, it will not matter that we die without confession! Is this not our land? What are the Spaniards doing in it?"[50] Some even mocked the Spaniards and emasculated them: "Swinish Spaniards, the fleet has arrived! Go to the shops, little girls, to buy ribbons and hairpieces!"[51] Regardless of the accuracy of his account, Sigüenza y Góngora's recollection of powerful words, public taunts, and protest chants as key aspects of the confrontation corroborates archival accounts of resistance in Mesoamerican communities.

Tumultos could erupt spontaneously, or they could result from coordinated plans. A conflict with the alcalde mayor fueled repeated riots in Achiutla in the first half of the seventeenth century. On one occasion in 1649, the alcaldes organized a very large demonstration, mobilizing more than fifteen hundred men and women of the community to travel to Teposcolula to protest before the Spanish judge.[52] A witness remarked that it was "customary for the alcaldes of the community to hate the alcalde mayor," an observation that, in part, explains why there was sustained opposition to the authority of the Spanish magistrate in the region. The mid-seventeenth-century rebellion in Nexapa following the murder of the alcalde mayor in Tehuantepec was another large-scale, coordinated action. Some leading members of Calpulapa, Nesiche, and Analco attempted to build a coalition against the highest-ranking local Spanish official, in letters to native authorities of other communities inviting them to participate in their conspiracy to kill don Joseph de Reynoso, their alcalde mayor, just as the people of Tehuantepec had when they murdered their Spanish magistrate.[53] The revolts in Tehuantepec, Nexapa, and Achiutla defy the notion of the spontaneous peasant revolt. Many local riots appear unplanned on the surface, but most resulted from decades of grievances and frustration.[54]

Insults and acts of resistance reflect the breakdown of sociopolitical relations within and among ethnic states. Legal records reveal the many reasons for indigenous revolts, the cultural and social values that shaped their actions, and the economic and political issues at stake. The following section examines a representative selection from the archives.

Colonial Economic Relations

Tribute and labor institutions were at the very core of native-Spanish interaction throughout the colonial period. From the time of the conquest, Spaniards demanded payment in goods and services from subjugated natives. Furthermore, the dramatic loss of life due to epidemics, warfare, and hazardous working conditions, among other threats, shifted the responsibility for tribute obligations onto a shrinking population base.

While the colonial tribute system had been built on preconquest institutions and practices, within a few decades the Spaniards had implemented changes that would dramatically alter economic relations in New Spain. Spanish officials had restructured the original tribute system by the 1570s by increasing tribute assessments and restricting the types of goods accepted as payment to maize, wheat, cloth, and gold or silver pesos.[55] As labor demands increased, people were required to work for longer periods and were forced to travel greater distances to work. For some groups, this meant new and potentially dangerous labor in silver mines or the *desague*, a project to drain the lake around Mexico City.[56] Other groups, which had been exempt from the obligation, were required to pay tribute for the first time.

The Annals of Juan Bautista reveal emerging tensions in the mid-sixteenth century over the excessive tribute demands in Mexico City. Based on his translation and analysis of this Nahuatl-language text, Luis Reyes García concludes that the conflicts "suggest the confrontation of two different economic modes of thought, the traditional indigenous versus the colonial Hispanic, that is to say, the system of economic redistribution versus mercantile capitalism."[57] Women and their labor were often at the center of clashes between traditional modes of production and colonial mercantile capitalism.

Women contributed a broad range of services and goods to meet tribute obligations. They cooked for men working on construction projects and worked alongside men in fields belonging to the community, local nobles, and Spaniards. They also ground corn and provided domestic labor in the homes of Spaniards and indigenous nobles. In many places, women's most valuable contributions continued to be spinning and weaving; however, over time Spaniards demanded not only indigenous clothing but also simpler cloth that would be sold to make household furnishings, bedding, curtains, awnings, and inexpensive clothing for African slaves and indigenous commoners.[58] Cotton textiles produced in Oaxaca were often resold for profit in markets in Mexico City or in the silver-mining regions in the north.[59]

At the same time, indigenous officials traditionally relied on commoner labor to finance the community's daily business and religious activities.[60] A Ñudzahui official confirmed the value of cloth in 1596 when he confessed to distributing cotton to women of the community for weaving because "the pueblo was impoverished and needed to raise money."[61] Even as Oaxacan communities began to pay tribute in money rather than goods, funds were often raised by cloth production and sale.[62] The Spanish demand for cash forced indigenous people and communities to participate in the emerging money economy of New Spain and the Atlantic World.

Through the tribute labor system and other semiformal arrangements, Spaniards and local magistrates especially profited from women's labor as weavers.[63] Spaniards contracted cloth production on a community basis by working through native officials and nobles. Spanish investors provided the cotton and negotiated the price of the finished product, and local officials took responsibility for organizing production, distribution, and collection of the finished goods. In one of many examples, a representative of a Spaniard traveled to the Zapotec town of Talea to collect cloth in 1676, accompanied by a different indigenous official in each distinct *barrio*.[64] In exchange for their role as intermediaries, the cabildo and/or nobles kept a portion of the payment collected from the Spanish investor, allegedly for community expenses.[65]

Using a system known as *repartimiento de efectos* (division of goods), Spanish magistrates and merchants distributed goods, including mules, oxen, cotton, and agricultural tools, to native communities or individuals and then collected payment for them, plus interest, at a later date.[66] Colonial cloth production was part of this system in Oaxaca, where Spaniards provided raw cotton (which they monopolized) and paid below-market rates for the finished cloth.[67] Although Spanish law prohibited alcaldes mayores from engaging in economic activities in their jurisdictions, the alcaldes circumvented these restrictions and came to monopolize the textile and cochineal dye trades.[68] In 1751 the Crown conceded that the repartimiento system was rife with abuses, but justified and enforced it as the only way to induce indigenous people to produce and consume goods.[69]

Legal or not, Spaniards took advantage of their relationships with local indigenous officials to acquire goods produced by women which they resold in urban centers, such as Mexico City and Oaxaca, where ties to the transatlantic exchange network were strongest. The lucrative trade in cloth and cochineal dye made the Villa Alta *alcaldía mayor* (post of alcalde mayor) one of the most profitable and attractive in New Spain.[70] Colonial commentators estimated that before 1787, when reforms were instituted, women produced between fifty thousand and two hundred thousand mantles each year in the Villa Alta district alone.[71] The alcalde mayores' responsibilities as tax collectors and their investment in local production blurred the lines between tribute and repartimiento goods.[72]

Merchants often established financial partnerships and agreements with alcaldes mayores; some specialized in importing cotton from coastal regions that the Spanish officials distributed to women to spin and weave.[73] Profiles of typical traders in Oaxaca illustrate the link between regional production and transatlantic trade networks. For example, one Spanish resident of the Ñudzahui town of Yanhuitlan who made a living trading cloth and local sugar, chocolate, and vanilla, left a modest estate valued at two hundred twenty pesos when he died in 1695.[74] On the other end of the spectrum was one of the most important merchants in the Mixteca Alta in the seventeenth century, who exchanged textiles from Spain and New Spain as well as sugar from Oaxaca. He also owned an agricultural estate where he raised sheep, a store where he sold goods, and multiple houses in Puebla and Teposcolula. The net worth of his estate in 1701 when he made his last will and testament was 53,727 pesos.[75] Several Spanish traders documented their vast mercantile networks, showing that local products were part of the international trade system. Francisco de Acosta, born in the North African town of Ceuta, resided in the Ñudzahui community of Teposcolula in the mid-seventeenth century, where he sold local goods, products imported from Spain and the Philippines, and slaves.[76]

Spanish and *mestiza* (a woman of native and Spanish descent) women also participated in trade. In the early seventeenth century, Isabel Jiménez, for example, invested in a mercantile company with her brother that exchanged cloth from western Oaxaca for Spanish wine in Veracruz, the principal port linking New Spain to Sevilla.[77] Similar cases are found in the Zapotec regions of eastern Oaxaca. In 1665 a Spanish captain named don Manuel de Pedraza shipped a hundred and thirty mantles along with other indigenous products from Villa Alta to his business partner in Mexico City.[78] Likewise, don Josef Martín de la Sierra, a resident and local official of Villa Alta, traded cloth and native cacao, vanilla, and wax in the 1680s and 1690s.[79]

By the late eighteenth century, the Spanish Crown had implemented reforms that outlawed the repartmientos de efectos. Intendant Mora y Peysal, a Spanish official who supported the legislation, conceded that cloth production through repartimiento had unjustly exploited women and noted that women who did not deliver the finished products on time were sometimes imprisoned.[80] A proponent of trade reform, he argued that indigenous people would continue to generate cash by selling in regional markets. Even when women produced cloth that they sold independently, however, they were forced to sell at unjustly low prices that were fixed by Spanish officials.[81]

Scholarship on repartimiento de efectos in New Spain has acknowledged that coercion was a fundamental part of the system. Some scholars have argued, however, that it allowed indigenous people to purchase goods and livestock that they would not have been able to buy without the advancement of credit.[82] Indigenous officials sometimes engaged in this system of production and trade to raise money for their communities. Missing from studies on Oaxaca is the recognition that the burden of production often fell on local women, not on the male officials who worked out the agreements with the alcalde mayor and Spanish merchants. Abuses in cloth production are but one example of the ways that colonial labor regimes exploited indigenous women. Conflicts over tribute and repartimiento de efectos were the result of changing economic systems, but the hardships were not evenly shared by all.

Tribute and Community

From the early colonial period on, nobles and commoners objected to the Spaniards' excessive demands for tribute and labor. The Nahua intellectual Chimalpahin described an uprising in Mexico City in 1564 after Jerónimo Valderrama imposed a royal tribute of four tomines during his *visita* (inspection tour). Tensions over tribute had been brewing since the early 1550s, and this new fee was the final straw. Chimalpahin reported the Mexicas' outrage and their violent response: "The Mexica, the men and the women, stoned the tecpan of San Juan because they did not consent to pay the tribute; they went about very angry, and they strongly protested" (*Ye Yhcuac yn tlateepachoque yn tecpan San Juan yn mexica yn toquichti yhuan yn cihua yn amo ciaya tlacallaquizque; cuallania, huel tlatohuaya*).[83] The mention of women is significant. According to Chimalpahin, the Tlatelolca rioted in the same year against the imposition of a headtax: "And in their annales, the Tlatelolca say that in this year of 7 Tecpatl began the tribute of one peso and two tomines per head; and the 11th day of October, in Tlatelolco they resisted the alcaldes, they stoned them" (*Auh yn tlatilulca, yn iuh ypan quitohua yn inxiuhpohual, ca quitohua ypan in yn VII Tecpatl xihuitl oncan otzintic y tlacallaquilli, cecen peso ypan oome tomin yn mocha tlacatl; yn Tlatilulco ypan yc XI mani metztli octubre yn oyxnamicoque yn alcaldesme, otetepacholloque*).[84] Protests against indigenous officials reveal commoners' exasperation over their leaders' failure to defend the community against Spanish demands.

The Nahuatl-language Annals of Juan Bautista discuss the controversies that led to the uprising in Mexico City and the events that followed. Although the Mexica cabildo had appealed repeatedly to the Royal Audiencia to reduce tribute, the Spanish judges would not reconsider. The cabildo's ineffectiveness made matters worse, and in 1564 several artisans petitioned the Royal Audiencia to consider charges against the governor and the cabildo officers alleging that they had committed idolatry and abused the repartimiento system by using laborers for personal service.[85] Artisans and scribes working in the church also insisted that their labor was a type of tribute and that they should not be obligated to provide additional service or pay anything more.[86] Moreover, Spaniards demanded that adolescent women and men pay tribute, which violated the rule that young people contribute only after they marry and thereby become adults. The Annals record the growing resentment and desperation of those saddled with paying tribute and providing labor. They include several examples of women organizing as a separate faction, including a group of widows who opposed the *zacate* (grass, hay) tribute.[87]

When the tlatoani and governor, don Luis and the Mexica cabildo announced that the Spaniards would not reduce the tribute and that the people were expected to meet their obligations, there was rebellion. Several men made impassioned speeches about the failure of the nobles and called for violent resistance. In what appears to have been a highly symbolic call to arms, "all of the elder women wept and they grew very angry" (*auh ixquich çihuatl yllamatzin chocaque yhuan cenca quallanque*).[88] Because elder women were considered moral authorities and keepers of tradition, this reaction signaled that defiance and outrage were justified. Soon a full-scale riot was under way on the streets and plazas near the ruler's palace. The rioters stoned the tecpan, and a group of women broke through one of the outer walls of the palace precinct. Don Luis escaped the chaos with his life only because Spaniards armed with swords dispersed the seething crowds and took several protesters as prisoners.

As some women and men became bolder in expressing their disdain for the cabildo officials, Mexica authorities became increasingly repressive over the following days and months. According to the Annals, two days after the riot, don Luis ordered the singing of the Chalca Women's Song, in which, according to Kay Read and Jane Rosenthal's translation and analysis, a ruler's concubine "[tries] to make a claim for a different relationship based on her historical lineage. Through titillation, humor, sometimes a few insults, a few veiled threats, some offers of help and reminders of his royal responsibilities the Chalcan songsters [tell] Axayacatl [the Mexica ruler] that they want their status improved."[89] This complex and provocative song contains multiple messages and must have been understood differently depending on one's perspective. In this case, it seems to have expressed the desire of don Luis and the members of the Mexica cabildo, who had been stripped of their autonomy and authority and thus symbolically reduced to concubines, to be considered equal partners in the viceroyalty. Like the Chalcan concubine who pleads that her "historical lineage" justifies reconsideration of her secondary status, don Luis, grandson of the legendary Mexica ruler Ahuitzotl, believed that equal status was his birthright. He must have understood the irony, for the cabildo had clearly expressed the hope that it would be considered an ally, not merely a subject, of the Spanish king. The song also may have warned the Spaniards that failure to create an alliance could lead to war.

Immediately following the song, beams were carried in from the market that could be used to tie up and whip prisoners "so that no one would speak badly of the governor" (*ynic ayac q[ui]chicoytoz gou[ernad]or*).[90] The Chalca Women's Song and the punishments were reminders for don Luis's critics that they had been conquered, both by his own noble forebears and the Spaniards. Some Mexica and Tlatelolca protesters were placed in stocks; some were given as many as two hundred lashes or were sold for periods of two or five years; others were imprisoned or banished from the altepetl.[91] The *tlacuilo* (scribe, painter) wrote that while the tribute was being debated, several women continued to resist:

And they whipped a poor woman who protested then and [as for] another poor woman who had left, an alguacil pursued her, shoving her. And through a window, the governor yelled to the alguacil to tie her up to the column. And there in the patio of the jail he mistreated people. And the alguacil kicked another poor woman, and blood flowed from her body.

Auh ce çihuatzintli tlananquiliaya niman oncan quimecahuitecque yhuan occe çihuatzintli hualquizca ce topille quitopeuhtinenca auh ventana hualtzatzic in gouernador quihualito xiccalaquican xiquilpican temimiltitech auh oncan nemimictiloc yn ithualco carçel. Auch oc no ce çihuatzintli quicuitlapanic çac alguazil niman oncan ezquiz yn nacayo.[92]

Later "again those who did not want to pay tribute were imprisoned, they put them in irons" *(auh ye no cepa huel onilpiloque yn amo quimanaznequi tlacalaquilli tepuztli quintlatlalilique)*.[93]

The tlacuilo, by focusing on the officials' harsh punishments of both men and women, clearly sympathized with the protestors. Tensions over tribute and subsequent uprisings were significant enough that indigenous scribes, including Chimalpahin and the authors of the Annals of Juan Bautista, recorded them in their histories as some of the most important events of their time. The strong animosities unleashed by the new tribute obligations left a lasting impression on Mexica social memory.

Although most conflicts involved native or Spanish officials, they sometimes erupted over disputes with local Iberians. In the Ñudzahui ñuu of Tlaxiaco in 1610, for example, the teniente found himself in the middle of a bitter struggle between the local population and the Cisneros family.[94] While investigating complaints about the family's abuses, he asked the governor and alcaldes to gather all the commoners so he could take their testimony. At the core of the dispute was the accusation that the Cisneroses were using three men to provide labor and tend sheep and one woman to grind maize for eight-day periods, paying them only a nominal wage.[95] In addition, several men and one woman asserted that the Cisneros's livestock was destroying their fields. The people became irate over the teniente's handling of the negotiations for compensation because the family patriarch refused to pay more than half of the damages that had been sought. Several people began to ridicule the teniente and make threatening battle cries by slapping their hands to their mouths.[96] The tension escalated into a riot in the presence of the cabildo officials, who made no attempt to stop the commoners from expressing their discontent. Rather than resolve the issues at hand, the exasperated teniente filed a request for punishment of the rioters. Again, the legal system and the intervention of Spanish authorities failed to deliver justice to the indigenous plaintiffs.

One case from Malinalco sheds light on how colonial tribute demands destabilized indigenous households, sometimes leaving women to support their children and communities on their own.[97] In the first half of the seventeenth century, demands for tribute and labor became so burdensome that many men fled Malinalco to avoid them, burdening abandoned wives with paying the tribute, tending the household's fields, and raising the children. Some who remained in the community tried to organize a campaign of resistance. In 1641 the governor, don Juan de Escobar, filed a criminal complaint against several individuals, including Jusepe Guexolotl, Juan Quauhnochitl, Miguel Tepexcatl, and Juan Tlacochi, accusing them of being rebellious for having persuaded fifty commoners to refuse to pay tribute. Additional charges were brought against these men and others for having collected money for a lawsuit against the governor over the labor tribute.[98] The Nahuatl surnames of the men betray their humble status, suggesting that the colonial system could aggravate class tensions. This case, like many others of the period, documents the dissolution of reciprocal ties between commoners and nobles, whose contested relationship dating to preconquest times was becoming increasingly strained by changes under Spanish rule. As married women assumed additional responsibilities in their husbands' absence, they, too, became more vocal in local politics and in matters concerning economic relations.

Factional disputes over tribute obligations sometimes culminated in violent uprisings in which women were involved. A detailed examination of a case from Tamasulapa in the late seventeenth-century shows that resentment over perceived injustices could fester for months or even years, and that commoner men and women engaged in dialogues about tribute with native and Spanish officials. In 1686 don Fulgencio de Santiago, the indigenous governor of Tamasulapa, and Pedro de Palma, an alcalde, informed the alcalde mayor that a group of about one hundred men and women had rebelled against another alcalde, Blas de Ayala, and taken his vara while he was overseeing their work in a wheat field.[99] One of the *tequitlatos* (tribute collectors), mocking the disgraced official, paraded the vara high above his head. A witness recalled that the tribute collectors had argued with Ayala because he always criticized how they did things and because he made the people work too much.

The cabildo officials from Tamasulapa recalled that many furious *yndias e yndios* had gathered at the municipal hall once before and that don Fulgencio had said at that time that they could not just take the staff away from an alcalde. Don Fulgencio asked them to put their grievances against Ayala in writing and promised that the cabildo would consider them. Following the uprising, a large group of *yndias y yndios* assembled before the alcalde mayor and insisted that they wanted another man, Juan Rodríguez, to serve as alcalde, but don Fulgencio explained that he could not appoint Rodríguez until he had examined the case against

Ayala. When they heard this, the men and women became very agitated and refused to leave until Juan Rodríguez was appointed. The alcalde mayor realized that he had no other choice if he wanted to maintain the peace, so he reluctantly gave the vara to Juan Rodríguez on the understanding that the arrangement was provisional. The people also charged that Ayala, mayordomo of the cofradía of Our Lady of the Rosary, had absconded with the confraternity's funds. The men and women brought out a wooden box that belonged to the cofradía and demanded that don Fulgencio open it to check the contents.

As tensions mounted in Tamasulapa, Spaniards in the community could see that only the intervention of the native authorities would calm the disgruntled crowd. The increasingly frustrated men and women returned to the convent, many carrying rocks and protesting loudly. The alcalde mayor, his scribe, and some friars fled for protection inside the convent, but some rioters used axes to try to break down the door.

Again, the alcalde mayor demanded that the governor, don Fulgencio, and the alcalde, Pedro de Palma, go out to pacify the angry crowd. Apparently they succeeded in dispersing the protesters long enough for the alcalde mayor and his group to go by horse to check the market. When the Spaniards returned to the municipal palace, the alcalde mayor announced that he intended to arrest the governor and alcalde for refusing to help resolve the matter. He also decided to take Ayala to Teposcolula after an elder delivered a threat from a group of men and women that they would set fire to the jail in Tamasulapa and burn Ayala in it if don Fulgencio was taken away from the community. The protestors insisted that if the alcalde mayor had something to say to "their cacique and governor," he could say it to him in their pueblo of Tamasulapa. Many men and women continued to shout and demonstrate as the Spaniards attempted to escort Ayala out of the jail. When the alcalde mayor ordered a Spaniard to tie up one of the native officials (likely don Fulgencio), the crowd began throwing stones, pelting the Spaniards with so many rocks that they were not able to arrest the governor and the alcalde and were forced to flee. By the time the rioting was over, one man was dead, many people were injured, and two houses, including Ayala's, had been set on fire. Fearing for the safety of the friars who remained in the convent, the alcalde mayor sent ten armed men to protect them.

When the alcalde mayor later dared to return to Tamasulapa, he discovered that the governor, the alcalde, and several other leaders of the uprising had gone into hiding. The Spanish magistrate ordered that the body of the man who had been killed be hung in the plaza and that three women who had played leading roles in the uprising be tied up and lashed fifty times. After further investigation, the alcalde mayor brought formal charges against ten men and seven women for taking the staff of office from Blas de Ayala and for disrespecting royal justice.[100] Don Fulgencio, cacique and governor, was arrested for failure to assist the alcalde mayor. The initial conflict that began when the tequitlatos took Ayala's vara occurred on June 4, 1686; the tumulto took place the following day. It was not until March 5, 1687, nine months later, that several nobles and officials appeared on behalf of the accused to post bond and secure their release from prison.[101]

The violence in Tamasulapa shows how the colonial system had placed native officials in a difficult position. On the one hand, traditional relations between nobles and commoners were conceived of in familial terms so that local rulers were considered parents ("the father, the mother") of the community, who ideally protected commoners from excessive Spanish demands. On the other hand, the Spaniards allowed the nobles to retain their positions of authority in their communities only as long as they delivered the required tribute payment on time. If they failed to do so, their own goods could be confiscated and they could be removed from office. In most instances, communities did their best to provide the required labor and tribute. However, if the people considered the demands unreasonable, they often simply refused to comply, sometimes even abandoning their settlement when they knew that the census taker would be coming.[102] This was a short-term solution at best.

At times local officials feared rebellions in their own communities. When the cabildo of Teposcolula failed to provide workers to serve in the Dominican convent in 1597, an alcalde argued with one of the friars and told him that the convent could find its own workers because the people were fed up with serving the Spaniards and the religious.[103] Clearly the irritated alcalde had grown tired of enforcing policies that benefited the Spaniards to the detriment of the community and its people.

Women and men might turn against their own leaders if those leaders failed to improve conditions. The spectacular demise of don Luis Santa María Cipac, last Mexica governor of Mexico Tenochtitlan, suggests the tragic fate that might befall nobles who could not negotiate effectively with Spanish officials. As discussed previously, don Luis had appealed to the Royal Audiencia to have the tribute reduced, but his futile attempts made him completely irrelevant and the target of a lawsuit.[104] Many of don Luis' critics suspected that he and other officials had sought only to protect their traditional privileges and had not represented the interests of the broader Mexica and Tlatelolca populations. According to Chimalpahin, people mocked the disgraced governor, calling him *Nanacacipactzin* (Mushroom Alligator). Evoking memories of the conquest, Chimalpahin commented:

The Mexica placed the nickname Nanacacipac on him to defame him, because he had accepted without contradiction that the Mexica pay the tribute, showing himself to be weak and cowardly; as if it were still in the time of the lord Moteucçomatzin, who did not confront the Spaniards and allowed them to imprison him and place him in irons in his own home without putting up resistance.

Ynic ytoca mochiuh Nanacacipac çan temahuizpololiztica ynic cahuiltocayotique mexica, çan ipampa yn quiceli ynic tlacallaquilli quimana mexica, ynic atle contradicion quichiuh, yece quemach nen tlapaltic chicahuac yezquia; yntla ocachi huey tlacpac catcaya yn itlahtocayo Moteuhcçomatzin, yn amo huel quimixnamic españoles, ye conilpico contetepoçotico yn çano ychan, yn atle ychicahualiz mochiuh.[105]

In the eyes of the enraged Mexica and Tlatelolca, don Luis resembled Moteucçoma, who had conceded to the Spaniards' unceasing demands for more wealth and services and who had suffered the humiliation of losing his autonomy and authority. The sobriquet "[hallucinogenic] mushroom" might mean that the people considered him to be deluded, confused, and disoriented rather than clear-headed, effective, and persuasive.

According to the Annals of Juan Bautista several months after the tribute uprising, when his palace had become a target of the people's anger, don Luis responded in a most dramatic manner. He outfitted himself for war, went up to the roof of his tecpan carrying his shield, and danced and made battle cries all night. His elaborate warrior costume, covered in precious feathers, would have evoked memories of Mexica imperial power and its control over vast resources through tribute and trade. Apparently in a state of utter despair, he fell from the roof to his death, bringing an end to Mexica glory on his own terms. In his final hours, he dramatically displayed his knowledge of traditional noble culture and asserted his masculinity by performing the dance of the ruler. He distinguished himself from Moteucçoma, who famously appeared on the roof of the palace to order the people to comply with Spanish demands, reminding them of their military glory perhaps to encourage continued resistance. In the new war with the Spaniards over labor, resources, and the privileges of the nobility, don Luis, like a warrior in battle, danced himself to death.

Protecting Lands and Resources

In skirmishes over land, water, and other natural resources women, as active members of the community, struggled to protect local interests. One such confrontation occurred in the Ñudzahui estancia of San Andrés, when several men from nearby Texupa, accompanied by don Gabriel, a noble, passed through town carrying wood that they had cut to build a church.[106] Following elite protocol, don Diego Pacheco, cacique of San

Andrés, invited don Gabriel to eat with him. As the nobles shared a meal, some local youth celebrating Carnival began to joke and tease the men from Texupa. Although the circumstances are not entirely clear, at some point the joking turned to fighting. According to fray Antonio de Almedina, vicar of Texupa, the people of San Andrés attacked the men from Texupa with clubs and shouted at them. Two men from Texupa died, and three or four were critically wounded. The following Saturday several armed men from Texupa came to San Andrés. They tried to take eight large wooden beams stored in the church patio, perhaps as compensation for the deaths of their men. Women from San Andrés fought off the intruders, shouting: "If you want to take our beams, pay us for the tortillas and piñol and [the cost of] the transportation to our husbands."[107] Their statement recognized the joint contributions of men and women to community projects, for like the men, the women had sacrificed their time and labor to obtain wood for their church.[108] They succeeded in protecting the resources of the community, acquired through their concerted effort, and drove the men away.

Conflicts over contested land were common among communities. Spanish attempts to resolve them sometimes only made matters worse. When the people of Sayultepec and the neighboring communities of Santiago Tillo and San Andrés Xinastla assembled to verify lands in 1683, bitter hostilities came to a head.[109] According to several witnesses, the people of San Matheo Susuquitepec refused to accept the alcalde mayor's decision awarding lands to San Juan Sayultepec. The men and women of Susuquitepec arrived at the site armed with clubs and rocks, assaulted and insulted several people, seized and broke officials' staffs, and imprisoned one of the magistrates.

Communities occasionally encountered outsiders who threatened to invade or damage their fields or other communal enterprises. In 1615 in the Ñudzahui estancia of San Felipe, a subject settlement of Teposcolula, violence erupted when several Spanish shepherds attempted to herd sheep through the community's salt beds, which were vital to San Felipe residents, who raised money to pay tribute by working them collectively.[110] When the Spaniards began to trespass, a large group of women ran out to defend the salt beds and drive the livestock away. One woman, Magdalena Naqua, tried to grab the reins of one of the shepherds' horses, but the mounted Spaniard began beating her. When her husband came to her defense, the Spaniard drew his dagger and stabbed him in the hand. Magdalena's husband later testified that the women who were present saved his life by fighting off the Spaniard. When the shepherds accused the women of having killed two hundred sheep, apparently in a ploy to have the community punished, the investigating official found no evidence to support their claim and dismissed the charges. The women's actions in San Felipe attest to the important role they played in defense of the estancia's resources.

A case from the Sierra Zapoteca provides another example of women fighting with neighboring rivals over contested lands. A large group of Bènizàa women from San Andrés Yaa attacked the people of San Melchor Betaza and Santo Tomás Lachita in 1728 when the latter began clearing lands that bordered their yetze to build a small ranch for the alcalde mayor.[111] For more than twenty years, the community of Yaa had maintained that the land, where a church had once stood, belonged to them, and they refused to accept the alcalde mayor's ruling that granted the land to Betaza and Lachita, insisting that only the Royal Audiencia should decide the case. They must have been doubly concerned that if the alcalde mayor resided next to their community, he would burden them with demands for goods and services and interfere in their business.

Nahua women played a leading role in an uprising in Ocuila in 1746 after learning that the Royal Audiencia had awarded disputed lands and water resources to the Jesuits, with whom the community had been engaged in several costly legal suits over resources.[112] While the court considered the case, the women prayed to Ocuila's patron saint, San Antonio, for protection. Members of the community were outraged when they learned that the Royal Audiencia had awarded the disputed lands to the Jesuits. They became agitated and the women, whose prayers had gone unanswered, began to throw rocks. The church bells tolled, calling the people to the center of town. As tensions escalated, the women stormed the Jesuits' refectory where they destroyed the kitchen, smashed the dishes, and trashed other belongings. That they vented their rage on the convent refectory was no coincidence since it was the site of much of their labor tribute to the church.[113] Furthermore, the sharing of food and drink continued to be a highly symbolic social and political act that represented cooperation and mutual support. By destroying the refectory, the women defied their obligation to work there and signaled the termination of their duties of sustaining and caring for the Jesuits, responsibilities that were central to reciprocal relations between the community and the Company of Jesus. By breaking the cooking pots and dishes in the refectory, they were quite literally breaking off their relationship with the Jesuits.

In addition to highlighting concerns over land and tribute, legal investigations resulting from colonial uprisings often reveal popular understandings of class relations and commoners' expectations of their nobles and rulers.

Protection of Local Officials

Witnesses who testified in the colonial courts frequently extolled the virtues of local rulers or nobles. Although their statements are not to be taken at face value, they do reveal cultural attitudes regarding the characteristics of an ideal leader. Noble birth, community service, a good reputation, and an exemplary life were highly valued. Within two generations after the conquest, the qualities attributed to rulers and nobles came to reflect a mixture of native and Spanish values, which had overlapped from the beginning. For example, in 1563 witnesses described don Francisco de Arellano, the Ñudzahui cacique and governor of Tecomastlahuaca, as "a good Christian, of a good life and fame" who "provides a good example to the commoners."[114] Bènizàa men and women of Yagayo used similar terms to characterize their cacique and governor and his father in 1696, recalling them as men who had served the community by holding office on several occasions, who lived peacefully and well, and who cared for the church and served the king.[115] In addition, social norms dictated that indigenous elites look after the landless or orphaned, the poorest of commoners. According to a questionnaire completed in the late sixteenth-century, it was customary for a native noble who saw a destitute, naked person to feed and clothe him.[116] Nobles often adopted the indigent and orphaned as dependents, employing them on their lands and in their households. As one Nahua governor testified in the mid-seventeenth century, people frequently came to him begging for assistance, and he hired them to work on his estate, which included agricultural lands, a wheat mill, and a bakery.[117]

Because class and political relations were conceived of in familial terms, Nahuas metaphorically referred to a ruler as "our father, our mother."[118] Like loving parents, nobles were expected to care and provide for the people of their community as though they were members of their household. In 1559 the Ñudzahui people of Tonaltepec praised don Domingo, the son of their cacique and heir to the rulership, affirming that he was a devoted Christian and a man of good repute, who "very much loved his macehuales."[119] In a community in the Mixteca Alta in 1563, witnesses testified that the cacique, don Francisco de Arellano, had never mistreated his people and that he "loved" the people of Igualtepec (a subject town) just as he "loved his own commoners."[120]

Conversely, unpopular leaders were characterized as exploitative and abusive. Although many charges of mistreatment by officials involved factional disputes, it is telling that such accusations were frequently rooted in terms of class conflict. In a typical case from the Mixteca Alta in 1596, people complained that the regidor forced them to contribute funds, allowed others to pay a fine to escape community labor service, and disparaged the commoners by calling them *perros esclavos* (slave dogs).[121] Similarly, in 1670 opponents of don Francisco de Chávez, the Bènizàa cacique of Lachichina, accused him of abusing and intimidating his macehuales.[122] Commoners frequently criticized native authorities who did not pay them fairly for their labor or provide them with food. The people of Malinalco asserted in 1635 that the cabildo officials underpaid them and "they never gave them meat to eat, only a little bit of cooked beans and two or three tamales to each one" when they forced them to sow wheat.[123] Failing to provide food did not simply mean inadequate compensation; recall that feeding was a fundamental act of caring for another person, giving such charges great symbolic weight.

Like good parents, Mesoamerican leaders defended their people and communities. The Nahuas spoke metaphorically of their rulers as "shade, protection" (*in pochotl, in ahuehuetl*; "the silk tree, the cypress"). Throughout the seventeenth century, the expectation was that nobles would protect their people and the community's interests. Throughout central and southern Mexico, local officials had always been responsible for organizing labor; however, by the mid-sixteenth century commoners increasingly complained that they were forced to work on Spanish estates and enterprises, which violated the basic premise of communal labor that commoners would not be sent outside of the pueblo to work. Thus in 1685 the people of Atlacomulco, a Mazahua community in central Mexico, praised don Francisco, who they believed as "their principal and cacique" would help free them from the excessive burdens of labor in the mines.[124] Charges that officials neglected their duty to guard the community from Spaniards' onerous demands demonstrate commoners' expectations of protection. In 1628 the people of San Jerónimo, a subject settlement of Coixtlahuaca, denounced their governor and fiscal (native church official) for routinely sending fifteen men and one woman each week to serve on the estate of the friars of Coixtlahuaca and for punishing those who did not comply.[125] These examples illustrate that colonial obligations undermined idealized relations between native nobles and commoners, and eroded the authority and wealth of indigenous elites.

In communities where the relationship between caciques, local officials, and community members remained mutually beneficial, men and women strongly opposed the imprisonment or removal of their leaders. Indeed this was the central issue that led to rioting in Tepozotlan in 1556 following the viceroy's order unseating the alguaciles of the estancias of Tepuxaco, Quahuila, Acpan, and Xobo.[126] When the men and women gathered, many said with "anger and resentment that they would not obey the mandate."[127] The frustrated crowd attacked the Tepozotlan alcaldes and a Spaniard with rocks, digging sticks, clubs, and cactus branches. The conflict involved Tepozotlan's relationship with several outlying settlements that the Spaniards had designated as estancias, meaning that they were subject to Tepozotlan's authority. The men and women of these so-called estancias rejected their subordinate status and insisted on their right to elect their own officials.

The very same issue that led to violence in Tepozotlan was at the heart of a dispute in the Mixteca Alta in 1583. Ñudzahui officials of Teposcolula notified the Spanish alcalde mayor that in the estancia of Santiago there were several "rebellious Indians, who were agitated and anxious, and who were friends of lawsuits and discord," including don Domingo, Domingo García, and Diego Pérez.[128] The men planned to travel to Mexico City to litigate their secession from the cabecera of Teposcolula and had collected money as well as tortillas and piñol from the women to sustain them on their trip. They insisted that the community should be designated a cabecera because it had a ruling couple, don Pedro and doña Juana, which made the community a yuhuitayu. Thus don Pedro and doña Juana should collect the tribute and send it directly to Mexico City rather than funnel it through Teposcolula. By Domingo García's own admission, the community leaders had been trying for three years to win Santiago's independence from Teposcolula. Although he denied having collected money, he admitted to having used some community funds to finance several trips to Mexico City. The fact that several witnesses from the estancia testified against don Domingo and the others suggests that some were not willing to continue supporting what appeared to be a losing cause. The financial burden of pursuing the case and internal factionalism had eroded community solidarity. Both doña Juana, the female ruler, and the commoner women who were pressed to provide provisions for trips to Mexico City and tribute to Teposcolula, had vested, although perhaps differing, interests in the outcome of the case.

Women participated in factional politics by resisting Spanish rulings that favored opposition groups. In 1639 a Spanish official reported that more than one hundred women had rebelled against royal authorities in a prominent Ñudzahui community in Oaxaca. He recalled that the shouting women ("with a few men among them") rushed out of the cacique's house and attacked a native official who was escorting a prisoner out of the community on orders from Spanish authorities. The angry crowd mobbed the magistrate, shouting insults and "offensive words" and managed to free the prisoner. The women began to beat and kick the magistrate and witnesses testified that they would have killed him if several Spaniards had not come to his rescue. Fearing that the uprising was not an isolated incident, the Spanish official stated that just a few days earlier the women had beaten another native magistrate and had broken his royal staff when he delivered several rulings against some of the cabildo officers. A Spanish resident who witnessed the onslaught verified the account and concluded: "The Indian women were rebellious, having lost respect for justice."[129] As in the case from Nuyoo that opened this chapter, women expressed their support for local officials whom they felt Spanish authorities had dismissed. Furthermore, women emasculated officials when they beat them, insulted them with "offensive words," seized their symbols of authority, and broke their staffs.

Cultural conflict was a root cause of many uprisings. For example, Franciscan friars of the convent of Calimaya filed a legal complaint in 1711 against the Nahuas of Chapultepec and Mexicalzingo accusing them of preventing the friars from saying mass, expelling the religious from the community, and intimidating them by "mistreating them with words and pushing and shoving them."[130] According to the friars, these "yndios" were "poorly instructed" and did not want their children baptized. When the teniente and some of his men went to Chapultepec to investigate, he brought a Franciscan friar to say mass. The friar asked the alcaldes to open the church and call the people to the service by ringing the bells, but the local officials refused to comply. Instead, they said that they would arrange for a friar to come from Toluca and cut the bell cord. The teniente promptly arrested the alcaldes. Not easily deterred, the friar set up his portable altar of San Miguel in the church cemetery and proceeded to say mass. Not a single Nahua man or woman was present. After the friar finished, the Spaniards mounted their horses and began taking their prisoners out of town. Just outside of the altepetl, many native men and women from Chapultepec and Mexicaltzingo ambushed them with rocks and clubs, badly injuring the Spaniards and freeing the alcaldes. The original source of tensions between the Franciscans and the communities of Chapultepec and Mexicaltzingo is not clear. However, this episode reveals communities' use of passive resistance in the locals' refusal to attend mass or have their children baptized and in the alcaldes' refusal to toll the bells to call the people before church and crown officials. Men and women of Chapultepec and Mexicaltzingo resorted to violence only when the Spaniards began to remove the alcaldes from the pueblo.

In the Ñudzahui ñuu of San Miguel, a sujeto of Teposcolula, women vehemently protested the imprisonment of their cacique, don Diego de San Miguel, and his removal from the community in 1719.[131] When the teniente arrived with an order from the Bishop of Oaxaca to arrest don Diego, the cacica and other women became frightened and agitated. Soon six or eight of them had gathered and begun to shout at the Spaniards that they should not take don Diego away. By the time the Spaniards left with their prisoner, the majority of women from the community had gathered to harass them, following them all the way to Teposcolula in defense of their cacique. The charges against don Diego are not known, although the order to arrest him came from the Bishop of Oaxaca so it may have concerned a spiritual matter. Interestingly, the women assumed that his troubles were financial, and they appealed to the Spaniards' monetary interests, offering to pay any debts the cacique might have to win his release. When that did not work, they threatened to refuse to pay tribute to the king. The women's defiance prompted Spanish officials in Teposcolula to summon all Spaniards to appear with their weapons. To quash their protest, many of the women were arrested and held in the Spaniards' homes.

Women's awareness of political developments in their communities is difficult to gauge given that they were not allowed to participate in formal political institutions or processes. However, incidental evidence in criminal cases sheds some light on this issue. For example, when a scuffle broke out in Yolotepec between an alcalde, the priest, and the priest's household staff, all the women rushed out of the municipal hall, where the people had gathered to hold an election, to protect the alcalde.[132] At least on this occasion, it appears that women were present at elections even if they did not participate in them. The women blamed the community's troubles on the two men and one woman who worked for the priest, so about twelve women rushed to the priest's house, locked him in a room, and then fought with his servants, throwing them all into the street and shouting that the community would be better off without them. One man and the woman fled the community, but the women seized the other man and demanded that the cacique punish him with lashes for spreading rumors, which he did. Spanish officials intervened in the conflict, arrested eight women, and imprisoned them. On their release, an interpreter read them a royal decree that ordered them to obey the priest and threatened to send them to an obraje if they refused to comply.

Riots might result from the mistreatment of any community member, not only high-ranking officials. On Easter Sunday, Pedro Sánchez, the alguacil mayor of the Ñudzahui community of Achiutla, ordered the *alguaciles menores* and some commoners to arrest don Andrés de Alabéz, a high-ranking Spaniard who had served as corregidor of the jurisdiction of Papaloticpac. At the time of the riot, don Andrés was alcalde mayor of the province of Igualapa.[133] He had come to Achiutla to administer justice in the community. When he attempted to force Pedro Sánchez to rent him a horse and he refused, Alabéz struck him. As the conflict escalated, Alabéz and his servants threatened to draw their swords and daggers. Domingo de Silva, a local Ñudzahui noble, shouted to the alguacil mayor

Rebellious Women 293

and the others to arrest Alabéz, whom he referred to as a *bellaco* (scoundrel). The Ñudzahui officials tied Alabéz's hands and took him and his two servants to jail. A friar who was present, fray Diego del Rio, began to argue with the agitated crowd, reminding them that don Andrés was a "great gentleman and was married to the niece of the marshall of Castille, their encomendero."[134] Interestingly, he appealed to Ñudzahui sensibilities of the importance of marriage alliances with prominent women as a source of power. Despite the friar's pleas and warnings, the Spaniard and his servants remained in custody.

When the alcalde mayor heard about the incident, he was furious that the alcaldes had not reported it to him directly. He arrested and imprisoned several men from the ñuu for initiating an uprising against the Spaniard. In their defense, the officials said that they had tried to resolve the conflict on their own. Several testified that they had wanted to free the Spaniard and his pages but the large crowd of macehuales had been so agitated that they did not dare do so. Of course, the alcaldes' account may have been a convenient excuse to detain the Spaniards for a time, but it also suggests that men and women would not tolerate officials who caved into the Spaniards when they threatened a member of the community. After several hours had passed, the alcaldes brought the Spanish prisoners and the offended Ñudzahui officials up on the roof of the municipal palace. There they negotiated peace among all parties in the presence of the community and the friar, who with don Andrés assured them that the matter would be dropped and that the alcaldes would not report it to the alcalde mayor. This assurance was probably given in exchange for a safe exit from the town; someone did report the uprising to the alcalde mayor, and there is little reason to believe that it was anyone from Achiutla.

CONCLUDING REMARKS

Records of uprisings in indigenous communities in New Spain, legal suits over tribute assessments, and other acts of resistance document the tensions created by colonial rule. Indigenous women had a stake in the survival of their communities and in the defense of their livelihoods, which at times led them to confront male officials, whether Spanish or native, often as a unified group. Such disputes demonstrate that colonial demands sometimes turned communities against Spaniards as well as turned indigenous groups against one another. This chapter has challenged the characterization of tumultos as spontaneous outbursts by showing that they were often the result of long-term struggles. Through periods of simmering tensions, as communities sought legal redress of their grievances, indigenous women and men developed a consciousness that guided their understanding of political and economic relations with colonial authorities.

Although Taylor notes women's widespread participation in tumultos, his study did not examine the motivations and concerns that drove women to riot. In fact, he surmises that "because men were more often traveling outside the community or working fields several miles from town, more women than men usually took part."[135] I argue that the reasons that women participated in uprisings were varied and complex; it was not simply the absence of men that forced them to challenge outsiders. In his study of women's opposition to colonial authorities and demands, Haskett notes: "The objectives of rioting were often as political in nature as otherwise, and there may have been more to some of these activities than meets the eye."[136]

This chapter has expanded on Haskett's observation and shown that indeed there was much more to women's actions. Records of conflicts shed light on women's gendered interests in the local organization of production, the processes of exploitation that developed with the expansion of the transatlantic economy, and the consolidation of colonial rule. Women and men expressed concerns in court proceedings and in local protests over the amount of tribute that they paid and the conditions in which they labored. Indigenous leaders recognized the value of women's labor and tribute contributions to their own communities and to the colonial regime. Petitions over tribute assessments were written on behalf of the men and women of the community, and many included complaints about excessive demands for labor and goods that women produced. Women's work complemented men's labor and was essential to the undertaking and completion of community projects. Heavy tribute burdens and exploitative production practices tied to the emerging transatlantic trade and the tribute system galvanized conflicts between commoners, local officials, and Spaniards. Both men and women sought to assert control over their labor by resisting the Spanish and native authorities who exploited them.

Legal suits and uprisings reveal women's concerns about the resources and lands that made life in their communities sustainable. Women's participation in collective enterprises often placed them at the scene of conflicts over land and resources with Spaniards and neighboring indigenous communities. Women held lands privately and as members of households, and therefore participated in efforts to recover losses that resulted from damages to their crops and to protect plots whose ownership was contested.

Cultural expectations of reciprocal relationships between nobles and commoners shaped indigenous responses to increasing economic burdens, dramatic changes, and challenges to local political authority. Whereas nobles and officials were expected to mediate demands for labor and tribute goods on behalf of commoners, commoners were in turn obligated to protect the status and authority of the community's leaders. Men and women both resisted the removal of respected magistrates from office and insisted that unpopular officials be ousted. Women's participation in riots and lawsuits over the autonomy and authority of local leaders had clear political implications. Their actions, which spoke to the right to exact tribute from other communities or to secede from cabeceras, affected the status of their pueblos in the colonial hierarchy. Defiant acts, such as breaking the vara of an officeholder from a rival faction or stoning Spanish officials, were overtly political gestures that revealed women's anger toward colonial authorities. Their participation in these conflicts illuminates their awareness of broader political and financial issues that defined the Spanish reorganization of native communities in the sixteenth century and beyond.

Finally, this chapter has challenged the common assumption that native women possessed little political influence in New Spain. While women were not allowed to hold cabildo offices, their participation in litigation, riots, and other acts of resistance had political significance. The testimony by women, and about women, who were accused of inciting and participating in rioting and who sought legal recourse for perceived injustices reveals a political consciousness that has been overlooked or undervalued.

CHAPTER TEN

Conclusion

Focusing specifically on the Nahua, Ñudzahui (Mixtec), Bènizàa (Zapotec), and Ayuuk (Mixe) peoples, the chapters of this book feature narratives about women's lives and experiences in the first two centuries of colonial rule in central and southern Mexico. They address a number of distinct but interrelated topics, including gender roles and identities, concepts of the body, women's labor and duties, the significance of marriage, nuptial customs and ceremonies, sexual attitudes, family structure, household-community relations, and women's participation in riots and other acts of civil disobedience. By focusing on women, rather than on a particular region or ethnic group, I have identified cross-cultural similarities and differences in gender ideology and relations among highland societies.

Throughout the work, I have sought to examine a broad range of sources that are available to historians and ethnohistorians of women in Mexico. My analysis of complex gender relations over time and across regions proceeds from an unusually rich and diverse corpus of original sources that come from more than a hundred communities. These include Ñudzahui-, Tíchazàa-, and mainly Nahuatl-language civil and criminal documents, published texts, linguistic materials, and Spanish legal records and other Spanish-language texts. I have also analyzed and interpreted preconquest and colonial pictorial manuscripts. Indigenous women are omnipresent in the colonial archive, and I hope that scholars will see the potential for future studies using the same types of sources that I have used.

Whereas much indigenous language–based research has studied change at the community level and has considered Spanish-native interactions through colonial institutions, this work contributes to that literature by examining social dynamics and cultural practices in households, mainly in rural communities. In his monumental study of the Nahuas, Lockhart comments: "One would like to know a great deal about what went on in the households and among kin . . . not only to appreciate Nahua humanity, but to learn how principles of social organization worked themselves out in everyday life, which would bring in turn a better understanding of these principles, their evolution over time, and conflicts between them."[1] My study sheds light on the dynamics between men and women in the household as they lived and worked, celebrated and struggled in their daily lives. By shifting the focus to the household, it illuminates women's important contributions to their families and communities. The interdependence of women and men, nobles and commoners, and households and communities becomes clearer with each successive chapter, as do the conflicts arising from failure to live up to the ideals of complementary and reciprocal relations.

This book contemplates the ways that gender identity was socially constructed in Mesoamerica through specific duties, behaviors, and bodily adornment. In central Mexico and Oaxaca, Nahuas and other indigenous groups conceived of the body as inherently unstable and linked the origins of personality to the calendar rather than to biology. Whereas in many European cultures the body served as the origin of gender identity and personal attributes, Mesoamericans seem to have downplayed it. Mesoamerican concepts of nahualism and tonalism reveal indigenous interpretations of the body as a dynamic entity that undermined the development of defining characteristics based on biological difference. Mesoamericans did not consider men to be more intelligent, rational, or capable, or women to be inherently emotional, nurturing, or immoral. The concept of the "weaker sex" did not dictate gender relations.

Despite the absence of essentialist ideology, throughout central Mexico and Oaxaca social constructions evolved over time to establish binary opposites. Labor, clothing, and speech genres demarcated male and female in native culture. Gender-specific clothing, hairstyles, forms of speaking, ways of sitting, and the tasks and tools associated with the gendered division of labor were among the most prominent markers of masculinity and femininity. These associations retained their significance throughout the colonial period, and ethnographies of the region demonstrate that they continue to do so today in many Mexican communities. Because of gender fluidity, cross-gendering was possible through the adoption of the clothing, speech patterns, and duties of the "opposite sex." Unfortunately, the historical record does not shed much light on how frequently this might have occurred or the circumstances under which reassignment was possible. Cecilia Klein, Pete Sigal, and Guilhem Olivier show that in certain ritual contexts Nahuas disrupted this gender binary and used gender ambiguity to signify disorder and creation.[2]

One's gender identity and social status dictated one's roles and responsibilities. Significantly, tribute duties corresponded to the idealized division of labor during the colonial period. Rituals that reinforced gender distinctions justified the organization of labor to the state and provided sacred significance to these socially constructed roles. Through encomienda (approximately from the 1520s to the 1560s) and repartimiento (from the 1560s on), women worked in the fields and homes of native nobles, local Spaniards, and ecclesiastics, performing tasks such as grinding corn and preparing tortillas. They often contributed to their households' tribute assessment in cloth and yarn, continuing to raise money by weaving and selling cloth in many regions even after Spanish tax collectors began to demand tribute payments in cash. Indigenous officials sometimes distributed cotton and wool to be spun into yarn and woven into cloth in order to raise funds for the community. Thus the local state, its ruling elite, and colonial authorities profited from the gendered division of labor (and by extension, a binary gender system) by making it the basis of the tribute system.

This book also underscores the symbolic, social, and economic value that the people of highland Mexico placed on goods produced by women, especially cloth and food. In Nahuatl metaphors, cloth symbolized life and food and drink represented sacred offerings. Throughout central Mexico and Oaxaca, cloth and food were exchanged at life-cycle rituals and included in offerings to deities and saints. Thus the fruits of women's labor were used to establish and maintain reciprocal relations among the people and between the people and their deities. Cloth and food also had significant economic value; both were used to pay tribute and to generate wealth for indigenous households and communities. Legal suits filed by cabildos seeking redress for the exploitation of women's (and men's) labor reveal the importance of women's contributions to both the household and the community. The recognition of the symbolic, social, and economic value of women's work accorded women prestige and enhanced their status.

The colonial economy created new opportunities for a relative few who, by virtue of their wealth, possession of the best lands, access to nominally compensated native labor, and connections with Spanish officials, stood to benefit. However, it placed increased burdens on the vast majority. By the mid-sixteenth century on, indigenous men were entering European trades as, for example, cobblers, tailors, blacksmiths, and weavers. The types of labor that women performed seem to have changed less. They continued to weave textiles on the backstrap loom for household production, trade, and tribute throughout the colonial period. Overtime, many traditional forms of elite craft production, including weaving and featherworking, were eclipsed by European and hybrid styles. It is difficult to document the impact that these changes had on women's work as artisans, but the overall picture suggests a decline in status, one cause of which was the increased demand for simple cloth which undercut production of the more intricately woven styles that brought prestige to weavers.

Female and male healers (Nahuatl *ticitl*) continued to care physically and spiritually for the sick and infirm. Female ticitl also specialized in midwifery and the care of infants and young children. The vital role of ritual and deity impersonation in healing practices made medical specialists, and especially female ticitl, a target of idolatry investigations, although the frequency and extent of investigations varied considerably according to the concerns of local ecclesiastics. Friars criticized female curers in the confessional because of their knowledge and use of abortifacients and because of the European belief that women were more easily deceived by the Devil. Once considered *in tlamatinime* (Nahuatl, "the wise ones"), female healers lost status as their expertise, skill, and authority were devalued and demonized by Catholic moral teachings and ideology.

Archival sources demonstrate that an idealized division of labor represented only the core of men and women's activities. The organization of labor was not entirely rigid and, in fact, there was a good deal of overlap in men and women's work. Beyond the tasks of weaving, spinning, and cooking, women worked alongside men as agriculturalists, market vendors, artisans, and healers. Women and men shared the burden of maintaining the household, jointly performing tasks such as sweeping, carrying water, and hauling firewood. Mothers and fathers raised their children together, each taking responsibility for socializing and training same-sex children in their proper roles. These fundamental patterns of household labor and child rearing continued throughout the colonial period.

The complementary division of labor defined the basis of marriage and the alliance of households that was established when a young man and a young woman were wed. Parents arranged marriage once their children had acquired the fundamental skills that would allow them to fulfill their roles and once they had become sexually active. Marriage allowed households to formalize cooperative labor arrangements and thereby replenish their human resources. Marriage marked the young couple's transition to adulthood, enabled the formation of proper families, and provided companionship. Furthermore, through marriage the nobility established or strengthened bonds with one another and with prominent families and individuals, including Spaniards, and produced legitimate heirs. Even after the introduction of Christian marriage, the people of highland Mexico continued to understand the significance of marriage in these terms. The testimony of indigenous witnesses in archival documents shows that these ideals shaped marital expectations and familial relations.

Friars attempted to promote marriage in the church as part of the larger evangelization campaign by celebrating elaborate ceremonies for nobles. Marriages of commoners followed, but the introduction of Christian marriage and the frequency of holy matrimony varied depending on region and the availability of friars. Throughout central Mexico and Oaxaca, the arrangement and celebration of nuptials retained many ancient aspects and meanings. Symbolic acts, including gift exchange, feasting and drinking, and the participation of household and community members invested marriage negotiations and ceremonies with rich cultural meaning. Often couples celebrated parallel rituals, even after indigenous elements, including references to the importance of fulfilling gendered labor duties, were incorporated into Christian ceremonies. This study reveals a great deal of continuity in the celebration and meaning of marriage in indigenous communities.

Perhaps one of the most profound social changes in the colonial period was the imposition of the Christian interpretation of marriage as a life-long, indissoluble sacrament. From the 1530s on, friars made strident efforts to enforce Catholic impediments to marriage, to eliminate divorce, and to eradicate polygyny among the indigenous peoples of highland Mexico, but the undertaking proved to be difficult. Native noblemen seemed especially reluctant to embrace the new morality. Friars resorted to violence, harsh punishments, and threats to enforce compliance with Catholic marriage doctrine. Although the practice of polygyny eventually faded away in most places, divorce proved to be much harder to eliminate. When their marriages failed, couples continued to separate and create new unions without formalizing their relationships with the church. In an attempt to end divorce and remarriage, friars emphasized in sermons that marriage in the church was indissoluble and instructed women to tolerate their husbands' abusive behavior rather than terminate their unions. This pressure forced some women to accept secondary status in marriage.

Violence in marriage sheds light on conflicts over gendered duties and sexual fidelity that undermined the idealized portrayal of marital relations as complementary and reciprocal in formal texts. Although wife beating occurred in indigenous societies, we should not dismiss the fact that women had social and institutional support in preconquest and colonial times that allowed them to seek recourse against their husbands' violent behavior. This fact would suggest that, despite the admonition in marriage sermons to accept abuse, women and men in indigenous communities did not condone or disregard wife beating; in fact, assault, especially when deemed excessive or unwarranted, was considered a serious and punishable crime.

The indigenous peoples of central Mexico and Oaxaca acknowledged the intimate desires of both men and women and developed a rich corpus of symbols to represent sex, fertility, and reproduction, including food and drink, flowers, feathers, reed mats, sight, and speech. Food, drink, sight, and speech clearly retained their potency during the colonial period and were evoked frequently in common narratives and formal texts. Because of the decline of pictorial writing and the lack of records of Nahuatl speech and rhetoric after the early seventeenth century, the symbolism of flowers and feathers is more difficult to trace over time. Indigenous peoples considered sexual relations as one of life's pleasures, but believed that excessive or illicit relations could cause illness and social discord.

Preconquest and colonial sources express particular concern with adultery. Infidelity was conceived of within a broad framework of immoral behavior, which included stealing, excessive drinking, vagrancy, and violence. Christian doctrine may have influenced native accounts that condemned adultery; nevertheless, the responses of spouses who had been betrayed suggest that infidelity was genuinely abhorred. Women used informal networks and called on local officials to punish their unfaithful husbands. It was reported in some communities that in ancient times adulterers were put to death. Spanish law accommodated this belief to some extent, granting men the right to kill their wives and lovers if they caught them in an adulterous act and lashed out in a fit of rage. It seems to have privileged men in this regard, asserting a husband's authority over his wife, and Spanish lawyers were quick to use this to defend their indigenous clients.

Colonial society also condemned rape as a sexual crime. However, indigenous officials and jealous husbands sometimes conflated the rape of a married woman with adultery. Consequently, women ran the risk being beaten by their husbands if they reported an assault. Some eighteenth-century rape cases from central Mexico show Spanish influence in terms of attitudes toward sexuality. Whereas native men and women had not placed a great deal of importance on virginity, by the eighteenth century some indigenous women began initiating legal suits over its loss in central Mexico, where Spanish influence was most pronounced in New Spain.

This study of sexuality identifies a double standard that granted men considerably more sexual freedom than women. Polygyny and concubinage, which institutionalized a man's right to multiple partners in preconquest times, were not options for women. In the colonial period, some men, who admitted to having lovers, beat their wives or in rare cases murdered them if they suspected that they were involved with other men. Some married men even beat their lovers if they simply suspected that the women had intentions to marry or had engaged in sex with another man. Marital and sexual relations affected social harmony within the household and the community, especially when family members and local magistrates intervened to stop an illicit affair or when infidelity became publicly known. The relative lack of charges or investigations of homosexuality suggests that same-sex relations were not a major concern in indigenous communities. If homosexual acts were perceived as immoral or criminal, they must have been punished outside of formal institutional channels. Adults did much of the moral policing of household members; thus matters of marriage and sexuality significantly shaped family relations.

Mesoamericans articulated a broad conception of family, emphasizing the joint life of those who lived together in a household and were bound by mutual obligations and shared privileges rather than consanguinity alone. The flexibility of the household, with its ability to expand and contract with the life cycle of the family, allowed indigenous communities to weather the debilitating challenges of demographic collapse, outmigration, and *congregación*, (congregation, a program undertaken by Spaniards to concentrate dispersed settlements into one) programs. There was considerable regional variation in household types, which were both nuclear and multifamily. The broad conceptualization of family and the limited role of the head diffused authority and power within indigenous households. Ritual kinship extended an individual's social network and created bonds between households. Women often turned to ritual kin for support in difficult times.

A careful analysis of indigenous labor patterns and household organization dispels the notion of a clear distinction between "public" and "private" spheres in which women were confined to the home. Many traditional female tasks were not carried out in a "private" setting. Duties such as laundry and cooking required women to leave the enclosed patio of the household complex. In her study of the relationship between Mexica women's duties in the home (sweeping, making offerings, cooking, and weaving) and men's activities and fate on the battlefield, Burkhart has shown that the labor of men and women was interconnected: "To approach Mexica culture with ready-made categories of 'public' and 'private' merely distorts the reciprocal images cast by these mirrored constructions of gender."[3] Moreover, my study has emphasized that much of women's labor did not produce food or cloth strictly for household consumption or for sale in the market. Rather, women frequently worked in their homes preparing food and weaving cloth for local nobles, cabildo officials, ecclesiastics, and resident Spaniards to fulfill their tribute and repartimiento responsibilities. Therefore, viewing women's labor as "housework" greatly oversimplifies the complexity of indigenous social, political, and economic relations.

The economic, sacred, and political functions of the household were integrated with those of the community. Constituent households managed the community's land and labor resources. Sacred rituals conducted in individual households and attended by the entire community diminished the boundaries between public and private space. Similarly noble households sponsored political functions that overlapped with those of the community. In preconquest and colonial times, the palace of an indigenous hereditary ruler symbolized and represented the local state, and members of the pueblo often convened there to conduct business, hold elections, and negotiate disputes. Commoners also invited cabildo officials and neighbors to their homes, for example, such as when they ordered their last will and testament or requested a grant of land. In terms of women's status, this interpretation suggests that women stood at the center of interhousehold interaction rather than being isolated in the domestic sphere. They played a key role in initiating social relationships with the members of other households and in supplying the essential items for establishing and maintaining these bonds.

The household performed economic, sacred, and political acts that continually reestablished its ties to the community, which relied on the unity and sum of its individual households to collectively pay tribute and miscellaneous fees used to finance construction projects, the church, religious festivals, and officials' salaries. Consequently, the cabildo had a direct stake in the smooth functioning of each household. Native magistrates attended to criminal and civil matters, intervened in marital conflicts, and prosecuted offenses, such as wife beating and adultery that threatened the household's stability.

While the lack of rigid public and private spheres and the nature of women's work brought women into contact with many men and other women, the rules of social behavior served to restrict women's activities. In the absence of strict boundaries between public and private space, codes of conduct and morality governed male-female interactions. Cases in which violent husbands attacked their wives because they found them talking to another man in public show that women were confined by social rules rather than gendered space. The intimacy of daily life in native communities allowed women to rally support from those who witnessed injustices or who simply heard about mistreatment through local gossip. However, a woman always had to conduct herself in such a way that she would not become the subject of malicious rumors.

A deeper understanding of women's economic contributions, and of the integration of the household and community, helps to explain women's participation in colonial riots. Like the men of their communities, women felt the increasing pressure of economic demands placed on them under colonial rule. Both men and women paid tribute in labor and kind, and were left to fend for themselves and their children when spouses were required to leave the community to perform labor duties. And they had a vested interest in protecting lands, water supplies, and natural resources threatened by encroachment from neighboring communities, Spanish religious institutions, and the growing Spanish and casta populations in the countryside, especially after the mid-seventeenth century. They also felt the sting of threats to the community when, for example, Spanish officials undermined political autonomy by arresting native officials or by removing them from office, or when ecclesiastics attempted to interfere with local religious practices. Some women who resisted Spanish and native authorities were labeled "rebellious," and many played active leadership roles in long-term struggles as well as in more spontaneous protests. Through their participation in legal suits, riots, and acts of civil disobedience, women expressed a political consciousness that harshly condemned certain colonial policies, institutions, and authorities.

By examining local dynamics and developments at the household level, we can appreciate the complexity of changes in the Atlantic World and their consequences for people who were pulled into the global economy. By focusing on mechanisms of indigenous production and the work of native women in Mexico, we decenter the traditional focus on the North Atlantic and Europe, challenge historical narratives of western progress and the civilizing influences of colonialism, and highlight women's economic contributions and agency in resisting abusive and exploitative practices. Indigenous peoples should not be consigned to the margins of Atlantic World studies, for it was the wealth that indigenous men and women produced in Mexico, Peru, and many other places that stimulated further European expansion, settlement, and immigration; financed the early African slave trade; and established patterns of economic production based on the exploitation of cheap labor and the extraction of natural resources.

This work shows that indigenous gender ideology, social organization, marital expectations, and sexual attitudes persisted as integral value systems that remained markedly different from the cultural attitudes, ideals, and practices of Spanish settlers and officials. Studies of marriage, family, and divorce in colonial Mexico have revealed Spanish honor ideology, marital expectations and relations, and marriage practices. Many of the fundamental concepts and practices they have uncovered simply do not appear in records generated in or by indigenous communities. Rarely do the sources used in my study mention the exchange of the promise of marriage (palabra de casamiento) or refer to mala vida (a phrase that often appears in complaints against abusive husbands). Nor do they do mention the payment of dowries or *arras* (monetary gift to the bride from the groom), and certainly none of the women studied here would have considered the elite Spanish practice of "private pregnancy" to preserve family and personal honor when they found themselves pregnant out of wedlock. Thus this study shows that Iberian honor ideology had a very limited impact on indigenous gender relations within communities during the first two centuries of colonial rule. However, there were also important points of convergence, especially in terms of sexual attitudes. In both the Hispanic and the indigenous communities of highland Mexico, there was a sexual double standard that more harshly condemned women's sexual activity outside of marriage and very strongly prohibited adultery. At least superficially, Spaniards and Mesoamericans had a similar division of labor, although we cannot assume that women's work was valued the same way among Iberians.

The many different findings in this work, considered together, suggest that the status of indigenous women declined in the first two centuries of colonial rule, as did the status of all native people, elites and commoners. Changing cultural ideals and economic practices eroded women's prestige as elite artisans, ritual specialists, and erudite healers. Women lost ground in certain legal contexts as their husbands increasingly came to represent them in court. Indeed, the overwhelming majority of indigenous people were suffering economic hardship by the mid-eighteenth century. However, loss of status and wealth was contingent on a number of factors, including proximity to Spanish populations, the permanent presence of friars, local tribute practices, economic conditions, and a variety of personal circumstances. To the best of their ability, women tried to assert their will, protect themselves, and defend their interests. They often worked with their husbands, or as members of households and communities, but in certain situations they challenged spouses, neighbors, community officials, and Spanish magistrates.

To illuminate the changes in rural highland Mexico examined in this book, let us return briefly to the account offered by Marcial de la Cruz of his wife, Catalina María, turning into a jaguar nahualli (Chapter 2), which neatly blends both traditional concepts and European introductions. The narrative involves a husband and wife whose reciprocal relationship was in jeopardy because he had been imprisoned for stealing a mule. Marcial describes his shock as Catalina transformed into a jaguar and then back again into his wife. He recalls that he recognized her by her huipilli and her market basket, suggesting the ways in which the body and social identity were constructed through clothing and labor (local native officials later confirmed her identity by her dress and basket when they found her body in a ravine). Marcial remembers hearing a voice speaking to him in Zapotec, so he is familiar with ancient beliefs in nahualli and shape-shifting, but he holds a rosary and makes his appeal to Spanish authorities in court.

Archival narratives such as Marcial's suggest that relationships between men and women could be complex and even contentious. Over the course of the colonial period, profound social, political, economic, and cultural change would distort the idealized portrayals of social relations of earlier texts and images, even as many fundamental principles, concepts, and practices continued to shape indigenous gender relations in highland Mexico.

EPILOGUE

The century that followed the period of this study (1750–1850) was a time of dramatic change in colonial Mexico. The Bourbon Reforms increased taxes and reorganized the colonial administrative system. Independence ushered in a century of political turmoil, economic decline, and "liberal" reform. Many indigenous communities and individuals were dispossessed of their lands, and many men and women in performing wage labor were reduced to debt peonage.

The Mexican Revolution (1910–1920) initiated sweeping changes that included land reform, protection of labor, and the expansion of education, but native women seem to have been the last to benefit from them. Revolutionary programs redistributed land to male heads of household, and women continued to make up the largest portion of the illiterate population in Mexico throughout the twentieth century. Neoliberal policies implemented at the end of the century appear to have only made matters worse for indigenous working-class Mexicans. Commenting on the impact of these neoliberal reforms, María Luisa, a worker in a Tijuana maquiladora who earns about forty-three dollars a week, remarks:

Everything has gone up in price, and we neither organize ourselves nor protest. The Indians of Mexico used to complain, and it wasn't possible to get away with such injustice because people knew that, even if it was only with sticks, the Indians were going to fight and defend their rights. But now it's like we are asleep. With impunity they devalue the money on us, and nobody says a thing.[4]

María Luisa's statement associates memories of native struggles against oppression and exploitation with Mexican history. However, the participation of indigenous women in acts of resistance remains little recognized and little understood.

Perhaps knowing some of the history of native women's status and responsibilities and their participation in acts of civil disobedience helps to explain the prominent role that women played in the Zapatista Army and in many other social movements at the turn of the twentieth century. It is interesting that, according to the Revolutionary Women's Laws, "Women will have the *rights* and *obligations* elaborated in the revolutionary laws and regulations." In fact, the idea of rights and obligations as an essential aspect of community membership is an ancient native concept, and the struggle to defend them has had a long historical trajectory among indigenous Mexican women. In Chiapas, Oaxaca, Tehuantepec, Guerrero, Nayarit, and many other places, indigenous women are struggling for social, economic, and political justice today just as they did in the past.

Glossary

Alcalde (**Spanish**)   Member of a Spanish-style municipal council who acted as a judge.
Alcalde mayor (**Spanish**)   Spanish judicial and administrative official in charge of a given jurisdiction; often synonymous with *corregidor*.
Alcaide (**Spanish**)   Jailer.
Alguacil (**Spanish**)   Constable.
Altepetl (**Nahuatl**)   Sovereign ethnic Nahua state; equivalent to Ñudzahui *ñuu* or Bènizàa *yetze*; called *pueblo* by Spaniards.
Amancebamiento (**Spanish**)   Cohabitation outside of wedlock.
Real Audiencia (**Spanish**)   "Royal Court"; high court that adjudicated civil and criminal matters.
Ayuuk (**Ayuuk**)   Term of self-ascription used by the group that resided and continues to reside in the Sierra Alta of eastern Oaxaca (commonly known as Mixe).
Beneyetze (**Tíchazàa**)   Commoner.
Bènizàa (**Tíchazàa**)   Ethnic group that resided and continues to reside in Oaxaca; speaker of the Tíchazàa language (popularly known as Zapotec).
Cabecera (**Spanish**)   Head town; municipal status assigned to larger towns.
Cabildo (**Spanish**)   Spanish-style municipal council; body of political officers.
Cacica (**Spanish**)   Female indigenous ruler; wife of a cacique.
Cacique (**Spanish**)   Male indigenous ruler; equivalent to *tlatoani* in Nahuatl, *yya toniñe* in Ñudzahui, and *coqui* in Tíchazàa; derived from Arawak.
Cihuatlanqui (**Nahuatl**)   "One who asks for women"; male or female who specializes in arranging marriage.
Coqui (**Tíchazàa**)   Bènizàa hereditary ruler.
Corregidor (**Spanish**)   Chief Spanish judicial and administrative officer of a given district; often synonymous with *alcalde mayor*.
Encomendero (**Spanish**)   One who holds a grant of encomienda.
Encomienda (**Spanish**)   Grant of labor and tribute of indigenous people of a

given community; usually given by the Crown as a reward for participation in the conquest.

Estancia (**Spanish**)   Outlying settlement.

Fiscal (**Spanish**)   Church steward; highest indigenous ecclesiastical position.

Gobernador (**Spanish**)   Governor; highest-ranking office on the indigenous cabildo.

Huipilli (**Nahuatl**)   Woman's shift or tunic.

Lienzo (**Spanish**)   Painted cloth produced in the early colonial period to support legal claims of rulers and communities.

Macehualli (**Nahuatl**)   Commoner.

Mixe (**Spanish**)   Term commonly used to describe the Ayuuk of Oaxaca.

Nahua (**Nahuatl**)   Ethnic group that resided and resides mainly in central Mexico and satellite communities north of the Valley of Mexico and in central Mexico and Guatemala; speaker of the Nahuatl language (popularly known as Aztec).

Nahualli (**Nahuatl**)   Man or woman with the ability to shape-shift into animals or natural phenomena; refers to both the person who possessed supernatural abilities and his or her assumed form.

Ñudzahui (**Ñudzahui**)   Indigenous ethnic group residing in Oaxaca; speaker of the Ñudzahui language (popularly known as Mixtec).

Ñuu (**Ñudzahui**)   Local ethnic Ñudzahui or Mixtec state; equivalent to Nahua altepetl or Bènizàa yetze.

Obraje (**Spanish**)   Workshop, often specializing in textile production.

Principal (**Spanish**)   Prominent member of an indigenous community.

Pulque (**Spanish**)   Beverage made from fermented maguey juice.

Regidor (**Spanish**)   Member of a Spanish-style municipal council.

Repartimiento (**Spanish**)   Labor draft based on indigenous mechanism of rotary labor service.

Repartimiento de efectos (**Spanish**)   Distribution of goods to native communities on credit.

Sujeto (**Spanish**)   Indigenous subject town subordinate to a cabecera.

Tequitlato (**Nahuatl**)   Tribute collector.

Tay ñuu (**Ñudzahui**)   Commoner.

Ticitl (**Nahuatl**)   Healer; midwife.

Tlacuilo (**Nahuatl**)   Painter; scribe.

Tlatoani (**Nahuatl**)   Hereditary ruler.

Tonalli (**Nahuatl**)   "Heat," "light," "life force"; a day sign that represents a person's destiny associated with his or her day of birth; one of three animistic entities that each person possessed.

Topile (**Nahuatl**)   Lesser official; holder of a staff of office.

Tumulto (**Spanish**)   Riot or spontaneous local uprising.

Vara (**Spanish**)   Staff of office distributed to indigenous officials by local Spanish alcalde mayor.

Visita (**Spanish**)   Inspection tour, visit; carried out by priests, royal officials, and crown appointed inspectors.

Xonaxi (**Tíchazàa**)   Bènizàa noblewoman; wife of hereditary ruler.

Yetze (**Tíchazàa**)   Bènizàa local ethnic state; equivalent to Nahua *altepetl* and Ñudzahui *ñuu*.

Yuhuitayu (**Ñudzahui**)   Ñudzahui complex political state formed by the marriage of a male and female who each rule a *ñuu*.

Yya dzehe toniñe (**Ñudzahui**)   Female hereditary ruler.

Yya toniñe (**Ñudzahui**)   Hereditary ruler.

Notes

CHAPTER ONE

1. The literature on Maya women in preconquest and colonial times suggests that there were significant similarities and differences that merit further consideration. See especially Clendinnen 1982; Hunt and Restall 1997; Sigal 2000; Joyce 2000; Few 2002; and Komisaruk 2013.
2. The main exceptions are Cline 1986; Kellogg 1995, 2005; Schroeder, Wood, and Haskett 1997; Terraciano 2001.
3. Especially relevant to this work are Arrom 1985; Behar 1989; Boyer 1995; Gutiérrez 1991; Lavrin 1978a, 1978b, 1989a, 1989b, 2008; Seed 1988; Stern 1995; Twinam 1999.
4. Of course, historians must also consider the context in which archival sources were created in order to detect women's voices from the historical record. For interesting discussions of the use of testaments for ethnohistory, see Kellogg and Restall 1998 and Christensen and Truitt 2016. See also Chaudhuri, Katz, and Perry's 2010 collection on writing women's history and Davis 1987 for a discussion of archival testimonies as narratives.
5. For an examination of the discrepancy between images of Nahua women performing rituals in pictorial manuscripts and discussions of their roles in alphabetic texts, see Brown 1983, who concludes that although women were often depicted participating in ceremonies, their roles were not elaborated in written texts.
6. Sousa 2010.
7. Lockhart 1982, 1991, esp. 1992; Lockhart, Berdan, and Anderson 1986; Anderson, Berdan, and Lockhart 1976; Cline 1986; Wood 1984, 2003; Schroeder 1991; Horn 1997; Haskett 1991a, 2005.
8. Lockhart 1981; Karttunen 1982, 1983; Karttunen and Lockhart 1976, 1978, 1980, 1987; Anderson 1997; Burkhart 1989; Sell and Burkhart 2004; Sell, Burkhart, and Poole 2006; Sell, Burkhart, and Wright 2008.
9. Many excellent works have been published since the 1970s, including Boyer 1995; Few 2002; Gauderman 2003; Gonzalbo Aizpuru 1991; Gonzalbo Aizpuru and Rabell Romero 1994, 1996; Lavrin 1978b; Lavrin 1989a; Lavrin 2008; Muriel 1982, 1992; Powers 2005; Seed 1988; Stern 1995; Silverblatt 1987; Twinam 1999.

10. For the Nahuas, see Cline 1986; Kellogg 1995; Schroeder, Wood, and Haskett 1997. For the Ñudzahui, see Terraciano 2001.

11. Most of the scholarship on women in pre-Hispanic Mexico focuses on the Maya and Nahua regions. See, for example, Dodds Pennock 2008; Klein 1994, 2000, 2001; McCafferty and McCafferty 1988, 1991; Joyce 2000; Rodríguez-Shadow 1997; Brumfiel 1991; Gero and Conkey 1991. For sexuality, see Lavrin 1989a; Olivier 2004; Sigal 2000, 2003, 2011.

12. Karttunen and Lockhart 1987, 146–147. (Here I rely on Karttunen and Lockhart's translation and transcription).

13. For a description of Nahua sociopolitical organization, see Lockhart 1992 (esp. chap. 2); Haskett 1991a; Horn 1997. Terraciano 2001 (esp. chaps. 4, 6) discusses Ñudzahui sociopolitical structures. I have identified the *yetze* (or *queche* as spelled in Córdova and in documents from the Valley of Oaxaca) in a survey of Tíchazàa-language records from the Villa Alta jurisdiction. For more on colonial administrative jurisdictions, see Gerhard 1972.

14. For a discussion of Nahuatl as a lingua franca, especially in the south of Mesoamerica, see Dakin 1981, 1982, 2009. Terraciano examines the use of Nahuatl as a lingua franca and in the transition to Ñudzahui-language writing in Oaxaca (2001, 45–48).

15. Both the Nahua and Ñudzahui states, altepetl and ñuu, respectively, were further subdivided into constituent parts that rotated responsibilities and privileges associated with the ethnic state. Sometimes two or more Nahua altepetl and Ñudzahui ñuu were unified through conquest, intermarriage among ruling elites, or military alliances to form complex states. In some instances, many of the small local kingdoms of highland Mexico formed larger confederations, which sometimes reached the proportion of "empires." Because Sierra Zapotec sociopolitical organization is less understood at this time, it is unclear whether the yetze was subdivided or whether multiple yetze could be combined to form more complex units. Michel Oudijk suggests that because the Bènizàa had recently migrated into the Sierra Alta, perhaps only fifty-two or fewer years prior to the conquest, they had yet to form large lordly establishments or develop elaborate systems of marriage alliance and state formation (2000, 224–225). Still less is known of the internal complexity of Ayuuk sociopolitical organization.

16. See Alvarado for the Ñudzahui (1962 [1593], fol. 188v) and Molina for the Nahuatl (1992 [1571], fol. 140v, Nahuatl to Spanish (N–S)). Also see Terraciano 2001 for a comparison of Nahua and Ñudzahui ruling traditions (165–169).

17. Gillespie 1989; Schroeder 1992.

18. Córdova 1987a, fol. 377. The general term for a male ruler was *coquitao* and for a male noble was *coqui* or *joana* in Tíchazàa. Oudijk notes that the glosses on the Lienzo of Tabaá, a colonial pictorial history and map painted on cloth, identifies the male rulers as *coque* and their wives as *xonaxi* (2000, 186).

19. Terraciano 2001, 3; Chance 1989, 16.

20. Lockhart 1992; Haskett 1991a; Horn 1997a; Terraciano 2001.

21. Lockhart and Schwartz 1983, 342.

22. Terraciano 2001, 3.

23. Chance 1989, 35.
24. Gibson 1952, 1964; Haskett 1991a; Lockhart 1992; Horn 1997a; Restall 1997; Terraciano 2001.
25. Rothenberg 1980; Deeds 1997.
26. For more on this discussion, see Monaghan 2001, 287.
27. Kellogg 1997, 125.
28. For the emergence of this debate, see Nash 1978, 1980, and McCafferty and McCafferty 1988. See also MacLachlan 1976.

CHAPTER TWO

1. AJVA-CR 1, 50, San Francisco Cajonos, 1684 (pre-2001 cataloging system). The case was initiated in 1684 when Catalina María was murdered; however, Marcial de la Cruz fled from authorities and did not confess to the crime until he returned to the community two years later.
2. See López Austin 1988, 1:305.
3. Sahagún 1996, bk. 7, fol. 7.
4. Sahagún 1996, bk. 5, fols. 19v–20.
5. Córdova 1987b [1578], fol. 216.
6. Sahagún 1996, bk. 5, fol. 19v.
7. Córdova 1987b [1578], fols. 215–216.
8. Sahagún 1996, bk. 10, fols. 11v–12.
9. Sahagún 1996, bk. 7, fols. 17v–19.
10. Klein 2001, 185.
11. Sahagún 1996, bk. 11, fol. 209v. Perhaps rabbits are associated with pulque because they often make their burrows in the ground near the base of the maguey plant, the source of the juice that is fermented to make the beverage (Sahagún 1996, bk. 11, fol. 14).
12. Karttunen 1983, 57.
13. Andrews 1975, 455.
14. Andrews and Hassig 1984, 246.
15. For example, among the entries in Molina 1992 are (1) *naualtia esconderse o ampararse con algo*; (2) *naualtia tlayoalli esconderse a la sombra de algo*; (3) *naualquixtia. sacar o echar fuera de algun lugar a otro con engaño y cautela*; (4) *naualcalaqui entrar disimulado con cautela y secretamente en algun lugar*; and (5) *naualitoa dezir algo cautelosamente para enlabiar, o embaucar a otros* (Nahuatl to Spanish (N–S), fol. 63r-v). On the Spanish side of the dictionary, nahual derivations also appear in conjunction with hiding oneself for mischievous or deceptive purposes. Molina uses a construction based on *nahual-* in his definition of *esconderse entre las yeruas o matas para espiar. nino, çacanahualtia, nino, xiuhnaualtia* and *esconderse para acechar. nino, nauallatia*" (Spanish to Nahuatl (S–N), fol. 58).
16. Because Spanish friars associated the nahualli with the Devil's ability to assume different shapes, they identified the concept with witches, sorcerers, and the

devil. Molina 1992 [1571] translated *nahualli* as *bruxa* (witch) (N–S, fol. 63v); he also listed nahualli among the definitions of *hechizero* (sorcerer) (S–N fol. 70r). See Musgrave-Portilla 1982; Olmos 1990; Molina 1992 [1571]; Sahagún 1996; Ruiz de Alarcón 1984.

In his Ñudzahui *Vocabulario* of 1593, Alvarado 1962 [1593] refers to nahuallis under the listings for *wizard* (*brujo*) and *sorcerer* (*hechizero*); the entries refer to the nahualli's supernatural abilities by specifying that these terms mean a "wizard who deceives by saying that he turns into a lion" (fol. 38v) and a "sorcerer who says he turns into a tiger" (fol. 122v).

Córdova's *Vocabulario en lengua çapoteca* (1987a [1578]) reveals an association between drinking and powerful ritual specialists with entries for "wizard or witch who drinks" (fol. 61v) and "to bewitch with drinks" (fol. 216v).

17. Sahagún 1996, bk. 3, fols. 9, 10v; Ruiz de Alarcón 1984, 83–88.
18. Sahagún 1996, bk. 3, fols. 12v–13v.
19. Ibid., fols. 16v, 19r-v.
20. See, for example, Klein's 1980 discussion of the male and female attributes of Tlaloc.
21. Sahagún 1996, bk. 3, fols. 19r-v, 20.
22. Sahagún 1996, bk. 4, fol. 28.
23. Sahagún 1996, bk. 4, fol. 57v.
24. Quiñones Keber 1995, 28.
25. Sahagún 1996, bk. 4, fol. 58.
26. Ibid., fol. 28. López Austin 1988 makes this observation (1:366). A systematic analysis of colonial cases of nahualism may suggest otherwise. See also Musgrave-Portilla 1982.
27. Ruiz de Alarcón 1984, 45–46.
28. López Austin 1988, 297.
29. Some colonial and modern sources suggest that the animal day sign under which a person was born determined his or her nahualli form, thereby equating nahualli with tonalli. As Ruiz de Alarcón understood the concept, a person's day sign determined his or her alternate form (1984, 45). The fusing of the two terms continues today. Like Ruiz de Alarcón, Rigoberta Menchú, the Nobel Peace Prize laureate and a Quiché Maya woman, equates the nahualli form and the day sign in her account of her life (1994, 18–20). However, the supernatural form cannot correspond with the day sign of one's birth date because according to colonial accounts, nahuallis were born on days named Rain, Wind, and Death, not on days named for animals. Furthermore, many accounts suggest that nahuallis could assume various guises, not just that of one day sign animal.

Other accounts provide contradictory evidence, suggesting that in some cases the nahualli assumed just one form. For example, in an incantation collected by Ruiz de Alarcón the speaker proclaims *ninahualocelotl* (I am an ocelot nahualli) (1984, 108). Similarly, the names of the gods of Amatlan employed a possessed singular form of nahualli. The name *Coyotl inahual* (Coyote is his nahualli) suggests a deity/ancestor hero who had only one alternate form. Other Amatlan

deities were said to have had specific "disguises" (*inaoal*) (Sahagún 1996, bk. 9, fols. 56v–58v).
30. Ruiz de Alarcón 1984, 46.
31. Sahagún 1996, bk. 4, fols. 20–22, passim.
32. Ibid., fols. 31–33v.
33. Ibid., fol. 37v.
34. Ibid., fol. 34.
35. Ibid., fol. 14v.
36. Acuña 1986, 2:88.
37. Acuña 1986, 2:316, 264, 305, 310, respectively.
38. Córdova 1987b [1578], fols. 202–203.
39. AGI-M 882, Lachirio, 1704, fol. 157r.
40. AGI-M 882, Yatoni, 1704, fol. 205r; AGI-M 882, Yatzona, 1704, fol. 92r-v. Don Francisco de Paz, governor, admits that he consulted Juan Jiménez, a local teacher of idolatry, when his five children were born. Felipe Méndez, an alcalde, states that he consulted don Juan de Vargas when his four children were born. Miguel de la Cruz consulted don Gaspar de Paz when one child was born and Juan Jiménez when the other two were born. Juan Bautista consulted don Gaspar when his children were born and ordered him to ritually bathe in order to strengthen the child (AGI-M 882, 1704, Taguí, fol. 189v). Pedro Méndez confessed that Juan Gonzalo, a maestro, gave this first child the name Yotela; the second, Bilalao; and the third, Cuachila. The towns that reported these traditions in the 1704–1705 investigation included Temascalapa, Yalahuí, Yaxoni, Yetzelálag, Reagui, and Latani.
41. AGI-M 882, 1704, Yacochi. The names of Jacinto Martín's sons may be according to birth order; however, he states that his own is a calendrical name, and I suspect that the names of his sons are as well.
42. AJT-CR 9, 27, Teposcolula, 1613; AJT-CR 12, 26, Teposcolula, 1630; AJT-CR 12, 12, Teposcolula, 1630; AJT-CR 1, 23, Ocotepec, 1569; AJT-CR 6, 33, Yanhuitlan, 1605.
43. Córdova 1987a [1578], fol. 282.
44. Ibid., 290.
45. Ibid., 277.
46. Sahagún 1996, bk. 10, fols. 122v–123. Anderson and Dibble 1950–1982 note that in a marginal gloss (bk. 10, 173–174) Sahagún changed *quititlani* to *quitlani*.
47. Sahagún 1996, bk. 6, fol. 170v.
48. Warfare may not have been as important metaphorically or symbolically among the Ñudzahui and Bènizàa peoples as it was among the Nahuas of central Mexico, especially the Mexica.
49. Sahagún 1996, bk. 6, fol. 148.
50. Ibid., fol. 170v.
51. Acuña 1986, 3:72.
52. Acuña 1986, 2:64.

53. Sahagún 1996, bk. 6, fol. 170.
54. Ibid., fol. 170v.
55. These symbols appear in the Codex Mendoza (fol. 70r), with Spanish glosses identifying each trade (Berdan and Anawalt 1992); the identification of the first symbol with the carpenter trade is tentative.
56. Berdan and Anawalt 1992, fol. 57r. See also accompanying text (fol. 56v).
57. Acuña 1986, 3:72.
58. Ibid., 75.
59. Motolinía 1950, 59–60, 132.
60. Sahagún 1996, bk. 3, fol. 25v. The *Relaciones geográficas* of Tzicaputzalco and Alahuiztlan mention that when a cacique died all of his belongings were buried with him, including four of his slaves (Acuña 1986, 2:270–271, 277). The *Relación* of Tlacotepec, a Tepuzteca community, also mentions the practice of burying slaves with a cacique (ibid., 301).
61. Acuña 1986, 2:295.
62. Ibid., 311.
63. Sahagún 1996, bk. 4, fol. 141v. See Sullivan 1966.
64. Sahagún 1996, bk. 5, fols. 141v–142.
65. In addition to the examples provided here, see the Nahuatl text in the Florentine Codex regarding goods presented to a baby girl (Sahagún 1996, bk. 4, fol. 170v, quoted previously). These terms are attested to and discussed in Cline 1986, 113; Lockhart 1992, 70; Kellogg 1995, 124.
66. Sahagún 1996, bk. 2, fol. 99v.
67. Sahagún 1996, bk. 6, fol. 77.
68. Ibid., fol. 77v.
69. Sahagún 1996, bk. 2, fol. 63v.
70. Sahagún 1996, bk. 6, fol. 199.
71. Ibid., fol. 199v.
72. Sahagún 1996, bk. 9, fol. 14.
73. Klein 2001, 236–237; López Austin 1988, 2:272–273. For negotiation of sex and gender in ancient Mesoamerica, see Joyce 2000 and 2001.
74. Ruiz de Alarcón 1984, 75–77. See Andrews and Hassig's 1984 commentary on the rhetorical conventions used in the incantations (259–302, esp. 259–261).
75. Ruiz de Alarcón 1984, 99.
76. Ibid., 102.
77. Sahagún 1996, bk. 6, fols. 144v, 151.
78. Ibid., fols. 70–80.
79. AGI-M 882, 1704, pts. 1, 2.
80. For detailed discussions of these investigations, see Tavárez 2011 and Alcina Franch 1993.
81. AJVA-CR 3, 117, Betaza y Lachitaa, 1703 (pre-2001 cataloging system).
82. AGI-M 882, Santo Domingo Roayaga, 1704, fols. 208–265.
83. Sahagún 1996, bk. 6, fols. 170–171v.
84. Sahagún 1996, bk. 9, fol. 39r-v.
85. Sahagún 1996, bk. 6, fol. 106v.

86. Olmos 1990, fol. 18.
87. Ibid., fol. 16.
88. Sahagún 1996, bk. 6, fol. 98.
89. It may be that these metaphors were used in nonsexual contexts as well; the compilation of additional examples should clarify issues of usage.
90. AJVA-CR 3, 117, Betaza y Lachitaa, 1703 (pre-2001 cataloging system).
91. Sahagún 1996, bk. 7, chap. 15.
92. Sahagún 1996, bk. 6, fol. 9v.
93. For a study of costume in pre-Hispanic codices, see Anawalt 1981.
94. For a discussion of gender differences in Nahuatl and Spanish, see Lockhart 1992, 321.
95. Reyes 1976 [1593], fol. 87.
96. Córdova 1987a [1578], fol. 301v.
97. Carochi 1983, bk. 1, chap. 4, fol. 15.
98. Carochi 1983, bk. 4, chap. 4, fol. 83v.
99. Carochi 1983, bk. 4, chap. 6, fol. 85r-v.
100. Reyes 1976, fol. 5.
101. Ibid., fols. 15–16.
102. Ibid., fol. 18.
103. Monaghan 2001; see also Klein 2001.
104. Klein 2001, 236.
105. Sahagún 1996, bk. 10, fol. 25.
106. The image may show a man dressed as a woman and a woman dressed as a man to indicate that each uses the speech convention of the opposite sex; however, the text does not refer explicitly to cross-dressing. For more on the Florentine Codex's treatment of the xochihua, see also Sigal 2007. For cross-dressing among North American tribes, see for example Blackwood 1984 and Roscoe 1991.
107. Codex Tudela 1980, fol. 62.
108. Sahagún 1996, bk. 7, fols. 20v, 25. The meaning of these verbs is to confuse or corrupt people.
109. Ibid.

CHAPTER THREE

1. AGN-I 23, 1, Coyoacan, 1538.
2. Córdova 1987b [1578], fol. 217.
3. See especially Arrom 1985, chap. 5. Among the grounds for divorce under canon law, according to Arrom, were these: if one spouse was guilty of excessive cruelty, physical abuse, or attempted murder against the other; if one spouse attempted to force the other to commit criminal acts; if one spouse was a heretic or pagan; if one spouse committed adultery; and if the husband abandoned his wife and did not support her for a number of years (208–209).
4. On this point, see Córdova 1987b [1578], fol. 217.
5. Most sources speak of polygyny as a privilege of nobles; however, the *Relación de Tezcoco* and the *Relaciones de los pueblos de Tecuicuilco* report that

commoners who could afford to maintain additional women also practiced it (Acuña 1986, 3:71–72; Acuña 1984, 3:93–94). For examples of commoners with multiple wives in the Cuernavaca *padrones*, see Cline 1993, 54, and for examples of polygyny among nobles in the Cuernavaca census, see Carrasco 1976, 48.

6. AGN-I 36 pt 1, 7, Coyoacan, 1539, provides an example of sororal polygyny; however, because most polygyny cases do not explicitly discuss the relationship between a man's multiple wives, it is unclear whether this was common or exceptional.

7. Motolinía 1971, 189. As Robert Ricard (1966, 111) notes, "the difficulty [of eradication] was all the greater because polygamy, as practiced there and in most of the country, was owing less to the sensual temperament of the natives than to economic and social factors." For an alternative interpretation of Motolinía's views on polygyny, see Sigal 2011, 70–79.

8. D'Emilio and Freedman 1988, 87.

9. Acuña 1985, 5(2), 167.

10. Ibid., 172. See also Acuña 1988, 10:220, 223.

11. Burkhart 1989, 156–157.

12. Sahagún 1996, bk. 6, fol. 110r-v.

13. For a discussion of the evolution of marriage practices in Tuscany and the importance of the marriage of the Virgin as a theme in Italian painting, see Klapisch-Zuber 1985, 178–212. On the promotion of Joseph and Mary as the model couple in New Spain, see Burkhart 1989 and Villaseñor-Black 2001.

14. For discussions of impediments to marriage, see Seed 1988; Lavrin 1989a; and Socolow 1989.

15. Motolinía 1950, 151.

16. Ricard 1966, 114. Mark Christensen (2010) demonstrates that indigenous church officials also produced their own texts, which were intended for local use and remained unpublished. These writings incorporated regional traditions and beliefs into the Christian narratives.

17. Molina 1984, 45–58.

18. Seed 1988 notes that the impediment of public honesty concerned a prior public engagement with a close relative of the intended spouse (85); however, Molina 1984 is much more general, asking only whether the bride or groom had exchanged the promise of marriage with any one else.

19. On this point, see Seed 1988.

20. AGN-I 23, 1, Coyoacan, 1538.

21. AGN-CR 686, 3, Acatepec, 1558.

22. Hackel 2005 finds similar cases of spousal homicide in his examination of the imposition of Christian marriage on California mission Indians (205–212).

23. The records often mention abandonment in passing, such as in the criminal case of Julian Martín, described as "a married man whose wife is absent and who lives as a fugitive from him in Taxco" (AGN-CR 139, 17, Malinalco, 1757).

24. AJT-CR 10, 7, Yanhuitlan, 1615.

25. Several women complained that their husbands had fled Malinalco to escape excessive tribute and labor burdens, leaving the women saddled with the burdens of raising their children and paying the tribute (AGN-CR 140, 1, Mali-

nalco, 1635). A petition filed in 1641 by several men of Malinalco who had left the altepetl because of grievances over labor demands confirmed these complaints (AGN-CR 139, 25, Malinalco, 1641). For another example of a person fleeing his community because of financial pressures, see the testimony of Pablo de la Cruz, a Mixtec of Santiago Tiñuu, who in 1685 explained that he had left his wife in order to go to the regional center of Yanhuitlan to seek work (AJT-CR 19, 5, Yanhuitlan, 1685).

26. AGN-CR 686, 3, Acatepec, 1558.
27. Acuña 1986, 3:65.
28. In his study of California Indians, Hackel 2005 comes to a similar conclusion that communal pressures would have deterred indigenous couples from divorcing, and that the Franciscans seem to have exaggerated the frequency of the dissolution of marriages (187).
29. Zorita 1994, 125.
30. AGN-CR 686, 3, Acatepec, 1558; AGN-CR 217, 10, Atengo, 1723.
31. Feria 1567, fol. 111.
32. Alva 1999, 155. (Here I use Sell and Schwaller's translation.)
33. On this point see Ricard 1966, who, on the basis of Antonio Tello's *Libro Segundo de la Crónica Miscelánea en que se trata de la Conquista Espiritual y Temporal de la Santa Provincia de Xalisco*, notes the challenges that fray Martín de Jesus, fray Juan de Padilla, and fray Antonio de Segovia, among others, faced in trying to convince the nobles to accept monogamy (111).
34. Durán 1994, 435.
35. Motolinía 1950, 149.
36. Alva 1999, 154–155. (Here I use Sell and Schwaller's translation.)
37. Alva 1999, 156–157. (Here I use Sell and Schwaller's translation.)
38. The original document is in AGN-T 637, 1, fols. 66–73. See the translation of this text in Restall, Sousa, and Terraciano 2005, 193–194.
39. The central Mexican doctrinas influenced church texts produced later for the missions. Hackel 2005 notes that the Franciscans threatened native witnesses with Hell in the afterlife if they lied about impediments (193).
40. Fray Juan de Estella accused Tomás of living with both María and Magdalena, leading to the charge of polygyny in this case. However, Tomás and María insisted that they did not reunite until after Magdalena's death.
41. Ricard 1966 discusses the differing factors that ecclesiastics considered in determining which wife should be recognized as legitimate (113–115).
42. On the church's negotiation over the impediments of blood and spiritual kinship, see Lavrin 1989a, 56.
43. Quoted in Don 2010, 41.
44. AGN-I 23, 1, Coyoacan, 1538.
45. AGN-I 36, part 1a, 7, Coyoacan, 1539.
46. AGN-I 36, part 1a, 7, Coyoacan, 1539; AGN-I 23, 1, Coyoacan, 1538.
47. See especially Ricard 1966; Gruzinski 1989a; Don 2010; Tavárez 2011.
48. The trial transcript is published in *Proceso Inquisitorial del Cacique de Tetzcoco don Carlos Ometochtzin (Chichimecatecotl)* (Biblioteca Enciclopédica del Estado de México 1980).

49. Biblioteca Enciclopédica del Estado de México 1980, 49.
50. AGN-I 40, 32, Iguala, 1540.
51. AGN-I 40, 33, Matlactlan, 1540.
52. AGN-I 36, part 1, 7, Coyoacan, 1539. For a discussion of native responses to the imposition of Christian marriage in California missions, see Hackel 2005, chap. 5.
53. Biblioteca Enciclopédica del Estado de México 1980, 15.
54. AGN-I 40, 32, Iguala, 1540.
55. Townsend 2006 uses "The Song of the Women of Chalco" as an entry point into an examination of the tensions created by polygynous relationships and the resentment that secondary wives and concubines might have felt.
56. On this point, see Seed 1988.
57. Lara 2008, 116.
58. Ricard 1966, 112. Ricard suggests that this had been the policy among the Franciscans as early as 1531 and among the Augustinians as early as 1534. Don Juan, the cacique of Matlactlan, may have been married as early as 1533 after having made such a compromise with fray Andrés de Olmos (AGN-I 40, 33, Matlactlan, 1540).
59. For an example of a baptized noble living with multiple wives, some baptized and others not, see the colonial census from Morelos translated in Cline (1993, 52). See also the 1540 case against don Juan, cacique of Iguala, who was charged with violating the sacrament of marriage by continuing to live with his multiple wives; he too must have been married in the 1530s (AGN-I 40, 32, Iguala, 1540).
60. Durán 1967, 1:5, 56.
61. For example, in the late seventeenth century, when it was time for Tomás Gonzalo to marry, his stepmother looked for a wife for him (AJVA-CR 1, 6.01, Lachirio, 1667). Similarly, Pedro de Castañeda, a Ñudzahui man of Teposcolula, accompanied his nephew to the house of his future bride to negotiate the marriage with her family in 1592 (AJT-CR 3, 23, Teposcolula, 1592).
62. Acuña 1986, 3:264.
63. Acuña 1984, 2:289. The account states that the man went to "dos viejos, los más antiguos" to discuss his desire to marry. Because of the importance of male and female pairs, especially as participants in life-cycle rituals, and because pictorial evidence shows old men and old women speaking at the marriage ceremony, it is possible that the two elders in this description are an old man and an old woman.
64. See, for example, AJT-CR 4, 5, Coixtlahuaca, 1596, fol. 3v, in which a Mixtec man states that he married his wife "with the condition that [she] had to go to make a life with him in the pueblo of Texupa, where he was born, and [his] father and mother, houses and lands."
65. See, for example, AGN-CR 217, 10, Atengo, 1723.
66. Ages at first marriage can only be approximated from colonial records in which witnesses rarely knew with certainty how old they were and qualified their ages with "más o menos" (more or less). The approximation of age twelve for marriage is based on criminal cases in which husbands and/or wives stated their

ages and the length of time they had been married. Occasionally, respondents to the *Relaciones geográficas* questionnaires reported later marriages in preconquest times. The *Relación de Ichcateupan* and the *Relación de Chichicapa* state that men and women did not marry before they reached thirty years of age because of the belief that early marriage shortened one's life. Both accounts allude to the belief, widespread among natives, that men had a fixed amount of semen and would suffer if it were expelled while they were very young or used up because of excessive sex. However, social prescriptions for moderate sexual activity, not late age at marriage, resolved the dilemma for men. I think that statements regarding very late marriage ages are not to be taken literally, being attempts to explain why people were healthier and lived longer in preconquest times. In fact, colonial pressures and severe demographic decline may have driven marriage age down. Hackel 2005 finds a downward trend in marriage age over time in California missions, although ages were a little higher and there was some age difference between the bride and groom (184–188).

Based on his analysis of early colonial censuses from the Morelos region, McCaa 1996 finds evidence that Nahua girls married at a young age, usually between ten and twelve, some as young as eight, and that boys married somewhat later (18–31). This suggests that age at marriage may have declined slightly over time but that marriage at a fairly young age was a well-established precolonial pattern.

67. Sahagún 1996, bk. 5, fol. 127.

68. In her study of marriage in late colonial Argentina, Susan Socolow finds that women, mainly of Spanish or mixed descent, married between the ages of fourteen and twenty-one while men married in their late twenties and later (1989, 212–213). Thomas Calvo also notes significant age differences among marriage partners in the Hispanic sectors of society in his study of colonial Guadalajara: "The 'elderly' peninsulars, over 25 years of age, married young creole girls under twenty-one, while the mulattos and natives did not wait that long" (1989, 289).

69. *Relación de Tezcoco* (Acuña 1986, 3:70); *Relación de Tecuicuilco* (Acuña 1984, 3:93); *Relación de Xalapa, Cintla, y Acatlan* (ibid., 2:289); *Relación de Justlahuaca* (ibid., 2:286); *Relación de Mixtepec* (Juxtlahuaca) (ibid., 294); *Relación de Ayusuchiquilazala* (Juxtlahuaca) (ibid., 301); *Relación de Xalapa* (Juxtlahuaca) (ibid., 307); *Relación de Puctla* (Juxtlahuaca) (ibid., 314–315).

70. Córdova 1987b, fol. 217.

71. This is observed throughout the *Relaciones geográficas* and in the colonial archival record. See for example the statement of respondents to the *Relación de Tetzcoco* (Acuña 1986, 3:70–71).

72. Sahagún 1996, bk. 4, fol. 109. See also Sahagún 1996, which lists the same days as considered good for marriages except *calli* (house) (bk. 2, fol. 14v).

73. There is a strong correlation between the numbers and fates in the Codex Laud and the Codex Vaticanus B. The Codex Borgia shows slightly more variation, probably reflecting regional differences, and yet the great continuity reveals a high degree of cultural conformity. The arrangement of the prognostication scenes varies in each manuscript. The Codex Borgia is divided into three rows read Boustrophedon style from bottom right to upper left. The Codex Laud is

divided into two rows read from bottom right to upper left. The Vaticanus B is also divided into two rows, with the marriage prognostication scenes arranged in one long row along the bottom and calendrical information arranged at the top. Other sections of the codices also pertain to marriage that are not discussed here but are considered in Boone 2006, 2007. I am grateful to John Pohl, who first introduced me to these sections of the codices in his art history graduate seminar on the Codex Borgia at UCLA.

74. Byland 1993. Byland credits Peter van der Loo for explaining this to him in a personal communication (xxix). Van der Loo's interpretation must be based on Córdova's 1987b description of how prognosticators determined whether a prospective couple would be compatible (fols. 216–217). Boone 2006 provides an excellent overview of the historiography of the marriage prognostication sections in the Borgia, Laud, and Vaticanus B codices.

75. This symbol may also represent the sun setting or rising. Boone 2006 refers to it as the sun-darkness symbol (78).

76. Anders, Jansen, and Reyes 1993, fol. 59.

77. Miller and Taube 1993, 92.

78. Acuña 1984, 2:286, 294–295, 302, 308, 320.

79. Córdova's 1978a [1578] Tíchazàa *Vocabulario* contains a revealing entry: "Echarse las suertes para los casamientos como hazian antiguamente" (to cast lots for marriages as they did in ancient times) (fol. 149).

80. Córdova 1987b, fols. 202–203, 216–217.

81. Acuña 1984, 3:93.

82. AGI-M 882, 1704. Bènizàa witnesses from Yalálag, Betaza, and Yacochi said that the native priest would cast lots to determine the most favorable day for marriage.

83. Molina 1992, fol. 129v. The term also appears as *cihuatlanques* with both the Nahuatl and Spanish plural forms in Karttunen and Lockhart 1987 (119).

84. Sahagún 1996, bk. 2, fol. 14v.

85. The couplet is in Sahagún 1996 (bk. 5, fol. 108); the illustration is on fol. 106.

86. *Huehuehyotl* can also mean old age or custom and propriety of elders.

87. Alvarado 1962 lists the following Ñudzahui terms for a male bride negotiator under *casamentero*: *tay yosinonoo, tay sasicandahui, tay yosaqndahui, tay ñohosahandahui* (fol. 45v). In his Tíchazàa dictionary, Córdova 1987a [1578] lists *checola, chacola, zecola,* and *huexija* under *casamentero* and *checolagonna* and *quiniça* under *casamentera* (fol. 74).

88. Acuña 1986, 2:64–65, 3:301.

89. Lavrin 1989a notes that Spanish and casta couples also gave personal gifts once they had exchanged the marriage promise, but this was not part of a larger cycle of reciprocal giving between households (61).

90. Acuña 1986, 3:270.

91. Ibid., 295.

92. Acuña 1984, 2:286, 294, 301, 307, 314–315).

93. Ibid., 307.

94. See the *Relación de Ichcateupan* (Acuña 2:264).
95. Codex Mendoza (Berdan and Anawalt 1992, fol. 61); Sahagún 1996, bk. 2, fols. 14v, 6, 109v; Acuña 1986 2:264.
96. Burkhart 1989, 82–83.
97. Taggart 1983, 63.
98. Acuña 1986, 2:264.
99. Sahagún 1996, bk. 1, fol. 7r-v.
100. Acuña 1986, 3:70–71. For an example of the Nahuatl-language speeches made by nobles at wedding ceremonies, see Karttunen and Lockhart 1987, 122–127.
101. See the descriptions of ceremonies in Juxtlahuaca (Acuña 1984, 2:286); Ayusuchiquilazala (ibid., 2:301); and Xalapa (ibid., 2:307).
102. Acuña 1984, 2:307.
103. Karttunen and Lockhart 1987, 122–123, 127, 110–113.
104. Ibid., 124–125. (Here I use Karttunen and Lockhart's translation.)
105. *Relación de Tezcoco* (Acuña 1986, 3:70–71); *Relación de Guaxilotitlan* (Acuña 1984, 2:215); *Relación de Justlahuaca* (ibid., 2:286).
106. Sahagún 1996, bk. 2, fol. 14v. The Nahuatl term *titici* (sing. *ticitl*, physician, prognosticator, healer) is used in the Spanish text. See also Sahagún 1996, bk. 6, fol. 112.
107. Burkhart 1989 notes the use of the term *nemecatiliztli* in sermons (154–156).
108. Although it is not explicitly stated here, the woman's garments probably contained symbols indicating that she was married. In the Triqui region of the Mixteca Alta today, for example, an unmarried woman's skirt is very plain and not well made. At marriage, she begins to wear a higher quality skirt embroidered with a rainbow band around the hip. Andrés and Marcelina Gutiérrez, Triquis from Copala, say that the Triqui also exchange clothing and literally dress the bride and groom for their new roles, as described in Sahagún's sixteenth-century account of Nahua marriage (personal communication, March 1996).
109. Acuña 1984, 2:286.
110. Ibid., 2:286.
111. Ibid., 2:215.
112. Sahagún 1996, bk. 6, fol. 132.
113. According to the *Relación de Cempoala* (Acuña 1986, 2:77) and the *Relación de Epazoyuca* (ibid., 2:86), the couple remained on the mat for three days. According to the *Relación de Tlacotepeque* (ibid., 2:301), they were left on the mat for an unspecified number of days.
114. Sahagún 1996, bk. 6, fol. 112v.
115. Ibid., fol. 113. The term *ilamatque* (old women) suggests that several of the groom's female relatives may have spoken at the huexiuhtlauana.
116. *Relación de Tezcoco* (Acuña 1986, 3:70–71); *Relación de Cempoala* (ibid., 77); *Relación de Epazoyuca* (ibid., 86); and Sahagún 1996, bk. 2, fol. 14v.
117. *Relación de Epazoyuca* (Acuña 1986, 2:86); Sahagún 1996, bk. 6, fol. 110. The Florentine Codex explains that the bride pasted red parrot feathers on

her arms and legs. Interestingly, women who were to become "aunts" (roughly equivalent to a godmother) also pasted red feathers on their arms and legs during the ritual kinship ceremony. Red, a color associated with heat and fertility in Mesoamerican thought and iconography, has maintained its symbolic meaning in native cultures today. In contemporary Triqui communities, according to Andrés and Marcelina Gutiérrez, who are Triquis from Copala, the huipiles of women of child-bearing age are bright red and those of older women are white, representing the fact that they are "cooling off" (personal communication, April 1996).

118. Acuña 1984, 2:294.
119. Ibid., 2:286.
120. Ibid., 2:301.
121. Ibid., 2:301.
122. Motolinía 1950, 150.
123. Cline 1993, 52.
124. For descriptions of marriage ceremonies in colonial New Mexico and in California, see Gutiérrez 1991, 259–270 and Hackel 2005, 195–197, respectively.
125. Motolinía 1950, 150.
126. Ibid., 148–149.
127. Motolinía 1950, 149 mentions an elaborately decorated marriage bed set up at the cacique's house on which the bride and groom greeted guests. This may have followed the indigenous custom of the married couple being seated on a mat during the marriage ceremony and the festivities that followed.
128. Motolinía 1950, 148.
129. Ibid., 149.
130. Don 2010, 35. Don notes that Ixtlilxochitl, his wife, and his mother were baptized at around the same time. She calls Nahua nobles' tactic of accommodating the friars while still maintaining traditional spiritual beliefs and practices the "arbitration of avoidance."
131. Tena 1998, 172–175.
132. Molina 1984 [1571], fols. 49, 50v, 51v, 56, 57. See also Alva 1999, 155.
133. Ibid., fols. 53v–54.
134. According to Lara 2008, Alberto Castellani reported that childless couples could request a "special exorcism" called "a prayer for those impeded in the marriage by a demon or mischief-maker" (119).
135. Alva 1999, fol. 47v. (Here I use Sell and Schwaller's translation.)
136. Feria 1567, fol. 109v.
137. Molina 1984 [1571], fol. 55v.
138. Ibid.
139. Ibid., fols. 55v–56.
140. Feria 1567, fol. 110v.
141. Ibid.
142. Ibid.
143. Klapisch-Zuber 1985, 178–212. Lara 2008 suggests that customs may have been adapted to incorporate indigenous practices into the Mozarabic Rite (118). See Lara 2008, 71, 121, for depictions of the binding of the hands.

144. Feria 1567, fol. 111.

145. Quoted in Burkhart 1996, 100. Boyer 1995 also finds evidence in ecclesiastical texts that priests tolerated a husband's corporal punishment of his wife when he had reasonable cause, as long as it did not become abusive (134).

146. Here I differ from Anderson 1997, who also notes similarities between *huehuetlahtolli* and Christian marriage texts but interprets them as evidence of continuity in marital roles and relations.

147. See also Sousa 2007.

148. Don 2010, 40.

149. Katzew 2011, 173.

CHAPTER FOUR

1. AJVA-CR 1, 4, Yalahui, 1651.
2. Ibid., fol. 5v.
3. Ibid., fol. 20.
4. *Penixitobi* is in Córdova 1987a [1578] for *soltero* or *soltera* (fol. 385). Under "donzella qualquiera que no aun casada," Córdova also lists *pinicocòni, chapacóla, cocónigolà,* and *cocònicobiba* (fol. 146). I have not found the use of any of these terms in the colonial record.
5. Sahagún 1996, bk. 6, fol. 110r-v. In a similar speech to a noble bride, the speaker reminds the young woman: "You are no longer to give yourself to childishness" (*ca aocmo in pipillotl in coconeyotl ticmomacaz*)" (Karttunen and Lockhart 1987, 110–111).
6. Ibid., fol. 113v.
7. Córdova 1987a [1578], fol. 415.
8. Boone 2000, 56–57, passim.
9. Karttunen and Lockhart 1987, 110–113, 122–123, 127.
10. Sahagún 1996, bk. 6, fols. 114–119v.
11. Ibid., fols. 112v–114.
12. Cline 1993, 55–56.
13. Ibid., 56.
14. Córdova 1987b [1578] lists the reasons for divorce among the Zapotecs, noting that childlessness was the primary cause (fol. 217). Monaghan 2001 observes that in contemporary indigenous communities the inability to have children often leads to divorce (fol. 292).
15. AGN-I 23, 1, Coyoacan, 1538.
16. AGN-CR 686, 3, Acatepec, 1558.
17. Many examples of this practice can be seen in the Nahuatl-language testaments from Culhuacan transcribed and translated in Cline and León-Portilla 1984.
18. AJT-CR 3, 30, Teposcolula, 1593; AJT-CR 3, 31, Teposcolula 1593.
19. Kellogg 1997, 139.
20. Terraciano 2001, 182.
21. It should be noted that the practice of women serving as witnesses to tes-

taments has not been observed in archival records from the Bènizàa or Ayuuk communities of Oaxaca. The picture is somewhat different in criminal records, where women continually appear as witnesses, plaintiffs, and defendants. Perhaps because of the spontaneous nature of crime, anyone who had seen a crime or who had information on the plaintiffs or defendants was called to testify regardless of whether they were male or female.

22. AGN-CR 11, 30, San Cristobal Coatepec, 1768.

23. Emphasis mine. AGN-CR 10, 16, Ecatepec, 1742.

24. On conceptions of honor among plebeians and slaves, see Boyer 1998; Johnson 1998; Lauderdale Graham 1998. Lipsett-Rivera 1998 examines cases of women defending their own honor.

25. AJT-CR 2, 1, Coixtlahuaca, 1578. For cases that provide similar scenes, see AJT-CR 14, 13, Tamazulapa, 1634, which discusses the attendance of Tomás de Aquino and his wife Andrea López together at ceremonies in Tamazulapa in 1634; also see AJVA-CR 4, 21, Tiltepec 1694, which recounts the journey of Magdalena Hernández and Marcos Pérez, an Ayuuk couple from Tiltepec, to Yaxila to celebrate the fiesta of the rosary in 1694.

26. AJT-CR 4, 31, Teposcolula, 1597.

27. For example, Francisco Martín went with his wife to visit their son in Texupa in 1592 (AJT-CR 3, 24, Texupa, 1592).

28. AJT-CR 3, 26, Coixtlahuaca, 1592.

29. AJT-CR 3, 52, Teposcolula, 1595; AJT-CR 5, 55, Yanhuitlan, 1601; AJT-CR 7, 38, Teposcolula, 1605; AJT-CR 7, 40, Teposcolula, 1606; AJT-CR 11, 8, Teposcolula, 1624; AJVA-CR 4, 17, Yaganisa, 1691; AJVA-CR 2, 7, Yagayo, 1670.

30. Restall, Sousa, and Terraciano 2005, 141. For a transcription and translation of the full text of don Géronimo's Ñudzahui-language testament, see Terraciano 2001, 376–379. The original document is in AJT-C 4, 417, Teposcolula, 1672–1691, fol. 16–16v (this citation follows the older cataloguing system at the AJT). The translation is Terraciano's.

31. Restall, Sousa, and Terraciano 2005, 142. For a transcription and translation of doña Lazara's testament, Terraciano 2001, 380–383. The original document is in AJT-C 4, 417, Teposcolula, 1672-1691, fol. 18–19 (this citation follows the older cataloguing system at the AJT). The translation is Terraciano's.

32. *Relación de Xalapa, Cintla y Acatlan* (Acuña 1984, 3:289).

33. Karttunen and Lockhart 1987, 108–111.

34. Sahagún 1996, bk. 6, fol. 113r-v.

35. Ibid., fol. 113.

36. Acuña 1986, 2:237.

37. Ibid., 270. Similar statements are found in the *Relación de Ichcateupan* (ibid., 2:264), *Relación de Alahuiztlan* (ibid., 2:277), and *Relación de Coatepeque* (ibid., 2:295).

38. Córdova 1987b [1578], fol. 217.

39. See, for example, AGN-CR 139, 17, Malinalco, 1757; AJT-CR 2, 25, Tamazulapa, 1580.

40. AGN-CR 236, 1, Culhuacan, 1696.

41. AJVA-CR 2, 2, Teotalsingo, 1667, fol. 3.
42. Cline and León-Portilla 1984, 82–83. (Here I use Cline and León-Portilla's translation.)
43. AJT-CR 4, 24, Tilantongo, 1596.
44. AJVA-CR 1, 4, Yalahuí, 1651.
45. AGN-CR 217, 10, Atengo, 1723. For more on marital expectations in colonial Mexico City for a broad cross-section of the population, see Arrom 1985, 229–230. Some of the examples explicitly refer to a woman's responsibilities of maintaining the household and taking care of her husband's clothing.
46. AGN-CR 630, 1, Quatitlan, 1619.
47. AJT-CR 14, 24, Tlaxiaco, 1636.
48. AJVA-CR 1, 54, Camotlan, 1685.
49. AGN-CR 131, 7, Coyoacan, 1643.
50. AGN-CR 730, 9, Tacuba, 1752. Lucas Antonio and all the other witnesses in the case later retracted their statements. Nevertheless, the fact that he concocted a story that they had been working together as evidence of their sexual intimacy, and his comment that they acted like husband and wife, are telling.
51. As an example, the *Relación* of the Nahua community of Chichicapa states that the town had "1,200 tributaries, that is, [each] husband and wife one tributary" (Acuña 1984, 2:74). The *Relación* of the Ñudzahui community of Nochistlan describes a similar arrangement: "This pueblo has very few Indians, because it has no more than 720 complete tributaries, each one being a husband and wife, not counting children" (ibid., 2:366).
52. This was the norm throughout central and southern Mexico and is specifically described in Acuña 1984 for Xocotipac, 2:148; Xaltepetongo, 2:151; Tanatepec, 2:158; and Nochistlan, 2:366. See also Acuña 1984, vol. 3; Acuña 1986, vols. 2 and 3.
53. For example, Diego López Cachi testified that he was born in Texupa but that he had "married Isabel Xaco in Coixtlahuaca" (AJT-CR 4, 5, Coixtlahuaca, 1596). For additional cases that refer to "casados" in terms of tribute duties, see AJT-CR 9, 18, Malinaltepec, 1613; AJT-CR 14, 34, Cuquila, 1637.
54. Carrasco 1984.
55. Schroeder 1992. See also Marcus 2001 for a comparative study of women's rise to rule in ancient states and Connell 2011 for a discussion of the importance of women in creation of noble lineages (62–63).
56. Herrera 2007.
57. See Terraciano 2001 (esp. chap. 6) for a discussion of the yuhuitayu, and Spores 1967, 1984 for examinations of dynastic rule and succession.
58. AJT-CR 2, 46, Teposcolula, 1583.
59. See Terraciano 2001 for a discussion of how Mixtec noblewomen were marginalized by the introduction of the cabildo and by changes among hereditary rulers (179–190).
60. Connell 2011, 74–76; see chap. 2 for a fuller discussion of the career of Valeriano.
61. AGN-CR 216, 4, Atlacomulco, 1685.

62. AGN-CR 140, 1, Malinalco, 1635. He was also accused of placing his sons in office.

63. AJT-CR 10, 11, Cuquila, 1615.

64. AJT-CR 14, 4, Teposcolula, 1633.

65. AGI-P 230A, R1, Nexapa and Tehuantepec, 1661.

66. I believe that Miguel de Illescas' connection was through his brother-in-law, don Esteban Maldonado, rather than his wife, Marta Hernández, who was not as high ranking as don Esteban. Furthermore, Marta's birthplace is unknown to me at this time. Miguel de Illescas did face serious opposition when factional disputes divided the community. His adversaries explained that they had imprisoned and whipped him, removed him from office, and confiscated his belongings because they were tired of the hardship that he caused them. They asserted that because Illescas was not a native of the community, he had them taking care of colts and mules and producing cochineal for the Spanish alcaldes mayores, "who always worked through [Illescas's] hands." The opposition to Illescas on the grounds that he was an outsider underscores the continued importance of local birth in the legitimation of rule in indigenous communities in the late colonial period.

67. Chance 2009, 116.

68. In her study of late colonial and early national Toluca, Kanter 2008 argues that matrilocal residence made men "powerless" (45–47); however, evidence suggests that the effects of matrilocality may have varied depending on class and marriage alliances.

69. See Terraciano 2001, chap. 6, for a full discussion of the yuhuitayu.

70. Oudijk 2000, 185–208, 311–318, figs. 28–37. Oudijk's masterful study of Bènizàa pictorial writing and history provides additional examples of the convention of depicting ruling couples in documents such as the Lienzo of Tiltepec, which is similar in format to the Lienzo of Tabaá but distinct in style and content (208–224, figs. 39a, b, 40).

71. AGN-T 2912, fc. 210, Caxhuacan, mid-eighteenth century.

72. Terraciano 2001, 241.

73. Osowski 2010, 104.

74. The move into adult status associated with marriage made men eligible for office. Terraciano notes that marriage was central to the construction of the Ñudzahui yuhuitayu. He finds no cases of a yuhuitayu ruler who had never married (2001, chap. 6).

75. AJVA-CR 5, 3, Yatzona, 1695.

76. Chance 2009.

77. AGN-CR 643, 7, San Juan Cuescomatepec, 1671. In addition to the cases discussed here, see AJT-CR 1, 111, Yanhuitlan, 1698, which involves a married Ñudzahui woman and a non-Indian tailor, probably a mestizo (this citation follows the older cataloguing system).

78. AJT-CR 1, 33, Tamazulapa, 1580.

79. AJT-CR 6, 46, Yanhuitlan, 1604. I suspect these were the circumstances surrounding the case in AJT-CR 18, 14, Yanhuitlan, 1609.

80. It may be that interracial couples who lived together were more often de-

nounced than were indigenous couples because of other political and economic concerns, and that therefore they appear more frequently in the record. For studies of interethnic sexual relations, see Gutiérrez 1991 for New Mexico (103–104, 285–292); Hackel 2005 for California mission areas (220–227); Landers 2005 for Spanish Florida; Carroll 2009 for New Spain; Restall 2009 for Yucatan (191–193, 221–222, 235–236, 257–277); Komisaruk 2013, for late colonial Guatemala (206–222).

81. AJT-CR 4, 34, Teposcolula, 1597. In her study of the Toluca region, Pizzigoni 2012 finds a similar arrangement in which financial need was at the center of the relationship. Juliana María confessed that she lived with Juan Domingo de la Cruz, calling herself a "fragile and poor woman, [who] went with him because he supported her and her two children" (128). See also Komisaruk 2013 for a discussion of the motivations, including financial, for seeking an informal union (211–218).

82. AGN-CR 641, 28, Ciudad de México, 1584.

83. There is an excellent literature on honor in colonial Latin America. See especially Seed 1988; Gutiérrez 1991; Twinam 1989, 1999; Johnson and Lipsett-Rivera 1998.

84. See AGN-CR 641, 28, Ciudad de México, 1584, which includes cases against Cristóbal de Medina, a vendor of silks and hats, and "an honest woman"; Juan Sarabia, a mestizo tailor, and "an honest woman"; Juan de Salinas, a solicitor, and "an honest woman"; Pedro de Malvenda, a mestizo, and "an honest woman." The file also includes a case against Gregorio Ruiz, a single Spanish cobbler, and Juana Ortíz, a Spanish woman. Someone tried to obliterate Juana Ortíz's name from the record, but it is possible to read it through the back of the page.

85. For cases in which local native officials prescribed punishments of whipping, see AJT-CR 2, 25, Tamazulapa, 1580; AGN-CR 140, 1, Malinalco, 1635; AGN-CR 590, 2, Lalopa, 1657. AJT-CR 10, 7, Yanhuitlan, 1615, provides an example of a Spanish alcalde mayor ordering a man and woman convicted of amancebamiento to pay a *tostón* (silver coin made in Mexico worth one-half *real*; there were eight reales to a peso) each for wax for the Holy Sacrament.

86. See AJT-CR 4, 34, Teposcolula, 1597, for example.

87. AGN-CR 236, 1, Culhuacan, 1696.

88. See, for example, AJT-CR 2, 15, Coixtlahuaca, 1577. In this case, Tomás Gerónimo translated from Chocho to Nahuatl, and Gabriel García translated from Nahuatl to Spanish.

89. Taylor 1979, 87–88; Stern 1995, 60–61. See also Kanter 2008 for discussion of violence in marriage in rural Mexico (chap. 3); Komisaruk 2013 for spousal conflict among multiethnic populations in the urban setting of Guatemala City (196–206); and Sousa 1997 for a discussion of wife beating in Oaxaca.

90. Not all the cases that I consulted were trials for wife beating. In some cases, an assault was mentioned only as incidental evidence.

91. This observation corroborates the conclusions of Taylor 1979, 83–84, and Stern 1995, 54.

92. The language in the records includes *por heridas* (for wounds) and *por malos tratos* (for mistreatment). For a discussion of changing attitudes toward

domestic violence in the United States on the basis of a woman being a mother, see Pleck 1987.

93. For discussions of the concept of mala vida, see Boyer 1989, 1995; Stern 1995, 268; Kanter 2008, 35–51.

94. See, for example: AJT-CR 9, 25.01, Teposcolula, 1613; AJVA-CR 4, 9, Tepantlali, 1688; AJVA-CR 6, 13, Yate, 1701. For discussions of motivations behind gendered violence, see also Stern 1995, 55–59; Kanter 2008, 39–45.

95. AJT-CR 5, 38, Teposcolula, 1600.
96. AGN-CR 686, 3, Acatepec, 1558.
97. AJVA-CR 4, 9, Tepantlali, 1688.
98. AJVA-CR 4, 19, Taguí, 1692.
99. AGN-CR 217, 10, Atengo, 1723.
100. AJT-CR 14, 13, Tamazulapa, 1634.
101. AJVA-CR 7, 10, Camotlan, 1706.
102. AJT-CR 7, 38, Teposcolula, 1605.
103. Stern 1995, 141.

104. Of course, because these cases were not prosecuted, it is much harder to know how often women simply tolerated abusive relationships for the sake of financial security, as tenuous as this was for indigenous families under colonial rule. Kanter 2008 provides an example of a woman who dropped adultery charges against her husband in the hope that he would return to the community and help support their household (49).

105. See, for example, AJVA-CR 4, 17, Yaganiza, 1691.

106. Stern 1995 also finds women's insistence on physical separation in Oaxaca: "In Oaxaca a stronger right of physical separation, backed by a stronger customary right of in-law surveillance and intervention, placed the husband's assertion of ownership on a somewhat softer cultural footing" (235).

107. In this case, Pedro continued to abuse Petrona once she returned home to him, and several days later she was found hanging in a tree on the outskirts of town.

108. AJT-CR 4, 24, Tilantongo, 1596. For additional cases in which the mother and/or father of the victim pressed charges, see AGN-CR 645, 1, Tonaltepec, 1559; AGN-CR 590, 2, Lalopa, 1657; AJT-CR 1, 23, Ocotepec, 1569; AJT-CR 4, 24, Tilantongo, 1596; AJT-CR 8, 12, Yanhuitlan, 1608; AJT-CR 11, 8, Teposcolula, 1632; AJVA-CR 1, 4, Yalahuí, 1651; AJVA-CR 1, 10, Huitepec, 1659; AJVA-CR 4, 16, Tonaguia, 1691; AJVA-CR 4, 19, Taguí, 1692; AJVA-CR 7, 10, Camotlan, 1706.

109. AJT-CR 1, 17, Yanhuitlan, 1577. For additional examples, see AGN-CR 686, 3, Acatepec, 1558 (uncle is plaintiff); AJT-CR 6, 39, Tonaltepec, 1603 (nephew, plaintiff); AJT-CR 7, 38, Teposcolula, 1605 (mother-in-law from a previous marriage is plaintiff); AJT-CR 10, 22, Yanhuitlan, 1608 (victim's adult son accuses stepfather).

110. Taylor 1979, 85.

111. See, for example, AJT-CR 3, 18, Teposcolula, 1590; AJT-CR 7, 38, Teposcolula, 1605; AJT-CR 10, 7, Yanhuitlan, 1615; AJT-CR 11, 28, Teposcolula, 1626; AGN-CR 590, 2, Lalopa, 1657.

112. AJT-CR 1, 61: 2, 12, Yanhuitlan, 1577. See also AJT-CR 11, 28, Teposcolula, 1626. In this case, the defendant's labor was sold for two years; he had attacked his wife with a knife and accidentally killed their baby, which she was holding at the time.

113. Many of the men who killed their wives fled to other regions to escape punishment, abandoning their homes and children. Also, the Audiencia in Mexico City issued sentences for homicide cases as well, so many cases ended with a notation that the case had been submitted to the Audiencia for final judgment.

114. Death sentences were issued in AJT-CR 10, 22, Yanhuitlan, 1616; AGN-CR 590, 2, Lalopa, 1657. Floggings and the sale of service were the punishments in AJT-CR 5, 38, Teposcolula, 1600; AJT-CR 7, 38, Teposcolula, 1605; AJVA-CR 1, 50, San Francisco Cajonos, 1684 (this citation follows the older cataloguing system).

115. Respectively, AJT-CR 1, 23, Ocotepec, 1569; AJVA-CR 4, 19, Camotlan, 1706.

116. AJT-CR 4, 24, Tilantongo, 1596.

117. Stern 1995, 235.

CHAPTER FIVE

1. AJT-CR 3, 30 and 3, 31, Teposcolula, 1593. For a similar example, see AJT-CR 8, 17, Teposcolula, 1610.
2. Burkhart 2001.
3. Molina 1992 glosses this term *cosas mundanas y terrenales* (N-S 124v). Although the term does not appear to have an explicitly sexual connotation in the gloss, the context of the passages that use *tlalticpacaiotl* suggests pleasure.
4. Sahagún 1996, bk. 6, fols. 75r-v.
5. Sahagún 1996, bk. 10, fol. 87.
6. Lavrin 1989a.
7. Sahagún 1996, bk. 6, fol. 98.
8. Ibid.
9. Ibid., fols. 98v–99v.
10. Sahagún 1996, bk. 6, fol. 99v.
11. Ibid., fol. 98v.
12. Ibid., fol. 97.
13. Ibid., fol. 98.
14. Ibid., fols. 97v–98.
15. Ibid., fol. 105v, and bk. 11, fol. 83. Aphrodisiacs were made from the scrapings of certain types of snakes and snails. The description of the snail implies an analogy between the snail who goes along exuding a sticky liquid and the man who causes his liquid to dry up by drinking too much aphrodisiac. Also note that the snail is said to live in the cornfields, a place associated with fertility.
16. AGN-I 40, 33, Matlactlan, 1540.
17. Cline 1993, 52–54.
18. Chimalpahin 1997, 136–139.
19. López Austin 1988, 1:293.

20. As Clendinnen 1991 points out, the Nahuas did not practice menstrual seclusion (158, 206). In fact, in Mesoamerica blood was considered a purifying substance.
21. Sahagún 1996, bk. 6, fol. 79. Note the use of *tlaticpac* for earthly pleasure rather than *tlalticpacaiotl*.
22. Sahagún 1996, bk. 9, fol. 32v.
23. Sahagún 1996, bk. 1, fol. 22. Note that pulque makers also fasted during production time.
24. Sigal 2011 offers a fascinating study of images and texts concerning Tlazolteotl.
25. Ixcuina is one manifestation of Tlazolteotl. See Sullivan 1982.
26. Sahagún 1996, bk. 1, fols. 6v-10.
27. For more on Xochiquetzal, see Sigal 2011, 105-107, 121-122, 125-128, 169-174, 246-247.
28. In colonial criminal records, native witnesses sometimes discredited defendants or other witnesses by accusing them of being a "vagabond." See, for example, AJT-CR 5, 23, Yanhuitlan, 1600; AJT-CR 14, 4, Teposcolula, 1633; AJVA-CR 1, 5, Totontepec, 1655; AJVA-CR 2, 17 bis, Ayutla, 1674.
29. Klein 2001, 206-211.
30. Sahagún 1996, bk. 6, fol. 79.
31. See also Ibid., fol. 79v, which uses *cuepa* in the construction *mitzonaviani-cuepaz* (He will turn you into an auiani).
32. Ibid., fol. 97v.
33. Andrews and Hassig 1984, 134-139.
34. I have followed Andrews and Hassig's 1984 reconstruction and translation of the Nahuatl. Note that Ruiz de Alarcón has *tlacolmiquiliztli*, but the tlaçol-miquiliztli proposed by Andrew and Hassig makes sense (353).
35. Sahagún 1996, bk. 5, fol. 21.
36. See Andrews and Hassig 1984, 353, n. 12.
37. For a discussion of contemporary Nahua explanations of the sources of disease and methods of healing, see Sandstrom 1991, 252-253, 321-322, passim.
38. *Ahuiani* (one who indulges in pleasure) is a term for a woman who danced and participated in temple rituals. The friars distorted the original meaning of the word when they adopted it for *prostitute*. Although I recognize the corruption of the term in Christian discourse, I use *prostitute* here because it conveys the intention of the colonial texts. Olivier 2004 considers whether prostitution existed in postclassic Mexico and concludes that the colonial concept distorts the role of the ahuiani as companions of warriors who were to be sacrificed. See also Flores Farfán and Elferink 2007 for a discussion of Nahua attitudes toward prostitution.
39. Sahagún 1996, bk. 10, fol. 39.
40. Ibid., fol. 40.
41. Acuña 1984, 2:101-102, 3:272-273, respectively, provide examples from Chinantla and Ucila. See Acuña 1984, 2:319, 3:144, respectively, for examples specifying that the priests in Juxtlahuaca and Teozacualco refrained from sex before their rituals.
42. Sahagún 1996, bk. 3, fol. 38v.

43. Acuña 1984, 3:93.

44. People of the communities of Talea, Yatoni, Yatzona, Temascalapa, Yalahuí, Yaxoni, Camotlan, Reagui, Yagalasi, Lachixila, Teotlasco, Comaltepec, and Chinantla were among the many that reported sexual abstinence among their ritual observances (AGI-M 882, 1704).

45. Sigal 2011, 180. I read more than five hundred criminal cases in the archives of Teposcolula, Villa Alta, and Central Mexico, and found only a single case of two men having been accused of homosexuality; however, the case is incomplete. The men denied the charges, and one of them asserted that the accuser was an enemy seeking retribution (AJT-CR, 6, 633, Texupa, 1693). Komisaruk 2013 also notes that she found no cases in the criminal archive concerning the prosecution of homosexuality in her study of late colonial Guatemala (221). Tortorici 2007 found one case from Michoacán alleging thirteen different acts of sodomy; he argues that the case provides evidence of a sodomitical subculture in rural Mexico. Sigal 2007 analyzes the representation of same-sex relations in the Florentine Codex.

46. Sahagún 1996, bk. 2, fol. 54v.

47. Sahagún 1996, bk. 4, fol. 53v.

48. Karttunen 1983, 337.

49. The Codex Telleriano-Remensis reports that those who were found guilty of adultery and robbery were executed on the day of Five Dog (Quiñones Keber 1995, fol. 12v). Significantly, a dog and other symbols of sex and discord, including a snake, are shown emerging from beneath the goddess Xochiquetzal in an illustration in the Codex Telleriano-Remensis (see Figure 5.3).

50. Sahagún 1996, bk. 6, fol. 97.

51. Ibid., fol. 98.

52. Ibid., fols. 97v–98.

53. Sahagún 1996, bk. 2, fol. 119v.

54. Ibid., fol. 84.

55. Ibid., fol. 78v.

56. Sahagún 1996, bk. 1, fols. 11v–12.

57. Sahagún 1996, bk. 4, fol. 6.

58. Acuña 1984, 3:272.

59. Acuña 1984, 2:101–102. The *Relaciones* of Tecuicuilco and Putla also conflate fasting and sexual abstinence (Acuña 1984, 3:93; 2:319, respectively).

60. AGI-M 882, 1704.

61. AJT-CR 3, 30, Teposcolula, 1593.

62. AJT-CR 11, 32, Tamazulapa, 1626.

63. AGN-CR 590, 2, Lalopa, 1657.

64. AJVA-CR 1, 6.01, Lachirio, 1667.

65. As Monaghan 1995 points out, food is (and was) often scarce in agricultural communities (39).

66. AJVA-CR 4, 19, Taguí, 1692.

67. For examples of couples drinking together at home, see AJT-CR 5, 55, Yanhuitlan, 1601; AJT-CR 14, 34, Cuquila, 1637. For examples of couples drinking with other people, see AJT-CR 7, 40, Teposcolula, 1575; AJT-CR 2, 37, Tlaxi-

aco, 1581; AJT-CR 3, 52, Teposcolula, 1595; AJT-CR 7, 38, Teposcolula, 1605; AJT-CR 11, 8, Teposcolula, 1624; AJVA-CR 4, 17, Yaganisa, 1691.

68. AJT-CR 9, 1, Tamazulapa, 1612. Don Agustín was married to doña María de Alvarado, a noblewoman from Camotlan in the Mixteca Baja. For example, in 1612, when don Agustín Maldonado confessed to committing adultery with Catalina Xañu, he admitted that, on the day of his arrest, he had promised to buy a little pulque for them to drink together that evening. Don Agustín's admission associates drinking with native courting customs and the intimate life of a couple.

69. Sahagún 1996, bk. 6, fol. 83.
70. Sahagún 1996, bk. 10, fols. 38v–39.
71. Peterson 1988, 284–285.
72. Burkhart 1989, 63–64.
73. Sahagún 1996, bk. 10, fol. 24.
74. AJT-CR 3, 6, Yanhuitlan, 1588.
75. AGN-CR 131, 7, Coyoacan, 1643.
76. Flowers were also associated with paradise and the afterlife (Burkhart 1992; Hill 1992; Taube 2004).
77. Sahagún 1996, bk. 5, fol. 15v. The Florentine Codex states that it was believed that people should smell only the edges of flowers. Interestingly, one Triqui man from Oaxaca told me that people should not smell the flowers in church because they belong to the saints (Andrés Gutiérrez, personal communication, May 1995).
78. Karttunen and Lockhart 1987, 124–125.
79. Acuña 1984, 2:307 (*Relación de Juxtlahuaca*).
80. Katzew 2011, 172–173.
81. Sahagún 1996, bk. 11, fol. 215.
82. Ibid.
83. Biblioteca Enciclopédica del Estado de México, 1980, 33.
84. The Spanish in Molina 1992 is *encantar, enlabiar a la muger para llevarla a otra parte, o hechizarla* (fol. 160). See also *xuchiuia. nite. dar bevezidos o hechizos paraque quiera bien el hombre a la muger* (fol. 161v).
85. Sahagún 1996, bk. 5, fol. 15r-v.
86. Arvey 1988, in analyzing flower imagery in the Florentine Codex, argues that the negative association of flowers reflected Christian influence. Considering the images and the Nahuatl-language terminology together, I would suggest that flowers also represented sexual excess and decadence in the postclassic period. Furthermore, as a carryover of the pictorial writing system, the images include symbols, such as flowers, that were meant to evoke specific Nahuatl terms, such as *xochihuia*. Arvey's discussion of the European influence on the poses of prostitutes is especially convincing.
87. Sahagún 1996, bk. 10, fol. 40.
88. Russo 2002.
89. Sahagún 1996, bk. 3, fol. 1v.
90. Sahagún 1996, bk. 6, fol. 120.
91. Acuña 1986, 2:86.
92. Monaghan 1995, 145.

93. In some Nahua myths, Ehecatl retrieves the bones of an ancient people from the underworld and scatters them on the surface of the earth to create humans (Miller and Taube 1993, 84).
94. See Sigal 2011 for an interpretation of this image (134–135). Sigal argues that the serpent represents Tlazolteotl's phallus and that in this case Tlazolteotl is regendered as both god and goddess.
95. Terraciano 2001, 166–169.
96. Córdova 1987a [1578], 149f.
97. Alvarado 1962, fol. 85.
98. Molina 1992, fol. 48.
99. AJT-CR 3, 30, Teposcolula, 1593.
100. AJT-CR 11, 32, Tamazulapa, 1626.
101. Sahagún 1996, bk. 6, fol. 97v. The meaning of *aoc cuelle tiquilvia* remains open to various interpretations. The Spanish translation in the original is "The man says to the woman that he can do no more."
102. Sahagún 1996, bk. 10, fol. 24v.
103. Ibid., fols. 24v–25.
104. Ibid., fol. 41. *Tecochtlacani* sic for *tecochtlaçani*. Native-language dictionaries also list various terms that mean "to seduce a woman with speech"; however, it is unclear if this is a Spanish concept or a native concept, or both. For example, Molina 1992 has an entry on the Spanish side of the dictionary, *enlabiar a la muger, o halagar a alguno con palabras blandas* (fol. 54). Córdova 1987a [1578] also provides Tíchazàa terms for the Spanish *enlabiar con palabras a la muger* (fol. 168v). Alvarado 1962 contains an entry, *enlabiar engañando* (fol. 99).
105. AJT-CR 3, 50, Tlaxiaco, 1594 (fol. 1v).
106. AGN-CR 216, 5, Amanalco, 1650.
107. AJT-CR 12, 22, Teposcolula, 1630 (fol. 7v). See also AJT-CR 13, 13, Achiutla, 1632, in which María López confesses that she had committed adultery with a local Ñudzahui man after he spoke "some words" to her, convincing her to have sex with him on the bank of a nearby river.
108. AGN-CR 141, 9, Ayapango, 1765.
109. AJT-CR 3, 18, Teposcolula, 1590.
110. AJT-CR 6, 27, Teposcolula, 1623.
111. AJT-CR 2, 13, Teposcolula, 1578.
112. AJT-CR 9, 1, Tamazulapa, 1612.
113. Sahagún 1996, bk. 6, fol. 101r-v.
114. Alvarado 1962, fol. 85.
115. Córdova 1987a [1578], fol. 289.
116. Sahagún 1996, bk. 3, fols. 12v–14.
117. Sahagún 1996, bk. 6, fol. 183r-v.
118. Sahagún 1996, bk. 10, fol. 39.
119. Ibid., fol. 40.
120. Ibid., fol. 40r-v.
121. Burkhart 1989, 46.
122. In addition to the metaphors discussed here, see Klein 1990, 1991; also

see Burkhart 1986, who discuss nets, snares, and entrails and the rabbit and deer, respectively, related to discourses on immorality.

123. Burkhart 1989, esp. chap. 3. Russell notes that in European folklore the Devil also favored noon; this would have contrasted sharply with Mesoamerican views of the moral order of the universe (Russell 1984, 171).

124. Taggart 1983.

125. See Burkhart 1988 for a discussion of the development of this association. See also Burkhart 1989, 83.

126. Taggart 1983, 63.

127. For contemporary examples of this ideology, see Taggart 1983. For the colonial period, see Burkhart 1989. These concepts are clearly conveyed in the speeches in the Florentine Codex (bk. 6).

128. Monaghan 1995, 136–137.

129. Ibid., 312.

130. Monaghan 1995, 164.

131. Córdova 1970, 102.

132. Ibid., 103.

133. Ibid., 102.

134. Ibid., 102–103.

135. Trexler 1995; Tortorici 2010.

136. Molina 1984, fols. 80–80v.

137. Molina 1984, fols. 33–33v.

138. Molina 1984, fol. 33.

139. On these concepts and practices among the Spanish population, see Seed 1988; Twinam 1989; Socolow 1989; Lavrin 1989a.

140. Molina 1984, fol. 33v.

141. Ibid.

142. Ibid., fols. 80v–81.

143. Ibid., fol. 80v.

144. Alva 1999, 63.

145. Ibid., 107.

146. Ibid., 63–67.

147. To use Gruzinski's 1989 term.

148. Alva 1999, 61, 67.

149. Ibid., 71.

150. Ibid., 105.

151. Ibid., 61.

152. Ibid., 77.

153. Ibid., 81.

154. Sahagún 1996, bk. 10, fols. 40v–41. See Klein 2000 for a discussion of changing views on the nature of the tzitzimime.

155. Sahagún 1996, bk. 10, fol. 40v.

156. See, for example, Taggart 1983, 58, 65; Monaghan 1995, 58,144; see also Russell 1984, 69, 71, for directional significance in Christianity.

157. Sousa 2002.

158. On the uses of *tlacatecolotl* and *tzitzimitl* as terms for the Devil in eccle-

siastical texts, see Burkhart 1989, 42–43. Tzitzimitl, which were believed to fall from the sky, were likened to fallen angels. Interestingly, Pohl 1998 notes a symbolic association between drunkenness, violence, and factionalism (represented by tzitzimime) on postclassic Tlaxcalan altars.

159. AGN-CR 686, 3, Acatepec, 1558.

160. Martín Tilantzin's statement reflects the Mesoamerican belief that repeated intercourse was necessary so that enough sperm could build up inside the womb to form a baby, making conception a cumulative process. On this and other Nahua beliefs about conception, see López Austin 1988, 1:296–299.

161. AGN-CR 590, 2, Lalopa, 1657. In the course of his confession before Spanish officials, Jacinto had the nerve to complain that local officials continued to whip him even after he had confessed to the crime.

162. AGN-CR 590, 2, Lalopa, 1657 (fol. 36).
163. AJT-CR 3, 6, Yanhuitlan, 1588.
164. AJT-CR 5, 36, Teposcolula, 1601.
165. AJT-CR 6, 46, Yanhuitlan, 1604.
166. AJT-CR 12, 22, Teposcolula, 1630.
167. AJT-CR 13, 22, Tamazulapa, 1632.
168. AJVA-CR 2, 2, Teotalsingo, 1667.
169. AJT-CR 21, 13, Xinastla, 1695.

CHAPTER SIX

1. AJT-CR 1, 81, Coixtlahuaca, 1596.
2. Ibid.
3. Spanish couples also routinely engaged in premarital sex once the promise of marriage (*palabra de casamiento*) had been exchanged (Lavrin 1989a, 61–64).
4. Sahagún 1996, bk. 3, fol. 34r-v.
5. Molina 1992, fol. 32v; Córdova 1987a [1578], fol. 277; Alvarado 1962 [1593], fol. 83v., respectively. Terraciano 2001, 301–302 briefly discusses the use of ñaha quachi and a related term *ñaha dzuchi* in religious and mundane texts.
6. Adultery in many societies is contingent on the woman's marital status only. See D'Emilio and Freedman 1988 for a historical survey of adultery and its punishments in the United States.
7. López Austin 1988 and Clendinnen 1991 define adultery based on the woman's marital status alone. Their studies focus more on the postclassic period, so it may be that indigenous concepts of adultery broadened overtime.
8. AJT-CR 9, 1, Tamazulapa, 1612.
9. AJT-CR 16, 25, Teposcolula, 1655.
10. AJVA-CR 5, 4, Yatzona, 1695.
11. AGN-CR 216, 5, Amanalco, 1650, fol. 262.
12. Lavrin 1989a, 50. Sex between two single adults outside of marriage was considered simple fornication.
13. Molina 1992, fol. 108v.
14. Molina 1992, fol. 5 (S-N).

15. Karttunen 1983, 304.

16. Since *xima* (to plane, shave, cut, do carpentry), is a transitive verb, this originally must have been a two-word expression, *xima* bearing a separate object, but with the passage of time and frequent use, the two became amalgamated. Probably all sense of the etymological origin was lost. Although the verb generally keeps the indefinite object *te-*, it can be found with a specific object, the offended spouse. Thus Sahagún 1996, bk. 5 has *oquitlaxin yn inamic* (he or she committed adultery against his or her spouse) (fol. 20v); the *n* still appears occasionally in texts, thus *tetlanximaz* in Sahagún 1996, bk. 4, fol. 53v.

17. Molina 1992, fol. 54v.

18. Sahagún 1996, bk. 6, 79.

19. Molina 1992, fol. 20.

20. Sahagún 1996, bk. 10, fol. 40r-v.

21. AJVA-CR 1, 21, Lachirio, 1665.

22. AJVA-CR, 6, 8, Yalahuí, 1699.

23. Sahagún's informants associated the two transgressions saying, "If someone here in dire straits had stolen, had committed adultery, had taken a paramour" (*intla aca ivivi onican oichtec, otetlaxin, anoçe omomecati*) to explain the context in which a certain expression would be used. The *onican* is a little puzzling here and would make more sense if it were *ohuican* (1996, bk. 6, fol. 190v).

24. Quiñones Keber 1995, fol. 12v. They were both killed on the day of Five Dog.

25. Sahagún 1996, bk. 4, fol. 32v.

26. Acuña 1984, 2:51.

27. Acuña 1984, 2:287. Pairing of the crimes of adultery and theft occurs in statements from other communities in the Juxtlahuaca jurisdiction, including Mixtepec (ibid., 2:295); Ayusuchiquilazala (ibid., 2:302); Xalapa (ibid., 2:308); and Zacatepec (ibid., 2:320).

28. AJT-CR 19: 3, Yanhuitlan, 1684. This document is transcribed, translated, and analyzed in more detail in Terraciano 1998.

29. Acuña 1984, 2:271.

30. AJT-CR 8, 17, Teposcolula, 1610.

31. AJT-CR 9, 27, Teposcolula, 1613.

32. AGN-CR 217, 10, Atengo, 1723.

33. AJT-CR 8, 14, Yanhuitlan, 1609. For an additional example, see AGN-CR 645, 1, Tonaltepec, 1559.

34. AJT-CR 13, 2, Teposcolula, 1631.

35. On this point, see also Sigal 2011, 212.

36. For example, Bènizàa couples prosecuted in the two following cases reported that they had been involved for three years: AJVA-CR 6, 9, Amatepec, 1699; AJVA-CR 1, 9, San Francisco Cajonos, 1659.

37. AJT-CR 9, 1, Tamazulapa, 1612.

38. AJVA-CR 1, 9, San Francisco Cajonos, 1659.

39. AJVA-CR 6, 9, Amatepec, 1699.

40. One Ñudzahui official was stabbed to death in 1630 when he attempted to apprehend a married man and his lover, whom he had caught together in a cave

(AJT-CR 12, 22, Teposcolula, 1630). A Mixe official also was killed when he tried to arrest an adulterous couple (AJVA-CR 6, 9, Amatepec, 1699).

41. See also *Relación de Coatepec* (Acuña 1986, 2:295).
42. Acuña 1986, 2:236.
43. For a history of the conflict between the couple see, AJT-CR 5, 40, Yanhuitlan, 1601; AJT-CR 6, 40, Yanhuitlan, 1603; AJT-CR 6, 33, Yanhuitlan, 1603.
44. It is possible that what is described here refers to the practice of punishing someone by holding his or her face in chile smoke, as depicted in the Codex Mendoza.
45. AGN-CR 590, 2, Lalopa, 1657.
46. Acuña 1984, 2:215.
47. See *Relación de Atlatlauca y Malinaltepec* (Acuña 1984, 2:51); *Relacíon de Coatepec* (ibid., 2:295); *Relación de Tlacotepec* (ibid., 2:301); *Relación de Cuezala* (ibid., 2:316); *Relación de Teloloapan* (ibid., 2:324); *Relación de Guaxilotitlan* (ibid., 2:215); *Relación de Cempoala* (ibid., 2:77); *Relación de Epazoyuca* (ibid., 2:86).
48. Sahagún 1996, bk. 4, fol. 93.
49. See, for example, *Relación de Tlacotepec* (Acuña 1986, 2:301); *Relación de Cempoala* (ibid., 2:77); *Relación de Epazoyuca* (ibid., 2:86).
50. Sahagún 1996, bk. 4, fol. 53v.
51. Sahagún 1996, bk. 1, fols. 6v–10.
52. Note that the Spanish gloss specifies that if a man had sex with a married woman they were both killed, suggesting that adultery was contingent on the woman's marital status. In colonial criminal records, it is clear that sex between a married man and a single woman or a widow still constituted adultery.
53. Phillips 1884, 642. *Historia Mexicana por sus pinturas* also states that death by strangulation was the punishment for lesbian activity and that male and female adulterers were put to death by stoning.
54. AGN-T 19, pt. 2a, 2, fol. 79.
55. Acuña 1984, 2:271.
56. Acuña 1986, 2:311.
57. Codex Tudela 1980, fols. 24v–25. Those who were caught committing adultery a second time were killed by stoning.
58. Acuña 1984, 2:256.
59. Acuña 1986, 2:236.
60. Acuña 1984, 2:308.
61. Ibid., 2:320.
62. Acuña 1986, 2:250.
63. Ibid, 2:305–306.
64. See, for example, AJT-CR 3, 30, Teposcolula, 1592, in which a married man and married woman were ordered not to see each other or continue their affair, and warned that if they were caught together again they would be given 100 lashes.
65. AJT-CR 9, 1, Tamazulapa, 1612.
66. AJVA-CR 1, 9, San Francisco Cajonos, 1659.
67. AJT-CR 9, 1, Tamazulapa, 1612.

68. AJT-CR 11, 32, Tamazulapa, 1626.
69. AGN-CR 131, 7, Coyoacan, 1643.
70. AJVA-CR 6, 14, Analco, 1701.
71. Perry 1990, 135.
72. Phillips 1884, 642.
73. Acuña 1984, 3:288.
74. AJT-CR 11, 9, Tamazulapa, 1624.
75. AJT-CR 13, 21, Teposcolula, 1632, fol. 2v. Additional materials related to this case are in AJT-CR 13, 22, Tamazulapa, 1632.
76. AJT-CR 13, 21, Teposcolula, 1632, fol. 12v.
77. AJVA-CR 1, 9, San Francisco Cajonos, 1659.
78. AJVA-CR 6, 14, Yahuibee, 1698.
79. AJT-CR 22, 08, Tlaxiaco, 1711–1713. Initially both Josefa de Rosa and Baltasar Melchor were sentenced to death; on appeal her sentence was reduced, but it was still harsh: two hundred lashes and her labor sold to an obraje for ten years.
80. Córdova 1987b, fol. 217.
81. AGN-CR 686, 3, Acatepec, 1558.
82. Ibid.
83. AGN-CR 590, 2, Lalopa, 1657.
84. AJT-CR 14, 22, Tlaxiaco, 1635.
85. AGN-I 40, 32, Iguala, 1540; AJVA-CR 2, 2, Teotalsingo, 1667; AJVA-CR 4, 5, Yatzona, 1687; AJVA-CR 5, 4, Yatzona, 1695.
86. Nouns based on these words (*forzamento* or *forzamiento*; *estupro*; *corrupción*; and *violación*) are found rarely or never in the sources that I consulted.
87. For examples of the use of *estupro* see AJT-CR 18, 34, Coyotepec, 1684; AGN-CR 216, 5, Amanalco, 1650; AGN-CR 11, 26, Ecatepec, 1748. In one instance, *estupro* had positive connotations: a witness stated that she saw "the couple very happy together and they told her that the man had raped her" (AGN-CR 139, 24, Malinalco, 1696, fol. 365v). Lavrin 1989a notes that *estupro* and *violación* were somewhat ambiguous terms (71–72). In her study of rape cases in Mexico from 1750 to 1850, Lipsett-Rivera 1996 finds that *estupro* is the closest to the modern English definition of rape. For examples of the use of *corromper*, see AGN-I 40, 32, Iguala, 1540; AGN-CR 216, 5, Amanalco, 1650.
88. AGN-CR 11, 26, Ecatepec, 1748; AGN-CR 705, 2, Tenango, 1763.
89. AGN-I 40, 32, Yguala, 1540; AJT-CR 5, 55, Yanhuitlan, 1601.
90. These could be constructions created to convey the sense of the Spanish *forzar*; perhaps in the future, as more Nahuatl-language criminal records come to light, it will be possible to attest to usage.
91. AJT-CR 3, 39, Teposcolula, 1594.
92. AJVA-CR 5, 16, La Oya, 1697.
93. AGN-CR 597, 7, Ayozingo, 1736.
94. AGN-CR 11, 26, San Cristobal Ecatepec, 1748.
95. AGN-CR 705, 2, Tenango, 1763.
96. AGN-CR 234, 6, Tizapan, 1763.
97. AGN-CR 597, 7, Ayozingo, 1736.

98. AJVA-CR 2, 1, Lachirio, 1666. It is possible that he was tried for rape and that the records have not survived.
99. Restall and Sigal 1992; Haskett 1994; Restall 1995; Chuchiak 2007; Sigal 2000.
100. AGN-CR 12, 13, Ecatepec, 1721.
101. AJT-CR 5, 55, Yanhuitlan, 1601.
102. AJT-CR 14, 11, Cuquila, 1633.
103. AJVA-CR 4, 23, Yaa, 1694.
104. AJVA-CR 5, 16, La Oya, 1697. There was considerable tension between Juliana Martín and her husband and Juliana's sister and her husband. Conflicting testimony suggests that Juliana complained to officials because she had argued with her sister's husband. One reason for the tension was the accusation by Juliana's sister that Juliana's husband had once tried to rape her by pulling up her huipilli.
105. AGN-CR 216, 5, Amanalco, 1650.
106. AGN-CR 597, 7, Ayozingo, 1736; AGN-CR 705, 2, Tenango, 1763.
107. AJT-CR 5, 55, Yanhuitlan, 1601; AJVA-CR 5, 4, Yatzona, 1695. See also AJT-CR 14, 11, Cuquila, 1633.
108. AJT-CR 18, 34, Coyotepec, 1684.
109. AGN-CR 216, 5, Amanalco, 1650. See also AGN-CR 234, 6, Tizapan, 1763, in which a native man was sentenced to four years in an obraje for the rape of the daughter of a Spaniard.
110. AGN-CR 139, 24, Malinalco, 1696.
111. Ibid.
112. Her brothers asserted that he had given her the marriage promise.
113. AGN-CR 597, 7, Ayozingo, 1736.
114. AGN-CR 216, 5, Amanalco, 1650.
115. Lipsett-Rivera 1996.
116. AGN-CR 10, 15, Ecatepec, 1674.
117. Ibid.
118. AGN-CR 11, 26, Ecatepec, 1748.
119. AGN-CR 234, 6, Tizapan, 1763.
120. In her study of late colonial Guatemala, Komisaruk 2013 finds suits filed by women seeking child support from ex-lovers, but notes that "issues of honor, *honra*, and promises of marriage played a relatively minor part" (228). I have not encountered any cases involving demands for child support in my research.
121. AGN-CR 10, 17, San Cristobal Ecatepec, 1743.
122. Lavrin 1989a, 63.
123. I have not located any suits over loss of virginity from the Mixteca Alta and only one case from Villa Alta from the eighteenth century (AJVA-CR 7, 5, Lachirio, 1702). Perhaps further research in ecclesiastical records will uncover more cases.

CHAPTER SEVEN

1. AGN-CR 10, 16, Ecatepec, 1742.

2. Sahagún 1996, bk. 10, fol. 1r-v.
3. AJVA-CR 3, 9, Yalala, 1678.
4. AJVA-CR 2, 17bis, Ayutla, 1674. See also AJVA-CR 4, 19, Tagui, 1692.
5. See, for example, AJT-CR 15, 19, Yanhuitlan, 1641, in which Pedro de Zárate's enemies discredit him by accusing him of failing to participate in the *tequio* (rotary tribute labor system).
6. For this reason, an outraged Joseph Luis assaulted a Bènizàa alcalde who had asked him why he had not helped with work on the church (AJVA-CR 5, 10, Yate, 1696).
7. See especially Gibson 1952, 1964; Lockhart 1992; Haskett 1991b; Terraciano 2001.
8. Molina 1992, fol. 90v, fol. 115r; Alvarado 1962, fol. 157v, fol. 198v; Córdova 1987a, fol. 287v, fol. 412r.
9. Sahagún 1996, bk. 10, fol. 7v.
10. See, for example, the groundbreaking work of McCafferty and McCafferty 1991.
11. Klein 1982.
12. Sahagún 1996, bk. 6, fol. 189.
13. Sahagún 1996, bk. 12, fol. 84r-v. Of course, it is possible that the Nahua authors embellished their description of the rulers when they recounted the fall of the Mexica Empire. Nevertheless, the point remains that their attention to the details of the rulers' garments reveals the symbolic importance of cloth.
14. Similar sentiments were expressed on a popular, informal level. For example, a Ñudzahui man testified in a criminal trial that he had seen the defendant intoxicated, "without a cape or hat, like a crazy person." The witness equated the drunken man's disheveled state and lack of appropriate clothing with insanity and disorder (AJT-CR 14, 24, Tlaxiaco, 1636, fol. 24v). Klein 2001 notes that the *Anales de Tlatelolco* describes how, when the city fell to the Spaniards, the ruler appeared wearing rags and women's clothing (193).
15. Sahagún 1996, bk. 6, fol. 170v; see illustrations on fol. 170r-v.
16. Sahagún 1996, bk. 4, fol. 67v.
17. Sahagún 1996, bk. 7, fol. 20r-v.
18. Sahagún 1996, bk. 12, fols. 51v–52. Today, in communities such as Chicahuastla, Oaxaca, the Virgin Mary is often dressed in indigenous women's clothing that is characteristic of the region.
19. Motolinía 1950, 96.
20. Ibid.
21. For examples of ancient textiles found in caves and other archaeological contexts, see Mastache 1996 and Ávila 1996.
22. Sahagún 1996, bk. 9, fols. 2–8.
23. Ibid., fols. 36v–37.
24. Sahagún 1996, bk. 12, fol. 4r-v. The cloaks included "the sun-covered style, the blue-knotted style, the style covered with jars, the one with painted eagles, the style with serpent faces, the style with the wind jewels, the style with turkey blood, or with whirlpools, the style with smoking mirrors."

25. Although he does not discuss female artisans specifically, Durand-Forest (1994) discusses the importance of crafts in the economy in general, and notes the artisan's high status.

26. Sahagún 1996, bk. 9, fol. 8.

27. Sahagún 1996, bk. 12, fol. 55r-v.

28. In the overwhelming majority of robbery cases, people complained that either cloth or livestock had been stolen from them. For examples that specify cloth among the stolen goods, see AJT-CR 5, 17, Teposcolula, 1598; AJT-CR 7, 2, Yanhuitlan, 1604; AJT-CR 7, 10, Teposcolula, 1604; AJT-CR 7, 16, Yanhuitlan, 1605; AJT-CR 7, 18, Teposcolula, 1605; AJT-CR 7, 22, Yanhuitlan, 1605; AJT-CR 7, 23, Yanhuitlan, 1605; AJT-CR 8, 5, Teposcolula, 1607; AJT-CR 12, 3, Teposcolula, 1628; AJT-CR 13, 18.01, Teposcolula, 1632; AJT-CR 14, 6, Teposcolula, 1633; AJVA-CR 1, 18, Villa Alta, 1665; AJVA-CR 2, 12, Talea, 1671; AJVA-CR 2, 17 bis, Ayutla, 1674; AJVA-CR 3, 10, Villa Alta, 1682.

29. In some regions of Mesoamerica, these symbols metaphorically represented the female body, and spinning was considered strictly women's work (see Sahagún 1996, bk. 6, fol. 199v for Nahua associations of the female body and spinning tools); however, evidence from the Zapotec Sierra shows that both men and women spun thread and yarn using the spindle whorl and a bowl. In several criminal cases officials noted that either a suspect or a household member was spinning thread when they arrived at the house to make the arrest. See, for example, AJVA-CR 2, 15, Yatzona, 1674; when officials went to arrest don Felipe de Santiago, they found him and his wife seeding (*escarmando*) and spinning cotton. Similarly, Pedro Méndez was spinning thread when officials apprehended him (AJVA-CR 4, 19, Taguí, 1692). Interestingly, in preconquest times a female slave who was to be sacrificed also spun cotton as she awaited her death (Sahagún 1996, bk. 9, fol. 36).

Concerning weaving see AJT-CR 2, 179, Teposcolula, 1603; AJT-CR 2, 244, Teposcolula, 1608.

30. See, for example, the Codex Osuna, fol. 38v, which shows a Spaniard issuing an order to Nahua men operating a footloom and a spinning wheel.

31. AJT-CR 7, 30, Yanhuitlan, 1606.

32. AJT-CR 12, 3, Teposcolula, 1628; AGN-CR 29, 2, Coyoacan, 1652; and AGN-CR 216, 5, Amanalco, 1650, provide references to indigenous button makers.

33. See Peterson 2003 for a discussion of the depictions of artisans in the Florentine Codex.

34. Sahagún 1996, bk. 10, fol. 67v. Note that this is one of the few loans that appear in this section of book 10. See also the construction with *candela, candelanamacac* (fol. 67).

35. AJT-CR 6, 27, Tepsocolula, 1623. Additional *expedientes* that refer to cobblers include AJT-CR 15, 03, Teposcolula, 1639; AJT-CR 16, 05, Teposcolula, 1646.

36. See Karttunen and Lockhart 1987, 152–153. In reality these activities were carried out by both women and men (although to a lesser extent) in colonial times.

37. See Karttunen and Lockhart 1987, 152–153; Sahagún 1996, bk. 10, fols. 22v–24, 29, 36v–37v, and *passim*.
38. Sahagún 1996, bk. 6, fols. 77v and 72.
39. Sahagún 1996, bk. 9, fol. 60.
40. See, for example, illustrations in Sahagún 1996, bk. 9, fols. 61r–67.
41. Sahagún 1996, bk. 10, fol. 15. Anderson and Dibble translate *toltecatl* as "craftsman"; however, gender is not indicated in the noun or in the preterit agentive nouns in the description of the *toltecatl* that follows (Anderson and Dibble 1950–1982, bk. 10, 25).
42. Sahagún 1996, bk. 10, fols. 29, 37.
43. Ibid., fols. 15v, 16v, 18v.
44. Ibid., fols. 15v, 37, 29.
45. Ibid., fol. 36v.
46. Ibid., fols. 36v and 15v.
47. Ibid., fol. 36v.
48. Ibid., fol. 15v.
49. Ibid., fols. 36v and 15v.
50. Ibid., fols. 16 and 36v.
51. Ibid., fol. 37. In his discussion of codices, King 1994 notes the association between writing and weaving in Ñudzahui verbs. He posits the similarities in meaning and in form of *taa* (to write), *tãã* (to weave or braid), *yaa* ([musical] performance), *ndaa* (to have a design/writing on something), and *naa* (type of drawn figure).
52. Sahagún 1996, bk. 4, fol. 6.
53. Sahagún 1996, bk. 9, fol. 63.
54. Sahagún 1996, bk. 10, fols. 15v, 16, and 37.
55. Sahagún 1996, bk. 10, fol. 23v.
56. Sahagún 1996, bk. 9, fol. 50.
57. Ecclesiastical raiment and devotional paintings made of feathers that combined European forms and native techniques are examples of the unique and stunning art produced by indigenous craftspersons in colonial times. See Russo 2002 for a discussion of the transformation of featherworking in colonial Mexico and Peterson 1993 for an examination of the integration of European and indigenous techniques and symbols in the colonial murals of Malinalco.
58. Charlton and Charlton 1994.
59. Long 2008.
60. For references to women grinding maize, making tortillas, and preparing piñol, see AJVA-CR 4, 23, Yaa, 1694; AJVA-CR 4, 19, Taguí, 1692; AJVA-CR 6, 6; Sogocho, 1698; AJVA-CR 6, 13, Yatee, 1701; AJVA-CR 6, 16, Tlahuitoltepec, 1701; AJVA-CR 7, 3, Totontepec, 1701; AJT-CR 2, 25, Tamazulapa, 1580; AJT-CR 3, 24, Texupa, 1592; AJT-CR 10, 22, Yanhuitlan, 1616; AJT-CR 12, 22, Teposcolula, 1630; AJT-CR 14, 11, Cuquila, 1634; AJT-CR 14, 22, Tlaxiaco, 1635; AJT-CR 16, 5, Teposcolula, 1646; AJT-CR 18, 8, 1681; AJT-CR 19, 13, Tamazulapa, 1686; AGN-CR 10, 3, Temascalapa, 1641; AGN-CR 140, 1, Malinalco, 1635; AGN-CR 139, 17, Malinalco, 1757; AGN-CR 139, 25, Malinalco, 1641.

61. AJT-CR 9, 27, Teposcolula, 1613 and AJVA-CR 4, 19, Taguí, 1692.
62. AJT-CR 10, 22, Yanhuitlan, 1616. See also AJT-CR 19, 13, Tamazulapa, 1686 and AGN-CR 139, 17, Malinalco, 1757.
63. When a Ñudzahui official of Tamazulapa sent Antón Dajo on an errand for the community in 1580, his wife made piñol and tortillas for him to take on his journey (AJT-CR 2, 25, Tamazulapa, 1580).
64. AJT-CR 9, 27, Teposcolula, 1613.
65. AGN-CR 139, 25, Malinalco, 1641.
66. AJVA-CR 1, 20, Lachirio, 1665. The case also mentions a male cook in the monastery.
67. AJT-CR 6, 27, Teposcolula, 1623 and AJT-CR 14, 1, Tamazulapa, 1633; see also AJT-CR 19, 13, Tamazulapa, 1686.
68. On this point see Taylor 1979, 53 and Wood 1997, 176.
69. For changes in alcoholic consumption in colonial Mexican villages, see Taylor 1979.
70. Sahagún 1996, bk. 6, fol. 58v.
71. Sahagún 1996, bk. 6, fols. 146v–147.
72. Sahagún 1996, bk. 9, fol. 25v.
73. A wonderful example of this pattern of household members sharing food and pulque with cabildo officials to make transactions official is a document concerning a grant of land to a Nahua woman named Ana that Lockhart has translated and analyzed in Lockhart 1991, 66–74.
74. Sahagún 1996, bk. 6, fol. 176v.
75. Sahagún 1996, bk. 6, fol. 170.
76. AJVA-CR 2, 1, Lachirio, 1666.
77. AGI-P 230A, R1, 12v, 1661. The incident took place in 1660, and the governor recalled the events in a trial in 1661.
78. Sahagún 1996, bk. 6, fol. 59v.
79. Sahagún 1996, bk. 6, fol. 260.
80. AJT-CR 2, 13, Teposcolula, 1578, fol. 2.
81. The following terms appear in Chapters 26–28 in bk. 6 of the Florentine Codex (Sahagún 1996, bk. 6, fols. 127–38v). Ticitl also is used throughout Ruiz de Alarcón's 1629 treatise (1984). In addition, he notes the word *temixiuitiani* for midwife, but he is puzzled that it is not used more often (1984, 159).
82. The midwife's advice is contained in the speech in Chapter 27 of bk. 6 of the Florentine Codex (Sahagún 1996, bk. 6, fols. 128v–136v).
83. Sahagún 1996, bk. 6, fol. 121v.
84. The midwife's methods are described in Chapter 2 of bk. 6 of the Florentine Codex (Sahagún 1996, bk. 6, fols. 137–138v).
85. Sahagún 1996, bk. 6, fols. 137r-v and Ruiz de Alarcón 1984, 160.
86. Sahagún 1996, bk. 6, fols. 138v–143v.
87. Tavárez 2011, 77–89.
88. Ruiz de Alarcón 1984, 160. Andrews and Hassig offer the interpretation of Cuato and Caxxoch as names for Tlazolteotl on pp. 220 and 227. See also n. 11 for the Sixth Treatise, ch. 1.

89. Ruiz de Alarcón 1984, 45.
90. Ruiz de Alarcón 1984, 45.
91. Ponce's *relación* has been reproduced in Andrews and Hassig 1984, 212–213.
92. Sahagún 1996, bk. 6, fol. 139–139v.
93. Sigal 2000, see especially Chapter 7.
94. Gutiérrez 1991, 33–35.
95. Sahagún 1996, bk. 10, fol. 38. The same Nahuatl terms are used in the description of the male physician but they are listed in a different order (Sahagún 1996, bk. 10, fol. 20).
96. Note that it is a female healer shown administering an enema to a patient.
97. Boone 2005, 12.
98. Ruiz de Alarcón 1984, 161–167. Ruiz de Alarcón translates *tetonaltique* as "women who return the fate or fortune to its place," but as Andrews and Hassig point out, the term is a preterit agentive noun that means "ones who have provided someone with a tonal" or "soul providers" (360).
99. Sahagún 1996, bk. 12, fol. 53v.
100. Another illustration of a smallpox victim with a speech scroll in front of his mouth is in the Codex Osuna, fol. 6v. The suffering man is labeled as a "cocoxqui" (sick person) and is shown in the Hospital de Indios.
101. Olmos 1990, 18–21.
102. Alva 1999, 103. (Here I use Sell and Schwaller's translation.)
103. Alva 1999, 103–105. (Here I use Sell and Schwaller's translation.)
104. See, for example, Ruiz de Alarcón 1984, 185.
105. Díaz Balsera 2007.
106. Ruiz de Alarcón 1984, 150.
107. AJT-CR 4, 21, Teposcolula, 1596. The Nahuatl term for medicine, *pactli*, appears in the Spanish-language criminal record.
108. AJVA-CR 2, 1, Lachirio, 1666.
109. Among other things, Gerónimo López was accused of confessing the men and women of the community and telling them not to confess all of their sins to the Catholic priests, baptizing children before the priests did and giving them Tíchazàa names, telling people not to practice Christianity, and leading local rituals, including heart sacrifice on deer. It seems that Catalina Pérez' son, don Diego Martín, was at the center of a factional dispute and it is probable that he fabricated the story about his uncle.
110. AJT-CR 4, 24, Tilantongo, 1596.
111. AJT-CR 3, 31, Teposcolula, 1593. As in colonial Mexico, "juries of matrons or midwives" in colonial New England examined women and provided expert testimony regarding miscarriages, stillbirths, infant deaths, infanticide, and pregnancy (Hull 1987, 77, 113). For cases in which Nahua midwives attest to miscarriage caused by assault or injury, see AGN-CR 630, 4, Tecamachalco, 1710 and AGN-CR 139, 17, Malinalco, 1757.

112. AJT-CR 6, 28, Teposcolula, 1603.
113. AJT-CR 7, 41, Yanhuitlan, 1606. For similar cases from the Nahua region involving charges of rape or loss of virginity, see, AGN-CR 730, 9, Tacuba, 1752 and AGN-CR 705, 2, Tenango, 1763.
114. For more on the continuation of traditional medicine in colonial times through an analysis of the Codex Cruz Badiano, see Gimmel 2008.
115. AGN-CR 590, 2, Lalopa, 1657, AGN-CR 645, 1, Tonaltepec, 1559, and AJT-CR 5, 23, Yanhuitlan, 1600.
116. For the Ñudzahuis, see Spores 1997 and Terraciano 2001. For the Nahuas, Lockhart 1992 provides examples of noblewomen who inherited and bequeathed palaces. On the Nahuas, see also Cline 1986, Haskett 1991a, and Horn 1997a. The picture in the Zapotec region is less clear.
117. See, for examples, bk. 6 of the Florentine Codex (Sahagún 1996) or the collection published as the Bancroft Dialogues (Karttunen and Lockhart 1987).
118. Sahagún 1996, bk. 6, fol. 77. See Burkhart 1997 for a discussion of the relationship between women's ritual roles in the household and men's performance on the battlefield.
119. Sahagún 1996, bk. 6, fols. 77v–78.
120. Sahagún 1996, bk. 6, fol. 77r-v.
121. AGN-CR 645, 1, Tonaltepec, 1559.
122. Kellogg 1997.
123. Sahagún 1996, bk. 7 and bk. 10.
124. Sahagún 1996, bk. 10, fol. 30r-v.
125. Sahagún 1996, bk. 10, fol. 30v.
126. Sahagún 1996, bk. 10, fol. 31.
127. Gillespie 1989. The writings of Nahua intellectual Chimalpahin make references to only two *cihuatlatoque* in his list of rulers of Chalco and their kingdoms, which covers approximately four hundred years of history (Schroeder 1992, 48).
128. On Ñudzahui ruling traditions see Terraciano 2001 and Spores 1967 and 1984.
129. Codex Sierra 1933. See also Terraciano 2001, 187–189.
130. The records of this case are dispersed in several different expedientes, AJT-C 1, 62, Chicahuastla, 1570; AJT-C 1, 06, Chicahuastla, 1560; and AJT-C 1, 54, Chicahuastla, 1568.
131. Terraciano 2001, 376–379. Original document is located in AJT-C 4, 417, Teposcolula, 1672, 16–16v. The translation is Terraciano's. It is not entirely clear whether don Gerónimo means to suggest that doña Lazara would turn over the tribute from the palace or from the community. I take it to mean the latter.
132. Terraciano 2001, 181.
133. Terraciano 2001, 186 and Spores 1997, 187.
134. Spores 1997 and Terraciano 2001.
135. Truitt 2010.
136. Ibid., 436.

137. Osowski 2010, 130, chapter 4.

138. AJT-CR 8, 21, Teposcolula, 1610.

139. For a list of market vendors and the taxes they paid in Coyoacan in the mid-sixteenth century, see the document reproduced in Anderson, Berdan and Lockhart 1976, 138–149. The original is in AGN-T 1735, exp. 2, fols. 117, 118, and 121. For a full discussion of markets see Hassig 1985.

140. On trade routes from the Mixteca Alta, see Terraciano 2001, 244.

141. AJT-CR 15, 22, Teposcolula, 1643.

142. AJT-CR 8, 5, Teposcolula, 1607. Juan Hernández also sold candles.

143. See AJT-CR 5, 17, Teposcolula, 1598; AJT-CR 7, 10, Teposcolula, 1604; AJT-CR 7, 2, Yanhuitlan, 1604; AJT-CR 14, 6, Teposcolula, 1633.

144. AJT-CR 7, 2, Yanhuitlan, 1604.

145. AJT-CR 7, 10, Teposcolula, 1604.

146. It is interesting that when Bernal Díaz del Castillo describes the market in Tenochtitlan, he only specifically refers to women twice: first, as the sellers of cooked foods and, second, as the fisherwomen (and men). His ambiguity might suggest that he could not distinguish a clear gender division of vendors and the types of goods that they sold in the market. See Díaz del Castillo 1963, 232–234.

147. See, for example, AJT-CR 6, 25, Teposcolula, 1602 which refers to "the Indian women who sell fruit" (fol. 3); AJT-CR 12, 33, Texupa, 1631; AJT-CR 19, 13, Tamazulapa, 1686; AJT-CR 8, 12, Yanhuitlan, 1608; and AJT-CR 12, 34, Teposcolula, 1631. For cases of women selling lime, see AJT-CR 16, 31, Tamazulapa, 1662 and AJT-CR 17, 38, Soyaltepec, 1680. For cases of women buying maize in the market, see AJT-CR 12, 22, Teposcolula, 1630; AJT-CR 15, 31, Teposcolula, 1645.

148. For cases of men selling meat, see AJT-CR 6, 29, Teposcolula, 1603 and AJT-CR 9, 25.01, Teposcolula, 1631. See also AGN-CR 217, 7, Metepec, 1634, in which one witness testifies: "It is common among the Indian men and women of this New Spain to sell in the markets and public plazas beef, raw and cooked, with which they sustain themselves and pay their tributes" (fol. 85). For men and women selling hay and hierba buena, see AJT-CR 12, 12, Teposcolula, 1630; AGN-CR 216, 5, Amanalco, 1650. For men selling cotton, see AJT-CR 7, 20, Suchitepec, 1605; AJT-CR 8, 3, Teposcolula, 1607; AJT-CR 12, 34, Teposcolula, 1631. Men selling cacao is mentioned in AJT-CR 8, 3, Teposcolula, 1607. However, it should be noted that in the Florentine Codex the illustration of the cacao vendor shows a woman.

149. Sahagún 1996, bk. 10, fols. 41–70.

150. AGN-CR 139, 19, Zumpaguacan, 1647.

151. AGN-CR 10, 3, Temascalapa, 1641.

152. Clendinnen comments on the importance of merchant women, noting: "[They] seem to have played something close to an equal role with their men, their exclusion from trading expeditions compensated for by the readiness of the men to trade as their proxies, and more by the women's special responsibilities as guardians of the warehoused goods, and of the rate and price of the goods' release on to the home market" (1991, 162–163). For additional examples of prominent female traders in the Mixteca, see Terraciano 2001, 244–245.

153. AJT-CR 9, 17, Yanhuitlan, 1613.

154. AJT-CR 9, 25.01, Tepsocolula, 1613. Such an arrangement is also implied in AJT-CR 6, 29, Teposcolula, 1603.

155. AGN-CR 10, 3, Temascalapa, 1641.

156. AJT-CR 7, 22, Yanhuitlan, 1605.

157. See, for example, AJT-CR 4, 3, Teposcolula, 1569; AJT-CR 7, 38, Teposcolula, 1605; AJT-CR 14, 8, Teposcolula, 1633; AJT-CR 14, 20, Tamazulapa, 1635; AJVA-CR 1, 10, Huitepec, 1659; AJVA-CR 6, 5, Taguí, Royaga, 1698; AGN-CR 139, 17, Malinalco, 1757.

158. Sahagún 1996, bk. 6, fol. 59v. An additional example is the Nahuatl proverb "Everybody gets up to go" (*Tlacaitlehua*), which describes the entire population harvesting and planting, implying that women cultivated fields alongside men (Sahagún 1996, bk. 6, fol. 194).

159. Cline 1993, 91.

160. AJT-CR 3, 49, Yanhuitlan, 1594.

161. AGN-CR 686, 3, Acatepec, 1558.

162. AJVA-CR 6, 5, Taguí, Royaga, 1698.

163. For a discussion of some taboos against women's participation in certain aspects of agricultural production in contemporary Mesoamerican communities, see Monaghan 2001, 289–290. Monaghan also provides examples of contexts in which men should avoid engaging in production.

164. AJVA-C 1, 9, Totontepec, 1676–1677.

165. AJVA-C 1, 9, Totontepec, 1676–1677.

166. AJVA-C 1, 9, Totontepec, 1676–1677.

167. Wood 1997, 175–176.

168. See, for example, AJVA-CR 4, 1, Ayutla, 1685; AJT-CR 5, 38, Teposcolula, 1600; AJT-CR 14, 34, Cuquila, 1637. Indigenous landholdings were scattered rather than concentrated in one contiguous plot. In addition to the permanent main household, small houses or huts were often built on outlying plots of land that provided shelter and storage space. Household members rotated between the various houses and lands, especially when crops were planted that needed to be guarded or when land claims were challenged. For a thorough discussion of landholding patterns in central Mexico and Oaxaca, see Gibson 1964; Spores 1967; Taylor 1972; Wood 1984; Cline 1986; Lockhart 1992; Horn 1997; Terraciano 2001.

169. AJT-CR 3, 26, Coixtlahuaca, 1592.

170. AJT-CR 11, 16, Izcatlan, 1625.

171. See, for example, AGN-CR 140, 4, Malinalco, 1626; AGN-CR 730, 9, Tacuba, 1752; AJT-CR 11, 16, Izcatlan, 1625; AJVA-CR 1, 10, Huitepec, 1659; AJVA-CR 7, 10, Camotlan, 1706.

172. AJT-CR 5, 23, Yanhuitlan, 1600.

173. AJT-CR 2, 13, Teposcolula, 1578; AJT-CR 14, 11, Cuquila, 1633; AJVA-CR 1, 20, Lachirio, 1665; AJVA-CR 10, 25, Lachirio, 1716.

174. AJT-CR 7, 38, Teposcolula, 1605; AJVA-CR 6, 14, Analco, 1701.

175. AJT-CR 3, 26, Coixtlahuaca, 1592.

176. AJVA-CR 10, 25, Lachirio, 1716. Clendinnen 1991 also recognizes the collaborative efforts of husbands and wives: "Women were also specialist trad-

ers, although some of those apparently independent woman market traders were probably the commercial end of a family chain of production, as when the saltseller sold the product of collective kin effort, or the fisherman's wife undertook the sale of the catch. Nonetheless, the crucial economic decision of price often lay in female hands" (162).

177. AJVA-CR 2, 15, Yatzona, 1674; AJVA-CR 4, 19, Tagui, 1692.

178. See, for example, Taylor 1972, chap. 2; Lockhart 1992, chap. 5; Spores 1997; Horn 1997, chaps. 5 and 8; Terraciano 2001, chap. 7.

179. AGN-CR 10, 13, San Juan Teotihuacan, 1757.

180. Anderson, Berdan and Lockhart 1976, 67.

181. AJT-CR 8, 12, Yanhuitlan, 1608. See also AGN-CR 140, 1, Malinalco, 1635, for an example of a governor and his wife who invested in wheat, a mill, and a bakery. Terraciano 2001 provides additional examples of Ñudzahui women who were entrepreneurs (chap. 7).

182. For a history of the silk trade in colonial Mexico, see Borah 1943. Terraciano 2001 discusses the production of silk to pay as tribute or to raise funds to pay tribute (126–129, 234).

183. Lockhart, Berdan, and Anderson 1986, 51, 52–53, 79–84.

184. AJVA-CR 2, 12, Talea, 1674.

185. AJT-CR 3, 3, Achiutla, 1587.

186. AJT-CR 2, 25, Tamazulapa, 1580.

187. References to silk bathers can be found in AJT-CR 7, 10, Teposcolula, 1604; AJT-CR 7, 23, Yanhuitlan, 1605.

188. AJVA-CR 1, 18, Villa Alta, 1665.

189. AJT-CR 18, 14, Tlaxiaco, 1682. See also AJT-CR 4, 397, Yanhuitlan, 1632.

190. AJVA-CR 12, 16, Solaga, 1729.

191. AJT-CR 9, 31, Yanhuitlan, 1614.

192. AJT-CR 8, 12, Yanhuitlan, 1608.

193. Whereas there are many cases in the Teposcolula archive that mention Spanish, Nahua, and Ñudzahui shepherds, I did not find a single reference in the documentation from the Villa Alta jurisdiction that I examined. For cases of Nahua shepherds who herded sheep in the Mixteca Alta, see AJT-CR 3, 42, Tlaxiaco, 1594; AJT-CR 11, 3, Tlaxiaco, 1623; AJT-CR 15, 32, Teposcolula, 1645.

194. AGN-T 400,1, Yanhuitlan, 1591. Don Gabriel noted that twenty of the goats belonged to his wife, doña María de Cháves.

195. AJT-CR 18, 14, Tlaxiaco, 1682.

196. See, for example, AJT-CR 7, 10, Teposcolula, 1604; AJT-CR 15, 31, Teposcolula, 1645; AJT-CR 18, 34, Coyotepec, 1684. Also, for a discussion of animal husbandry by women in a modern Zapotec community, see Stephen 1991, 78–80, 196–199.

197. Burkhart 1997.

198. For women carrying water see AJVA-CR 2, 16, Betaza, 1674; AJT-CR 8, 1, Yanhuitlan, 1607. Men also commonly carried water.

199. For women carrying firewood, see AJVA-CR 6, 8, Yalahuí, 1699; AJT-

CR 3, 18, Teposcolula, 1590; AGN-CR 630, 4, Tecamachalco, 1710. For men carrying firewood, see AJVA-CR 12, 5, Analco, 1726; AJT-CR 11, 16, Izcatlan, 1625; AJT-CR 14, 24, Tlaxiaco, 1636; AGN-CR 630, 4, Tecamachalco, 1710. For women going to neighbors' homes for coals to start a fire, see AJVA-CR 5, 4, Yatzona, 1695; AJT-CR 14, 20, Tamazulapa, 1635. For men going out for coals to start a fire, see AJVA-CR 5, 4, Yatzona, 1695.

200. For an example of a man sweeping the household patio, see AJT-CR 6, 46, Yanhuitlan, 1604.

201. AJT-CR 14, 8, Teposcolula, 1633; AJVA-CR 12, 5, Analco, 1726; AGN-CR 641, 27, Cd. de México, 1581; AGN-CR 139, 17, Malinalco, 1757. The bulk of washing was probably left for women. The men in the cases just listed may not have had a woman living in their households to wash for them, but this is not clearly stated in the documentary record.

202. See, for example, AJT-CR 9, 25.01, Teposcolula, 1613.

203. Terraciano 2001, 236.

204. AJT-CR 7, 30, Yanhuitlan, 1606.

205. AJT-CR 8, 4, Teposcolula, 1607.

206. AJT-CR 8, 12, Yanhuitlan, 1608.

207. AGN-CR 235, 15, Tacubaya, 1644.

208. AJT-CR 22, 08, Tlaxiaco, 1701. As it turned out, Baltasar Melchor and Josefa de Rosa were not married, although they told Diego Rodríguez that they were; she was actually married to a third man who traveled with them, whom she and Baltasar later killed. The native tradition of hiring husband and wife teams became a part of Mexican custom in general. In 1736, don Francisco Sánchez Carballo and his wife, doña María A. de Herrera Ramírez, employed a mestizo couple, Juan de Piñeda and Marta María; Juan transported goods as a carrier; Marta worked as a cook (AGN-CR 597, 7, Ayozingo, 1736).

209. The Spaniards greatly restricted the number of nobles' dependents, in part undermining their control over commoners' labor. Also, it should be noted that although nobles were exempt from manual labor, they accompanied tribute laborers when they went to work on Spanish enterprises and construction projects.

210. References to tribute labor used to roof churches are in AJVA-CR 4, 16, Tonaguia, 1691; and AJVA-CR 5, 10, Yatee, 1696. Mention of tributaries repairing the walls and cleaning the patio of the convent of Teposcolula are from AJT-CR 12, 22, Teposcolula, 1630; AJT-CR 16,4, Teposcolula, 1646.

211. See AJT-CR 19, 13, Tamazulapa, 1686; AJT-CR 13, 22, Tamazulapa, 1632; AJT-CR 12, 6, Yanhuitlan, 1628.

212. Borah and Cook 1960; Cook and Borah 1968.

213. One exception is Cline, who briefly describes the importance of textiles and food as tribute items (1993, 76–81).

214. AJVA-CR 5, 10, Yatee, 1696.

215. AJT-CR 3, 24, Texupa, 1592.

216. AJT-CR 14, 11, Cuquila, 1633.

217. AJT-CR 15, 7, Teposcolula, 1639.

218. AJT-CR 8, 19, Tlaxiaco, 1610. The indigenous officials complained that

Cisneros and his son paid the woman only a nominal amount and paid the men three tomines each. Also, they forced other men to guard their livestock and did not pay them.

219. AJT-CR 12, 6, Yanhuitlan, 1628.
220. AJT-CR 12, 6, Yanhuitlan, 1628, fol. 12v.
221. AGN-T 1871, 1, Quauhtla, 1593.
222. AJT-CR 10, 12, Teposcolula, 1615.
223. AJT-CR 12, 6, Yanhuitlan, 1628.
224. AJT-CR 14, 34, Cuquila, 1637.
225. AJT-CR 9, 7, Nuyoo, 1612, 1613.
226. AJVA-CR 1, 7, Tonaguia, 1654.
227. AJVA-CR 5, 7, Yagayo, 1696. They also complained that he wanted to pay seven reales instead of the customary nine for the cloth, and that he wanted to collect the tribute in April instead of June.
228. AJT-CR 14, 4, Teposcolula, 1633.
229. AJT-C 18, 11, Yolomecatl, 1705.
230. Burkhart 1997, 26.

CHAPTER EIGHT

1. Sahagún 1996, bk. 2, fol. 102v. Interestingly, the accompanying illustration shows a man presenting the tamales to a couple. A second image in the passage depicts three men, three women, and three children gathered around eating the tamales, showing the five tamales that were dedicated to the hearth fire.

2. Lockhart 1992 explains: "Not only do any lineages tend to remain unnamed and undiscussed in Nahuatl sources; no word appears that would have approximately the same scope as English "family" (59). Lockhart further observes that the main term for "relatives" in Nahuatl was *huanyolque* (those who live with one) (156). See Lockhart 1992 for a discussion of Nahua kinship in colonial times. Kellogg 1995 traces significant changes in family structure and terminology in Mexico City in the sixteenth and seventeenth centuries (chap. 5).

3. Alvarado 1962, fol. 109v and Córdova 1987a, fol. 194v. In these entries, first-person possession is marked in the Ñudzahui language by the suffix *-ndi* and in Tíchazàa by *-a*.

4. Lockhart 1992, 59.

5. Terraciano 2001 finds that the Ñudzahui concept of family also emphasized joint residence based on his analysis of bequests of land (224). For a similar point regarding Yucatec Maya definitions of family, see Restall 1997, 99.

6. Monaghan 1995 examines "marriage, gift exchange, cargo service and communal labor, pooling and distribution, sacrifice and revelation" and even "envious acts" as "forms of sociation" which "culminate in . . . two 'summating images' of Nuyooteco society, Nuyoo as an association of households, and Nuyoo as a 'great house'"(15). Sandstrom 1991 addresses similar issues focusing on culture and ethnic identity in his study of a modern-day Nahua community. Stephen 1991 addresses the importance of overlapping networks and ethnic identity in her study

of Zapotec women in Teotitlan in the Valley of Oaxaca, although she does not explore the definition of community as explicitly as Monaghan does.

7. Information on the layout of the household complex is most detailed for central Mexico because this region has received the most attention from archaeologists and because descriptions and drawings of Nahua households are abundant in the colonial archival record. Lockhart 1992, provides a full discussion of Nahua household structure (chap. 3).

Although a systematic synthesis of household layouts in Oaxaca has not been undertaken, the scattered evidence suggests that, like Nahuas, Ñudzahui, Bènizàa, and Ayuuk families lived in compounds consisting of multiple separate structures arranged around a patio and enclosed by a wall. Archaeological evidence from the Valley of Oaxaca shows that palaces consisted of multiple dwellings, arranged around a series of patios; for example, the sites of Yagul and Mitla, which were established by Bènizàa people and then later occupied and elaborated by Ñudzahui communities in the postclassic period, have similar palaces with multiple patios (Bernal 1966). Archival documents describe similar household arrangements occupied by Ñudzahui nobles of the Mixteca Alta; for example, the compound of the cacique of Yanhuitlan was said to have nine patios, surrounded by separate houses in which the community's nobles lived (AGN-T 400, 1). Evidence from archival records shows that Ñudzahui commoners lived in less elaborate household compounds; nevertheless they frequently refer to patios, and sometimes they explicitly mention the wall that enclosed the patio or separate houses, including special houses for saints. For references to patios or household oratories in the Mixteca Alta, see AJT-CR 3, 3, Achiutla, 1587; AJT-CR 5, 36, Teposcolula, 1601; AJT-CR 9, 2, Nuyoo, 1612; AJT-CR 10, 46, Teposcolula, 1623; AJT-CR 11, 3, Tlaxiaco, 1623; AJT-CR 11, 28, Teposcolula, 1626; AJT-CR 12, 7, Teposcolula, 1628; AJT-CR 13, 22, Temascalapa, 1632; AJT-CR 14, 34, Cuquila, 1637; AJT-CR 14, 20, Tamazulapa, 1635; AJT-CR 14, 27.01, Teposcolula, 1639; AJT-CR 18, 31, Teposcolula, 1681.

Archival records from the Villa Alta jurisdiction sometimes explicitly refer to two or more houses, each occupied by a married couple, sharing a central patio. See, for example, AJVA-CR 2, 15, Yatzona, 1674; AJVA-CR 3, 2, San Francisco Cajonos, 1676; AJVA-CR 3, 5, Yatzona, 1676; AJVA-CR 5, 8, Lachixila, 1696; AJVA-CR 5, 12, San Francisco Cajonos, 1696; AJVA-CR 5, 17, Mocton, 1697; AJVA-CR 6, 8, Yalahuí, 1699; AJVA-CR 7, 10, Camotlan, 1706. General references to household patios are found in AJVA-CR 1, 9, San Francisco Cajonos, 1659; AJVA-CR 1, 10, Huitepec, 1659; AJVA-CR 1, 17, Chichicastepec, 1665; AJVA-CR 1, 20, Lachirio, 1665; AJVA-CR 3, 13, Yate, 1684; AJVA-CR 4, 16, Tonaguia, 1691; AJVA-CR 4, 19, Taguí, 1692; AJVA-CR 5, 1, Totontepec, 1694; AJVA-CR 6, 12, Suchila, 1700. The discussion of separate houses for worship in documents from Bènizàa and Ayuuk communities further reveals the use of multihouse compounds in the Villa Alta jurisdiction. See, for example, AJVA-CR 2, 10, Lachichina, 1670, and the many references in AGI-M 882, 1704.

8. Terraciano 2001, 160.

9. See, for example, the illustration of an assembly in the patio of the royal

palace in the Codex of Yanhuitlan in Jiménez Moreno and Mateos Higuera 1940, plate 2.

10. Sahagún 1996, bk. 11, fols. 240v–241v. See also the Codex Mendoza illustration of Moteucçoma's palace (Codex Mendoza 1992, 3: fol. 69r).

11. Sahagún 1996, bk. 11, fols. 240–241v.

12. Ibid., fol. 241v. For an example of a surviving palace from the Mixtec region that bears specific decorative motifs conveying political and religious authority, see Terraciano 2001, 160–164, and Kiracofe 1995.

13. Lockhart 1992, 64.

14. Evans 1998, 171–172.

15. Goody 1972, 122.

16. Offner 1984, 136.

17. Harvey 1986, 284.

18. Carrasco 1976, 45.

19. Cline 1993, 58–69. Kanter 2008 finds that by the late colonial period, nuclear family residences predominated (63 percent) in Tenango del Valle (55).

20. For a case in which two men abandoned their wives to escape community tribute payments, see AGN-CR 140, 1, Malinalco, 1635. Abandonment is discussed in greater detail in Chapter 3.

21. I use the terms *patrivirilocal* and *patriuxorilocal* with some reservation. The *patri-* traces the location to the father and, as discussed earlier, I believe that indigenous people considered the household to have been established by and belonged to the married couple. However, these are the terms used in the existing literature, and I use them here with the qualification that *patri-* should be read to indicate the mother and father.

22. Harvey 1986, 283.

23. Carrasco 1976, 50–52. The breakdown of affinal relations was as follows: ten were brothers of a married woman; eleven were sisters of a married woman; and fifteen were more distant relatives.

24. Cline 1993, 62–69. Patrivirilocal residence occurred in 11 percent and 20 percent of the cases in Quauhchichinollan and the second section of Huitzillan, respectively; it did not occur at all in the first section of Huitzillan.

25. Colonial criminal records provide information that can be used to reconstruct residence patterns in central Mexico and Oaxaca and to test conclusions based on early censuses. Witnesses often stated their places of birth and residence if one differed from the other. Some mentioned their natal communities in the course of their testimony or specifically stated that they lived with their in-laws. However, the presentation of birth and residence information for both husband and wife depended on the particular case in which they were plaintiffs, defendants, or witnesses and whether they had married exogamously. Sometimes residence information was noted when a witness had occasion to discuss postmarital living arrangements, and these cases did not involve necessarily community exogamy. Although references to residence are incidental and scattered, they provide data that suggest observable patterns.

26. Examples of patrivirilocal residence are described in AGN-CR 29, 2, Coyoacan, 1652; AGN-CR 217, 10, Atengo, 1723; AGN-CR 10, 16, Ecatepec,

1742; AGN-CR 139, 17, Malinalco, 1757. A patriuxorilocal case is mentioned in AGN-CR 216, 4, Atlacomulco, 1685.

27. For cases of patrivirilocality among commoners in the Mixteca Alta, see AJT-CR 1, 52, Teposcolula, 1575; AJT-CR 4, 31, Teposcolula, 1597; AJT-CR 11, 16, Izcatlan, 1625. References to patriuxorilocal commoner residences are found in AJT-CR 5, 40, Yanhuitlan, 1601; AJT-CR 14, 22, Tlaxiaco, 1635; AJT-CR 15, 3, Teposcolula, 1639.

Patrivirilocal residences among Bènizàa commoners are described in AJVA-CR 1, 4, Yalahuí, 1651; AJVA-CR 2, 7, Yagayó, 1670; AJVA-CR 2, 12, Talea, 1674; AJVA-CR 2, 16, Betaza, 1674; AJVA-CR 3, 2, San Francisco Cajonos, 1676; AJVA-CR 4, 17, Yaganiza, 1691; AJVA-CR 6, 8, Yalahuí, 1699; AJVA-CR 6, 13, Yate, 1701. Patriuxorilocal cases in Bènizàa communities of the Villa Alta include AJVA-CR 1, 4, Yalahuí, 1651; AJVA-CR 1, 20, Lachirio, 1665; AJVA-CR 2, 16, Betaza, 1674; AJVA-CR 3, 5, Yatzona, 1676; AJVA-CR 5, 12, San Francisco Cajonos, 1696.

Evidence of patrivirilocal residence among Ayuuk commoners can be found in AJVA-CR 1, 10, Huitepec, 1659; AJVA-CR 1, 17, Chichicastepec, 1665; AJVA-C 1, 7, Totontepec, 1630; AJVA-CR 5, 17, Mocton, 1697; AJVA-CR 3, 15, Metepec, 1685. Patrivirilocal residence in a Chinantec community is mentioned in AJVA-CR 5, 8, Lachixila, 1696. Patriuxorilocal residence among Ayuuk commoners is mentioned in AJVA-CR 3, 15, Metepec, 1685.

28. AJVA-CR 2, 15, Yatzona, 1674. For members of Yatzona's ruling family for which evidence exists, there were five community exogamous marriages and patrivirilocal arrangements. Don Felipe de Santiago, the cacique of Yatzona, married doña Petrona de los Ángeles, cacica of Santa María; don Miguel de Santiago, the cacique's brother, married Cecilia Méndez of Temascalapa; don Juan de Santiago, the cacique's nephew, married doña María de la Cruz of Lachixila; and don Baltasar de Zavala, the cacique's son, married Magdalena Hernández of Reagui. All of the couples lived in Yatzona.

By this time several of the men and women of the ruling lineage were called cacique and cacica. In this case, for example, doña María de Santiago (also known as doña María de los Ángeles), the daughter of don Gabriel de los Ángeles; doña Lucía de Vargas, a relative of don Gabriel; and doña Magdalena de Santiago, granddaughter of don Gabriel, were each identified as cacica de Yatzona. Don Felipe and don Gabriel's nephews, don Felipe de Santiago, don Pablo de Vargas, and don Miguel de Santiago, were each referred to as cacique of Yatzona. It is unclear whether communities had multiple rulers in preconquest times, or whether use of the titles cacique and cacica by multiple individuals reflects some reorganization of complex communities in colonial times, especially after *congregación* (congregation; a program undertaken by Spaniards to concentrate dispersed settlements into one). It may also be that usage of the terms became more flexible during the colonial period. On the unique use of *cacique* in Villa Alta, see Chance 1989, 125–126.

For additional examples of patrivirilocal residence among Bènizàa nobles, see AJVA-CR 1, 22, San Francisco Yate, 1666; AJVA-CR 2, 1, Lachirio, 1666; AJVA-CR 2, 7, Yagayó, 1670; AJVA-CR 2, 15, Yatzona, 1674; AJVA-CR 3, 5, Yatzona, 1676; AJVA-CR 7, 5, Lachirio, 1702; AJVA-CR 7, 10, Camotlan, 1706. Patriuxorilocal arrangements among Bènizàa nobles are mentioned in AGI-P 230A, R1, 1660; AJVA-CR 2, 16, Betaza, 1674.

29. Spores 1984, 72. For examples of patriuxorilocality among Ñudzahui nobles, see AJT-CR 10, 11, Cuquila, 1615; AJT-CR 14, 4, Teposcolula, 1633. Patrivirilocal noble residences in the Mixteca are described in AGN-CR 645, 1, Tonaltepec, 1559; AJT-CR 9, 1, Tamazulapa, 1612.

30. Cline 1993 argues that the lack of married sons may explain in part patriuxorilocal residence (63).

31. AJT-CR 4, 5, Coixtlahuaca, 1596, fol. 3v.

32. AJT-CR 5, 40, Yanhuitlan, 1601. In a personal communication, Lockhart notes that some well-off people were muleteers. It is impossible to determine the young man's economic status from the information in the criminal docket; he may have been reasonably wealthy, and the reason for the matrivirilocal arrangement may solely have been his frequent absences.

33. Kanter 2008 provides a few examples of men who joined their wives' parents' households in late colonial Toluca because they did not have lands in their home communities; however, she notes that matrilocal residence was rare in the region at this time (45–47).

34. Offner 1984, 139; Harvey 1986, 292; Cline 1993, 69.

35. Taylor 1979, especially p. 107; Stern 1995; Kanter 2008, 33.

36. Kanter 2008, 45–47. This line of argumentation is especially important in studies of North American native women. See, for example, Diane Rothenberg's 1980 study of Seneca women and Theda Perdue's 1989 article on Cherokee women, which argue that women enjoyed high status because these societies were matrilineal and matrilocal. In response, in her essay on Iroquois women, Nancy Shoemaker emphasizes that "matrilineal" must not be equated with "matriarchal" (Shoemaker 1991).

37. Spores 1984, 72.

38. AJT-CR 5, 40, Yanhuitlan, 1601.

39. AGN-CR 140, 1, Malinalco, 1635; AGN-CR 216, 4, Atlacomulco, 1685; AJT-CR 10,11, Cuquila, 1615; AJT-CR 14, 4, Teposcolula, 1633; AGI-P 230A, R1, 1660.

For a discussion of noble marriage alliances in ancient Mexico, see Carrasco 1984. For royal marriages in the Mixteca Alta, see also Spores 1967, 139–141; Terraciano 2001, chap. 6.

40. AJT-CR 4, 31, Teposcolula, 1597. For an example of a Bènizàa couple who returned to the wife's parents' home for a social visit and drinking, see AJVA-CR 4, 17, Yaganiza, 1691.

41. AJT-CR 11, 16, Izcatlan, 1625. Catalina's husband, Jacinto de Castañeda, was supposed to go with her, but did not because he was drunk. A similar case is found in AJT-CR 4, 5, Coixtlahuaca, 1596.

42. AJVA-CR 7, 10, Camotlan, 1706.

43. Sahagún 1996, bk. 6, fols. 110, 113.

44. Offner 1984, 136; Harvey 1986, 280–282; Cline 1993, 58, 63.

45. AJVA-C 1, 9, Totontepec, 1676–1677.

46. AJVA-CR 6, 9, Amatepec, 1699.

Notes to Chapter Eight 359

47. See, for example, AGN-CR 139, 25, Malinalco, 1641; AJT-CR 19, 5, Yanhuitlan, 1685; AJT-CR 22, 08, Tlaxiaco, 1701.

48. See, for example, AJT-CR 8, 21, Teposcolula, 1610; AJVA-CR 6, 13, Yate, 1701.

49. See, for example, AJT-CR 9, 27, Teposcolula, 1613; AJT-CR 18, 14, Tlaxiaco, 1682; AJVA-CR 3, 4, Talea, 1676.

50. See the midwife's speech, for example, in which she addresses the newborn as "my precious child, my youngest child" (*notlaçopiltzin, noxocoiouh*) (Sahagún 1996, bk. 6, fol. 146v.). In a marriage speech, a noble addresses the bride: "O, my daughter" (*nochpochtze*) and invokes the pair: "O, my youngest children, my children" (*O, noxocoyohuane nopilhuane*) (Karttunen and Lockhart 1987, 110). Karttunen and Lockhart 1987 discuss the use of kinship terminology in the Bancroft Dialogues, (43–49). See also Lockhart 1992, 188. In his study of Nahuatl kinship terminology, Lockhart 1992 notes that the many instances in which lineal kinship terms are used for collateral relatives, the shared origins of the words for father and uncle, and the proximity of the terms for child and niece/nephew of a woman suggest that "inclusiveness is emphasized over precise descent" (76).

51. AJT-CR 2, 34, Chalcatongo, 1581 (transcribed and translated in Terraciano 2001, 372–375). For examples of the use of *hermano* in Spanish-language criminal records, see, AJT-CR 3, 7, Yanhuitlan, 1588, fol. 1v; AJT-CR 4, 12, Teposcolula, 1596, fol. 1r-v; AJT-CR 5, 36, Teposcolula, 1601; AJT-CR 6, 25, Teposcolula, 1602, fol. 2-2v; AJVA-CR, 1, 9, San Francisco Cajonos, 1659; AGN-CR 140, 4, Malinalco, 1626, fol. 117v.

52. Córdova 1987a, fol. 301v.

53. Reyes 1976, fol. 88.

54. See AJVA-CR 3, 9, Yalálag, 1678, for just one of many examples of the household head organizing labor. In this case, the household head orders his brother to check the household's maize field. The extent to which the household head was seen as an authority remains unclear from the perspective of criminal records. Lockhart 1991 discusses a case in which a woman and her husband promise not to misbehave and to accept the household head's punishment if they do (90); a full discussion of the document can be found in Lockhart 1991, 66–74. The couple's statement may have been a formality more than a reflection of the nature of interaction among household members.

55. In preconquest times among the Nahua, Ñudzahui, and Bènizàa people, it seems that men and women had both calendrical and personal names. Birth order names were also used by Nahuas (mainly for women) and Bènizàas (for both men and women according to Córdova). Lockhart, in his study of the evolution of naming patterns among the Nahuas of central Mexico, finds that with the introduction of Spanish names, indigenous naming patterns went through various stages. By the mid-sixteenth century, all those who had been baptized had a Spanish first name, and high noblemen and noblewomen adopted the honorific titles of don and doña, respectively. Roughly between 1550 and 1650, indigenous people increasingly used Christian first and last names. Among commoners especially, the last name was a second first name rather than a Spanish surname, so names such as Ana María, María Magdalena, and Barbara Agustina were

quite common. Noblewomen also frequently had two first names. Noblemen tended to have Spanish surnames, and many adopted the names of prominent local Spaniards. Second names were not generally passed on to succeeding generations, except among dynastic rulers and colonial governors for whom particular surnames functioned as lineage names. After about 1650, an elaborate naming system emerged in which each person's rank was clearly indicated by his or her name. For a full discussion of Nahua naming patterns, see Lockhart 1992, 117–130 and Horn 1997b.

Terraciano traced similar patterns in Ñudzahui communities. He found that in the Mixteca Alta changes occurred about twenty years later than they did in central Mexico. Calendrical names were used as second names in the Mixteca Alta until around the 1640s. For a discussion of the evolution of Ñudzahui and Chocho names, see Terraciano 2001, 150–157.

Bènizàa and Ayuuk naming patterns await future study. Córdova 1987b described the importance of calendrical and birth order names in his 1578 grammar.

56. AGN-T 1735, exp. 2, fol. 108. This illustration is also reproduced with brief commentary in Lockhart 1992, 353–355; Horn 1997a, 113–114.

57. Lockhart 1992 notes that in the Nahuatl-language record *calli* mainly refers to the physical structure (60).

58. AGN-T 165, 4, fol. 15. For additional depictions of native households, see the Códice de Santa María Asunción and the Códice Vergara. These early sixteenth-century manuscripts use glyphic conventions similar to those described here. Also, they show the married couple facing each other with their children linked to them by a series of lines. For an analysis of the pictorial writing in these codices, see Williams 1984.

59. Durán 1994, plate 1. See also plate 2, which shows seven caves, each inhabited by a husband and wife and extended relations.

60. See Wood 1997 and Kanter 1995. Based on their study of early nineteenth-century Nahuatl-language testaments from the Metepec jurisdiction of the Toluca Valley, Melton-Villanueva and Pizzigoni 2008 conclude that men did not predominate in landholding and identify some women who were wealthy (372).

61. Terraciano 2001, 216.

62. Testaments in AJVA Tíchazàa-language civil records for Bènizàa communities and Nahuatl-language civil records for Ayuuk communities reveal evidence of women's landholding in the Sierra Alta.

63. For discussions of colonial tribute systems in central Mexico, see, Gibson 1964 (esp. chaps. 8, 9); Hassig 1985; Haskett 1991b; Lockhart 1992; Cline 1993. Hicks 1984 studies rotational labor in preconquest times. Tribute collection and disputes in the Mixteca Alta are discussed in Spores 1967, 1984; Terraciano 2001.

64. Although spinning was a task largely associated with women, references to men performing this labor are made in the archival record. Clear statements about Bènizàa men spinning are made in AJVA-CR 2, 15, Yatzona, 1674; AJVA-CR 4, 19, Taguí, 1692. In a dispute over tribute labor brought by the sujetos of Coixtlahuaca in 1628, witnesses complained that the governor distributed wool

and cotton for the "comun y yndias" to spin. Also one male witness from Iztepec stated that his profession was spinning wool yarn (AJT-CR 7, 30, Yanhuitlan, 1606). See Chapter 7 for a discussion of the overlap in labor performed by men and women.

References to women weaving locate this activity in the household complex. Cases that mention women weaving in the patio include AJT-CR 5, 36, Teposcolula, 1601; AJT-CR 5, 547, Teposcolula, 1681 (the latter follows the older archival cataloguing system). Also see illustrations of women weaving in the patio in the Florentine Codex in Sahagún 1996, bk. 10, fols. 2, 4, 37.

65. AJVA-CR 2, 12, Talea, 1674; AJVA-CR 6, 12, Suchila, 1700; AJT-CR 6, 27, Teposcolula, 1623.

66. References to pulquerías are made in AJT-CR 3, 49, Yanhuitlan, 1594; AJT-CR 6, 25, Teposcolula, 1602; AJT-CR 7, 38, Teposcolula, 1605; AJT-CR 8, 15, Teposcolula, 1609; AJT-CR 8, 17, Teposcolula, 1610; AJT-CR 10, 39, Teposcolula, 1618; AJT-CR 11, 8, Teposcolula, 1624; AGN-CR 29, 2, Coyoacan, 1652; AGN-CR 235, 18, Mexicalcingo, 1722; AJVA-CR 4, 1, Ayutla, 1685; AJVA-CR 6, 12, Suchila, 1700. Taylor 1979 notes the prominence of female pulquería proprietors and pulque distributors (38, 53).

67. Cline and León-Portilla 1984, 132. (Here I use Cline and León-Portilla's translation.)

68. AJT-CR 13, 21, Teposcolula, 1632.

69. AJT-CR 4, 3, Teposcolula, 1596. See also the case in which Juan García and his wife brought atole to a sick and delirious friend (AJT-CR 3, 26, Coixtlahuaca, 1592).

70. AGN-CR 29, 1, Tacubaya, 1639, fol. 2.

71. Information on the training of Ñudzahui and Bènizàa children in preconquest times either was never written down or has not survived. We can only assume that, like the Nahuas, the Ñudzahui and Bènizàa had formal institutions at the community level and informal mechanisms at the household level. The dedication of children to the temple is described in Sahagún 1996, bk. 6, fols. 176–183.

72. Karttunen and Lockhart 1987, 152–154.

73. Sahagún 1996, bk. 9, fols. 12v–15v.

74. Karttunen and Lockhart 1987, 156. (Here I use Karttunen and Lockhart's translation.)

75. AJT-CR 11, 32, Tamazulapa, 1626. See also the case of Andrés Jacobo mentioned previously. Jacobo, a noble of Tacubaya, assumed the care of his brother's children after the death of their father; he trained his nephew to read while his nieces mainly stayed with their mother (AGN-CR 29, 1, Tacubaya, 1639). Pizzigoni 2012 finds expression of concern for children's education and religious training in a testament from Toluca (132).

76. García Icazbalceta states that some of the girls remained in the school with the *beatas* after they had learned Christianity. However, this experiment was apparently short-lived; according to García Icazbalceta, this school was gone before 1540 (1896, 92).

77. Terraciano 2001, 284.

78. AJVA-CR 1, 20, Lachirio, 1665.

79. Sahagún 1996, bk. 6, fols. 74v–106. The Florentine Codex contains samples of the parents' speech to a noble daughter and the father's speech to a noble son. Similar advice is found in the model speeches of the Bancroft Dialogues; see for example, the grandmother's speech, on how children were raised in preconquest times, made in the presence of her grandsons (Karttunen and Lockhart 1987, 149–157).

80. Sahagún 1996, bk. 6, fols. 106–114. The Bancroft Dialogues also provide a speech delivered by the groom's mother to her son (Karttunen and Lockhart 1987, 116–117).

81. AJT-CR 7, 22, Yanhuitlan, 1605.

82. AJT-CR 11, 9, Tamazulapa, 1624.

83. AJT-CR 8, 21, Teposcolula, 1610.

84. Karttunen and Lockhart 1987, 158.

85. Kanter 2008 finds evidence only of fathers beating their children in late colonial Toluca, and she mentions no other forms of discipline. Whether this is typical of the later period, unique to the region, or an issue of sources remains to be seen (56).

86. AJVA-CR 4, 12, San Andrés Yaa, 1689. Baltasar Martín, the girls' father, also gave María Martín twelve reales to restore peace and begged her not to go to the alcalde mayor. He did not contest the officials' actions until Magdalena died about six months later of fevers. Even then he did not question their authority in punishing the girls; he only argued that they had punished them too harshly by giving them so many lashes.

87. AJT-CR 10, 46, Teposcolula, 1623. Pedro Cumaa's age is not specified in the document; he is described simply as a *muchacho*.

88. Monaghan 1995 notes that in the modern Mixtec community of Nuyoo the people of the household are responsible for the actions of other household members. He provides an example in which a man accidentally burned his own house and plot and damaged neighboring fields. The man was killed in the accident, so his brother was forced to pay for the damages (35–36).

89. AJVA-CR 3, 2, San Francisco Cajonos, 1676.

90. AJVA-C 1, 9, Totontepec, 1676–1677.

91. AJVA-CR 1, 10, Huitepec, 1659. In this case, Catalina López's father-in-law was an alcalde, and he had whipped her publicly.

92. AGI-P 230A, R1, Capulalpa, 1660.

93. AGN-CR 217, 10, Atengo, 1723.

94. AJT-CR 13, 18.01, Teposcolula, 1632. He agreed that he and his wife would work at the rate of a peso and a half a month for twenty-six months to repay Inés. His wife promised to pay the balance if Sebastián abandoned Inés's house.

95. AJVA-CR 4, 77, Yatzona, 1688. For more on the life and struggles of don Joseph, see Yannakakis 2008.

96. Oratories are mentioned in AGN-CR 29, 2, Coyoacan, 1652; AGN-CR 10, 15, Ecatepec, 1674; AGN-CR 139, 17, Malinalco, 1757; AJT-CR 18, 3,

Teposcolula, 1681; AJVA-CR 2, 10, Lachichina, 1670; many times in AGI-M 882, 1704.

97. Lockhart 1992, 239, and Terraciano 2001, 309–310.
98. See Lockhart 1992, 66–67, 235–251, for a general discussion of saints.
99. AGN-CR 29, 2, Coyoacan, 1652.
100. AGN-CR 139, 17, Malinalco, 1757.
101. AJT-CR 18, 3, Teposcolula, 1681.
102. Ruiz de Alarcón 1984.
103. Tavárez 2011 discusses this campaign in significant detail (esp. chap. 7).
104. AGI-M 882, Yaa, 1704.
105. AGI-M 882, Yoeche, 1704. The instruments were collected by fray Francisco de Orozco and burned.
106. AGI-M 882, Betaza, 1704.
107. Tavárez 2011, 204.
108. The Spanish-language testament is reproduced and translated in Restall, Sousa and Terraciano 2005, 106–113. See Terraciano 2001, 284–285, for a discussion of don Gabriel's last will and testament; also see Terraciano 2001, 309, for additional examples of Ñudzahui elites who owned Christian relics and images.
109. AJVA-CR 6, 7, Yatzona, 1699. Just a few years later, don Felipe would be investigated for idolatry, although his real troubles stemmed from his aggressive defense of communal interests against the economic interests of the alcaldes mayores (Tavárez 2011, 216).
110. Osowski 2010. Osowski discusses a fascinating case of a prominent Nahua woman named doña María de los Dolores, who served for a time as governor of Xochimilco. She had a santocalli attached to her home that opened to the plaza. Inside was a large image of Santo Cristo el Redentor, religious paintings, and offerings. In an attempt to undermine her authority, the alcalde mayor had her santocalli nailed shut (122–124).
111. AGI-M 882, Talea, 1704.
112. AGI-M 882, Yatoni, 1704.
113. As Tavárez 2011 notes, "teachers of idolatry" led ceremonies in both the collective and elective ritual sphere—that is, ceremonies organized for the benefit of the entire community and others for the well-being of individuals or families.
114. AGI-M 882, Yalálag, 1704.
115. AJVA-CR 1, 20, Lachirio, 1665.
116. AGI-M 882, Yacoche, 1704.
117. AGI-M 882, Yoeche, 1704.
118. AGI-M 882, San Pablo Cajonos, 1704.
119. AGI-M 882, Betaza, 1704.
120. Ibid. It is unclear whether he has the skulls of his grandmothers and grandfathers; I suspect that he had both, given the importance of female ancestor deities in Mesoamerican religion.
121. AGI-M 882, Yatee, 1704.

122. Osowski 2010, 117. See also Taylor 2010, 36, 38, 169–172; Taylor 2011, pt. 3.
123. Evans 1998.
124. Lockhart 1992, 102.
125. Ibid., 102–110.
126. Ibid., 16.
127. On Ñudzahui sociopolitical organization, see Terraciano 2001, esp. chaps. 4, 6.
128. AJT-CR 7, 30, Yanhuitlan, 1606. People of Tocaçahuala met at the cacique's house in Yanhuitlan to participate in the procession of penitents.
129. One Bènizàa priest stated that the number of sacrifices the community made depended on whether the alcaldes were "good" and "punctual" (AGI-M 882, Betaza, 1704, fol. 142v).
130. AJVA-CR 1, 16, Tiltepec, 1661. In a similar example, a group also met to drink pulque at the house of the *alguacil mayor* (head constable) in Metepec in 1685 (AJVA-CR 3, 15, Metepec, 1685).
131. AJVA-CR 5, 17, Mocton, 1697.
132. AJVA-CR 3, 5, Yatzona, 1676.
133. AJVA-CR 3, 117, Betaza and Lachitaa, 1703 (this citation follows the older cataloguing system of this archive).
134. AJVA-CR 1, 119, Tabaá, 1703 (this citation follows the older cataloguing system).
135. AJVA-CR, unindexed, San Francisco Cajonos, 1704 (this citation follows the older cataloguing system).
136. Sometimes the notary specifically stated that he had come to the testator's house, as did the notary who noted in a Ñudzahui-language testament written in 1581: "I came to the house of the woman named Catalina and a testament was written" (*niquihidi huey ñaa nani cathalina yidaa memoriaña*) (AJT-CR 1, 25, Achiutla, 1581).
137. There are many examples of Nahua women as witnesses to testaments reproduced in a collection of sixteenth-century testaments from Culhuacan (Cline and León-Portilla 1984). See also Lockhart 1992, 370; Horn 1997, 162. For the Mixteca Alta, see Terraciano 2001, 50.
138. AJVA-CR 2, 112, Totontepec, 1701 (this citation follows the older cataloguing system).
139. Berdan and Anawalt 1992, fols. 67v–69r.
140. Gómez de Cervantes 1944, 135; quoted in Lockhart 1991, 69.
141. AGN-CR 140, 4, Malinalco, 1626.
142. Sahagún 1996, bk. 2, fol. 101r-v.
143. AJVA-CR 5, 1, Totontepec, 1694.
144. Ibid.; see the testimony of Juan de Escobar and Gaspar Sánchez.
145. AJT-CR 2, 37, Tlaxiaco, 1581.
146. Nutini 1976 discusses the occurrence and importance of compadrazgo relations that transcend community boundaries in modern-day rural Tlaxcala. He shows that extracommunal compadrazgo relations allow neighboring com-

munities to avoid disputes over land and water rights, avert conflict within the community and allow the community to create regional factions, and enable migrant workers to establish kin ties that sustain them when they are outside of the community (see also Nutini and Bell 1980; Nutini 1984).

147. For an example of a cacique with compadres in neighboring communities, see AJVA-CR 6, 5, Taguí, Royaga, 1698; for cases of commoners, see, for example, AJVA-CR 1, 4, Yalahuí, 1651; AJVA-CR 1, 15, Yetzelálag, 1661; AJVA-CR 3, 9, Yalálag, 1678; AJVA-CR 5, 1, Totontepec, 1694.

148. AJT-CR 2, 37, Tlaxiaco, 1581.

149. AGN-CR 29, 2, Coyoacan, 1652. For an additional case of compadres celebrating together, see AGN-CR 217, 10, Atengo, 1723.

150. For additional cases of men and women who traveled to other communities to visit their comadres and compadres, see AJT-CR 6, 46, Yanhuitlan, 1604; AJVA-CR 7, 10, Camotlan, 1706; AJVA-CR 4, 19, Taguí, 1692.

151. AJVA-CR 3, 9, Yalálag, 1678.

152. AGN-CR 590, 2, Lalopa, 1657.

153. For examples of dialogues in which the speaker(s) use *compadre* and *comadre*, see AJT-CR 6, 46, Yanhuitlan, 1604; AJT-CR 8, 12, Yanhuitlan, 1608; AJVA-CR 1, 4, Yalahuí, 1651; AJVA-CR 5, 15, San Francisco Cajonos, 1697.

154. AJT-CR 6, 36, Teposcolula, 1603, fol. 2v.

155. AJVA-CR 3, 9, San Francisco Cajonos, 1678.

156. AGN-CR 140, 4, Malinalco, 1626.

157. AGN-CR 590, 2, Lalopa, 1657; AJT-CR 3, 276, Teposcolula, 1613.

158. AJVA-CR 2, 17 bis, Ayutla, 1674.

159. AJVA-CR 3, 9, Yalálag, 1678; AJT-CR 6, 46, Yanhuitlan, 1604.

160. Melton-Villanueva and Pizzigoni 2008, 379–380.

161. Pizzigoni 2012, 183.

162. AJVA-CR 1, 4, Yalahuí, 1651.

163. Ibid., fol. 4v.

164. AGN-CR 217, 10, Atengo, 1723.

165. AJT-CR 8, 21, Teposcolula, 1610.

166. AJT-CR 21, 13, Xinastla, 1695.

167. AJT-CR 11, 9, Tamazulapa, 1624.

168. AGN-CR 10, 13, San Juan Teotihuacan, 1757. This case is an example of ritual kin relations between Nahuas and Spaniards. Miguel García was a Spanish muleteer, and his compadres were Nahua farmers.

169. AJT-CR 6, 36, Teposcolula, 1603.

170. AGN-CR 630, 4, Tecamachalco, 1710.

171. AJT-CR 19, 5, Yanhuitlan, 1685, fol. 5.

172. AJT-CR 6, 46, Yanhuitlan, 1604. For additional examples of commoners presenting compadres as witnesses, see AGN-CR 140, 4, Malinalco, 1626; AGN-CR 730, 15, Tacuba, 1745.

173. AGN-CR 29, 1, Tacubaya, 1639.

174. AJVA-CR 3, 26, Yatzona, 1687; AJVA-CR 5, 3, Yatzona, 1695; see

AJVA-CR 2, 12, Talea, 1674, for another example of a compadre who serves as a witness.
175. Pizzigoni 2012, 184.
176. Burkhart 1997, 52.

CHAPTER NINE

1. AJT-CR 9: 7, 9, 12, Nuyoo, 1612, 1613.
2. Ibid. Also included in the contingent were several native officials from nearby communities and a seventeen-year-old mulatto slave.
3. Taylor 1979, 116.
4. In my sampling of cases, I do not consider millenarian movements, although women often played a major leadership role in these popular forms of resistance. In his study of a major eighteenth-century Tzeltal revolt that grew out of a millenarian movement inspired by the visions of a young woman, Gosner concludes that women did not engage in the fighting. See Taylor 1979, chap. 4; Gosner 1992, 1997.
5. Codex Selden (Añute) sections concerning Six Monkey are discussed in Boone 2000, 72–75, and Jansen and Pérez Jiménez 2007. Jansen and Pérez Jiménez propose decolonizing the names of the codices by referring to them with the names of their place of origin (27–28, 202–206, 283–285). I provide both names here because some readers will be unfamiliar with the term *Añute* at this time.
6. These examples are provided in Kellogg 2005, 24. Klein 1994 analyzes how different texts and images portray women's role in the famous battle between the Mexica and the Tlatelolca. She concludes: "In Aztec ideology, those who fought with their femininity were simply part of a discursive strategy that bolstered not just the sovereignty of the state itself but, concomitantly, the power and authority of men" (146).
7. Duran 1994, 555.
8. Lockhart 1993, 266–267 (I use Lockhart's translation).
9. For studies of tensions over cabecera/sujeto status in the Zapotec Sierra, see Romero Frizzi 2010 and Yannakakis 2010. For conflicts in the Mixteca over cabecera/sujeto designations, see Terraciano 2001, 124–130.
10. Yannakakis 2010 cautions: "We should be careful not to position the pueblo as historical actor but rather specify who within the pueblo was utilizing the legal system and who was constructing and deploying the legal strategies to pursue an objective" (146). She makes an excellent point; however, in cases in which Spanish officials complained that the entire community rioted, it is difficult to identify internal factions.
11. AJT-CR 15, 19, Yanhuitlan, 1641. Note related documents in 15, 18 and 15, 20.
12. Ana de Meneses was the widow of Gaspar de Meneses, a literate officeholder (he was able to sign his name), who appears in the historical record in 1603 as an alguacil mayor of Teposcolula and in 1631 and 1632 as an alcalde. Together Ana and Gaspar de Meneses had purchased sheep that they raised. They used the proceeds from the livestock to purchase silver candlesticks, ornaments,

an altar cloth, and other things for the church and to sponsor church festivities (AJT-C 9,11, San Felipe Ixtapa, 1640).

13. Unfortunately, the record is incomplete; if Ana de Meneses was called to clear her name or that of Pedro de Zarate, her testimony is now lost.

14. AJT-CR 13, 36, Teposcolula, 1633; AJT-CR 14, 05, Teposcolula, 1633.

15. Juana de Mendoza was charged again with rebelliousness in 1639 (AJT-CR 15, 10, Teposcolula, 1639).

16. AJT-CR 13, 34, Teposcolula, 1633.

17. AJT-CR 13, 34, Teposcolula, 1633, fol. 2–2v.

18. Haskett 1997.

19. Haskett 1997, 151.

20. For examples of letters to the Crown, see Restall, Sousa and Terraciano 2005, 64–71, and Lockhart and Otte 1976, 163–172.

21. Ruiz Medrano 2010a, 6.

22. On the emergence and evolution of the legal and political system in New Spain, see Gibson 1952, 1964; Borah 1983; Lockhart 1992; Kellogg 1995; Restall 1997; Terraciano 2001; Owensby 2008; Yannakakis 2008, 2010; Romero Frizzi 2010; Connell 2011.

23. Ruiz Medrano 2010a provides an interesting case study of the work of a procurador named Agustín Pinto in early Mexico (48–61). See also Connell 2011, esp. chap. 1.

24. Kimberly Gauderman has demonstrated that indigenous market women were quite adept at using the legal system to defend their rights to participate in commerce in colonial Quito (2003, chap. 5).

25. *Códice Tepetlaoztoc (Códice Kingsborough) Estado de México*, Edición facsimilar, (Toluca, El Colegio Mexiquense, 1994), fol. 12, lámina B. For a discussion of the case, see Gibson 1964, 78–80.

26. See, for example, ibid., fol. 12, lámina A.

27. AJT-CR 13, 30, Tlaxiaco, 1633.

28. AJT-C 11, 11, Teposcolula, 1641.

29. AJT-CR 9: 7; 9: 9; 9: 12, Nuyoo, 1612. For another case concerning spinning, see AJT-CR 12, 6, Yanhuitlan, 1628; AJVA-CR 5, 3, Yatzona, 1695. Similar issues were raised in a dispute in the Zapotec community of Yatzona in 1695. One group opposed the town council officials, complaining that they had distributed cotton to the women to spin into thread and weave into mantas.

30. This case is discussed in Terraciano 2001, 240.

31. AJT-CR 9, 23, Teposcolula, 1613, fol. 1.

32. AGN-T 2935, 79, Teposcolula, 1647.

33. Chance 1989, 110.

34. AGI-P 230A, R1, Nexapa, Tehuantepec, 1661. For secondary scholarship on these uprisings, see Díaz Polanco 1992a, 1992b; Díaz Polanco and Sánchez 1992; Owensby 2008, chap. 8.

35. Reyes García 2001, 210–213.

36. Quoted in Owensby 2008, 283.

37. AJT-CR 5, 10, Tlaxiaco, 1598.

38. See also Taylor 1979, 115.

39. Chimalpahin 1997, 216; Reyes García 2001, 216. The term also appears in Molina 1992, S-N 11v.
40. Molina 1992, S-N 7v. A form of *comonia* is used in the Annals of Juan Bautista to describe the uprising in 1564 against don Luis and the Mexica cabildo (Reyes García 2001, 214).
41. These terms are attested to in Chimalpahin 1997, 216; Reyes García 2001, 214, 216.
42. Forms based on *qualania* are in Reyes García 2001, 214, 216; Chimalpahin 1997, 216. For references to *netenhuiteco*, see Reyes García 2001, 214, 216. This act is also described in Spanish-language documents.
43. AJVA-CR 12, 12, Villa Alta, 1728.
44. For more on insults in later colonial riots, see Taylor 1979, 115, passim.
45. AJVA-CR 12, 12, Villa Alta, 1728.
46. AGI-P 230A, R1, Nexapa and Tehuantepec, 1661, fol. 23r.
47. AJT-CR 2, 25, Teposcolula, 1719.
48. AJT-CR 25, 28, Tillo, Yanhuitlan, 1722.
49. Ibid., 70.
50. Ibid., 65.
51. Ibid., 72.
52. AJT-CR 16,12, Achiutla, 1649.
53. AGI-P 230A, R1, Nexapa and Tehuantepec, 1661.
54. On this point see, Owensby 2008, chap. 8.
55. Gibson 1964, chap. 8, esp. 198–202.
56. For an excellent article on Nahua resistance to the obligation to provide labor in mines, see Haskett 1991b. According to Chimalpahin 2006, 50,000 indigenous commoners died working on the desague project (294–295).
57. Reyes García 2001, 33.
58. Villanueva 1985.
59. Hamnett 1971, 3.
60. For examples of communities that distributed cotton for women to spin and weave, see AJT-CR 9, 7, 9: 9, and 9: 12, Nuyoo, 1612, 1613; AJT-CR 12, 6, Yanhuitlan, 1628; AJT-CR 14, 34, Cuquila, 1637; AJVA-CR 5, 3, Yatzona, 1695.
61. AJT-CR 4, 10, Coixtlahuaca, 1596.
62. Acuña 1984, 1,33, 1, 370, and 2, 248.
63. For a related discussion, see Villanueva 1985; Terraciano 2001; Chance 1989.
64. AJVA-CR 3, 4, Talea, 1676. For an example from a Mixe community, see AJVA-CR 1, 7, Tonaguia, 1654.
65. Yannakakis 2008 highlights the critical role of native officials as intermediaries in civil and religious matters in the Villa Alta jurisdiction.
66. This institution is also sometimes called *repartimiento de comercio, repartimiento de mercancias,* or *reparto de efectos.* On the connection between rebellion and the alcalde mayor's use of repartimiento de efectos, see Taylor 1979, 134–135.
67. For the Mixteca Alta, see Pastor 1987; Romero Frizzi 1990; Terraciano

2001. For the Sierra Zapoteca, see Chance 1989; Hamnett 1971; Baskes 2000; Yannakakis 2008.

68. Terraciano 2001, 240; Chance 1989, 103.
69. Chance 1989, 104.
70. Hamnett 1971, 68; Baskes 2000, 28.
71. These estimates are discussed in Hamnett 1971, 76.
72. Baskes 2000, 36–37.
73. For examples, see Romero Frizzi 1990, 445–477. See Hamnett 1971 and Baskes 2000 for a discussion of the relationship between Spanish officials and merchants, who often served as *aviadores*, or financial guarantors of alcaldes mayores, and their ability to collect tribute for the crown.
74. Romero Frizzi 1990, 446.
75. Ibid., 475–476.
76. Ibid., 463.
77. Ibid., 456.
78. AJVA-CR 1, 18, Villa Alta, 1665.
79. AJVA-CR 3, 10, Villa Alta, 1682. Chance 1989 notes that de la Sierra was the *alguacil perpetuo* of the villa (101). For an additional example, see AJVA-CR 3, 13, Yatee, 1684.
80. Hamnett 1971, 79.
81. Chance 1989, 109. According to the Bishop of Oaxaca who had visited the Bixanos region in 1779, a woman's profit for a week of work might be four or five reales.
82. Patch 2013; Baskes 2000; Romero Frizzi 1990.
83. Chimalpahin 1998, 216.
84. Ibid.
85. Chap. 1, Connell 2011, provides a full discussion of the case and the significance of the suit for the evolution of the relationship between the indigenous cabildo and the Audiencia. Complaints against the cabildo began as early as 1555, but it was not until 1564 that the Audiencia decided to investigate. The case is also treated in Ruiz Medrano's 2010b study of the role of Nahua nobles and friars in the conspiracy of the encomenderos against the crown.
86. Gibson 1964, 197, 517–518, note 21.
87. Reyes García 2001, 216–219, 258–259, 282–285.
88. Ibid., 214–215.
89. Read and Rosenthal 2006, 318.
90. Reyes García 2001, 220–221.
91. Ibid., 244–245, 258–259.
92. Ibid., 258–259.
93. Ibid., 258–259.
94. AJT-CR 8, 19, Tlaxiaco, 1610.
95. The men were paid only three tomines for their labor; the woman earned even less.
96. The Florentine Codex has a passage that describes war captives who make the same motions and shouts as discussed here. Lockhart 1993, 216.
97. AGN-CR 139, 25 and 26, Malinalco, 1641.

98. AGN-CR 139, 26, Malinalco, 1641.

99. AJT-CR 19, 13, Tamasulapa, 1686.

100. The case named Domingo Hernández, Bernavel de la Cruz, Juan Matias, Juan de la Cruz, Domingo de la Cruz, Lorenzo Juárez, Francisco de la Cruz, Domingo de Estrada, Domingo de Vega, doña Lucía de Guzman, Gracía Hernández, Inés de Mendoza, Agustina de la Cruz, Gracía de Santo Domingo, María Juárez, Magdalena García, "Indian men and Indian women, natives of the pueblo of Tamasulapa."

101. Many of the patterns observed in the Tamasulapa case appear in a late seventeenth century riot in the Zapotec Sierra community of Santiago Yagayo. Although many of the details are now lost, the records state that the people rebelled when the alcalde mayor, capitan don Juan Manuel, sent a Spaniard named Joseph de Marabel to the town to collect tribute. As in other riots from central Mexico and Oaxaca, the people showed their disrespect for the alcalde mayor's representative and, by extension for royal justice, by seizing and breaking his staff and trying to tie him up. Several people, including town officials, were punished for this with flogging (AJVA-CR 5, 7, Yagayo, 1696).

102. Gibson 1964, 210.

103. AJT-CR 3, 22, Teposcolula, 1597. Tensions between the alcalde and the priest escalated further. When the friar heard the alcalde's response, he accused him of being drunk. The alcalde returned the insult and then punched the priest. Apparently officials had grown tired of the friars' demands and their constant harping on the natives for drinking.

104. Connell argues that one of the underlying issues in these conflicts in Mexico Tenochtitlan was the matter of succession.

105. Tena 1998, 220–221.

106. AJT-CR 3, 24, Texupa, 1592.

107. Ibid., fol. 7v.

108. Incidentally, one of the women also berated the men from Texupa for bringing oxen into the church patio. The church served as a symbol of the community, and the women were protecting it against this desecration.

109. AJT-CR 18, 28, Sayultepec, 1683.

110. AJT-CR 10, 12, Teposcolula, 1615.

111. AJVA-CR, 12, 12, Villa Alta, 1728.

112. AGN-CR 18, 3, Ocuila, 1746.

113. Ibid.

114. AJT-CR 1, 25, Tecomastlahuaca, 1563, fol. 2.

115. AJVA-CR 5, 7, Yagayo, 1696, fol. 22v.

116. *Relación geografica de Minas de Tasco*, Acuña, 1986, 2:126.

117. AGN-CR 139, 25, Malinalco, 1641.

118. Kellogg 1997.

119. AGN-CR 645, 1, Tonaltepec, 1559, fol. 63.

120. AJT-CR 1, 25, Tecomastlahuaca, 1563.

121. AJT-CR 4, 10, Coixtlahuaca, 1596. It was common throughout central and southern Mexico to pay a fine in lieu of performing tribute labor. When

questioned, the regidor explained that the community was poor and needed the money.
122. AJVA-CR 2, 10, Lachichina, 1670.
123. AGN-CR 140, 1, Malinalco, 1635, fol. 21.
124. AGN-CR 216, 4, Atlacomulco, 1685. For a discussion of native resistance to Spanish demands for mining labor, see Haskett 1991b.
125. AJT-CR 12, 6, Yanhuitlan, 1628.
126. AGN-CR 686, 6, Tepozotlan, 1556.
127. AGN-CR 686, 6, Tepozotlan, 1556, fol. 55.
128. AJT-CR 2, 46, Teposcolula, 1583.
129. AJT-CR 14, 30, Teposcolula, 1639.
130. AGN-CR 217, 4, Chapultepec, Mexicaltzingo, 1711.
131. AJT-CR 2, 25, Teposcolula, 1719.
132. AJT-CR 43, 37.01, Teposcolula, 1754.
133. AJT-CR 12, 14, Achiutla, 1629.
134. AJT-CR 12, 14, Achiutla, 1629, fol. 2.
135. Taylor 1979, 116.
136. Haskett 1997, 148. On this point, see also Gosner 1997.

CHAPTER TEN

1. Lockhart 1992, 85.
2. Klein 1980, 2001; Sigal 2011; Olivier 2004.
3. Burkhart 1997, 52.
4. Quoted in Iglesias Prieto 1997, 25–26.

References

ARCHIVES
Archivo General del Estado de Oaxaca, Oaxaca, (AGEO)
Archivo General de la Nación, México, (AGN)
Archivo General de las Indias, Sevilla (AGI)
Archivo Judicial de Teposcolula, Oaxaca (AJT)
Archivo Judicial de Villa Alta, Oaxaca (AJVA)
Civil (C)
Criminal (CR)
Inquisición (I)
México (M)
Patronato (P)
Tierras (T)

A NOTE ON SOURCES
The judicial archive in Oaxaca that houses the AJVA and AJT collections has been moved and reorganized since I began research for this project. I have updated all but a few citations and have noted when a citation refers to the older cataloguing system.

WORKS CITED
Acuña, René. 1984–1988. *Relaciones geográficas del siglo XVI,* vols. 2 and 3: Antequera; vols. 4 and 5: Tlaxcala; vols. 6–8: México. Mexico City: Universidad Nacional Autónoma de México.

Alcina Franch, José. 1993. *Calendario y religión entre los zapotecos.* Mexico City: Universidad Nacional Autónoma de México.

Alva, Bartolomé de. 1999. *A Guide to Confession Large and Small in the Mexican Language, 1634.* Translated and edited by Barry D. Sell and John Frederick Schwaller, with Lu Ann Homza. Norman: University of Oklahoma Press.

Alvarado, fray Francisco de. 1962 [1593]. *Vocabulario en lengua mixteca.* Ed-

ited by Wigberto Jiménez Moreno. Mexico City: Instituto Nacional de Antropología e Historia.
Anawalt, Patricia. 1981. *Indian Clothing Before Cortés: Mesoamerican Costumes from the Codices*. Norman: University of Oklahoma Press.
Anderson, Arthur J. O. 1997. "Aztec Wives." In *Indian Women of Early Mexico*. Edited by Susan Schroeder, Stephanie Wood, and Robert Haskett, 55–85. Norman: University of Oklahoma Press.
Anderson, Arthur J. O., Frances Berdan, and James Lockhart, eds. and trans. 1976. *Beyond the Codices: The Nahua View of Colonial Mexico*. UCLA Latin American Studies Series, 27. Berkeley: University of California Press.
Anderson, Arthur J. O., and Charles E. Dibble, trans. 1950–1982. *Florentine Codex: General History of Things of New Spain*. 13 parts. Salt Lake City: University of Utah Press.
Andrews, J. Richard. 1975. *Introduction to Classical Nahuatl*. Austin: University of Texas Press.
Arrom, Silvia Marina. 1985. *The Women of Mexico City, 1790–1857*. Stanford, CA: Stanford University Press.
Arvey, Margaret Campbell. 1988. "Women of Ill-Repute in the Florentine Codex." In *The Role of Gender in Precolumbian Art and Architecture*. Edited by Virginia E. Miller, 179–204. Lanham, MD: University Press of America.
Ávila, Alejandro B. de. 1996. "Textiles arqueológicos y contemporáneos de Oaxaca." *Arqueología Mexicana*, 3 (17):34–41.
Baskes, Jeremy. 2000. *Indians, Merchants, and Markets: A Reinterpretation of the Repartimiento and Spanish-Indian Economic Relations in Colonial Oaxaca, 1750–1821*. Stanford, CA: Stanford University Press.
Behar, Ruth. 1989. "Sexual Witchcraft, Colonialism, and Women's Powers: Views from the Mexican Inquisition." In *Sexuality and Marriage in Colonial Latin America*. Edited by Asunción Lavrin, 178–206. Lincoln: University of Nebraska Press.
Berdan, Frances F. 1982. *The Aztecs of Central Mexico: An Imperial Society*. New York: Holt, Rinehart, and Winston.
Bernal, Ignacio. 1966. "The Mixtecs in the Archeology of the Valley of Oaxaca." In *Ancient Oaxaca: Discoveries in Mexican Archeology and History*. Edited by John Paddock, 345–366. Stanford, CA: Stanford University Press.
Biblioteca Enciclopédica del Estado de México. 1980. *Proceso Inquisitorial del Cacique de Tetzcoco don Carlos Ometochtzin (Chichimecatecotl)*. Mexico City: Patrimonio Cultural y Artístico del Estado de México.
Blackwood, Evelyn. 1984. "Sexuality and Gender in Certain Native American Tribes: The Case of Cross-Gender Females." *Signs: Journal of Women in Culture and Society*, 10 (11):27–42.
Boone, Elizabeth Hill. 2000. *Stories in Red and Black: Pictorial Histories of the Aztecs and Mixtecs*. Austin: University of Texas Press.
———. 2005. "*In tlamatinime*: The Wise Men and Women of Aztec Mexico." In *Painted Books and Indigenous Knowledge in Mesoamerica: Manuscript Studies in Honor of Mary Elizabeth Smith*. Edited by Elizabeth Hill Boone, 9–25. New Orleans, LA: Middle American Research Institute, Tulane University.

———. 2006. "Marriage Almanacs in the Mexican Divinatory Codices." *Anales del Instituto de Investigaciones Estéticas*, 28 (29):71–92.
———. 2007. *Cycles of Time and Meaning in the Mexican Books of Fate*. Austin: University of Texas Press.
Borah, Woodrow. 1943. *Silk Raising in Colonial Mexico*. Ibero-Americana, 20. Berkeley: University of California Press.
———. 1983. *Justice by Insurance: The General Indian Court of Colonial Mexico*. Berkeley: University of California Press.
Borah, Woodrow, and S. F. Cook. 1960. *Indian Population of Central Mexico, 1531–1570*. Ibero-Americana, 43. Berkeley: University of California Press.
Boyer, Richard E. 1989. "Women, *La Mala Vida*, and the Politics of Marriage." In *Sexuality and Marriage in Colonial Latin America*. Edited by Asunción Lavrin, 252–286. Lincoln: University of Nebraska Press.
———. 1995. *Lives of the Bigamists: Marriage, Family, and Community in Colonial Mexico*. Albuquerque: University of New Mexico Press.
———. 1998. "Honor among Plebians." In *The Faces of Honor: Sex, Shame, and Violence in Colonial Latin America*. Edited by Lyman L. Johnson and Sonya Lipsett-Rivera, 152–178. Albuquerque: University of New Mexico Press.
Brown, Betty Ann. 1983. "Seen but Not Heard: Women in Aztec Ritual—The Sahagún Texts." In *Text and Image in Pre-Columbian Art*. Edited by Janet C. Berlo, 119–153. Oxford, UK: B.A.R. Press.
Brumfiel, Elizabeth M. 1991. "Weaving and Cooking: Women's Production in Aztec Mexico." In *Engendering Archaeology: Women and Prehistory*. Edited by Joan M. Gero and Margaret W. Conkey, 224–251. Oxford, UK: Basil Blackwell.
Burkhart, Louise M. 1986. "Moral Deviance in Sixteenth-Century Nahua and Christian Thought: The Rabbit and the Deer." *Journal of Latin American Lore* 12 (2):107–139.
———. 1988. "The Solar Christ in Nahuatl Doctrinal Texts of Early Colonial Mexico." *Ethnohistory* 35 (3):234–256.
———. 1989. *The Slippery Earth: Nahua-Christian Moral Dialogue in Sixteenth-Century Mexico*. Tucson: University of Arizona Press.
———. 1992. "Flowery Heaven: The Aesthetic of Paradise in Nahuatl Devotional Literature." *RES: Anthropology and Aesthetics* 21 (Spring):88–109.
———. 1996. *Holy Wednesday: A Nahua Drama from Early Colonial Mexico*. Philadelphia: University of Pennsylvania Press.
———. 1997. "Mexica Women on the Home Front: Housework and Religion in Aztec Mexico." In *Indian Women of Early Mexico*. Edited by Susan Schroeder, Stephanie Wood, and Robert Haskett, 25–54. Norman: University of Oklahoma Press.
———. 2001. "Gender in Nahuatl Texts of the Early Colonial Period: Native 'Tradition' and the Dialogue with Christianity." In *Gender in Pre-Hispanic America: A Symposium at Dumbarton Oaks, 12 and 13 October 1996*. Edited by Cecelia Klein, 87–107. Washington, DC: Dumbarton Oaks Research Library and Collection.
Byland, Bruce E. 1993. Introduction to and commentary on *Codex Borgia: A Full*

Color Restoration of the Ancient Mexican Manuscript. Edited by Gisele Díaz and Alan Rodgers. New York: Dover Publications.

Carochi, Horacio. 1983. *Arte de la lengua mexicana con la declaración de los adverbios della.* Facsimile of 1645 edition with introduction by Miguel León-Portilla. Mexico City: Universidad Nacional Autónoma de México, Instituto de Investigaciones Filológicas, Instituto de Investigaciones Históricas.

Carrasco, Pedro. 1976. "The Joint Family in Ancient Mexico: The Case of Molotla." In *Essays on Mexican Kinship.* Edited by Hugo G. Nutini, Pedro Carrasco, and James M. Taggart, 45–64. Pittsburgh: University of Pittsburgh Press.

———. 1984. "Royal Marriages in Ancient Mexico." In *Explorations in Ethnohistory: Indians of Central Mexico in the Sixteenth Century.* Edited by H. R. Harvey and Hanns J. Prem, 41–81. Albuquerque: University of New Mexico Press.

Carroll, Pat. 2009. "Black Aliens and Black Natives in New Spain's Indigenous Communities." In *Black Mexico: Race and Society from Colonial to Modern Times.* Edited by Ben Vinson III and Matthew Restall, 72–95. Albuquerque: University of New Mexico Press.

Chance, John K. 1989. *Conquest of the Sierra: Spaniards and Indians in Colonial Oaxaca.* Norman: University of Oklahoma Press.

———. 2009. "Marriage Alliances among Colonial Mixtec Elites: The Villagómez Caciques of Acatlan-Petlalcingo." *Ethnohistory* 56 (1):91–123.

Charlton, Thomas, and Cynthia Otis Charlton. 1994. "Aztec Craft Production in Otumba, 1470–1570: Reflections on a Changing World." In *Chipping Away on Earth: Studies in Prehispanic and Colonial Mexico in Honor of Arthur J. O. Anderson and Charles E. Dibble.* Edited by Eloise Quiñones-Keber, 241–251. Lancaster, CA: Labyrinthos.

Chaudhuri, Nupur, Sherry J. Katz, and Mary Elizabeth Perry, eds. 2010. *Contesting Archives: Finding Women in the Sources.* Foreword by Antoinette Burton. Urbana: University of Illinois Press.

Chimalpáhin, Domingo. 1997. *Las ocho relaciones y el memorial de Colhuacan, II.* Paleografía y traducción, Rafael Tena. Mexico City: Cien de México, Consejo Nacional Para la Cultura y las Artes.

———. 2006. *Annals of His Time: Don Domingo de San Antón Muñón Chimalpahin Quauhtlehuanitzin.* Edited and Translated by James Lockhart, Susan Schroeder, and Doris Namala. Stanford, CA: Stanford University Press.

Christensen, Mark Z. 2010. "The Tales of Two Cultures: Ecclesiastical Texts and Nahua and Maya Catholicisms." *The Americas,* 66 (3):353–377.

Christensen, Mark, and Jonathan Truitt, eds. 2016. *Native Wills from the Colonial Americas: Dead Giveaways in a New World.* Salt Lake City: The University of Utah Press.

Chuchiak, John F. 2007. "The Sins of the Fathers: Franciscan Friars, Parish Priests, and the Sexual Conquest of the Yucatec Maya, 1545–1808." *Ethnohistory,* 54 (1):69–127.

Clendinnen, Inga. 1982. "Yucatec Maya Women and the Spanish Conquest: Role and Ritual in Historical Reconstruction." *Journal of Social History,* 15:427–442.

———. 1991. *The Aztecs: An Interpretation.* Cambridge: Cambridge University Press.

Cline, S. L. 1986. *Colonial Culhuacan, 1580–1600: A Social History of an Aztec Town.* Albuquerque: University of New Mexico Press.

———, ed. and trans. 1993. *The Book of Tributes: Early Sixteenth-Century Nahuatl Censuses from Morelos.* Nahuatl Studies Series 4. Los Angeles, CA: UCLA Latin American Studies Center Publications,

Cline, S. L., and Miguel León-Portilla, eds. 1984. *The Testaments of Culhuacan.* Nahuatl Studies Series 1. Los Angeles, CA: UCLA Latin American Studies Center Publications.

Codex Becker II (Códice Becker II). La Gran Familia de los reyes mixtecos: Libro explicativo de los codices llamados Egerton y Becker II. 1994 [undated]. Commentary by Maarten E. R. G. N. Jansen. Vienna: Akademische Druckund Verlagsanstalt; Madrid: Sociedad Estatal Quinto Centenario; Mexico City: Fondo de Cultura Económica.

Codex Borbonicus (Códice Borbónico). 1991 [undated]. Introducción y explicación por Ferdinand Anders, Maarten Jansen, y Luis Reyes García. Vienna: Akademische Druckund Verlagsanstalt; Madrid: Sociedad Estatal Quinto Centenario; Mexico City: Fondo de Cultura Económica.

Codex Borgia (Códice Borgia). 1993 [undated]. Introducción y explicación por Ferdinand Anders, Maarten Jansen, y Luis Reyes García. Vienna: Akademische Druckund Verlagsanstalt; Madrid: Sociedad Estatal Quinto Centenario; Mexico City: Fondo de Cultura Económica.

Codex Kingsborough. Códice Tepetlaoztoc (Códice Kingsborough) Estado de México. 1994 [undated]. Edición facsimilar con estudio preliminar por Perla Valle P. Toluca, Mexico: El Colegio Mexiquense.

Codex Laud (Códice Laud). 1994 [undated]. Introducción y explicación por Ferdinand Anders, Maarten Jansen, y Luis Reyes García. Vienna: Akademische Druckund Verlagsanstalt; Madrid: Sociedad Estatal Quinto Centenario; Mexico City: Fondo de Cultura Económica.

Codex Magliabechiano. 1970 [undated]. Edited by Ferdinand Anders. Graz, Austria: Akademische Druckund Verlagsanstalt.

Codex Mendoza. 1992 [undated]. Facsimile with commentary by Frances F. Berdan and Patricia Anawalt. 4 vols. Berkeley: University of California Press.

Codex Nuttall (Códice Zouche-Nuttall). 1992 [undated]. Introducción y explicación por Ferdinand Anders, Maarten Jansen, y Luis Reyes García. Vienna: Akademische Druckund Verlagsanstalt; Madrid: Sociedad Estatal Quinto Centenario; Mexico City: Fondo de Cultura Económica.

Codex Osuna (Códice Osuna). Pintura del gobernador, alcaldes, y regidores de México: Códice Osuna. 1973 [undated]. Madrid: Ministerio de Educación y Ciencia, Dirección General de Archivos y Bibliotecas.

Codex Sierra. Códice Sierra: Traducción al español\de su texto nahuatl, y explicación de sus pinturas jeroglíficas por el doctor Nicolás León. 1933 [undated]. Mexico City: Imprenta del Museo Nacional de Arqueología, Historia y Etnografía.

Codex Telleriano-Remensis. 1995 [undated]. Facsimile with commentary by

Eloise Quiñones Keber and foreword by Emmanuel Le Roy Ladurie. Austin: University of Texas Press.

Codex Tudela (Códice Tudela). 1980 [undated]. Introducción y explicación por José Tudela de la Orden con un prologo de Donald Robertson y un epilogo de Wigberto Jiménez Moreno y la reproducción autorizada de tablas de Ferdinand Anders y S. Jeffrey K. Wilkerson. Madrid: Ediciones Cultura Hispanica del Instituto de Cooperación Iberoamericana.

Codex Vaticanus B (Códice Vaticano B). 1993 [undated]. Introducción y explicación por Ferdinand Anders, Maarten Jansen, y Luis Reyes García. Vienna: Akademische Druckund Verlagsanstalt; Madrid: Sociedad Estatal Quinto Centenario; Mexico City: Fondo de Cultura Económica.

Codex Vindobonensis (Códice Vindobonensis). 1992 [undated]. Introducción y explicación por Ferdinand Anders, Maarten Jansen, y Luis Reyes García. Vienna: Akademische Druckund Verlagsanstalt; Madrid: Sociedad Estatal Quinto Centenario; Mexico City: Fondo de Cultura Económica.

Codex Yanhuitlan (Códice de Yanhuitlán). 1940 [undated]. Edición en facsimile y con estudio preliminar por Wigberto Jiménez Moreno y Salvador Mateos Higuera. Mexico City: Museo Nacional.

Connell, William F. 2011. *After Moctezuma: Indigenous Politics and Self-Government in Mexico City, 1524–1730.* Norman: University of Oklahoma Press.

Cook, S. F., and Woodrow Borah. 1968. *The Population of the Mixteca Alta, 1520–1960.* Ibero-Americana, 50. Berkeley: University of California Press.

Córdova, fray Juan de. 1987a [1578]. *Vocabulario en lengua çapoteca.* Mexico City: Ediciones Toledo.

———. 1987b [1578]. *Arte en lengua zapoteca.* Republished as *Arte del idioma zapoteco por el P. Fr. Juan de Cordova* in 1886 with an introduction. Mexico City: Ediciones Toledo.

Córdova, Pedro de. 1970 [1544]. *Christian Doctrine for the Instruction and Information of the Indians.* Translated and with an introduction by Sterling Stoudemire. Coral Gables, FL: University of Miami Press.

Dakin, Karen. 1981. "The Characteristics of a Nahuatl Lingua Franca." *Texas Linguistics Forum,* 18:55–67.

———. 1982. *La evolución del protonáhuatl.* Mexico City: Universidad Nacional Autónoma de México.

———. 2009. "Algunos documentos nahuas del sur de Mesoamérica." In *Visiones del encuentro de dos mundos en América: Lengua, cultura, traducción y transculturación.* Edited by Karen Dakin, Mercedes Montes de Oca, and Claudia Parodi, 247–269. Mexico City: Universidad Autónoma de México y Universidad de California Los Angeles Centro de Estudios Coloniales Iberoamericanos.

Davis, Natalie. 1987. *Fiction in the Archives: Pardon Tales and Their Tellers in Sixteenth-Century France.* Stanford, CA: Stanford University Press.

Deeds, Susan. 1997. "Double Jeopardy: Indian Women in Jesuit Missions of Nueva Vizcaya." In *Indian Women of Early Mexico.* Edited by Susan Schroeder, Stephanie Wood, and Robert Haskett, 255–272. Norman: University of Oklahoma Press.

D'Emilio, John, and Estelle B. Freedman. 1988. *Intimate Matters: A History of Sexuality in America.* New York: Harper and Row.

Díaz Balsera, Viviana. 2007. "Nombres que conservan el mundo: Los nahualtocaitl y el Tratado sobre idolatrías de Hernando Ruiz de Alarcón." *Colonial Latin American Review,* 16 (2):159–178.

Díaz del Castillo, Bernal. 1963. *The Conquest of New Spain.* Translated by J. M. Cohen. London: Penguin Books.

Díaz Polanco, Héctor. 1992a. "Sociedad colonial y rebellion indigena en el Obispado de Oaxaca (1660)." In *El fuego de la disobediencia: Autonomía y rebelión india en el Obispado de Oaxaca.* Edited by Héctor Díaz Polanco, 17–52. Mexico City: Centro de Investigaciones y Estudios Superiores en Antropología Social.

———, ed. 1992b. *El fuego de la disobediencia: Autonomía y rebelión india en el Obispado de Oaxaca.* Mexico City: Centro de Investigaciones y Estudios Superiores en Antropología Social.

Díaz Polanco, Héctor, and Consuelo Sánchez. 1992. "El vigor de la espada restauradora: La repression de las rebeliones indias en Oaxaca (1660–61)." In *El fuego de la disobediencia: Autonomía y rebelión india en el Obispado de Oaxaca.* Edited by Héctor Díaz Polanco, 53–80. Mexico City: Centro de Investigaciones y Estudios Superiores en Antropología Social.

Dodds Pennock, Caroline. 2008. *Bonds of Blood: Gender, Lifecycle and Sacrifice in Aztec Culture.* New York: Palgrave Macmillan.

Don, Patricia Lopes. 2010. *Bonfires of Culture: Franciscans, Indigenous Leaders, and Inquisition in Early Mexico, 1524–1540.* Norman: University of Oklahoma Press.

Durán, fray Diego. 1967 [1581]. *Historia de las indias de Nueva España e islas de tierra firme.* 2 vols. Mexico City: Editorial Porrua.

———. 1994. *The History of the Indies of New Spain.* Translated, annotated, and with an introduction by Doris Heyden. Norman: University of Oklahoma Press.

Durand-Forest, Jacqueline de. 1994. "The Aztec Craftsman and the Economy." In *Chipping Away on Earth: Studies in Prehispanic and Colonial Mexico in Honor of Arthur J. O. Anderson and Charles E. Dibble.* Edited by Eloise Quiñones-Keber, 173–176. Lancaster, CA: Labyrinthos.

Evans, Susan Toby. 1998. "Sexual Politics in the Aztec Palace: Public, Private, and Profane." *RES* 33 (Spring):166–183.

Feria, Pedro de. 1567. *Doctrina Christiana en lengua Castellana y Çapoteca: Compuesta por el muy reverend padre fray Pedro de Feria, provincial de la Orden de Sancto Domingo, en la provincia de Sanctiago de la Nueva Hespaña.* Mexico City: Casa de Pedro Ocharte.

Few, Martha. 2002. *Women Who Live Evil Lives: Gender, Religion, and the Politics of Power in Colonial Guatemala.* Austin: University of Texas Press.

Flores Farfán, José Antonio, and Jan G. R. Elferink. 2007. "La prostitución entre los nahuas." *Estudios de Cultura Náhuatl,* 38:265–282.

García Icazbalceta, Joaquín. 1896. *Obras de d. J. García Icazbalceta.* Mexico City: Imprenta de V. Agüeros.

Gauderman, Kimberly. 2003. *Women's Lives in Colonial Quito.* Austin: University of Texas Press.
Gerhard, Peter. 1972. *A Guide to the Historical Geography of New Spain.* Cambridge: Cambridge University Press.
Gero, Joan M., and Margaret W. Conkey, eds. 1991. *Engendering Archaeology: Women and Prehistory.* Oxford, UK: Basil Blackwell.
Gibson, Charles. 1952. *Tlaxcala in the Sixteenth Century.* New Haven: Yale University Press.
———. 1964. *The Aztecs Under Spanish Rule: A History of the Indians of the Valley of Mexico, 1519–1810.* Stanford, CA: Stanford University Press.
Gillespie, Susan. 1989. *The Aztec Kings: The Construction of Rulership in Mexica History.* Tucson: University of Arizona Press.
Gimmel, Millie. 2008. "Hacia una reconsideración del Códice de la Cruz Badiano: nuevas propuestas para el estudio de la medicina indígena e el período colonial." *Colonial Latin American Review* 17 (2):273–283.
Gómez de Cervantes, Gonzalo. 1944 [1599]. *La vida económica y social de la Nueva España al finalizar del siglo XVI.* Prólogo y notas de Alberto María Carreño. Biblioteca histórica Mexicana de obras ineditas, 19. Mexico City: Antigua Librería Robredo, de José Porrúa y Hijos.
Gonzalbo Aizpuru, Pilar, ed. 1991. *Familias novohispanas, siglos XVI al XIX.* Mexico City: Seminario de Historia de la Familia, Centro de Estudios Históricos, El Colegio de México.
Gonzalbo Aizpuru, Pilar, and Cecilia Rabell Romero, eds. 1994. *La familia en el mundo Iberoamericano.* Mexico City: Instituto de Investigaciones Sociales, Universidad Nacional Autónoma de México.
———. 1996. *Familia y vida privada en la historia de Iberoamérica.* Mexico City: El Colegio de México, Universidad Nacional Autónoma de México.
Goody, Jack. 1972. *Domestic Groups.* Reading, MA: Addison-Wesley.
Gosner, Kevin. 1992. *Soldiers of the Virgin: The Moral Economy of a Colonial Maya Rebellion.* Tucson: University of Arizona Press.
———. 1997. "Women, Rebellion, and the Moral Economy of Maya Peasants in Colonial Mexico." In *Indian Women of Early Mexico.* Edited by Susan Schroeder, Stephanie Wood, and Robert Haskett, 217–230. Norman: University of Oklahoma Press.
Gruzinski, Serge. 1989. "Individualization and Acculturation: Confession among the Nahuas of Mexico from the Sixteenth to the Eighteenth Century." In *Sexuality and Marriage in Colonial Latin America.* Edited by Asunción Lavrin, 96–115. Lincoln: University of Nebraska Press.
Gutiérrez, Ramón A. 1991. *When Jesus Came, the Corn Mothers Went Away: Marriage, Sexuality, and Power in New Mexico, 1500–1846.* Stanford, CA: Stanford University Press.
Hackel, Steven W. 2005. *Children of Coyote, Missionaries of Saint Francis: Indian-Spanish Relations in Colonial California.* Chapel Hill, NC: University of North Carolina Press. Published for the Omohundro Institute of Early American History and Culture, Williamsburg, Virginia.

Hamnett, Brian R. 1971. *Politics and Trade in Southern Mexico, 1750–1821.* London: Cambridge University Press.
Harvey, H. R. 1986. "Household and Family Structure in Early Colonial Tepetlaoztoc: An Analysis of the Códice de Santa María Asunción." *Estudios de Cultura Nahuatl,* 18:275–294.
Haskett, Robert S. 1991a. *Indigenous Rulers: An Ethnohistory of Town Government in Colonial Cuernavaca.* Albuquerque: University of New Mexico Press.
———. 1991b. "'Our Suffering with the Taxco Tribute': Involuntary Mine Labor and Indigenous Society in Central New Spain." *Hispanic American Historical Review,* 71 (3):447–475.
———. 1994. "'Not a Pastor, but a Wolf': Indigenous-Clergy Relations in Early Cuernavaca and Taxco." *The Americas,* 50 (3):293–336.
———. 1997. "Activist or Adulteress? The Life and Struggle of Doña Josefa María of Tepoztlan." In *Indian Women of Early Mexico.* Edited by Susan Schroeder, Stephanie Wood, and Robert Haskett, 145–163. Norman: University of Oklahoma Press.
———. 2005. *Visions of Paradise: Primordial Titles and Mesoamerican History in Cuernavaca.* Norman: University of Oklahoma Press.
Hassig, Ross. 1985. *Trade, Tribute, and Transportation: The Sixteenth-Century Political Economy of the Valley of Mexico.* Norman: University of Oklahoma Press.
Hernández, fray Benito. 1567, 1568. *Doctrina en lengua misteca.* Mexico City: Pedro Ocharte.
Herrera, Robinson A. 2007. "Concubines and Wives: Reinterpreting Native-Spanish Intimate Unions in Sixteenth-Century Guatemala." In *Indian Conquistadors: Indigenous Allies in the Conquest of Mesoamerica.* Edited by Laura E. Matthews and Michel R. Oudijk, 127–144. Norman: University of Oklahoma Press.
Hicks, Frederick. 1984. "Rotational Labor and Urban Development in Prehispanic Tetzcoco." In *Explorations in Ethnohistory: Indians of Central Mexico in the Sixteenth Century.* Edited by H. R. Harvey and Hanns J. Prem, 147–174. Albuquerque: University of New Mexico Press.
Hill, Jane. 1992. "The Flower World of Old Uto-Aztecan." *Journal of Anthropological Research* 48 (2):117–144.
Horn, Rebecca. 1997a. *Postconquest Coyoacan: Nahua-Spanish Relations in Central Mexico, 1519–1650.* Stanford, CA: Stanford University Press.
———. 1997b. "Gender and Social Identity: Nahua Naming Patterns in Postconquest Central Mexico." In *Indian Women of Early Mexico.* Edited by Susan Schroeder, Stephanie Wood, and Robert Haskett, 105–122. Norman: University of Oklahoma Press.
Hull, N. E. H. 1987. *Female Felons: Women and Crime in Colonial Massachusetts.* Urbana: University of Illinois Press.
Hunt, Marta Espejo-Ponce, and Matthew Restall. 1997. "Work, Marriage, and Status: Maya Women of Colonial Yucatan." In *Indian Women of Early Mexico.* Edited by Susan Schroeder, Stephanie Wood, and Robert Haskett, 231–252. Norman: University of Oklahoma Press.

Iglesias Prieto, Norma. 1997. *Beautiful Flowers of the Maquiladora: Life Histories of Women Workers in Tijuana*. Translated by Michael Stone with Gabriel Winkler. Austin: University of Texas Press.

Jansen, Maarten, and Gabina Aurora Pérez Jiménez. 2007. *Encounter with the Plumed Serpent: Drama and Power in the Heart of Mesoamerica*. Boulder: University of Colorado Press.

Johnson, Lyman L. 1998. "Dangerous Words, Provocative Gestures, and Violent Acts." In *The Faces of Honor: Sex, Shame, and Violence in Colonial Latin America*. Edited by Lyman L. Johnson and Sonya Lipsett-Rivera, 127–151. Albuquerque: University of New Mexico.

Joyce, Rosemary A. 2000. *Gender and Power in Prehispanic Mesoamerica*. Austin: University of Texas Press.

———. 2001. "Negotiating Sex and Gender in Classic Maya Society." In *Gender in Pre-Hispanic America: A Symposium at Dumbarton Oaks, 12 and 13 October 1996*. Edited by Cecelia Klein, 109–142. Washington, DC: Dumbarton Oaks Research Library and Collection.

Kanter, Deborah E. 1995. "Native Female Land Tenure and its Decline in Mexico, 1750–1900." *Ethnohistory*, 42 (4):607–616.

———. 2008. *Hijos del Pueblo: Gender, Family, and Community in Rural Mexico, 1730–1850*. Austin: University of Texas Press.

Karttunen, Frances. 1982. "Nahuatl Literacy." In *The Inca and Aztec States*. Edited by George A. Collier, Renato I. Rosaldo, and John D. Wirth, 395–417. New York: Academic Press.

———. 1983. *An Analytical Dictionary of Nahuatl*. Austin: University of Texas Press.

Karttunen, Frances, and James Lockhart. 1976. *Nahuatl in the Middle Years: Language Contact Phenomena in Texts of the Colonial Period*. University of California Publications in Linguistics, 85. Berkeley: University of California Press.

———. 1978. "Textos en náhuatl del siglo XVIII: Un documento de Amecameca, 1746." *Estudios de Cultura Náhuatl*, 13:153–175.

———. 1980. "La estructura de la poesía náhuatl vista por sus variantes." *Estudios de Cultura Náhuatl*, 14:15–65.

———, eds. 1987. *The Art of Nahuatl Speech: The Bancroft Dialogues*. Los Angeles: UCLA Latin American Center Publications.

Katzew, Ilona. 2011. "'Remedo de la ya muerta América': The Construction of Festive Rites in Colonial Mexico." In *Contested Visions in the Spanish Colonial World*. Edited by Ilona Katzew, 151–175. Los Angeles: Museum Associates.

Kellogg, Susan. 1984. "Aztec Women in Early Colonial Courts: Structure and Strategy in a Legal Context." In *Five Centuries of Law and Politics in Central Mexico*. Edited by Ronald Spores and Ross Hassig, 25–38. Vanderbilt University Publications in Anthropology, 30. Nashville, TN: Vanderbilt University Press.

———. 1995. *Law and the Transformation of Aztec Culture, 1500–1700*. Norman: University of Oklahoma Press.

———. 1997. "From Parallel and Equivalent to Separate and Unequal: Tenochca Mexican Women, 1500–1700." In *Indian Women of Early Mexico*. Edited by Susan Schroeder, Stephanie Wood, and Robert Haskett, 123–143. Norman: University of Oklahoma Press.

———. 2005. *Weaving the Past: A History of Latin America's Indigenous Women from the Prehispanic Period to the Present*. Oxford, UK: Oxford University Press.

Kellogg, Susan, and Matthew Restall, eds. 1998. *Dead Giveaways: Indigenous Testaments of Colonial Mesoamerica and the Andes*. Salt Lake City: University of Utah Press.

King, Mark. 1994. "Hearing the Echoes of Verbal Art in Mixtec Writing." In *Writing without Words: Alternative Literacies in Mesoamerica and the Andes*. Edited by Elizabeth Boone and Walter Mignolo, 102–136. Durham, NC: Duke University Press.

Kiracofe, James B. 1995. "Architectural Fusion and Indigenous Ideology in Early Colonial Teposcolula: The Casa de la Cacica: A Building at the Edge of Oblivion." *Anales de Instituto de Investigaciones Estéticas*, 66:45–84.

Klapisch-Zuber, Christiane. 1985. *Women, Family, and Ritual in Renaissance Italy*. Translated by Lydia Cochrane. Chicago: University of Chicago Press.

Klein, Cecelia F. 1980. "Who Was Tlaloc?" *Journal of Latin American Lore*, 6 (2):155–204.

———. 1982. "Woven Heaven, Tangled Earth: A Weaver's Paradigm of the Mesoamerican Cosmos." In *Ethnoastronomy and Archaeoastronomy in the American Tropics*. Edited by Anthony F. Aveni and Gary Urton. *Annals of the New York Academy of Sciences* 385:1–35.

———. 1990/1991. "Snares and Entrails: Mesoamerican Symbols of Sin and Punishment." *RES: Anthropology and Aesthetics*, 19/20:81–103.

———. 1994. "Fighting with Femininity: Gender and War in Aztec Mexico." In *Gender Rhetorics: Postures in Dominance and Submission in History*. Edited by Richard C. Trexler, 107–146. Binghamton: Center for Medieval and Early Renaissance Studies, State University of New York.

———. 2000. "The Devil and the Skirt: An Iconographic Inquiry into the Prehispanic Nature of the Tzitzimime." *Estudios de Cultura Nahuatl*, 31:17–62.

———. 2001. "None of the Above: Gender Ambiguity in Nahua Ideology." In *Gender in Pre-Hispanic America: A Symposium at Dumbarton Oaks, 12 and 13 October 1996*. Edited by Cecelia F. Klein, 183–253. Washington, DC: Dumbarton Oaks Research Library and Collection.

Komisaruk, Catherine. 2013. *Labor and Love in Guatemala: The Eve of Independence*. Stanford, CA: Stanford University Press.

Landers, Jane. 2005. "Africans and Native Americans on the Spanish Florida Frontier." In *Beyond Black and Red: African-Native Relations in Colonial Latin America*. Edited by Matthew Restall, 53–80. Albuquerque: University of New Mexico Press.

Lara, Jaime. 2008. *Christian Texts for Aztecs: Art and Liturgy in Colonial Mexico*. Notre Dame, IN: University of Notre Dame Press.

Lauderdale, Graham. 1998. "Honor among Slaves." In *The Faces of Honor: Sex, Shame, and Violence in Colonial Latin America*. Edited by Lyman L. Johnson and Sonya Lipsett-Rivera, 201–228. Albuquerque: University of New Mexico.

Lavrin, Asunción. 1978a. "In Search of the Colonial Woman in Mexico: The Seventeenth and Eighteenth Centuries." In *Latin American Women: Historical Perspectives*. Edited by Asunción Lavrin, 23–59. Westport, CT: Greenwood Press.

———, ed. 1978b. *Latin American Women: Historical Perspectives*. Westport, CT: Greenwood Press.

———. 1989a. "Sexuality in Colonial Mexico: A Church Dilemma." In *Sexuality and Marriage in Colonial Latin America*. Edited by Asunción Lavrin, 47–92. Lincoln: University of Nebraska Press.

———, ed. 1989b. *Sexuality and Marriage in Colonial Latin America*. Lincoln: University of Nebraska Press.

———. 2008. *Brides of Christ: Conventual Life in Colonial Mexico*. Stanford, CA: Stanford University Press.

Lipsett-Rivera, Sonya. 1996. "The Intersection of Rape and Marriage in Mexico, 1750–1856." Paper presented at the Berkshire Conference on the History of Women, Raleigh, NC, June 2–4.

———. 1998. "A Slap in the Face of Honor." In *The Faces of Honor: Sex, Shame, and Violence in Colonial Latin America*. Edited by Lyman L. Johnson and Sonya Lipsett-Rivera, 179–200. Albuquerque: University of New Mexico Press.

Lockhart, James. 1991. *Nahuas and Spaniards: Postconquest Central Mexican History and Philology*. Stanford: Stanford University Press.

———. 1992. *Nahuas After the Conquest: A Social and Cultural History of the Indians of Central Mexico, Sixteenth through Eighteenth Centuries*. Stanford, CA: Stanford University Press.

———, ed. and trans. 1993. *We People Here: Nahuatl Accounts of the Conquest of Mexico*. Berkeley: University of California Press.

Lockhart, James, Frances Berdan, and Arthur Anderson. 1986. *The Tlaxcalan Actas: A Compendium of the Records of the Cabildo of Tlaxcala (1545–1627)*. Salt Lake City: University of Utah Press.

Lockhart, James, and Enrique Otte, eds. 1976. *Letters and People of the Spanish Indies, Sixteenth Century*. Cambridge: Cambridge University Press.

Lockhart, James, and Stuart B. Schwartz. 1983. *Early Latin America: A History of Colonial Spanish America and Brazil*. Cambridge Latin American Series, 46. Cambridge: Cambridge University Press.

Long, Janet. 2008. "Tecnología alimentaria prehispánica." *Estudios de Cultura Nahuatl* 39:127–136.

López Austin, Alfredo. 1988. *The Human Body and Ideology: Concepts of the Ancient Nahua*. Vols. 1 and 2. Translated by Thelma Ortiz de Montellano and Bernard Ortíz de Montellano. Salt Lake City: University of Utah Press.

MacLachlan, Colin M. 1976. "The Eagle and the Serpent: Male over Female in Tenochtitlan." *Proceedings of the Pacific Coast Council on Latin American Studies*, 5:45–56.

Marcus, Joyce. 2001. "Breaking the Glass Ceiling: the Strategies of Royal Women in Ancient States." In *Gender in Pre-Hispanic America: A Symposium*

at Dumbarton Oaks, 12 and 13 October 1996. Edited by Cecelia F. Klein, 305–340. Washington, DC: Dumbarton Oaks Research Library and Collection.
Mastache, Guadalupe. 1996. "El tejido en México antiguo." *Arqueología Mexicana*, 3 (17):17–25.
McCaa, Robert. 1996. "Matrimonio infantil, *cemithualtin* (familias complejas) y el antiguo pueblo nahua." *Historia mexicana*, 46 (1):3–70.
McCafferty, Sharisse D., and Geoffrey G. McCafferty. 1988. "Powerful Women and the Myth of Male Dominance in Aztec Society." *Archaeological Review from Cambridge*, 7 (1):45–59.
———. 1991. "Spinning and Weaving as Gender Identity in Post-Classic Mexico." In *Textile Traditions of Mesoamerica and the Andes: An Anthology*. Edited by Margot Schevill, Janet Berlo, and Edward B. Dwyer, 19–44. New York: Garland Publishing.
Melton-Villanueva, Miriam, and Caterina Pizzigoni. 2008. "Late Nahuatl Testaments from the Toluca Valley: Indigenous-Language Ethnohistory in the Mexican Independence Period." *Ethnohistory*, 55 (3):361–391.
Menchú, Rigoberta. 1994. *I, Rigoberta Menchú: An Indian Woman in Guatemala*. Translated by Ann Wright. London: Verso Press.
Miller, Mary, and Karl Taube. 1993. *The Gods and Symbols of Ancient Mexico and the Maya: An Illustrated Dictionary of Mesoamerican Religion*. London: Thames and Hudson.
Molina, Alonso de. 1984 [1569]. *Confesionario mayor en la lengua mexicana y castellana*. Introducción por Roberto Moreno. Mexico City: Universidad Nacional Autónoma de México.
———. 1992 [1571]. *Vocabulario en lengua castellana y mexicana y mexicana y castellana*. Mexico City: Editorial Porrua.
Monaghan, John Desmond. 1995. *The Covenants of Earth and Rain: Exchange, Sacrifice, and Revelation in Mixtec Sociality*. Norman: University of Oklahoma Press.
———. 2001. "Physiology, Production, and Gendered Difference: The Evidence for Mixtec and Other Mesoamerican Societies." In *Gender in Pre-Hispanic America: A Symposium at Dumbarton Oaks, 12 and 13 October 1996*. Edited by Cecelia F. Klein, 285–304. Washington, DC: Dumbarton Oaks Research Library and Collection.
Motolinía, fray Toribio de Benavente. 1950. *History of the Indians of New Spain*. Edited and Translated by Elizabeth Andras Foster. Berkeley, CA: Cortes Society.
———. 1971. *Memoriales, o Libro de las cosas de la Nueva España y de los naturales de ella*. Mexico City: Universidad Nacional Autonoma de México, Instituto de Investigaciones Historicas.
Muriel, Josefina. 1982. *Cultura femenina novohispana*. Mexico City: Universidad Autónoma de México.
———. 1992. *Las mujeres de Hispanoamérica: Época colonial*. Madrid: Editorial MAPFRE.
Musgrave-Portilla, L. Marie. 1982. "The Nahualli or Transforming Wizard in Pre- and Postconquest Mesoamerica." *Journal of Latin American Lore*, 8 (1):3–62.

Nash, June. 1978. "The Aztecs and the Ideology of Male Dominance." *Signs: Journal of Women in Culture and Society*, 4 (2):349–362.

———. 1980. "Aztec Women: The Transition from Status to Class in Empire and Colony." In *Women and Colonization: Anthropological Perspectives*. Edited by Mona Etienne and Eleanor Leacock, 134–147. New York: Praeger.

Nutini, Hugo G. 1984. *Ritual Kinship: Ideological and Structural Integration of the Compadrazgo System in Rural Tlaxcala*. Vol. II. Princeton, NJ: Princeton University Press.

———. 1976. "The Demographic Functions of Compadrazgo in Santa María Belén Azitzimititlán and Rural Tlaxcala." In *Essays on Mexican Kinship*. Edited by Hugo G. Nutini, Pedro Carrasco, and James M. Taggart, 219–236. Pittsburgh: University of Pittsburgh Press.

Nutini, Hugo G, and Betty Bell. 1980. *Ritual Kinship: The Structure and Historical Development of the Compadrazgo System in Rural Tlaxcala*. Vol. I. Princeton, NJ: Princeton University Press.

Offner, Jerome A. 1984. "Household Organization in the Texcocan Heartland." In *Explorations in Ethnohistory: Indians of Central Mexico in the Sixteenth Century*. Edited by H. R. Harvey and Hanns J. Prem, 127–146. Albuquerque: University of New Mexico Press.

Olivier, Guilheim. 2004. "Homosexualidad y prostitución entre los nahuas y otros pueblos del posclásico." In *Mesoamérica y los ámbitos indígenas de la Nueva España*. Edited by Pablo Escalante Gonzalbo, 301–338. México City: El Colegio de México.

Olmos, fray Andrés de. 1990. *Tratado de hechicerías y sortilegios*. Con introducción por Georges Baudot. Mexico City: Universidad Nacional Autónoma de México.

Osowski, Edward W. 2010. *Indigenous Miracles: Nahua Authority in Colonial Mexico*. Tucson: University of Arizona Press.

Oudijk, Michel. 2000. *Historiography of the Benizaa: The Postclassic and Early Colonial Periods (1000–1600 A.D.)*. Leiden, The Netherlands: Research School of Asian, African, and Amerindian Studies, Universiteit Leiden.

Owensby, Brian P. 2008. *Empire of Law and Indian Justice in Colonial Mexico*. Stanford, CA: Stanford University Press.

Pastor, Rodolfo. 1987. *Campesinos y reformas: La mixteca, 1700–1856*. Mexico City: El Colegio de México.

Patch, Robert W. 2013. *Indians and the Political Economy of Colonial Central America, 1670–1810*. Norman: University of Oklahoma Press.

Perdue, Theda. 1989. "Cherokee Women and the Trail of Tears." *Journal of Women's History*, 1 (1):14–30.

Perry, Mary Elizabeth. 1990. *Gender and Disorder in Early Modern Seville*. Princeton, NJ: Princeton University Press.

Peterson, Jeanette Favrot. 1988. "The Florentine Codex Imagery and the Colonial Tlacuilo." In *The Work of Bernardino de Sahagún: Pioneer Ethnographer of Sixteenth-Century Aztec Mexico*. Edited by J. Jorge Klor de Alva, H. B. Nicholson, and Eloise Quiñones Keber, 273–293. Austin: University of Texas Press.

———. 1993. *The Paradise Garden Murals of Malinalco: Utopia and Empire in Sixteenth-Century Mexico*. Austin: University of Texas Press, 1993.

———. 1994. "Lengua o Diosa? The Early Imaging of Malinche." In *Chipping Away on Earth: Studies in Prehispanic and Colonial Mexico in Honor of Arthur J. O. Anderson and Charles E. Dibble*. Edited by Eloise Quiñones Keber, 187–202. Lancaster, CA: Labyrinthos Press, 1994.

———. 2003. "Crafting the Self: Identity and the Mimetic Tradition in the Florentine Codex." In *Sahagún at 500: Essays on the Quincentenary of the Birth of Fr. Bernardino de Sahagún, O.F.M.* Edited by John Schwaller, 223–253. Berkeley: Academy of American Franciscan History.

Phillips, Henry, Jr. 1884. "Notes on the Codex Ramirez [Historia mexicana por sus pinturas] with a translation of the same." *Proceedings of the American Philosophical Society*, 21 (116):616–651.

Pizzigoni, Caterina. 2012. *The Life Within: Local Indigenous Society in Mexico's Toluca Valley, 1650–1800*. Stanford, CA: Stanford University Press.

Pleck, Elizabeth. 1987. *Domestic Tyranny: The Making of Social Policy Against Family Violence from Colonial Times to the Present*. New York: Oxford University Press.

Pohl, John M. D. 1994. "Weaving and Gift Exchange in the Mixtec Codices." In *Cloth and Curing: Continuity and Change in Oaxaca*. Edited by Grace Johnson and Douglas Sharon, 3–13. San Diego: San Diego Museum of Man.

———. 1998. "Themes of Drunkenness, Violence, and Factionalism in Tlaxcala Altar Paintings." *RES: Anthropology and Aesthetics* 33 (Spring):184–207.

Powers, Karen Viera. 2005. *Women in the Crucible of Conquest: The Gendered Genesis of Spanish American Society, 1500–1600*. Albuquerque: University of New Mexico Press.

Read, Kay A., and Jane Rosenthal. 2006. "The Chalcan Woman's Song: Sex as a Political Metaphor in Fifteenth-Century Mexico." *The Americas*, 62 (3):313–348.

Restall, Matthew. 1995. "'He Wished It in Vain': Subordination and Resistance among Maya Women in Post-Conquest Yucatan." *Ethnohistory*, 42 (4):577–594.

———. 1997. *The Maya World: Yucatec Culture and Society, 1550–1850*. Stanford, CA: Stanford University Press.

———. 2009. *The Black Middle: Africans, Mayas, and Spaniards in Colonial Yucatan*. Stanford, CA: Stanford University Press.

Restall, Matthew, and Pete Sigal. 1992. "'May They Not Be Fornicators Equal to These Priests': Postconquest Yucatec Maya Sexual Attitudes." *UCLA Historical Journal* 12:91–121.

Restall, Matthew, Lisa Sousa, and Kevin Terraciano, eds. and trans. 2005. *Mesoamerican Voices: Native-Language Writings from Colonial Mexico, Oaxaca, Yucatan, and Guatemala*. New York: Cambridge University Press.

Reyes, fray Antonio de los. 1976 [1593]. *Arte en lengua mixteca*. Vanderbilt University Publications in Anthropology, 14. Nashville: Vanderbilt University Press.

Reyes García, Luis. 2001. *¿Como te confundes? ¿Acaso no somos conquistados?: Anales de Juan Bautista*. Mexico City: Centro de Investigaciones y Estudios Superiores en Antropología Social and Biblioteca Lorenzo Boturini, Insigne y Nacional Basílica de Guadalupe.

Ricard, Robert. 1966 [1933]. *The Spiritual Conquest of Mexico: An Essay on the Apostolate and the Evangelizing Methods of the Mendicant Orders in New Spain: 1523–72.* Translated by Lesley Byrd Simpson. Berkeley: University of California Press.

Robertson, Donald. 1959. *Mexican Manuscript Painting of the Early Colonial Period: The Metropolitan Schools.* New Haven, CT: Yale University Press.

Rodríguez-Shadow, María J. 1997. *La mujer Azteca.* Mexico City: Universidad Autónoma del Estado de México.

Romero Frizzi, María de los Ángeles. 1990. *Economía y vida de los españoles en la Mixteca Alta: 1519–1720.* Mexico City: Instituto Nacional de Antropología e Historia.

———. 2010. "The Power of the Law: The Construction of Colonial Power in an Indigenous Region." In *Negotiation within Domination: New Spain's Indian Pueblos Confront the Spanish State.* Edited by Ethelia Ruiz Medrano and Susan Kellogg, 107–135. Boulder: University Press of Colorado.

Roscoe, Will. 1991. *The Zuni Man-Woman.* Albuquerque: University of New Mexico Press.

Rothenberg, Diane. 1980. "Mothers of the Nation: Seneca Resistance to Quaker Intervention." In *Women and Colonization: Anthropological Perspectives.* Edited by Mona Etienne and Eleanor Leacock. New York: Praeger.

Ruiz de Alarcón, Hernando. 1984. *Treatise on the Heathen Superstitions That Today Live among the Indians Native to This New Spain, 1629.* Edited and translated by J. Richard Andrews and Ross Hassig. Norman: University of Oklahoma Press.

Ruiz Medrano, Ethelia. 2010a. *Mexico's Indigenous Communities: Their Lands and Histories, 1500–2010.* Translated by Russ Davidson. Boulder: University Press of Colorado.

———. 2010b. "Fighting Destiny: Nahua Nobles and Friars in the Sixteenth-Century Revolt of the Encomenderos against the King." In *Negotiation within Domination: New Spain's Indian Pueblos Confront the Spanish State.* Edited by Ethelia Ruiz Medrano and Susan Kellogg, 45–77. Boulder: University Press of Colorado.

Russell, Jeffrey Burton. 1984. *Lucifer: The Devil in the Middle Ages.* Ithaca, NY: Cornell University Press.

Russo, Alessandra. 2002. "Plumes of Sacrifice: Transformations in Sixteenth-Century Mexican Feather Art." *RES* 42 (Autumn):226–250.

Sahagún, fray Bernardino de. 1996. *Historia Universal de las cosas de Nueva España: Codice Laurenziano Mediceo Palatino 218, 219, 220.* Florence: Giunti.

Sandstrom, Alan. 1991. *Corn Is Our Blood: Culture and Ethnic Identity in a Contemporary Aztec Indian Village.* Norman: University of Oklahoma Press.

Schroeder, Susan. 1991. *Chimalpahin and the Kingdoms of Chalco.* Tucson: University of Arizona Press.

———. 1992. "The Noblewomen of Chalco." *Estudios de Cultura Náhuatl,* 22:45–86.

Schroeder, Susan, Stephanie Wood, and Robert Haskett, eds. 1997. *Indian Women of Early Mexico.* Norman: University of Oklahoma Press.

Seed, Patricia. 1988. *To Love, Honor, and Obey in Colonial Mexico: Conflicts over Marriage Choice, 1574–1821*. Stanford, CA: Stanford University Press.
Sell, Barry D., and Louise M. Burkhart, eds. 2004. *Nahuatl Theater, Volume I: Death and Life in Colonial Nahua Mexico*. Foreword by Miguel León-Portilla. Norman: University of Oklahoma Press.
Sell, Barry D., Louise M. Burkhart, and Stafford Poole, eds. 2006. *Nahuatl Theater, Volume II: Our Lady of Guadalupe*. Norman: University of Oklahoma Press.
Sell, Barry D., Louise M. Burkhart, and Elizabeth R. Wright, eds., 2008. *Nahuatl Theater, Volume IV: Spanish Golden Age Drama in Mexican Translation*. Foreword by John Frederick Schwaller. Norman: University of Oklahoma Press.
Shoemaker, Nancy. 1991. "The Rise or Fall of Iroquois Women." *Journal of Women's History*, 2 (Winter):39–57.
Sigal, Pete. 2000. *From Moon Goddesses to Virgins: The Colonization of Yucatecan Maya Sexual Desire*. Austin: University of Texas Press.
———, ed. 2003. *Infamous Desire: Male Homosexuality in Colonial Latin America*. Chicago: University of Chicago Press.
———. 2007. "Queer Nahuatl: Sahgagún's Faggots and Sodomites, Lesbians and Hermaphrodites." *Ethnohistory* 54 (1):9–34.
———. 2011. *The Flower and the Scorpion: Sexuality and Ritual in Nahua Culture*. Durham, NC: Duke University Press.
Silverblatt, Irene. 1987. *Moon, Sun, and Witches: Gender Ideologies and Class in Inca and Colonial Peru*. Princeton, NJ: Princeton University Press.
Socolow, Susan M. 1989. "Acceptable Partners: Marriage Choice in Colonial Argentina." In *Sexuality and Marriage in Colonial Latin America*. Edited by Asunción Lavrin, 209–246. Lincoln: University of Nebraska Press.
Sousa, Lisa. 1997. "Women and Crime in Colonial Oaxaca: Evidence of Complementary Gender Roles in Mixtec and Zapotec Societies." In *Indian Women of Early Mexico*. Edited by Susan Schroeder, Stephanie Wood, and Robert Haskett, 199–214. Norman: University of Oklahoma Press.
———. 2002. "The Devil and Deviance in Native Criminal Narratives from Early Mexico." *The Americas*, 59 (2):161–179.
———. 2007. "Tying the Knot: Nahua Nuptials in Colonial Mexico." In *Religion in New Spain: Varieties of Colonial Religious Experience*. Edited by Susan Schroeder and Stafford Poole, 33–45. Albuquerque: University of New Mexico Press.
———. 2010. "Spinning and Weaving the Threads of Native Women's Lives." In *Contesting Archives: Finding Women in the Sources*. Edited by Nupur Chaudhuri, Sherry Katz, Mary Elizabeth Perry, and Ula Taylor, 75–88. Urbana-Champaign: University of Illinois Press.
———. 2016. "The Testament of Gerónimo Flores, 1660: A Nahuatl-Language Writing from a Mixe Community in Colonial Mexico." In *Native Wills from the Colonial Americas: Dead Giveaways in a New World*. Edited by Mark Christensen and Jonathan Truitt, 180–194. Salt Lake City: University of Utah Press.
Spores, Ronald. 1967. *Mixtec Kings and Their People*. Norman: University of Oklahoma Press.

———. 1984. *The Mixtecs in Ancient and Colonial Times*. Norman: University of Oklahoma Press.

———. 1997. "Mixteca Cacicas: Status, Wealth, and the Political Accomodation of Native Elite Women in Early Colonial Oaxaca." In *Indian Women of Early Mexico*. Edited by Susan Schroeder, Stephanie Wood, and Robert Haskett, 185–197. Norman: University of Oklahoma Press.

Spores, Ronald, and Ross Hassig. 1984. *Five Centuries of Law and Politics in Central Mexico*. Vanderbilt University Publications in Anthropology, 30. Nashville: Vanderbilt University.

Stephen, Lynn. 1991. *Zapotec Women*. Austin: University of Texas Press, 1991.

Stern, Steve J. 1995. *The Secret History of Gender: Women, Men, and Power in Late Colonial Mexico*. Chapel Hill, NC: University of North Carolina Press, 1995.

Sullivan, Thelma D. 1966. "Pregnancy, Childbirth, and the Deification of the Women Who Died in Childbirth." *Estudios de Cultura Nahuatl*, 6:63–95.

———. 1976. *Compendio de la gramatica nahuatl*. Mexico City: Universidad Nacional Autonoma de México, Instituto de Investigaciones Historicas.

———. 1982. "Tlazolteotl-Ixcuina: The Great Spinner and Weaver." In *The Art and Iconography of Late Post-Classic Central Mexico*. Edited by Elizabeth Hill Boone, 7–35. Washington, DC: Dumbarton Oaks.

Taggart, James M. 1983. *Nahuat Myth and Social Structure*. Austin: University of Texas Press.

Taube, Karl A. 2004. "Flower Mountain: Concepts of Life, Beauty, and Paradise among the Classic Maya." *RES: Anthropology and Aesthetics* 45 (Spring):69–98.

Tavárez, David. 2011. *The Invisible War: Indigenous Devotions, Discipline, and Dissent in Colonial Mexico*. Stanford, CA: Stanford University Press.

Taylor, William. 1972. *Landlord and Peasant in Colonial Oaxaca*. Stanford, CA: Stanford University Press.

———. 1979. *Drinking, Homicide, and Rebellion in Colonial Mexican Villages*. Stanford, CA: Stanford University Press.

———. 2010. *Shrines and Miraculous Images: Religious Life in Mexico before the Reforma*. Albuquerque: University of New Mexico Press.

———. 2011. *Marvels and Miracles in Late Colonial Mexico: Three Texts in Context*. Albuquerque: University of New Mexico Press.

Tena, Rafael, trans. 1998. *Las ocho relaciones y el memorial de Colhuacan, Domingo Chimalpahín*. Mexico City: Consejo Nacional para la Cultura y las Artes.

Terraciano, Kevin. 1994. "Nahuatl and Mixtec Writing in Sixteenth-Century Oaxaca." In *Chipping Away on Earth: Studies in Prehispanic and Colonial Mexico in Honor of Arthur J. O. Anderson and Charles Dibble*. Edited by Eloise Quiñones Keber, 105–117. Culver City, CA: Labyrinthos Press.

———. 1998. "Crime and Culture in Colonial Mexico: The Case of the Mixtec Murder Note." *Ethnohistory*, 45 (4):709–745.

———. 2001. *The Mixtecs of Colonial Oaxaca: Ñudzahui History, Sixteenth through Eighteenth Centuries*. Stanford, CA: Stanford University Press.

Terraciano, Kevin, and Lisa Sousa. 2003. "The 'Original Conquest' of Oaxaca: Nahua and Mixtec Accounts of the Spanish Conquest." *Ethnohistory*, 50 (2):349–400.
Tortorici, Zeb. 2007. "'Heran Todos Putos': Sodomitical Subcultures and Disordered Desire in Early Colonial Mexico." Ethnohistory 54 (1):35–67.
———. 2010. "Contra natura: Sin, Crime, and "Unnatural" Sexuality in Colonial Mexico, 1530–1821." Ph.D. diss., Department of History, University of California, Los Angeles.
Townsend, Camilla. 2006. "'What in the World Have You Done to Me, My Lover?': Sex, Servitude, and Politics among the Pre-Conquest Nahuas as Seen in the Cantares Mexicanos." *The Americas* 62 (3):349–389.
———, ed. and trans., 2010. *Here in This year: Seventeenth-Century Annals of the Tlaxcala Puebla Valley*. Stanford, CA: Stanford University Press.
Trexler, Richard C. 1995. *Sex and Conquest: Gendered Violence, Political Order, and the European Conquest of the Americas*. Ithaca, NY: Cornell University Press.
Truitt, Jonathan. 2010. "Courting Catholicism: Nahua Women and the Catholic Church in Colonial Mexico City." *Ethnohistory* 57 (3):415–444.
Twinam, Ann. 1989. "Honor, Sexuality, and Illegitimacy in Colonial Spanish America." In *Sexuality and Marriage in Colonial Latin America*. Edited by Asunción Lavrin, 118–155. Lincoln: University of Nebraska Press.
———. 1999. *Public Lives, Private Secrets: Gender, Honor, Sexuality and Illegitimacy in Colonial Spanish America*. Stanford, CA: Stanford University Press.
Villanueva, Margaret A. 1985. "From Calpixqui to Corregidor: Appropriation of Women's Cotton Textile Production in Early Colonial Mexico." *Latin American Perspectives*, 44, 12 (1):17–40.
Villaseñor-Black, Charlene. 2001. "Love and Marriage in the Spanish Empire: Depictions of Holy Matrimony and Gender Discourses in the Seventeenth Century." *The Sixteenth Century Journal* 32, (3):637–668.
Williams, Barbara J. 1984. "Mexican Pictorial Cadastral Registers: An Analysis of the Códice de Santa María Asunción and the Codex Vergara." In *Explorations in Ethnohistory: Indians of Central Mexico in the Sixteenth Century*. Edited by H. R. Harvey and Hanns J. Prem, 103–125. Albuquerque: University of New Mexico Press.
Wood, Stephanie. 1984. "Corporate Adjustments in Colonial Mexican Towns: Toluca Region, 1550–1810." Ph.D. diss., Department of History, University of California, Los Angeles.
———. 1997. "Matters of Life at Death: Nahuatl Testaments of Rural Women, 1589–1801." In *Indian Women of Early Mexico*. Edited by Susan Schroeder, Stephanie Wood, and Robert Haskett, 165–182. Norman: University of Oklahoma Press.
———. 2003. *Transcending Conquest: Nahua Views of Spanish Colonial Mexico*. Norman: University of Oklahoma Press.
Yannakakis, Yanna. 2008. *The Art of Being In-Between: Native Intermediaries, Indian Identity, and Local Rule in Colonial Oaxaca*. Durham, NC: Duke University Press.

———. 2010. "*Costumbre*: A Language of Negotiation in Eighteenth-Century Oaxaca." In *Negotiation within Domination: New Spain's Indian Pueblos Confront the Spanish State*. Edited by Ethelia Ruiz Medrano and Susan Kellogg, 137–171. Boulder: University Press of Colorado.

Zorita, Alonso de. 1994. *Life and Labor in Ancient Mexico: The Brief and Summary Relation of the Lords of New Spain*. Edited by Benjamin Keen. Norman: University of Oklahoma Press.

Index

Page numbers followed by "f" or "t" indicate material in figures or tables.

Achiutla, 6f, 209, 214, 266, 271, 274–275, 292–293, 337n107
adultery, 149–150; as cause of violence, 103, 107–108, 110, 148, 167–168; circumstances of, 154–156; community responses to, 118, 156–158, 204, 250–251, 332n104; depicted in manuscripts, 114–116 (115f); and drinking, 336n68; effects on household, 92, 151–153; gender and, 168–169, 339nn6–7, 341n52; as grounds for divorce, 51, 319n3; informal unions, 99–102; investigations of, 122–124, 132–134; mutilation as punishment for, 162, 165f; Nahuatl terms for, 150; native beliefs on, 112, 151–154; as offense to God, 146; proneness to, 28f, 42, 119, 150–151 (151f); public versus illicit, 153; punishments for, 156–167 (159t, 160f–161f, 163f–165f); versus rape, 171–173; reed mat symbol, 132; as theft, 153, 340n27; and "trash goddess," 71–72
afterlife, 37, 90, 138, 321n39
agriculture: commercial, 213, 277, 288; by couples, 212–213, 216; cyclical nature of, 216; and gender, 31, 36–37, 39, 178, 190, 211–212,
351n163; landholding patterns, 351n168; as offerings, 1, 2f
ahuiani ("one who indulges in pleasure"; prostitute), 111, 124f, 127f, 128f, 334n38. *See also* prostitutes/harlots
Ahuitzotzin, 182
alcohol, use of, 22, 23f, 120, 123–124 (124f), 125f, 191. *See also* drunkenness
Alva, fray Bartolomé de, 56–58, 79, 140–142, 200–201
Alvarado, fray Francisco de, 131, 135, 225, 316n16
Alvarado, Magdalena de, 266–267
Amanalco, 5f, 133, 173
amancebamiento (cohabitation), 99–102 (101t), 331n85
ancestor worship, 61, 245–246
Andrews, J. Richard, 23, 334n34, 348n98
animals, 25–26 (25f), 214–215, 286, 358n32
Annals of Juan Bautista, 275–276, 279, 281, 285
Anunciación, fray Juan de la, 52
aphrodisiacs, 333n15
Arrom, Silvia Marina, 319n3
Arvey, Margaret Campbell, 336n86
Atlacomulco, 5f, 94, 289

autosacrifice, 75
Axayacatl (Axayacatzin), 113, 280
Ayutla, 63, 89, 158, 159t, 167

backward-facing feet, significance of, 114, 115f, 116f
Bancroft Dialogues, 362nn79–80
banishment, 101
Betaza, 6f, 39–41, 43, 67, 245, 247, 287, 318, 324n82, 364n129
bigamy, 50
birth. *See* pregnancy and childbirth
birth date, 15, 24, 27–29 (28f)
birth rituals, 26–27, 29–36 (34f, 35f, 36f), 39, 42, 46
body paint, 43, 65, 71–72, 78, 82, 117
Boone, Elizabeth, 199
Bourbon Reforms, 306
Boyer, Richard E., 327n145
Brown, Betty Ann, 313n5
Burkhart, Louise, 136–137, 215, 223, 260–261

cabeceras (head towns), 11, 93–94
cabildo (municipal council), 4, 11, 29, 40–41, 54, 88, 94–95, 99, 102, 106, 157, 207, 208, 212–213, 221, 242–243, 249–251, 258, 266–267, 270–272, 276, 279–282, 284, 288–293, 295, 298, 303
cacicas (female indigenous hereditary ruler; wife of a *cacique*), 1, 75, 94–95, 207–208
caciques (male indigenous hereditary ruler), 56, 75, 94, 207–208, 217
Cajonos, 6f, 19, 156, 166, 168, 214, 249, 256
calendar days, 28 (28t), 30; calendrical names, 29–30, 51, 64, 67, 95, 317n41
calendar readers. See *tonalpouhque*
Calvo, Thomas, 323n68
Camotlan, 6f, 92, 105, 121, 231
Carochi, Horacio, 45

Carrasco, Pedro, 93, 228–229
Castellani, Alberto, 326n134
Catholic church: baptism, 62–63; confession, 79, 133, 138, 140–147, 200, 299; as gendered space, 41; incorporation of local practices, 320n16; interpreting birth rituals, 36–37; persecution of female healers, 200–202; promoting monogamy, 77, 149; replacing native temples, 241; and sexuality, 52–61, 80–81, 136–146 (143f); "spiritual conquest," 59; using public punishment, 59. *See also* marriage in Catholic church; polygyny
caves, 112, 182, 236f, 246
Chalca Women's Song, 280, 322n55
Chalco, 5f, 77, 93
Chance, John, 95
chastity, 117–118
Chicahuastla, 6f, 207, 344n18
Chicome Coatl, 1, 2f
childlessness, 86–87, 326n134, 327n14; exorcism for childlessness, 326n134
children, 163, 239–243 (240f), 343n120
chiles as weapon, punishment, 163, 240f, 242, 262, 272
Chimalpáhin, don Domingo, 77, 113, 278–279, 281, 284–285, 349n127
Christensen, Mark, 320n16
cihuapilli (Nahua noblewoman), 9–10, 12
cihuatlanque (marriage negotiator), 68–70
Citlal, 211
class endogamy, 64
Clendinnen, Inga, 334n20, 339n7, 350n152, 351–352n176
Cline, Sarah L., 76, 211, 228–229
cloth/clothing, 183f, 184f, 344n14; and Christian iconography, 181–182; consolidating alliances with, 182; cosmos made of, 179;

fulfilling tribute, 221, 222f; as gender marker, 33, 34f, 35f, 42–43, 47–48; grabbing of, 170; in marriage rituals, 73–74; for newborns, 181; offerings of, 181–182; representing people, intercourse, 42–43; rulers' attire at surrender, 180; as trade goods, 209; types of cloth, 209–210; as unit of exchange, 182–183; worn-out body compared to, 179–180. *See also* weaving, spinning
Coanacochtzin (ruler of Tetzcoco), 180
Coatlicue, 126, 136
cobblers, 184
cochineal dye, 213, 238f, 277
codices: Becker II, 95, 96f; Borbonicus, 159, 162, 163f; Borgia, 64–67 (66f), 150–151 (151f), 160, 323–324n73; Florentine, 2f, 8, 23f, 24, 25f, 27, 27f, 29, 31–34 (34f), 35f, 37–38, 47–48 (47f), 68, 69f, 74, 86, 117, 119–120, 123–126 (124f, 125f), 127f, 128f, 132, 135, 142–143 (143f), 149, 152–153, 158, 170, 177–178, 179f, 181–190 (183f, 184f, 185f, 187f, 188f, 189f), 193–201 (195f, 196f, 197f, 201f), 206, 210, 227, 237–239; Kingsborough/Tepetlaoztoc, 268, 269f, 270; Laud, 64–65, 67 (67f), 130, 131f, 323–324n73; Magliabechiano, 199, 200f; Mendoza, 33, 36f, 71–74 (72f), 81, 114, 116f, 131, 158, 159t, 160f, 162, 221, 222f, 239, 240f, 242, 251, 252f, 253f; Nuttall, 44 (44f), 129–130 (130f); Santa María Asunción, 228–229; Selden, 263–264 (264f); Sierra, 207; Telleriano-Remensis, 24, 114–116 (115f), 121f, 153, 159–162 (159t, 161f), 335n49; Tudela, 48, 157, 159t, 162, 165f; Vaticanus B, 64–65, 67, 68f, 323–324n73; Vergara, 228, 360n58; Vindobonensis, 127, 129f
Coixtlahuaca, 6f, 88, 148, 168, 206, 212, 216, 219, 221, 289, 322n64, 360n64
community membership, 15
compadrazgo (ritual kinship), 254–259, 364–365n146
compadre, comadre, 256–258
complementary relations, 1, 13–15, 20, 31, 39–42, 74, 80, 89, 90, 97, 137, 168, 199, 215, 224, 297, 299–300
conception beliefs, 112–113, 132, 323n66, 339n160
concubinage, 59–62, 64, 113, 117, 132, 280
Confesionario mayor (Molina), 53–54
contamination, 112–114, 117, 120
cooking, 190–193; breaking of pots, 287; for feast days, 225; in gendered division of labor, 89, 206, 216, 219; girls learning, 239–240; and labor obligations, 268, 276; like metalworking, 188–189 (189f); marketing, 210, 350nn146, 148; and marriage, 92, 100, 103, 122; noblewomen and, 205–206; prestige of, 223; and regulating resources, 190; Spanish, 191; and women's gear, 37; as women's work, 31, 39, 177, 178–179, 190
coqui/coquitao (Bènizàa *cacique*), 11, 95, 244, 309, 314n18
Córdova, fray Juan de: on birth order names, 359n55; on calendar usage, 29; on divorce, 51, 64, 87, 90, 168, 327n14; kin terms, 233; on prognostication, 67, 324n74; on sexual prohibitions, 138–139; *Vocabulario en lengua çapoteca*, 316n16; words for house, 225–226; words for relatives, 45; words for sex, 131, 135
Cortés, Hernando, 180

cotton: noble's clothing of, 56; offerings of, 181, 202; supplies of, 190; and Tlazolteotl, 65–66; as trade goods, 209–210, 277; as tribute goods and labor, 207, 221, 262, 270–271, 276–277; wives and husbands growing, 212–213. See also weaving, spinning
Coyoacan, 5f, 50, 59, 124, 233, 245, 256
criminal records, 15, 39–42, 110–111
cross-dressing, 22, 118, 126, 319n106
cross-gender, 46–48 (47f), 118. See also *xochihua*
cuana betao (sacred herb), 41
Cuauhtemoc, 180, 264–265
Cuernavaca, 5f, 86, 267
Culhuacan, 5f, 88, 90
Cuquila, 6f, 94, 172, 219, 221

dancing, 22, 40, 255, 285
day signs, 24–29 (28t), 120, 316n29
death and afterlife, 37
Devil, the, 137, 142–145 (143f), 299
Díaz del Castillo, Bernal, 350n146
division of labor by gender, 1–2 (2f), 12–13, 31–39 (34f–36f), 51, 80, 92; in Bènizàa rituals, 39–42
divorce, native, 51, 55–56, 87, 90, 106–107, 319n3, 321n28; separation, legal, 106–107
dogs, 29, 62, 119, 214, 247
Don, Patricia, 77, 82–83
dowry, 70
drunkenness, 22, 23f; as part of marriage ritual, 74, 89; punishments for, 158, 160; and sex, 123–124 (124f), 125f. See also alcohol, use of
Durán, fray Diego, 56, 63, 199, 234, 264
dyes, 185, 213, 238f, 239, 277

earth as female, 1, 2f
Ecatepec, 5f, 170, 175, 177

Ehecatl, 130, 337n93
encomienda system, 11, 178, 216–218, 298, 369n85
Epazoyuca, 5f, 29, 127, 158, 159t
epidemics, 12, 155, 217–218, 228
essentialism, 20, 30, 297

family. See household
fasting, meaning of, 120
fathers, 21, 115–116, 119
feathers: in colonial times, 346n57; feathered serpent, 129–130, 130f, 131f; featherworkers, 33, 40, 185–188 (188t), 190, 205, 241; headdresses, 44–45; symbolism of, 126–127, 136, 181, 122, 246, 285; at weddings, 325–326n117
female rulers, 1, 75, 94–95, 207–208. See also *cacicas*
Feria, fray Pedro de, 56, 80–81
fishing, 239 (240f), 350n146
flowers, 75, 124–128 (127f, 128f), 132–133, 136, 336nn77, 86. See also *xochihua*
food: feasts, 70, 74–75, 78, 192; meaning of sharing, 122, 191–192; preparation of, 1, 2f, 32; and sex, reproduction, 119–124 (121f, 124f). See also agriculture; cooking

García, Luis Reyes, 276
García y Guzmán, don Gerónimo (*cacique* of Teposcolula), 89, 207, 349n131
Gauderman, Kimberly, 367n24
gender, 14–15, 24, 30–31, 39–47 (44f), 74–75; ambiguity, 22, 24, 26, 30, 49, 114, 297. See also complementary relations; division of labor by gender
gift exchange, among nobles, 45, 95, 113, 181, 192; meaning of, 71, 78; as offerings, 1, 179; in ritual, 32, 63, 70–71, 73, 75, 77–78, 255, 300
god impersonators, 117

Gómez de Cervantes, Gonzalo, 254
Gosner, Kevin, 366n4
Guzmán, don Gabriel de (*cacique* and governor of Yanhuitlan), 123, 215, 241, 246
Guzmán, doña Lazara de (*cacica* of Teposcolula), 89, 207, 349n131

Hackel, Steven W., 320n22, 321nn28, 39, 323n66
hair, 43, 114, 116
hallucinogens, use of, 22
Harvey, Herbert R., 228–229
Haskett, Robert, 267, 294
Hassig, Ross, 23, 334n34, 348n98
healers, 32, 71, 73, 107, 192–193, 194t, 198–204 (201f, 203t), 223, 239, 251, 258, 299, 305. *See also* midwives; *ticitl*
hearth, 75
Historia de las Indias . . . (Durán), 234
History of the Indians of New Spain (Motolinía), 36
homosexuality, 48, 118, 138, 335n45, 341n53
honest woman (*mujer honesta*), 101
honor, 9, 28, 88, 101, 134, 169, 175, 206, 223, 227, 238, 243, 305
household, 259–261; as basic social unit, 4, 225–226, 242; composition of, 227–233; conflict resolution in, 250–254 (252f, 253f); economic dimension of, 233, 235–239 (238f); men's and women's roles, duties, 14, 32, 215–216, 233; as moral unit, 239–244 (240f); physical layout of, 226–227; political nature of, 248–250; relations within, 233, 234f, 235f; as sacred space, 244–248; socialization of children in, 239–242 (240f)
Huauhquiltamalqualiztli, 225–226, 238
Huehuecoyotl, 65

huehuetlahtolli (speech of the elders), 204–205, 327n146
huexiuhtlahuana ceremony (in-laws get drunk ceremony), 74, 89
Huitzilopochtli, 23, 126
hunger, sexual desire as, 119
hunting, 31, 38

Icazbalceta, García, 361n76
ichpochtli (Nahua unmarried woman), 85, 149
idolatry, 39–42, 61, 67, 245–248
Iguala, 5f, 61–62, 87, 203
illegitimate birth, 152–153
impotence, 86–87; *tetzicatl*, Nahuatl term for, 86
incest, 57–60
indias ladinas (acculturated indigenous woman), 101
indigents, care of, 288
infants, 26–27 (27f), 32–37 (34f–36f), 42, 245. *See also* pregnancy and childbirth
infidelity. *See* adultery
in-laws, 74, 104–105, 332n106
interracial couples, 100–101 (101t), 330–331n80
Ixnextli, 114–116 (115f)
Ixtlilxochitl (*cacique* of Tetzcoco), 77, 326n130

Jansen, Maarten, and Gabina Aurora Pérez Jiménez, 366n5
jewelry as gender neutral, 43
Jewish marriage practices, 80
Juxtlahuaca, 6f, 70, 74–75, 153, 159t, 163, 334n41

Kanter, Deborah E., 330n68, 332n104, 358n33, 362n85
Karttunen, Frances, 23
Katzew, Ilona, 83
Kellogg, Susan, 14, 87, 206
King, Mark, 346n51
kin terms, use of, 232–233

Klein, Cecelia, 22, 47, 114, 179, 297, 366n6
Komisaruk, Catherine, 335n45

labor: forced work, 289; by gender, 1–2 (2f), 12–13, 31–39 (34f–36f), 51, 80, 92; lawsuits over women's labor, 268–271; organization of, 178–179; selling of as punishment, 102, 333n112. *See also* cobblers; *encomienda*; *repartimiento*; tribute system; weaving, spinning
Lachirio, 6f, 29, 152, 171, 191, 202, 212, 241, 247, 322n61
Lalopa, 6f, 94, 122, 144–145
land ownership, 12, 15, 95, 98f, 306
Lara, Jaime, 326n143
Lavrin, Asunción, 324n89
lawsuits by indigenous communities, 267–272 (269f)
Lienzo of Tabaá, 95, 97f
Lipsett-Rivera, Sonya, 174
Lockhart, James, 226, 245, 296–297, 358n32, 349n116, 354n2, 359n50
López Austin, Alfredo, 113, 339n7
lunar eclipse, 21
luxury materials, 45

macehuales (Nahua commoners), 270, 288–289
Macuilxochitl, 120
Magdalena, María, 152, 156, 362n86
maguey, 19, 112–113, 180, 315n11
maize production, 209–210, 212–213, 217–219, 268–270 (269f)
mala vida (bad life), 103
Malinalco, 5f, 94, 173, 191, 245, 254, 257, 281–282, 289
Malinche, 180
marriage in Catholic church, 81, 82f; age at first marriage, canon law, 52; colonial indigenous texts, 148–149; compared to indigenous practice, 50–54, 77–82; consanguinity and marriage, 57–59; date of earliest, 76–77 (78f); dispensations, 58–59; as display of power, 76–77; and free will, 54, 58; indigenous-Christian marriage, 75–82; as indissoluble, 81; lack of recourse for abuse, 81; for procreation, 78–79; Spanish couples, 323n68
marriage in Mesoamerica: abandonment, 55, 320nn23, 25; age at, 64, 322–323n66; as alliance, 93; arranged, 63–71; as basic social unit, 40, 85–89, 233–235 (234f, 235f); bride price, 70; burdens of, 89–90; Carrasco's types of, 93; children as purpose of, 86–87; clothing for, 325n108; conflicts with church, 54–63; economic dimensions of, 89–93; informal unions, 99–102; as initiation rite, 85; legal separation, 106–107; marriage procession, 71–72 (72f); political dimensions of, 93–99 (96f–98f); political status through marital ties, 93–99 (96f, 97f, 98f); postponement, 100; prognostication, 64–68 (65f–68f); reciprocity, 89; serial monogamy, 51; social life of married couple, 87–88; temporary separations, 106; wives punished with husbands, 244. *See also* household; polygyny; violence in marriage
Matlactlan, 5f, 52, 61, 113
McCaa, Robert, 323n66
Melton-Villanueva, Myriam, 257
men/boys: apprenticeships, 40, 241; bathing ritual for newborns, 28, 32–37 (34f–36f), 42, 181, 191; semen, 112–113, 132, 323n66, 333n15; sharing in domestic labor, 216; speech forms of, 45–46. *See also* division of labor by gender; gender
Menchú, Rigoberta, 316n29
Mendoza, don Francisco de, 206, 249
Mendoza, Juana de, 266–267

Mendoza, doña María de, 266–267
Meneses, Ana and Gaspar de, 266–267, 366–367n12
merchants, indigenous, 38, 182–183 (183f), 209–211, 216, 224, 242, 350n152; Spanish, 214, 276–278
metaphors, 42–43, 118–124
Mexican Revolution, 306
Mexico City, 274–276, 278–281
Mexico Tenochtitlan, 5f, 10–11, 77, 87, 94, 113, 180–182, 208, 251–254 (252f, 253f), 264, 272, 284, 350n146
midwives, 32, 193; and birth rituals, 31–36 (34f–36f), 42, 191, 197–198, 347n81; as expert witnesses, 203–204; as healers, 193, 199–201 (200f, 201f), 202–203; as juries, 348n111; overseeing pregnancy, 194–195 (194t, 195f); use of abortifacients, 200–201, 299. See also *ticitl*
millenarian movements, 366n4
moderation, 119
Molina, fray Alonso de: *Confesionario mayor*, 53–54, 57, 138–140, 200; dictionary, 23, 69, 126, 131, 150, 170, 272–273, 315–316n15; investigation of don Carlos Ometochtzin Chichimecatecuhtli, 59; marriage advice, 52, 53, 78–82 (82f)
Monaghan, John, 46, 129, 137, 226, 327n14, 351n163, 354n6, 362n88
Moquihuixtli, 113
morality, Christian, 16, 51, 56–57, 60–62, 82, 111, 136–138, 141–142, 144–147, 152, 158–159, 168, 299, 303; household as moral unit, 222, 226, 239–244, 250, 260; indigenous, 2, 7, 10, 16, 22, 27, 65, 71, 112, 114, 117–118, 123, 125 (125f), 132, 137, 150–151, 154, 158–159, 162, 166, 170, 175, 177, 192, 213, 272, 279; moral support of ritual kin, 256–259

Mora y Peysal, Antonio, 278
Moteucçoma (*cacique* of Mexico Tenochtitlan), 182, 251–252 (253f), 285
mothers. *See* pregnancy and childbirth
Motolinía, fray Toribio de Benavente, 76–77, 181, 326n127

nahuallis (ability to transform the body)/*nahualism* (belief in the ability of certain individuals to transform the body), 19, 20–26 (23f, 25f), 48, 315–316nn15–16, 29; companion animal, 26
Nahua sexual beliefs, 110–118 (115f, 116f), 150–151
naming and bathing rituals, 26–27 (27f), 32–37 (34f–36f), 42
Nanacacipactzin (Mushroom Alligator). *See* Santa María Cipac, don Luis
neoliberal policies, 306–307
New Fire ceremony, 21–22, 181
nobles, Mesoamerican: alliances of, by, 93, 241; community protection of, 288–293; couples, 95, 96f; dependents of, 353n209; given leniency, 56–57, 167; noblewomen, 205–206, 329n59, 349n116; as parents of community, 284, 288–289; sociopolitical organization of, 248–250; under Spanish rule, 282, 284, 289. See also *cacicas*; *caciques*
noses, biting off of, 162, 165f
ñuu, 10, 262, 314n15
Nuyoo, 6f, 129, 137, 262–263, 270, 272, 291, 354n6, 362n88

Oaxaca, 6f, 11–12, 271–272, 290–291
Offner, Jerome A., 228
Olivier, Guilhem, 297, 334n38
Olmos, fray Andrés de, 42, 160, 200
Ololiuhqui, 22, 202. See also *cuana betao*

Ometochtzin Chichimecatecuhtli, don Carlos (of Tetzcoco), 59–63, 126
oquichtlatquitl (men's gear), 37
orphans, 170, 238–239, 288
Osowski, Edward, 96–97, 208, 246, 363n110
Otomi, 3
Oudijk, Michel, 97f, 314nn15, 18

"pacification" timeline, 11
palaces, 9, 227–228, 248, 253f, 260, 272–274
Panquetzaliztli, 120, 182
patriarchy, 14–15, 208
patrivirilocality, patriuxorilocality, 229–231, 356–358nn21–29
Paz, don Francisco de (*cacique* of Yatzona), 259, 317n40
Pedraza, don Manuel de, 214, 278
penicoconi (Tíchazàa, unmarried young woman), 149
penixitobi (Tíchazàa, unmarried young man), 85
Pérez, Catalina, 192, 202, 214, 348n109
Peterson, Jeanette, 123
Pizzigoni, Caterina, 257, 331n81, 361n75
Pohl, John M. D., 339n158
pole flyers/*voladores*, 61
pollution, marriage, 71–72
polygamy, 320n7
polygyny, 12, 51–54, 56–63 (60f), 113, 228, 300; sororal polygyny, 320n6
Ponce, Pedro, 197
population centers, precolonial, 10
pregnancy and childbirth: celebrations of, 86, 126–127; conception beliefs, 339n160; death in childbirth, 197–198 (197f); illegitimacy, 152–153; importance of procreation, 78–79; infants, 26–27 (27f), 32–37 (34f–36f), 42, 245; intercourse during, 195; labor, 39, 195–198 (196f, 197f); males mimicking, 198–199; mother's visual experience during, 21; and Quetzalcoatl, 129–130 (130f, 131f); rituals of, 31–36 (34f–36f), 42; stillbirths, 87, 245; women's warfare, 39. *See also* midwives
primordial couple, 127, 129f
procurer/procuress, 48, 126, 128f, 132–133, 136; *tetlanochili*, Nahuatl term for, 142–143 (143f)
prognostication, birth, 26–29 (27f, 28t), 119; casting lots, 29, 67, 199, 200f, 247; healing, 119, 202, 203t; marriage, 64–68 (65f–68f), 87, 150, 151f, 323–324nn73–74
prostitutes/harlots, 117; *ahuiani*, 111, 334n38; depiction of, 336n86; Florentine Codex on, 123, 124f, 126, 127f, 135; and flowers, 126, 127f, 128f; and procurers, 48, 126, 128f, 132–133, 136

Quautla, 5f, 219, 220f
Quecholli, 120
Quetzalcoatl, 23–24, 129–130 (130f), 135, 199, 200f

rabbits, 22, 23f, 315n11
rape, 61, 169–175; *estupro*, 342n87; *violación*, 342n87
Read, Kay, 280
rebellions, 265–266, 271–272, 275, 278–287, 291–292
reciprocity: between bride's and groom's families, 70, 73–74; between commoners and nobles, 282; within community, 13; between community and church, 287; between humans and deities, 191; within marriage, 39, 79–82, 89–93, 149
reed mats: *petate*, 110, 132; sexual connotations of, 72, 118, 124, 131–132; as thrones, 46, 95, 96f, 131, 219, 251–252 (252f, 253f)
Relaciones geográficas: on abstinence, fasting, 118, 120–121; on adul-

tery, 153, 158–159 (159t), 166; on ancient religious customs, 117–118; on arranged marriage, 63, 66–67; on burying slaves, 318n60; on marriage practices, 52, 55, 70, 71; on newborn rituals, 32–34; on sacred calendar, 29; on semen belief, 323n66
repartimiento system, 178, 218, 271, 279, 298, 303; *de efectos*, 276–279; mining, 267
Revolutionary Women's Laws, 307
Reyes, fray Antonio de los, 45–46, 233
Reynoso, don Joseph de, 193, 275
Ricard, Robert, 320n7, 321n41, 322n58
Rio, fray Diego del, 293
riots, women's participation: in Achiutla incident, 292–293; in Chapultepec/Mexicalcingo incident, 290; in Mexico City incidents, 274, 278–281, 284–285; in Nuyoo incident, 262–263; in Ocuila incident, 287; in San Andrés Yaa/Betaza/Lachita incident, 287; in San Felipe (*estancia* of Teposcolula) incident, 286–287; in San Matheo Susuquitepec/San Juan Sayultepec incident, 286; in Santiago Tiyyu uprising, 273–274; in Sayultepec and Santiago Tillo incident, 286; in Tamasulapa incident, 282–284; in Teposcolula incidents, 290–292; in Tepoztlan incident, 289–290; in Texupa/San Andrés incident, 285–286; women's roles in, 273–274, 293–294; women's roles in warfare in preconquest times, 263–265
ritual kinship and compadrazgo, 254–259, 364–365n146
Roman marriage practices, 80
Rosenthal, Jane, 280
Ruiz de Alarcón, Hernando: on gender-based insults, 38; on medical practices, 117, 197, 199, 201–204 (203t); on *nahualli*, 25–26, 316n29; on sacred objects, 245; on *tetonaltique*, 348n98; on *ticitl*, 347n81
Ruiz Medrano, Ethelia, 268, 367n23, 369n85
rulers, terminology and roles, 11, 206–208. See also *cacicas*; *caciques*
Russo, Alessandra, 126, 346n57

sacred calendars, 26–29 (27f)
sacred objects, 245–246
sacrifices: of animals, 40–41, 181, 246–247, 250, 348n109; autosacrifice, 75; of humans, 22, 37, 42, 117, 151, 191, 345n29
Sahagún, fray Bernardino de, 52, 59
San Martín Quetzalmazatzin Chichimecateuctli, Tomás de (*cacique* of Itztlacozauhcan Amaquemecan Chalco), 77
San Pablo y Alvarado, Domingo de (*cacique* of Yanhuitlan), 258
Santa María Cipac, don Luis (aka Nanacacipactzin "Mushroom Alligator"), 271, 279–280, 284–285
Santiago, Fulgencio de (governor of Tamasulapa), 282–284
santocalli, 244–245
Sasayu, Cecilia, 209, 242, 257
scholarship on gender roles in Mesoamerica, 3–4, 8–9, 296
Schroeder, Susan, 93
seamstresses, 184, 186–187, 187t, 188t
Sebastiana Ana, 90, 101–102
Seed, Patricia, 320n18
semen, 112–113, 132, 323n66, 333n15
sex: abstinence from, 117–118; appetite, 111–112; contamination from, 112–118 (115f–116f); fornication, 339n12; premarital, 149, 339n3; sexual diseases, 126; sight and sexual power, 134–136; sodomy, 335n45

sexual symbols and metaphors, 118–119; eye contact, sexual power of, 135–136; flowers, feathers, reed mats, 124–132 (125f, 127f–131f); food and drink, 119–124 (121f, 124f); posture, 131–132, 160f; speaking and sexual power, 132–134; speech, sight, and seduction, 132–136
Shoemaker, Nancy, 358n36
shoes, European-style, 184
siblings, elite, 94–95
Sierra, Josef Martín de la, 278
Sigal, Pete, 118, 147, 198, 297
Sigüenza y Góngora, don Carlos de, 274
silk, 209–210, 213–214, 271, 352n182
Silva, Domingo de, 173, 292
sitting posture and gender, 46
Six Monkey (Ñudzahui ruler), 263–264 (264f)
skulls, 65, 245, 247, 363n120
sky as male, 1, 2f
slaves/slavery: African slave trade, 304; clothing for, 276; as punishment for adultery, 159t, 162–163; rape case in Lachirio, 171; sacrifice of, 37, 42, 318n60, 345n29
smallpox epidemics, 199–200, 201f, 348n100
Socolow, Susan, 323n68
Sosa, Andrés de, 146
Sotomayor, Pedro de, 262
spinning. *See* weaving, spinning
Spores, Ronald, 230
Stern, Steve, 102, 105, 109, 332n106
stonings, 158–159 (159t), 160f, 162–163 (163f), 272–273, 208, 287
strangulation executions, 159–162 (159t), 341n53
sujetos, 93–94

Tabaá, 6f, 95, 97f, 249, 314n18
Taggart, James, 137

Tagui, 6f, 29, 106, 122, 211–212, 317n40, 345n29, 360n64
tailors, 184, 185f. *See also* weaving, spinning
Talea, 6f, 214, 246, 276, 335n44
Tamazulapa, 6f, 122, 132, 146, 149, 155, 166–167, 191, 218, 241, 257, 282–284, 370nn100, 101, 328n25
Tapia, Andrés de, 193
Tavárez, David, 245, 363n113
Taylor, William, 102, 107, 263, 294
"teachers of idolatry" ("*maestros de idolatrias*"), 40, 245–246, 363n113
tecpan, tecpancalli, teccalli (palace), 227, 248
Tehuantepec, 209, 271, 275, 307
telpochtli (unmarried young man), 85
Temascalapa, 6f, 84, 210, 317n40, 335n44, 357n28
temascalli (sweatbath), 195–197 (197f)
Teotihuacan, 5f, 90, 157, 159t, 162, 213
Tepetlaoztoc, 5f, 228–229, 268–270 (269f)
Teposcolula, 6f, 12, 30, 94, 100, 105, 110, 122, 132, 134, 145, 153–154, 170, 184, 191, 202, 204, 207, 209–210, 216, 219, 221, 239, 242, 255, 266, 270–271, 275, 277, 283–284, 286, 290–292, 322n61, 333n112
tequio, 344n5
Terraciano, Kevin, 88, 93, 131, 208, 237, 330n74, 354n5, 360n55
testaments, 7, 9, 15, 88–89, 91, 204, 207, 210–212, 215, 226, 232–233, 238, 243, 245–246, 250, 257, 259, 277, 303
Tetlepanquetzaltzin, 180
Tetzcoco, 5f, 32, 59, 61–62, 73, 76–78, 126, 180
Texupa, 6f, 207, 219, 230, 285–286, 322n64
theft, adultery as, 153, 340n27
Tíchazàa doctrina (1567), 56

ticitl, 32, 193, 347n81. *See also* healers; midwives
Tilantongo, 6f, 107, 204
Tilantzin, Martín, 54–55, 144, 169, 339n160
Tiltepec, 6f, 249, 328n25, 330n70
Titlacahuan, 24, 124
tlalticpacaiotl (earthly pleasure), 111, 333n3
Tlatelolco, 5f, 113, 180, 265, 279
tlatoani (ruler), 11, 77, 180, 182, 219, 246
tlatocacioatl (ruling woman), 206–207. See also *cacicas*
Tlaxiaco, 6f, 92, 133, 168–169, 215–216, 219, 270, 272, 281, 344n14, 352n193
Tlazolteotl, 66, 71–72, 114, 130, 337n94
tonalism, 19, 25–26 (25f)
tonalli ("heat"; "light"; "life force"), 25, 27 (27f), 71, 113, 126; as "shadow," 126
tonalpouhque (calendar reader), 26–30 (27f), 64
tools: in birth rituals, 31–36 (34f–36f); *cihuatlatquitl*, 37–38; and gender formation, 37–38; *oquichtlatquitl*, 37; women's gear, 37, 345n29
tortillas, 40, 190–191, 237
Tortorici, Zeb, 335n45
Totontepec, 6f, 212, 250
Townsend, Camilla, 322n55
tribute system, 216–223 (220f, 222f); couple as unit, 75, 92–93; and gendered labor, 32; head tax, 217, 237; and individual work ethic, 177; native appeals against excess, 271; precolonial, 11, 13, 235; Spanish restructuring of, 275; uprisings, unrest over, 278–287, 291–292; women in, 12, 219–223, 266–267, 276, 329n51
Triqui region, 325n108

Truitt, Jonathan, 208
turkeys, 70, 214, 246–247

umbilical cord burial, 33–34
uxoricide, 102–104, 107–108

"vagabonds," 334n28
vagina as a cave, 112
Valderrama, Jerónimo, 278
Valencia, fray Martín de, 77
Valeriano, don Antonio, 94
Van der Loo, Peter, 324n74
vara (staff of office), 270, 282–284, 295
Villa Alta, 6f, 12
violence in marriage. *See* uxoricide; wife beating
virginity, 85, 139, 149
Virgin Mary in indigenous clothing, 344n18
voladores. See pole flyers

warriors: men as, 32, 37; and polygyny, 52; women as, 263–267, 274, 286–287, 290–294
washing, 43, 78, 117, 142, 353n201
weaving, spinning, 153, 276–277; *comadres* help with, 257; as community duty, 178–179f; disputes with Spaniards over, 262, 268, 270–271, 276, 367n29; European competition, 190, 299; in gendered division of labor, 80, 89, 91, 185, 205; and goddess Tlazolteotl-Ixcuina, 130, 131f; by men, 183–185 (184f, 185f), 345n29, 360–361n64; metaphors of, 38, 42, 48, 179–180; in Nahuatl, 186–188 (187t, 188t); noblewomen supervising, 206; passed from mother to daughter, 239; prestige of, 223; as "public" work, 237; raising money for pueblos, 276; for room and board, 232; by sacrificed slaves, 345n29; Spanish tools for, 183–184; as tribute,

weaving, spinning (*continued*)
221, 298; as women's duty from birth through afterlife, 1, 32–34, 37–38, 84; and women's gear, 37, 345n29; writing as, 346n51
wheat, 191, 213, 217–218, 288
"wicked old man," 126, 128f
widows, widowers, 232, 257
wife beating, 84–85, 102–110, 154, 231, 327n145, 332n92; responses to, 104–108
witnesses: of legal documents, 15; women as, 327–328n21
women: ban on cochineal trade by, 213–214; bathing ritual for newborns, 28, 32–37 (34f–36f), 42; changes in legal identity of, 87–88; childbirth as warfare, 39; collecting alms, 97; compensation for labor of bride, 70; defeated warriors as, 38; defending their honor, 328n24; as featherworkers, 186, 205; as landowners, 237; leadership, 204–208, 265–267; menstruation, 334n20; as moral authorities, 279; performing Christian rituals, 41; as plaintiffs, 251–254 (252f, 253f); protecting church, 370n108; in religious life, 208; running pulque taverns, 238; semiautonomous financial status, 106; sexual desires of, 111–112; and Spanish legal authorities, 208, 265–268, 270–275; as specialist traders, 351–352n176; speech forms of, 45–46; submission in marriage, 80–81; use of Catholic doctrine, 62; using Spanish legal system, 267–272 (269f); as vendors and merchants, 209–211; as warriors, 263–267, 274, 286–287, 290–294. *See also cacicas;* midwives; weaving, spinning; wifebeating
women/girls: children as fragments of mother, 21; legal status of, 12; matrilocality, 95, 230, 330n68, 358n33, 36; and tribute system, 12, 219–223, 266–267, 276, 329n51
Wood, Stephanie, 212
writing and weaving, 346n51

Xilo, 186
Xiuhtlati, 186
xochihua (one who possesses flowers), 47–48 (47f). *See also* cross-dressing; cross-gender
Xochipilli, 120
Xochiquetzal, 114–116 (115f), 121 (121f), 202, 335n49
xonaxi (Bènizàa noblewoman), 11, 95

Yaa, 6f, 172, 245, 247, 272, 287
Yalálag, 43, 67, 247, 324n82, 359n54
Yanhuitlan, 6f, 30, 95, 107, 123, 145, 154, 157, 172, 204, 210, 212, 214–215, 227, 231, 241–242, 246, 249, 258–259, 265–267, 277, 330n77, 331n85
Yannakakis, Yanna, 366n10, 368n65
Yatzona, 6f, 29, 99, 212, 241, 244, 246, 249, 259, 335n44, 345n29, 357n28, 360n64
yetze (Bènizàa local ethnic state), 10–11, 217, 309, 314n15
yuhuitayu (Ñudzahui complex state), 88, 93, 96, 127, 129f, 330n74

Zapatista Army, 307
Zorita, Alonso de, 55
Zumárraga, fray Juan de, 50, 59

The authorized representative in the EU for product safety and compliance is:
Mare Nostrum Group
B.V Doelen 72
4831 GR Breda
The Netherlands

www.ingramcontent.com/pod-product-compliance
Lightning Source LLC
Chambersburg PA
CBHW031749220426
43662CB00007B/339